W9-CFC-310

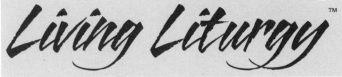

Living Liturgy™

Using this book for small group sharing

Groups using *Living Liturgy*™ for prayer and faith-sharing
might begin with the following general format and then adjust
it to fit different needs.

OPENING PRAYER
- Begin with a hymn
- Pray the opening prayer for the Sunday or solemnity

GOD'S WORD
- Proclaim the gospel
- Observe a brief period of silence

INDIVIDUAL STUDY, REFLECTION, PRAYER
- Read and consider "Reflecting on the Gospel" or "Living
  the Paschal Mystery"
- Spend some time in reflection and prayer

FAITH-SHARING
- Use the "Assembly & Faith-sharing Groups" spirituality
  statements (and the specific liturgical ministry statements
  if they apply)
- Consider what ways the gospel is challenging you to *live*
  the liturgy you will celebrate on Sunday

CONCLUDING PRAYER
- Pray the "Model Prayer of the Faithful"
- Pray the Our Father at the end of the intercessions
- Conclude with a hymn

Using this book for personal prayer

The best preparation for Sunday celebration of Eucharist is prayer. Here are two suggested approaches for an individual to use this book for personal prayer.

Daily Prayer

MONDAY
- Read the gospel prayerfully

TUESDAY
- Read the gospel again
- Reflect on the statements from "Assembly and Faith-sharing Groups" and let your reflection lead you to prayer

WEDNESDAY
- Read again the gospel
- Read "Reflecting on the Gospel" and let it lead you to prayer

THURSDAY
- Read and study "Living the Paschal Mystery"
- Pray the "Model Prayer of the Faithful"

FRIDAY
- Pray the responsorial psalm
- Read "Appreciating the Responsorial Psalm"

SATURDAY
- Read the gospel and first reading
- Read and study "Focusing the Gospel"
- Reflect on how you have been able to live this gospel during the week

SUNDAY
- Enter fully into the celebration of Eucharist
- Enjoy a day of rest

Prayer as Time and Opportunity Permit

A daily routine of study and prayer is not always possible.
As time and opportunity permit:
- Read the gospel prayerfully
- Reflect on "Living the Paschal Mystery"
- Pray the "Model Prayer of the Faithful"

Living Liturgy™

Living Liturgy™

Spirituality, Celebration, and Catechesis for Sundays and Solemnities

Year C • 2010

Joyce Ann Zimmerman, C.PP.S.
Kathleen Harmon, S.N.D. de N.
Christopher W. Conlon, S.M.

LITURGICAL PRESS
Collegeville, Minnesota

www.litpress.org

Design by Ann Blattner. Art by Annika Nelson.

ISSN 1547-089X

ISBN 978-0-8146-2747-1

CONTENTS

# CONTRIBUTORS

Joyce Ann Zimmerman, C.PP.S. is the director of the Institute for Liturgical Ministry in Dayton, Ohio and is the founding editor and columnist for *Liturgical Ministry*. She is an adjunct professor of liturgy, liturgical consultant, and frequent facilitator of workshops on liturgy. She has published numerous scholarly and pastoral liturgical works. She holds civil and pontifical doctorates of theology.

Kathleen Harmon, S.N.D. de N. is the music director for programs of the Institute for Liturgical Ministry in Dayton, Ohio and is the author of the *Music Notes* column for *Liturgical Ministry*. An educator and musician, she facilitates liturgical music workshops and cantor formation programs, and is a parish director of music. She holds a graduate degree in music and a doctorate in liturgy.

Christopher W. Conlon, S.M. is a Marianist priest who works with faculty and staff and has taught Scripture at the University of Dayton. He has been an educator for over a half century and is a highly respected homilist, a frequent workshop presenter, and a spiritual director. He holds a graduate degree in religious education and the licentiate in theology.

USING THIS RESOURCE

A while ago it was reported that a *Bat Mitzvah* cost in excess of $10,000,000. A five-year-old's birthday party cost in excess of $100,000. We are aware of statistics that tell us the average wedding today costs in excess of $50,000. In all these examples and many others, we find the number of zeros in cost figures to be staggering! It seems there is no limit to what we spend on a single day—both in terms of monetary costs as well as time and energy spent in preparation. By comparison, the cost of an issue of *Living Liturgy*™ is modest, indeed. Even the time it takes to prepare for a Sunday or solemnity or holiday liturgy is modest by comparison. Yet, this money spent and time and energy expended are really for far more than a single day—we have eyes on eternity. Our goal is not personal satisfaction but eternal glory with all the angels and saints. Our focus is not on ourselves but on the God of creation, salvation, and holiness who chooses to be present to us each and every day. The only cost of this gift-presence is our own surrender.

This eleventh volume of *Living Liturgy*™ continues its original purpose: to help people prepare for liturgy and live a liturgical spirituality (that is, a way of living that is rooted in liturgy) that opens their vision to their baptismal identity as the Body of Christ and shapes their living according to the rhythm of paschal mystery dying and rising. The paschal mystery is the central focus of liturgy, of the gospels, and of this volume.

A threefold dynamic of daily living, prayer, and study continues to determine the basic structure of *Living Liturgy*™, captured in the layout under the headings "Spirituality," "Celebration," and "Catechesis." This threefold dynamic is lived by the three authors; this is why each year the new volume is fresh with new material. The features don't always change, but the content does.

A note about music suggestions on the Catechesis page: because a number of the music suggestions made in *Living Liturgy*™ are drawn from resources published annually, some suggestions made at the time a volume of *Living Liturgy*™ was being written and published may no longer appear in the resources cited. Also, our intention here is not to provide a complete list of music suggestions for each Sunday or solemnity (these are readily available in other publications) but to make a few suggestions with accompanying catechesis; thus, we hope this is a learning process.

During Ordinary Time of the 2010 liturgical year, we read from Luke's gospel where one recurring theme is concern for the poor. What a contrast to the expense of some of our secular celebrations! What a contrast to focusing on ourselves and our own grandiose desires and expectations! Rather than lavishness on a day for a person, Luke insists on God's lavish care for us, especially the poor and downtrodden, each and every day of our lives. This care is not for a day but now and for all eternity. Let's listen to Luke's invitation this year to model our own lives after God's life and love and care.

PREPARATION FOR SUNDAY: LITTLE COST IN MONEY AND TIME

PASCHAL MYSTERY STILL CENTRAL FOCUS

SPIRITUALITY, CELEBRATION, AND CATECHESIS

A NOTE ABOUT MUSIC SUGGESTIONS

GOD'S LAVISH CARE

✝ INTRODUCTION to the Gospel of Luke

Luke, who lived in Antioch, wrote his gospel for a Gentile community somewhere between 80 and 85 A.D. The people for whom he wrote never saw Jesus and probably never even knew anyone who did. Consequently, a problem facing the community was maintaining faithful continuity with the teaching and spirit of Jesus. Luke's response to this problem was the post-resurrection story on the road to Emmaus, where the two disciples realized that they had experienced the presence of Jesus after they heard him explain what the Scriptures said and recognized him in the breaking of the bread.

The gospel begins in Galilee from where Jesus sets about preaching and then "sets his face" toward Jerusalem where he will meet suffering and death; the gospel, then, is structured around this resolute journey to Jerusalem. The Acts of the Apostles (considered to be the second part of Luke's gospel) picks up in Jerusalem after Jesus' death and tells of his ascension to heaven and the coming of the Spirit upon the disciples. Filled with this Spirit of the risen Jesus, the disciples go out to preach and live the Good News. Whereas Jesus began his preaching in Galilee and was crucified in Jerusalem, the disciples—filled with the Spirit of Jesus—began their preaching and healing in Jerusalem and went forth from there to the four corners of the world to preach the Good News. Moreover, the preaching of the Good News does not die with the martyrdom of great apostles like Peter and Paul (highlighted in the Acts) but is taken up all over the known world. Now, in our own day, we are also called to continue the preaching of the Good News by the way we live as followers of Jesus, filled with this same Spirit.

Jesus born in a stable and placed in a manger, the shepherds who visited him, the elderly Simeon and Anna who recognized him in the temple, the Good Samaritan, the Prodigal Son, the Widow of Naim: the narratives around these people are among the best known and loved stories in the whole New Testament, and they are stories unique to the Gospel of Luke. Such people as the poor, outcasts, and sinners who figure so prominently in Luke lead us to refer to the third gospel as the gospel of mercy. A few more examples illustrate this further. Whereas in Matthew's gospel Jesus calls us to "be perfect, just as your heavenly Father is perfect" (Matt 5:48), Luke replaces "perfect" with "merciful" (Luke 6:36). Luke 15 contains three familiar parables of mercy (the lost sheep, lost coin, and Prodigal Son; the last two are unique to Luke) that compare God to those who go out of their way to help the lost. We are called to be compassionate like the rich merchant who forgave a servant who owed him much (but who, in turn, refused to forgive the much smaller debts that fellow servants owed him). Likewise this gospel is also called the gospel of prayer (Jesus often goes off by himself to pray) and of women (because of the prominent role of women in this gospel; for example, the angel appears to Mary). It is precisely these people who play such significant roles that highlight Luke's message: salvation is for all, God cares for the poor, God's care and mercy are wonderfully shown through the life and ministry of Jesus.

ABBREVIATIONS

LITURGICAL RESOURCES

BofB	*Book of Blessings*. International Commission on English in the Liturgy. Collegeville: Liturgical Press, 1989.
BLS	*Built of Living Stones: Art, Architecture, and Worship*. Guidelines of the National Conference of Catholic Bishops, 2000.
CCC	*Catechism of the Catholic Church*. USCCB, 2004.
GIRM	General Instruction of the Roman Missal (2002).
GNLYC	General Norms for the Liturgical Year and the Calendar
ILM	Introduction to the Lectionary for Mass
L	*Lectionary*
NT	New Testament
OT	Old Testament
SC	*Sacrosanctum Concilium*. The Constitution on the Sacred Liturgy. Vatican II.

MUSICAL RESOURCES

BB	*Breaking Bread*. Portland, OR: Oregon Catholic Press, annual.
CBW3	*Catholic Book of Worship III*. Ottawa, Ontario: Canadian Conference of Catholic Bishops, 1994.
CH	*The Collegeville Hymnal*. Collegeville: Liturgical Press, 1990.
G2	*Gather*. 2nd edition. Chicago: GIA Publications, Inc., 1994.
GC	*Gather Comprehensive*. Chicago: GIA Publications, Inc., 1994.
GC2	*Gather Comprehensive*. 2nd edition. Chicago: GIA Publications, Inc., 2004.
HG	*Hymns for the Gospels*. Chicago: GIA Publications, Inc., 2001.
JS2	*Journeysongs*. 2nd edition. Portland, OR: Oregon Catholic Press, 2003.
LMGM	*Lead Me, Guide Me*. Chicago: GIA Publications, Inc., 1987.
OFUV	*One Faith/Una Voz*. Portland, OR: Oregon Catholic Press, 2005.
PMB	*People's Mass Book*. Schiller Park, IL: World Library Publications, 2003.
RS	*Ritual Song*. Chicago: GIA Publications, Inc., 1996.
SS	*Sacred Song*. Collegeville: Liturgical Press, annual.
VO	*Voices As One*. Schiller Park, IL: World Library Publications, 1998.
VO2	*Voices As One*, vol. 2. Schiller Park, IL: World Library Publications, 2005.
W3	*Worship*. 3rd edition. Chicago: GIA Publications, Inc., 1986.
WC	*We Celebrate*. Schiller Park, IL: World Library Publications, 2008.
WS	*Word and Song*. Schiller Park, IL: World Library Publications, annual.
GIA	GIA Publications, Inc.
LTP	Liturgy Training Publications, Inc.
OCP	Oregon Catholic Press
WLP	World Library Publications

Season of Advent

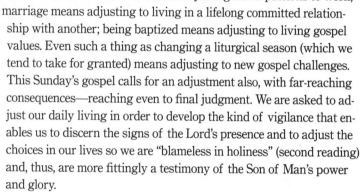

✝ SPIRITUALITY

GOSPEL ACCLAMATION
Ps 85:8

℟. Alleluia, alleluia.
Show us Lord, your love;
and grant us your salvation.
℟. Alleluia, alleluia.

Gospel

Luke 21:25-28, 34-36; L3C

Jesus said to his disciples:
"There will be signs in the sun,
    the moon, and the stars,
    and on earth nations will be in
        dismay,
    perplexed by the roaring of the
        sea and the waves.
People will die of fright
    in anticipation of what is
        coming upon the world,
    for the powers of the heavens
        will be shaken.
And then they will see the Son of
    Man
    coming in a cloud with power and
        great glory.
But when these signs begin to happen,
    stand erect and raise your heads
    because your redemption is at hand.

"Beware that your hearts do not
        become drowsy
    from carousing and drunkenness
    and the anxieties of daily life,
    and that day catch you by surprise
        like a trap.
For that day will assault everyone
    who lives on the face of the earth.
Be vigilant at all times
    and pray that you have the strength
    to escape the tribulations that are
        imminent
    and to stand before the Son of Man."

Reflecting on the Gospel

Adjustments are a fact of life. We make them all day long, usually without even thinking about it. For example, we adjust the volume on the TV, radio, or iPod; we pay attention to adjustable mortgage rates; we adjust our schedules to accommodate someone in need. Other adjustments take more thought and energy and have more far-reaching consequences. For example, moving from an apartment or house to another means rearranging furniture or perhaps even buying other more suitable furniture as well as adjusting travel patterns to work; marriage means adjusting to living in a lifelong committed relationship with another; being baptized means adjusting to living gospel values. Even such a thing as changing a liturgical season (which we tend to take for granted) means adjusting to new gospel challenges. This Sunday's gospel calls for an adjustment also, with far-reaching consequences—reaching even to final judgment. We are asked to adjust our daily living in order to develop the kind of vigilance that enables us to discern the signs of the Lord's presence and to adjust the choices in our lives so we are "blameless in holiness" (second reading) and, thus, are more fittingly a testimony of the Son of Man's power and glory.

The source of the vigilance the gospel admonishes is found in these two actions: God's call and our response. The redemption at hand promised in the gospel is God's work (the first reading reveals God's plan of redemption through the coming of the Savior), but it also calls for a response from us (in the second reading Paul exhorts us to do our part by growing in love, living in ways pleasing to God, and being faithful to the teachings of Christ). Moreover, the very discernment of signs of the Lord's presence is already a response, already a factor in the end-time judgment. We have nothing to fear when we live as if the end times were now, as if Christ is present in all his glory now.

One sign of the Son of Man's presence is that we are growing in love. Despite appearances to the contrary (disaster and destruction generated both by natural forces and human choices), God's plan and purpose are directed toward redemption and life. We need to read the right signs—new life in the midst of seeming destruction, the glory of the Son of Man coming into the darkness, the love of Christ growing in our hearts.

Living the Paschal Mystery

Vigilance for the many ways Christ is present to us involves dying to self. This means that our focus is not on our own wants and needs but on the Christ who chooses to be intimately present to us. Our prayer for strength might be that Jesus help us see his presence in the people around us. This is pretty easy (with a practical reminder to ourselves) when the other person is pleasant or cooperative or helpful. The dying happens when the other is cranky or threatening or not to our liking. How can we see Christ in the other when the other doesn't conform to our image of Christ? This is the question raised by the "anxieties of daily life." The dying comes in growing in our image of who Christ is! The dying comes in forming the habit of seeing Christ in *all* others because Christ came to redeem *all*. The rising comes in constant vigilance, for Christ comes in many ways. The real challenge comes in adjusting to all these presences of Christ in our lives.

Focusing the Gospel

Key words and phrases: signs, dismay, Son of Man coming, redemption is at hand, anxieties of daily living, Be vigilant

To the point: Despite appearances to the contrary (disaster and destruction generated both by natural forces and human choices), God's plan and purpose are directed toward redemption and life. We need to read the right signs—new life in the midst of seeming destruction, the glory of the Son of Man coming into the darkness, the love of Christ growing in our hearts (see second reading).

Connecting the Gospel

to the first and second reading: The redemption at hand promised in the gospel is God's work, but it also calls for a response from us. The first reading reveals God's plan of redemption through the coming of the Savior. In the second reading Paul exhorts us to do our part by growing in love, living in ways pleasing to God, and being faithful to the teachings of Christ.

to our experience: It's easier to get caught up in external signs and events such as cosmic disasters than it is to do the hard work of recognizing in our daily living what needs to change in us. Making changes like these are signs of redemption.

Connecting the Responsorial Psalm

to the readings: Christ challenges us in the gospel for this first Sunday of Advent not to "become drowsy" but to remain "vigilant" while we await his final coming at the end of time. "Pray," he says, "that you have the strength," and this is just what Paul does for us in the second reading ("May the Lord . . . strengthen your hearts"). The final coming of Christ stands in some unknown future, but we are to conduct ourselves now with the holiness (second reading) that will enable us to "stand erect" when we at last see him face to face (gospel). The verses we sing this Sunday from Psalm 25 are a humble request to be guided by God along the path of righteousness. They are our confident assertion of God's friendship and constancy along the way, and our prayer that God will indeed keep us alert and strong until the day of Christ's coming.

to psalmist preparation: As you sing this psalm refrain, you model the posture of the church during these days of Advent—heads up and eyes lifted for the coming of Christ. Use the refrain every day as part of your personal prayer. At the end of the week reflect on how this has kept you ready for the coming of Christ and helped you spot his arrival.

ASSEMBLY & FAITH-SHARING GROUPS

- What helps me see the signs of God's redemption is . . . What distracts me from seeing the signs of God's redemption is . . .
- The anxieties of my daily living are . . . These keep me from . . .
- What helps me love as Christ loves is . . .

PRESIDERS

- I am a sign for my parish of Christ's love when I . . .

DEACONS

- The "do so even more" (see second reading) to which Advent calls me is . . .

HOSPITALITY MINISTERS

- I see the gathering of the assembly as a sign of Christ's presence among us whenever . . .

MUSIC MINISTERS

- Leading the music of the assembly helps create openness to God's redemption when . . .

ALTAR MINISTERS

- My service at the altar draws the assembly to focus on the signs of God's presence whenever I . . .

LECTORS

- My proclamation itself is a sign of God's call to redemption whenever . . .

EXTRAORDINARY MINISTERS OF HOLY COMMUNION

- My life—as Christ's Eucharist for others—reveals Christ's coming when I . . . I nourish and strengthen others until Christ comes in glory whenever I . . .

Model Act of Penitence

Presider: Our God is coming—not just in our anticipation of Christmas as we begin Advent but at the end of time when Christ will come in great power to save us. We pause at the beginning of this celebration to open our hearts to the signs of Christ's coming among us . . . [pause]

Lord Jesus, you are the Son of Man who comes in great power and glory: Lord . . .

Christ Jesus, you are the promise of our redemption and our peace: Christ . . .

Lord Jesus, you are the love that strengthens our hearts: Lord . . .

Homily Points

• At this point in the year it is almost winter with shorter daylight hours, changing weather patterns, and increased busy-ness as we shop, bake, clean, decorate, etc. New seasons always call for adjustments—not just in clocks, clothing, and calendars but also in the way we approach each other and the tasks of Christian living before us.

• This gospel calls us to look to the signs of the times for Christ's coming. The second reading reminds us that who and how we live today are some of the very signs we must discern. To be sure, Christ will come at the end of time with judgment and redemption. But this ought not make us miss his many presences now with their challenge of growing in holiness and loving as he does.

• The "anxieties of life" often enough blind us to the genuine signs of Christ's presence and saving actions. This time of year is filled with all kinds of distractions. The Advent season invites us to a more balanced perspective on what we are really about: continually opening ourselves to Christ's presence. Thus Advent calls us to do deeper discernment about our lives and this very discernment is already a way to prepare for Christ's comings now and in future glory.

Model Prayer of the Faithful

Presider: Our caring God is ever present to us, and so we are encouraged to make known our needs.

Response:

Lord,— hear our prayer.

Cantor:

we pray to the Lord,

That all members of the church faithfully witness by the goodness of their lives that Christ is already present among us . . . [pause]

That all world leaders govern with the justice that leads to lasting peace . . . [pause]

That the poor and all those in any need receive from the generosity of others what they need . . . [pause]

That each of us here grow in discerning the signs of redemption within and among us . . . [pause]

Presider: O God, you come to save us: hear these our prayers of need that we might be ready to meet you when you come. We ask this through Christ our Lord. **Amen.**

OPENING PRAYER
Let us pray

Pause for silent prayer

All-powerful God,
increase our strength of will for doing
    good
that Christ may find an eager welcome at
    his coming
and call us to his side in the kingdom of
    heaven,
where he lives and reigns with you and the
    Holy Spirit,
one God, for ever and ever. **Amen.**

FIRST READING
Jer 33:14-16

The days are coming, says the LORD,
    when I will fulfill the promise
      I made to the house of Israel and Judah.
In those days, in that time,
    I will raise up for David a just shoot;
      he shall do what is right and just in the
        land.
In those days Judah shall be safe
    and Jerusalem shall dwell secure;
    this is what they shall call her:
    "The LORD our justice."

RESPONSORIAL PSALM

Ps 25:4-5, 8-9, 10, 14

℟. (1b) To you, O Lord, I lift my soul.

Your ways, O LORD, make known to me;
    teach me your paths,
guide me in your truth and teach me,
    for you are God my savior,
    and for you I wait all the day.

℟. To you, O Lord, I lift my soul.

Good and upright is the LORD;
    thus he shows sinners the way.
He guides the humble to justice,
    and teaches the humble his way.

℟. To you, O Lord, I lift my soul.

All the paths of the LORD are kindness and
        constancy
    toward those who keep his covenant
        and his decrees.
The friendship of the LORD is with those
        who fear him,
    and his covenant, for their instruction.

℟. To you, O Lord, I lift my soul.

SECOND READING

1 Thess 3:12–4:2

Brothers and sisters:
May the Lord make you increase and
        abound in love
    for one another and for all,
    just as we have for you,
    so as to strengthen your hearts,
    to be blameless in holiness before our
        God and Father
    at the coming of our Lord Jesus with all
        his holy ones. Amen.

Finally, brothers and sisters,
    we earnestly ask and exhort you in the
        Lord Jesus that,
    as you received from us
    how you should conduct yourselves to
        please God
    —and as you are conducting
        yourselves—
    you do so even more.
For you know what instructions we gave
    you through the Lord Jesus.

About Liturgy

Advent and redemption: The future is in God's hands and God will bring it to fulfillment. What we do know is the outcome (God comes with redemption) and how it is achieved (through intimacy with Christ). Advent is a special liturgical season that begins with looking to the future, comes to a climax in looking to the past, and bears fruit in the present. Advent is a season when we bring to mind and celebrate the three comings of Christ and redemption.

Christ's first coming (that we celebrate on Christmas) *fulfilled* the Old Testament prophecies that God's Messiah would come to restore all things new. Christ's birth as the incarnate Son fulfilled these promises. Jesus' public ministry showed us how God's new reign would come about: by repenting and believing in the Gospel. His death and resurrection assured us that salvation is surely at hand, but it is only at Christ's second coming that the fullness of God's glory and justice will be *revealed*. We find ourselves in an age straddling the first and second comings of Christ, at a time when we need to be *strengthened* now. The third coming of Christ is *now*, when Christ comes, first and foremost, in sacraments but no less through each other. Our Advent vigilance and waiting doesn't just look back to the first coming or forward to the Second Coming. The first coming bears fruit and the Second Coming is not frightening to the extent that our vigilance and waiting is in the here and now, recognizing Christ in the many sacramental comings of our everyday lives.

The challenge of Advent and our Christian living is to heighten our expectation of the coming of Christ so that we can be attentive to Christ's presence already among us. Attentive waiting is already a presence that is redemptive.

About Liturgical Music

Appropriate music for Advent: An important principle guiding music during the season of Advent is found in GIRM 313: "In Advent the organ and other musical instruments should be used with a moderation that is consistent with the season's character and does not anticipate the full joy of the Nativity of the Lord." In others words, a certain restraint should mark the music during this season. This restraint does not have the penitential character of Lent. Instead, its intent is to express a kind of "fasting" before the "feasting" that enables us to enter more consciously into the waiting that marks Advent. We may certainly sing songs that express joy and expectation (many of the Advent readings do this very thing), but the music overall should be characterized by a sense of holding back until the time for full celebration arrives.

Songs for the first two weeks of Advent: During the first two weeks of Advent the focus of the liturgy is not on the infant Christ's coming in Bethlehem but on the risen Christ's final coming in judgment at the end of history. It is important that the music we sing these two weeks reflects this focus and that we hold off singing songs oriented toward the coming of the newborn Christ until the final two weeks of Advent. Examples of songs that focus on the Second Coming include "Hail to the Lord's Anointed"; "Wake, O Wake, and Sleep No Longer"; "Lift Up Your Heads, O Mighty Gates"; "The King Shall Come When Morning Dawns"; "Soon and Very Soon"; and "Ride On, Jesus, Ride."

NOVEMBER 29, 2009
FIRST SUNDAY OF ADVENT

✝ SPIRITUALITY

GOSPEL ACCLAMATION
Luke 3:4, 6

℟. Alleluia, alleluia.
Prepare the way of the Lord, make
    straight his paths:
all flesh shall see the salvation of God.
℟. Alleluia, alleluia.

Gospel

Luke 3:1-6; L6C

**In the fifteenth year of the reign
    of Tiberius Caesar,
  when Pontius Pilate was
      governor of Judea,
  and Herod was tetrarch of
      Galilee,
  and his brother Philip tetrarch
      of the region of Ituraea
      and Trachonitis,
  and Lysanias was tetrarch of
      Abilene,
  during the high priesthood of
      Annas and Caiaphas,
  the word of God came to John
      the son of Zechariah in the
      desert.
John went throughout the whole region
    of the Jordan,
  proclaiming a baptism of repentance
      for the forgiveness of sins,
  as it is written in the book of the
      words of the prophet Isaiah:
  *A voice of one crying out in the
      desert:
  "Prepare the way of the Lord,
      make straight his paths.
  Every valley shall be filled
      and every mountain and hill
          shall be made low.
  The winding roads shall be made
      straight,
      and the rough ways made smooth,
      and all flesh shall see the salvation
          of God."***

Reflecting on the Gospel

Mathematics tells us that the shortest distance between two points is a straight line. Yet, how often do we humans move in very circuitous ways? If we want to drive to the top of a steep mountain, going straight up usually doesn't get us there—we use switchbacks so the grade isn't so steep. Sometimes we go out of our way to avoid another person, especially when there is ill will between this person and us. At other times we might take a roundabout way home to enjoy a gorgeous, sunny spring evening a bit more. The gospel for this Sunday, contrary to our sometimes roundabout ways, gives us clear instructions: make straight our path to the Lord. The gospel also makes clear the means to make that path straight: repentance and forgiveness.

Sometimes we don't understand or are unaware of the critical importance of repentance and forgiveness in our relationships with each other. Baruch's prophecy of a glorious future was fulfilled when Israel returned from exile (first reading and psalm). Isaiah's prophecy of future glory quoted in the gospel ("all flesh shall see the salvation of God") is fulfilled when we return to God through repentance and forgiveness. "[R]epentance for the forgiveness of sins" is an essential requirement for us to "see the salvation of God." What is at stake in our making a straight path to the Lord is our very salvation.

The salvation of God is progressively revealed in repentance (our work) and forgiveness (God's work). The meandering paths and winding roads of our lives are straightened and the valleys filled and mountains brought low when our lives are characterized by attitudes of repentance. To repent means to change one's mind, one's life; this is how we reach the fullness that is promised and our true home: by increasing our love for one another, discerning "what is of [true] value," and by being "filled with the fruit of righteousness" (see second reading). Our work of repentance is a matter of turning ourselves toward the God who embraces us in mercy and forgiveness and welcomes us home.

Living the Paschal Mystery

Last Sunday's gospel directed our attention to the end times and gave us a glimpse of those times, both in terms of the calamities that will befall those who are not ready as well as the promise of safety and security for those who are vigilant. This Sunday both the gospel and first reading give us a glimpse of the fullness of the end days. Our natural tendency is to want to get to the fullness and bypass the hard work of daily dying to self that is required to reach the glory and joy that is promised.

Let's be honest: it's not just the busy-ness of Christmas preparations now in full December fury that distract us from our ongoing work of repentance and forgiveness. Every day of the year we tend to be distracted by mountains of work, paths of indecision, valleys of doubt and fear. This would be a good Sunday of Advent to take some special time to reflect on God's forgiveness and mercy and how it is God who gives sure direction to our lives and will eventually bring us home to eternal glory if we are faithful partners in the gospel. Our Advent watchfulness and waiting include taking time to rest in the security of God's nearness. Part of the work of Advent is smoothing our relationships with each other so that we can see the nearness of God—within each other.

Focusing the Gospel

Key words and phrases: repentance, forgiveness, all flesh shall see the salvation of God

To the point: Baruch's prophecy of a glorious future was fulfilled when Israel returned from exile (first reading and psalm). Isaiah's prophecy of future glory quoted in the gospel ("all flesh shall see the salvation of God") is fulfilled when we return to God through repentance and forgiveness. "[R]epentance for the forgiveness of sins" is an essential requirement for us to "see the salvation of God."

Connecting the Gospel

to the second reading: Isaiah in the gospel admonishes us to "[p]repare the way of the Lord," so that, as Paul says, "a good work in you will continue" to completion in "the day of Christ Jesus." Repentance and forgiveness are ways we prepare the way of the Lord.

to Catholic culture: When we hear the words "repentance" and "forgiveness" of sins" some immediately think of confession and the sacrament of penance. The gospel points us to repentance and forgiveness as a way of life.

Connecting the Responsorial Psalm

to the readings: Psalm 126 celebrated Israel's return from exile in Babylon. God intervened and those who had gone forth weeping returned home rejoicing. Over time Israel came to use this psalm any time the community felt endangered or threatened. The remembrance of God's past saving actions became the source of confidence that God would again intervene to save them.

Advent is the season when we look as did Jerusalem toward the redemption coming on our behalf from the hand of God (first reading). Truly "the one who began a good work in [us] will . . . complete it" (second reading). Luke tells us this redemption will take place in real history ("In the fifteenth year of . . . when . . .") and that it will demand choices and changes (gospel). This Advent may we recognize what God is doing. May we make the choices and changes redemption requires. May we make Psalm 126 our story and our song.

to psalmist preparation: Psalm 126 invites the community to take the long view of history. It reminds them that what God has done in the past God will do in the future. In singing it you embody the messianic hope that marks the church. What or who helps keep this hope alive in you? When this hope feels shaken, what or who revives it for you?

**ASSEMBLY &
FAITH-SHARING GROUPS**

- John's call to "repentance for the forgiveness of sins" is real for me in my relationship with . . .
- I feel an urgency for repentance and forgiveness when . . .
- For me, salvation looks like . . . feels like . . . sounds like . . .

PRESIDERS

- During this Advent the "good work" (second reading) that Christ is completing *in* me is . . .; the "good work" that Christ is completing *through* me is . . .

DEACONS

- I recognize my ministry as a "partnership for the gospel" (second reading) when . . .

HOSPITALITY MINISTERS

- My hospitality—at home or at church— goes beyond mere busy-ness to preparing the way of the Lord when I . . .

MUSIC MINISTERS

- The music I sing helps the assembly prepare the way of the Lord when . . .

ALTAR MINISTERS

- As I consider John's preaching, the really important Advent preparations in my life are about straightening up and smoothing out . . .

LECTORS

- The "word of God came to" me when . . . I am God's word coming to others when I . . .

**EXTRAORDINARY MINISTERS
OF HOLY COMMUNION**

- A way the Eucharist reveals the "salvation of God" for me is . . . When I receive Holy Communion I am called to embody this same salvation for others by . . .

Model Act of Penitence

Presider: Our lives are constantly filled with the ups and downs, the mountains and valleys, of everyday living, challenging us to keep focused on the God who comes to save us. We pause now to recognize God's mercy and forgiveness . . . [pause]

> Lord Jesus, you are the light and glory of God: Lord . . .
> Christ Jesus, you are the salvation of God: Christ . . .
> Lord Jesus, you offer us mercy and forgiveness: Lord . . .

Homily Points

• Paving the way for someone can mean either removing obstacles or filling in absences and gaps. For example, sometimes we must change expectations, as when we remove prejudices in order to receive persons as they really are. Other times we must create expectations, as when a parent keeps the memory and presence of an absent parent alive so the absent parent isn't a stranger to the children upon return. In both examples, expectations pave the way for acceptance.

• The gospel clearly reminds us that the expectation of Christ's coming with salvation is paved by our own attitudes toward one another, especially of repentance and forgiveness. *When* does God call us to repentance and forgiveness? Now, at this precise moment in history. *How* does God call us to repentance and forgiveness? Through human messengers who render a concrete call to conversion. *Who* does God call to repentance and forgiveness? All and each of us.

• The practice of repentance and forgiveness—in concrete here-and-now ways—not only paves the way for deeper reception of one another, but also for our recognizing the presence of God among us.

Model Prayer of the Faithful

Presider: Recognizing and responding to God's call to repentance and forgiveness, we ask God for the grace we need.

Response:

Lord,———— hear our prayer.

Cantor:

we pray to the Lord,

That the church faithfully announce the salvation of God through the ministry of forgiveness and mercy . . . [pause]

That all peoples of the world hear the call to repentance and open themselves to the presence of a merciful God . . . [pause]

That the rough ways of the poor be made smooth by the mercy and compassion of this community . . . [pause]

That each of us here take sufficient time during this busy Advent season to be mindful of what God is asking of us . . . [pause]

Presider: Saving God, you are merciful and forgiving: hear these our prayers that one day we might dwell with you in everlasting glory. We ask this through Christ our Lord. **Amen.**

OPENING PRAYER
Let us pray

Pause for silent prayer

God of power and mercy,
open our hearts in welcome.
Remove the things that hinder us from
    receiving Christ with joy,
so that we may share his wisdom
and become one with him
when he comes in glory,
for he lives and reigns with you and the
    Holy Spirit,
one God, for ever and ever. **Amen.**

FIRST READING
Bar 5:1-9

Jerusalem, take off your robe of mourning
    and misery;
    put on the splendor of glory from God
      forever:
wrapped in the cloak of justice from God,
    bear on your head the mitre
    that displays the glory of the eternal
      name.
For God will show all the earth your
    splendor:
    you will be named by God forever
    the peace of justice, the glory of God's
      worship.

Up, Jerusalem! stand upon the heights;
    look to the east and see your children
gathered from the east and the west
    at the word of the Holy One,
    rejoicing that they are remembered by
      God.
Led away on foot by their enemies they
    left you:
    but God will bring them back to you
    borne aloft in glory as on royal thrones.
For God has commanded
    that every lofty mountain be made low,
and that the age-old depths and gorges
    be filled to level ground,
    that Israel may advance secure in the
      glory of God.
The forests and every fragrant kind of
    tree
    have overshadowed Israel at God's
      command;
for God is leading Israel in joy
    by the light of his glory,
    with his mercy and justice for company.

RESPONSORIAL PSALM

Ps 126:1-2, 2-3, 4-5, 6

R̸. (3) The Lord has done great things for us; we are filled with joy.

When the LORD brought back the captives of Zion,
    we were like men dreaming.
Then our mouth was filled with laughter,
    and our tongue with rejoicing.

R̸. The Lord has done great things for us; we are filled with joy.

Then they said among the nations,
    "The LORD has done great things for
      them."
The LORD has done great things for us;
    we are glad indeed.

R̸. The Lord has done great things for us; we are filled with joy.

Restore our fortunes, O LORD,
    like the torrents in the southern desert.
Those who sow in tears
    shall reap rejoicing.

R̸. The Lord has done great things for us; we are filled with joy.

Although they go forth weeping,
    carrying the seed to be sown,
they shall come back rejoicing,
    carrying their sheaves.

R̸. The Lord has done great things for us; we are filled with joy.

SECOND READING

Phil 1:4-6, 8-11

Brothers and sisters:
I pray always with joy in my every prayer
    for all of you,
      because of your partnership for the
        gospel
    from the first day until now.
I am confident of this,
    that the one who began a good work
      in you
    will continue to complete it
    until the day of Christ Jesus.
God is my witness,
    how I long for all of you with the
      affection of Christ Jesus.
And this is my prayer:
    that your love may increase ever more
      and more
    in knowledge and every kind of
      perception,
    to discern what is of value,
    so that you may be pure and blameless
      for the day of Christ,
    filled with the fruit of righteousness
    that comes through Jesus Christ
    for the glory and praise of God.

About Liturgy

Advent penance service: Many parishes offer communal penance liturgies at least twice a year, during Advent and Lent. The readings this Sunday remind us that this sacrament is not primarily about lists of sins but about repentance, changing one's heart. Just as with all the sacraments, we repeat the ritual as a way of appropriating the insight of the sacrament, namely, to "take off" the robes of sin and "put on the splendor" of the gospel attitudes of repentance and forgiveness (see first reading).

Penitential rite: Sometimes people claim that they have no need for the sacrament of penance because every Sunday Mass begins with a penitential rite. Two points by way of response might be made to such objections. First of all, the penitential rite isn't the same as the sacrament of penance and so it doesn't replace in our Christian practice the need for this special sacrament of forgiveness and healing. Second, the "penitential rite" really isn't primarily about the forgiveness of sins as such but is about celebrating God's mercy and offer of salvation that always leads us to praise and thanksgiving.

Although it is always good to acknowledge our sinfulness and beg for God's mercy, it is telling that the Sacramentary gives us other choices for the introductory rites, and it is good pastoral practice to choose carefully among them according to the liturgical season and/or festival. For example, since Lent focuses our attention specifically on the work of being penitential, on the Sundays of Lent the strongest option among the choices for the penitential rite would be to use the *Confiteor* ("I confess to almighty God . . ."). On other Sundays of the year another choice would be more appropriate, especially since every Sunday is a celebration of resurrection, a little Easter (even the Sundays of Lent!). To protect and preserve that sense, it would be pastorally effective to reserve the *Confiteor* for Lent, using form C the rest of the year.

About Liturgical Music

Music suggestions: As with the first Sunday of Advent, the songs we sing this day need to focus on the final coming of Christ and the completion of redemption at the end of time. An excellent entrance hymn that interrelates Christ's final coming with John the Baptist's call to repentance is Genevieve Glen's "Arise, Stand on the Height," found in *Voices from the Valley* [OCP]. Two very fine hymns that speak of all three comings of Christ (in the Incarnation, in sacraments, and in the Second Coming) are Herman G. Stuempfle's "O Christ at Your Appearing," found in *Awake Our Hearts to Praise!* [GIA], and Carl Daw's "For the Coming of the Savior" [SS]. A hymn that relates particularly well to the first reading and the psalm is Genevieve Glen's "When Christ in Majesty Returns," found in *The Listening Heart* [OCP]. Delores Dufner's "Wait When the Seed Is Planted," in *The Glimmer of Glory in Song* [GIA], would be a good choice for the preparation of the gifts or Communion on any Sunday. Good verse-refrain choices for Communion include Francis Patrick O'Brien's "Maranatha, Come" [GC2, SS], Paul Page's "Lord, Come," in *Mantras for the Season* [WLP], and Kathy Powell's "Maranatha, Lord Messiah" [GC2, SS].

✝ SPIRITUALITY

GOSPEL ACCLAMATION
cf. Luke 1:28

℞. Alleluia, alleluia.
Hail, Mary, full of grace, the Lord is with you;
blessed are you among women.
℞. Alleluia, alleluia.

Gospel   Luke 1:26-38; L689

The angel Gabriel was sent from
    God
    to a town of Galilee called
        Nazareth,
    to a virgin betrothed to a
        man named Joseph,
    of the house of David,
    and the virgin's name was
        Mary.
And coming to her, he said,
    "Hail, full of grace! The Lord is
        with you."
But she was greatly troubled at what was
        said
    and pondered what sort of greeting this
        might be.
Then the angel said to her,
    "Do not be afraid, Mary,
    for you have found favor with God.
Behold, you will conceive in your womb and
        bear a son,
    and you shall name him Jesus.
He will be great and will be called Son of
        the Most High,
    and the Lord God will give him the throne
        of David his father,
    and he will rule over the house of Jacob
        forever,
    and of his Kingdom there will be no end."

Continued in Appendix A, p. 261.

See Appendix A, p. 261, for the other readings.

Reflecting on the Gospel

What's in a yes? Many possibilities! Sometimes a yes simply means I agree. Sometimes it's a vote in favor of something. Sometimes it's a distracted "Yes, yes, yes, I hear you." Sometimes it's an indication of approval. And sometimes it bespeaks something as serious as a life commitment: yes, I'll marry you; yes, I'll sign this loan and begin a new business; yes, I'll adopt this child. But who ever uttered a yes that changed not only that person's life but the course of history and the lives of all who have lived since? Who ever uttered a yes and became the mother of God? What a yes!

The quality of Mary's yes goes beyond her being overshadowed by the Holy Spirit and giving birth to the Son of God. Mary's yes is indicative of her faithful cooperation with God's plan of salvation both before and after the birth of Jesus. We might surmise that her yes didn't come all of a sudden out of nowhere. Mary's yes to Gabriel is indicative of how Mary must have lived her daily life from the moment of her own conception—being in tune with God's word, no doubt through the habit of a virtuous life and union with God through prayer.

This solemnity challenges us to say yes to whatever challenging word God sends our way and thus we, too, participate in God's ongoing plan of salvation. Mary participated in God's work of salvation in these ways: she was overshadowed by the Holy Spirit, the child born to her is the Son of God, and she said yes to God. We, too, have our "annunciation" by which the Spirit dwells within us, we bear Christ in the world today, and we are called to speak an ongoing yes to God. In these ways we, like Mary, participate in God's work of salvation. Our "annunciations" are in the ordinary, everyday circumstances that present us with the choice to say yes to God.

God's announcement of a divine word to us probably won't come in such an extraordinary way as an angel appearing to us. God's word does come to us through the ordinary people and circumstances of our everyday lives. God's word comes to us at liturgy and when we take personal time to pray. God's word comes to us at times of repentance and forgiveness. The challenge is to recognize God's word and respond with a faithful yes, as Mary responded to God and lived her whole life in cooperation with the divine plan of salvation. As Mary bore the Son of God, we are also to bear Christ within us—by our faithfully saying yes to God.

Living the Paschal Mystery

We don't know how many children St. Anne, the mother of Mary, bore, but we do believe that from the moment of conception Mary was free from sin. This is a privilege accorded her because she bore the Son of God, but it no doubt is also a privilege because she was always open to God's word for her and the direction her life should take. None of us live our lives without sin, but nonetheless, we can say yes to God's plan of salvation as Mary did. In our own times of prayer we can listen for the annunciation of a divine word, and we, too, can say "May it be done to me according to your word." Living the paschal mystery simply means conforming our will to God's. It means saying yes.

Focusing the Gospel

Key words and phrases: Holy Spirit . . . overshadow you, child to be born . . . Son of God, May it be done to me

To the point: Mary participated in God's work of salvation in these ways: she was overshadowed by the Holy Spirit, the child born to her is the Son of God, and she said yes to God. We, too, have our "annunciation" by which the Spirit dwells within us, we bear Christ in the world today, and we are called to speak an ongoing yes to God. In these ways we, like Mary, participate in God's work of salvation.

Model Act of Penitence

Presider: Mary, conceived without sin, faithfully said yes to God. We pause at the beginning of this celebration to examine our faithfulness in saying yes to God . . . [pause]

Lord Jesus, you are the holy One, the Son of God: Lord . . .

Christ Jesus, you are the incarnate One, the Son of Mary: Christ . . .

Lord Jesus, you are the Savior of the world: Lord . . .

Model Prayer of the Faithful

Presider: As surely as God showed favor to Mary, God will favor us and re-spond to the needs we now name in our prayer.

Response:

Lord, hear our prayer.

Cantor:

we pray to the Lord,

That Mary's motherhood be a model for how all members of the church live their yes to God . . . [pause]

That all peoples of the world share in the salvation of God . . . [pause]

That those who are unable to say yes to God's will be touched by the divine Word and be encouraged to say yes . . . [pause]

That we ourselves might participate in God's plan of salvation through our hearing God's word and saying yes to God's will . . . [pause]

Presider: Saving God, Mary the sinless one conceived and bore your only-begotten Son: hear these our prayers that we might draw closer to you and one day share in your everlasting glory. We ask this through that same Son, Jesus Christ our Lord. **Amen.**

FOR REFLECTION

• What helps me to respond to God with "May it be done to me" is . . .

• Like Mary, I have been invited to partici-pate in God's work of salvation for others when . . . by . . .

• One way I bear Christ in the world is . . .

Homily Points

• Mary's annunciation was extraordi-nary and dramatic: an angel appears and she conceives in any but an ordinary way. Our own annunciations are almost always quite ordinary and easy to miss. They are, however, so important in the overall plan of salvation.

• Mary's conception without sin and her holiness of life do not set her so apart from us that she cannot model for us the way we, too, are called to respond to God. Our "annunciations" come in the everyday events that draw us to say yes to God.

✚ SPIRITUALITY

GOSPEL ACCLAMATION
Isa 61:1 (cited in Luke 4:18)

℞. Alleluia, alleluia.
The Spirit of the Lord is upon me,
because he has anointed me
to bring glad tidings to the poor.
℞. Alleluia, alleluia.

Gospel

Luke 3:10-18; L9C

The crowds asked John the Baptist,
    "What should we do?"
He said to them in reply,
    "Whoever has two cloaks
    should share with the person
        who has none.
And whoever has food should do
    likewise."
Even tax collectors came to be
    baptized and they said to him,
"Teacher, what should we do?"
He answered them,
    "Stop collecting more than what
        is prescribed."
Soldiers also asked him,
    "And what is it that we should do?"
He told them,
    "Do not practice extortion,
    do not falsely accuse anyone,
    and be satisfied with your wages."

Now the people were filled with
    expectation,
    and all were asking in their hearts
    whether John might be the Christ.
John answered them all, saying,
    "I am baptizing you with water,
    but one mightier than I is coming.
I am not worthy to loosen the thongs of
    his sandals.
He will baptize you with the Holy Spirit
    and fire.
His winnowing fan is in his hand to
    clear his threshing floor
    and to gather the wheat into his barn,
    but the chaff he will burn with
        unquenchable fire."
Exhorting them in many other ways,
    he preached good news to the people.

Reflecting on the Gospel

"Rain, rain, go away, come again another day, so little N. can go out and play" is a children's chant that has been around for generations. The implication is that there is much more to do for children outdoors; cooped up inside the house, they often ask, "What should we do?" They are really asking about how they find something to do inside that is as interesting and wide open as the great outdoors. Outside, creativity abounds, expectations of finding new and interesting things are abundant, such as everything from discovery of a tiny new bug to learning how to do a new trick on a bike or skateboard. The question, "What should we do?" has a built-in set of expectations—if what we do is to be satisfying, it must fulfill our expectations and involve more than we are and are doing now.

In the gospel three groups of people ask the same question, "What should we do?" John exhorts them to define their obligations in right relation to others, just as John himself defines his role in relation to Jesus. The gospel, further, pivots on the people's "expectation." To whom were their expectations led? The Christ (the Messiah), yes, but also for another "who"—our neighbor. The "good news" is that our relationship with others makes visible our relation to Jesus. "What should we do?"

John's loaded answers about right living (his effective proclamation of the Good News) fill the people "with expectation." Their seeking "the Christ"—that is, the Messiah, the anointed one of God—means that they were seeking a new life. John answers them by using himself as the model for the ultimate answer to the question, "What should we do?" John denies being "the Christ" himself and announces that "one mightier than I is coming." Just like John, our lives are about others. And by being about others, we actually exceed ourselves and point people to the presence of Christ. Thus, the explicit question about what we are to do points to our natural desire for finding the ultimate One. We define ourselves not in terms of what we do but who we are in relation to Other and others. The *relationship* to others is the key, not what we or they do.

Living the Paschal Mystery

When we've ordered our lives in the minimal things—fulfilling the requirements of our state in life and job or ministry—then we can seek the greater things, the greater One. Our being baptized in the Holy Spirit means that we already share in divine life. This means that we are enabled to relate to Christ not as One "out there" but as One who is in our midst, one who is near. Relationships to others take on a whole new meaning because through them we enter into a unique relationship with the divine One.

In our daily living we, too, point to the One who is to come, first by doing well what is expected of us. Second and more important, we point to the One who is to come by being who we have become in Christ: the presence of Christ. We ourselves are to be the "mighty one" for others. Because of God's indwelling, the doing and being collapse into one: whatever it is we do, we always do so as bearers of Christ because we are "in Christ Jesus" (second reading). For this reason—we are the presence of the risen Christ for each other—nothing we do is small or inconsequential. Everything we do brings the Lord near to those around us.

Focusing the Gospel

Key words and phrases: What should we do? expectation, the Christ, good news for the people

To the point: In the gospel three groups of people ask the same question, "What should we do?" John exhorts them to define their obligations in relation to others, just as John himself defines his role in relation to Jesus. The gospel, further, pivots on the people's "expectation." To whom were their expectations led? The Christ (the Messiah), yes, but also for another "who"—our neighbor. The "good news" is that our relationship with others makes visible our relation to Jesus. "What should we do?"

Connecting the Gospel

to the first and second readings: These two readings open up for us what is at the basis of our relationships with each other and of the "good news to the people": "the LORD . . . is in your midst" (first reading) and "The Lord is near" (second reading).

to our experience: With so much to do in these hectic, final days before Christmas, we may find ourselves asking, "What should we do?" The gospel pushes us to answer the question on a deeper level than organizing busy holiday preparations.

Connecting the Responsorial Psalm

to the readings: It is easy to see the connection between this Sunday's readings and the verses from Isaiah we sing as the responsorial psalm. The first reading proclaims God "is in your midst." The second reading affirms "the Lord is near." The gospel portrays John the Baptist announcing "one mightier than I" is coming. No wonder we shout in the psalm refrain: "Cry out with joy and gladness, for among you is the great and Holy One of Israel."

But all is not joy and gladness in the gospel reading. John challenges his hearers to change their behavior. And he announces that when the Messiah does arrive he will sort the wheat from the chaff and burn what he does not want. Nonetheless, John's audience hears his exhortations as "good news." They hear the call to conversion and the imminence of judgment as heralds of the coming of the Holy One of Israel. They know the promise of renewal (first reading) is about to be fulfilled. May we with them give thanks, know peace (second reading), and sing for joy (psalm).

to psalmist preparation: How does your manner of living announce the presence of the Holy One?

ASSEMBLY & FAITH-SHARING GROUPS
- If I could ask John the Baptist, "What should I do?" he would say to me . . .
- Usually I define my life and myself according to . . .
- In order to define my life and myself more deeply in relation to Christ and others I would need to . . .

PRESIDERS
- My manner of living and preaching helps my parishioners know that they should . . .

DEACONS
- My service of others helps them understand that they are Christ for me when . . .

HOSPITALITY MINISTERS
- "Your kindness should be known to all" (second reading). What is known about me through my ministry is . . .

MUSIC MINISTERS
- "What should we do?" More than simply singing, at liturgy I lead others to . . . when . . .

ALTAR MINISTERS
- When I recollect that I, too, am serving—at the altar, in my daily life—"one mightier than I," then my service becomes . . .

LECTORS
- The last time the word of God made me "filled with expectation" and "asking in [my] heart" was . . .

EXTRAORDINARY MINISTERS OF HOLY COMMUNION
- Knowing that I distribute the Body or Blood of the One whose sandals "I am not worthy to loosen" challenges me to . . .

Model Act of Penitence

Presider: The gospel for today three times asks, "What should we do?" We pause at the beginning of this celebration and ask the same question of ourselves—in this busy time before Christmas, what is the Lord asking of us? . . . [pause]

Lord Jesus, you are the Christ, the Son of God: Lord . . .

Christ Jesus, you are the mighty One who dwells among us: Christ . . .

Lord Jesus, you are the Good News of salvation: Lord . . .

Homily Points

• "So-and-so is a tough act to follow." How often do we utter this when we are judged and measured against the accomplishments of another? Siblings struggle in school with comparisons, or athletes are often measured against the star player. Judgments usually include measurement against a perceived norm or expectation. In the gospel, John calls the people to measure themselves by another criterion—their relationship with others.

• To the question, "What should we do?" John's answer doesn't focus on accomplishments, but on relationships. Further, by his pointing beyond himself to Christ he models the very "norm" he sets up.

• For followers of Jesus the question, "What should we do?" is replaced by "How shall we be?"—kind, just, and loving toward each other. Or, still yet, the question is replaced by "*Who* shall we be?"—Christ for each other, that Christ who is the measure of all.

Model Prayer of the Faithful

Presider: As we rejoice in the coming of our Savior, we are emboldened to ask God for what we need.

Response:

Lord,   hear our prayer.

Cantor:

we pray to the Lord,

That all members of the church, baptized with the Holy Spirit and fire, point to the Christ who dwells among us . . . [pause]

That all peoples of the world come to salvation and rejoice in God's care and goodness . . . [pause]

That the poor and the lonely be embraced by the loving care and concern of this community . . . [pause]

That we each define ourselves as those in relationship to Christ our savior . . . [pause]

Presider: Mighty God, you sent John to announce the coming of your Son into the world: hear these our prayers that we might recognize his presence among us today. We ask this through that same Christ our Lord. **Amen.**

ALTERNATIVE OPENING PRAYER

Let us pray

Pause for silent prayer

Father of our Lord Jesus Christ,
ever faithful to your promises
and ever close to your Church:
the earth rejoices in hope of the Savior's
       coming
and looks forward with longing
to his return at the end of time.
Prepare our hearts and remove the
       sadness
that hinders us from feeling the joy and
       hope
which his presence will bestow,
for he is Lord for ever and ever. **Amen.**

FIRST READING

Zeph 3:14-18a

Shout for joy, O daughter Zion!
    Sing joyfully, O Israel!
Be glad and exult with all your heart,
    O daughter Jerusalem!
The LORD has removed the judgment
       against you,
    he has turned away your enemies;
the King of Israel, the LORD, is in your
       midst,
    you have no further misfortune to fear.
On that day, it shall be said to Jerusalem:
    Fear not, O Zion, be not discouraged!
The LORD, your God, is in your midst,
    a mighty savior;
he will rejoice over you with gladness,
    and renew you in his love,
he will sing joyfully because of you,
    as one sings at festivals.

RESPONSORIAL PSALM
Isa 12:2-3, 4, 5-6

R⃒. (6) Cry out with joy and gladness: for among you is the great and Holy One of Israel.

God indeed is my savior;
    I am confident and unafraid.
My strength and my courage is the LORD,
    and he has been my savior.
With joy you will draw water
    at the fountain of salvation.

R⃒. Cry out with joy and gladness: for among you is the great and Holy One of Israel.

Give thanks to the LORD, acclaim his name;
    among the nations make known his
        deeds,
    proclaim how exalted is his name.

R⃒. Cry out with joy and gladness: for among you is the great and Holy One of Israel.

Sing praise to the LORD for his glorious
    achievement;
    let this be known throughout all the
        earth.
Shout with exultation, O city of Zion,
    for great in your midst
    is the Holy One of Israel!

R⃒. Cry out with joy and gladness: for among you is the great and Holy One of Israel.

SECOND READING
Phil 4:4-7

Brothers and sisters:
Rejoice in the Lord always.
I shall say it again: rejoice!
Your kindness should be known to all.
The Lord is near.
Have no anxiety at all, but in everything,
    by prayer and petition, with
        thanksgiving,
    make your requests known to God.
Then the peace of God that surpasses all
    understanding
    will guard your hearts and minds in
        Christ Jesus.

About Liturgy

Ministry of the assembly: We hear much these days about the visible liturgical ministries (hospitality ministers, music ministers, altar ministers, lectors, eucharistic ministers). We also know that these ministries require preparation and formation. Rarely do we hear, however, about the ministry of the assembly itself. All these visible ministers—the presiders and deacons, and all the others who are present at any liturgy—together make up the *assembly*. We might think that the assembly is just *there* to pray and the visible ministers have all the *doing*. This isn't a very accurate assessment of the role of the assembly. A most important ministry at any liturgy is the *ministry of the assembly.*

To be sure, there is a *doing* on the part of the assembly: standing, sitting, kneeling, singing, responding, acclaiming, professing, etc. Sometimes we might fall into the trap of presuming that this is all the assembly does and this is all there is to participation. The most fruitful role of the assembly *comes out of* the doing. First and foremost, the liturgical assembly is the Body of Christ gathered around the Head. The assembly, then, makes visible the church, makes visible Christ. One fundamental role of the assembly is to be present to one another, to relate to each other as the presence of the risen Christ. This relational ministry of the assembly makes concrete and visible how we live our everyday lives: relating to each other as members of the Body of Christ. The ministry of the assembly is to be the Body of Christ made visible. Our very being there together to celebrate this most sacred act of praise and thanksgiving to God is, in itself, a kind of preaching the Good News. We learn from each other so that we might live what we preach.

About Liturgical Music

Music suggestions: This Sunday the focus of Advent turns from looking toward the return of Christ at the end of time to remembering his coming two thousand years ago. Accordingly, the texts of the songs we sing need to change focus. Appropriate hymns available in most hymnals include "O Come, O Come, Emmanuel"; "On Jordan's Bank"; "Savior of the Nations, Come"; "Come, O Long Expected Jesus"; "People, Look East"; and "Creator of the Stars of Night" (also titled "O Lord Who Made the Stars of Night"). Songs less widely available but also expressing the imminent expectation of the Christ Child's arrival include "Each Winter as You Grow Older" [G1, G2, GC, RS]; "Awake! Awake, and Greet the New Morn" [RS, WC, WS, W3, CBW3, SS]; and "Lift Up Your Heads" [GC2]. Since this is Gaudete Sunday, Delores Dufner's "Nations, Hear the Prophets Word," in *Sing a New Song* [OCP], would make an excellent choice for either the entrance or the recessional song.

✝ SPIRITUALITY

GOSPEL ACCLAMATION
Luke 1:38

R̸. Alleluia, alleluia.
Behold, I am the handmaid of the Lord.
May it be done to me according to your word.
R̸. Alleluia, alleluia.

Gospel

Luke 1:39-45; L12C

Mary set out
and traveled to the hill country
in haste
to a town of Judah,
where she entered the house of
Zechariah
and greeted Elizabeth.
When Elizabeth heard Mary's
greeting,
the infant leaped in her womb,
and Elizabeth, filled with the
Holy Spirit,
cried out in a loud voice and
said,
*"Blessed are you among women,
and blessed is the fruit of your
womb.*
And how does this happen to me,
that the mother of my Lord should
come to me?
For at the moment the sound of your
greeting reached my ears,
the infant in my womb leaped for joy.
Blessed are you who believed
that what was spoken to you by the
Lord
would be fulfilled."

Reflecting on the Gospel

TV show genres seem to be broadcast in cycles. For a few seasons dramas are most popular; sitcoms, game shows, and reality shows all seem to have their periodic appeal. Once in a while a spate of science fiction invades the airwaves. Here it seems that the most outlandish characters, with the most supernatural powers and the most enduring goodness, have greatest audience appeal. But in our wildest fictive imaginations we could not best the plan God has for our salvation!

In the gospel Mary "set[s] out" to visit the elderly Elizabeth who also is pregnant according to the word of Gabriel, so the meeting of these two women naturally promises something unusual! Mary was overshadowed by the Holy Spirit and the Son of God became incarnate within her; Elizabeth was "filled with the Holy Spirit" and announced the presence of her Lord. What imagination could come up with this scene? And who could best their blessedness and their power to change the course of history?

The gospel, in fact, announces two "incarnations": Jesus in the womb of Mary, and the Holy Spirit who filled Elizabeth. Although Elizabeth extols Mary for her belief in what would happen to her, it was also Elizabeth's belief that enabled her to conceive John as well as recognize the presence of the Savior in her midst through Mary. Our own belief enables the "incarnation" within us of both the presence of the risen Christ and the Holy Spirit. Blessed are they, and blessed are we to whom God comes and within whom God dwells.

On this last Sunday before Christmas we are gently led into the depths of the Christmas mystery. Jesus' incarnation was no Hallmark card. Already on this Sunday we are reminded that his life was one of obedience to his Father ("Behold, I come to do your will"; second reading) that meant offering his body for our salvation. Mary and Elizabeth show us the way to *our* being overshadowed by the Spirit by their offering their own bodies in cooperating with God's plan of salvation. Always our encounters with God lead to an annunciation of God's presence, an incarnation of that presence within each of us, and an unprecedented blessedness as we share in the very life of God.

Living the Paschal Mystery

God's plan of salvation is fulfilled by Christ's obedience to the Father's will (see second reading). The way the mystery moves from annunciation to fulfillment is by obedience. The same dynamic defines our Christian way of living: we are overshadowed by the Holy Spirit in baptism when, in the midst of the Christian community, the Lord's presence is announced. But our own annunciation only comes to fulfillment when we spend our lives incarnating Christ for others through the power of the Holy Spirit within us.

Think about this: doing God's will is an incarnation and annunciation! The circumstances of our surrender won't be as spectacular as Mary's and Elizabeth's, but our own surrender is no less fruitful. In our helping hand, God is present. In our visits to the sick and elderly, God is present. In our disciplining and forming our children, God is present. In all our daily dying to self, God is present. This is incarnation: God is present. This is the depths of the Christmas mystery: we, too, incarnate the divine presence! And this is no science fiction—it is God's plan of salvation.

Focusing the Gospel

Key words and phrases: Mary, Elizabeth, filled with the Holy Spirit, fruit of your womb, Blessed, believed

To the point: The gospel, in fact, announces two "incarnations": Jesus in the womb of Mary, and the Holy Spirit who filled Elizabeth. Although Elizabeth extols Mary for her belief in what would happen to her, it was also Elizabeth's belief that enabled her to conceive John as well as recognize the presence of the Savior in her midst through Mary. Our own belief enables the "incarnation" within us of both the presence of the risen Christ and the Holy Spirit. Blessed are they, and blessed are we to whom God comes and within whom God dwells.

Connecting the Gospel

to the second reading: Mary and Elizabeth's willingness to do God's will is brought to completion in Christ's "Behold, I come to do your will." They offered their bodies, and so did he.

to our experience: We all know that the birth of a child is not so much the end of a pregnancy as the beginning of a lifetime. So it is with Jesus' birth. Indeed, his birth and self-sacrifice ushered in more than a lifetime—they incarnated for us an eternity of salvation.

Connecting the Responsorial Psalm

to the readings: Psalm 80 was a lament the whole Israelite community raised at times of national destruction. The community begged God to "look down from heaven" and see their suffering, to "rouse . . . power and come to save" them. The "man of your right hand" prayed for in verse 18 was the king who represented them all. Like many laments this one contains a note of penitence. The people asked to be returned to God ("make us turn to you") so that they would no longer "withdraw" from divine love and presence. Like all laments this one rose on a note of faith: Israel begged God to act in their favor because they believed beyond doubt that God would.

For us the request that God show us the divine face (refrain) has been answered by the enfleshing of Christ in the womb of Mary (gospel). The request that God save us has been fulfilled by Christ offering his very body that we be consecrated (second reading). What remains for us is the call to believe as did Israel (first reading) and Mary and Elizabeth (gospel), that God will continue to come to save us. As we near this year's celebration of the birth of Christ, may we sing with their hope and confidence.

to psalmist preparation: As you prepare to sing this psalm, you might spend some time reflecting on where you see the face of God and where you struggle to see it. Is there any way you need to "turn" toward God so that you might better see?

**ASSEMBLY &
FAITH-SHARING GROUPS**

- I recognize Christ and the Holy Spirit "incarnated" in others when . . . in myself when . . .
- My blessing for believing in the Lord's word is . . .
- Like Elizabeth, I am amazed that "my Lord" should come to me and dwell within me. I express and share my joy by . . .

PRESIDERS

- Presiding demands more than sacrifices or offerings (see second reading). The will of God that Christ is inviting me to *live* now is . . .

DEACONS

- My diaconal service helps others to trust and believe that "what was spoken to [them] by the Lord would be fulfilled" by . . .

HOSPITALITY MINISTERS

- As Elizabeth welcomed and greeted Mary, she witnessed the presence of the Lord. In my ministry of hospitality I have witnessed *in* others and *to* others the presence of the Lord when . . .

MUSIC MINISTERS

- God comes to me through the singing of the assembly when . . .

ALTAR MINISTERS

- Serving others empties me of . . . so that Christ may be born in me.

LECTORS

- When I believe that the word is spoken by the Lord and will be fulfilled, my proclamation and living are like . . . When I doubt that word, my proclamation and living are like . . .

**EXTRAORDINARY MINISTERS
OF HOLY COMMUNION**

- Each communicant's *Amen* professes his or her willingness to do God's will and consecrates him or her in Christ (see second reading). My response to such belief is . . .

Model Act of Penitence

Presider: Believing the angel Gabriel, Mary sets out to visit her cousin Elizabeth who, "filled with the Holy Spirit," announces that her Lord is present. As we prepare for this liturgy let us open ourselves to God's presence . . . [pause]

> Lord Jesus, you are the One conceived by the power of the Holy Spirit: Lord . . .
> Christ Jesus, you are the blessed Fruit of Mary's womb: Christ . . .
> Lord Jesus, you obediently offered your body on the cross for our salvation: Lord . . .

Homily Points

• We live in a very logical society: we want proofs, we love our technological gimmicks, we avoid risks when we aren't sure something is trustworthy. But curiously, we are also a people of belief: we place our trust in surgeons, we act on the advice of certain persons, we take a risk whenever we try or do something new. We recognize that human growth and especially human relationships always entail a certain amount of trust and self-surrender. Nothing about what Mary and Elizabeth did was logical; they relied solely on their belief that God's word would be fulfilled and trusted in and surrendered to that word.

• The incarnation is more than a past historical event in which Mary and Elizabeth participated. God's presence among us is continued by the power of the Spirit and the obedience of the Son. Our own participation in God's work of salvation places each of us in a long line of followers of Christ who believe, do God's will, and offer themselves for the good of others. In this is our own blessedness.

• Elizabeth called Mary "[b]lessed . . . among women." We are perhaps uncomfortable thinking of ourselves as "blessed," but this is so precisely because we give ourselves over in the act of believing. Part of the work of belief is accepting our own goodness, our "incarnating" Christ and the Spirit in our lives, and recognizing in the relationships among us the very presence and blessedness of God.

Model Prayer of the Faithful

Presider: Because we believe in God's word and presence to us, let us pray for our needs.

Response:

Lord, hear our prayer.

Cantor:

we pray to the Lord,

May all members of the church faithfully announce the nearness of God by the goodness of their lives . . . [pause]

May all peoples of the world live in peace and justice, and thus announce the blessedness of God . . . [pause]

May the poor receive what they need to grow in belief in God's goodness . . . [pause]

May each of us celebrate the Christmas mystery with joyful sharing of God's presence with family and friends . . . [pause]

Presider: Gracious God, you visit your people in so many ways: hear these our prayers that our lives might always announce your nearness. We ask this through Christ our Lord. **Amen**.

FIRST READING
Mic 5:1-4a

Thus says the LORD:
You, Bethlehem-Ephrathah
    too small to be among the clans of
        Judah,
from you shall come forth for me
    one who is to be ruler in Israel;
whose origin is from of old,
    from ancient times.
Therefore the Lord will give them up, until
    the time
    when she who is to give birth has borne,
and the rest of his kindred shall return
    to the children of Israel.
He shall stand firm and shepherd his flock
    by the strength of the LORD,
    in the majestic name of the LORD, his
        God;
and they shall remain, for now his
    greatness
    shall reach to the ends of the earth;
    he shall be peace.

RESPONSORIAL PSALM

Ps 80:2-3, 15-16, 18-19

R̞. (4) Lord, make us turn to you; let us see your face and we shall be saved.

O shepherd of Israel, hearken,
  from your throne upon the cherubim,
    shine forth.
Rouse your power,
  and come to save us.

R̞. Lord, make us turn to you; let us see your face and we shall be saved.

Once again, O LORD of hosts,
  look down from heaven, and see;
take care of this vine,
  and protect what your right hand has
    planted,
  the son of man whom you yourself
    made strong.

R̞. Lord, make us turn to you; let us see your face and we shall be saved.

May your help be with the man of your
    right hand,
  with the son of man whom you yourself
    made strong.
Then we will no more withdraw from you;
  give us new life, and we will call upon
    your name.

R̞. Lord, make us turn to you; let us see your face and we shall be saved.

SECOND READING

Heb 10:5-10

Brothers and sisters:
When Christ came into the world, he said:
  "Sacrifice and offering you did not
    desire,
  but a body you prepared for me;
  in holocausts and sin offerings you took
    no delight.
  Then I said, 'As is written of me in the
    scroll,
  behold, I come to do your will, O God.'"

First he says, "Sacrifices and offerings,
  holocausts and sin offerings,
  you neither desired nor delighted in."
These are offered according to the law.
Then he says, "Behold, I come to do your
    will."
He takes away the first to establish the
    second.
By this "will," we have been consecrated
  through the offering of the body of
    Jesus Christ once for all.

About Liturgy

Announcing the Christmas mystery: Opportunities for us to announce the Christmas mystery abound. Here are two clusters of possibilities.

First, with respect to the ritual "tangibles." The way we enhance the sacred space for Christmas, the music we choose, the way people who come (especially those who have been away from church for a while) are greeted all beg us to think about how we want to announce the Christmas mystery. Is the focus almost entirely on a Babe who was born long ago? If so, there is the real danger that Christmas will come and go without affecting us and the way we live. Our Christmas preparations and celebrations must lead us to the deeper mystery: Christmas is a salvation feast that reminds us this Babe whose birth we celebrate was obedient even to death on a cross. The mystery of birth always enfolds the mystery of death. Our environment, music, hospitality, etc., all must affect us in such a way that we are led to announce the Christmas mystery as God's presence to humanity and make that presence known in the goodness of our daily living.

Second, with respect to the liturgy itself. Liturgy always makes demands on us: the word proclaimed, the homily's challenge, the Creed's demands, the intercession's follow-through, Communion's unity. All preparation for liturgy must open the space for the Spirit to work within the community so that liturgy, truly, transforms us into being better and more fruitful presences of Christ. The deepest and most lasting joy of Christmas spills beyond the liturgy into making the world a better place to be, a place of peace and good will to all. The liturgy itself must be celebrated in such a way as to lead us to announce in our daily living that we believe with all our hearts that the Lord is come and dwells within each of us.

About Liturgical Music

Music suggestions: Herman G. Stuempfle's "The Night Will Soon Be Ending," in *Awake our Heart to Praise!* [GIA], combines the sense of hope in the imminent dawn of Christ with the reality of our ongoing struggle with darkness: "The night will soon be ending; the dawn cannot be far. . . . Yet nights will still bring sadness and rob our hearts of peace. . . . God dwells with us in darkness and makes the night as day." This hymn would be a fitting choice for the entrance procession; if the procession will not be long enough to accommodate all verses, the choir alone could sing it as a prelude. "See How the Virgin Waits" [JS2, OFUV] would be appropriate during the preparation of the gifts, as would "Emmanuel" [PWB, WC, WS] for Communion.

John A. Dalles's "We Blew No Trumpet Blasts to Sound," in *Swift Currents and Still Waters* [GIA], would make a thought-provoking post- Communion hymn as we enter this last week of Advent : "We blew no trumpet blasts. . . . We built no bonfire. . . . We spread no welc'ming canopy. . . . [instead] We hurried through another week, unheeding, and unmoved. . . . Dear God, how unprepared we were to welcome Jesus, then. We pray you, help us not to miss your priceless gift again."

DECEMBER 20, 2009
FOURTH SUNDAY OF ADVENT

Season of Christmas

To whom are you like,

glad Babe, fair little One,

whose mother is a virgin,

whose Father is hidden,

who even the Seraphim are not able to look upon?

Tell us who you are like,

O Son of the gracious One!

—St. Ephraim the Syrian
Nineteen Hymns on the Nativity of Christ in the Flesh
Hymn IX

SPIRITUALITY

The Vigil Mass

GOSPEL ACCLAMATION

R̸. Alleluia, alleluia.
Tomorrow the wickedness of the earth will be
   destroyed:
the Savior of the world will reign over us.
R̸. Alleluia, alleluia.

Gospel

Matt 1:1-25; L13 ABC

The book of the
   genealogy of Jesus
   Christ,
   the son of David,
      the son of
         Abraham.

Abraham became the
   father of Isaac,
   Isaac the father of
      Jacob,
   Jacob the father of
      Judah and his
      brothers.
Judah became the
   father of Perez and Zerah,
   whose mother was Tamar.
Perez became the father of Hezron,
   Hezron the father of Ram,
   Ram the father of Amminadab.
Amminadab became the father of
   Nahshon,
   Nahshon the father of Salmon,
   Salmon the father of Boaz,
   whose mother was Rahab.
Boaz became the father of Obed,
   whose mother was Ruth.
Obed became the father of Jesse,
   Jesse the father of David the king.

Continued in Appendix A, p. 262

or Matt 1:18-25 in Appendix A, p. 262.

See Appendix A, p. 263, for the other readings.

Reflecting on the Gospel and Living the Paschal Mystery

Key words and phrases: birth of Jesus Christ, through the Holy Spirit, *Emmanuel . . .* "God is with us."

To the point: How much Joseph must have loved Mary, since he was "unwilling to expose her to shame"! How much Joseph must have loved God, since he did all that "the angel of the Lord commanded him." Isaiah in the first reading describes how much *God loves us* by using espousal imagery to portray the intimate relationship God wishes to have with us. Jesus is the very incarnation of God's love and presence, for he is "*Emmanuel . . .* 'God is with us.'"

Reflection: DNA research and testing have come a long way in the past few decades. It has been used to prove some prisoners were wrongly convicted. It has been used to match organ donors. It has been used to verify paternity. We human beings have a DNA identity that is unique and so telling that it reveals our bloodline with almost 100 percent certainty. The longer reading of the gospel selection for the Vigil Mass of Christmas includes the genealogy of Jesus—kind of Matthew's account of Jesus' DNA. Matthew wants to identify Jesus as the son of David, whose descendant says Paul (in the second reading) is to be the savior. But the first reading reminds us that this Son cannot be traced only by human ancestral lines—not even by our advanced DNA testing. This Son fulfills God's promise through Isaiah that God "will not be silent." The *Word* God speaks in Jesus is unprecedented—he is the very incarnation of divinity.

How much Joseph must have loved Mary, since he was "unwilling to expose her to shame"! How much Joseph must have loved God, since he did all that "the angel of the Lord commanded him." Joseph (and Mary) model for us the depths of love to which we humans are really capable. They show us a love that is kind and merciful, gentle and compassionate, just and peaceful. How we long for this love! At the same time we celebrate Joseph's and Mary's faithfulness, the mystery of Christmas turns us toward the mighty deeds of God worked through them. Joseph and Mary were instruments of God's love borne anew into the world.

Isaiah in the first reading describes how much *God loves us* by using espousal imagery to portray the intimate relationship God wishes to have with us. Jesus is the very incarnation of God's love and presence, for he is "*Emmanuel . . .* 'God is with us.'" The mystery we celebrate is not only beyond the science of DNA testing, it is really beyond our wildest imagination. This mystery reveals our creator God's intimate love for us creatures, shows us how God prepared for our salvation from the very beginning, and how God desires to be one with us creatures. This day we celebrate God's love for us and the divine presence to us.

All the readings for the Vigil Mass are still anticipatory of Jesus' birth. This would be even appropriate on Christmas day itself because the readings remind us that we always anticipate the coming of Christ; his coming is never completed. In this sense we celebrate Christmas every day, each time we cooperate with the Spirit who dwells within each of us, who overshadows us, who enables us to say yes to God. Our own yes is an incarnation of God's love for us that was so lavishly portrayed on that first Christmas night. Our own yes is an announcement of the intimate relationship God desires with each of us. Christmas celebrates the love of God for us expressed in the mightiest deed of salvation: *Emmanuel*—"God is with us."

✠ SPIRITUALITY

Mass at Midnight

GOSPEL ACCLAMATION
Luke 2:10-11

R⁊. Alleluia, alleluia.
I proclaim to you good news of great joy:
today a Savior is born for us,
Christ the Lord.
R⁊. Alleluia, alleluia.

Gospel

Luke 2:1-14; L14ABC

In those days a decree went
   out from Caesar Augustus
   that the whole world should
   be enrolled.
This was the first enrollment,
   when Quirinius was
   governor of Syria.
So all went to be enrolled,
   each to his own town.
And Joseph too went up from
   Galilee from the town of
   Nazareth
to Judea, to the city of David that is
   called Bethlehem,
because he was of the house and
   family of David,
to be enrolled with Mary, his
   betrothed, who was with child.
While they were there,
   the time came for her to have her child,
   and she gave birth to her firstborn son.
She wrapped him in swaddling clothes
   and laid him in a manger,
because there was no room for them
   in the inn.

Continued in Appendix A, p. 263.

See Appendix A, p. 264, for the other readings.

Reflecting on the Gospel and Living the Paschal Mystery

Key words and phrases: Joseph too went up, she gave birth, glory of the Lord shone, Glory to God, on earth peace

To the point: Contrasting images abound in this gospel. On the one hand, it speaks of the hardship of a long journey from Nazareth to Bethlehem undertaken in obedience to an earthly ruler, of the poverty of a manger crib, of the inhospitality suffered by stranger travelers. On the other hand, the gospel speaks of angels appearing, of praise-filled glory given tongue, of unbounded joy and peace proclaimed. Of such is Christmas: a festival of contrasts. The bridge between these contrasts is obedience—both human and divine.

Reflection: If there is any time of year that we might call a time of lights, surely it is now, in December. Many TV stations ask viewers to send in pictures of their outdoor Christmas decorations and announce the number of light bulbs—sometimes up to several million. We ooh and ah over lights—the more the better. How heart-warming it is to drive through our neighborhoods to look at the outdoor light displays. Even in totally strange neighborhoods we feel welcome. How heart-wrenching it is to turn onto a street that is dark, where no one has displayed the warmth of welcome. Isaiah (in the first reading) announces that "The people who walked in darkness have seen a great light." Far more than lights on a string, this Light we welcome into our midst is a divine person, "the appearance of the glory of our great God" (second reading).

Only twice a year (now, and at the Easter Vigil) does the church gather in the deep darkness of night to celebrate the mystery of salvation. At night—when most are asleep and all is quiet—does God burst into mortal human dominion from "His dominion [that] is vast and forever peaceful" (first reading). At night, in the quiet, is the time when perhaps we are most able to hear the mighty Word of God in our humble midst and join with the heavenly choir to speak God's glory. At night, in the rest, are we perhaps best able to contemplate all God does for us by becoming incarnate, by dwelling among us.

On this night we celebrate the joy of a divine birth. No wonder contrasting images abound in this gospel, for who ever heard of a divine birth? On the one hand, the gospel speaks of the hardship of a long journey from Nazareth to Bethlehem undertaken in obedience to an earthly ruler, of the poverty of a manger crib, of the inhospitality suffered by stranger travelers. On the other hand, the gospel speaks of angels appearing, of praise-filled glory given tongue, of unbounded joy and peace proclaimed. Of such is Christmas: a festival of contrasts. The bridge between these contrasts is obedience—both human and divine. Mary and Joseph were obedient to God's will for salvation. Jesus was obedient to the same will as he "deliver[ed] us" and "cleanse[d] for himself a people as his own" (second reading). We are invited, then, not only to hear the "Glory to God in the highest" but also invited to our own life of obedience to God's will by "liv[ing] temperately, justly, and devoutly" (second reading).

Mary gave birth "to her firstborn son." In this she also gave birth to a way of life—this birth is more than about one life; it is about the life of all. Our own obedience to God, our faithfulness in following Jesus, is a birth of justice and peace for our world. It is our own incarnation of God's reign of favor.

SPIRITUALITY

Mass at Dawn

GOSPEL ACCLAMATION
Luke 2:14

R℣. Alleluia, alleluia.
Glory to God in the highest,
and on earth peace to those
on whom his favor rests.
R℣. Alleluia, alleluia.

Gospel

Luke 2:15-20; L15ABC

When the angels went away
    from them to heaven,
  the shepherds said to one
        another,
  "Let us go, then, to Bethlehem
  to see this thing that has
        taken place,
  which the Lord has made
        known to us."
So they went in haste and found
    Mary and Joseph,
  and the infant lying in the manger.
When they saw this,
  they made known the message
  that had been told them about this
        child.
All who heard it were amazed
  by what had been told them by the
        shepherds.
And Mary kept all these things,
  reflecting on them in her heart.
Then the shepherds returned,
  glorifying and praising God
  for all they had heard and seen,
  just as it had been told to them.

See Appendix A, p. 264, for the other readings.

Reflecting on the Gospel and Living the Paschal Mystery
Key words and phrases: Let us go; found . . . the infant; returned, glorifying and praising God

To the point: It didn't take much for shepherds to abandon their sheep and follow up on the preposterous message of angels! They saw the infant for themselves and then they "returned, glorifying and praising God." To whom or what did they return? To their sheep? To their former way of a shepherding life? Maybe to some shepherds who didn't go with them to find the infant? Yes, most likely, but with a difference. Their encounter with this infant stirred in them hearts now raised in glory and praise of God. This simple encounter with a humble "infant lying in a manger" changes lives.

Reflection: Childlike playfulness never quite abandons even the most mature and serious of us adults. When pleasantly surprised, we might react with bodily glee and even wriggle in delight. At an NFL game one Sunday afternoon when snow was falling rather heavily, one of the big, burly players scooped up some snow, squeezed it into a ball, and threw it at one of his teammates with the camera capturing the most mischievous grin on his face. The unexpected often causes us to act out of character. The shepherds in this gospel surely met with the unexpected: angels appearing to them in the heavens. They could have ignored this as a figment of their imaginations. Maybe the darkness and stars were playing tricks on them during this long, winter night. But, no, something had stirred in their hearts. An announcement of the in-breaking of God's presence arouses more in us than a curious response. The shepherds responded "in haste" to this strange message they heard from angels. Their willingness to act out of character and follow divine promptings brought them to an infant who was divine presence. It brought them face to face with a revelation that they had to make known.

It didn't take much for shepherds to abandon their sheep and follow up on the preposterous message of angels! They saw the infant for themselves and then they "returned, glorifying and praising God." To whom or what did they return? To their sheep? To their former way of a shepherding life? Maybe to some shepherds who didn't go with them to find the infant? Yes, most likely all this, but when they returned they were different. Their encounter with this infant stirred in them hearts now raised in glory and praise of God. This simple encounter with a humble "infant lying in a manger" changes lives.

We, too, are changed by our encounters with this Savior born to us. We are now called "the holy people" (first reading), those "justified by his grace" and "heirs in hope of eternal life" (second reading). The issue, however, isn't that we are changed automatically by divine encounter; the issue is that we must recognize and respond to divine encounter. Unlike the shepherds who had angels appear to them, our encounters are much more modest but no less real. We encounter the Savior in the sick and suffering to whom we extend a healing hand, in the child who needs moral guidance, in the beleaguered parent who needs an encouraging word, in a lonesome youth who needs a friend. The presence of these human beings we encounter each day changes, us, too. We need to reflect upon the mystery of divine presence coming to us every day in human flesh.

✠ SPIRITUALITY

Mass during the Day

GOSPEL ACCLAMATION
R. Alleluia, alleluia.
A holy day has dawned upon us.
Come, you nations, and adore the Lord.
For today a great light has come upon the earth.
R. Alleluia, alleluia.

Gospel

John 1:1-18; L16ABC

In the beginning was the
    Word,
    and the Word was with
        God,
    and the Word was God.
He was in the beginning
    with God.
All things came to be
    through him,
    and without him nothing
        came to be.
What came to be through
    him was life,
    and this life was the light of the
        human race;
the light shines in the darkness,
    and the darkness has not
        overcome it.

A man named John was sent from God.
He came for testimony, to testify to the
    light,
    so that all might believe through him.
He was not the light,
    but came to testify to the light.

Continued in Appendix A, p. 265

or John 1:1-5, 9-14 in Appendix A, p. 265.

See Appendix A, p. 265–266, for the other readings.

Reflecting on the Gospel and Living the Paschal Mystery

Key words and phrases: In the beginning, the Word was God, Word became flesh, made his dwelling among us

To the point: How lofty a meditation this gospel offers us on this Christmas day when we celebrate the birth of Jesus! From the very beginning this new Life we celebrate was God, was the source of created life, was the light that dispelled the darkness of nothingness. But John doesn't stay with these lofty thoughts. He also affirms that "the Word became flesh and made his dwelling among us." This divine One who was "[i]n the beginning" before all creation deigned to take on our humanity, to dwell among us not as a deity but as one who gave himself in suffering and death so that we might have "purification from sins" (second reading).

Reflection: "In the beginning . . ." Sometimes this phrase brings to mind something easy to remember, such as the happiness and bliss of a wedding day, the optimism on the first day of a new job, teary-eyed parents as they send their little one off to school for the first time. Sometimes this phrase leaves the mind in a fog, as when we try to remember the first time we tried to print our name or what we wore on our very first night of Halloween trick or treating. Some things, such as our first steps or first words, simply can't be remembered. Video cameras now might bring images of a birth or blowing out a first birthday cake candle, but these images are new information for us—our minds don't really *remember* these early life events. This gospel opens with the words, "In the beginning." None of us can reach back the incalculable stretch of years to this beginning, because there really wasn't a beginning: God is eternal, has no beginning. The image, however, is telling: from all eternity "was the Word," and this is the evangelist's way of giving an account of Jesus' participation in divinity. Indeed, "the Word was God."

How lofty a meditation this gospel offers us on this Christmas day when we celebrate the birth of Jesus! From the very beginning this new Life we celebrate was God, was the source of created life, was the light that dispelled the darkness of nothingness. But John doesn't stay with these lofty thoughts. He also affirms that "the Word became flesh and made his dwelling among us." This divine One who was "[i]n the beginning" before all creation deigned to take on our humanity, to dwell among us not as a deity but as one who gave himself in suffering and death so that we might have "purification from sins" (second reading).

But the act of self-giving of this divine One comes full circle, for from "his fullness we have all received." Indeed, through him we "become children of God." Through this birth we ourselves are rebirthed into divine life itself. The One who took on our human flesh and dwelled among us is the "Father's only Son," he who chooses to be present to us in such an intimate way that we are made more perfectly into his image and likeness through the "grace and truth" he brings. The "glad tidings" (first reading) this birth brings is the Good News of salvation, the good news that God dwells among us and is present to us in a whole new way.

Our salvation is nothing less than our own openness to the inpouring of God's divine life within us, made possible by this birth. Our salvation is nothing less than the grace and truth of our own lives, lived in the simple acts of care and love for each other. Our minds don't remember "[i]n the beginning," but the goodness of our lives does make present that time of beginning, when God loved us so much to give us life.

Model Act of Penitence

Presider: Today we celebrate the birth of the incarnate Son of God, Jesus our Savior. As we prepare to celebrate this liturgy, may we open our hearts to God's loving presence to us as beloved sons and daughters . . . [pause]

Lord Jesus, you were born of Mary: Lord . . .

Christ Jesus, you are *Emmanuel*, God with us: Christ . . .

Lord Jesus, you are the Prince of peace: Lord . . .

Model Prayer of the Faithful

Presider: As we celebrate the God who gives *the* gift of the Son, we are encouraged to ask for what we need.

Response:

Lord, hear our prayer.

Cantor:

we pray to the Lord,

For the people of God, the continued presence of divine Love in the world . . . [pause]

For all peoples of the world, called from darkness into the Light . . . [pause]

For the poor and the lonely, the sick and the suffering, all the beloved children of God . . . [pause]

For each of us here, called to act with justice and to live in peace . . . [pause]

Presider: O saving God, you sent your only-begotten Son into the world to be your presence among us: hear these our prayers that we might one day enjoy everlasting life with you and your incarnate Son, Jesus Christ our Lord. **Amen.**

ALTERNATIVE OPENING PRAYER

(from the Mass during the Day)

Let us pray

Pause for silent prayer

God of love, Father of all,
the darkness that covered the earth
has given way to the bright dawn of your
    Word made flesh.
Make us a people of this light.
Make us faithful to your Word,
that we may bring your life to the waiting
    world.
Grant this through Christ our Lord. **Amen.**

FOR REFLECTION

• I am called to continue Jesus' incarnation in the world by . . .
• I encounter the closeness of Emmanuel, "God with us," in . . .
• God's self-gift to us is the divine Son. My gift of self to others is . . .

Homily Points

• Society acts as if Christmas is merely a day: Christmas carols are off the air by December 26, Christmas trees are already at the curb, department store Christmas decorations are already gone. However, the Christmas readings clearly tell us that Christmas is a lifetime.

• Christmas celebrates the Light in the darkness, the Word dwelling among us, the people who come to adore. These are not images for a day, but rather are invitations into the very mystery of how God's love is present to us each day.

• The God who did not make the universe in a day ("[i]n the beginning") never ceases sending divine Love into our world. Emmanuel not only came at a specific moment in history; Emmanuel is among us throughout all time. Even more: we are the human flesh that continues to make Emmanuel present.

✝ SPIRITUALITY

GOSPEL ACCLAMATION
Col 3:15a, 16a

℟. Alleluia, alleluia.
Let the peace of Christ control your hearts;
let the word of Christ dwell in you richly.
℟. Alleluia, alleluia.

Gospel   Luke 2:41-52; L17C

Each year Jesus' parents went to
    Jerusalem for the feast of Passover,
  and when he was twelve years old,
  they went up according to festival
    custom.
After they had completed its days, as
    they were returning,
  the boy Jesus remained behind in
    Jerusalem,
  but his parents did not know it.
Thinking that he was in the caravan,
  they journeyed for a day
  and looked for him among their
    relatives and acquaintances,
  but not finding him,
  they returned to Jerusalem to look for
    him.
After three days they found him in the
    temple,
  sitting in the midst of the teachers,
  listening to them and asking them
    questions,
  and all who heard him were astounded
  at his understanding and his answers.

Continued in Appendix A, p. 266.

Reflecting on the Gospel

Dad and four-year-old Adam were at a family funeral. As is usually the case at such occasions, reminiscing abounded among the gathered family members, especially about all the fun when the family gathered at the family home. Dad asked who lived in that house now and discovered it was one of the cousins who was also present for the funeral. Dad asked if he could visit the home and property, explaining that he wanted to show his son where he played when he was his son's age. Dad wanted to show his son firsthand what he valued from his own childhood: happy memories of playtime with extended family, rootedness in home and land, the importance of tradition. This feast and these readings remind us that being a "holy" family isn't a matter of being obsessively religious and pietistic. It is a matter of valuing the memories, families, and traditions that make us who we are.

The gospel opens with a telling detail: the Holy Family goes to Jerusalem each year at Passover, the Jewish feast that recalls Israel's identity as the family of God's people. Mary and Joseph consciously formed Jesus in the traditions and memories of the family of Israel. We, too, belong to a larger family, for we are "the children of God" (second reading). This larger family is not something abstract but very concrete: our being members of God's holy family is expressed in our own nuclear families, where we build our identities from the traditions of goodness and values we pass on from generation to generation.

The model the Holy Family provides us is one of fidelity to traditions and obedience to who they were. They teach us that holiness means we are "in [our] Father's house," because there we learn our religious traditions and form the memories that make us who we are as members of the larger family of God. They teach us that we really belong to God, and everything about our living must reflect that we are most at home "in [our] Father's house."

The Holy Family also models for us the importance of the nuclear family for nourishing and strengthening our religious identity. In our everyday family living we are called to the same obedience to which Mary and Joseph called Jesus, for it is in giving ourselves over to God's will that we, too, advance in "wisdom and age and favor before God" and all those who know us. Our nuclear families are the school of holiness, for there we learn the memories and traditions that make us who we are.

Living the Paschal Mystery

The familiarity of family life can sometimes blind us to see the goodness in each other. This feast reminds us to open our eyes and be "astonished" at the goodness of each other rather than anxious about our own concerns. Families grow in strength when each person in the family—from parents to the smallest child to anyone extended the hospitality of family—is treated as a member of God's family and, therefore, holy.

This is challenging when sometimes all we can see is each other's faults. It takes a great deal of dying to self to get beyond the normal, everyday annoyances that are part of family life and see others as holy and deserving of our honor, love, and respect. Mary and Joseph were not free from family struggles; after all, they lost Jesus on a trip! And when they found him they had to struggle to understand who he was and who he was meant to become. In doing so, they were able to help Jesus grow in wisdom, age, and grace. In this same way we help each other in our families grow to full maturity as members of the household of God.

Focusing the Gospel

Key words and phrases: went to Jerusalem, Passover, advanced in wisdom and age and favor

To the point: The gospel opens with a telling detail: the Holy Family goes to Jerusalem each year at Passover, the Jewish feast that recalls Israel's identity as the family of God's people. Mary and Joseph consciously formed Jesus in the traditions and memories of the family of Israel. We, too, belong to a larger family, for we are "the children of God" (second reading). This larger family is not something abstract but very concrete: our being members of God's holy family is expressed in our own nuclear families, where we build our identities from the traditions of goodness and values we pass on from generation to generation.

Connecting the Gospel

to the first reading: Hannah models returning to God the most treasured of what God has given her when she hands Samuel over to Eli in the temple at Shiloh. Mary and Joseph are learning to do the same when Jesus stays in his "Father's house."

to our experience: Like Mary and Joseph in this gospel story, we often do not understand events as they are unfolding. We must ponder their meaning as we continue on with the ordinary affairs of daily life. In this way making memory (pondering) becomes a means of grace.

Connecting the Responsorial Psalm

to the readings: On this feast of the Holy Family the psalm refrain identifies as blessed those who dwell in the house of the Lord. Hannah and Elkanah (first reading), Mary and Joseph (gospel) show us that to dwell in the house of the Lord means to keep God and God's law as the center of one's life. Both sets of parents are faithful to the cultic demands of the covenant with God. They travel regularly to Jerusalem for the temple celebrations. They are faithful to prayer—to offering sacrifice, to persisting in petition, to contemplating what of God's ways they do not yet understand. Above all they acknowledge that the offspring given them belong to God, Hannah and Elkanah without hesitation, Mary and Joseph with as yet incomplete understanding.

This feast calls us to the same focus: to stay centered on God, faithful to communal worship and personal prayer, and steadfast in granting God first place in the hearts of the children given to our care. Thus will we who "are God's children" (second reading) dwell in God's house and be called blessed.

to psalmist preparation: The context of the readings suggests the "dwelling place" you sing about in this responsorial psalm is not a building but a way of life. When you sing the refrain for the first time during the Liturgy of the Word, can you look upon the assembly as the "blessed" who are faithful to this way of life? What difference might this make in the way you sing and the manner you gesture?

**ASSEMBLY &
FAITH-SHARING GROUPS**

- My most treasured family memories are . . . They shape me in holiness in that . . .

- The religious traditions I value most are . . . because . . .

- My family calls me to holiness by . . . My family models holiness when . . .

PRESIDERS

- I am helping families realize that "we are God's children now" (second reading) by . . .

DEACONS

- My ministry enriches my family by . . . My ministry has distracted me from my family when . . .

HOSPITALITY MINISTERS

- My hospitality—whether with my family or the parish family—helps others be comfortable in God's house when . . .

MUSIC MINISTERS

- My music ministry leads the assembly to experience themselves as God's holy family when . . .

ALTAR MINISTERS

- What my ministry of service has taught me about being a holy family is . . .

LECTORS

- I model what it truly means to listen to and ponder God's word as did the Holy Family when . . .

**EXTRAORDINARY MINISTERS
OF HOLY COMMUNION**

- I model holiness by the manner in which I distribute Holy Communion by . . .

Model Act of Penitence

Presider: We gather here as God's holy family called to model our values and behaviors on those of Jesus, Mary, and Joseph. Let us prepare ourselves to celebrate this liturgy by opening our hearts to continue to grow in the holiness to which we have been called . . . [pause]

Lord Jesus, you show us the way to holiness: Lord . . .

Christ Jesus, you call us to grow in wisdom and grace: Christ . . .

Lord Jesus, you were faithful to the will of both your heavenly Father and of Mary and Joseph: Lord . . .

Homily Points

• We often hear people say, "Oh, you're just like your mother [or your father]." We learn (often subconsciously) our behavior patterns and values within a family. Our identity within our own families is passed on through memory, often revealed in the stories we tell. Our identity is also (and even especially) passed on through our behavior—our memories made flesh.

• As son, Jesus was learning from Mary and Joseph; but he was also listening to a deeper voice. This gospel story shows us two sources for learning behaviors and values. Jesus dwelt in his "Father's house" as well as in the house of Joseph and Mary in Nazareth.

• We gather around the word in our "Father's house" to refresh our memories of Jesus' behavior that speak to our experience and challenge us to growth in goodness and gospel values.

Model Prayer of the Faithful

Presider: Let us ask the God who forms us into a holy family to give us all we need.

Response:

Cantor:

For all members of the community of the church, the family of God . . . [pause]

For the peoples of the world, the family of humanity . . . [pause]

For families suffering loss, division, or hardship . . . [pause]

For ourselves gathered here, the parish family . . . [pause]

Presider: Gracious God, you gave us your Son who calls us to be your children: hear these our prayers that our families may be strengthened in our dedication to you and one day be with you for ever and ever. **Amen.**

OPENING PRAYER
Let us pray

Pause for silent prayer

Father,
help us to live as the holy family,
united in respect and love.
Bring us to the joy and peace of your
   eternal home.

Grant this through our Lord Jesus Christ,
   your Son,
who lives and reigns with you and the
   Holy Spirit,
one God, for ever and ever. **Amen.**

FIRST READING
1 Sam 1:20-22, 24-28

In those days Hannah conceived, and at
   the end of her term bore a son
   whom she called Samuel, since she had
      asked the LORD for him.
The next time her husband Elkanah was
   going up
   with the rest of his household
   to offer the customary sacrifice to the
      LORD and to fulfill his vows,
   Hannah did not go, explaining to her
      husband,
   "Once the child is weaned,
   I will take him to appear before the LORD
   and to remain there forever;
   I will offer him as a perpetual nazirite."

Once Samuel was weaned, Hannah
   brought him up with her,
   along with a three-year-old bull,
   an ephah of flour, and a skin of wine,
   and presented him at the temple of the
      LORD in Shiloh.
After the boy's father had sacrificed the
   young bull,
   Hannah, his mother, approached Eli and
      said:
   "Pardon, my lord!
As you live, my lord,
   I am the woman who stood near you
      here, praying to the LORD.
I prayed for this child, and the LORD
   granted my request.
Now I, in turn, give him to the LORD;
   as long as he lives, he shall be dedicated
      to the LORD."
Hannah left Samuel there.

RESPONSORIAL PSALM
Ps 84:2-3, 5-6, 9-10

℟. (cf. 5a) Blessed are they who dwell in
your house, O Lord.

How lovely is your dwelling place, O LORD
   of hosts!

My soul yearns and pines for the courts
of the LORD.
My heart and my flesh cry out for the
living God.

R̦. Blessed are they who dwell in your
house, O Lord.

Happy they who dwell in your house!
Continually they praise you.
Happy the men whose strength you are!
Their hearts are set upon the
pilgrimage.

R̦. Blessed are they who dwell in your
house, O Lord.

O LORD of hosts, hear our prayer;
hearken, O God of Jacob!
O God, behold our shield,
and look upon the face of your
anointed.

R̦. Blessed are they who dwell in your
house, O Lord.

SECOND READING
1 John 3:1-2, 21-24

Beloved:
See what love the Father has bestowed
on us
that we may be called the children of
God.
And so we are.
The reason the world does not know us
is that it did not know him.
Beloved, we are God's children now;
what we shall be has not yet been
revealed.
We do know that when it is revealed we
shall be like him,
for we shall see him as he is.

Beloved, if our hearts do not condemn us,
we have confidence in God and receive
from him whatever we ask,
because we keep his commandments
and do what pleases him.
And his commandment is this:
we should believe in the name of his
Son, Jesus Christ,
and love one another just as he
commanded us.
Those who keep his commandments
remain in him, and he in them,
and the way we know that he remains
in us
is from the Spirit he gave us.

*See Appendix A, pp. 266–267, for
optional readings.*

About Liturgy

Choice of readings: The revised Lectionary on some festivals has provided readings for all three years of the Lectionary cycle. The feast of the Holy Family is one such festival. In order to plumb the riches of the Lectionary the *Living Liturgy*™ team has chosen to go with the proper readings now given for each year; hence, these reflections are based on the readings that may be used for year C.

Strengthening family life: The church provides us with two celebrations helpful for strengthening family life immediately following our celebration of Christmas. First (and since these are weekday celebrations many may not be aware of them), the liturgical calendar celebrates three special feast days immediately after Christmas: December 26, the feast of St. Stephen, the first martyr; December 27, the feast of St. John the Evangelist; December 28, the feast of the Holy Innocents. All three of these feasts remind us that following Christ has its demands, even to the point of giving one's life in order to remain faithful to our Christian discipleship. Naturally, family life has its demands but none of these exceed our strength if we remember that God has given us the gift of the divine Son who dwells within each of us because of our baptism.

Second, the liturgical calendar gives us this feast of the Holy Family. Although the gospel passages about the Holy Family are scanty, we know that life wasn't easy for Jesus, Mary, and Joseph. They model for us a family life not beyond our reach but one that is very real and built on caring for each other.

About Liturgical Music

Music suggestion: Delores Dufner's "What Feast of Love," found in the collection *Sing a New Church* [OCP], exemplifies a way of introducing an excellent eucharistic text for the Christmas season via use of a traditional text and tune. Using "What Child Is This?" Dufner moves from the gift of Jesus in his birth at Bethlehem to his ongoing gift of self in the Eucharist. Because of their long familiarity with the original, any assembly will sing this new hymn with ease. Singing it will also entice them to reflect on the traditional text with deepened insight. Dufner suggests that cantor(s) or choir only sing the first four lines of each verse and the assembly respond with the refrain ("This, this is Christ the King . . ."). Depending on the length of the Communion procession, either sing only Dufner's text (perhaps with instrumental interludes to lengthen it) or sing the traditional text followed with Dufner's eucharistic verses. Unlike the traditional refrain, Dufner's refrain changes text with each repetition, so the assembly will need copies in hand.

DECEMBER 27, 2009
THE HOLY FAMILY OF JESUS, MARY, AND JOSEPH

✠ SPIRITUALITY

GOSPEL ACCLAMATION

℟. Alleluia, alleluia.
In the past God spoke to our ancestors through
    the prophets;
in these last days, he has spoken to us through
    the Son.
℟. Alleluia, alleluia.

Gospel

Luke 2:16-21; L18ABC

**The shepherds went in haste to
    Bethlehem and found Mary
    and Joseph,
    and the infant lying in the
    manger.
When they saw this,
    they made known the
    message
    that had been told them
    about this child.
All who heard it were amazed
    by what had been told them by the
    shepherds.
And Mary kept all these things,
    reflecting on them in her heart.
Then the shepherds returned,
    glorifying and praising God
    for all they had heard and seen,
    just as it had been told to them.**

**When eight days were completed for
    his circumcision,
    he was named Jesus, the name given
        him by the angel
    before he was conceived in the womb.**

See Appendix A, p. 267, for the other readings.

Reflecting on the Gospel

Most parents are so proud of their newborn that they naturally wish to show off their infant. No doubt Mary and Joseph were proud parents also and only too willing to show off Jesus even to these stranger-shepherds. Mary and Joseph heard the shepherds' message and rejoiced when the shepherds were "glorifying and praising God."

Because Mary's conception and giving birth happened under such extraordinary circumstances, we might think that Mary took all this for granted and that it was easy for her. Not so! The salvation events the incarnation unleashed are neither easy to understand nor to embrace. Yet the shepherds did hear the message of the angels and then they made it known. Mary, in turn, heard their good news, took it into her heart, and reflected on it. Mary shows us the way: we, too, must adopt a contemplative stance before God and the mystery of salvation. Mary's ongoing yes to God wasn't really very easy at all. The only way she continued to be faithful was that she took a contemplative stance: reflecting, pondering, praying.

It is important that we have a Marian feast this close to Christmas. It not only gives Mary her just due as the mother of God, but it also is a feast that encourages us in our own yes to God. Mary was human, like us. Her need for reflection to align herself with God's plan is a model for our own Christian living. The mystery of the incarnation and salvation is too big to celebrate during one week of the year and too deep for us to grasp easily. Like Mary, we must ponder these things in our hearts so that, as children of God (see second reading), we can continually glorify and praise God for the wonders of salvation.

How kindly God looked upon Mary and bestowed blessing and peace on her (see first reading)! God does the same with us: we are no longer "slaves" to sin but "heirs" to God's very life. The mystery of the incarnation that Mary models for us is that God's life dwells within each of us. But in our busy, everyday living we can easily lose sight of that Life within us. We can easily get distracted from a contemplative stance that helps us appreciate God's abiding presence to us. It is only by making a conscious effort to ponder, like Mary, the way we live and how God's grace is guiding us that we are able to face the inevitable difficulties of daily living with the sureness of blessing and strength.

Living the Paschal Mystery

Like Mary, we also must "give flesh" to the Savior, ponder his presence within us, and then let that presence guide us in the way we respond to the daily tasks and events we face. The way our busy daily living takes shape is that we usually act first, then (sometimes) take time to ponder the effects of our actions. Authentic gospel living turns this around: we must first ponder God's presence and guidance, then act in light of gospel values. This solemnity so closely following Christmas helps us realize that the joy of Christmas is ongoing only when we ourselves are the incarnation of Christ for others and are the bearers of his message of Good News. We "give flesh" to the Savior in the simple, ordinary demands of our daily living when they are done with a contemplative stance. Our actions flow from gospel values that first shape us and that we learn through pondering God's deeds on our behalf. Thus is the Word made flesh in our lives.

Focusing the Gospel

Key words and phrases: shepherds, made known the message, Mary . . . reflecting on them in her heart

To the point: The salvation events the incarnation unleashed are neither easy to understand nor to embrace. Yet the shepherds did hear the message of the angels and then they made it known. Mary, in turn, heard their good news, took it into her heart, and reflected on it. Mary shows us the way: we, too, must adopt a contemplative stance before God and the mystery of salvation.

Model Act of Penitence

Presider: Today we honor Mary the mother of God. The mystery of the incarnation is so great that Mary "kept all these things, reflecting on them in her heart." Let us pause a moment for our own reflection as we prepare to celebrate this mystery . . . [pause]

Lord Jesus, you are the Son of God and Son of Mary: Lord . . .

Christ Jesus, you are worthy of all glory and praise: Christ . . .

Lord Jesus, you are the Savior of the world: Lord . . .

Model Prayer of the Faithful

Presider: God sent the Son to bring us salvation and peace. Let us pray that we and all peoples in our world may be blessed this year.

Response:

Lord, hear our prayer.

Cantor:

we pray to the Lord,

That all members of the church be people of prayerful contemplation, pondering God's blessings and saving deeds . . . [pause]

That all peoples of the world enjoy peace and receive justice during this new year . . . [pause]

That those who are poor receive what they need this year through the generosity of others who ponder God's word . . . [pause]

That each of us during this coming year live the Gospel with renewed vigor and insight . . . [pause]

Presider: God of peace and justice, you bless us and are gracious to us beyond measure: hear these our prayers that we might live in peace with you for ever and ever. **Amen.**

FOR REFLECTION

- As I celebrate and pray about the Christmas mystery, what continues to amaze me about it is . . .
- My daily living—among family, neighbors, and coworkers—makes "known the message" about this mystery whenever I . . .
- If I am to imitate and develop Mary's reflective stance found in the gospel, I must . . .

Homily Points

• Often in our daily lives past experience guides our actions. For example, we get up and go to work because we know we will get a paycheck. What do we do when we face a situation that is beyond our experience? What enables us to try something new? What during this new year will we do that's new?

• Mary finds herself in the midst of an event that is well beyond human experience. Her response is to ponder the mystery in the depths of her heart. This same event calls us to reflect on the mystery made known also to us, so that it moves us to Gospel living. Here is our New Year's resolution: make room every day to ponder the Mystery.

SPIRITUALITY

GOSPEL ACCLAMATION
Matt 2:2

℟. Alleluia, alleluia.
We saw his star at its rising
and have come to do him homage.
℟. Alleluia, alleluia.

Gospel   Matt 2:1-12; L20ABC

When Jesus was born in Bethlehem of Judea,
in the days of King Herod,
    behold, magi from the east arrived in
        Jerusalem, saying,
"Where is the newborn king of the Jews?
We saw his star at its rising
    and have come to do him homage."
When King Herod heard this,
    he was greatly troubled,
    and all Jerusalem with him.
Assembling all the chief priests and the
        scribes of the people,
    he inquired of them where the Christ was
        to be born.
They said to him, "In Bethlehem of Judea,
    for thus it has been written through the
        prophet:
And you, Bethlehem, land of Judah,
    are by no means least among the
        rulers of Judah;
since from you shall come a ruler,
    who is to shepherd my people Israel."
Then Herod called the magi secretly
    and ascertained from them the time of
        the star's appearance.
He sent them to Bethlehem and said,
    "Go and search diligently for the child.
When you have found him, bring me word,
    that I too may go and do him homage."
After their audience with the king they set
        out.

Continued in Appendix A, p. 267.

Reflecting on the Gospel

Children love stories, and the more imaginative the better. Witness how popular the Harry Potter series has been. Parents and caretakers enjoy telling such stories to children who listen with rapt attention. As children age, however, they come to see how many of the stories of childhood were fairy tales and they move beyond them. This gospel is a wonderful story, and it's easy to get caught up in the imaginative details of the narrative: stars and kings, journeys and searches, newborn Baby and gifts. But like small children, we must move beyond these enticing details to get to the challenge of the message that is there.

The point of the gospel is even more amazing than the imaginative details it includes: God chooses to manifest the mystery of Christ Jesus to all the nations. This, of course, includes each of us today: we are to both search for the Christ as well as manifest his presence for others. Our task-response, note, is not only to search for the Christ among us but also to manifest that divine presence. In other words, we are to *be* the revelation of his presence, and this is possible for we are "members of the same body" and "copartners in the promise" (second reading). We are to *be* the story of the manifestation of Christ to all the world.

The three magi from the East were wise men; yet they followed the light of a star from the far regions of the East to Bethlehem in search of a "newborn king." What enabled them to see that light and receive the insight to follow it to their journey's end? It appears from the very beginning of their journey they were single-minded about their purpose. They journeyed to "do him homage"; they brought him gifts. Seeing is possible when we are single-minded, when our goal is clear and we prepare well and never lose sight of why we undertake the journey.

The light of the glory of God's presence is all around us. Unlike the magi, we don't have to undertake an arduous journey. We need only do two things: be single-minded about seeking God's presence and arm ourselves with whatever we need to reach our journey's end. The real challenge of the gospel is that we do not seek the light outside ourselves, but within. We ourselves have become the story; we ourselves are the guiding light; we ourselves manifest divine presence.

Living the Paschal Mystery

Simply because God's generosity in offering us divine presence is so lavish, our response must be just as lavish. God has given us great treasures, two of which are mystery so deep: the gift of the only-begotten Son as the divine presence that dwells among us, and the gift of our own selves being "members of the same body" (see second reading) with the power to manifest that divine presence for others. Our response can be no less than the total gift of ourselves as story made real in our relationships with others.

At baptism we become "coheirs" and "copartners" in Christ. We are copartners, therefore, in Jesus' saving ministry. Clearly, seeing the revelation of Christ among us requires of us a unique kind of seeing. We do not "look at" the light; we become the Light. We do not simply "see" the glory of divine presence; we become the glory of that divine presence. The challenge of daily living is that all our actions and decisions reflect the goodness of the revelation that has been given to us. We must consistently cooperate with God's revelation of divine presence.

Focusing the Gospel

Key words and phrases: magi, king, star, the Christ, child, gifts

To the point: This gospel is a wonderful story, and it's easy to get caught up in the imaginative details of the narrative: stars and kings, journeys and searches, newborn Baby and gifts. The point of the gospel is even more amazing: God chooses to manifest the mystery of Christ Jesus to all the nations. This, of course, includes each of us today. But our task-response is not only to search for the Christ among us but also to *be* the revelation of his presence, for we are "members of the same body" and "copartners in the promise" (second reading).

Connecting the Gospel

to the first reading: The first reading announces the light and glory of the presence of God come upon all nations. When we raise our eyes to see this glory, we become "radiant at what [we] see." We shine with the glory of God.

to our experience: All major occasions include some form of gift-giving: births, birthdays, anniversaries, weddings; even at funerals we send cards and flowers. It is not surprising that the magi bring gifts to the "newborn king"— gold, frankincense, and myrrh. Their greatest gift, however, was their coming to pay him homage.

Connecting the Responsorial Psalm

to the readings: Historically, the purpose of Psalm 72 from which this responsorial psalm is taken was to intercede for the king of Israel who represented God. The people asked God to endow the king with divine judgment so that justice might reign, the poor and afflicted be rescued, and peace blossom for all time. Then light would shine from Jerusalem and all nations would recognize and pay homage to the true King, the Lord God (first reading).

Liturgically, the Lectionary uses these verses from Psalm 72 to identify Christ as the fulfillment of Israel's prayer: this newborn Babe is the King par excellence, God's justice and mercy in the flesh come to rescue the poor and bring peace to all nations. Those who "see" recognize who he is and come to adore him (gospel). In the second reading Paul tells us the revelation made known in the coming of Christ is complete and universal. Nonetheless, leading all people to see and recognize Christ requires action on our part: we are "copartners in Christ." And so our singing of this psalm is more than just a celebration of what God has done for salvation. It is also a commitment on our part to spread the Good News of God's saving work to all nations.

to psalmist preparation: When you sing this responsorial psalm, you reveal who Christ is: the justice, peace, and mercy of God in human flesh. You also participate in the church's prayer that all peoples recognize who Christ is and come to adore him. What might you do this week to be the justice of God in human flesh for someone? Who needs you to be the mercy of God made flesh?

**ASSEMBLY &
FAITH-SHARING GROUPS**

- The magi's journey began with God's first reaching out to them through the star; my faith journey began with God's first reaching out to me through . . .

- I search for Christ when . . . I am the revelation of Christ for others when . . .

- Like the magi, as I encounter the great mystery of my "newborn king," the gift I offer him is . . .

PRESIDERS

- When Christ's light shines in and through my ministry it looks like . . .

DEACONS

- My servant ministry leads others to the light of Christ when . . .

HOSPITALITY MINISTERS

- My ministry communicates how all are "coheirs, members of the same body, and copartners in the promise in Christ Jesus" (second reading) whenever I . . .

MUSIC MINISTERS

- I offer homage to the "newborn king" through my music making when I . . .

ALTAR MINISTERS

- I experience being a copartner with Christ by serving at the altar when . . .

LECTORS

- My manner of proclamation gives light to those searching for the "newborn king" whenever I . . .

**EXTRAORDINARY MINISTERS
OF HOLY COMMUNION**

- I am radiant with the light of Christ when I distribute Holy Communion because . . .

Model Act of Penitence

Presider: The magi followed the star to the newborn King and offered him homage. Let us prepare ourselves to offer God homage in this liturgy by examining how well we have followed God's light in our own lives . . . [pause]

Lord Jesus, your presence was revealed by the light of a star: Lord . . .

Christ Jesus, you received homage from the magi: Christ . . .

Lord Jesus, you are light for all nations: Lord . . .

Homily Points

• In terms of physics, light is a property external to us. It is provided by the sun, by candles, by electric lamps. The gospel also bespeaks an external light: the star guiding the magi to the presence of Christ. At the same time, the feast points to an internal Light—one that is divine and that makes of us a source of light for others.

• In the story, the magi received the light that guided them to new and wonderful possibilities from the star in the heavens. We don't look outside to the heavens for the light of God's guidance, but we look to the light of God's word and to the light of Christ's Spirit shining within us to gain the insight that enables us to seek and find divine presence.

• The story in the gospel that starts with imaginative details ends with the very real challenge for us to become the story. Our fidelity to the word of God and the Spirit of Christ within us becomes light leading others to the Christ. The Word is still being made flesh and dwells among us and within us through the light of our faithful living of the original story.

Model Prayer of the Faithful

Presider: God is the source of all light and goodness. We are confident as we pray.

Response:

Lord,   hear   our prayer.

Cantor:

we pray to the Lord,

That all members of the church grow in being the light of Christ for others . . . [pause]

That all peoples walk in the radiance of God's light and peace . . . [pause]

That the sick and the suffering be lifted up by our goodness and generosity . . . [pause]

That each of us here may open ourself to the many ways Christ's light comes to us . . . [pause]

Presider: Generous God, you lavish us with all good things: hear these our prayers that we might one day enjoy with you the fullness of your light, life everlasting. We ask this through Christ our Lord. **Amen.**

OPENING PRAYER

Let us pray
[that we will be guided by the light of faith]

Pause for silent prayer

Father,
you revealed your Son to the nations
by the guidance of a star.
Lead us to your glory in heaven
by the light of faith.

We ask this through our Lord Jesus Christ, your Son,
who lives and reigns with you and the Holy Spirit,
one God, for ever and ever. **Amen.**

FIRST READING
Isa 60:1-6

Rise up in splendor, Jerusalem! Your light has come,
    the glory of the Lord shines upon you.
See, darkness covers the earth,
    and thick clouds cover the peoples;
but upon you the LORD shines,
    and over you appears his glory.
Nations shall walk by your light,
    and kings by your shining radiance.
Raise your eyes and look about;
    they all gather and come to you:
your sons come from afar,
    and your daughters in the arms of their nurses.

Then you shall be radiant at what you see,
    your heart shall throb and overflow,
for the riches of the sea shall be emptied out before you,
    the wealth of nations shall be brought to you.
Caravans of camels shall fill you,
    dromedaries from Midian and Ephah;
all from Sheba shall come
    bearing gold and frankincense,
    and proclaiming the praises of the LORD.

RESPONSORIAL PSALM

Ps 72:1-2, 7-8, 10-11, 12-13

R℣. (cf. 11) Lord, every nation on earth will adore you.

O God, with your judgment endow the
    king,
    and with your justice, the king's son;
he shall govern your people with justice
    and your afflicted ones with judgment.

R℣. Lord, every nation on earth will adore you.

Justice shall flower in his days,
    and profound peace, till the moon be no
        more.
May he rule from sea to sea,
    and from the River to the ends of the
        earth.

R℣. Lord, every nation on earth will adore you.

The kings of Tarshish and the Isles shall
    offer gifts;
    the kings of Arabia and Seba shall
        bring tribute.
All kings shall pay him homage,
    all nations shall serve him.

R℣. Lord, every nation on earth will adore you.

For he shall rescue the poor when he cries
    out,
    and the afflicted when he has no one to
        help him.
He shall have pity for the lowly and the
    poor;
    the lives of the poor he shall save.

R℣. Lord, every nation on earth will adore you.

SECOND READING

Eph 3:2-3a, 5-6

Brothers and sisters:
You have heard of the stewardship of
    God's grace
    that was given to me for your benefit,
    namely, that the mystery was made
        known to me by revelation.
It was not made known to people in other
    generations
    as it has now been revealed
    to his holy apostles and prophets by the
        Spirit:
    that the Gentiles are coheirs, members
        of the same body,
    and copartners in the promise in Christ
        Jesus through the gospel.

About Liturgy

Gift of worship: Each Sunday when the Christian assembly gathers for liturgy, many gifts are clearly given to God: the gift of time and talent shown in the various ministries; the gift of money and food goods for those in need and the upkeep of the parish; the gift of ourselves to each other by our presence and full, conscious, and active participation. All of this is good. At the same time we must never forget that we gather on Sunday *in response to* God's prior gifts to us summed up in the Son and our share in divine life. Thus our Sunday celebration most of all ought to be characterized by thankfulness for all God has given us and praise (homage) for this God who chooses to be so intimately present to us.

It is all too easy for our Sunday celebrations to be subtly focused on ourselves. Although we can never be passive at Sunday Mass (and our greeting each other, hospitality, offerings are an important and indispensable part of the time spent in worship), we must never forget, however, that we are there first and foremost to give God praise and thanksgiving. The purpose of Sunday worship is just that: *worship.* Threaded through the speaking and singing, gestures and postures, relating and responding must be an attitude of awe, reverence, and deep-felt gratitude for God's lavish generosity to us in so many ways. In the end the only lasting gift we can really give God is ourselves in worship and self-emptying service of others.

About Liturgical Music

Hymn suggestion: Although the Christmas season celebrates our jubilation at Christ's birth, the liturgy never lets us stray far from the looming presence of the paschal mystery implications of his birth. Ruth Duck's "O Radiant Christ, Incarnate Word," in the collection *Dancing in the Universe* [GIA], captures both the confidence we feel in the revelation brought by Christ and the struggle we experience with letting that revelation guide human affairs: "Our bartered, busy lives burn dim, too tired to care, too numb to feel . . . Come, shine upon our shadowed world . . . illumine all we say and do . . . lead the peoples to your peace, as stars once lead the way to you." The text is set to a specifically commissioned tune (David Cherwien's RADIANT LIGHT) in which the shifts from C major to minor then back to major aptly express the light-darkness-light shifts in the text itself. As this tune will be unknown to most assemblies, the choir only might sing the hymn during the preparation of the gifts. Otherwise, as Duck herself suggests, choose a familiar tune such as WAREHAM for the assembly to sing.

✠ SPIRITUALITY

R⁊. Alleluia, alleluia.
John said: One mightier than I is coming;
he will baptize you with the Holy Spirit and with
    fire.
R⁊. Alleluia, alleluia.

Gospel

Luke 3:15-16, 21-22; L21C

The people were filled with
    expectation,
    and all were asking in their hearts
    whether John might be the Christ.
John answered them all, saying,
    "I am baptizing you with water,
    but one mightier than I is coming.
I am not worthy to loosen the thongs of
    his sandals.
He will baptize you with the Holy Spirit
    and fire."

After all the people had been baptized
    and Jesus also had been baptized and
        was praying,
    heaven was opened and the Holy
        Spirit descended upon him
    in bodily form like a dove.
And a voice came from heaven,
    "You are my beloved Son;
    with you I am well pleased."

Reflecting on the Gospel

Show-and-tell is generally a popular time in elementary school classrooms and this for at least two reasons. First, education research has revealed that we learn best by concrete, hands-on experiences. When the children can see and touch some object, their curiosity is roused, questions come easily, and they are usually eager to run home after school and tell others about the experience. Second, show-and-tell is popular because it boosts the self-esteem of the little one doing the explaining in front of the class. Something significant to the child is shared with others, and the interest of the classmates encourages the child and makes him or her feel important. Show-and-tell is a manifestation of good learning technique and the worth of an individual. This Sunday's gospel tells of a kind of show-and-tell on the part of both Jesus and us. It manifests who we are and how we have been gifted.

As Jesus was baptized by John, so must we be baptized—not just in the waters of repentance and forgiveness but by the Holy Spirit and fire, which calls us to give ourselves (see second reading) for the good of others. Thus the gospel speaks of two baptisms. The first is the event this feast celebrates: the baptism Jesus received at the hands of John. The second is the baptism that we receive "with the Holy Spirit and fire." Jesus' baptism revealed him as "beloved Son"; our own baptism reveals us as ones who are saved, renewed, justified, and heirs of eternal life (see second reading). This feast, then, is an epiphany not only of who Jesus is but also of who we are.

We are baptized with the Spirit who is the divine presence within us. We are also baptized with fire that burns within us so that we are ignited with ardor, commitment, intensity, energy, drive toward a goal—by the very goodness of our lives, being a faithful divine presence for others. Our baptism, then, is a dynamic and energetic embracing of our own graced identity as God's own people (see second reading) expressed through a Gospel way of life. The fire with which we are baptized surely must make us "eager to do what is good" (second reading).

Living the Paschal Mystery

Being baptized by "the Holy Spirit and fire" means that we share in Jesus' mission, including the total gift of ourselves. Who we are manifests God's presence in the very dying to self we do each day as we conform ourselves to God's will. Like the simple show-and-tell time in the classroom mentioned above, we learn from experiencing and encountering the Divine through others. In this our own self-esteem is boosted when we realize that *we ourselves* are God's presence for another.

The gift of divine life and its attendant call to self-giving discipleship does make demands on us. Taking our baptism seriously means that the ritual moment is just the beginning of a lifetime of openness to God's continuing grace "training" us to be faithful to who God has made us to be. God's giving us a share in divinity is so gracious that the only response is dying to self in fidelity to our baptismal call. Further, living our baptism and the paschal mystery means that while our life manifests dying for the sake of others, we also manifest the hope that is sure because God's ultimate gracious act toward us is the offer of everlasting life, a promise already being fulfilled.

Focusing the Gospel

Key words and phrases: baptize you with the Holy Spirit and fire, Jesus also had been baptized, beloved Son

To the point: The gospel speaks of two baptisms. The first is the event this feast celebrates: the baptism Jesus received at the hands of John. The second is the baptism we receive "with the Holy Spirit and fire." Jesus' baptism revealed him as "beloved Son"; our own baptism reveals us as ones who are saved, renewed, justified, and heirs of eternal life (see second reading). This feast, then, is an epiphany not only of who Jesus is but also of who we are.

Connecting the Gospel

to the first and second readings: One effect of our baptism is that our "guilt is expiated" (first reading) and we are "saved . . . through the bath of rebirth" (second reading). Another effect is that God "gathers the lambs" (first reading) into a new and most intimate relationship with Godself—that of being heirs of divine life (see second reading).

to religious experience: Baptism is more than a ritual moment on a specific day; it is a gift of divine life that God continuously sustains with yet more gifts to which we must respond daily.

Connecting the Responsorial Psalm

to the readings: The verses from Psalm 104 used for this responsorial psalm recite the many ways God's glory is revealed: God generates the heavens, rules water and wind, creates all that roams earth and swims seas, gives all creatures their food in due season, and, above all, continuously sends the Spirit, the breath of life and renewal.

The first and second readings proclaim that in Christ the fullness of God's glory has appeared. His identity is confirmed at his baptism: "You are my beloved Son" who will "baptize . . . with the Holy Spirit and fire" (gospel). The power of God has become fully manifest in Christ who cleanses us from sin and recreates us as a people "eager to do . . . good" (second reading). What better response can we make than "O bless the Lord, my soul"? May this response express our acknowledgment of our baptismal identity and our willingness to enter with Christ into the way of living to which this identity calls us.

to psalmist preparation: The numerous signs of God's glory that you enumerate in these psalm verses are external revelations of the even greater glory God works within us through our baptism in Christ. What might you do this week to renew your awareness of the power and grace of baptism? What might you do to bless God for this power and grace?

ASSEMBLY & FAITH-SHARING GROUPS
- Jesus heard who he was ("beloved Son") when he prayed; I realize and remember who I am in faith when I . . .
- Having been baptized "with the Holy Spirit and fire" means to me . . .
- My daily living manifests what I believe about my baptism whenever I . . .

PRESIDERS
- I remind the assembly of their baptismal dignity whenever I . . . and I call them to baptismal responsibility whenever I . . .

DEACONS
- When I baptize others, I am most aware of my own baptismal dignity and responsibility when I . . .

HOSPITALITY MINISTERS
- My manner of greeting those who gather respects their baptismal dignity when I . . .

MUSIC MINISTERS
- My ministry helps the assembly sing together as the one baptized community when . . .

ALTAR MINISTERS
- Serving at the altar is an expression of my baptismal dignity when . . .

LECTORS
- The manner of my proclamation calls forth the dignity and duty of baptism when . . .

EXTRAORDINARY MINISTERS OF HOLY COMMUNION
- When others come forward in procession to receive Holy Communion, I see in them . . . They see in me . . .

Model Rite of Blessing and Sprinkling Holy Water

Presider: Jesus' identity as beloved Son of God was manifested at his baptism. Through our own baptism we share in this divine identity that is manifested in the good works of our own lives. We ask God to bless this water and we sprinkle it, asking God to strengthen us to be faithful disciples of Jesus.

[*continue with form B of the blessing of water*]

Homily Points

• What, really, is the Holy Spirit's "fire"? We have several expressions that might give us a hint at its meaning. For example, a coach works to get a team "all fired up" before a game, a boss tries to "light a fire under" a staff to undertake a new project, someone intent on a mission has a "fire in the belly." All these expressions point to ardor, commitment, intensity, energy, drive toward a goal. Our baptism is meant to instill in us all this dynamism as well.

• Baptism transforms our identity and confers on us a mission. We are the Body of Christ entrusted with cooperating with the Spirit of Christ in making present God's reign by which the world is saved, renewed, and justified. Baptism initiates us into an inspired, dynamic way of life.

• The mission of Jesus is continued through his disciples, those who are baptized "with the Holy Spirit and fire." The very enthusiasm with which we ought to live our baptism is both a revelation of what it means to be a disciple of Jesus and an invitation to continue his saving mission. Baptism, then, is hardly a single or simple yes; it is an ongoing and total commitment to a way of living.

Model Prayer of the Faithful

Presider: Our baptism confers on us the gift of divine identity and requires of us faithful discipleship. We pray for the strength to live out our baptism.

Response:

Lord, hear our prayer.

Cantor:

we pray to the Lord,

May the church, the Body of Christ, be filled with the dynamism of the Spirit . . . [pause]

May all peoples, the children of God, faithfully receive the offer of God's salvation . . . [pause]

May the poor, the beloved of God, receive more abundantly the gifts of this world . . . [pause]

May each of us, the presence of the risen Christ, be faithful to our baptismal commitment . . . [pause]

Presider: Gracious God, you give all good gifts: hear these our prayers that one day we may share in the fullness of eternal life. We ask this through Christ our Lord. **Amen.**

OPENING PRAYER

Let us pray
[that we will be faithful to our baptism]

Pause for silent prayer

Almighty, eternal God,
when the Spirit descended upon Jesus
at his baptism in the Jordan,
you revealed him as your own beloved
Son.
Keep us, your children born of water and
the Spirit,
faithful to our calling.

We ask this through our Lord Jesus Christ,
your Son,
who lives and reigns with you and the
Holy Spirit,
one God for ever and ever. **Amen.**

FIRST READING
Isa 40:1-5, 9-11

Comfort, give comfort to my people,
says your God.
Speak tenderly to Jerusalem, and proclaim
to her
that her service is at an end,
her guilt is expiated;
indeed, she has received from the hand of
the LORD
double for all her sins.

A voice cries out:
In the desert prepare the way of the LORD!
Make straight in the wasteland a
highway for our God!
Every valley shall be filled in,
every mountain and hill shall be made
low;
the rugged land shall be made a plain,
the rough country, a broad valley.
Then the glory of the LORD shall be
revealed,
and all people shall see it together;
for the mouth of the LORD has spoken.

Go up onto a high mountain,
Zion, herald of glad tidings;
cry out at the top of your voice,
Jerusalem, herald of good news!
Fear not to cry out
and say to the cities of Judah:
Here is your God!
Here comes with power
the Lord GOD,
who rules by a strong arm;
here is his reward with him,
his recompense before him.
Like a shepherd he feeds his flock;
in his arms he gathers the lambs,
carrying them in his bosom,
and leading the ewes with care.

RESPONSORIAL PSALM

Ps 104:1b-2, 3-4, 24-25, 27-28, 29-30

R℣. (1) O bless the Lord, my soul.

O LORD, my God, you are great indeed!
    You are clothed with majesty and glory,
robed in light as with a cloak.
    You have spread out the heavens like a
        tent-cloth.

R℣. O bless the Lord, my soul.

You have constructed your palace upon
        the waters.
    You make the clouds your chariot;
you travel on the wings of the wind.
    You make the winds your messengers,
and flaming fire your ministers.

R℣. O bless the Lord, my soul.

How manifold are your works, O LORD!
    In wisdom you have wrought them all—
        the earth is full of your creatures;
the sea also, great and wide,
    in which are schools without number
of living things both small and great.

R℣. O bless the Lord, my soul.

They look to you to give them food in due
        time.
When you give it to them, they gather it;
    when you open your hand, they are
        filled with good things.

R℣. O bless the Lord, my soul.

If you take away their breath, they perish
        and return to the dust.
When you send forth your spirit, they are
        created,
    and you renew the face of the earth.

R℣. O bless the Lord, my soul.

SECOND READING

Titus 2:11-14; 3:4-7

Beloved:
The grace of God has appeared, saving all
    and training us to reject godless ways
        and worldly desires
    and to live temperately, justly, and
        devoutly in this age,
    as we await the blessed hope,
    the appearance of the glory of our
        great God
    and savior Jesus Christ,
    who gave himself for us to deliver us
        from all lawlessness
    and to cleanse for himself a people as
        his own,
    eager to do what is good.

Continued in Appendix A, p. 268.

About Liturgy

Symbols of baptism: The symbols of the baptismal rite put into focus the primary gift of baptism—a share in divine life that is for us a new identity:

Water—plunged into the baptismal waters, we are plunged into Christ's death; rising, we share in divine life. Water brings both death (to our old selves) and a rebirth of life (new life in God).

Chrism—anointed with chrism, we share in the threefold office of Christ—priest, prophet, ruler. Our being anointed with chrism is a consecration of ourselves to conform our life to Christ's.

White garment—clothed in a white garment, we are reminded of our new, risen life in Christ. We are to live unstained until we enjoy eternal life with God.

Lighted candle—enlightened by Christ, we are also to be the light of Christ dispelling sin and darkness in the world. We ourselves are manifestations that in Christ the light of salvation has come into the world.

Although all these symbols also imply the demands of discipleship (*water*—dying to self; *chrism*—conforming ourselves to Christ; *white garment*—living lives worthy of who we are; *lighted candle*—overcoming the darkness of evil), they primarily help us understand who we become in baptism—members of the Body of Christ sharing in divine identity. Moreover, greater awareness and appreciation of our identity eases the way for us to be more faithful in our discipleship.

About Liturgical Music

Service music for Ordinary Time: The celebration of the Baptism of the Lord is the hinge Sunday marking the changeover from the Christmas season to Ordinary Time. Because the feast stands as a turning point and faces both directions, it would be appropriate either to sing the service music used during Christmas season one last time or to begin using the Ordinary Time setting. Some examples of service music suitable for Ordinary Time—that is, settings that are well written musically and possess acclamatory energy without being overly festive—are Vermulst's "People's Mass," Owen Alstott's "Heritage Mass," the St. Louis Jesuits' Mass, and the Danish Mass.

Hymn suggestion: A hymn text extraordinarily appropriate for this Sunday when we return to Ordinary Time is Herman Stuempfle's "The Hills Are Still, the Darkness Deep," found in *The Word Goes Forth* [GIA]. Stuempfle brings us down from the glories of Christmas and plants us firmly in the reality of ordinary life. The song of angels no longer fills the sky but instead a "hungry cry"; shepherds once roused by glorious light have returned to "cold and lonely vigil"; the kings have departed, leaving Mary to tend a Child in the night. The final verse captures the challenge of Ordinary Time: "O God, when glory fades away, And duties fill the night, the day: By grace unseen but present still, Give strength to heart and hand and will." This would make an excellent text for the assembly to sing after Communion as an act of quiet renewal of their baptism and its meaning for daily life.

Ordinary Time I

✝ SPIRITUALITY

GOSPEL ACCLAMATION
See 2 Thess 2:14

R7. Alleluia, alleluia.
God has called us through the Gospel
to possess the glory of our Lord Jesus Christ.
R7. Alleluia, alleluia.

Gospel   John 2:1-11; L66C

There was a wedding at Cana in
    Galilee,
    and the mother of Jesus was there.
Jesus and his disciples were also
    invited to the wedding.
When the wine ran short,
    the mother of Jesus said to him,
    "They have no wine."
And Jesus said to her,
    "Woman, how does your concern
        affect me?
My hour has not yet come."
His mother said to the servers,
    "Do whatever he tells you."
Now there were six stone water jars there
        for Jewish ceremonial washings,
    each holding twenty to thirty gallons.
Jesus told them,
    "Fill the jars with water."
So they filled them to the brim.
Then he told them,
    "Draw some out now and take it to the
        headwaiter."
So they took it.
And when the headwaiter tasted the
    water that had become wine,
    without knowing where it came from
    —although the servers who had drawn
        the water knew—,
    the headwaiter called the bridegroom
        and said to him,
    "Everyone serves good wine first,
    and then when people have drunk
        freely, an inferior one;
    but you have kept the good wine until
        now."
Jesus did this as the beginning of his
    signs at Cana in Galilee
    and so revealed his glory,
    and his disciples began to believe in him.

Reflecting on the Gospel

Plenty of love is evident at a wedding. Of course, there's the love between the bride and groom. And there's the love between the parents—as a couple as well as for their son or daughter. There's grandparents' and godparents' love. Usually the maid of honor and best man have such a close relationship with the couple that we might speak of love far more than friendship. The gospel this Sunday is about a "wedding at Cana." Mary and Jesus are guests there. As with all weddings, we might presume that love abounds.

This wedding, however, is quite different. It is far more than a story about the couple and their big day. It is really a story about God's big day!

Why does John begin with a wedding story? What, really, is the wedding? What, really, is the sign? This first manifestation of why Jesus came among us summarizes his whole saving mission, and so John uses this occasion at the beginning of Jesus' public life to give us an overview of the meaning and purpose of Jesus' whole life. All Jesus' life and actions are directed toward his saving work, culminating in his death and resurrection—and our response to this is "to believe in him." Our believing is our own action of entering into Jesus' saving work. The wedding feast was an opportunity for epiphany and belief.

John uses the wedding as a metaphor to manifest to us that there is new wine among us. The readings taken together intimate that the marriage is between heaven and earth, divinity and humanity, God and us. The sign is how obedience leads to glory, dying to rising, believing to abundance. The purpose of using wedding imagery runs deep: the sign "revealed [Jesus'] glory." If water changed to wine can reveal Jesus' glory, how much more can changed hearts reveal it!

The first reading gives us a hint about why Jesus had to reveal his glory: so that we might "be called by a new name," that is, God's "Delight" and "Espoused." The epiphany of Jesus' glory is a sign of the persistence of God's overtures of love to us—God reveals glory to us in many ways to make sure we catch it—and the depths of God's love, so much that we are espoused to God.

Living the Paschal Mystery

Belief entails a *Who* rather than a *what*. Our own encounters with Jesus (in prayer, through others, in struggling with daily dying) are truly epiphanies of God's glory that also invite *us* to respond to divine presence with belief. These epiphany signs might come in many ways—through others in a cry for help, in a lonely person's plea for companionship, in the spontaneous laughter of delight, in the beauty of nature. The challenge for us is to see these as revelations of God's glory, as epiphanies of God's love for us, and an opportunity to respond in belief.

Yes, these common, ordinary signs of God's love and glory are all around us. By *responding* to other people (recognizing them as revelations of God to us) we also become signs of God's in-breaking, epiphanies for others. We ourselves are the good wine kept until after Jesus' ascension when we take up Jesus' mission as disciples. Living the paschal mystery means that we empty ourselves in order to be filled with the goodness of God's glory.

Focusing the Gospel

Key words and phrases: wedding, Do whatever he tells you, signs, revealed his glory, began to believe

To the point: Why does John begin with a wedding story? What, really, is the wedding? What, really, is the sign? This first manifestation of why Jesus came among us summarizes his whole saving mission. The marriage is between heaven and earth, divinity and humanity, God and us. The sign is how obedience leads to glory, dying to rising, believing to abundance.

Connecting the Gospel

to the first reading: By using espousal imagery the first reading expresses God's intense and intimate love for Israel. John places the first manifestation of Jesus in the context of a wedding celebration. God's espousal love for all humanity is coming to fulfillment in Jesus.

to our experience: Few of us ever witness a dramatic sign like that reported in this gospel. Nevertheless, we are surrounded by many signs of God's transforming love for us. We have only to see to believe.

Connecting the Responsorial Psalm

to the readings: The verses from Psalm 96 used for this Sunday divide thematically. In the first two strophes we are commanded to sing to God, bless God's name, announce God's wondrous deeds to all the world. In the second two strophes we invite all nations to join us in our praise and worship of God. We know from the history of salvation that we have much to proclaim. The Israelites had learned that God's gifts always surpassed their wants and dreams (first reading). The gospel shows us that Jesus' actions also surpass all human expectations. In singing this psalm we announce that we see the works God is doing in Christ and want to tell all the world.

to psalmist preparation: You can sing about the saving acts of God only if you recognize them. Sometimes these saving acts come in extraordinary ways, but most often they come in the quiet events of ordinary, everyday living. The trick is to see them so that you can believe. How is Christ turning the ordinary water of your life into the wine of salvation?

**ASSEMBLY &
FAITH-SHARING GROUPS**

- The many signs of God's love for me are . . . I respond by . . .
- "Do whatever he tells you" challenges me because . . .
- Jesus reveals his glory to me in . . . by . . . through . . .

PRESIDERS

- I am a sign of God's love for the community when I . . . because . . .

DEACONS

- I become aware of and respond to the needs of others in these ways . . .

HOSPITALITY MINISTERS

- My manner of welcoming expresses God's "Delight" (first reading) in those who gather by . . .

MUSIC MINISTERS

- In my music making I am a sign that leads others to believe more deeply in Jesus when . . .

ALTAR MINISTERS

- Jesus' glory is revealed in the self-emptying that my service demands. I see self-emptying as a sharing in Jesus' glory because . . .

LECTORS

- That I am God's "Delight" (first reading) was announced to me through . . . I announce this to others by . . .

**EXTRAORDINARY MINISTERS
OF HOLY COMMUNION**

- Those who have been living signs (Eucharist) of Jesus' glory for me are . . .

CELEBRATION

Model Act of Penitence

Presider: Jesus performed his first public sign at the wedding feast at Cana. We pause at the beginning of this celebration to reflect on the signs of Jesus' glory in our own lives and to ask God during this liturgy to increase our belief . . . [pause]

Lord Jesus, you are the sign of God's love for us: Lord . . .

Christ Jesus, you are the new Wine that leads us to glory: Christ . . .

Lord Jesus, you are the One who calls us to belief and discipleship: Lord . . .

Homily Points

• A successful and enjoyable wedding celebration demands lots of preplanning and hard work by many people. Yet we've all had experiences of some of these people becoming so caught up in the celebration itself that they lose sight of details needing attention. It is interesting that it is Mary in the gospel who noticed a need. But it is even more interesting that she went to Jesus to meet this need.

• Jesus' initial reaction to Mary's request seems to indicate a preoccupation with ultimate rather than immediate concerns: "My hour has not yet come." Mary helps Jesus redefine the "hour." It is *now*. His task is at hand.

• The wedding celebration the gospel speaks about is not simply a past, historical event. There is a wedding celebration going on *now* between God and us. As it was with Jesus, our task is also obedience and self-giving. Our taking up this task is already a participation in the eternal wedding banquet.

Model Prayer of the Faithful

Presider: We are confident to make our needs known to the God who is always attentive to these needs.

Response:

Lord, hear our prayer.

Cantor:

we pray to the Lord,

That all members of the church be attentive to God's overtures of love . . . [pause]

That world leaders always be attentive to the needs of those under their care . . . [pause]

That the poor share in the abundant wine of God's gifts through the generosity of this community . . . [pause]

That all of us gathered here respond with obedience and self-giving to God's gift of Self to us . . . [pause]

Presider: O God, your love for us is overwhelming. Hear these our prayers that one day we might share forever at your heavenly wedding banquet. We ask this through Christ our Lord. **Amen.**

ALTERNATIVE OPENING PRAYER

Let us pray

Pause for silent prayer

Almighty and ever-present Father,
your watchful care reaches from end to
end
and orders all things in such power
that even the tensions and the tragedies
of sin
cannot frustrate your loving plans.
Help us to embrace your will,
give us the strength to follow your call,
so that your truth may live in our hearts
and reflect peace to those who believe in
your love.
We ask this in the name of Jesus the Lord.
Amen.

FIRST READING

Isa 62:1-5

For Zion's sake I will not be silent,
for Jerusalem's sake I will not be quiet,
until her vindication shines forth like the
dawn
and her victory like a burning torch.

Nations shall behold your vindication,
and all the kings your glory;
you shall be called by a new name
pronounced by the mouth of the LORD.
You shall be a glorious crown in the hand
of the LORD,
a royal diadem held by your God.
No more shall people call you "Forsaken,"
or your land "Desolate,"
but you shall be called "My Delight,"
and your land "Espoused."
For the LORD delights in you
and makes your land his spouse.
As a young man marries a virgin,
your Builder shall marry you;
and as a bridegroom rejoices in his bride
so shall your God rejoice in you.

RESPONSORIAL PSALM

Ps 96:1-2, 2-3, 7-8, 9-10

R⁊. (3) Proclaim his marvelous deeds to all the nations.

Sing to the LORD a new song;
  sing to the LORD, all you lands.
Sing to the LORD; bless his name.

R⁊. Proclaim his marvelous deeds to all the nations.

Announce his salvation, day after day.
  Tell his glory among the nations;
among all peoples, his wondrous deeds.

R⁊. Proclaim his marvelous deeds to all the nations.

Give to the LORD, you families of nations,
  give to the LORD glory and praise;
  give to the LORD the glory due his name!

R⁊. Proclaim his marvelous deeds to all the nations.

Worship the LORD in holy attire.
  Tremble before him, all the earth;
say among the nations: The LORD is king.
  He governs the peoples with equity.

R⁊. Proclaim his marvelous deeds to all the nations.

SECOND READING

1 Cor 12:4-11

Brothers and sisters:
There are different kinds of spiritual gifts
      but the same Spirit;
  there are different forms of service but
      the same Lord;
  there are different workings but the
      same God
  who produces all of them in everyone.
To each individual the manifestation of
      the Spirit
  is given for some benefit.
To one is given through the Spirit the
      expression of wisdom;
  to another, the expression of knowledge
      according to the same Spirit;
  to another, faith by the same Spirit;
  to another, gifts of healing by the one
      Spirit;
  to another, mighty deeds;
  to another, prophecy;
  to another, discernment of spirits;
  to another, varieties of tongues;
  to another, interpretation of tongues.
But one and the same Spirit produces all
      of these,
  distributing them individually to each
      person as he wishes.

About Liturgy

Eucharist's epiphanies: Year C in the Lectionary cycle is the only one in which the three traditional themes of epiphany occur on three consecutive Sundays: epiphany to the magi, Jesus' baptism, and the sign at the wedding feast at Cana. Yet, each time we celebrate liturgy God manifests divine Self to us in a number of ways. For example, in the *introductory rites* we are given an opportunity to be aware that God calls us into divine presence and asks us to be attentive to and respond to that epiphany. In the *Liturgy of the Word* God speaks to us—sometimes in terms of promise and fulfillment, sometimes exhorting us to right living, sometimes assuring us with divine love, sometimes challenging us to change our ways—and in the epiphany of word invites a response of a renewed commitment to follow Jesus as disciples. In the *Liturgy of the Eucharist* Christ becomes substantially present to us in the consecrated Bread and Wine and gives his very Body and Blood for our food and drink. This epiphany shows us God's tremendous love for us and God's desire for intimacy; it also shows our own dignity, as we ourselves are and are becoming the very Body of Christ. In the *concluding rite* we are sent forth to be the epiphany of God's presence in our everyday lives.

The Sunday Eucharist is a most sublime epiphany of God. Moreover, through our being transformed by the ritual action, we are reminded over and over again to be the presence of Christ in our world. God loves us so much as to send the Son to be our Savior; God trusts us so much as to send us to be the manifestation of God's presence!

About Liturgical Music

Selecting seasonal service music: Just as changes in art and environment cue the assembly about a change in liturgical seasons, so must the service music assist the parish to enter into the character of each season and into the unfolding rhythms of the liturgical year. For this to happen a parish needs to have a set of service music in place for each season, which over time becomes recognizable as part of celebrating that season.

Selecting such seasonal service music must begin by considering the liturgical year, both as a whole and in its individual seasons. Why does the church follow a liturgical year? What relationship exists between the unfolding seasons and solemnities of the liturgical year and the identity and mission of the church? Why, in the midst of the busy commercialism of pre-Christmas do we have the four weeks of Advent? Why each year do we enter into the renewal period of Lent prior to the resurrection celebration of the weeks of Easter? What is the purpose of Ordinary Time and what formative influence does it bear on our growth in Christian living?

These questions are worth reflection and discussion among music ministers, parish staff, and the parish at large, for their answers will form the theological basis for the musical decisions to be made.

✝ SPIRITUALITY

GOSPEL ACCLAMATION
See Luke 4:18

℟. Alleluia, alleluia.
The Lord sent me to bring glad tidings to the
    poor,
and to proclaim liberty to captives.
℟. Alleluia, alleluia.

Gospel   Luke 1:1-4; 4:14-21;
L69C

Since many have undertaken to
    compile a narrative of the
    events
  that have been fulfilled among
    us,
  just as those who were
    eyewitnesses from the
    beginning
  and ministers of the word have
    handed them down to us,
  I too have decided,
  after investigating everything
    accurately anew,
  to write it down in an orderly
    sequence for you,
  most excellent Theophilus,
  so that you may realize the certainty
    of the teachings
  you have received.

Jesus returned to Galilee in the power
    of the Spirit,
  and news of him spread throughout
    the whole region.
He taught in their synagogues and was
    praised by all.

He came to Nazareth, where he had
    grown up,
  and went according to his custom
  into the synagogue on the sabbath day.
He stood up to read and was handed a
    scroll of the prophet Isaiah.
He unrolled the scroll and found the
    passage where it was written:
  The Spirit of the Lord is upon me,
    because he has anointed me
    to bring glad tidings to the poor.

Continued in Appendix A, p. 268.

Reflecting on the Gospel

We place a great premium on reading in our society, and rightly so. Many toddlers' games are geared toward learning the alphabet and recognizing simple words. Computer programs teach reading to youngsters and speed reading to people of all ages. Yes, reading is so important. Yet, are there any children's games that teach *hearing*? Are there any computer programs that sharpen one's hearing? In this Sunday's gospel, Jesus reads aloud to the people in the Nazareth synagogue. The hearers must have *heard*, for after Jesus' proclamation in the synagogue, they "looked intently at him." What were they expecting from Jesus? An explanation of what they had just heard, yes. But Jesus moves his hearers beyond receiving mere explanation of the word to encountering him as the Word made flesh.

The synagogue hearers' expectations were fulfilled in two ways: *hearing* God's word and *encountering* God's word in the very person of Jesus. In the very proclamation, Jesus also announces his saving mission: to meet the needs of the poor, the captives, the blind, the oppressed. He identifies himself with the word that makes a difference, changes lives, fulfills expectations. Jesus' word is an active word that brings to life the "glad tidings" of God's care for us. Our own hearing and encountering the Word today invites us to participate in these saving deeds as, through us, the Word continues to be made flesh.

Just as the people of Nehemiah's time listened intently as Ezra proclaimed the law, the people in today's gospel focus on Jesus in the synagogue. Their intense anticipation is met by Jesus' dramatic assertion that the Scripture passage from Isaiah "is fulfilled" in their hearing. In the first reading Ezra read from the book of the law; in the gospel Jesus *is* the book, the Good News, the Word made flesh. Ezra interpreted what he read; in the gospel Jesus himself *is* the interpretation. Ezra's word was an inspiring word that had power and moved the people to worship and praise; Jesus' word is a creative word fulfilled *in him* and continues in the gospel, where *we ourselves* encounter Jesus and are moved to be disciples. The feasting, joy, and new strength on the holy day when Ezra read the law are now fulfilled in a new order in which the feasting is on Jesus and the strength comes from our sharing in the same Spirit.

Living the Paschal Mystery

Jesus is enfleshed today in the lives of those who encounter him, the gospel's very fulfillment, throughout the ages. Now we—our own lives—announce the meaning of the word proclaimed and enfleshed. We can do so because, like Jesus, in our baptism we also have been anointed with the Spirit. By our baptism we have received a share in Jesus' saving deeds. As his followers, we make present his saving mystery.

Living the paschal mystery means that we continually look for the poor, captive, blind, and oppressed among us. We don't have to look very far! "Today this passage has been fulfilled" is now true only when we respond to those around us who need a nourishing, strengthening, joyful word. This means that God's word isn't something we hear only on Sunday, but it becomes a living word in our hearts, inspiring us to be living gospels in our very selves. As we gradually grow into being anointed by the Spirit, we, like Jesus, are the fulfillment of the Scriptures.

Focusing the Gospel

Key words and phrases: stood up to read, bring glad tidings, looked intently at him, fulfilled in your hearing

To the point: After Jesus' proclamation in the synagogue, the hearers "looked intently at him." What were they expecting from Jesus? An explanation of what they had just heard, yes. But Jesus moves his hearers beyond receiving mere explanation of the word to encountering him as the Word made flesh. In this he also announces his saving mission: to meet the needs of the poor, the captives, the blind, the oppressed. Our hearing the Word today invites us to participate in these saving deeds as, through us, the Word continues to be made flesh.

Connecting the Gospel

to the first reading: Both the first reading and the gospel indicate the value the Israelites placed upon the word of God proclaimed in a public gathering. For them the very proclamation of God's law and word revealed the holiness and presence of God.

to our experience: Media inundates us with words. New technologies such as text messaging often reduce words to mere information sending. Word as proclamation is far more than swapping information in abbreviated forms; proclamation is presence, power, invitation to action, fullness.

Connecting the Responsorial Psalm

to the readings: The responsorial psalm proclaims that the word of God is perfect, trustworthy, right, and clear. The word of God refreshes the soul, rejoices the heart, and enlightens the eye. In the first reading this word is the law read by Ezra to the assembled people who weep at its hearing. In the gospel this word from the prophet Isaiah is announced by Jesus to the synagogue gathering who "look intently at him" for its interpretation. His interpretation is a stunner: this word is his very person "fulfilled in your hearing."

Jesus' interpretation takes our understanding of the psalm to a new level. The word of God given in the Law and the Prophets expresses God's will for human salvation. Jesus reveals that he is this will, the Word-will of God in flesh and bone, bringing Good News to the poor, restoring sight to the blind, and granting freedom to the oppressed. The Word, which is trustworthy and clear, which rejoices the heart and enlightens the eye, is the very person of Christ. Such a Word is truly salvation for the world. This is the Word/Law about which we sing.

to psalmist preparation: The word of God you sing of in this responsorial psalm is fulfilled in the person of Christ. As you pray the psalm in preparation this week, you might substitute the name of Christ for the words "law," "decree," "precept," etc. How does this deepen your personal relationship with Christ? How might this affect your singing of the psalm for the assembly?

ASSEMBLY & FAITH-SHARING GROUPS
- The expectations that motivate me in my everyday living are . . .
- What I expect from the word of God is . . . What I expect from the Word Jesus is . . .
- I continue Jesus' mission to the poor, captives, blind, and oppressed whenever I . . .

PRESIDERS
- I preach with power that excites expectation to encounter the Word whenever . . .

DEACONS
- My ministry to the poor, captives, blind, and oppressed looks like this . . .

HOSPITALITY MINISTERS
- My manner of greeting people prepares them to expect encounter with the Word made flesh when . . .

MUSIC MINISTERS
- I find music at liturgy enables the assembly to encounter Christ in the gospel when . . . I find myself pulled into this encounter when . . .

ALTAR MINISTERS
- My serving at the altar makes me more mindful of the needs of others because . . .

LECTORS
- My prayerful hearing of God's word moves me to . . . it helps me proclaim better in that . . .

EXTRAORDINARY MINISTERS OF HOLY COMMUNION
- I live with integrity the words I announce to communicants, "Body/Blood of Christ," when . . .

Model Act of Penitence

Presider: Jesus announced that the word he read in the synagogue was fulfilled in him. At the beginning of this celebration let us open ourselves to God's word and pray that it be fulfilled in each of us . . . [pause]

Lord Jesus, you ministered with the power of the Spirit: Lord . . .

Christ Jesus, you are the fulfillment of God's word: Christ . . .

Lord Jesus, you are glad tidings for the poor: Lord . . .

Homily Points

• In January, when we celebrate Martin Luther King Jr.'s birthday, the media always replay a clip of his famous "I Have a Dream" speech. Even these many years later we are moved and challenged by what he said. The power of his words derive from the integrity of what he said, how he lived, and what he called us to. He is a model for us of a response by word and deed to the challenge Jesus gives us in this gospel.

• In Hebrew the word *dabar* is never simply a spoken word, but it always includes action. For example, at creation when God said, "Let there be . . .," there was. In Jesus, the Word is action fulfilled, for in him God's plan of love is enfleshed in his care and compassion for the poor, the captives, the blind, the oppressed—indeed, anyone who came to him.

• The poor we encounter today include not only those who lack material necessities but also those without inner satisfaction. The imprisoned are not only those in cells but also those held captive by their own fears. The blind are not only those who lack physical sight but also those who fail to see their own dignity and goodness. The oppressed are not only those held down by injustice but also those downtrodden by false expectations. Like Jesus, we are sent to preach the "glad tidings" to all those we encounter—not simply by uttering words but by the action of changing the world around us.

Model Prayer of the Faithful

Presider: Let us pray that through us the glad tidings of God's love and care be brought to all people.

Response:

Lord,___ hear our prayer.

Cantor:

we pray to the Lord,

That all church leaders inspire others to do good works . . . [pause]

That leaders in our society collaborate to free those unjustly imprisoned . . . [pause]

That the poor be helped and the oppressed be lifted up . . . [pause]

That the word of God be effectively fulfilled in each of us . . . [pause]

Presider: O God, you desire that all people live in peace and abundance: hear these our prayers that one day we might live in the everlasting joy of eternal life. We ask this through Christ our Lord. **Amen.**

ALTERNATIVE OPENING PRAYER
Let us pray

Pause for silent prayer

Almighty Father,
the love you offer
always exceeds the furthest expression of
    our human longing,
for you are greater than the human heart.
Direct each thought, each effort of our life,
so that the limits of our faults and
    weaknesses
may not obscure the vision of your glory
or keep us from the peace you have
    promised.

We ask this through Christ our Lord.
    Amen.

FIRST READING
Neh 8:2-4a, 5-6, 8-10

Ezra the priest brought the law before the
    assembly,
    which consisted of men, women,
    and those children old enough to
        understand.
Standing at one end of the open place that
        was before the Water Gate,
    he read out of the book from daybreak
        till midday,
    in the presence of the men, the women,
    and those children old enough to
        understand;
    and all the people listened attentively to
        the book of the law.
Ezra the scribe stood on a wooden
        platform
    that had been made for the occasion.
He opened the scroll
    so that all the people might see it
    —for he was standing higher up than
        any of the people—;
    and, as he opened it, all the people rose.
Ezra blessed the Lord, the great God,
    and all the people, their hands raised
        high, answered,
    "Amen, amen!"
Then they bowed down and prostrated
        themselves before the Lord,
    their faces to the ground.
Ezra read plainly from the book of the law
        of God,
    interpreting it so that all could
        understand what was read.
Then Nehemiah, that is, His Excellency,
        and Ezra the priest-scribe
    and the Levites who were instructing
        the people
    said to all the people:
    "Today is holy to the Lord your God.

Do not be sad, and do not weep"—
    for all the people were weeping as they
       heard the words of the law.
He said further: "Go, eat rich foods and
     drink sweet drinks,
    and allot portions to those who had
       nothing prepared;
    for today is holy to our LORD.
Do not be saddened this day,
    for rejoicing in the LORD must be your
      strength!"

RESPONSORIAL PSALM
Ps 19:8, 9, 10, 15

R̸. (cf. John 6:63c) Your words, Lord, are
Spirit and life.

The law of the LORD is perfect,
    refreshing the soul;
the decree of the LORD is trustworthy,
    giving wisdom to the simple.

R̸. Your words, Lord, are Spirit and life.

The precepts of the LORD are right,
    rejoicing the heart;
the command of the LORD is clear,
    enlightening the eye.

R̸. Your words, Lord, are Spirit and life.

The fear of the LORD is pure,
    enduring forever;
the ordinances of the LORD are true,
    all of them just.

R̸. Your words, Lord, are Spirit and life.

Let the words of my mouth and the
     thought of my heart
    find favor before you,
O LORD, my rock and my redeemer.

R̸. Your words, Lord, are Spirit and life.

SECOND READING
1 Cor 12:12-14, 27

Brothers and sisters:
As a body is one though it has many parts,
    and all the parts of the body, though
       many, are one body,
    so also Christ.
For in one Spirit we were all baptized into
     one body,
    whether Jews or Greeks, slaves or free
       persons,
    and we were all given to drink of one
      Spirit.
Now the body is not a single part, but
     many.
You are Christ's body, and individually
     parts of it.

or 1 Cor 12:12-30

See Appendix A, p. 269.

About Liturgy

Eucharistic word and its fulfillment: Each Sunday during the Liturgy of the Word we hear God's word proclaimed. Would that this word so moved us that, like the people of Ezra's time, we would prostrate ourselves before the presence of God! Yet, even when our hearing the word is less enthusiastic, God still fulfills it.

The Liturgy of the Word always opens onto the Liturgy of the Eucharist. There is a very real pastoral danger that we focus during this part of the Mass only on receiving Communion. Important as that moment is, we cannot neglect the eucharistic prayer. In this prayer narrative we hear the story of God's faithful deeds in bringing about our salvation. Now, with our twenty-twenty hindsight, we are hearing a narrative of salvation *already fulfilled in Christ* and in this are encouraged and strengthened to respond to the word that we have just heard. We come forward in the Communion procession, toward the altar-table that is a symbol of the messianic banquet, to feast and have our fill at God's table, knowing that God nourishes us to be the fulfillment of the word in our daily lives.

Coming to Communion without paying due attention to the Liturgy of the Word and the salvation narrative of the eucharistic prayer is like coming late for a banquet and missing all the conversation that brings the joy and satisfaction to the meal. This gospel challenges us to prepare well for Sunday liturgy—not just to reflect on the readings but also occasionally to read prayerfully the eucharistic prayers so that they are truly *prayers*. Eucharistic Prayer IV borrows words from this Sunday's gospel, and it would be a good choice to begin our prayerful reflection on these beautiful narratives of salvation.

About Liturgical Music

The gospel acclamation: Both the first reading and the gospel this Sunday relate occasions when the word of God is proclaimed in the midst of the community. This offers a good opportunity to examine the meaning and importance of the gospel acclamation. While we remain seated during the proclamation of the first and second readings, we stand for the proclamation of the gospel, and we greet this proclamation by singing the acclamation. This important liturgical element announces our belief that the person of Christ becomes present in our midst in the proclamation of the gospel (GIRM 62). The accompanying verse sung by cantor or choir is often taken from the gospel text and acts as an invitation to open our hearts to truly hear what will be proclaimed and let ourselves be transformed by it (like a "liturgical *hors d'oeuvre*" offered to whet our appetites for the main course to come). The most suitable gesture during the singing of the acclamation would be to turn our bodies toward the Book of the Gospels as it is carried to the ambo (see GIRM 133).

JANUARY 24, 2010
THIRD SUNDAY IN ORDINARY TIME

✝ SPIRITUALITY

GOSPEL ACCLAMATION
Matt 4:18

℟. Alleluia, alleluia.
The Lord sent me to bring glad tidings to the
    poor,
to proclaim liberty to captives.
℟. Alleluia, alleluia.

Gospel   Luke 4:21-30; L72C

Jesus began speaking in the
    synagogue, saying:
    "Today this Scripture
        passage is fulfilled in
        your hearing."
And all spoke highly of him
    and were amazed at the
        gracious words that
        came from his mouth.
They also asked, "Isn't this the son of
    Joseph?"
He said to them, "Surely you will quote me
    this proverb,
    'Physician, cure yourself,' and say,
    'Do here in your native place
    the things that we heard were done in
        Capernaum.'"
And he said, "Amen, I say to you,
    no prophet is accepted in his own native
        place.
Indeed, I tell you,
    there were many widows in Israel in the
        days of Elijah
    when the sky was closed for three and a
        half years
    and a severe famine spread over the
        entire land.
It was to none of these that Elijah was sent,
    but only to a widow in Zarephath in the
        land of Sidon.
Again, there were many lepers in Israel
    during the time of Elisha the prophet;
    yet not one of them was cleansed, but
        only Naaman the Syrian."
When the people in the synagogue heard this,
    they were all filled with fury.
They rose up, drove him out of the town,
    and led him to the brow of the hill
    on which their town had been built,
    to hurl him down headlong.
But Jesus passed through the midst of them
    and went away.

Reflecting on the Gospel

Water coolers have achieved something of iconic status as gathering places. Around them are shared anecdotes of life and love, good times and bad, frivolous gossip and serious information. Whether something is true or not depends largely on the speaker's integrity. In unimportant tales and consequential descriptions alike we desire the truth. This Sunday's gospel continues Jesus' teaching in the synagogue, and he speaks words of truth. The gospel challenges us to stand pat on the truth of God's word, even to stake our life on it—as Jesus did. God is clear on the divine purpose: salvation for all at all costs, even if this means the life of the divine Son.

As long as Jesus announces glad tidings, the crowd responds positively. But when Jesus challenges their narrowness with the examples of Elijah's and Elisha's outreach to Gentiles (Sidon and Syria), they grow furious. The response of the crowd registers increasing resistance—from amazement (at his "gracious words") to skepticism ("Isn't this the son of Joseph?") to fury (they wanted "to hurl him down headlong" from "the brow of the hill"). Jesus challenged the crowd because the Good News is always broader than selective preferences or limited understanding—yes, salvation would be for Gentiles as well as Jews. While the gospel is always Good News, it is not always comfortable, because it ever stretches us beyond where we are now.

The demise of the prophets came about because they forced choices; the challenge of the gospel is also that it forces choices. The comforting thing about God's word is that we have always had the reassurance that God will protect and deliver us (see first reading). The disturbing thing is that the protection and deliverance don't always come as quickly as we might like or in the way we might like.

Jeremiah ended up in a cistern, and some of the prophets were killed; Jesus ended up on the cross. Prophets may be rejected and destroyed, but God's word is always enduring. One symbol of this is that Jesus does escape the crowd in this gospel, demonstrating that, like God's word, the gospel will prevail. And what is our response to the challenge of the gospel? Amazement or fury? Welcoming Jesus or expelling him from our midst? Growing in discipleship or stagnating in narrowness?

Living the Paschal Mystery

If we never meet doubt or opposition over values in our daily living, then we must examine how committed to the gospel we are. Most of us aren't called to preach the Good News "professionally." All of us, however, because of our baptism, are committed to living it. Living the gospel is what must shape our everyday choices and responses. This means, for example, that if the chatter around the water cooler at work grows uncharitable or coarse, we have the courage to walk away. Another example: if prejudice exists among our friends and acquaintances, we have the courage to extol the dignity of the minority. Dying to oneself means that we place gospel values before any others and are willing to stake our lives on them. We might not always concretely experience God's protection and deliverance in the given moment, but we know from Jesus' life that it is there when it really counts—leading us to life everlasting.

Focusing the Gospel

Key words and phrases: amazed, gracious words, filled with fury, drove him out

To the point: As long as Jesus announces glad tidings, the crowd responds positively. But when Jesus challenges their narrowness with the examples of Elijah's and Elisha's outreach to Gentiles (Sidon and Syria), they grow furious. While the gospel is always Good News, it is not always comfortable, because it ever stretches us beyond where we are now. Our response: amazement or fury, welcoming Jesus or expelling him from our midst, growing in discipleship or stagnating in narrowness.

Connecting the Gospel

to the first reading: There are at least two points of contact between the first reading and the gospel. The first is the presentation of Jeremiah and Jesus as prophets who are rejected. The second is God's promise of protection and deliverance.

to our experience: So much of our contemporary culture is based on what is popular, for example, *American Idol,* Nielson ratings, political polls, marketing samples, etc. Jesus based his message not on popular reaction but on the truth of God's word.

Connecting the Responsorial Psalm

to the readings: Psalm 71, from which the verses of the responsorial psalm are taken, is a lament prayed by a righteous person undergoing persecution. Out of a confidence instilled at birth, the psalmist cries for help and sings of hope in God, the "rock of refuge" who will act to rescue. This is the confidence that enables both Jeremiah and Jesus to remain faithful to their identity and mission. Jeremiah faces crushing opposition for speaking God's message to the people (first reading). God, fully aware of the terrible price Jeremiah is paying, promises him protection and deliverance. Jesus speaks words of divine judgment and incurs the wrath of his hearers (gospel). This time he slips away unhurt, but it will not always be so.

Remaining faithful to the mission appointed by God means facing persecution and death. What gives us courage to do so is the sure knowledge that we are known and loved by God who will remain with us and will ultimately deliver us. Such is the knowledge expressed in this psalm. Such was Jesus' knowledge. Such is ours as we sing.

to psalmist preparation: The confidence of this psalm is a perfect counterbalance to the reality of persecution about which the first reading and the gospel speak. If you choose to be faithful to the mission you share with Christ, you will know rejection. But you will also know in an ever-deepening way the intimate presence of the God who guides and protects you. Are you willing to take the risk?

**ASSEMBLY &
FAITH-SHARING GROUPS**

- Words of Jesus that are amazing and "gracious" to me are . . .
- Words of Jesus that I would rather not hear are . . .
- My response to the gospel usually is . . .

PRESIDERS

- I am comfortable preaching the gospel when . . . I am uncomfortable preaching the gospel when . . .

DEACONS

- The views of God and salvation that have been stretched in me because of my experiences in ministry are . . .

HOSPITALITY MINISTERS

- My ministry of welcoming extends beyond those I know to include outsiders when . . .

MUSIC MINISTERS

- The music I sing challenges me and the assembly to live the gospel more radically when . . .

ALTAR MINISTERS

- The demands of my service amaze me when . . . infuriate me when . . .

LECTORS

- I heed or dismiss a passage from Scripture based on . . .

**EXTRAORDINARY MINISTERS
OF HOLY COMMUNION**

- My distributing Holy Communion stretches me beyond narrowness to the wide reach of God's embrace when . . .

Model Act of Penitence

Presider: Jesus was sent to announce the Good News of salvation to Jews and Gentiles alike. Let us open ourselves at the beginning of this celebration to the wideness of God's offer of salvation . . . [pause]

Lord Jesus, you are the gracious Word of salvation spoken to all: Lord . . .

Christ Jesus, you are the prophetic Word that challenges us to grow: Christ . . .

Lord Jesus, you are the Word that endures forever: Lord . . .

Homily Points

• We find it easy to speak to people when we have pleasant things to say, and they are obviously glad to hear them. On the other hand, we tend to shy away from delivering words of confrontation, criticism, challenge. Neither do we ourselves like to hear such negative remarks. Yet at the same time, we realize that growth often results from what we really don't want to hear.

• Jesus speaks gracious words that are encouraging. Just as boldly, he speaks words that are challenging and confrontational. His concern was always to speak words of salvation that call people to new life.

• In practice, probably most of us are not left feeling challenged or furious by the proclamation of the gospel itself. The real challenge comes when we are nudged (sometimes not so gently) to *live* the gospel. What increases our capacity to be nudged? What determines our response?

Model Prayer of the Faithful

Presider: The God whose Word constantly calls us to growth will give us all that we need for salvation. And so we pray.

Response:

Lord,—— hear our prayer.

Cantor:

we pray to the Lord,

That all members of the church have the courage to speak only the truth of God's word . . . [pause]

That leaders of nations speak just, encouraging, peaceful words . . . [pause]

That the poor and the suffering may have their burdens lifted by those who have heard and heeded God's word . . . [pause]

That each of us risk being prophets in our own native places . . . [pause]

Presider: Saving God, you are with us through all trials and challenges: hear these our prayers that we might always speak only the truth of your word and live it faithfully. We ask this through Christ our Lord.

ALTERNATIVE OPENING PRAYER
Let us pray

Pause for silent prayer

Father in heaven,
from the days of Abraham and Moses
until this gathering of your Church
in prayer,
you have formed a people in the image of
your Son.
Bless this people with the gift of your
kingdom.
May we serve you with our every desire
and show love for one another
even as you have loved us.

Grant this through Christ our Lord.
Amen.

FIRST READING
Jer 1:4-5, 17-19

The word of the LORD came to me, saying:
Before I formed you in the womb I knew
you,
before you were born I dedicated you,
a prophet to the nations I appointed you.

But do you gird your loins;
stand up and tell them
all that I command you.
Be not crushed on their account,
as though I would leave you crushed
before them;
for it is I this day
who have made you a fortified city,
a pillar of iron, a wall of brass,
against the whole land:
against Judah's kings and princes,
against its priests and people.
They will fight against you but not
prevail over you,
for I am with you to deliver you, says
the LORD.

RESPONSORIAL PSALM
Ps 71:1-2, 3-4, 5-6, 15, 17

R꞉. (cf. 15ab) I will sing of your salvation.

In you, O LORD, I take refuge;
let me never be put to shame.
In your justice rescue me, and deliver me;
incline your ear to me, and save me.

R꞉. I will sing of your salvation.

Be my rock of refuge,
a stronghold to give me safety,
for you are my rock and my fortress.
O my God, rescue me from the hand of the
wicked.

R꞉. I will sing of your salvation.

For you are my hope, O Lord;
   my trust, O God, from my youth.
On you I depend from birth;
   from my mother's womb you are my
     strength.

R̸. I will sing of your salvation.

My mouth shall declare your justice,
   day by day your salvation.
O God, you have taught me from my
    youth,
   and till the present I proclaim your
     wondrous deeds.

R̸. I will sing of your salvation.

SECOND READING
1 Cor 13:4-13

Brothers and sisters:
Love is patient, love is kind.
It is not jealous, it is not pompous,
   it is not inflated, it is not rude,
   it does not seek its own interests,
   it is not quick-tempered, it does not
     brood over injury,
   it does not rejoice over wrongdoing but
     rejoices with the truth.
It bears all things, believes all things,
   hopes all things, endures all things.

Love never fails.
If there are prophecies, they will be
    brought to nothing;
   if tongues, they will cease;
   if knowledge, it will be brought to
     nothing.
For we know partially and we prophesy
    partially,
   but when the perfect comes, the partial
     will pass away.
When I was a child, I used to talk as a
    child,
   think as a child, reason as a child;
   when I became a man, I put aside
     childish things.
At present we see indistinctly, as in a
    mirror,
   but then face to face.
At present I know partially;
   then I shall know fully, as I am fully
     known.
So faith, hope, love remain, these three;
   but the greatest of these is love.

or 1 Cor 12:31–13:13

See Appendix A, p. 269.

About Liturgy

Liturgy of the Word: When we claim that God's word is enduring, we are saying more than the fact that it is proclaimed throughout the world every Saturday evening and Sunday (and weekdays, too!). The mere *saying* or *proclaiming* God's word isn't what makes it enduring; it is *receiving, internalizing,* and *living* God's word that makes it enduring. God's word endures as each of us is transformed, realizing ever more perfectly the spread of God's reign. God's word endures *in us.*

On Sundays the Lectionary selections almost always include both a prophetic word and a comforting word. First challenge: we must truly hear God's word and not let it simply go over our heads. The best way to *hear* (receive) God's word is not to come to liturgy cold; if this is our first hearing, we probably won't get much out of the Liturgy of the Word. A good spiritual practice for all of us is to read the Scriptures well in advance of Sunday so that we can be thinking about them as we go through our normal everyday routines.

Second challenge: we must hear God's word in terms of how it challenges each of us *personally.* This means that almost every Sunday we will hear something in the word that calls us to change (internalize the word) some behavior or attitude. We must help ourselves get into the habit of truly *listening* for that personal word to us. Let our prayer during the rest of the Mass then be one in which we beg God's help to live this word.

Third challenge: we must let that internalized word help us see what we need to address (living the word) in our personal lives and in the world. Sometimes our world is so complex that we don't even recognize the hurts and injustices around us. God's enduring word within us helps us see our world with new eyes—God's eyes. We will no longer be able to take things for granted; we will begin to understand that hearing God's word each Sunday makes demands on us.

About Liturgical Music

Music suggestions: In this Sunday's gospel, Jesus meets with mixed reactions when he challenges his hearers to broaden their perspective about those to whom God offers salvation. "Christus Paradox" [RS] expresses well such mixed reactions to Christ, the "peace-maker and sword-bringer" whom we "both scorn and crave," and works well during the preparation of the gifts. "You Walk along Our Shoreline" [GC2, PMB, RS, SS, WC, WS], a good choice for the preparation of the gifts or the recessional, reminds us that as disciples "We cannot fish for only Those lives we think have worth. We spread your net of gospel Across the water's face, Our boat a common shelter For all found by your grace." "Make Us True Servants" [PMB, WC, WS], suitable for the recessional, calls us to be prophets who "cry out the way, Telling the nations of mercy's new day. Let us break barriers of hatred and scorn, speaking of hope to all people forlorn."

✠ SPIRITUALITY

GOSPEL ACCLAMATION
Matt 4:19

R℟. Alleluia, alleluia.
Come after me
and I will make you fishers of men.
R℟. Alleluia, alleluia.

Gospel   Luke 5:1-11; L75C

While the crowd was
   pressing in on Jesus
   and listening to the
   word of God,
he was standing
   by the Lake of
   Gennesaret.
He saw two boats there
   alongside the lake;
the fishermen had disembarked and
   were washing their nets.
Getting into one of the boats, the one
   belonging to Simon,
he asked him to put out a short
   distance from the shore.
Then he sat down and taught the
   crowds from the boat.
After he had finished speaking, he said
   to Simon,
   "Put out into deep water and lower
      your nets for a catch."
Simon said in reply,
   "Master, we have worked hard all
      night and have caught nothing,
   but at your command I will lower the
      nets."
When they had done this, they caught a
   great number of fish
   and their nets were tearing.
They signaled to their partners in the
   other boat
   to come to help them.
They came and filled both boats
   so that the boats were in danger of
      sinking.

Continued in Appendix A, p. 270.

Reflecting on the Gospel

All of us at times give in to our impulses. Retail stores count on this when they place certain items near the checkout counters—in our face as we stand waiting in line. Sometimes acting on impulse is just fun, as when we skip along the hopscotch boxes some child has chalked on the sidewalk. Sometimes acting on impulse has implications, as when we agree to do something and then find how much time and energy the task will take. Rarely if ever does acting on impulse have lifelong implications. The gospel this Sunday seems to be about impulses: Jesus commands the fisherman to put out their nets in spite of laboring all night catching nothing; the fishermen leave all and follow Jesus. These impulses certainly have lifelong implications!

What precipitated the radical response of the first disciples who "left everything and followed" Jesus? Clearly, Jesus' words and actions. To fishermen who had labored fruitlessly all night, Jesus says try again and leads them to a great catch. To a sinful Peter who considers himself unworthy of Jesus' company, Jesus says follow me, and transforms his life's purpose. More than one miracle has occurred in this gospel.

Jesus "taught the crowds." The miracle of the great catch makes concrete the Good News of Jesus' teaching: God's intervention overturning the futility of mere human work, the superabundance of God's actions on our behalf, the invitation to follow in Jesus' footsteps. The miracle of the catch is the bridge to the second miracle: hearing the Good News and living it. The miracle enabled the disciples to see more deeply into the truth of Jesus' teaching. It's the power of Jesus' Good News that drew them to follow him. Today we are the miracle that makes the Good News visible when we allow God to work in and through us.

Following Jesus can hardly be an impulse decision, although the gospel account might make it seem that way. Between the miracle of the great catch and the disciples leaving everything to follow Jesus stands Peter's recognition that he is "a sinful man." Their encounter with Jesus helped the disciples see themselves for who they were and opened up the willingness to change their life course. They would still be fishermen—but now their catch would be human beings to whom they would tell the Good News of God's presence. Jesus is the net God lowers into the sea of humanity, knowing full well there will be a great catch.

Living the Paschal Mystery

For most of us, Jesus does not come in dramatic and miraculous ways and bid us to follow him; rather, he comes in the ordinary events of daily living. The gospel invites us to look at the simple ways we live, the ways we have changed our purpose in life to follow Jesus—for example, in the generosity of so many volunteers, in the faithfulness of husbands and wives, in the unselfishness of pastoral workers, in the uncomplaining suffering of the sick, in the gracious wisdom of the elderly, we see faithful followers of Jesus living his teachings. Our yes response is to imitate these good behaviors, and by doing so we are faithful followers. Living the paschal mystery means we respond to God in these little, everyday things. The astonishing thing about this Good News is that we are all made worthy followers simply because God calls.

Focusing the Gospel

Key words and phrases: word of God, Put out into deep water, caught a great number, I am a sinful man, they left everything and followed him

To the point: What precipitated the radical response of the first disciples who "left everything and followed" Jesus? Clearly, Jesus' words and actions. To fishermen who had labored fruitlessly all night, Jesus says try again and leads them to a great catch. To a sinful Peter who considers himself unworthy of Jesus' company, Jesus says follow me and transforms his life's purpose. More than one miracle has occurred in this gospel.

Connecting the Gospel

to the first reading: In responding to God's call, our personal worthiness is not the issue, for all humanity is sinful, as both Isaiah and Peter declare. All that matters are the call of God, the mission God gives, and our fidelity to it.

to our experience: Contemporary culture sets up standards of acceptability: body shape, fashions, job performance, etc. The Good News is that God calls us precisely as we are and works through our humanity.

Connecting the Responsorial Psalm

to the readings: Confronted with the Holy, both Isaiah (first reading) and Peter (gospel) immediately acknowledge their sinfulness. Their encounters with the Holy and their subsequent conversions are not entirely private or personal events. Rather, the experience thrusts them into public mission. Isaiah instantly asks to be sent as prophet; Peter leaves everything to become a "catch[er] of men." A similar narrative unfolds in the verses of Psalm 138 used for the responsorial psalm. The psalmist cried to God for help and was rescued. She or he now tells the story before heaven and earth, drawing "all the kings of the earth" to come and glorify God.

Every time we gather to celebrate the Eucharist, we, too, encounter the Holy in the person of Christ. We, too, discover our need for conversion and find forgiveness. And we, too, are called to tell the story. May we do so not only in the singing of this psalm but, like Peter and the first disciples, in the very living of our lives.

to psalmist preparation: In this psalm you tell the whole story of salvation: the human being's cry for help, God's saving response, the subsequent proclamation of what God has done. Telling the story is one thing; however, living it is another. In what way this week might you call for God's help? In what way might you experience God's response? In what way might you tell others?

ASSEMBLY & FAITH-SHARING GROUPS

• When I feel I have ministered fruitlessly, the words of Jesus I hear are . . .

• When I feel unworthy to be a follower of Jesus, the words of Jesus I hear are . . .

• The miracles Jesus has worked in my life are . . . They have moved me to . . .

PRESIDERS

• The manner of my preaching and living calls forth from others a radical response to the words of Jesus when . . .

DEACONS

• My fidelity to diaconal service models for others Jesus' words put into action when . . .

HOSPITALITY MINISTERS

• The manner of my welcome helps others to feel worthy to be in God's presence when . . .

MUSIC MINISTERS

• I experience my music ministry as a way of following Christ because . . . What I have to leave behind to do this is . . .

ALTAR MINISTERS

• Peter became a "catcher of men" because of Jesus' words and actions. I became a minister of the altar because . . .

LECTORS

• The disciples didn't just follow Jesus; they "left everything." What I have to leave behind in order to follow him is . . .

EXTRAORDINARY MINISTERS OF HOLY COMMUNION

• My encounters with Jesus in the Body of Christ have changed me from . . . to . . .

Model Act of Penitence

Presider: In the gospel today Jesus teaches the crowds and calls Peter, James, and John to follow him. Let us pause to prepare ourselves to hear what Jesus teaches us today and to follow him more faithfully . . . [pause]

Lord Jesus, you are the Word of God: Lord . . .

Christ Jesus, you are the power of the Spirit transforming our lives: Christ . . .

Lord Jesus, you call us to follow you and preach your Gospel: Lord . . .

Homily Points

• As human beings we are often impulsive. We hear a pitch for a new product and we run out to buy it. We hear a motivational speaker and we sign on the dotted line. Yet how often the new product ends up sitting on our shelf, how quickly we drop out of trends or fads. The gospel narrative relates what might appear to be an impulsive response on the part of the first disciples, yet we know they grew into a lifelong commitment of being faithful followers of Jesus.

• Jesus' own words and actions were not impulse decisions but flowed from the clarity of his mission and the consistent, radical orientation of his whole life toward service of his Father and others. The disciples were "caught" by the integrity of Jesus' words and actions.

• The miracle of the great catch is dramatic and sensational, as is the radical response of the first disciples who leave everything to take on a new way of life. For our part, we rarely if ever experience such dramatic miracles or such all-encompassing life changes. But our ordinary daily living can nonetheless flow from a similar integrity of our own words and actions—our own radical response to Jesus.

Model Prayers of the Faithful

Presider: The God who calls us to discipleship will give us what we need to be faithful. And so we pray.

Response:

Lord,—— hear our prayer.

Cantor:

we pray to the Lord,

That all members of the church grow in their commitment to follow Jesus faithfully . . . [pause]

That all leaders of nations, by the integrity of their words and actions, inspire concern for others . . . [pause]

That those who feel lowly be raised to a greater appreciation of their God-given dignity . . . [pause]

That each of us be a source of strength to one another as we strive to live the gospel . . . [pause]

Presider: O God, you come in many different ways, calling us to be disciples. Hear these our prayers that we might one day share everlasting life with you. We ask this through Christ our Lord. **Amen.**

Let us pray
[with reverence in the presence of
the living God]

Pause for silent prayer

In faith and love we ask you, Father,
to watch over your family gathered here.
In your mercy and loving kindness
no thought of ours is left unguarded,
no tear unheeded, no joy unnoticed.
Through the prayer of Jesus
may the blessings promised to the poor in
     spirit
lead us to the treasures of your heavenly
     kingdom.

We ask this in the name of Jesus the Lord.
     Amen.

FIRST READING
Isa 6:1-2a, 3-8

In the year King Uzziah died,
     I saw the Lord seated on a high and
          lofty throne,
     with the train of his garment filling the
          temple.
Seraphim were stationed above.

They cried one to the other,
     "Holy, holy, holy is the LORD of hosts!
All the earth is filled with his glory!"
At the sound of that cry, the frame of the
          door shook
     and the house was filled with smoke.

Then I said, "Woe is me, I am doomed!
For I am a man of unclean lips,
     living among a people of unclean lips;
     yet my eyes have seen the King, the
          LORD of hosts!"
Then one of the seraphim flew to me,
     holding an ember that he had taken
          with tongs from the altar.

He touched my mouth with it, and said,
     "See, now that this has touched your
          lips,
     your wickedness is removed, your sin
          purged."

Then I heard the voice of the Lord saying,
     "Whom shall I send? Who will go for
          us?"
"Here I am," I said; "send me!"

RESPONSORIAL PSALM
Ps 138:1-2, 2-3, 4-5, 7-8

℟. (1c) In the sight of the angels I will sing your praises, Lord.

I will give thanks to you, O Lord, with all
   my heart,
      for you have heard the words of my
         mouth;
      in the presence of the angels I will sing
         your praise;
I will worship at your holy temple
   and give thanks to your name.

R︎. In the sight of the angels I will sing
your praises, Lord.

Because of your kindness and your truth;
   for you have made great above all things
      your name and your promise.
When I called, you answered me;
   you built up strength within me.

R︎. In the sight of the angels I will sing
your praises, Lord.

All the kings of the earth shall give
      thanks to you, O Lord,
   when they hear the words of your mouth;
and they shall sing of the ways of the Lord:
   "Great is the glory of the Lord."

R︎. In the sight of the angels I will sing
your praises, Lord.

Your right hand saves me.
   The Lord will complete what he has
      done for me;
your kindness, O Lord, endures forever;
   forsake not the work of your hands.

R︎. In the sight of the angels I will sing
your praises, Lord.

SECOND READING
1 Cor 15:3-8, 11

Brothers and sisters,
   I handed on to you as of first
         importance what I also received:
      that Christ died for our sins
      in accordance with the Scriptures;
      that he was buried;
      that he was raised on the third day
      in accordance with the Scriptures;
      that he appeared to Cephas, then to the
         Twelve.
After that, he appeared to more
   than five hundred brothers at once,
   most of whom are still living,
      though some have fallen asleep.
After that he appeared to James,
   then to all the apostles.
Last of all, as to one born abnormally,
   he appeared to me.
Therefore, whether it be I or they,
   so we preach and so you believed.

or 1 Cor 15:1-11

See Appendix A, p. 270.

About Liturgy
"Lord, I am not worthy . . ." At Mass our response to the invitation to Holy Communion includes the words, "Lord, I am not worthy." This Sunday's gospel challenges us to utter these words, not simply as a confession of sinfulness or a way to debase our own dignity as daughters and sons of God, but as a simple statement of recognizing our own status as creatures before God's all-powerful and divine holiness. The amazing generosity of Jesus' self-offering of his Body and Blood for our nourishment and drink is that God doesn't focus on our unworthiness but raises us up to share in divinity. Communion should always be a kind of wake-up call in which we praise and thank God for the call to holiness and also resolve to be faithful to God's call to continue Jesus' mission. Sharing in God's holiness is also sharing in God's mission.

About Liturgical Music
Music suggestions: Songs about the call to discipleship would be suitable this Sunday, as would songs that speak of how encounter with Christ transforms us and changes our lives. The bilingual "Pescador de Hombres," found in many hymnals, flows directly from the gospel story and would be a good choice for Communion. Christopher Walker's "Out of Darkness" [BB, JS2, OFUV] would work well for the entrance, the preparation of the gifts, or Communion. In Michael Ward's "Here I Am, Lord" [PMB] we can hear the sinful Peter saying to Jesus, "What joy it is to stand amid your glory. Let me always stay in your presence, O God" (verse 2). This verse-refrain song would be suitable for Communion. In "Lead Me, Guide Me," included in most hymnals, we speak to Jesus about our weakness and our need for his strength and power, praying to be led by him all along the way of discipleship. This hymn could be sung for Communion or as a recessional.

FEBRUARY 7, 2010
FIFTH SUNDAY IN ORDINARY TIME

SPIRITUALITY

GOSPEL ACCLAMATION
Luke 6:23ab

R/. Alleluia, alleluia.
Rejoice and be glad,
your reward will be great in heaven.
R/. Alleluia, alleluia.

Gospel   Luke 6:17, 20-26; L78C

Jesus came down with the Twelve
  and stood on a stretch of level ground
  with a great crowd of his disciples
  and a large number of the people
  from all Judea and Jerusalem
  and the coastal region of Tyre and Sidon.
And raising his eyes toward his disciples he
    said:
  "Blessed are you who are poor,
    for the kingdom of God is yours.
  Blessed are you who are now hungry,
    for you will be satisfied.
  Blessed are you who are now weeping,
    for you will laugh.
  Blessed are you when people hate you,
    and when they exclude and insult you,
    and denounce your name as evil
    on account of the Son of Man.
Rejoice and leap for joy on that day!
Behold, your reward will be great in heaven.
For their ancestors treated the prophets in
    the same way.
  But woe to you who are rich,
    for you have received your consolation.
  Woe to you who are filled now,
    for you will be hungry.
  Woe to you who laugh now,
    for you will grieve and weep.
  Woe to you when all speak well of you,
    for their ancestors treated the false
      prophets in this way."

Reflecting on the Gospel

Seth was about to "graduate" from preschool. He proudly put his paper mortarboard on his head and marched with his schoolmates to the stage. As he received his diploma Seth solemnly shook hands with the principal. After the ceremony his family rushed to him and each said, "Congratulations." He smiled and said thank you to each, then looked to his mom and dad and asked, "What does that big word mean?" to which they answered, "Good job!" While this answer works in this and many other situations, sometimes something much deeper is intended, which is closer to the original meaning of congratulations. From the Latin, congratulations actually means "to be pleased with" or "graced with." When we offer our congratulations, we are saying that we rejoice with the accomplishment of the other, which "enlarges" both of us and expresses a relationship. The Beatitudes of this Sunday's gospel express something of the same thing: they announce God's pleasure in and relationship to the poor, hungry, sorrowful, those who are hated and excluded and insulted.

The Greek word for "blessed" is *makárioi*, which functions as a kind of congratulatory note. It means someone is fortunate because he or she is the recipient of divine favor. Blessedness, by its very nature, bears the fruit of the kingdom of God because it is of God. With the Beatitudes, Luke highlights God's generosity. Blessedness isn't a matter of social status, satisfaction, possessions, respect, etc.; it is a matter of keeping our eyes glued on Jesus.

Luke seems in this gospel to be exalting the downtrodden simply because they are downtrodden, and cursing the comfortable simply because they are comfortable. While it is true that God has special care for the poor and downtrodden, it is equally true that having possessions is not in itself cause for condemnation. What really is at the heart of this gospel is the manner of life that makes present the kingdom and assures us that our "reward will be great in heaven." The model of this manner of life and the source of the blessedness it brings is Jesus himself.

All are blessed who open themselves to the favor God grants. First, then, comes God's grace, favor, graciousness. From this comes a relationship with God and our acknowledgment that we have been chosen by God, blessed by God. Then comes a manner of living that is consistent with our relationship. The "kingdom of God" is ours when our living is in line with Jesus, when all our actions are "on account of the Son of Man." Our reward, indeed, is great—because it is God who blesses.

Living the Paschal Mystery

Most of us live just barely getting by—we never have enough time, enough money, enough energy. We tend to keep our focus on *now* and, to a large extent, this is necessary. The Beatitudes, however, invite another stance. Even in being caught up in the cares of everyday living, we can still keep our eyes on Jesus Christ and what we are really seeking—everlasting glory with him in the time to come. We Christians are not so much *now* people as *future* people. This is why social status, or what people think of us, or possessions, lead to woes—they turn our eyes from the future glory that awaits us when we keep our eyes on Christ. It is our relationship to God that motivates us to live the blessing that is given us. It is our relationship with God that motivates us to reach out to others with good "on account of the Son of Man."

Focusing the Gospel

Key words and phrases: Blessed are you, kingdom of God, on account of the Son of Man, woe, now

To the point: Luke seems in this gospel to be exalting the downtrodden simply because they are downtrodden, and cursing the comfortable simply because they are comfortable. What really is at the heart of this gospel is the manner of life that makes present the kingdom and assures us that our "reward will be great in heaven." The model of this manner of life and the source of the blessedness it brings is Jesus himself.

Connecting the Gospel

to the first reading: Blessedness, by its very nature, bears good things because it is of God. For Jeremiah, blessedness brings the lushness that water can bring to a desert. For Jesus, blessedness brings the unimaginable reward of belonging to God.

to our experience: Although we in our society are proud that we do not have classes or castes that separate, in fact we do have distinctions that separate, not least among them being the rich and the poor, the haves and the have-nots. We discover the presence of God's kingdom when people come together across what divides and share both gifts and needs, so that everyone is on "level ground."

Connecting the Responsorial Psalm

to the readings: Jewish Wisdom literature portrays two ways of living: as faithful to the law of God or as unfaithful. The first way brings blessings and fruitfulness, the second waste and destruction. Psalm 1 introduces the entire collection of psalms by deliberately reminding the Israelites of the call to be faithful to the way of God in the midst of all the ups and downs, the losses and deliverances, the laments and joys that characterize human history (as the ensuing psalms reveal).

In the first reading Jeremiah uses the same imagery as Psalm 1 to make the same point. Those who turn from God will be dry and barren; those who trust in God will be deep-rooted and green. In the gospel Jesus specifies this blessedness and cursedness in concrete but surprising ways. The psalm refrain helps us get to the core: blessed are those who trust, hope in, and keep their focus on God. Regardless of appearances these are the ones prospering. In singing this psalm we express our choice to follow the way of God and know blessedness both here and now and forever in eternity.

to psalmist preparation: As you prepare to sing this responsorial psalm you might spend some time reflecting on those people who model blessedness for you. How does their manner of living show that they "hope in the Lord" (refrain)? How does their manner of living help you remain faithful to the way of God?

**ASSEMBLY &
FAITH-SHARING GROUPS**
- Jesus is the source of blessedness for me when . . . through . . .
- The manner of life to which the Beatitudes call me is . . . Those who model this for me are . . .
- My manner of life reveals the presence of God's kingdom when . . .

PRESIDERS
- What keeps me on "level ground" with those for whom I minister is . . .

DEACONS
- My service to those in need reveals them as blessed when . . .

HOSPITALITY MINISTERS
- My manner of greeting helps people feel they are on "level ground" before God when . . . with each other when . . .

MUSIC MINISTERS
- I hear Jesus calling me blessed in my music-making when . . .

ALTAR MINISTERS
- My doing the lowly tasks of ministering at the altar reminds me how blessed I am when . . .

LECTORS
- My manner of proclaiming God's word is an announcement of blessedness when . . .

**EXTRAORDINARY MINISTERS
OF HOLY COMMUNION**
- My recognizing each communicant as blessed enables me to . . .

Model Act of Penitence

Presider: Today we hear Luke's version of the Beatitudes. Let us prepare ourselves to celebrate this liturgy by pausing to reflect on how we have lived our blessedness . . . [pause]

Lord Jesus, you are the source of blessing and salvation for all: Lord . . .

Christ Jesus, you are the promise and the fulfillment of the kingdom of God: Christ . . .

Lord Jesus, your words bring challenge and joy: Lord . . .

Homily Points

• When we hear the phrase "blessed ones," we don't generally put ourselves in that crowd. The gospel, however, moves us beyond a narrow understanding of blessedness to seeing it in terms of a manner of living possible for all of us because of Jesus, who dwells within and among us.

• The kingdom of God is among us when we, rich and poor alike, seek to live the way Jesus did, in fidelity and obedience to his Father. His way of relating to all people shows us that he himself is the source of blessedness.

• The Beatitudes are lofty sayings, but Jesus delivers them "on . . . level ground." The Beatitudes are challenging, yes, but they are not pie-in-the-sky impossibilities; rather, they are played out in the concreteness of responding to the needs of the people around us. We can make the values and vision of Jesus our own way of life because he dwells among us here, showing us how—in and through one another.

Model Prayer of the Faithful

Presider: As people called to a life of blessedness, we pray for all we need.

Response:

Lord,——— hear our prayer.

Cantor:

we pray to the Lord,

That the church may always be the continued blessing of Christ's presence in the world . . . [pause]

That the peoples of the world may all share equally in the abundance with which God has blessed creation . . . [pause]

That the poor, hungry, weeping, and excluded may be the blessed children of God inheriting the fullness of God's kingdom . . . [pause]

That all of us gathered here may faithfully follow the way of life Jesus modeled for us . . . [pause]

Presider: Gracious God, you bless all who come to you: hear these our prayers that one day we might enjoy the fullness of life with you in heaven. We ask this through Christ our Lord. **Amen.**

OPENING PRAYER
Let us pray

Pause for silent prayer

God our Father,
you have promised to remain for ever
with those who do what is just and right.
Help us to live in your presence.

We ask this through our Lord Jesus Christ,
     your Son,
who lives and reigns with you and the
     Holy Spirit,
one God, for ever and ever. **Amen.**

FIRST READING
Jer 17:5-8

Thus says the LORD:
     Cursed is the one who trusts in human
          beings,
          who seeks his strength in flesh,
          whose heart turns away from the
          LORD.
     He is like a barren bush in the desert
          that enjoys no change of season,
          but stands in a lava waste, a salt and
          empty earth.
     Blessed is the one who trusts in the
          LORD,
          whose hope is the LORD.
     He is like a tree planted beside the
          waters
          that stretches out its roots to the
          stream:
     it fears not the heat when it comes;
          its leaves stay green;
     in the year of drought it shows no
          distress,
          but still bears fruit.

RESPONSORIAL PSALM
Ps 1:1-2, 3, 4, 6

R⁀. (40:5a) Blessed are they who hope in
the Lord.

Blessed the man who follows not
   the counsel of the wicked,
nor walks in the way of sinners,
   nor sits in the company of the insolent,
but delights in the law of the LORD
   and meditates on his law day and night.

R⁀. Blessed are they who hope in the Lord.

He is like a tree
   planted near running water,
that yields its fruit in due season,
   and whose leaves never fade.
Whatever he does, prospers.

R⁀. Blessed are they who hope in the Lord.

Not so the wicked, not so;
   they are like chaff which the wind
      drives away.
For the LORD watches over the way of the
   just,
   but the way of the wicked vanishes.

R⁀. Blessed are they who hope in the Lord.

SECOND READING
1 Cor 15:12, 16-20

Brothers and sisters:
If Christ is preached as raised from the
   dead,
   how can some among you say there is no
      resurrection of the dead?
If the dead are not raised, neither has
   Christ been raised,
   and if Christ has not been raised, your
      faith is vain;
   you are still in your sins.
Then those who have fallen asleep in
   Christ have perished.
If for this life only we have hoped in
   Christ,
   we are the most pitiable people of all.

But now Christ has been raised from the
   dead,
   the firstfruits of those who have fallen
      asleep.

About Liturgy

Christ's presence in liturgy: The Constitution on the Sacred Liturgy outlines four presences of Christ in liturgical celebration: Christ "is present . . . in the person of his minister . . . in the eucharistic species . . . in the word . . . when the Church prays and sings . . ." (SC 7). Our natural tendency is to focus on the sublime and substantial presence of Christ in the eucharistic species, but the constitution makes clear that this is not the only presence of Christ. Perhaps for too long now we have been neglecting Christ's presence in the word, the presider, and the assembly, yet these presences are also clearly presented in this Sunday's gospel.

We open ourselves to a much broader and richer experience of Christ when we also look for him in the presider, in eating and drinking the consecrated Bread and Wine, in the proclamation of the word, and in the assembled community itself, which is the Body of Christ being led, challenged, nourished, and offered dignity. Moreover, when we are able to recognize Christ in these other presences at Mass, we have begun to form ourselves to see Christ's presence in the everyday people and circumstances of our lives. In this way we already begin to live the blessedness of which Jesus speaks in this gospel. Liturgy teaches us that Christ is present in many ways.

About Liturgical Music

Music suggestions: Since the gospel readings for this and next Sunday are part of a single unit (Luke's Sermon on the Plain), singing a relevant hymn or choir piece both weeks would be an effective way to express this interrelationship. For example, "Choose Life" [WC; choral octavo WLP #7936] reiterates the content of these readings: "I have set before you life and death, the blessing and the curse. Choose life . . . that you may live" (Deut 30:15-20). Since the text is a direct address to the people, the piece needs to be sung by cantor or choir rather than by the assembly themselves. It could be sung as a choral prelude this Sunday and as a choir-only piece during the preparation of the gifts next Sunday.

Season of Lent

✝ SPIRITUALITY

GOSPEL ACCLAMATION
See Ps 95:8

If today you hear his voice,
harden not your hearts.

Gospel   Matt 6:1-6, 16-18; L219

Jesus said to his disciples:
  "Take care not to perform righteous
        deeds
    in order that people may see them;
    otherwise, you will have no recompense
        from your heavenly Father.
When you give alms,
    do not blow a trumpet before you,
    as the hypocrites do in the synagogues
        and in the streets
    to win the praise of others.
Amen, I say to you,
    they have received their reward.
But when you give alms,
    do not let your left hand know what your
        right is doing,
    so that your almsgiving may be secret.
And your Father who sees in secret will
    repay you.

"When you pray,
    do not be like the hypocrites,
    who love to stand and pray in the
        synagogues and on street corners
    so that others may see them.
Amen, I say to you,
    they have received their reward.
But when you pray, go to your inner room,
    close the door, and pray to your Father in
        secret.
And your Father who sees in secret will
    repay you.

"When you fast,
    do not look gloomy like the hypocrites.
They neglect their appearance,
    so that they may appear to others to be
        fasting.
Amen, I say to you, they have received their
    reward.
But when you fast,
    anoint your head and wash your face,
    so that you may not appear to be fasting,
    except to your Father who is hidden.
And your Father who sees what is hidden
    will repay you."

See Appendix A, p. 271, for other readings.

Reflecting on the Gospel

Motivation is a powerful force. If we want something badly enough, we are willing to go to almost any ends to achieve it. Parents shape children by motivating them with various rewards; teachers motivate learners with gold stars on papers and grades; companies motivate employees with bonuses; gratitude is a kind of motivation. In all these cases, motivation is a bridge between people that establishes, builds, strengthens relationships and behavioral outcomes, and it is powerful, indeed.

Yet in the gospel Jesus seems to ask us to undertake our Lenten penance without any of the usual motivation we like, especially "the praise of others" that is so powerfully moving. Gospel motivation for undertaking penance is that the Father in heaven sees and "repays" us—with new life, a share in divine life, a deeper relationship with God and each other that transforms us *now* (see second reading) to perform "righteous deeds." Much is at stake during Lent. Most important, what is at stake is growing in our relationship with God and each other, which in turn changes how we behave and what we do.

Jesus counsels us three times to give alms, pray, and fast "in secret" where only God knows what we are doing. But the words of the prophet Joel in the first reading call us to public penance as a community. We are to act "in secret" but also to "work[ ] together" to "be reconciled" (second reading) with God and one another. In fact, then, we never truly act "in secret." Our private Lenten practices have bearing on God's "blessing" (first reading) of the community. "In secret," as used in the gospel, raises a question about the motivation for our acts of Lenten penitence. All the readings together answer our question: we undertake Lenten practices because they transform self (through God's gift of new life) and, consequently, transform the community (because of who we become, how we relate to one another in community, and by our "righteous deeds").

Our strongest motivation for undertaking Lenten penance is the deepening of our relationships. Lent directs us inward to self-transformation, which opens us to new relationships with God and each other. Any transformation presupposes that we set right our relationships. In other words, our Lenten practices include the kind of inward renewal that changes how we relate to God and others. Changed behaviors and "righteous deeds" flow from our changed relationships.

Living the Paschal Mystery

We must take care that we don't live these next six weeks like the other weeks of the year. Now we are in a special kind of "training"—we are redoubling our efforts to learn what gospel living means. Extra time faithfully spent in prayer, emptying ourselves through fasting so we hunger for God, being attentive to others—this is how we die to ourselves and live faithfully the gospel.

Because our own transformation deepens our relationships, good choices for Lenten practices are those that really change us, and not just during Lent. In other words, simply "giving up" something and forgetting about the practice when Lent is over doesn't really help us do what the gospel is asking of us. Our Lenten penance must be directed to *transformation* (conversion) of self that lasts beyond Lent. Transformation makes a difference in our lives and relationships.

Focusing the Gospel

Key words and phrases: in secret, Father . . . will repay you

To the point: In the gospel Jesus counsels us three times to give alms, pray, and fast "in secret" where only God knows what we are doing. But the words of the prophet Joel in the first reading call us to public penance as a community. We are to act "in secret" but also to "work[ ] together" to "be reconciled" (second reading) with God and one another. In fact, then, we never truly act "in secret." Our private Lenten practices have bearing on God's "blessing" (first reading) of the community.

Model Prayer of the Faithful

Presider: As we begin this solemn time of discipline and conversion, let us pray that we will grow in our love for God and each other.

Response:

Lord, hear our prayer.

Cantor:

we pray to the Lord,

That all members of the church enter into this Lenten season with a spirit willing to change and a heart open to God's mercy . . . [pause]

That all peoples of the world work toward reconciliation and forgiveness . . . [pause]

That those who are poor and in need be lifted up by our Lenten almsgiving . . . [pause]

That our Lenten practices transform us and renew the communities in which we live . . . [pause]

Presider: Gracious and merciful God, you hear the prayers of those who call out to you: be near us during Lent, keep us faithful in our resolve, and lead us to new life. We ask this through Christ our Lord. **Amen.**

OPENING PRAYER

Let us pray

Pause for silent prayer

Lord,
protect us in our struggle against evil.
As we begin the discipline of Lent,
make this season holy by our self-denial.

Grant this through our Lord Jesus Christ,
    your Son,
who lives and reigns with you and the Holy
    Spirit,
one God, for ever and ever. **Amen.**

FOR REFLECTION

• During this Lent the "righteous deeds" that I need to do for renewal of myself are . . .

• My Lenten practices also transform the community because . . . when . . . if . . .

Homily Points

• In a society that applauds rugged individualism, we often discount the import our behavior has for others. When we change ourselves, however, we change the communities in which we live and work.

• The practices of Lent we undertake "in secret" must draw us beyond ourselves to the quality of life within community—both the community of the church and the community of the world.

✚ SPIRITUALITY

GOSPEL ACCLAMATION
Matt 4:4b

One does not live on bread alone,
but on every word that comes forth from
the mouth of God.

Gospel   Luke 4:1-13; L24C

Filled with the Holy Spirit, Jesus
    returned from the Jordan
and was led by the Spirit into the
    desert for forty days,
to be tempted by the devil.
He ate nothing during those days,
    and when they were over he was
    hungry.
The devil said to him,
    "If you are the Son of God,
    command this stone to become bread."
Jesus answered him,
    "It is written, *One does not live on bread
    alone.*"
Then he took him up and showed him
    all the kingdoms of the world in a single
    instant.
The devil said to him,
    "I shall give to you all this power and glory;
    for it has been handed over to me,
    and I may give it to whomever I wish.
All this will be yours, if you worship me."
Jesus said to him in reply,
    "It is written:
    *You shall worship the Lord, your God,
    and him alone shall you serve.*"
Then he led him to Jerusalem,
    made him stand on the parapet of the
    temple, and said to him,
    "If you are the Son of God,
    throw yourself down from here, for it is
    written:
    *He will command his angels
        concerning you, to guard you,*
and:
    *With their hands they will support you,
    lest you dash your foot against a stone.*"
Jesus said to him in reply,
    "It also says,
    *You shall not put the Lord, your God, to
    the test.*"
When the devil had finished every
    temptation,
    he departed from him for a time.

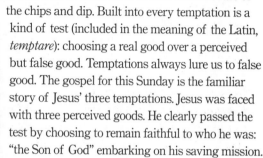

Reflecting on the Gospel

Temptations by their very nature are luring—they present us with a seeming good we do not presently have but want. Without a powerfully attractive lure, temptations simply don't exist. For example, if a tray of veggies and a tray of chips and dip are placed before us, few of us would be "tempted" by the veggies. Let's face it: the real temptation and need for resistance derives from the lure of the chips and dip. Built into every temptation is a kind of test (included in the meaning of the Latin, *temptare*): choosing a real good over a perceived but false good. Temptations always lure us to false good. The gospel for this Sunday is the familiar story of Jesus' three temptations. Jesus was faced with three perceived goods. He clearly passed the test by choosing to remain faithful to who he was: "the Son of God" embarking on his saving mission.

Jesus was "led by the Spirit into the desert . . . to be tempted." Each temptation put to him by the devil involved some misguided personal gain: seeking easy solutions to human hungers, pursuing "power and glory," defying death. By resisting these temptations Jesus shows us that our true gain is found not in satisfying ourselves but in something better—utter fidelity to God. Temptations always present us with the choice between personal gain and something even better: the goodness and holiness that comes from serving God and doing good for others. This same choice between self-satisfaction and fidelity to God frees us, like Jesus, to be who we are meant to be, persons "led by the Spirit."

Not even the Son of God was exempt from being tested! We can expect no less in our own lives. Temptation isn't an indication of sinfulness; rather, it is an occasion for showing that our lives are turned to God, in whom we find our very identity and being. Like Jesus, temptations and our very resistance to them strengthen us in our choices for goodness and holiness. In making these choices we are continually choosing who we want to be: those who faithfully serve God by doing good for others. Temptations' lure to self-satisfaction is overcome by an even stronger lure: growth in holiness and transformation into ever more beloved sons and daughters of God. Lent is a focused time to take the test of who we want to be. Let us pray that we all pass it well!

Living the Paschal Mystery

The ritual act of professing our faith during Sunday Mass is no substitution for *living* it in our daily lives. When we are tested by temptations, our faith is put to the test, too, and we are faced with a choice of who we are and how we want to live. Lent is a time to examine our choices.

Just as God led Israel to a "land flowing with milk and honey" (first reading), so will God lead us to salvation if we "call on the name of the Lord" (second reading). For us, though, our desert is the demands of everyday living, and our salvation is found on the cross. Each day we take up our cross and lay down our life for the sake of others, we are building strength to resist temptation and come to greater faith. Our simple acts of kindness are helping us resist temptation. Our doing well whatever the task at hand helps us resist temptation. Our complimenting another or offering a word of encouragement helps us resist temptation.

We don't have to go out into a desert to find temptation! But we do need God's nearness to resist it. And that God has promised us.

Focusing the Gospel

Key words and phrases: led by the Spirit, to be tempted, God . . . alone shall you serve

To the point: Jesus was "led by the Spirit into the desert . . . to be tempted." Each temptation put to him by the devil involved some misguided personal gain: seeking easy solutions to human hungers, pursuing "power and glory," defying death. By resisting these temptations Jesus shows us that our true gain is found not in satisfying ourselves but in something better—utter fidelity to God. This choice frees us, like Jesus, to be who we are meant to be, persons "led by the Spirit."

Connecting the Gospel

to the first and second readings: The recap of salvation history that Moses recites for the people (see first reading) reminds us that God always works on our behalf, "enriching all who call upon him" (second reading). This is our assurance that reliance on God is better than whatever any temptation can offer us.

to our experience: People often grow discouraged because they have to face temptations over and over. As human beings we will never eliminate temptations, but our resistance to them strengthens us in our relationship with God, self, and others.

Connecting the Responsorial Psalm

to the readings: Temptation is never absent from *our* lives, just as it was not even absent from the life of Jesus who was led by the Spirit directly into its face (gospel). Even when vanquished by Jesus' response, Satan departs only "for a time." The very psalm quoted by Satan as part of the temptation is for Jesus, however, a prayer of unshakable confidence in God who is always present in times of "trouble" (responsorial psalm). The God who forged a people and brought them out of Egypt through the desert to a land of milk and honey (first reading) will not now abandon Christ—or us—in the desert.

As we enter this Lenten period of fasting and prayer, we can be certain that as it was with Jesus so it will be with us. Satan will not be idle. The more faithful we are to prayer, fasting, and doing good for others, the more will we be tempted simply to give it all up for the sake of easier rewards. The psalm reminds us that when this happens we need only call with Jesus "on the name of the Lord" (second reading) and sing with him our confidence in the God who guards and delivers us.

to psalmist preparation: The gospel reading suggests a specific shape to the "trouble" you sing about in the responsorial psalm: the temptation at the beginning of Lent to abandon fidelity to God when the task is too hard, the time too long, and more alluring prospects offer themselves. In this psalm Christ shares with the assembly his certainty of God's presence and protection, and you are his voice. What might you say to Christ during this week to help you prepare for such a ministry?

**ASSEMBLY &
FAITH-SHARING GROUPS**

- I am most prone to temptation when . . . I am best able to resist temptation when . . .
- The misguided personal gain I am most tempted to pursue is . . .
- What strengthens my fidelity to God is . . .

PRESIDERS

- The way I lead and comfort those in the desert of temptation is . . .

DEACONS

- My openness to being "led by the Spirit" takes me to . . .

HOSPITALITY MINISTERS

- The grace of hospitality is meant to nurture and support those facing trials and temptations. Some I know who need this now are . . .

MUSIC MINISTERS

- Sometimes in my very music making I am tempted to turn from God by . . . What keeps me faithful to God is . . .

ALTAR MINISTERS

- The temptations I face within my ministry are . . . Relying on God in such times means to me . . .

LECTORS

- My manner of proclaiming the word helps people to be "led by the Spirit" when . . .

**EXTRAORDINARY MINISTERS
OF HOLY COMMUNION**

- My manner of distributing Holy Communion helps communicants focus on their real hungers by . . .

Model Act of Penitence

Presider: In the gospel today the Spirit leads Jesus into the desert to be tempted. We don't need to travel to a physical desert to be tempted—we find our desert in the demands of everyday living. Let us ask God to pardon us for the times we have given in to temptation . . . [pause]

Confiteor: I confess . . .

Homily Points

• The lure of temptations is that they always pull us toward something desirable; but temptations also pull us away from something even better. For example, an inordinate desire for "power and glory" hurts our relationships with family and friends. In the gospel Jesus is tempted three times but always resists because he chooses what is better: fidelity to his identity and mission.

• All three of the temptations the devil set before Jesus were directed toward Jesus' very identity as the Son of God. If he had given in to the devil and, ultimately, worshiped him, Jesus would have betrayed who he was and what he had been sent to do.

• When we resist temptations, we are really acting in consonance with who we are as baptized followers of Jesus. Our very identity is tied into our choice to remain faithful to God. Being true to ourselves means opening ourselves to being "led by the Spirit" more deeply into our Christian identity. This is truly the work of our Lenten journey.

Model Prayer of the Faithful

Presider: We pray for the strength to resist temptation and to grow in fidelity to God.

Response:

Lord, hear our prayer.

Cantor:

we pray to the Lord,

That all members of the church enter into the desert of Lent in fasting and prayer and receive the strength to resist temptation . . . [pause]

That peoples of the world come to the salvation God offers through the death and resurrection of the Son . . . [pause]

That those who are hungry receive nourishment, those who are downtrodden be lifted up, those who face death be comforted . . . [pause]

That those preparing for the initiation sacraments be led by the Spirit into new life . . . [pause]

That each of us enter into Lent with seriousness of purpose and resolve of will to grow in our baptismal identity . . . [pause]

Presider: Merciful God, you send your Spirit to strengthen us in times of need: hear these our prayers that we always remain faithful to you and one day enjoy eternal life with you. We ask this through Christ our Savior. **Amen.**

RESPONSORIAL PSALM

Ps 91:1-2, 10-11, 12-13, 14-15

℟. (cf. 15b) Be with me, Lord, when I am in trouble.

You who dwell in the shelter of the Most
      High,
   who abide in the shadow of the
         Almighty,
say to the LORD, "My refuge and fortress,
   my God in whom I trust."

℟. Be with me, Lord, when I am in trouble.

No evil shall befall you,
   nor shall affliction come near your tent,
for to his angels he has given command
      about you,
   that they guard you in all your ways.

℟. Be with me, Lord, when I am in trouble.

Upon their hands they shall bear you up,
   lest you dash your foot against a stone.
You shall tread upon the asp and the viper;
   you shall trample down the lion and the
      dragon.

℟. Be with me, Lord, when I am in trouble.

Because he clings to me, I will deliver him;
   I will set him on high because he
      acknowledges my name.
He shall call upon me, and I will answer
      him;
   I will be with him in distress;
I will deliver him and glorify him.

℟. Be with me, Lord, when I am in trouble.

SECOND READING

Rom 10:8-13

See Appendix A, p. 271.

About Liturgy

Creed and intercessions: The general intercessions we pray at Mass are a kind of practical continuation of the profession of faith already begun in the Creed. The name used now for this time of intense prayer that concludes the Liturgy of the Word is "Prayer of the Faithful," and this name suggests that this prayer, then, is a "profession" of our faithful relationship to God that spills over to faithful relationship with each other.

The format used for the prayer of the faithful in *Living Liturgy*™ involves the assembly in two ways. First of all, the prayers are short—only giving an *announcement* of a general intention that flows from the readings. The slight pause indicated by the ellipses is time for *each of us to pray with all our hearts*. Thus, the first involvement is in genuine prayer for the needs of the church, the world, the less fortunate, and our own parish or liturgical community. Second, the prayer of the faithful isn't finished when we respond *Amen* to the presider's concluding collect. In fact, the prayer we pray during Mass is only the beginning of our responsibility to those for whom we pray. In this prayer we also make a commitment to actually die to self—get involved in helping God's reign become a reality in our world. This prayer is a commitment to fidelity to doing good for others.

First readings during Lent: The Old Testament readings during Lent provide a thumbnail of salvation history and, because they have their own purpose, won't necessarily accord with the gospel. The Lectionary is instructing us in God's ways and mighty deeds in the first reading and asking for a faith response in the gospels.

About Liturgical Music

Hymn suggestion: Sylvia Dunstan's "From the River to the Desert" [*Hymns for the Gospels*, GIA] narrates in poetic form the story of Christ's temptation in the desert. Following the pattern of the gospel story, verses 2 to 4 unfold as a dialogue between Satan and Jesus. Verse 5 is a prayer begging Jesus who "knows our weakness" to plead for us for whom "your grace is all we need." The text is a lengthy one that must be sung in its entirety. If there is sufficient time, this would be a suitable song during the preparation of the gifts. Otherwise, the choir alone could sing it as a prelude. An effective way for them to sing it would be for a soloist to sing verse 1 to set the scene, antiphonal sections to sing verses 2 to 4 to express the dialogue between Satan and Christ, and the full choir to sing the final verse as a communal prayer.

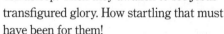

✝ SPIRITUALITY

GOSPEL ACCLAMATION

cf. Matt 17:5

From the shining cloud the Father's voice is
    heard:
This is my beloved Son, hear him.

Gospel   Luke 9:28b-36; L27C

Jesus took Peter, John, and James
    and went up the mountain to
        pray.
While he was praying his face
        changed in appearance
    and his clothing became
        dazzling white.
And behold, two men were
        conversing with him, Moses
        and Elijah,
    who appeared in glory and spoke of
        his exodus
    that he was going to accomplish in
        Jerusalem.
Peter and his companions had been
        overcome by sleep,
    but becoming fully awake,
    they saw his glory and the two men
        standing with him.
As they were about to part from him,
        Peter said to Jesus,
    "Master, it is good that we are here;
    let us make three tents,
    one for you, one for Moses, and one
        for Elijah."
But he did not know what he was
        saying.
While he was still speaking,
    a cloud came and cast a shadow over
        them,
    and they became frightened when
        they entered the cloud.
Then from the cloud came a voice that
        said,
    "This is my chosen Son; listen to
        him."
After the voice had spoken, Jesus was
        found alone.
They fell silent and did not at that time
    tell anyone what they had seen.

Reflecting on the Gospel

Most of us live far too hectic lives—we are busy from morning to night with work, chauffeuring kids, cleaning, meals, answering e-mail, and a hundred other things. When we might finally sit down in the evening to relax a little, we often doze off while reading or watching a TV program. We might wake with a start when the book drops out of our hand, or wake up when a commercial comes on with its louder volume to find we've missed half the TV program. Peter, John, and James in this gospel must have been really tired after their climb up the mountain, for they fell asleep. Then they awaken to see Jesus' transfigured glory. How startling that must have been for them!

Luke's account of the transfiguration event is the only one that includes the necessity of the passion on the journey to glory ("his exodus that he was going to accomplish in Jerusalem"). Peter awakens from sleep to see Jesus' glory and wants to stay there ("it is good that we are here; let us make three tents"). "But he did not know what he was saying." To share in the glory of Jesus, disciples must walk the journey of Jesus: offer their very lives for the sake of others. These three apostles were privileged to awaken from sleep to see Jesus' transfigured glory. But they clearly missed the most important point: this transfigured glory foreshadows his risen glory. Luke's insight is that glory always presupposes embracing passion.

Jesus' transfiguration—in all its glory—cannot erase the stark reality of self-offering. Simply put, glory comes only through embracing the passion. This is the paradox of the paschal mystery: that something as desirable as a share in Jesus' transfigured glory only comes through our embracing something as demanding as dying to self for the good of others. Even in this glorious moment of transfiguration—which gives us encouragement and hope on our Lenten journey—we are reminded that the only way to remain in that glory is to die to self. We have to come down off the mountain and walk our own journey through death to glory.

Living the Paschal Mystery

Baptism is our covenant with the Lord. Rather than animal offerings and "smoking fire pot and flaming torch" (first reading), the sign of our covenant with God is water, chrism, white garment, and lighted candle. Luke's allusions to Jesus' death in Jerusalem prompt an allusion to our being plunged into Jesus' dying and rising in the baptismal waters. We are invited this Sunday to see our baptism in light of the transfiguration.

Baptism isn't simply a ritual we perform but a covenant with God that we live out the rest of our lives. During Lent as we walk with the elect through their final preparation for baptism we, too, prepare to renew our covenant with God at Easter. This means that we not only already share in God's life and look forward to that day when we will share eternal glory with God but we also embrace the suffering and death.

Let's face it: constant dying to self gets tiresome! This Sunday we are given a glimpse of glory to help ease the discouragement of a lifetime of self-emptying. This tells us something about how we might keep Sundays holy. If each Sunday were a day of rest, a time to be good to ourselves, to do something special that is uplifting, to enter into a moment of glory, we would be better fortified to continue dying to self.

Focusing the Gospel

Key words and phrases: his exodus . . . in Jerusalem, saw his glory, good that we are here, did not know what he was saying

To the point: Luke's account of the transfiguration event is the only one that includes the necessity of the passion on the journey to glory ("his exodus that he was going to accomplish in Jerusalem"). Peter awakens from sleep to see Jesus' glory and wants to stay there. "But he did not know what he was saying." To share in the glory of Jesus we must walk the journey of Jesus: offer our very lives for the sake of others.

Connecting the Gospel

to the second reading: Paul assures us that we will be conformed to Jesus' glory. This promise strengthens us to be subjected to Christ and "stand firm in" him.

to our experience: Early on—from the "terrible twos"—subjecting our will to another is challenging. As Christians, our whole lives are spent learning obedience to Christ ("listen to him"). This obedience is the dying to self that conforms us to Christ and grants us new life and glory.

Connecting the Responsorial Psalm

to the readings: Psalm 27 proclaims that those who seek the Lord will see the Lord. Such confidence enables the faithful to wait for salvation with courage and stoutheartedness. Nonetheless, as the middle verses of the psalm reveal, such confidence does not exempt one from anxiety. The righteous and obedient Abraham must sit through a "terrifying darkness" before hearing God's word of promise (first reading). Peter, James, and John are overcome by darkness and fear after seeing Christ glorified and remain silent about what they have seen (gospel).

As we journey through Lent—and through all of Christian life—we, too, have moments of revelation and periods of darkness. There are moments when we see the transfigured Christ and know his glory to be our future (second reading). And there are long periods when, as if asleep (gospel) or in a trance (first reading), we can neither see nor speak but only wait in hope. These verses from Psalm 27 capture both sides of our experience and frame them with faith.

to psalmist preparation: As you prepare to sing these verses from Psalm 27, read the entire psalm and spend some time with it in prayer. The psalm is shot through with images of danger and death, all the while maintaining its confidence in God's promise of salvation. As a baptized person the danger you face is the struggle with evil and the death to self this entails. How are you being called this Lent to die to yourself? How are you experiencing transformation because of it?

ASSEMBLY & FAITH-SHARING GROUPS

- It's easiest for me to give myself for the good of others when . . . It is hardest for me to give myself for the good of others when . . .
- Like Peter, I must awake from sleep and see . . .
- I have experienced a share in Jesus' transfigured glory when . . .

PRESIDERS

- While Jesus prayed his appearance changed. What I hope to change in myself this Lent so I can be a better presider is . . .

DEACONS

- My service is a revelation of Jesus' transfigured glory when . . .

HOSPITALITY MINISTERS

- My hospitality reminds the assembly their "citizenship is in heaven" (second reading) when I . . .

MUSIC MINISTERS

- I find my ministry transforming me more gloriously into the Body of Christ when . . . The dying to self that makes this transformation possible is . . .

ALTAR MINISTERS

- The self-emptying of serving is . . . The glory of serving is . . .

LECTORS

- My manner of proclaiming helps others listen to Jesus when . . .

EXTRAORDINARY MINISTERS OF HOLY COMMUNION

- My manner of distributing Holy Communion helps others experience their share in Jesus' transfigured glory when . . .

Model Act of Penitence

Presider: In today's gospel we witness Jesus transfigured in glory. We pause to reflect on the times when we have closed our eyes to this glory because of sin and ask God's pardon and mercy . . . [pause]

Confiteor: I confess . . .

Homily Points

• Often, achieving something good or strengthening something we love demands self-sacrifice. So, for example, athletes or musicians don't hesitate to put in arduous hours of practice. Or how often is it necessary for us to let go of our own desires if we wish to deepen our relationships with others we care about. This kind of self-sacrifice that we do every day is the dying to self demanded by the gospel.

• Surprisingly, a gospel that shows us Jesus' glory offers us two touch points with Jesus' passion. First, the three apostles who witness the transfiguration (Peter, John, and James) are the same ones Jesus takes aside with him in Gethsemane. Second, Moses and Elijah speak of Jesus' "exodus," that is, his "passing" over from this life to risen glory. Jesus' transfigured glory foreshadows both dying and rising.

• Some of us awake from sleep refreshed and ready to go. Others of us can hardly get out of bed. None of us has awakened to the sight Peter saw: Jesus transformed in glory. But even Peter was foggy in understanding what he was seeing—that glory demands dying. The dying the gospel invites us to reflect on is not an end-of-life event. Rather, it is the daily dying to self that conforms us to Christ and leads to our ultimate glory.

Model Prayer of the Faithful

Presider: We pray to the God of glory that we might have the strength to die to self for the good of others.

Response:

Lord, hear our prayer.

Cantor:

we pray to the Lord,

That all members of the church embrace dying to self as the road to eternal glory . . . [pause]

That all peoples of the world be open to the glory of salvation that God offers . . . [pause]

That those who cannot see through their suffering to the glory awaiting them be comforted by the nearness of God . . . [pause]

That we gathered here awaken to the glory of Christ and be strengthened in our Lenten practices . . . [pause]

Presider: Glorious God, you make known your salvation through the presence of your transfigured Son: hear these our prayers that one day we might share in your eternal glory. We ask this through that same Son, Jesus Christ our Lord. **Amen.**

OPENING PRAYER

Let us pray

Pause for silent prayer

God our Father,
help us to hear your Son.
Enlighten us with your word,
that we may find the way to your glory.

We ask this through our Lord Jesus Christ,
    your Son,
who lives and reigns with you and the
    Holy Spirit,
one God, for ever and ever. **Amen.**

FIRST READING
Gen 15:5-12, 17-18

The Lord God took Abram outside and
    said,
    "Look up at the sky and count the stars,
        if you can.
Just so," he added, "shall your descendants
    be."
Abram put his faith in the LORD,
    who credited it to him as an act of
        righteousness.

He then said to him,
    "I am the LORD who brought you from
        Ur of the Chaldeans
    to give you this land as a possession."
"O Lord GOD," he asked,
    "how am I to know that I shall possess
        it?"
He answered him,
    "Bring me a three-year-old heifer, a
        three-year-old she-goat,
    a three-year-old ram, a turtledove, and a
        young pigeon."
Abram brought him all these, split them
    in two,
    and placed each half opposite the other;
    but the birds he did not cut up.
Birds of prey swooped down on the
    carcasses,
    but Abram stayed with them.
As the sun was about to set, a trance fell
    upon Abram,
    and a deep, terrifying darkness
        enveloped him.

When the sun had set and it was dark,
    there appeared a smoking fire pot and a
        flaming torch,
    which passed between those pieces.
It was on that occasion that the LORD made
    a covenant with Abram,
    saying: "To your descendants I give this
        land,
    from the Wadi of Egypt to the Great
        River, the Euphrates."

RESPONSORIAL PSALM

Ps 27:1, 7-8, 8-9, 13-14

℟. (1a) The Lord is my light and my salvation.

The LORD is my light and my salvation;
 whom should I fear?
The LORD is my life's refuge;
 of whom should I be afraid?

℟. The Lord is my light and my salvation.

Hear, O LORD, the sound of my call;
 have pity on me, and answer me.
Of you my heart speaks; you my glance
 seeks.

℟. The Lord is my light and my salvation.

Your presence, O LORD, I seek.
 Hide not your face from me;
do not in anger repel your servant.
 You are my helper: cast me not off.

℟. The Lord is my light and my salvation.

I believe that I shall see the bounty of the
 LORD
 in the land of the living.
Wait for the LORD with courage;
 be stouthearted, and wait for the LORD.

℟. The Lord is my light and my salvation.

SECOND READING

Phil 3:17–4:1

Join with others in being imitators of me,
 brothers and sisters,
 and observe those who thus conduct
 themselves
 according to the model you have in us.
For many, as I have often told you
 and now tell you even in tears,
 conduct themselves as enemies of the
 cross of Christ.
Their end is destruction.
Their God is their stomach;
 their glory is in their "shame."
Their minds are occupied with earthly
 things.
But our citizenship is in heaven,
 and from it we also await a savior, the
 Lord Jesus Christ.
He will change our lowly body
 to conform with his glorified body
 by the power that enables him also
 to bring all things into subjection to
 himself.

Therefore, my brothers and sisters,
 whom I love and long for, my joy and
 crown,
 in this way stand firm in the Lord.

or Phil 3:20–4:1, see Appendix A, p. 271.

About Liturgy

Parish baptisms: Easter is the preferred time for baptisms, especially for those who have embraced the conversion process of the Rite of Christian Initiation of Adults (RCIA). In most parishes, however, it is not practical to baptize *only* during the season of Easter, especially the infants. Liturgical renewal has encouraged us to celebrate baptisms occasionally at Sunday Mass when the community is gathered. One reason for this is so that we understand that baptism is a *community* event, not some privatized ritual that is happening to this individual. Baptism is an initiation into the Body of Christ, the Christian community. When the parish gathers weekly to celebrate the Lord's resurrection, it is fitting that we share in the reception of an infant or young child into the church community.

Celebrating baptisms occasionally during Sunday Mass also reminds each of us that our own baptism is ongoing—it is not finished and over with at the last prayer of the baptismal ritual but continues in our daily dying and rising with Christ. These necessary reminders that we already share in Christ's glory encourage and strengthen us to continue with our daily dying to self.

This being said, there ought not to be so many baptisms at the Easter Vigil or during the year at Sunday Mass that we lose sight of the primary purpose of both these liturgical celebrations, which is to *enact* the death and resurrection of Jesus. Although baptism, like all sacraments, does make present the paschal mystery in its very enactment, its purpose is primarily initiation, a different emphasis from our weekly and yearly celebration of the paschal mystery. This poses some pastoral challenges that ought to be given careful consideration.

About Liturgical Music

Music suggestions: A number of hymns exist that are specific to the transfiguration of Jesus proclaimed every year on the second Sunday of Lent: "'Tis Good, Lord, to Be Here" [in many hymnals]; "Christ upon the Mountain Peak" [W3]; "Jesus, Take Us to the Mountain" [HG]; "Transfigure Us, O Lord" [BB]; "Transform Us" [HG, GC2, RS]; "From Ashes to the Living Font" [GC2, PM, RS, WC, WS]. A good choice this year would be one that explicitly relates Jesus' transfiguration to his passion and death.

Because both the first reading and the gospel use contrasting images of light and darkness, a good choice for the entrance procession would be "O Sun of Justice" [RS, W3. CBW3]. The text speaks of the light of Christ dispelling darkness and bringing new life. The chant melody (JESU DULCIS MEMORIA) could be accompanied with simple tone chimes or bells playing open chords or chord clusters at the places of primary rhythmic impulse.

✠ SPIRITUALITY

GOSPEL ACCLAMATION
Matt 4:17

Repent, says the Lord;
the kingdom of heaven is at hand.

Gospel   Luke 13:1-9; L30C

Some people told Jesus about the
        Galileans
    whose blood Pilate had mingled with
        the blood of their sacrifices.
Jesus said to them in reply,
    "Do you think that because these
        Galileans suffered in this way
    they were greater sinners than
        all other Galileans?
By no means!
But I tell you, if you do not repent,
    you will all perish as they did!
Or those eighteen people who were
        killed
    when the tower at Siloam fell on
        them—
    do you think they were more guilty
    than everyone else who lived in
        Jerusalem?
By no means!
But I tell you, if you do not repent,
    you will all perish as they did!"

And he told them this parable:
    "There once was a person who had a
        fig tree planted in his orchard,
    and when he came in search of fruit
        on it but found none,
    he said to the gardener,
    'For three years now I have come in
        search of fruit on this fig tree
    but have found none.
So cut it down.
Why should it exhaust the soil?'
He said to him in reply,
    'Sir, leave it for this year also,
    and I shall cultivate the ground
        around it and fertilize it;
    it may bear fruit in the future.
If not you can cut it down.'"

*See Appendix A, pp. 272–274, for optional
readings.*

Reflecting on the Gospel

The first part of this Sunday's gospel leaves a lot of room for us to fill in the blanks! We don't know anything about the two tragic events reported in the gospel. Jesus doesn't reply to the people by filling in more information; rather, he uses these probably fairly recent events that are very much on the minds of people as a "teachable moment."

These events involve tragic death, and Jesus uses these tragedies to make absolute that unless we repent, we also will die. Then in the parable of the fig tree, Jesus reveals the patience of God with us, despite our slowness to repent. How merciful is our God (see psalm)! This is God's work of mercy: to take what

is almost dead and coax it to new life. This is our work of repentance: to turn from sinfulness toward God's transforming mercy.

Jesus redirects the people from idle speculation about the meaning of the tragic fate of others to the serious work of their own repentance. As the second reading reminds us, "standing secure" in the graciousness of the new life God offers us does not mean that, because

God gives us everything needed for our journey toward salvation, we don't need to cooperate with God to "cultivate" and "fertilize" our spiritual lives. We "grumble" our way through life—we judge others, fail to live up to our baptismal commitments, do not heed all the warnings given us. Jesus is quite clear in his message: "bear fruit" or be "cut . . . down." Our encouragement is that God is ever patient, ever merciful. God never gives up on us.

Living the Paschal Mystery

Suffering for suffering's sake is not what transforms us so that we can bear fruit—the dying that leads to new life is how we bear fruit. The dying that repentance requires forestalls meaningless dying; the dying we do in order to bear fruit is the result of cultivating an attitude of openness to constant transformation; the "fertilizer" is the charity, fasting, and prayer of our Christian penance.

Repentance is changing one's mind, letting go of the narrowness of our own perception of how life should be and embracing the expansiveness of God's plan for salvation. Repentance, in terms of changing one's mind, is really the same as conversion. The dying to self of repentance and coming to new life through God's gracious mercy characterize our Christian living, and make real and concrete our baptismal commitment. If we wish to bear fruit we must die to ourselves. Here is an interesting paradox: if we don't bear fruit, we die, but we must die to bear fruit. The choice before us is about dying: meaningless dying (selfishness) or fruitful dying (to self for the sake of others).

The gospel parable says for "three years" the owner of the fig tree had been waiting for good fruit. God waits more than three years for us to bear fruit—God waits each and every day of our lives for us to bear fruit. The good news is that God never gives up on us. God continually cultivates and fertilizes—especially by the ongoing proclamation of God's word and the invitation to God's table. All we need do is respond by dying to self. God does bring forth new life in us.

Focusing the Gospel

Key words and phrases: if you do not repent, For three years, leave it for this year also, cultivate . . . fertilize, bear fruit

To the point: The first two events reported in the gospel involve tragic death, and Jesus makes absolute that unless we repent, we also will die. Then in the parable of the fig tree, Jesus reveals the patience of God with us, despite our slowness to repent. How merciful is our God (see psalm)! This is God's work of mercy: to take what is almost dead and coax it to new life. This is our work of repentance: to turn from sinfulness toward God's transforming mercy.

Connecting the Gospel

to the second reading: Paul recounts incidents from Israel's history that, like the tragic events told in the gospel, call us to immediate and radical repentance. We can never "stand[ ] secure" but must always be alert to receive God's gracious acts on our behalf.

to our experience: Tragedy survived (for example, a near-fatal auto accident, a heart attack) is often experienced as a "wake-up call." Lent, with its call to repentance, affords us the same reappraisal of what really leads us to new life.

Connecting the Responsorial Psalm

to the readings: God sees the sufferings of the people Israel and "come[s] down to rescue them" (first reading). Thus, says God, am I to be remembered. But the people, traveling from slavery in Egypt to freedom in the Promised Land, do not remember; they "desire evil things" and are "struck down" (second reading). Thus Jesus' stark command in the gospel: repent or perish, bear fruit or be cut down; and Paul's warning in the First Letter to the Corinthians: do not take salvation for granted.

The responsorial psalm, however, reassures us that God will never renege on the work of salvation. No human fickleness will ever change the behavior of God who "pardons all . . . iniquities." Despite our recalcitrance, I AM continues to act for our redemption. Even in the gospel reading Jesus grants one more chance before final judgment is rendered. Our part of the bargain is to respond to such fidelity with willingness to be converted and transformed. May our singing about this God whose mercy knows no bounds motivate our repentance and keep us faithful to our Lenten journey.

to psalmist preparation: While the gospel commands the assembly to repent and the second reading warns them not to take salvation for granted, the responsorial psalm reminds them of God's mercy and compassion. The message, however, is not "do what you will and know you'll be forgiven" but "how can we not be faithful to this God who loves us so much." How can this message motivate your own repentance? How can it help you remain faithful to the Lenten journey?

ASSEMBLY & FAITH-SHARING GROUPS

- When I hear "repent [or] you will all perish" my first response is . . . What I understand Jesus is asking of me is . . .
- This Lent, how God is cultivating and fertilizing my life is . . . The fruit I hope to bear in the future is . . .
- I have experienced God's mercy . . .

PRESIDERS

- The gardener defends the fruitless tree and offers to cultivate and fertilize it. In my ministry I have been like this gardener when . . .

DEACONS

- My service ministry is a witness to God's mercy in that . . .

HOSPITALITY MINISTERS

- My welcoming the members of the assembly opens them to better receive God's mercy when . . .

MUSIC MINISTERS

- The repentance I need to do in order that my music ministry be more faithful to Christ is . . .

ALTAR MINISTERS

- My serving others cultivates repentance and conversion in me by . . .

LECTORS

- No matter what the Scripture reading, my proclamation announces God's mercy because . . .

EXTRAORDINARY MINISTERS OF HOLY COMMUNION

- The manner of my distributing Holy Communion witnesses to the new life God brings when . . .

Model Act of Penitence

Presider: In today's gospel Jesus lays before us the choice to repent or perish. We pause now to acknowledge our lack of repentance and ask God to pardon and heal us . . . [pause]

    Confiteor: I confess . . .

Homily Points

• Global warming is a serious issue. At both poles the glaciers are rapidly melting and the temperature of the oceans is rising alarmingly. Many scientists say that unless we do something quickly, we will reach a critical point of no return, and the lack of action will result in the destruction of life as we know it. In our spiritual lives, too, we can reach a point of no return. As in nature, so in our lives: the choice is to repent or perish.

• Aspects of the readings contradict one another. On the one hand, we are admonished: repent now or perish (see both gospel and second reading). On the other hand, God gives the fig tree one more chance (gospel). Perhaps the point is that it is not God's mercy that runs out (see psalm) but our time. Repent now, not because God is losing patience, but because with each passing moment we are losing opportunity.

• One of the purposes of Lent is to provide opportunities to pause and reflect on various aspects of our lives, to assess our need for repentance, and to respond anew to God's offer of mercy. Our strength and encouragement for such hard spiritual work is that God never reaches a point of no return in offering us divine mercy.

Model Prayer of the Faithful

Presider: We pray to God for all we need to be faithful to the work of conversion, repenting of all that takes us away from God.

Response:

Lord, hear our prayer.

Cantor:

we pray to the Lord,

That the church be a source of encouragement and strength for all those seeking God's mercy . . . [pause]

That all peoples repent of sinfulness so that God's reign of peace may be established . . . [pause]

That those dead because of sin may repent and be given new life . . . [pause]

That those preparing to receive the initiation sacraments at Easter may continue to turn toward Christ to receive his offer of new life . . . [pause]

That each of us be faithful to the hard work of repentance so that we might share in God's everlasting life . . . [pause]

Presider: Merciful God, you call sinners to repentance: hear these our prayers that we might change from our sinful ways and receive life everlasting. We ask this through Christ our Lord. **Amen.**

Let us pray

Pause for silent prayer

God of all compassion, Father of all goodness,
to heal the wounds our sins and selfishness bring upon us
you bid us turn to fasting, prayer, and sharing with our brothers.
We acknowledge our sinfulness, our guilt is ever before us:
when our weakness causes discouragement,
let your compassion fill us with hope
and lead us through a Lent of repentance to the beauty of Easter joy.

Grant this through Christ our Lord.
    Amen.

FIRST READING
Exod 3:1-8a, 13-15

Moses was tending the flock of his father-in-law Jethro,
    the priest of Midian.
Leading the flock across the desert, he came to Horeb,
    the mountain of God.
There an angel of the LORD appeared to Moses in fire
    flaming out of a bush.
As he looked on, he was surprised to see that the bush,
    though on fire, was not consumed.
So Moses decided,
    "I must go over to look at this remarkable sight,
    and see why the bush is not burned."

When the LORD saw him coming over to look at it more closely,
    God called out to him from the bush, "Moses! Moses!"
He answered, "Here I am."
God said, "Come no nearer!
Remove the sandals from your feet,
    for the place where you stand is holy ground.
I am the God of your fathers," he continued,
    "the God of Abraham, the God of Isaac, the God of Jacob."
Moses hid his face, for he was afraid to look at God.
But the LORD said,
    "I have witnessed the affliction of my people in Egypt
    and have heard their cry of complaint against their slave drivers,
    so I know well what they are suffering.
Therefore I have come down to rescue them

from the hands of the Egyptians
and lead them out of that land into a
good and spacious land,
a land flowing with milk and honey."

Moses said to God, "But when I go to the
Israelites
and say to them, 'The God of your
fathers has sent me to you,'
if they ask me, 'What is his name?'
what am I to tell them?"
God replied, "I am who am."
Then he added, "This is what you shall tell
the Israelites:
I AM sent me to you."

God spoke further to Moses, "Thus shall
you say to the Israelites:
The LORD, the God of your fathers,
the God of Abraham, the God of Isaac,
the God of Jacob,
has sent me to you.

"This is my name forever;
thus am I to be remembered through all
generations."

RESPONSORIAL PSALM
Ps 103:1-2, 3-4, 6-7, 8, 11

R̸. (8a) The Lord is kind and merciful.

Bless the LORD, O my soul;
and all my being, bless his holy name.
Bless the LORD, O my soul,
and forget not all his benefits.

R̸. The Lord is kind and merciful.

He pardons all your iniquities,
heals all your ills.
He redeems your life from destruction,
crowns you with kindness and
compassion.

R̸. The Lord is kind and merciful.

The LORD secures justice
and the rights of all the oppressed.
He has made known his ways to Moses,
and his deeds to the children of Israel.

R̸. The Lord is kind and merciful.

Merciful and gracious is the LORD,
slow to anger and abounding in
kindness.
For as the heavens are high above the
earth,
so surpassing is his kindness toward
those who fear him.

R̸. The Lord is kind and merciful.

SECOND READING
1 Cor 10:1-6, 10-12

See Appendix A, p. 272.

About Liturgy

Year C Lenten gospels: During year C of the Lectionary three-year cycle a common thread runs through the gospels from the third to the fifth Sundays of Lent—that of repentance. Not only is this an important Lenten theme but it is an important theme in Luke's gospel as well.

The act of penitence and confession of sins: During Lent we have been suggesting the use of the *Confiteor* (I confess to almighty God . . .) for the act of penitence at the beginning of Mass. If we consider all the helpful choices we have for the introductory rites and use them well, we can establish a rhythm at the beginning of Mass that captures something of the rhythm of Christian living. Using the *Confiteor* during Lent (and on Fridays for daily Mass at other times of the year) reminds us that we still must overcome our sinful ways and are in need of repentance and reconciliation. Acknowledging God's gifts to us in bringing us to salvation and our sometimes refusal (like Israel of old) of those gifts foster a genuine humility in us.

Using the Rite of Blessing and Sprinkling Holy Water during Easter (and on a few other appropriate Sundays during the year, for example, the feast of the Baptism of the Lord) reminds us that we are the redeemed Body of Christ, plunged into baptismal waters that bring us a share in divine life. Using the *Kyrie* tropes as a litany of praise during Ordinary Time reminds us that the Lord Jesus has walked the journey before us and showed us the way through death to new life. The rhythm, then, flows among repentance and reconciliation, celebration of divine life, and praise for Jesus' example of dying and rising.

About Liturgical Music

Music suggestions: The U.S. Bishops' pastoral additions to GIRM allow for the singing of seasonal hymns for the entrance and Communion processions during Advent, Christmas, Lent, and Easter. During Lent, however, we can inadvertently make the Communion procession a penitential rite if what we sing, be it a hymn or a psalm, speaks only of sinfulness and the need for conversion. The Communion procession is an eschatological moment, a celebration of arriving at the messianic banquet where all is forgiven, all healed, all made one in Christ. The Communion song, then, always needs an element of joy, praise, or thanksgiving. In terms of this Sunday an appropriate Communion song would be one in which we sing both our need for repentance and our thanksgiving for God's mercy. "There's a Wideness in God's Mercy" [found in most hymnals] expresses both these themes. These themes are implied in "Come, You Sinners, Poor and Needy" [RS, W3] in which choir or cantor call us to repentance and we respond with the refrain: "I will arise and go to Jesus, he will embrace me in his arms; In the arms of my dear Savior, O there are ten thousand charms."

✝ SPIRITUALITY

GOSPEL ACCLAMATION
Luke 15:18

I will get up and go to my Father and shall say
    to him:
Father, I have sinned against heaven and against
    you.

Gospel   Luke 15:1-3, 11-32; L33C

Tax collectors and sinners were
    all drawing near to listen to
    Jesus,
  but the Pharisees and scribes
      began to complain, saying,
  "This man welcomes sinners
      and eats with them."
So to them Jesus addressed this
    parable:
"A man had two sons, and the
    younger son said to his father,
  'Father give me the share of your estate
      that should come to me.'
So the father divided the property between
    them.
After a few days, the younger son collected
    all his belongings
  and set off to a distant country
  where he squandered his inheritance on
      a life of dissipation.
When he had freely spent everything,
  a severe famine struck that country,
  and he found himself in dire need.
So he hired himself out to one of the local
    citizens
  who sent him to his farm to tend the
      swine.
And he longed to eat his fill of the pods on
    which the swine fed,
  but nobody gave him any.
Coming to his senses he thought,
  'How many of my father's hired workers
      have more than enough food to eat,
  but here am I, dying from hunger.
I shall get up and go to my father and I
    shall say to him,
  "Father, I have sinned against heaven
      and against you.

Continued in Appendix A, p. 274.

*See Appendix A, pp. 275–276, for optional
readings.*

Reflecting on the Gospel
Most young adults chomp at the bit to leave home and get out on their own, thinking this is the way they can do what they want. No more adults in authority telling them what to do—they are quite capable of ordering their own lives (so they think). Frequently these young folks find out just how expensive living is, and paying for rent, food, utilities, transportation, etc., isn't as easy as it looks. Some of them, quite chagrined, are forced to move back home to get out of debt and begin again. So we readily identify from experience with the prodigal son in the gospel who is chomping at the bit to leave home. He is even bold enough to ask for his share of the inheritance! How little he knows about life; and how little he knows his father!

The gospel begins with the Pharisees and scribes complaining that Jesus welcomes and eats with sinners—how little they understand God! So Jesus tells a parable. When the prodigal son came "to his senses" and returned home, the most he hoped from his father was to be given a place as a servant and adequate food to eat. But the merciful father was prodigious: he embraced him, clothed him in dignity, and honored him with a feast. Sinners though we are, our merciful Father longs to embrace and celebrate with us. We have only to return to him.

Expecting, hoping, anticipating minimal response from his father, the son returned home to receive lavishly from his father. The father didn't even answer the son's plea for minimal acceptance; he simply began the concrete events of showing mercy and welcome. The point: Jesus' welcome of sinners makes visible the love and mercy of God our Father, a love and mercy we all need because we all are sinful. Further, the "ministry of reconciliation" (second reading) given us by God places us in the role of the merciful father, reminding us of not only the value but also the necessity of forgiveness. Forgiveness brings us to accept others (and ourselves) as weak human beings who often hurt others and cause them anguish. We are like the prodigal father when we are compassionate and forgiving toward those who have harmed us. Then we are like our merciful God who treats us in just this same way.

The father is a model of mercy and reconciliation. It is the father who models for us paschal mystery living. It is the father in the parable who models for us the mercy of our heavenly Father—mercy that not only forgives and reconciles but offers a feast as well.

Living the Paschal Mystery
Our human tendency is to think we can make a go of life on our own. If we are happy to settle for minimums, some of us can muddle through life reasonably happy. This parable reminds us that God offers us much more.

If we choose to die to self ("coming to [our] senses") and return to God, we are greeted with forgiveness and feasting. Even more, at our heavenly Father's Feast we aren't simply welcomed back as the sons and daughters we were, but we are transformed into more perfect sons and daughters sharing in divine life. We feast on much more than a fattened calf; the Feast to which we are invited is nothing less than the Body and Blood of the Son. Receiving God's forgiveness and mercy, and offering the same to one another, is how we pass from Wednesday ashes to Easter feasting.

Focusing the Gospel

Key words and phrases: complain . . . welcomes sinners, coming to his senses, father . . . embraced him, robe, ring, feast

To the point: The Pharisees and scribes are complaining that Jesus welcomes sinners—how little they understand God! So Jesus tells a parable. When the prodigal son came "to his senses" and returned home, the most he hoped from his father was to be given a place as servant and adequate food to eat. But the merciful father was prodigious: he embraced him, clothed him in dignity, and honored him with a feast. Sinners though we are, our merciful Father longs to embrace and celebrate with us. We have only to return to him.

Connecting the Gospel

to the first and second readings: God moves from giving us what is adequate to giving what is superabundant. In the first reading God replaces manna with the yield of the Promised Land. In the second reading the "old things have passed away" as God makes us a whole "new creation" in Christ.

to our experience: How easily we maintain the mind set of the Pharisees and scribes in this gospel! We so struggle to forgive ourselves and one another. The readings this Sunday call us to put on the mind of Christ who shows in word and deed how merciful God is toward those who sin.

Connecting the Responsorial Psalm

to the readings: The verses of this responsorial psalm move back and forth between first-person declaration ("I will bless . . ."; "I sought the Lord . . .") and direct address ("Glorify the Lord . . ."; "Look to him . . ."). This grammatical structure implicates us directly in the psalm and the readings. We are the ones who have tasted the goodness of the Lord and now call upon the lowly to cry for help and be saved. We are the Israelites once enslaved in Egypt who, having survived the terrible desert journey, now feast in the land of God's deliverance (first reading). We are the prodigal son once distant and dissipated who, having crossed the terrain of regret and repentance, now feast at our father's table (gospel). We are the ones who, having become a new creation in Christ (second reading), are now ambassadors of the message: repent, come home, the feast is ready and—oh, so good—it is God.

to psalmist preparation: In this psalm you call those who have abandoned God or sinned in any way to repent, come home, and feast on God's mercy. When in your own life have you repented, come home, and tasted God's goodness?

ASSEMBLY & FAITH-SHARING GROUPS

- The people who regularly help me to "come to my senses" and get my life back on track are . . .
- I have experienced the prodigious mercy of God when . . .
- I forgive as God forgives when . . .

PRESIDERS

- The *more* I have received from the Father is . . . This has led me to minister to others as prodigal father because . . .

DEACONS

- My service ministry embodies the prodigal mercy of God when . . .

HOSPITALITY MINISTERS

- The Pharisees and scribes complain about whom Jesus welcomes. I (we as parish) need to be more inclusive toward . . .

MUSIC MINISTERS

- My music making draws the assembly into God's offer of mercy when . . .

ALTAR MINISTERS

- My serving becomes an expression of mercy and compassion when . . .

LECTORS

- My proclamation enables the assembly to hear and receive the words of a merciful God when . . .

EXTRAORDINARY MINISTERS OF HOLY COMMUNION

- The father is the one who goes out to both sons and invites them to the feast. Imitating this compassionate father, the one I need to invite back to the Feast is . . .

Model Act of Penitence

Presider: In today's parable of the prodigal son, we encounter God as the merciful Father who always welcomes back repenting children with forgiveness and feasting. To prepare ourselves to celebrate this eucharistic feast, let us repent of our sinfulness . . . [pause]

> *Confiteor:* I confess . . .

Homily Points

• We humans tend to act out of a "contractual" frame of mind, that is, we give with expectations of equal return. For example, an expensive gift requires an expensive gift in return; or if we invite friends to dinner, we expect to be invited back. Forgiveness and mercy, however, must arise from a very different frame of mind because they are purely gratuitous. The embrace of the merciful father is undeserved yet fully and freely given.

• While traditionally this parable is called "The Prodigal Son," in fact it is about a prodigal father. It is the father who first reaches out and then puts aside all convention and lavishly receives the son back into the family. This is how God acts toward us.

• Coming to understand mercy and forgiveness from God's perspective changes our attitude toward ourselves and others. We become able to accept ourselves and others as weak, limited, even sinful. This acceptance enables us to relate differently. We move from "contractual" eye-for-an-eye dealings with one another to imitation of God's gratuitous self-giving. Jesus modeled perfectly for us this kind of forgiveness by eating with sinners and through his answer to the Pharisees and scribes.

Model Prayer of the Faithful

Presider: Aware of God's mercy and forgiveness, let us pray with confidence to this prodigal Father.

Response:
Lord, hear our prayer.

Cantor:
we pray to the Lord,

That the church be quick to open her arms to repentant sinners, welcoming them back to the Feast of the Lord . . . [pause]

That world leaders govern in such a way that nations are led to extend forgiveness and mercy, and come to peace . . . [pause]

That those in any need receive from our compassion and mercy . . . [pause]

That each of us be an ambassador of reconciliation in our families, among our friends, and in our places of work . . . [pause]

Presider: Merciful God, you forgive sinners and welcome them back to your love and care: hear these our prayers that we might one day be with you at your everlasting banquet table. We ask this through Christ our Lord. **Amen**.

Let us pray

Pause for silent prayer

Father of peace,
we are joyful in your Word,
your Son Jesus Christ,
who reconciles us to you.
Let us hasten toward Easter
with the eagerness of faith and love.

We ask this through our Lord Jesus Christ,
    your Son,
who lives and reigns with you and the
    Holy Spirit,
one God, for ever and ever. **Amen**.

FIRST READING
Josh 5:9a, 10-12

The LORD said to Joshua,
    "Today I have removed the reproach of
        Egypt from you."

While the Israelites were encamped at Gilgal
        on the plains of Jericho,
    they celebrated the Passover
    on the evening of the fourteenth of the
        month.
On the day after the Passover,
    they ate of the produce of the land
    in the form of unleavened cakes and
        parched grain.
On that same day after the Passover,
    on which they ate of the produce of the
        land, the manna ceased.
No longer was there manna for the
        Israelites,
    who that year ate of the yield of the
        land of Canaan.

RESPONSORIAL PSALM
Ps 34:2-3, 4-5, 6-7

R. (9a) Taste and see the goodness of the Lord.

I will bless the LORD at all times;
   his praise shall be ever in my mouth.
Let my soul glory in the LORD;
   the lowly will hear me and be glad.

R. Taste and see the goodness of the Lord.

Glorify the LORD with me,
   let us together extol his name.
I sought the LORD, and he answered me
   and delivered me from all my fears.

R. Taste and see the goodness of the Lord.

Look to him that you may be radiant with
    joy,
   and your faces may not blush with
     shame.
When the poor one called out, the LORD
    heard,
   and from all his distress he saved him.

R. Taste and see the goodness of the Lord.

SECOND READING
2 Cor 5:17-21

Brothers and sisters:
Whoever is in Christ is a new creation:
   the old things have passed away;
   behold, new things have come.
And all this is from God,
   who has reconciled us to himself
     through Christ
   and given us the ministry of
     reconciliation,
   namely, God was reconciling the world
     to himself in Christ,
   not counting their trespasses against
     them
   and entrusting to us the message of
     reconciliation.
So we are ambassadors for Christ,
   as if God were appealing through us.
We implore you on behalf of Christ,
   be reconciled to God.
For our sake he made him to be sin who
    did not know sin,
   so that we might become the
     righteousness of God in him.

or, these readings from year A:

1 Sam 16:1b, 6-7, 10-13a
Ps 23:1-3a, 3b-4, 5, 6
Eph 5:8-14
John 9:1-41 *or*
John 9:1, 6-9, 13-17, 34-38

See Appendix A, pp. 274–276.

About Liturgy

Sin affects the whole Body: As each of us grows in our awareness of being members of the Body of Christ, we also grow in our understanding that there is no such thing as a "private" sin. The prodigal son returned to his merciful father and declared that he had "sinned against heaven and against" his father. Each time we choose the death-dealing blow of sin, we have "sinned against heaven and against" all other members of the Body. In the Body we are a unity in Christ.

There can be many motivations for repentance besides "dying from hunger" and dire necessity. One strong motivation might be our genuine Christian love for one another; if we sin, we weaken the Body. At the same time, when we repent and seek reconciliation, we make the Body stronger. Repentance and a worthy reception of the Sacrament of Penance help us pass from death to life.

This is about the time in Lent when most parishes offer Lenten communal penance liturgies. Part of our preparation for this wonderful opportunity to repent and be forgiven ought to be a serious consideration of how our sin affects those with whom we live, work, and spend our leisure time. It is too easy simply to go to confession and list one's sins, being assured of God's forgiveness through the sacramental ministry of the ordained priest. Perhaps recognizing how we hurt others and reaching out to seek their forgiveness, too, might be the best deterrent for sin and the most fruitful motivation to repent.

About Liturgical Music

Music suggestions: A good entrance hymn this Sunday would be "Eternal Lord of Love" [CBW3, G1, G2, GC, JS2, RS]. The image in the first verse of God watching and leading the church on its "pilgrim way of Lent" identifies the church with the Israelites on their journey to the Promised Land, but it is also reminiscent of the journey home of the prodigal son, with the father compassionately watching for his return. To all—the Israelites in the desert, the prodigal son returning home, us on our Lenten journey—the conclusion of the first verse beautifully applies, "Moved by your love and toward your presence bent: Far off yet here the goal of all desire." Herman Stuempfle's "Far from Home We Run Rebellious" [HG] retells the gospel story of our return home after having abandoned God's love for false treasures and empty, self-centered dreams. This hymn would be very effective during the preparation of the gifts.

MARCH 14, 2010
FOURTH SUNDAY OF LENT

✝ SPIRITUALITY

GOSPEL ACCLAMATION
Ps 84:5

Blessed are those who dwell in your house, O Lord, they never cease to praise you.

Gospel   Luke 2:41-51a; L543

Each year Jesus' parents went to
    Jerusalem for the feast of
    Passover,
    and when he was twelve years
        old,
    they went up according to festival
        custom.
After they had completed its days,
    as they were returning,
    the boy Jesus remained behind in
        Jerusalem,
    but his parents did not know it.
Thinking that he was in the caravan,
    they journeyed for a day
    and looked for him among their relatives
        and acquaintances,
    but not finding him,
    they returned to Jerusalem to look for
        him.
After three days they found him in the
    temple,
    sitting in the midst of the teachers,
    listening to them and asking them
        questions,
    and all who heard him were astounded
    at his understanding and his answers.
When his parents saw him,
    they were astonished,
    and his mother said to him,
    "Son, why have you done this to us?
Your father and I have been looking for you
    with great anxiety."
And he said to them,
    "Why were you looking for me?
Did you not know that I must be in my
    Father's house?"
But they did not understand what he said to
    them.
He went down with them and came to
    Nazareth,
    and was obedient to them.

or Matt 1:16, 18-21, 24a in Appendix A, p. 277.

See Appendix A, p. 277, for the other readings.

Reflecting on the Gospel

We have many terms for weak persons (for example, "backbone of a jellyfish," "milk toast"), and all of them imply that we hold people whom we consider weak in less than high regard. Joseph is not prominent in today's gospel passage—he is not even mentioned by name. Yet, we celebrate a solemnity in honor of Joseph. He is the patron of the universal church. We might not know much about Joseph, but the church is telling us to look deeper.

Joseph is truly no weak person; he was chosen to be the foster father of Jesus, and by his very silence teaches us much about the strength needed for our salvation journey. The readings seem to downplay the role of Joseph by directing our attention to God as the Father of Jesus (gospel) and David as the ancestor of Jesus (first reading). Nonetheless, Joseph had a significant role to play in the unfolding of God's saving events. Consequently, he is a model for our own living: his faith (see second reading) enabled him to respond to God's initiatives even when he didn't understand fully what God was asking of him. Four times in the gospel we read about Jesus' parents looking for him. How tenacious and strong was Joseph in his faith! How good was he as Jesus' foster father!

No doubt Joseph's fidelity to Jewish custom instilled in Jesus a desire for "his Father's house." When Jesus returned home with Mary and Joseph to Nazareth and "was obedient to them," we can surmise it was Joseph who taught Jesus the obedience that would prepare him for the more demanding obedience to his Father in heaven, an obedience that led him to Jerusalem and the cross.

Joseph's quiet strength no doubt had a great influence on Jesus. By Joseph's willingness to let Jesus acknowledge his rightful claim—Son of David and Son of God—Joseph models for us the very dying to self that is an embodiment of the paschal mystery. Joseph died to self so that Christ's mission could be accomplished. His dying led to the new life that he shares now with his foster Son in life eternal. Joseph is surely deserving of the honor we grant him on this festival. He is a strong and good man.

Living the Paschal Mystery

Joseph models more for us than the dying to self and rising to divine life of the paschal mystery (as significant as that is). He also models that the ordinary way we live our baptismal commitment to enter into the dying and rising of Jesus is through fulfilling faithfully the regular demands of Christian living. Living the paschal mystery means nothing less than being faithful to an everyday yes to God. It doesn't mean we have to do big, heroic things. It does mean that we are faithful to God's will even when we don't understand fully what God is asking of us.

The quiet strength of Joseph reminds us that our Christian living doesn't have to be in big, showy ways. Joseph-like Christian living is searching diligently for Jesus in our own lives. This might mean renewing our efforts to be faithful to daily prayer. It might mean seeing Jesus in the person who annoys us by recalling that the other is a member of the Body of Christ, too. It might mean that we believe more strongly that we ourselves are the Body of Christ so that we can be God's presence to others. Joseph teaches us that dignity isn't in extolling what we do but in quietly knowing who we are—sharers in God's plan of salvation.

Focusing the Gospel

Key words and phrases: did not know it, your Father and I, my Father's house, they did not understand

To the point: The readings seem to downplay the role of Joseph by directing our attention to God as the Father of Jesus (gospel) and David as the ancestor of Jesus (first reading). Nonetheless, Joseph had a significant role to play in the unfolding of God's saving events. Consequently, he is a model for our own living: his faith (see second reading) enabled him to respond to God's initiatives even when he didn't understand fully what God was asking of him.

Model Act of Penitence

Presider: We take a day during our Lenten penance to honor St. Joseph, one who was ever faithful to God's plan of salvation. As we prepare to celebrate this liturgy, let us examine our own faithfulness to Christian living . . . [pause]

Lord Jesus, you are the foster Son of Joseph to whom you were obedient: Lord . . .

Christ Jesus, you astounded the teachers in the temple with your answers: Christ . . .

Lord Jesus, you taught us obedience to your Father in heaven: Lord . . .

Model Prayer of the Faithful

Presider: Let us ask St. Joseph to intercede for us as we make our needs known before God.

Response:

Lord, hear our prayer.

Cantor:

we pray to the Lord,

Through the intercession of St. Joseph, may the church be a model of Christian dying to self . . . [pause]

Through the intercession of St. Joseph, may world leaders be obedient to God's laws of righteousness and justice . . . [pause]

Through the intercession of St. Joseph, may the weak and lonely find strength and solace in God . . . [pause]

Through the intercession of St. Joseph, may each of us come to new life in God . . . [pause]

Presider: Father in heaven, you are attentive to the needs of your faithful children: through the intercession of St. Joseph hear our prayers that one day we might enjoy everlasting life with you. We ask this through Christ our Lord. **Amen**.

FOR REFLECTION

• As foster father, Joseph taught the boy Jesus the religious ways of his people. The people who inspire my faith in modest, unassuming ways are . . .

• The things God asks of me that I don't fully understand are . . . What helps me respond to God is . . .

• We honor Joseph for his life of faith. My life of faith looks like . . .

Homily Points

• Heroism is not dependent on event, age, status, duration. Rather, our recognition of someone as a hero is determined by that person's seeing and responding to a need without regard to personal cost. So it was with Joseph.

• Scriptures record very little about Joseph. Yet he is acclaimed universally by the church. His faith was such that he could support and guide Mary and Jesus as he supports and guides us today. Joseph's personal cost was his surrender to God even when not understanding fully. So it is with us.

✚ SPIRITUALITY

GOSPEL ACCLAMATION
Joel 2:12-13

Even now, says the Lord,
return to me with your whole heart;
for I am gracious and merciful.

Gospel   John 8:1-11; L36C

Jesus went to the Mount of Olives.
But early in the morning he arrived
        again in the temple area,
    and all the people started coming
        to him,
    and he sat down and taught them.
Then the scribes and the Pharisees
    brought a woman
    who had been caught in adultery
    and made her stand in the middle.
They said to him,
    "Teacher, this woman was caught
    in the very act of committing adultery.
Now in the law, Moses commanded us to
        stone such women.
So what do you say?"
They said this to test him,
    so that they could have some charge to
        bring against him.
Jesus bent down and began to write on
        the ground with his finger.
But when they continued asking him,
    he straightened up and said to them,
    "Let the one among you who is without
        sin
    be the first to throw a stone at her."
Again he bent down and wrote on the
        ground.
And in response, they went away one by
        one,
    beginning with the elders.
So he was left alone with the woman
        before him.
Then Jesus straightened up and said to her,
    "Woman, where are they?
Has no one condemned you?"
She replied, "No one, sir."
Then Jesus said, "Neither do I condemn
        you.
Go, and from now on do not sin any more."

*See Appendix A, pp. 278–280, for optional
readings.*

Reflecting on the Gospel

A common way parents deal with misbehaving children is to put them in a "time out" corner where they can cool down and (in the case of older children) think about changing their bad behavior. Often we adults need a cooling-off period when someone frustrates or angers us, so we take a walk, turn on the TV, do something different to occupy our minds. In the gospel for this Sunday about the woman caught in adultery, Jesus seems to be giving the crowd who brought the adulterous woman before him two cooling off periods; the image used is that he "bent down" and wrote "on the ground." He ignored their "test." He gave them time to think. Jesus turns the accusation away from the woman and toward her

accusers, who were obstinate in their "test": "Let the one among you who is without sin . . ."

A story that begins with deathly accusation ends with divine mercy. Where the community's condemnation would have led the adulterous woman to death, Jesus' mercy leads her to new life. A story that begins with human testing of the divine ends with a divine invitation to repent. Where narrow focus on application of a law is an excuse for testing the fidelity of Jesus to Jewish covenantal law, Jesus reveals a new order in which all are called to repentance and an experience of divine mercy. Jesus' desire for us is not death but new life.

The crowd brings before Jesus a woman caught in adultery, condemns her, and demands her life. Jesus doesn't condemn the woman. He does condemn her act ("sin no more"), then calls her to repent and choose a new way of living. Lent calls us to the same kind of encounter with Jesus so that we face our own sinfulness, hear his invitation to embrace a new way of living, and make the right choice. Central to this gospel is not simply the adulterous woman or even the crowd that comes to a realization of their own sinfulness. Taking a central place is encounter with Jesus who calls us to repentance and offers us divine mercy. We are quick to condemn each other; Jesus assures us, "Neither do I condemn you." We need only acknowledge our sinfulness and turn toward God. This is repentance. It rests in divine encounter and results in truth: our sinfulness, God's mercy, the promise of new life.

Living the Paschal Mystery

The gospel reminds us that we encounter Jesus at our own risk: we will be confronted with the truth of our own sinfulness. But encounter with Jesus also brings hope: in the confrontation and invitation to repent Jesus offers new life (see first reading).

We begin the last third of the Lenten season. Even if we haven't been all that faithful to our chosen Lenten practices, it isn't too late now to resolve to open ourselves to an encounter with Jesus so that we can approach Easter with a renewed spirit seeking new life. Like the crowd in the gospel, we often find it easier to focus on the sins of others than on our own weaknesses. Also like the crowd in the gospel, we can encounter Jesus and face the truth of ourselves. Lent is a time to encounter Jesus, turn from our sinfulness in repentance, and seek divine mercy. The remarkable good news of this gospel is that by facing and repenting of our own sinfulness we establish new relations with those around us. Acknowledgment of our own sins and how we have hurt others builds us into stronger members of Christ's Body.

Focusing the Gospel

Key words and phrases: woman . . . caught in adultery, Neither do I condemn you, do not sin any more

To the point: The crowd brings before Jesus a woman caught in adultery, condemns her, and demands her life. Jesus doesn't condemn the woman. He does condemn her act ("sin no more"), then calls her to repent and choose a new way of living. Lent calls us to the same kind of encounter with Jesus so that we face our own sinfulness, hear his invitation to embrace a new way of living, and make the right choice.

Connecting the Gospel

to the first reading: Jesus' response to the woman caught in adultery dramatically shows how God always opens a way, "doing something new" (first reading).

to our experience: We often condemn other people. The gospel challenges us to recognize and judge inappropriate behaviors but always to respect the dignity of the other by helping them make right choices about their way of living.

Connecting the Responsorial Psalm

to the readings: The first reading from Isaiah recounts God's mighty acts in restoring Israel as a nation after the Babylonian captivity. As Isaiah asserts, this restoration will make the exodus look as if it were nothing ("Remember not the events of the past . . . I am doing something new!"). The gospel reading recounts God's acting again to do something new in Jesus. Salvation becomes personalized in the adulterous woman whom Jesus does not condemn but grants new life, both physically and spiritually.

God constantly revolutionizes our expectations by saving us in newer, deeper ways. Psalm 126 is our "pinch me" response: we are not dreaming; this salvation is really happening. The readings remind us, however, that the challenge is not just to see but to believe. We must let this new righteousness take possession of us (second reading). We must change our ways and let go of our judgments (gospel). Only then can we "forget what lies behind" and look toward the future (second reading). Only then can we realize the past we sing about is just the beginning.

to psalmist preparation: As you sing this psalm you do not just retell past events, you establish hope for the future. The great things God has already done are as nothing compared to what God is yet to do for us in Christ. In what way this week might you let Christ take possession of you (second reading) so that you can sing of this hope with conviction?

ASSEMBLY & FAITH-SHARING GROUPS

• What is satisfying to me in pointing out the sins of others is . . . What helps me stop this and face my own sinfulness is . . .
• When Jesus has said to me "Neither do I condemn you," I have felt . . .
• What helps me choose to change my way of living is . . .

PRESIDERS

• Times when I have turned condemnation to a call for mercy and repentance are . . .

DEACONS

• My service is one of non-condemnation and mercy when . . .

HOSPITALITY MINISTERS

• My hospitality—whether at liturgy or at home—is about extending Jesus' mercy ("Neither do I condemn you") whenever I . . .

MUSIC MINISTERS

• My music making helps others encounter Jesus and hear his call to conversion of life when . . .

ALTAR MINISTERS

• My serving helps me make good choices about the way I live when . . .

LECTORS

• My reflecting on the word leads me to see new possibilities for my living when . . .

EXTRAORDINARY MINISTERS OF HOLY COMMUNION

• Looking on the face of communicants draws me to extend greater compassion and mercy toward others by . . .

Model Act of Penitence

Presider: Jesus does not condemn the adulterous woman in today's gospel but commands her to sin no more. As we begin this liturgy, let us acknowledge our own sinfulness and receive God's mercy . . . [pause]

    Confiteor: I confess . . .

Homily Points

• How many mistakes do we allow others before we write them off? We are quick to condemn another for behavior unacceptable to us; we are much slower to believe they can change. It's even harder to reach out and offer them opportunities to change.

• Jesus and the crowd in the gospel are alike in that they both name the woman an adulteress and hold her accountable for her behavior. They are different, however, in what they exact from her. The crowd demands her death; Jesus offers her a choice that brings new life.

• We need to hear of new possibilities if we are to move out of the prison of past behaviors. Jesus continually offers us new choices and opportunities to change through his word in the gospel and the community of the church. The work of Lent (indeed, of all Christian life) is to hear Jesus and respond by making choices that will lead us to new life.

Model Prayer of the Faithful

Presider: God continually calls us to new life. Let us pray for what we need to be faithful.

Response:

Lord, hear our prayer.

Cantor:

we pray to the Lord,

For God's mercy, that all members of the church turn from their sinfulness and embrace new life . . . [pause]

For God's mercy, that all peoples of the world share in salvation . . . [pause]

For God's mercy, that the unrepentant seek forgiveness . . . [pause]

For God's mercy, that each of us encounter Jesus in one another . . . [pause]

Presider: Merciful God, hear these our prayers that we might share in the new life of your Son Jesus Christ our Lord. **Amen.**

OPENING PRAYER
Let us pray

Pause for silent prayer

Father,
help us to be like Christ your Son,
who loved the world and died for our
    salvation.
Inspire us by his love,
guide us by his example,
who lives and reigns with you and the
    Holy Spirit,
one God, for ever and ever. **Amen.**

FIRST READING
Isa 43:16-21

Thus says the LORD,
    who opens a way in the sea
    and a path in the mighty waters,
who leads out chariots and horsemen,
    a powerful army,
till they lie prostrate together, never to rise,
    snuffed out and quenched like a wick.
Remember not the events of the past,
    the things of long ago consider not;
see, I am doing something new!
    Now it springs forth, do you not
        perceive it?
In the desert I make a way,
    in the wasteland, rivers.
Wild beasts honor me,
    jackals and ostriches,
for I put water in the desert
    and rivers in the wasteland
    for my chosen people to drink,
the people whom I formed for myself,
    that they might announce my praise.

RESPONSORIAL PSALM
Ps 126:1-2, 2-3, 4-5, 6

R̸. (3) The Lord has done great things for us; we are filled with joy.

When the LORD brought back the captives
    of Zion,
    we were like men dreaming.
Then our mouth was filled with laughter,
    and our tongue with rejoicing.

R̸. The Lord has done great things for us; we are filled with joy.

Then they said among the nations,
    "The LORD has done great things for
        them."
The LORD has done great things for us;
    we are glad indeed.

R̸. The Lord has done great things for us; we are filled with joy.

Restore our fortunes, O LORD,
    like the torrents in the southern desert.
Those that sow in tears

shall reap rejoicing.

℟. The Lord has done great things for us; we are filled with joy.

Although they go forth weeping,
   carrying the seed to be sown,
they shall come back rejoicing,
   carrying their sheaves.

℟. The Lord has done great things for us; we are filled with joy.

SECOND READING
Phil 3:8-14

Brothers and sisters:
I consider everything as a loss
   because of the supreme good of
      knowing Christ Jesus my Lord.
For his sake I have accepted the loss of all
   things
   and I consider them so much rubbish,
   that I may gain Christ and be found in
      him,
   not having any righteousness of my
      own based on the law
   but that which comes through faith in
      Christ,
   the righteousness from God,
   depending on faith to know him and the
      power of his resurrection
   and the sharing of his sufferings by being
      conformed to his death,
   if somehow I may attain the
      resurrection from the dead.

It is not that I have already taken hold of it
   or have already attained perfect maturity,
   but I continue my pursuit in hope that I
      may possess it,
   since I have indeed been taken
      possession of by Christ Jesus.
Brothers and sisters, I for my part
   do not consider myself to have taken
      possession.
Just one thing: forgetting what lies behind
   but straining forward to what lies
      ahead,
   I continue my pursuit toward the goal,
   the prize of God's upward calling, in
      Christ Jesus.

or, these readings from year A:

Ezek 37:12-14
Ps 130:1-2, 3-4, 5-6, 7-8
Rom 8:8-11
John 11:1-45 *or*
John 11:3-7, 17, 20-27, 33b-45

See Appendix A, pp. 278–280.

About Liturgy

Why communal dimension of sin and repentance? One of the major challenges of the liturgical renewal of the last four decades has been to shift from approaching liturgy as private prayer to liturgy as a communal celebration of the paschal mystery. Although some still lament the demise of liturgy as private devotional time, most in the church today appreciate the communal dimension of liturgy.

One challenge is to see this communal dimension as resting in a common identity that runs far deeper than our doing the same things together. Not since the early period of the church has there been such an emphasis on our baptismal identity as the Body of Christ. Herein rests the communal dimension of liturgy: through baptism we are plunged into the saving death/resurrection mystery of Christ; as the Body of Christ we are called to embrace that same death and resurrection. Because we share a common identity, everything we do affects the other members of the Body. When we do good, we build up the Body. Conversely, when we sin we weaken the Body. For this reason sin and repentance can never be mere individual acts; our own sinfulness and repentance affect all others in the Body.

This communal dimension of sin and repentance requires that we constantly nurture our bonds in the Body of Christ in order for us to come to greater realization of how our actions affect others. In other words, our common identity as Body of Christ must become so real for us that we not only believe it in our heads but live it every day. One practical way to bring this home to ourselves is that each time we receive Communion and hear "The body of Christ," we hear this acclamation as a statement of our own identity, too, in addition to acknowledging the real presence of Christ in the Eucharist; let our "Amen" be an affirmation of who we are and a promise that we grow in our awareness of solidarity with each other—in both grace and repentance.

About Liturgical Music

Music suggestions: Any Lenten hymns in which we acknowledge our need for God's mercy and forgiveness are appropriate on this Sunday, but those that also call us to give up condemning one another are particularly suitable. "The Master Came" [GC, GC2, RS, W3], set to the forceful tune ICH GLAUB AN GOTT, would be a good entrance song, as would "Help Us Accept Each Other" [RS, W3], set to the metrically strong tune ELLACOMBE. "Help Us Forgive, Forgiving Lord" [HG], set to a gentler tune, would work well during the preparation of the gifts. "Forgive Our Sins [As We Forgive]" [GC, GC2, PMB, JS2, RS, W3, WC] acknowledges our need for God's grace to put into practice these challenging words from the Our Father. Its style and tempo make it suitable for the preparation of the gifts. "As We Forgive" [WC] draws even more of its text from the Our Father, adding at verse 3: "Our Father in heaven, heal our jealous hearts. May we not judge, lest we be judged; help us to practice mercy." This refrain-verse song can be led by cantor or choir and would be suitable during the preparation of the gifts.

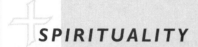

SPIRITUALITY

GOSPEL ACCLAMATION
John 1:14ab

The Word became flesh and made his dwelling
     among us
and we saw his glory.

Gospel   Luke 1:26-38; L545

The angel Gabriel was sent from God
  to a town of Galilee called Nazareth,
  to a virgin betrothed to a man named
     Joseph,
  of the house of David,
  and the virgin's name was Mary.
And coming to her, he said,
  "Hail, full of grace! The Lord is with you."
But she was greatly troubled at what was said
  and pondered what sort of greeting this
     might be.
Then the angel said to her,
  "Do not be afraid, Mary,
  for you have found favor with God.
Behold, you will conceive in your womb and
     bear a son,
  and you shall name him Jesus.
He will be great and will be called Son of
     the Most High,
  and the Lord God will give him the throne
     of David his father,
  and he will rule over the house of Jacob
     forever,
  and of his Kingdom there will be no end."
But Mary said to the angel,
  "How can this be,
  since I have no relations with a man?"
And the angel said to her in reply,
  "The Holy Spirit will come upon you,
  and the power of the Most High will over-
     shadow you.
Therefore the child to be born
  will be called holy, the Son of God.
And behold, Elizabeth, your relative,
  has also conceived a son in her old age,
  and this is the sixth month for her who
     was called barren;
  for nothing will be impossible for God."
Mary said, "Behold, I am the handmaid of
     the Lord.
May it be done to me according to your
     word."
Then the angel departed from her.

See Appendix A, p. 280, for the other readings.

Reflecting on the Gospel

Most of us handle with relative ease the many changes in plans that are part of the ordinary give-and-take of daily living. Someone may unexpectedly drop in, so we take the time to listen. A neighbor's car may have broken down, so we take the time to chauffeur. The family's been saving money for a special vacation, but a relative dies and we spend the vacation money to travel to the funeral. We might grumble a bit, but we take such change of plans pretty much in stride, even when the changes disrupt the steady flow of our daily living. We can hardly imagine the upset in her life plans the annunciation caused Mary!

The change of plans announced by Gabriel weren't as simple as a mild inconvenience of time and energy. Gabriel announced to Mary a change of plans that would demand total surrender of her very self for the rest of her life. The annunciation account begins with Mary's life and future already established—she is betrothed and expecting a typical married life. The message of the angel changed all this. Mary surrendered her plans, her life, and her body to the will of God. From this dying to self, Life comes not only to her but through her to the whole world.

The repentance fundamental to a good Lent involves some kind of "change of plans" in our own lives. None of us, however, has been asked to surrender plans, life, body to God quite in the way Mary did. At the same time we must not downplay the significance of our own acts of repentance and the surrender of our own plans (wills) to God. Even in our little, everyday, imperfect ways of saying yes to God, the divine One is conceived in us and Life comes not only to us but also through us to the whole world. This is the unthinkable of this solemnity: God brought forth the Life of the divine Son through the willing yes of Mary; God continues to bring forth the Life of the divine Son through the willing yes of each of us.

This solemnity that usually comes during Lent is a wonderful gift the church gives us to encourage us in our fledgling acts of Lenten changes in our plans so that we are more perfectly conformed to God's desires for us. Mary's conception of Jesus was a singular privilege that came from her surrendering her plans, her life, and her body to the will of God. The amazingly good news of this solemnity is that God offers us the same Life that God offered Mary. Like Mary, we also must surrender our plans, our lives, and our bodies so that Jesus Christ can become incarnate in the world through us. May it be done to all of us "according to [God's] word."

Living the Paschal Mystery

Mary probably had no idea at any point in her life that two thousand years later people would be celebrating her surrender to God's plans. Mary was a simple maiden who, without understanding fully how or why, gave herself over to God. She was overshadowed by "the power of the Most High." The challenge in our own lives is to let God take over, to let God do the work, to let "the power of the Most High" overshadow us. We don't have to have all the answers to God's plan for us; we just need to say yes, like Mary. Only by dying can we come to new life and help bring that Life to the whole world.

Focusing the Gospel

Key words and phrases: virgin betrothed, you will conceive, Son of God, I am the handmaid

To the point: The annunciation account begins with Mary's life and future already established—she is betrothed and expecting a typical married life. The message of the angel changed all this. Mary surrendered her plans, her life, and her body to the will of God. From this dying to self, Life comes not only to her but through her to the whole world.

Model Act of Penitence

Presider: Mary surrendered her plans, her life, and her body to God and Jesus was conceived and born of her who said yes. As we prepare to celebrate this liturgy, let us ask God for the strength to say yes in our own lives . . . [pause]

Lord Jesus, you were conceived by the power of the Holy Spirit: Lord . . .

Christ Jesus, you are holy, the Son of God: Christ . . .

Lord Jesus, you are the Savior who brings life to all: Lord . . .

Model Prayer of the Faithful

Presider: Our loving God hears our prayers and grants us our needs.

Response:

Lord, hear our prayer.

Cantor:

we pray to the Lord,

That all members of the church may surrender their lives to God for the sake of the life of the world . . . [pause]

That all in the world might surrender their wills to God so that they can be saved . . . [pause]

That those who are poor and in need may receive strength through the intercession of Mary . . . [pause]

That each of us here may grow in the fullness of life that God offers . . . [pause]

Presider: O saving God, you bring us life in abundance: hear these our prayers that one day we might enjoy life everlasting with you. We ask this through Christ our Lord. **Amen.**

ALTERNATIVE OPENING PRAYER
Let us pray
[that we may become more like Christ who chose to become one of us]

Pause for silent prayer

Almighty Father of our Lord Jesus Christ, you have revealed the beauty of your power by exalting the lowly virgin of Nazareth and making her the mother of our Savior. May the prayers of this woman bring Jesus to the waiting world and fill the void of incompletion with the presence of her child, who lives and reigns with you and the Holy Spirit, one God, for ever and ever. **Amen**.

FOR REFLECTION

• The message of the angel Gabriel changed what Mary had planned and expected for her future. Times when my plans/life had to be changed to follow God's ways are . . .

• Times when I have experienced new life by dying to self are . . .

• It is said, "Imitation is the highest form of flattery." I honor Mary this day by imitating her virtue of . . .

Homily Points

• We know little about the details of Mary's life, but what we do know enables us to regard her as someone who faced the same human situations we do: she was a young maiden from a small village, she was engaged, she was expecting a child, she dealt with unexpected changes of plans, she felt the pain of seeing her child suffer. In all of this, she remained ever faithful to God.

• God took Mary's ordinariness and did extraordinary things: she conceived and bore God's very Son. God takes our own ordinariness and does extraordinary things as well: consecrates us (see second reading) through our baptism to receive divine life—the very life dwelling within us that dwelt within Mary.

✠ SPIRITUALITY

GOSPEL ACCLAMATION
Phil 2:8-9

Christ became obedient to the point of death,
even death on a cross.
Because of this, God greatly exalted him
and bestowed on him the name which is above
     every name.

Gospel at the procession with
palms
Luke 19:28-40; L37C

Jesus proceeded on his
      journey up to Jerusalem.
As he drew near to Bethphage
      and Bethany
   at the place called the
      Mount of Olives,
   he sent two of his disciples.
He said, "Go into the village
      opposite you,
   and as you enter it you will find a colt
      tethered
   on which no one has ever sat.
Untie it and bring it here.
And if anyone should ask you,
   'Why are you untying it?'
   you will answer,
   'The Master has need of it.'"
So those who had been sent went off
   and found everything just as he had
      told them.
And as they were untying the colt, its
      owners said to them,
   "Why are you untying this colt?"
They answered,
   "The Master has need of it."
So they brought it to Jesus,
   threw their cloaks over the colt,
   and helped Jesus to mount.
As he rode along,
   the people were spreading their cloaks
      on the road;
   and now as he was approaching the
      slope of the Mount of Olives,
   the whole multitude of his disciples
   began to praise God aloud with joy
   for all the mighty deeds they had seen.

Gospel at Mass   Luke 22:14–23:56; L38ABC
or Luke 23:1-49 *in Appendix A, pp. 281–284.*

Reflecting on the Gospel

This Sunday is unusual for so many reasons: we begin the holiest of Christian weeks; we wear red vestments even before we put away for another year the red-violet ones of Lent; we fill the sparse environment of Lent with fresh greens; we have two gospel proclamations; we carry palms in procession; we proclaim a passion account. But perhaps most unusual is that in Luke's passion account Jesus hands himself over, not to his executioners, but to his Father: "Father, into your hands I commend my spirit." This is the utter confidence of an innocent man.

On five occasions in Luke's passion account Jesus is declared innocent (three times by Pilate, once by the Good Thief, once by the centurion at the foot of the cross). Jesus died, not because of guilt, but because of his infinitely compassionate love for us. Even in the midst of great suffering, he extended his compassion to others (to the servant whose ear was cut off, to the weeping women, to the Good Thief). His compassion was so total that he willingly emptied himself "to the point of death" (second reading). We enter into this holiest week of the year, praying that our self-emptying for the good of others could be so total! We pray that our compassion might increase and abound so that we have the same utter confidence in God's presence and care as did Jesus.

The first reading from Isaiah challenges us to allow the word to "rouse" us. The word that rouses us is no less than the power of innocence and compassion. As we've moved through the Lenten season we've been invited to lay aside more and more of our sinful ways, repent and change our lives, and so come to a new innocence before God and each other. The second reading reminds us that Jesus laid aside his divinity and even his life for our sake. Jesus lays down high standards for us!

Jesus' innocence conditions how he approaches others with compassion. His innocence is an invitation and challenge for us to take up our own cross and participate in self-emptying dying—not just during this holiest of weeks, but during every week of our lives. The real pity of this Holy Week would be that we miss the opportunity to empty ourselves, take up our own crosses, and follow Jesus through death to new life. The real triumph of this week would be that we are roused to self-emptying, humility, obedience, mercy, and compassion that confess in our everyday lives and in all our actions that "Jesus Christ is Lord" (second reading), and thereby witness to and glorify God (passion gospel).

Living the Paschal Mystery

For most of us Holy Week unfolds like many other weeks; we still contend with work, school, preparing meals, doing laundry, cranky folks, the usual triumphs and setbacks. Palm Sunday begins an extraordinary week—a week that concentrates in a few days the ultimate meaning of our whole lives. We must slow ourselves down and make choices so that this week doesn't go by without our taking the time to enter into its meaning. We celebrate in the liturgies what we live every day—all the dying to self that characterizes truly faithful disciples of Jesus. We are invited to proceed in innocence by being compassionate toward others. This means doing our usual tasks with joy, being kind to those cranky folks around us, meeting setbacks as paths to learning. This innocence is possible when we commend ourselves into God's hands.

Focusing the Gospel

Key words and phrases: not guilty; Father, into your hands I commend my spirit

To the point: On five occasions in Luke's passion account Jesus is declared innocent (three times by Pilate, once by the Good Thief, once by the centurion at the foot of the cross). Jesus died, not because of guilt, but because of his infinitely compassionate love for us. Even in the midst of great suffering, he extended his compassion to others (to the servant whose ear was cut off, to the weeping women, to the Good Thief). His compassion was so total that he willingly emptied himself "to the point of death" (second reading). We enter into this holiest week of the year, praying that our self-emptying for the good of others could be so total!

Connecting the Gospel

to the first reading: Isaiah foretells how completely Jesus freely chose his passion: "I have not rebelled," "have not turned back," "my face I did not shield," "set my face like flint."

to our experience: Our culture freezes heroes in the past by building monuments and museums to their memory. By contrast, we do more than remember the death and resurrection of Jesus: we make these present in our liturgy and life.

Connecting the Responsorial Psalm

to the readings: The whole of Psalm 22 is a masterpiece of poetry and theology. The psalmist struggles with an increasing sense of being abandoned (from "My God, my God, why have you abandoned me," to "all who see me scoff at me," to violent imagery of destruction and death) while also experiencing deepening intimacy with God (the one who is far away and does not answer is also the one who has been present "from my mother's womb"). The psalmist begs to be saved from suffering and violence, then offers God lengthy praise. Most lament psalms end with one or two short verses of praise, but here the praise continues for nearly one-third of the text. Furthermore, the psalmist invites an ever-widening circle to join in the praise: first the psalmist's immediate family, then all of Israel, then all nations, then generations yet unborn, and finally, even the dead.

Psalm 22 helps us understand the passion, both Christ's and ours. God is not distant from the suffering, but very near. And the depth of the suffering can be the wellspring of the most profound praise. May our singing of these verses from Psalm 22 give us the courage we need to enter Holy Week aware of both the sorrow and the praise to which it will lead.

to psalmist preparation: To help yourself sing this psalm well, take some time to pray the full text of Psalm 22. You sing not only about Christ's suffering but also about his transformation into new life through his suffering and death. You sing about your own transformation as well, for through baptism you have been incorporated into Jesus' death and resurrection. How willing are you to undergo this transformation? How willing are you to invite the assembly to do so?

ASSEMBLY & FAITH-SHARING GROUPS

- Jesus "emptied himself" (second reading) in his passion and death. Occasions calling me to self-emptying are . . .
- The innocence of Jesus touches me in that . . . his compassion touches me in that . . .
- I am innocent of . . . I am compassionate because . . .
- To assure that I walk with Jesus during these holy days I need to . . .

PRESIDERS

- What is emptied in me while ministering is . . . What is exalted in me because of this self-emptying is . . .

DEACONS

- When my ministry brings me face to face with the suffering of others, what enables me to extend the compassion of Jesus is . . .

HOSPITALITY MINISTERS

- My hospitality can be more compassionate in that . . .

MUSIC MINISTERS

- Holy Week places many extra demands on my time and energy. Meeting these demands calls me to self-emptying by . . .

ALTAR MINISTERS

- The self-emptying that is required by my ministry witnesses to compassion when . . .

LECTORS

- My proclamation of the word rouses people to greater self-emptying for the good of others when . . .

EXTRAORDINARY MINISTERS OF HOLY COMMUNION

- The manner of my distributing Holy Communion encourages others to greater compassion when . . .

Model Act of Penitence [used only with the Simple Entrance]

Presider: Let us begin this solemn Holy Week by resolving to enter into these liturgies with fervor, admit our sinfulness, and ask for God's strength and mercy . . . [pause]

   Confiteor: I confess . . .

Homily Points

• How do we let the power of the passion account move us when it is so familiar to us? The only way is to slow down, reflect, pray. The only way is to allow the innocence of one Man to wash over us so we become more innocent ourselves.

• We grow in innocence through imitating Jesus' compassion for others, and our daily lives provide many occasions for such compassion. As we see more clearly the needs of others, love them more totally, and empty ourselves for their sake, we become the innocence and compassion of the One whom we celebrate today.

Model Prayer of the Faithful

Presider: Let us pray that we enter into this Holy Week with fervor and unite ourselves with Christ's suffering and death so that we might share in his Easter joy.

Response:

Lord, hear our prayer.

Cantor:

we pray to the Lord,

That all members of the church always be models of self-emptying compassion . . . [pause]

That all peoples in the world come to salvation . . . [pause]

That those who are scorned and those who suffer might be comforted by the love and compassion of this community . . . [pause]

That each of us enter fervently into the mystery of salvation we celebrate this week . . . [pause]

Presider: Saving God, you sent your only-begotten Son to save us from our sins: strengthen our resolve to surrender ourselves to your will and come to salvation. We ask this through that same Son, Jesus Christ our Lord. **Amen**.

OPENING PRAYER

Let us pray

Pause for silent prayer

Almighty, ever-living God,
you have given the human race Jesus
    Christ our Savior
as a model of humility.
He fulfilled your will by becoming man
and giving his life on the cross.
Help us to bear witness to you
by following his example of suffering
and make us worthy to share in his
    resurrection.

We ask this through our Lord Jesus Christ,
    your Son,
who lives and reigns with you and the
    Holy Spirit,
one God, for ever and ever. **Amen.**

FIRST READING

Isa 50:4-7

The Lord GOD has given me
    a well-trained tongue,
that I might know how to speak to the
    weary
    a word that will rouse them.
Morning after morning
    he opens my ear that I may hear;
and I have not rebelled,
    have not turned back.
I gave my back to those who beat me,
    my cheeks to those who plucked my
        beard;
my face I did not shield
    from buffets and spitting.

The Lord GOD is my help,
    therefore I am not disgraced;
I have set my face like flint,
    knowing that I shall not be put to
        shame.

RESPONSORIAL PSALM

Ps 22:8-9, 17-18, 19-20, 23-24

℞. (2a) My God, my God, why have you abandoned me?

All who see me scoff at me;
    they mock me with parted lips, they
        wag their heads:
"He relied on the LORD; let him deliver him,
    let him rescue him, if he loves him."

℞. My God, my God, why have you abandoned me?

Indeed, many dogs surround me,
    a pack of evildoers closes in upon me;
they have pierced my hands and my feet;
    I can count all my bones.

R̸. My God, my God, why have you
abandoned me?

They divide my garments among them,
    and for my vesture they cast lots.
But you, O Lord, be not far from me;
    O my help, hasten to aid me.

R̸. My God, my God, why have you
abandoned me?

I will proclaim your name to my brethren;
    in the midst of the assembly I will
        praise you:
"You who fear the Lord, praise him;
    all you descendants of Jacob, give glory
        to him;
    revere him, all you descendants of
        Israel!"

R̸. My God, my God, why have you
abandoned me?

SECOND READING
Phil 2:6-11

Christ Jesus, though he was in the form
        of God,
    did not regard equality with God
    something to be grasped.
Rather, he emptied himself,
    taking the form of a slave,
    coming in human likeness;
    and found human in appearance,
    he humbled himself,
    becoming obedient to the point of
        death,
    even death on a cross.
Because of this, God greatly exalted him
    and bestowed on him the name
    which is above every name,
    that at the name of Jesus
    every knee should bend,
    of those in heaven and on earth and
        under the earth,
    and every tongue confess that
Jesus Christ is Lord,
    to the glory of God the Father.

✠ CATECHESIS

About Liturgy

"*. . . sweat became like drops of blood . . .*" The only time we hear the story of Jesus' struggle when praying in the Mount of Olives is on Palm Sunday with one of the three synoptic passion accounts. This year, in the account from Luke, includes a provocative detail: "He was in such agony and he prayed so fervently that his sweat became like drops of blood falling on the ground." It is tempting to think that because Jesus was the divine Son of God, the decision to be faithful to God's will even to suffering and death was easy. This scene tells us otherwise. Because it is only one tiny part of the whole passion account, Jesus' agony in the garden can easily be overlooked. Yet, this detail indicates precisely to what extent we must struggle to enter into these Holy Week liturgies—conform ourselves to God's will even if it costs us our very life. Add to this reflection the fact that for Jews, blood is the seat of life, and we see how in the very decision to be faithful to his Father's will, Jesus' life already was ebbing out. Decision making is not easy. Decision making that demands the self-emptying proclaimed in the passion is even more difficult. Just as an angel strengthened Jesus to say "not my will but yours be done," so will we be strengthened to make the same commitment of self-sacrifice.

Participation in the passion gospels: The passion accounts proclaimed on Palm Sunday and Good Friday are lengthy and call for effort to pay attention and enter into the accounts. We participate best not by reading along ourselves but by being roused by the word of the proclamation to live the self-emptying and fidelity of Jesus. In this way these accounts are not just long gospels we hear twice a year during Holy Week, but they become the very meaning of our lives.

Some assembly members claim that they feel more engaged in the gospel reading when they use both senses of hearing and sight, and prefer to read along with the passion account. The issue here isn't more active involvement as it is surrender to the word of God being proclaimed. An example might help: when a young man proposes marriage to his lady love, he doesn't give her a text to read while he speaks his proposal to make sure she pays attention. The quality of his voice, intensity of his eye contact, eagerness of his body language all convey that something important is happening. This is the kind of engagement demanded by the proclamation of the gospel. It is entirely relational—between lector and assembly and between Christ and Christian—rather than an exercise in hearing and reading.

About Liturgical Music

Music suggestion: Since the procession (or solemn entrance) that opens this Sunday's liturgy is meant to symbolize the assembly's full-bodied willingness to enter into the mystery of the cross and resurrection, it needs to be done with as many assembly participants as possible. Leading the music will take logistical planning, especially if the procession begins in a place other than the church. To support the singing the choir might flank the beginning and end of the procession, or be divided into smaller groups and placed at strategic points among the processors. Another option is to begin with everyone standing in place to sing a well-known Christ the King hymn, then processing in profound silence to the door of the church (or into the body of the church). Participants need to process slowly and reflectively, letting each step truly be a choice to move closer to the cross. Processing in silence will take some catechesis of the assembly, but doing it can move them from historical reenactment of Jesus' entry into Jerusalem to actual enactment of their here-and-now choice to walk with Jesus to the cross.

Easter Triduum

Grant me no more
than to be a sacrifice for God . . .
I am God's wheat and I am being ground
by the teeth of wild beasts
to make a pure loaf for Christ. . . .
Entreat Christ for me
that by these means
I may become God's sacrifice. . . .
only let me get to Jesus Christ! . . .
Let me imitate
the Passion of my God.

—Ignatius of Antioch, *Letter to the Romans* 2:2; 4:1, 2; 5:3; 6:3

Reflecting on the Triduum

Living into sacrifice and discipleship: Saint Ignatius was an early second-century bishop of Antioch who, during a persecution of that city, was captured, bound, and led to Rome to face being devoured by wild beasts in the coliseum. What is so striking about the seven letters he wrote to various churches on his journey to Rome and impending martyrdom is the sheer joy he takes in dying for Christ. For Ignatius, this is the way to true discipleship: he prays in his letter to the Romans (3:2) that he desires more than anything else not to be *called* a Christian, but to *be* one. Self-sacrifice is the way to live our Christian vocation because that is how we conform ourselves to Christ who gave his all for our salvation.

To be sure, few of us are called to be martyrs. In fact, "sacrifice" is something from which we all tend to recoil. Giving up something we want, delaying our own gratification, or self-sacrificing ourselves for the sake of others all too often aren't things we choose to do. These next days of entering into Jesus' paschal mystery through the Triduum liturgies and our own everyday living can be a clarion call to us, reminding us that we were created in God's image, and that means we love with an unselfish love, we give without counting the cost, we sacrifice without recoiling. These are days in which we relearn the deepest meaning of sacrifice.

In ancient Israel sacrifice was the backbone of the people's religious expression. Sacrifice originated as an act of worship and a way for a people to draw near to God. Although there were both animal and grain offerings, perhaps the most symbolic and telling for us during these days of the Triduum are the animal sacrifices. A pure, unblemished animal would be offered to God. The surrender of a prized, living thing impresses on us that sacrifice is intimately related to *life*. And here's the twist: the animal's life is sacrificed—its dying is an offering to God—so that life might return to the people as a gift from God. Death brings new life. Further, since blood was considered to be the seat of life, the sprinkling of the sacrificed animal's blood upon the people was key: this symbolized the return of life from God to them. Spilling blood made possible receiving blood (life).

All sacrifice, then, required a surrendering of life for the sake of the people. This observation offers a context for interpreting these three days: Jesus surrendered his life for the sake of the people so that we might live. **Holy Thursday/Good Friday:** each time we share in Eucharist we don't have the blood sprinkled upon us, but we actually take the Blood *within us* for the sake of our own life and, ultimately, for the sake of another. Jesus' sacrifice of life brings us new life and invites a sacrifice of our own lives. **Holy Saturday/Easter Sunday:** at the Vigil we hear the story of salvation in the readings—we hear of God's mighty deeds on our behalf, how much God has continually been faithful in offering us life. Our life of self-sacrifice has prepared us to burst with the joy of new, risen life we celebrate. We can dare to sing unending alleluias only when we have surrendered to the unending demands of sacrifice—giving our own selves for the sake of others. Jesus is the model.

Living the Paschal Mystery

No, we are not all called to be martyrs. But we are called to be disciples and in that conform ourselves to Christ. In little ways of self-sacrifice—being patient with others and ourselves when we are tired, taking some time to visit a lonely person, doing without something we don't need but would like to have and using the money to help fill the St. Vincent de Paul box—we are strengthened as disciples who are better able to witness to God's love and care. These sacred days are a gift of life indeed. The life we receive is no less than divine life.

TRIDUUM

"Triduum" comes from two Latin words (*tres* and *dies*) that mean "a space of three days." But since we have four days with special names—Holy Thursday, Good Friday, Holy Saturday, and Easter Sunday—the "three" may be confusing to some.

The confusion is cleared up when we understand how the days are reckoned. On all high festival days the church counts a day in the same way as Jewish people count days and festivals; that is, from sundown to sundown. Thus, the Triduum consists of *three* twenty-four-hour periods that stretch over four calendar days.

Therefore, the Easter Triduum begins at sundown on Holy Thursday with the Mass of the Lord's Supper and concludes with Easter evening prayer at sundown on Easter Sunday; its high point is the celebration of the Easter Vigil (GNLYC no. 19).

SOLEMN PASCHAL FAST

According to the above calculation, Lent ends at sundown on Holy Thursday; thus, Holy Thursday itself is the last day of Lent. This doesn't mean that our fasting concludes on Holy Thursday, however; the church has traditionally kept a solemn forty-hour fast from the beginning of the Triduum (Holy Thursday evening, thus the solemn fast is contiguous with the Lenten fast) until the fast is broken at Communion during the Easter Vigil.

✠ SPIRITUALITY

GOSPEL ACCLAMATION
John 13:34

I give you a new commandment, says the Lord: love one another as I have loved you.

Gospel   John 13:1-15; L39ABC

Before the feast of Passover, Jesus knew
    that his hour had come
    to pass from this world to the Father.
He loved his own in the world and he loved
    them to the end.
The devil had already induced Judas, son
    of Simon the Iscariot, to hand him
    over.
So, during supper,
    fully aware that the Father had put
        everything into his power
    and that he had come from God and was
        returning to God,
    he rose from supper and took off his
        outer garments.
He took a towel and tied it around his
    waist.
Then he poured water into a basin
    and began to wash the disciples' feet
    and dry them with the towel around his
        waist.
He came to Simon Peter, who said to him,
    "Master, are you going to wash my feet?"
Jesus answered and said to him,
    "What I am doing, you do not understand
        now,
    but you will understand later."
Peter said to him, "You will never wash my
    feet."
Jesus answered him,
    "Unless I wash you, you will have no
        inheritance with me."
Simon Peter said to him,
    "Master, then not only my feet, but my
        hands and head as well."
Jesus said to him,
    "Whoever has bathed has no need except
        to have his feet washed,
        for he is clean all over;
    so you are clean, but not all."
For he knew who would betray him;
    for this reason, he said, "Not all of you
        are clean."

Continued in Appendix A, p. 285.
See Appendix A, p. 285, for the other readings.

Reflecting on the Gospel and Living the Paschal Mystery

Key words and phrases: he loved them to the end, unless I wash you, I have given you a model to follow

To the point: If we should be so bold as to receive the very Body and Blood of Christ for our nourishment, then we should be so humble as to be at the loving service of others, daily outpouring the love of God that has first been given us.

Reflection: Toward the end of this Holy Thursday gospel we hear Jesus say, "I have given you a model to follow." The action he desires of us isn't simply to clean the feet of folks! It is far more than that and requires far more of us than a simple cleaning job. When he had completed his servant task of footwashing, Jesus asked his disciples, "Do you realize what I have done for you?" It takes us a whole lifetime to realize and live what Jesus modeled and expects of his followers: a sacrifice of self so total that love becomes personified by self-giving action.

The profound message Jesus proclaimed by his action is the extent of his love—"he loved them to the end." Jesus' self-sacrificing love is not simply a word, but it is deeds for the sake of others. Loving is being humble servant; loving is spilling out our very body and blood for others. Jesus makes clear that being servant and giving one's body and blood really are the same thing: the true servant disciple gives self to others for their good. Pouring forth one's body and blood is indeed an act of Eucharist—it is giving oneself for another's life. In this sense, serving others, Eucharist, and love all meld into one action, an action that Jesus modeled so perfectly for us.

In John's gospel we don't have an account of the institution of the Eucharist; on this sacred night we read the account recorded in Paul's First Letter to the Corinthians: "This is my body that is for you . . . This cup . . . is my blood." By giving his Body and Blood as our nourishment—by inviting us even in this life to share already in the messianic banquet—Jesus models for us a most profound service: the sacrifice of his very Body and Blood. As if he knew this would be too much for us to sacrifice, he showed us another, much more manageable model: stoop and wash the feet of others, be their servant, and in this way love them and bring them new life. No, John doesn't record the institution of the Eucharist; he does record for us its ultimate meaning and demand.

This sacred night with its ritual of footwashing is a profound reminder of what our Christian living is all about. Jesus invites each of us to be washed and, indeed, we have been washed in the waters of baptism. This plunges us deeply into Jesus' saving mystery. This demands of us that we, too, become servants to all. In this gospel Jesus shows us that love—sacrificing self unreservedly for the good of others—is down-to-earth practical.

Jesus raises humble service of others to a new level as a symbol of love. The simple gesture of Jesus in the gospel reminds us that love knows no bounds, excludes no one, is a remarkable gesture of self-sacrifice. Yes, Jesus loved us to the end. But the end isn't the cross. The end is the ongoing invitation to stand at the messianic table and be nourished by the Body and Blood of Christ. We come to the table worthily when we do as the Master has done: empty ourselves in self-sacrifice for the good of others.

Model Act of Penitence

Presider: Each time we gather to celebrate Eucharist, Jesus' great gift of self to us, we experience Jesus' self-sacrificing love. Tonight we ritualize Jesus' self-giving love in the washing of feet. Let us prepare for this liturgy—and for the celebration of these three days of the paschal Triduum—by opening our hearts to hear God's word and be fed at God's table . . . [pause]

Lord Jesus, you stoop to wash our feet: Lord . . .

Christ Jesus, you give us your Body and Blood as our nourishment: Christ . . .

Lord Jesus, you model for us love in both word and deed: Lord . . .

Homily Points

• Many of us anguish over the demise of so many sports and other prominent figures as positive role models. All too many lead lives of debauchery and drugs, infidelity and promiscuity, selfishly used riches and criminal waste. These are hardly role models for us. This gospel gives us a very different kind of role model.

• On this evening when we celebrate the institution of the Eucharist, we hear in the gospel what we don't expect. The gospel is not about nourishment by food but about nourishment through humble, loving service. By washing feet, Jesus is challenging us to tirelessly spend ourselves for the good of others.

• What Jesus models for us is hardly easy. This is what Eucharist is: giving oneself for others. Not just a Sunday event, the celebration of Eucharist aptly describes our ordinary daily lives: "Unless I wash you . . ." Our daily lives are about letting Jesus wash us with his love, so we can wash others with our love.

Model Prayer of the Faithful

Presider: We confidently make our needs known to a loving and self-sacrificing God.

Response:

Cantor:

That all members of the church follow Jesus in selflessly serving others . . . [pause]

That all people of the world share in God's gift of salvation . . . [pause]

That the hungering of the world be fed physically, emotionally, and spiritually . . . [pause]

That all of us here see in the servant-love modeled by Jesus at the Last Supper an invitation to generous self-giving for the good of others . . . [pause]

Presider: Loving God, you sent your Son to model for us self-giving love: hear these our prayers that we might follow his example and live our lives for others, and one day enjoy life with you forever at the messianic banquet of love. We ask this through that same Son, Jesus Christ our Lord. **Amen.**

FOR REFLECTION

• Footwashing is a metaphor for sacrificing for the good of others. This metaphor is made concrete in my daily living whenever I . . .

• How Jesus' life encourages me to give of myself for the good of others is . . .

• The way serving others (footwashing) and being nourished at the eucharistic table are connected for me is . . .

✝ SPIRITUALITY

GOSPEL ACCLAMATION
Phil 2:8-9

Christ became obedient to the point of death,
even death on a cross.
Because of this, God greatly exalted him
and bestowed on him the name which is above
     every other name.

Gospel   John 18:1–19:42; L40ABC

Jesus went out with his disciples
     across the Kidron valley
     to where there was a garden,
     into which he and his disciples
        entered.
Judas his betrayer also knew the
     place,
     because Jesus had often met there with
        his disciples.
So Judas got a band of soldiers and guards
     from the chief priests and the Pharisees
     and went there with lanterns, torches,
        and weapons.
Jesus, knowing everything that was going to
     happen to him,
     went out and said to them, "Whom are
        you looking for?"
They answered him, "Jesus the Nazorean."
He said to them, "I AM."
Judas his betrayer was also with them.
When he said to them, "I AM,"
     they turned away and fell to the ground.
So he again asked them,
     "Whom are you looking for?"
They said, "Jesus the Nazorean."
Jesus answered,
     "I told you that I AM.
So if you are looking for me, let these men
        go."
This was to fulfill what he had said,
     "I have not lost any of those you gave me."
Then Simon Peter, who had a sword, drew
     it,
     struck the high priest's slave, and cut off
        his right ear.
The slave's name was Malchus.
Jesus said to Peter,
     "Put your sword into its scabbard.
Shall I not drink the cup that the Father
     gave me?"

Continued in Appendix A, pp. 286–287.
See Appendix A, p. 288, for the other readings.

Reflecting on the Gospel and Living the Paschal Mystery
Key words and phrases: carrying the cross himself, they took his clothes, It is finished, immediately blood and water flowed out

To the point: The cross of Jesus is not so much an instrument of suffering as it is an opportunity to offer self-sacrificing love—again and again. Even on Good Friday—the day we commemorate Jesus' passion and death and seeming end—we cannot lose sight of what God has in store: God's overwhelming love that leads to everlasting exaltation.

Reflection: John's passion account is quite different from those of Matthew, Mark, and Luke. In the three Synoptic accounts the focus is on the suffering Jesus, the one falsely accused who goes to an undeserved death. We hear from Matthew's gospel the soul-searing cry, "My God, My God, why have you forsaken me?" We can identify more easily with this Jesus—the one who suffers, feels abandoned, remains silent before his accusers. The Jesus of John's passion is much more challenging to us.

In this gospel Jesus is the one in charge who chooses his destiny. It almost seems like he is arranging his own death. When the soldiers and guards come to the garden to get Jesus, he goes out to meet them and identifies himself as the one they are looking for. In his conversation with the high priest, Jesus is bold, almost accusatory in his answers—so bold, in fact, that he receives a slap from an indignant temple guard. In John, Jesus carries the cross *himself*—this is *his* destiny and he chooses to walk to it. Finally, it is Jesus who announces, "It is finished."

Jesus is the paschal victim; he was sacrificed for us and "it was our infirmities that he bore" (first reading). By choosing his destiny to give up his own life, Jesus makes it possible for us to receive life. The greatly unexpected turn of this sacrifice is that by dying, Jesus is raised to new life. The communion with God made possible by the sacrifice of the old covenant is raised to new heights: now the sacrifice is the very Son of God, and the life that is returned is God's very life. This is the new covenant—one sealed in the blood of the divine Son. This is the new covenant—self-giving that never ends, love that is ever outpoured. Even after Jesus has "handed over the spirit," he still gives, for when his side is pierced life-giving blood and water pour forth. Self-sacrifice knows no bounds; it never runs dry.

The cross of Jesus is not so much an instrument of suffering as it is an opportunity to offer self-sacrificing love—again and again. Even on Good Friday—the day we commemorate Jesus' passion and death and seeming end—we cannot lose sight of what God has in store: God's overwhelming love that leads to everlasting exaltation.

Good Friday is more than a step to resurrection; it is a day on which we celebrate Jesus' obedience, his kingship, the everlasting establishment of his reign, his side being opened and himself being poured out so that we can be washed in his very blood and water. The real scandal of the cross isn't suffering and death; the real scandal of the cross is that death is vindicated by Jesus' self-sacrificing love. Death has no power over God. Jesus, our High Priest, offered himself obediently and willingly and "became the source of salvation for all" (second reading). This sacrifice is death that brings life.

Homily Points

• Few people are born with a silver spoon in their mouths and live their whole lives with no pain, suffering, difficulties. And although few of us would deliberately seek adverse situations, these come our way in ordinary daily living. We learn to cope and also learn that adversity strengthens us and helps us become wise. In this way, the daily crosses we carry are also opportunities for growth and ways to learn self-giving.

• What happened to Jesus on that first Good Friday encapsulated his whole life. Jesus died to self every time he responded compassionately to those who were suffering or in need, every time he reached out in forgiveness to sinners, every time he challenged religious leaders obstinate about new understandings of the law. His daily living and ministry were already an entry into his death on the cross.

• In daily life we all face the cross in many forms: exhaustion, disappointment, discouragement—sometimes even in great suffering and tragedy. We find our strength in Jesus, who understands because he first suffered and ultimately laid down his life for us. The cross is not about suffering, it is about being transformed by great love. A cross always offers an opportunity to grow in love. Jesus teaches us the kind of love that we can undertake—love for the good of another. This is a parent's love, a teacher's love, a caregiver's love, our love . . .

Suggestions for Music

Singing the solemn prayers: Just as the Easter Vigil is the mother of all vigils, so the Good Friday solemn prayers are the mother and model of all prayers of the faithful. Because of their solemnity they are meant to be sung, using the simple chant given in the Sacramentary, and to include short periods of silent prayer after each statement of intention. If it is not possible that these prayers be sung, they should be spoken with solemnity with time allowed for the appropriate silent pauses.

Music during the veneration of the cross: As the title of this part of today's liturgy—"Veneration of the Cross"—indicates, what we honor in this procession is not the One crucified but the cross that embodies the mystery of his—and our—redemptive triumph over sin and death. Because we are not *historicizing* or reenacting a past event but *ritualizing* the meaning of this event for our lives here and now, this procession is not one of sorrow or expiation but of gratitude, of triumph, and of quiet and confident acceptance (the very sentiments expressed in the responsorial psalm).

The music during this procession needs, then, to sing about the mystery and triumph of the cross rather than about the details of Jesus' suffering and death. Examples of appropriate music include "We Acclaim the Cross of Jesus" [PMB, WC, WS]; "O Cross of Christ, Immortal Tree" [CBW3, PMB, WC, SS]; "Behold, Before Our Wond'ring Eyes" [BB, JS2]; Ricky Manalo's "We Should Glory in the Cross" [JS2; choir octavo OCP #11355CC]; Francis Patrick O'Brien's "Tree of Life and Glory" [GIA G-5452]; "We Venerate Your Cross/Tu Cruz Adoramos' [OFUV]; "Only This I Want" [BB, GC, GC2, JS2]. Gerard Chiusano's choral setting of the entrance antiphon for Holy Thursday, "We Should Glory in the Cross" (OCP octavo #10884), would be an excellent piece for the choir to sing. If already sung as part of the Holy Thursday liturgy, repeating it would emphasize the unity of these celebrations.

OPENING PRAYER

Let us pray

Pause for silent prayer

Lord,
by shedding his blood for us,
your Son, Jesus Christ,
established the paschal mystery.
In your goodness, make us holy
and watch over us always.

We ask this through Christ our Lord.
Amen.

FOR REFLECTION

• The cross of self-sacrifice I must yet take up and carry is . . .

• I model for others Jesus' obedience as the paschal victim whenever I . . . Such obedience gives life to others by . . .

• My self-sacrificing love is expressed best when . . .

✠ SPIRITUALITY

Gospel Luke 24:1-12; L41ABC

At daybreak on the first day of the week
the women who had come from
Galilee with Jesus
took the spices they had prepared
and went to the tomb.
They found the stone rolled
away from the tomb;
but when they entered,
they did not find the body of
the Lord Jesus.
While they were puzzling over
this, behold,
two men in dazzling garments
appeared to them.
They were terrified and bowed
their faces to the ground.
They said to them,
"Why do you seek the living
one among the dead?
He is not here, but he has been raised.
Remember what he said to you while he
was still in Galilee,
that the Son of Man must be handed
over to sinners
and be crucified, and rise on the third
day."
And they remembered his words.
Then they returned from the tomb
and announced all these things to the
eleven
and to all the others.
The women were Mary Magdalene,
Joanna, and Mary the mother of
James;
the others who accompanied them
also told this to the apostles,
but their story seemed like nonsense
and they did not believe them.
But Peter got up and ran to the tomb,
bent down, and saw the burial cloths
alone;
then he went home amazed at what
had happened.

Readings continued in Appendix A, pp. 289–294.

Reflecting on the Gospel and Living the Paschal Mystery

Key words and phrases: puzzling over this, terrified, he has been raised, seemed like nonsense

To the point: After two thousand years, the story of Jesus' resurrection is still as puzzling, terrifying, and seemingly nonsensical to us as it was to those early disciples. The resurrection doesn't call forth understanding; it calls forth belief. We can only be amazed at what God offers to those of us who have chosen to believe and follow Jesus through death to new life.

Reflection: The Easter Vigil is the climax of our whole liturgical year. This is the night we celebrate light, recapitulate the story of salvation, solemnize initiation sacraments and renewal of baptismal promises, ring out our joyous Easter alleluias. This night, of all nights, we celebrate new life. And as we anticipate the proclamation of the Easter gospel—our first hearing this year of the story of resurrection—we enter into Luke's world and experience in our hearts the puzzlement, wonderment, and, yes, maybe even a little of the nonsense that the proclamation announces. This is the night in which we, too, are invited to remember that Jesus would "be crucified, and rise on the third day." Is our own belief any less challenged by this event than those women who took burial spices to the tomb so long ago?

This is the night when the stones of our Lenten penance are rolled away and we are invited to peer into the empty space and see ourselves in "dazzling garments." This is the night we announce all these things to anyone who will hear—even though sometimes we are still puzzled at the seeming nonsense. This is the night God surprises humanity yet another time: he who is dead has risen!

This is the night when Jesus passes from death to life. This is the night we remember that we, too, "were indeed buried with him through baptism into death" (epistle). This is the night we celebrate that we "live in newness of life." This is the night when we don't "seek the living one among the dead," because our seeking need go no further than our own selves. By Jesus' resurrection we share in God's divinity; we ourselves become the life and presence of the risen One.

This is the night when sacrifice makes sense. Sacrificial death is for communion with God. This is the night when Christ's sacrifice and our own self-sacrificing surrender come together into one grand celebration of God's gift of Self to us. This is the night—just this one night—when we can ignore the sting of death because life is so abundant.

This is the night when the announcement of salvation cannot be contained. And so this night has its challenge: the new life isn't simply for our own gain but so that God can renew creation. "Let there be light," God creatively spoke so long ago. This is the night when God speaks again, and now the light is the risen Son. And so the challenge of this night is that we bring light to a world still darkened by disbelief and "slavery to sin" (epistle). We bring risen life in the simple smile, helping hand, and listening ear. We bring risen life in the kind word, the self-sacrificing surrender to another, and the daily dying to self.

The utter amazement of this night is that while we celebrate Jesus' resurrection we also celebrate our own new life. No wonder our alleluias cannot be contained. He is risen!

Homily Points

• Puzzles are intriguing. People will sit for hours, losing all track of time, until they solve one. When "the women" came to the tomb, they were puzzled over the rolled-back stone and missing body. But this was a puzzle they could never have figured out. Its solution needed to be experienced: "[H]e has been raised."

• Puzzled, the apostles didn't believe the story of the women. Yet Peter "got up and ran to the tomb"; his lack of belief didn't seem to stifle his hope. Did Peter run to the tomb because he remembered Jesus saying to him and the other apostles that he would "rise on the third day"?

• Sometimes things happen in our daily living and we see no possible life coming from them. Later, through remembering, we realize that our "Good Friday" experience led to new growth and stronger life. Just as in working puzzles we look at pieces and then look again and again to see where they fit, by remembering and reflecting on life's experiences we grasp what the disciples were led to regarding the resurrection: remembering brings us an encounter with the risen Lord. This is what we do each Easter and, indeed, every day: we remember; we believe, we receive new life. Alleluia!

Model Prayer of the Faithful

Presider: On this joyous night when we celebrate the new life of the risen Jesus, let us ask God to bring us new life.

Response:

Lord, hear our prayer.

Cantor:

we pray to the Lord,

That the Alleluia! the church sings this night ring throughout the world and through all time . . . [pause]

That our broken world be led to the new life offered in the risen Jesus . . . [pause]

That the newly baptized radiate Christ's new life within them and remain faithful to their promises . . . [pause]

That all of us gathered here share the new life of the risen Jesus through the good we do for others . . . [pause]

Presider: Redeeming God, you raised your Son to new life that we might share in his glory: hear these our prayers that all of us share in everlasting life. We ask this through that same risen Son, Jesus Christ our Lord. **Amen.**

OPENING PRAYER

Let us pray

Pause for silent prayer

Lord God,
you have brightened this night
with the radiance of the risen Christ.
Quicken the spirit of sonship in your Church;
renew us in mind and body
to give you whole-hearted service.

Grant this through our Lord Jesus Christ,
    your Son,
who lives and reigns with you and the Holy
    Spirit,
one God, for ever and ever. **Amen.**

FOR REFLECTION

• The way I understand resurrection is . . . One way I experience resurrection in my daily living is . . .

• The light of risen life was brought to me when . . . by . . . I am bringing the light of risen life to . . . when I . . .

• Obstacles to my experiencing new life are . . . Aids to my experiencing new life are . . .

GOSPEL ACCLAMATION
cf. 1 Cor 5:7b-8a

℟. Alleluia, alleluia.
Christ, our paschal lamb, has been sacrificed;
let us then feast with joy in the Lord.
℟. Alleluia, alleluia.

Gospel

John 20:1-9; L42ABC

On the first day of the week,
    Mary of Magdala came to the
        tomb early in the morning,
    while it was still dark,
    and saw the stone removed from
        the tomb.
So she ran and went to Simon Peter
    and to the other disciple whom
        Jesus loved, and told them,
    "They have taken the Lord from the
        tomb,
    and we don't know where they put him."
So Peter and the other disciple went out
    and came to the tomb.
They both ran, but the other disciple ran
    faster than Peter
    and arrived at the tomb first;
    he bent down and saw the burial cloths
        there, but did not go in.
When Simon Peter arrived after him,
    he went into the tomb and saw the
        burial cloths there,
    and the cloth that had covered his head,
    not with the burial cloths but rolled up
        in a separate place.
Then the other disciple also went in,
    the one who had arrived at the tomb
        first,
    and he saw and believed.
For they did not yet understand the
    Scripture
    that he had to rise from the dead.

or

Luke 24:1-12; L41C *in Appendix A, p. 295*

or, at an afternoon or evening Mass

Luke 24:13-35; L46 *in Appendix A, p. 295.*

See Appendix A, p. 296 for the other readings.

Reflecting on the Gospel and Living the Paschal Mystery

Key words and phrases: we don't know where they put him, saw and believed, did not yet understand, rise from the dead

To the point: Seeing and believing in Jesus' resurrection is as much a challenge for us today as it was for the disciples who were eyewitnesses. The challenge really lies in seeing and believing that risen life comes through our own self-sacrificing love of others. When we do this we, too, are eyewitnesses.

Reflection: Even on this day when the gospel announces the risen Lord, we feel the contradictions that the resurrection mystery arouses—seeing and believing on the one hand, misunderstanding and confusion on the other. This mystery defies all human understanding. These Easter stories tell us that the resurrection isn't something we understand but something we believe and live.

We might take our clue to entering into the mystery from the second reading (from 1 Corinthians). Lent has been the time when we cleared out the old yeast (of "malice and wickedness") "so that [we] may become a fresh batch of dough." Like Christ, our "paschal lamb [who] has been sacrificed," we, too, must be willing to give ourselves up in the self-sacrifice "of sincerity and truth." Inasmuch as we are the dough, we must be willing to allow others to feast on us. When Paul invites the Corinthians, "let us celebrate the feast," it is truly a startling invitation: as Jesus gave his body on the cross and gives his Body and Blood to us as nourishment, so must we do the same for others. The only way to open ourselves to the new life that God promises through the resurrection of Jesus Christ is to open ourselves to the needs of others in self-giving. If we try to *understand* this resurrection mystery we will miss it. The readings today invite us to *live* the mystery by self-sacrifice; in this way God gives us the new life that Jesus' resurrection offers.

The gospel identifies three characters: Mary of Magdala, Peter, and the "disciple whom Jesus loved." By not being named, John can function symbolically—all of us are the "disciple whom Jesus loved." Instead of trying to understand we simply "run" to the mystery and embrace it so that we, like John, can enter into it and see and believe. In John's gospel seeing and believing aren't mental exercises but actions that express one's inner disposition. Our belief in the resurrection is a matter of a willingness to embrace self-sacrifice, allowing others to "feast" on us.

Even on this Easter day when we rejoice in the risen life of Jesus, we are reminded that resurrection has its cost: self-emptying for the sake of others. The paradox of Christianity is that dying to self isn't something to avoid, but it is the way we remove the stone that blocks our own hearts from receiving new life. We have the next fifty days of Easter to help us grasp in our hearts and daily living that when we reach out to others we are actually living Jesus' risen life. We need only take the time to contemplate this mystery and recognize the good with which God blesses us. We need to see beyond the obvious—an empty tomb and the demands of self-emptying—to the glory that God has bestowed through Christ Jesus.

The alleluia that bursts forth with the news of resurrection captures a heartfelt cry that we be willing to identify ourselves with the dying and rising Christ. Let the feast begin!

Model Act of Penitence

Presider: On this day when we celebrate with joy the resurrection of Jesus from the dead, we will also renew our baptismal promises. Let us prepare ourselves to renew this commitment to the risen Lord by surrendering ourselves to God's loving presence in this celebration . . . [pause]

Lord Jesus, you are the Resurrection and the Life: Lord . . .

Christ Jesus, you are the Paschal Lamb sacrificed for us: Christ . . .

Lord Jesus, you are the Feast of love poured forth for us: Lord . . .

Homily Points

• Adults often run with purpose: they jog for exercise, run when they see a toddler about to wander onto a busy street, run down a trauma center hall toward a loved one. In the gospel Peter and John ran with a purpose, too: to see the empty tomb for themselves.

• Belief in the resurrection, however, is not a short run to an immediate object. Rather, coming to faith in the resurrection is the journey of a lifetime, a lifetime peering not into empty tombs but at the good works of those who are fully alive through the power of the resurrection. We can never completely understand the resurrection, but we can live it.

• So, on this Easter Sunday, we must run with a purpose: to encounter the risen Lord in one another. How do we encounter this risen Lord today? His presence is manifested through us in our manner of doing good works: forgiving one another, caring for those in need, being a healing presence for those troubled, encouraging people toward new purpose of life, working for justice and peace. Our purpose: not just to believe in the resurrection, but to *be* it.

Model Prayer of the Faithful

Presider: On this Easter day when we celebrate Jesus' resurrection, let us pray that the power of his risen life become evident in our lives.

Response:

Lord, hear our prayer.

Cantor:

we pray to the Lord,

May all members of the church express their seeing and believing in the resurrection by self-emptying love for others . . . [pause]

May all leaders of the world enable others to share in the abundance of new life God offers . . . [pause]

May all those in need have their fill of the new life of the risen Lord . . . [pause]

May we here who feast at the table of the Lord be strengthened to bring Jesus' risen life to others . . . [pause]

Presider: God of risen life, you give us all good things: hear these our prayers that one day we might enjoy life everlasting with you, sharing forever in your banquet of love. We ask this through your resurrected Son, our Lord Jesus Christ. **Amen.**

OPENING PRAYER

Let us pray

Pause for silent prayer

God our Father,
by raising Christ your Son
you conquered the power of death
and opened for us the way to eternal life.
Let our celebration today
raise us up and renew our lives
by the Spirit that is within us.

Grant this through our Lord Jesus Christ,
    your Son,
who lives and reigns with you and the Holy
    Spirit,
one God, for ever and ever. **Amen.**

FOR REFLECTION

• During Lent I tried to give myself for others in self-sacrifice in these ways . . . The way I see those efforts bursting forth into new life is . . .

• The times in my life when I have run to find the risen Jesus (like Peter and the other disciple did) are . . . The times I have run away are . . .

• "Seeing" and "believing" in Jesus' resurrection means to me . . . The way I try to live this mystery is . . .

Season of Easter

✝ SPIRITUALITY

GOSPEL ACCLAMATION
John 20:29

R꒭. Alleluia, alleluia.
You believe in me, Thomas, because you have
    seen me, says the Lord;
blessed are those who have not seen me,
    but still believe!
R꒭. Alleluia, alleluia.

Gospel   John 20:19-31; L45C

On the evening of that first day of
    the week,
when the doors were locked,
        where the disciples were,
    for fear of the Jews,
    Jesus came and stood in their midst
    and said to them, "Peace be with
        you."
When he had said this, he showed
    them his hands and his side.
The disciples rejoiced when they saw the
    Lord.
Jesus said to them again, "Peace be with
    you.
As the Father has sent me, so I send you."
And when he had said this, he breathed on
    them and said to them,
    "Receive the Holy Spirit.
Whose sins you forgive are forgiven them,
    and whose sins you retain are retained."

Thomas, called Didymus, one of the
    Twelve,
    was not with them when Jesus came.
So the other disciples said to him, "We
    have seen the Lord."
But he said to them,
    "Unless I see the mark of the nails in
        his hands
    and put my finger into the nailmarks
    and put my hand into his side, I will not
        believe."

Now a week later his disciples were again
    inside
    and Thomas was with them.
Jesus came, although the doors were locked,
    and stood in their midst and said, "Peace
        be with you."

Continued in Appendix A, p. 296.

Reflecting on the Gospel

The popularity of roller coasters at amusement parks, haunted houses at Halloween, horror shows at the theaters all attest to the fact that sometimes we like the thrill of a good fright. Fear overtakes us when we perceive mortal harm, face the unknown, encounter what is utterly different and threatening. When the fear is caused by temporary or unreal situations such as those mentioned above, our fears are quickly allayed: we climb out of the coaster car with our stomach back where it belongs, emerge from the haunted house all in one piece, leave the theater to reenter familiar and safe surroundings. A sense of well-being and peace comes over us as we laugh at the entertaining good time and its now dissipated fears. Sometimes, however, the fears are real and not so easily swept away, like the fear of the disciples in this Sunday's gospel. They were well aware of Jesus' fate. Their fears were well grounded, the locked doors a sensible protection. Unlike the peace we make in face of roller coasters, haunted houses, or horror shows, the disciples could not make their own peace. They had no power. Did they?

Into this scene filled with palpable fear, the risen Lord appears, and three times he addresses the gathered disciples, "Peace be with you." What is this peace he brings? It is a peace that allays fears, empowers forgiveness, and prompts us to accept the reality of suffering and death as doorways to new life. The peace Jesus brings prompts us to face death rather than cower from it. The peace Jesus brings prompts us to set right our relationships. This peace is new life: the Spirit breathed into us by the risen Lord. It is not a peace we can make for ourselves. It is a peace that is the gift of the risen Lord.

Peace is the wholeness and well-being of the gift of the Spirit breathed upon us and dwelling within us. This peace bestows on us the life and power of Jesus himself, and with it we can make a difference in our world, establish God's reign, continue Jesus' ministry of bringing salvation to all. The condition of this gift of peace, however, is belief. Belief is not merely an exercise in intellectual consent but a commitment of self to acceptance of the Life that is given us. We know *to whom and what* our belief is directed: to Jesus and the gift of new life. We know *how* we receive new life: through Jesus' gift of the breath of the Holy Spirit dwelling within us. We know the *fruit* of this new life: peace and forgiveness.

Living the Paschal Mystery

Our greeting of others must also be one of peace since we, too, share in the Lord's risen life. As with the disciples, Jesus allays our fears and offers us a whole new relationship with him—not one where we need to touch his wounds but one in which we utter with joyful conviction, "My Lord and my God!" We also enter into a whole new relationship with each other as we continue the works of Jesus that lead others to believing. These works include forgiveness, yes, but also caring for others, accepting them for who they are, easing pain and suffering. Any good we do brings new, risen life to others; our ministry of goodness brings salvation. We are empowered to do so through the Holy Spirit. All we need do is surrender to God's action within us. We have these fifty days of Easter to come to greater belief, deepen our relationships, forgive, spread peace. We have our whole lifetime to manifest the good works of our belief.

Focusing the Gospel

Key words and phrases: peace, breathed . . . the Holy Spirit, forgive, have life

To the point: Three times in the gospel the risen Lord addresses the gathered disciples, "Peace be with you." What is this peace he brings? It is a peace that allays fears, empowers forgiveness, and prompts us to accept the reality of suffering and death as doorways to new life. This peace is new life: the Spirit breathed into us by the risen Lord.

Connecting the Gospel

to the second reading: The risen Lord "holds the keys to death." He unlocks the doors to new life not only for himself who is "alive for ever and ever" but also for us. We who believe in him as the gospel bids do not live in fear but in the peace his risen life brings.

to our experience: We usually use the term "peace" in reference to absence of war or struggle. The peace of which the gospel speaks, however, can be known even in the midst of war or struggle—because it is a peace that comes to us only through the risen Lord.

Connecting the Responsorial Psalm

to the readings: The psalmist in Psalm 118 invites an ever-widening circle to join in praising God for mercy and deliverance. This is our mission as the Body of Christ, to "write down what [we] have seen, and what is happening, and what will happen" (second reading). What has happened and will continue to happen is God's victory over death (second reading), disease (first reading), and sin (gospel). God takes what is flawed, useless, and inconsequential—the rejected stone (psalm), our failing lives (psalm), our diseased bodies (first reading), our doubting hearts (gospel)—and makes them the cornerstone of faith and forgiveness. This is resurrection, done "by the Lord" and "wonderful in our eyes." This is what we see happening and what we proclaim to the world.

to psalmist preparation: In singing Psalm 118 you call the church to recognize and give thanks for the enduring mercy of God. You can give a "joyful shout" only because you have had personal experience of God's saving intervention, because you have been "hard pressed and falling" and known God's help. What story will you be telling when you sing?

ASSEMBLY & FAITH-SHARING GROUPS

- Where God is calling me to receive the peace of the risen Lord is . . . to extend this peace is . . .
- The peace I receive when offering forgiveness is . . . The peace I gain when receiving forgiveness is . . .
- I experience peace in the midst of suffering and struggle when . . .

PRESIDERS

- I am most often called to be a peacemaker when . . . and I respond by . . .

DEACONS

- The peace of Christ I invite the assembly to share with one another is most evident in my daily living when . . .

HOSPITALITY MINISTERS

- My hospitality unlocks doubting hearts to believe in the presence and peace of the risen Lord by . . .

MUSIC MINISTERS

- My music making embodies the joy and peace of the risen Lord when . . .

ALTAR MINISTERS

- Genuine service is a "sign and wonder" (first reading) of the resurrection. A way I experienced new life in serving others was . . .

LECTORS

- My manner of proclaiming the word announces peace when . . .

EXTRAORDINARY MINISTERS OF HOLY COMMUNION

- Distributing Holy Communion is a sign of forgiveness given and received when . . .

Model Rite of Blessing and Sprinkling Holy Water

Presider: Dear friends, as we ask God to bless this water that reminds us of our baptism, let us ask for deeper faith in the risen Lord . . . [pause]

[continue with form C of the blessing of water]

Homily Points

• Jesus was born in a period called the *Pax Romana*—but this Roman peace was wrought through force and domination; any uprising was quickly suppressed by the Roman army. How often we human beings continue to impose peace by vanquishing enemies!

• The risen Lord brings a different kind of peace wrought by vanquishing death and forgiving enemies. If we wish truly to share in the peace the risen Lord offers, we must ourselves pass through death to new life. This means that our lives must be marked by self-giving, forgiveness, and genuine care and concern for others—even those whom we perceive as our enemies.

• When we live in this way, the peace we know is deeply internal. Even in the midst of daily struggles, tensions, and fears, we can still have a sense of peace. Beneath the turmoil flows the deeper peace of acceptance: of self (with our strengths and weaknesses), of others (with their strengths and weaknesses), and of the reality that growth and new life require dying to former ways of behaving.

Model Prayer of the Faithful

Presider: Let us place our needs before our God, confident that the one who raised Jesus to new life will give us new life and peace.

Response:

Lord, hear our prayer.

Cantor:

we pray to the Lord,

That the church may always be a font of the peace of the risen Christ . . . [pause]

That all peoples of the world may receive the Spirit of God and live in peace . . . [pause]

That those facing struggle, tension, or suffering may experience the peace of the risen Christ . . . [pause]

That each of us gathered here may be peace-bearers, quick to forgive others . . . [pause]

Presider: Ever-creating God, you always breathe within us the new life of the Spirit: hear these our prayers that one day we might share that life with you for ever and ever. **Amen.**

Let us pray

Pause for silent prayer

God of mercy,
you wash away our sins in water,
you give us new birth in the Spirit,
and redeem us in the blood of Christ.
As we celebrate Christ's resurrection
increase our awareness of these blessings,
and renew your gift of life within us.

We ask this through our Lord Jesus Christ,
    your Son,
who lives and reigns with you and the
    Holy Spirit,
one God, for ever and ever. **Amen**.

Acts 5:12-16

Many signs and wonders were done
    among the people
    at the hands of the apostles.
They were all together in Solomon's
    portico.
None of the others dared to join them, but
    the people esteemed them.
Yet more than ever, believers in the Lord,
    great numbers of men and women, were
    added to them.
Thus they even carried the sick out into
    the streets
    and laid them on cots and mats
    so that when Peter came by,
    at least his shadow might fall on one or
    another of them.
A large number of people from the towns
    in the vicinity of Jerusalem also
    gathered,
    bringing the sick and those disturbed
    by unclean spirits,
    and they were all cured.

Ps 118:2-4, 13-15, 22-24

R℟. (1) Give thanks to the Lord for he is
good, his love is everlasting.
    or:
R℟. Alleluia.

Let the house of Israel say,
    "His mercy endures forever."
Let the house of Aaron say,
    "His mercy endures forever."
Let those who fear the LORD say,
    "His mercy endures forever."

R℟. Give thanks to the Lord for he is good,
his love is everlasting.
    or:
R℟. Alleluia.

I was hard pressed and was falling,
    but the Lord helped me.
My strength and my courage is the Lord,
    and he has been my savior.
The joyful shout of victory
    in the tents of the just.

R̸. Give thanks to the Lord for he is good,
his love is everlasting.
    or:
R̸. Alleluia.

The stone which the builders rejected
    has become the cornerstone.
By the Lord has this been done;
    it is wonderful in our eyes.
This is the day the Lord has made;
    let us be glad and rejoice in it.

R̸. Give thanks to the Lord for he is good,
his love is everlasting.
    or:
R̸. Alleluia.

SECOND READING
Rev 1:9-11a, 12-13, 17-19

I, John, your brother, who share with you
    the distress, the kingdom, and the
        endurance we have in Jesus,
    found myself on the island called
        Patmos
    because I proclaimed God's word and
        gave testimony to Jesus.
I was caught up in spirit on the Lord's day
    and heard behind me a voice as loud as
        a trumpet, which said,
    "Write on a scroll what you see."
Then I turned to see whose voice it was
        that spoke to me,
    and when I turned, I saw seven gold
        lampstands
    and in the midst of the lampstands one
        like a son of man,
    wearing an ankle-length robe, with a
        gold sash around his chest.

When I caught sight of him, I fell down at
        his feet as though dead.
He touched me with his right hand and
        said, "Do not be afraid.
I am the first and the last, the one who
        lives.
Once I was dead, but now I am alive
        forever and ever.
I hold the keys to death and the
        netherworld.
Write down, therefore, what you have
        seen,
    and what is happening, and what will
        happen afterwards."

About Liturgy

First reading from Acts and the Easter Lectionary: During these eight Sundays of Easter the first reading deviates from the norm: rather than being taken from the Old Testament, it is always taken from the Acts of the Apostles. This first book of the New Testament after the four gospels records for us the reception of Easter faith in the early Christian community. Although these first readings don't accord with the gospels for these Sundays in the usual way—either by a parallel theme or account, a promise-fulfillment motif, or a contrast—they do in one sense accord with the gospel.

The Easter Lectionary presents eight gospels that form a marvelous progression and whole: the first three Sundays of Easter all present appearance accounts of the risen Jesus; the Fourth Sunday of Easter is Good Shepherd Sunday, on which we are assured of Jesus' continued care and love; the fifth through seventh Sundays of Easter prepare us to be disciples who receive the Holy Spirit and carry on the saving ministry of Jesus; the eighth Sunday is Pentecost, on which we celebrate the giving and receiving of the Holy Spirit. We move in these eight gospels from celebrating the risen Lord to being given the power (the Holy Spirit) to continue the works of Jesus.

The selections from the Acts of the Apostles simply record for us how those first Christians received the Spirit and carried forward Jesus' mission. We see in this "mini-history" how the new life of Jesus' resurrection re-created these people. These accounts from Acts, then, make concrete what the gospels promise and help us see how we make risen life real in our own lives.

About Liturgical Music

Music suggestions: The hymns we sing over the course of the Sundays of Easter are an effective means of reinforcing the thematic progression that unfolds in the Lectionary readings (see above). The first three Sundays call for hymns that allow us simply to exult over Christ's resurrection (most Easter hymns fall into this category). On the fourth Sunday we need to sing songs that assure us of Christ's ongoing presence, of his tender nurturing, of his active support as we strive to live out our discipleship—hymns such as "The King of Love My Shepherd Is" and "Sing of One Who Walks Beside Us." For the final Sundays we need to sing texts that call us to our mission of bringing Christ's risen life to all people, such as "We Know That Christ Is Raised," "Christ Is Alive," "Now We Remain," and "Go to the World."

APRIL 11, 2010
SECOND SUNDAY OF EASTER
or DIVINE MERCY SUNDAY

✝ SPIRITUALITY

GOSPEL ACCLAMATION

R̷. Alleluia, alleluia.
Christ is risen, creator of all;
he has shown pity on all people.
R̷. Alleluia, alleluia.

Gospel   John 21:1-19; L48C

At that time, Jesus revealed
   himself again to his disciples
   at the Sea of Tiberias.
He revealed himself in this way.
Together were Simon Peter,
   Thomas called Didymus,
   Nathanael from Cana in Galilee,
   Zebedee's sons, and two others
      of his disciples.
Simon Peter said to them, "I am
   going fishing."
They said to him, "We also will
   come with you."
So they went out and got into the boat,
   but that night they caught nothing.
When it was already dawn, Jesus was
   standing on the shore;
   but the disciples did not realize that it
      was Jesus.
Jesus said to them, "Children, have you
   caught anything to eat?"
They answered him, "No."
So he said to them, "Cast the net over the
   right side of the boat
   and you will find something."
So they cast it, and were not able to pull
   it in
   because of the number of fish.
So the disciple whom Jesus loved said to
   Peter, "It is the Lord."
When Simon Peter heard that it was the
   Lord,
   he tucked in his garment, for he was
      lightly clad,
   and jumped into the sea.
The other disciples came in the boat,
   for they were not far from shore, only
      about a hundred yards,
   dragging the net with the fish.

Continued in Appendix A, p. 297.

Reflecting on the Gospel

Children are wonderful, complete human beings who never cease to delight us with their antics and frustrate us with their immaturity. All societies have exacting laws that protect children, not only because they are unable to do so themselves, but also because children are our future. They are our progeny. Good parents spend years guiding and teaching their children. Parents never cease to be parents—they can always lend one more helping hand, lead children to ever greater growth, help them always learn, bring them to the realization of new possibilities. In this Sunday's gospel Jesus addresses the adult, capable, fishermen disciples as "children." The appearance of the risen Jesus to them on the seashore is a presence bringing new life, challenging them to growth. Easter life is a constant invitation to growth, a constant opening to God's unexpected gifts of abundance, a constant invitation to faithful response, which in itself is growth leading to new life. These "children" disciples yet need to grow.

It would seem as though the disciples are still missing the point of the resurrection and how it changes one's life, because Peter and several other disciples revert to what is familiar—they go fishing. On their own they catch nothing. It is only in response to Jesus' command from the seashore that they cast their nets and pull in a great catch.

The two scenes in the gospel capture two different but interrelated aspects of the Easter mystery. The first scene (miraculous catch of fish) dramatizes what God gives us—abundance of new life. The second scene (encounter between Jesus and Peter) dramatizes our response—love that overflows in faithfully following the risen Christ even to the point of death. We can give our lives because we have first been given life by God. While discipleship is demanding, God always gives us what we need, is always there to nourish and encourage us. True, following Jesus isn't easy; it means that we must be willing to sacrifice ourselves—even to the point of death—for the sake of our beloved. At the same time, this dying to self is the only way to share in the abundance of new life Jesus offers us. Three times Jesus asks Peter if he loves him and three times Peter responds, "you know that I love you." But Peter is yet to find out that following Jesus always leads to death.

We share in the abundance of the fruit of this new life when we follow Jesus' commands. We share in new life only if we are willing to share in its cost: following Jesus even to death—dying to self. Heeding Jesus' call and sharing in risen life means that our own love must be so great that we feed and care for Jesus' flock, glorify God by dying to self, and all this because we choose to follow Jesus.

Living the Paschal Mystery

Risen life has its demands—but Jesus gives us all we need in terms of abundance and nourishment in order to meet those demands. The incredible thing about our God is that God provides us with all we need, beginning with offering us new life. Accepting the abundance that God offers means that by following Jesus we ourselves become Jesus' risen presence, those who lead others to him. Every day we must take care that our actions announce God's blessings at the same time that they speak of God's goodness and care. Leading others to Jesus doesn't mean doing big things; it means doing the little things well and so reflecting the new Life dwelling within us.

Focusing the Gospel

Key words and phrases: there were so many, Yes . . . I love you, death, Follow me

To the point: The two scenes in the gospel capture two different but interrelated aspects of the Easter mystery. The first scene (miraculous catch of fish) dramatizes what God gives us—abundance of new life. The second scene (encounter between Jesus and Peter) dramatizes our response—love that overflows in faithfully following the risen Christ even to the point of death. We can give our lives because we have first been given life by God.

Connecting the Gospel

to the first reading: The first reading records how the early believers wholeheartedly responded to Jesus' invitation to follow him: despite opposition, they were faithful to teaching in Jesus' name and joyfully "suffer[ed] dishonor for the sake of the name."

to our experience: Everything about our consumer society bespeaks our desire for abundance. We are never satisfied with the things we have but always want the newest, what's bigger and better, more. We can easily overlook that God is already offering us what lastingly satisfies: the unexpected and overflowing abundance of new life in Christ.

Connecting the Responsorial Psalm

to the readings: Although probably written before the Babylonian exile, the superscription or "title" given Psalm 30—"a song for the dedication of the temple" (cf. New American Bible)—indicates that it came to be used at Chanukah, the annual festival commemorating the reconsecration of the temple after it had been desecrated by the Seleucid army. The psalm is a song of thanksgiving to God for restoration after destruction.

What is the restoration we celebrate this Sunday? Most obviously, Jesus' resurrection from death. But also Peter's restoration to loving relationship with Jesus after his denial of him before the passion (gospel). Once fearful of speaking up in Jesus' name, Peter now rejoices in the very suffering that doing so will bring him (first reading). With joy he joins the crowds in heaven who cry out in praise of the "Lamb that was slain" (second reading). In singing Psalm 30, we make Peter's restoration our restoration. We celebrate that we, too, have been "brought up from the netherworld" of sin, infidelity, and fear of death to a new life of courageous witness to the power of Jesus' resurrection.

to psalmist preparation: In singing this responsorial psalm you not only celebrate deliverance from death but also accept the mission of proclaiming what God has done. The apostles accepted this mission knowing full well what it would cost (first reading). What is the cost to you? What is the reward?

**ASSEMBLY &
FAITH-SHARING GROUPS**

- My net has been filled by the risen Lord with . . . What I have learned about God through such abundance is . . .
- How I have responded to God's abundance to me is . . .
- At this point in my life following Jesus means to me . . .

PRESIDERS

- The way my ministry dramatizes the abundance God gives me is . . . The way my ministry models my response to God's generous giving is . . .

DEACONS

- My ministry is about tending Jesus' flock. When I do it out of obligation my service is like . . . When I do it out of love my service is like . . .

HOSPITALITY MINISTERS

- Hospitality is concerned with feeding and tending Jesus' flock. The dying to self that this demands is . . . The glory I experience while generously tending to others is . . .

MUSIC MINISTERS

- Jesus leads, nourishes, challenges me in my ministry by . . . I lead, nourish, and challenge the assembly through my ministry by . . .

ALTAR MINISTERS

- The abundance I have received from Jesus that leads me to serving him and others is . . .

LECTORS

- Good proclamation demands this kind of dying to self . . .

**EXTRAORDINARY MINISTERS
OF HOLY COMMUNION**

- The ways I feed and tend to God's flock (my family and my parish) are . . .

Model Rite of Blessing and Sprinkling Holy Water

Presider: Dear friends, as we ask God to bless this water, may it remind us of our baptismal commitment to follow the risen Lord faithfully as his disciples . . . [pause]

[continue with form C of the blessing of water]

Homily Points

• "Gone fishing!" This saying can be used either literally or metaphorically. Sometimes it indicates someone really has gone fishing, like the disciples in the gospel. At other times, it means someone has taken a break from the demands of work. Little did Peter know that this fishing trip would end by immersing him even more fully in the demands of a different kind of work!

• Peter's new work is to be a shepherd ("Tend my sheep") who gathers and feeds the hungers of the people for whom Jesus has given his life. The demands of this new work are total, for Peter will meet opposition (because of his teaching and "speaking in the name of Jesus"; see first reading) and in the end give his own life for the flock.

• Like Peter, we shepherd others, for example, when we offer a sense of direction to someone who feels lost or is fearful of taking a step in a new direction. We offer nourishment when we speak encouraging words to someone who feels distraught or downtrodden. We give our life for others when, despite opposition, we speak out against injustice. We can do all these things for others because we have experienced God's abundant love for us.

Model Prayer of the Faithful

Presider: We pray now to the God who tends to our needs abundantly.

Response:

Lord, hear our prayer.

Cantor:

we pray to the Lord,

That the church might always feed the hungry and tend those in need with love . . . [pause]

That all peoples of the world share equitably in the abundance God offers everyone . . . [pause]

That the newly baptized be faithful to their call to follow the risen Lord . . . [pause]

That each of us here respond to the gift of Easter new life by dying to self for the good of others . . . [pause]

Presider: Tender and loving God, you offer us abundance of new life: hear these our prayers that one day we might share in your everlasting life. We ask this through your resurrected Son, Jesus Christ our Lord. **Amen.**

ALTERNATIVE OPENING PRAYER
Let us pray

Pause for silent prayer

Father in heaven, author of all truth,
a people once in darkness has listened to
    your Word
and followed your Son as he rose from the
    tomb.
Hear the prayer of this newborn people
and strengthen your Church to answer
    your call.
May we rise and come forth into the light
    of day
to stand in your presence until eternity
    dawns.

We ask this through Christ our Lord.
    Amen.

FIRST READING
Acts 5:27-32, 40b-41

When the captain and the court officers had
        brought the apostles in
    and made them stand before the
        Sanhedrin,
    the high priest questioned them,
    "We gave you strict orders, did we not,
    to stop teaching in that name?
Yet you have filled Jerusalem with your
        teaching
    and want to bring this man's blood
        upon us."
But Peter and the apostles said in reply,
    "We must obey God rather than men.
The God of our ancestors raised Jesus,
    though you had him killed by hanging
        him on a tree.
God exalted him at his right hand as
        leader and savior
    to grant Israel repentance and
        forgiveness of sins.
We are witnesses of these things,
    as is the Holy Spirit whom God has given
        to those who obey him."

The Sanhedrin ordered the apostles
    to stop speaking in the name of Jesus,
        and dismissed them.
So they left the presence of the Sanhedrin,
    rejoicing that they had been found
        worthy
    to suffer dishonor for the sake of the
        name.

RESPONSORIAL PSALM
Ps 30:2, 4, 5-6, 11-12, 13

℟. (2a) I will praise you, Lord, for you have
rescued me.
    or:
℟. Alleluia.

I will extol you, O LORD, for you drew me
    clear
    and did not let my enemies rejoice over
       me.
O LORD, you brought me up from the
    netherworld;
    you preserved me from among those
       going down into the pit.

R7. I will praise you, Lord, for you have
rescued me.
    or:
R7. Alleluia.

Sing praise to the LORD, you his faithful
    ones,
    and give thanks to his holy name.
For his anger lasts but a moment;
    a lifetime, his good will.
At nightfall, weeping enters in,
    but with the dawn, rejoicing.

R7. I will praise you, Lord, for you have
rescued me.
    or:
R7. Alleluia.

Hear, O LORD, and have pity on me;
    O LORD, be my helper.
You changed my mourning into dancing;
    O LORD, my God, forever will I give you
       thanks.

R7. I will praise you, Lord, for you have
rescued me.
    or:
R7. Alleluia.

SECOND READING
Rev 5:11-14

I, John, looked and heard the voices of
    many angels
    who surrounded the throne
    and the living creatures and the elders.
They were countless in number, and they
    cried out in a loud voice:
    "Worthy is the Lamb that was slain
      to receive power and riches, wisdom
        and strength,
      honor and glory and blessing."
Then I heard every creature in heaven and
    on earth
    and under the earth and in the sea,
    everything in the universe, cry out:
    "To the one who sits on the throne
      and to the Lamb
      be blessing and honor, glory and
        might,
      forever and ever."
The four living creatures answered,
    "Amen,"
    and the elders fell down and worshiped.

✠ CATECHESIS

About Liturgy

Eucharist is God's gift asking for a response: Each time we share in the eucharistic banquet we are invited to be aware of God's gracious gifts to us. The gift of Eucharist is already a share in Christ's risen life. By eating and drinking Christ's very Body and Blood we are transformed into being more perfect members of the Body of Christ. This means that we follow Christ more perfectly as we are more identified with him—follow him even to death. Thus, the gift of Eucharist requires of us a response in kind. Jesus' gift of self to us means that we respond with the gift of self to others.

Far from a privatized action, Eucharist is the action of the whole church through which we share in God's abundant life and are called to bring that life to others. Integral to Eucharist is a call to charity and just actions on behalf of the whole world. One way to evaluate the quality of our eucharistic celebrations is not by simply focusing on the elements of the rite itself (as important as that task is!) but by focusing on how Christ's life is lived in the community. If the liturgical assembly doesn't become more loving, more charitable, more just by receiving God's abundance, then clearly those celebrations are not doing what they are supposed to do. Suitable questions to ask by way of evaluation: How do we visibly love one another more? How are we making a difference in our neighborhoods, city, nation, world? Do we relate the general intercessions as prayers of the faithful that extend beyond the celebration of Eucharist and demand a commitment of life from us?

About Liturgical Music

A note to the music director about maintaining Easter festivity: One of the challenges of the Easter season is maintaining the musical festivity for seven weeks. Often the choir and other music ministers are exhausted from the Triduum alone. The Triduum is the climax of the liturgical year and needs to be celebrated as such. But how is that done without letting the rest of the season become like Haydn's Farewell Symphony, where the musicians gradually slip out until only two violinists are left to finish? The answer lies in how the year as a whole is planned.

When the musical planning for the year is begun, it is best to start with the Triduum and Easter season. Then plan backward from this high point and utilize rehearsals throughout the whole year to prepare the choir for it. A second suggestion is to work over time toward a festive Easter repertory the choir can sing every year. Choose music that is aesthetically and liturgically substantial so that it will not tire, and concentrate on helping the choir sing it better each year. This does not mean that new music will never be introduced but that it will be introduced more judiciously and with the long view in mind.

✠ SPIRITUALITY

GOSPEL ACCLAMATION
John 10:14

℟. Alleluia, alleluia.
I am the good shepherd, says the Lord;
I know my sheep, and mine know me.
℟. Alleluia, alleluia.

Gospel

John 10:27-30; L51C

Jesus said:
"My sheep hear my voice;
I know them, and they follow me.
I give them eternal life, and they shall
never perish.
No one can take them out of my hand.
My Father, who has given them to me,
is greater than all,
and no one can take them out of the
Father's hand.
The Father and I are one."

Reflecting on the Gospel

Hands are strong symbols. Two clasped hands are the logo for the United Way. A child walking hand in hand with an adult is sometimes featured on commercials for Hallmark cards. A child who falls and receives a bump or scratch runs to embracing hands for comfort. Anyone who has sat with a very ill or dying person knows how important the touch of a hand is—a loving caress, a gentle stroke, the massage of soothing cream. Medical massage therapy is a respected alternative medical practice. All these images and countless others remind us that hands are a symbol for connectedness, care, hope. This Sunday's very brief gospel includes the Good Shepherd's reassuring words, "No one can take them out of my hand."

The gospel conveys Jesus' great, tender care and concern for his "sheep." This care does not keep his followers from "violent abuse" (first reading) or "great distress" (second reading). It does assure them of protection in the midst of persecution ("no one can take them out of my hand") and of eternal life ("they shall never perish"). But this assurance only comes when we followers of Jesus "hear [his] voice" and live out of the personal relationship God offers us.

By juxtaposing hearing and following the gospel intimates that hearing Jesus is already following him. We follow first by listening. The call to follow is a call to faithful obedience (the root word for obedience means "to hear"). In other words, hearing Jesus—heeding his voice—is already an act of following. Heeding Jesus' voice is already our participation in proclaiming the Gospel. But probably most important, hearing Jesus' voice is already our participation in eternal life. Ultimately this promise of eternal life is the reassurance and care that Jesus offers: by hearing Jesus' voice and following him we will not perish, but we already share in Jesus' eternal life. No better care than this could the Good Shepherd offer!

Living the Paschal Mystery

Most of our reflections on the paschal mystery revolve around reminders that being plunged into the dying and rising mystery of Christ through our baptism means we must die to self if we wish to share in Jesus' eternal life. We look for opportunities in our daily living to die to self and thus transform what appear to be ordinary, human actions into extensions of the ministry of the Good Shepherd himself. For example, comforting the sick and dying isn't simply a caring human action; in the context of our baptismal commitment it is an expression of Jesus' love for us and the dignity of the other as a member of the Body of Christ.

This is true and surely the heart of the mystery. This Sunday, however, we might turn this around and rest a bit in what the Good Shepherd offers us when we live the paschal mystery: eternal life, the assurance that we will never perish. For all our efforts to die to self for the good of others, they do not equal the gift of self that Jesus gives us. Sometimes we are so caught up in the effort of dying that we do forget that new life is already within us and among us. This is a good Sunday to bask in Jesus' care and protection; listen to his voice calling us to his loving, embracing hands; and rejoice in the goodness showered upon us who are faithful to his call. This, too, is living the paschal mystery.

Focusing the Gospel

Key words and phrases: My sheep, hear my voice, follow me, eternal life, No one can take them out of my hand

To the point: The gospel conveys Jesus' great, tender care and concern for his "sheep." This care does not keep his followers from "violent abuse" (first reading) or "great distress" (second reading). It does assure them of protection in the midst of persecution ("no one can take them out of my hand") and of eternal life ("they shall never perish"). But this assurance only comes when we followers of Jesus "hear [his] voice" and live out of the personal relationship God offers us.

Connecting the Gospel

to the first and second readings: Jesus' promise that no one will be taken out of his or the Father's hand is realized in both the first and second readings. Despite "violent abuse" and "persecution," Paul and Barnabas are kept safe to continue spreading the "word of the Lord." Those who have "washed their robes . . . in the blood of the Lamb" will survive "the time of great distress" to worship God day and night.

to our experience: We often experience that protection comes from a power or source outside ourselves. The readings reveal that our greatest protection comes from the Life that dwells within us.

Connecting the Responsorial Psalm

to the readings: Psalm 100 is part of a set (Pss 93, 95–100) that celebrates God's sovereignty over all things. Peoples of the ancient Near East acclaimed a god powerful because of specific acts, the greatest of which was creation. The Israelites believed their God acted not only to create the world but also to create them as a people. All forces inimical to Israel as a community—from natural disasters to human enemies—quelled before the power of God, who arranged all events in the cosmos to support Israel's coming together as a people.

In Christ, God has shown the ultimate creative power by overcoming death with resurrection. Out of this act God has formed a new people beyond the boundaries of the community of Israel (first reading), a people "no one could count, from every nation, race, people, and tongue" (second reading). No hostility or persecution can prevail against this people for they are held in God's hand (gospel). In singing Psalm 100 we are recognizing who we are because of Christ's death and resurrection: a people created by God, protected by God, and shepherded by God to eternal life.

to psalmist preparation: The "know[ing]" spoken of in the second strophe of the responsorial psalm refers to "hearing" and "following" the shepherd. What do you hear Christ saying? Where is he asking you to follow? What gives you confidence to respond?

ASSEMBLY & FAITH-SHARING GROUPS

- The places and ways I hear Jesus' voice are . . .
- Where Jesus my Good Shepherd is asking me to follow him is . . .
- When I hear Jesus say "No one can take them out of my hand," my first response is . . .

PRESIDERS

- In my ministry, I instill in others a confidence in God's care and protection by . . .

DEACONS

- My service models Jesus' tender care and concern when . . .

HOSPITALITY MINISTERS

- My hospitality mediates to the assembly that the Good Shepherd "know[s] them" when . . .

MUSIC MINISTERS

- My music making is a shepherding activity that opens the assembly to listen to Jesus' voice when . . .

ALTAR MINISTERS

- My unobtrusive service is a voice of Jesus saying . . .

LECTORS

- My manner of proclamation helps the assembly to hear and heed the voice of the Shepherd when . . .

EXTRAORDINARY MINISTERS OF HOLY COMMUNION

- My manner of distributing Holy Communion helps others experience the care and concern of the Good Shepherd when . . .

Model Rite of Blessing and Sprinkling Holy Water

Presider: Dear friends, this water we ask God to bless reminds us of our baptism and of the care and concern God has for us. Let us open our hearts to the Good Shepherd and prepare ourselves to hear and follow him more faithfully . . . [pause]

[continue with form C of the blessing of water]

Homily Points

• Shepherds separate sheep into folds by training them to recognize the specific sound of a bell worn by a lead sheep. At night shepherds often gather many folds into one keep for protection. In the morning the sheep of each fold fall into line by following the sound of the bell worn by their leader.

• The Good Shepherd trains us to hear and recognize his voice. His voice is not a tinkling sound, however, but a living word embodied in the way he lived, taught, and journeyed through death to risen life.

• The Good Shepherd speaks his living word to us in many ways. We hear the living word of the Good Shepherd and open ourselves to wherever he leads each Sunday when we gather for Eucharist. We hear the living word of the Good Shepherd within our community as we experience and share the demands of discipleship. We hear the living word of the Good Shepherd in the challenging words of others, in the demands for just acts in daily living, and in the cry of the poor and suffering. Even when this Voice leads us beyond safety and security, the hand of the Good Shepherd holds us tight and guides us to new life.

Model Prayer of the Faithful

Presider: Our loving God shepherds us with care and protection and so we are confident that these needs we place before God will be heard.

Response:

Lord, hear our prayer.

Cantor:

we pray to the Lord,

That all members of the church hear the voice of the Good Shepherd and follow him through faithful gospel living . . . [pause]

That leaders of nations shepherd their people with the justice and care that leads to peace and well-being . . . [pause]

That those who are perishing through sickness, depression, or hopelessness might know the care and nearness of the Good Shepherd . . . [pause]

That each one of us here might shepherd others faithfully to the risen life that Jesus offers all of us . . . [pause]

Presider: Loving God, you shepherd your people with unfailing care: hear these our prayers that one day we might all enjoy eternal life with you. We ask this through our Good Shepherd and Savior, Jesus Christ our Lord. **Amen.**

OPENING PRAYER

Let us pray

Pause for silent prayer

Almighty and ever-living God,
give us new strength
from the courage of Christ our shepherd,
and lead us to join the saints in heaven,
where he lives and reigns with you and the
     Holy Spirit,
one God, for ever and ever. **Amen.**

FIRST READING

Acts 13:14, 43-52

Paul and Barnabas continued on from
     Perga
   and reached Antioch in Pisidia.
On the sabbath they entered the
     synagogue and took their seats.
Many Jews and worshipers who were
     converts to Judaism
   followed Paul and Barnabas, who spoke
     to them
   and urged them to remain faithful to the
     grace of God.

On the following sabbath almost the whole
     city gathered
   to hear the word of the Lord.
When the Jews saw the crowds, they were
     filled with jealousy
   and with violent abuse contradicted
     what Paul said.
Both Paul and Barnabas spoke out boldly
     and said,
   "It was necessary that the word of God
     be spoken to you first,
   but since you reject it
   and condemn yourselves as unworthy
     of eternal life,
   we now turn to the Gentiles.
For so the Lord has commanded us,
   I have made you a light to the Gentiles,
   that you may be an instrument of
     salvation
   to the ends of the earth."

The Gentiles were delighted when they
heard this
and glorified the word of the Lord.
All who were destined for eternal life came
to believe,
and the word of the Lord continued to
spread
through the whole region.

The Jews, however, incited the women of
prominence who were worshipers
and the leading men of the city,
stirred up a persecution against Paul
and Barnabas,
and expelled them from their territory.
So they shook the dust from their feet in
protest against them,
and went to Iconium.
The disciples were filled with joy and the
Holy Spirit.

RESPONSORIAL PSALM
Ps 100:1-2, 3, 5

R̸. (3c) We are his people, the sheep of his
flock.
or:
R̸. Alleluia.

Sing joyfully to the Lord, all you lands;
serve the Lord with gladness;
come before him with joyful song.

R̸. We are his people, the sheep of his
flock.
or:
R̸. Alleluia.

Know that the Lord is God;
he made us, his we are;
his people, the flock he tends.

R̸. We are his people, the sheep of his
flock.
or:
R̸. Alleluia.

The Lord is good:
his kindness endures forever,
and his faithfulness, to all generations.

R̸. We are his people, the sheep of his
flock.
or:
R̸. Alleluia.

SECOND READING
Rev 7:9, 14b-17

See Appendix A, p. 298.

About Liturgy

Hinge Sunday in Easter Lectionary: Traditionally known as "Good Shepherd Sunday," this Fourth Sunday of Easter is something of a hinge Sunday. On the one hand, the image of a loving, caring shepherd bids us look back to the first three Sundays of Easter on which the gospels all record appearance accounts of the risen Jesus; these Sundays assure us that Jesus is alive and continues to be present to us, teach us, and care for us. On the other hand, the image of a loving, caring shepherd bids us look forward to the next three Sundays and Pentecost; Jesus prepares us to be disciples by "knowing" us. No matter what demands our discipleship make on us (at least the demand of dying to self), we are assured on this Sunday (as on all Sundays) that Jesus will never let us "perish." Such reassurance gives the hope and courage we need to be faithful to Jesus' call to follow.

Hands as sacramental symbol: Because the hands are such a powerful symbol, it ought to come as no surprise to us that hands are used as a symbol in all our Catholic sacraments. Four of the sacraments (baptism, confirmation, sacrament of the sick, holy orders) expressly call for an imposition of the hands that includes actual physical touch. The other three sacraments (Eucharist, penance, marriage) use extended hands (and, sometimes, in face-to-face confession the confessor might actually touch the head of the penitent during absolution). This latter gesture of extended hands usually signifies an *epiklesis*, which means calling down the Holy Spirit in blessing and/or consecration. In all cases the symbolic gesture with hands conveys the intimacy with which God chooses to be connected with us.

About Liturgical Music

Hymn suggestion: Jesus already began calling the church to mission in last Sunday's gospel ("Feed my lambs"). In the coming weeks this call to mission will become even more intense. This week's readings couch the hardships of the mission with the Shepherd's promise of protection. The hymn "I Know That My Redeemer Lives" [found in many hymnals] is particularly appropriate, especially the verse, "Christ lives to silence all my fears; He lives to wipe away my tears; Christ lives to calm my troubled heart; He lives all blessings to impart." Not all hymnals include this verse, in which case a cantor could interpolate it between other verses sung by the assembly. In this case, the song might work best as a hymn of praise after Communion. It would be good to vary the manner in which the other verses are sung. For example, the choir could sing the verses with the strongest texts SATB; everyone could sing the verses with the gentlest texts a cappella.

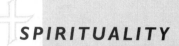

SPIRITUALITY

GOSPEL ACCLAMATION
John 13:34

R℟. Alleluia, alleluia.
I give you a new commandment, says the Lord:
love one another as I have loved you.
R℟. Alleluia, alleluia.

Gospel

John 13:31-33a, 34-35; L54C

When Judas had left them, Jesus said,
  "Now is the Son of Man glorified, and
    God is glorified in him.
If God is glorified in him,
  God will also glorify him in himself,
  and God will glorify him at once.
My children, I will be with you only a
    little while longer.
I give you a new commandment: love
    one another.
As I have loved you, so you also should
    love one another.
This is how all will know that you are
    my disciples,
  if you have love for one another."

Reflecting on the Gospel

Sometimes novels, plays, and movies use flashbacks as a literary technique to help tell the story, fill in details that are helpful for viewers to understand the unfolding tale, and/or remind viewers of previous incidents. The gospel this Sunday functions in the Lectionary as something of a flashback for us. The gospel's context is Jesus' farewell discourse to his disciples at the Last Supper—an event that took place *before* Jesus' suffering, death, and resurrection. Now we read this gospel *after* those events and hear Jesus' words in a new light. Death simultaneously reveals Jesus' glory and the full measure of his love for us: Jesus is willing to suffer and die not only that he might live but also that all of us might share in that same glory and new life.

This flashback also helps us understand more clearly Jesus' final command to his disciples: "love one another." The "new commandment" Jesus gives is not simply to "love" but to love *as he has loved us*. With respect to loving, "how far?" is the question. Jesus' commandment to love requires a new way of living: regard for the other without counting the cost to ourselves. Jesus' death simultaneously reveals the full measure of his love and his glory. Our death—dying to self—reveals the full measure of our love for others and leads to a share in Jesus' glory. Love is the doorway to glory.

Jesus doesn't ask of us anything that he himself hasn't already done to the fullest: the Good Friday–Easter events make clear the extent of Jesus' love for us—he will lay down his very life so that we might have a share in his risen life. As disciples we are commanded to love as the Master loved; if our love is to imitate his, then our love must also include the willingness to lay down our lives for others. The kind of love that Jesus commands leads to self-emptying dying to self.

Glory and love are promised to us—but we share in them only if we take up Jesus' mission. As the gospel says, Jesus was with the disciples only a little while longer; through our own self-sacrificing love we continue his mission of love whereby God is glorified. Loving one another, then, isn't just a nice idea shown in a flashback to a pleasant meal with friends and supporters. Loving one another is the very way we live.

Living the Paschal Mystery

The gospels tell us over and over in so many ways that love means self-sacrifice. We live the paschal mystery only when our own lives emulate the love of Jesus: giving one's all for the sake of another. In many human ways we already do this and could think of no other way to act: most parents sacrifice plenty for their children, we readily respond to others' tragedies with gifts of money and service, we reach out to the perfect stranger on the street who is in need. In so many ways we already act out of the love that Jesus commands in this gospel. Perhaps this gospel flashback reminds us that we need only do the everyday things we are already doing with new meaning: we share in Jesus' mission when we love. On the other hand, if an examination of our lives suggests that perhaps we are not as self-sacrificing as Jesus, then this gospel is an invitation to love more completely. What is at stake is a share in Jesus' everlasting life and glory. This is worth loving for!

Focusing the Gospel

Key words and phrases: glorify, new commandment, love, As I have loved you

To the point: The "new commandment" Jesus gives is not simply to "love" but to love as he has loved us. Jesus' commandment to love requires a new way of living: regard for the other without counting the cost to ourselves. Jesus' death simultaneously reveals the full measure of his love and his glory. Our death—dying to self—reveals the full measure of our love for others and leads to a share in Jesus' glory.

Connecting the Gospel

to the second reading: We cooperate with God to bring about a "new heaven and a new earth" when we fulfill Jesus' new commandment to love in the measure that Jesus loved—by giving our all.

to our experience: We experience many kinds of love in our everyday living. Not all expressions of love demand "dying." But if being loving persons is our way of life, then when love costs more of us, we are better able to respond.

Connecting the Responsorial Psalm

to the readings: Paul and Barnabas are highly energetic and immensely successful in their mission to the Gentiles. All this they credit to God working in them (first reading). John relays his vision of a new heaven and a new earth, God working to "make all things new" (second reading). Jesus speaks of his glorification, God's final work to complete the mission for which he was sent (gospel). In the responsorial psalm we command these works and more to give God thanks and to proclaim the power of God's might and the splendor of God's kingdom to all peoples. One work remains: that we who are God's people love one another as Jesus has loved us (gospel). This, too, will be God's work and the one that will most definitively declare who God is and who we are because of God. May our surrender to this new and final commandment be the praise we sing.

to psalmist preparation: The manner in which you sing this responsorial psalm needs to invite the members of the assembly to see themselves as a work of God, a new creation giving God praise. What might you do this week to help yourself see the assembly in this way? To see yourself in this way? How is this way of seeing a living out of Jesus' commandment to love one another as he has loved us?

ASSEMBLY & FAITH-SHARING GROUPS

- As I understand it, the newness of Jesus' commandment to love is . . .
- Loving one another glorifies God because . . . An instance where my love glorified God was . . .
- Love costs me most when . . .

PRESIDERS

- My ministry reveals the full measure of my love for Jesus whenever I . . . It reveals the full measure of my love for the people to whom I minister when . . .

DEACONS

- A recent example when my ministry glorified God was . . .

HOSPITALITY MINISTERS

- Hospitality is a way of loving another. What dies in me when I extend hospitality is . . . My hospitality glorifies God by . . .

MUSIC MINISTERS

- My collaboration in the ministry of music is an act of loving others as Jesus loves when . . . It is a sign to the assembly of such love when . . .

ALTAR MINISTERS

- When my service is an expression of love it feels and looks like . . . When it is not done in love it feels and looks like . . .

LECTORS

- The dying to self I must do to proclaim God's love is . . .

EXTRAORDINARY MINISTERS OF HOLY COMMUNION

- Distributing Holy Communion extends the full measure of God's love in these ways . . .

Model Rite of Blessing and Sprinkling Holy Water

Presider: Dear friends, this water reminds us of our baptism and the full measure of love and life God gives us. May our sprinkling of this water call us to self-giving love for which Jesus is the model . . . [pause]

[continue with form C of the blessing of water]

Homily Points

• Parents rightfully glory in the achievements of their children. Teachers glory in the accomplishments of their students. We all glory in a job well done. We humans need and respond well to these experiences of glory. But the glory Jesus speaks of in the gospel goes well beyond good feelings and well-being. It is new, risen life.

• The way to the glory of new, risen life is to obey Jesus' "new commandment" of love, a love that does not count cost even when that cost is dying. We are strengthened and encouraged to love in this way because Jesus has shown us the way: "As I have loved you."

• When we receive the love of others, our capacity to love is expanded and greater possibilities for newness of life are opened up. The "glory" promised to those who keep Jesus' new commandment of love is not only that of future, eternal life but also that of a glory experienced now in the goodness of each other and our relationships with one another.

Model Prayer of the Faithful

Presider: Jesus commands us to love as he has loved. Let us pray to be faithful to this command.

Response:

Lord, hear our prayer.

Cantor:

we pray to the Lord,

That the church always model the self-sacrificing love of Jesus . . . [pause]

That all peoples glorify God by loving one another . . . [pause]

That those deprived of love or dignity be embraced and lifted up by the love of this faith community . . . [pause]

That each of us grow in loving to the full measure that we have been loved by Jesus . . . [pause]

Presider: Loving God, you hear our prayers and grant our needs: help us to take up your Son's command to love so that our world might reflect your glory. We ask this through that same Son, Jesus Christ our Lord. **Amen.**

OPENING PRAYER

Let us pray

Pause for silent prayer

God our Father,
look upon us with love.
You redeem us and make us your children
     in Christ.
Give us true freedom
and bring us to the inheritance you
     promised.

We ask this through our Lord Jesus Christ,
     your Son,
who lives and reigns with you and the
     Holy Spirit,
one God, for ever and ever. **Amen.**

FIRST READING
Acts 14:21-27

After Paul and Barnabas had proclaimed
     the good news to that city
     and made a considerable number of
          disciples,
     they returned to Lystra and to Iconium
          and to Antioch.
They strengthened the spirits of the
     disciples
     and exhorted them to persevere in the
          faith, saying,
     "It is necessary for us to undergo many
          hardships
     to enter the kingdom of God."
They appointed elders for them in each
     church and,
     with prayer and fasting, commended
          them to the Lord
     in whom they had put their faith.
Then they traveled through Pisidia and
     reached Pamphylia.
After proclaiming the word at Perga they
     went down to Attalia.
From there they sailed to Antioch,
     where they had been commended to the
          grace of God
     for the work they had now
          accomplished.
And when they arrived, they called the
     church together
     and reported what God had done with
          them
     and how he had opened the door of
          faith to the Gentiles.

RESPONSORIAL PSALM
Ps 145:8-9, 10-11, 12-13

℟. (cf. 1) I will praise your name forever,
my king and my God.
     or:
℟. Alleluia.

The Lord is gracious and merciful,
  slow to anger and of great kindness.
The Lord is good to all
  and compassionate toward all his
    works.
Ry. I will praise your name forever, my
king and my God.
  or:
Ry. Alleluia.

Let all your works give you thanks, O
  Lord,
  and let your faithful ones bless you.
Let them discourse of the glory of your
    kingdom
  and speak of your might.
Ry. I will praise your name forever, my
king and my God.
  or:
Ry. Alleluia.

Let them make known your might to the
    children of Adam,
  and the glorious splendor of your
    kingdom.
Your kingdom is a kingdom for all ages,
  and your dominion endures through all
    generations.
Ry. I will praise your name forever, my
king and my God.
  or:
Ry. Alleluia.

SECOND READING
Rev 21:1-5a

Then I, John, saw a new heaven and a new
    earth.
The former heaven and the former earth
    had passed away,
  and the sea was no more.
I also saw the holy city, a new Jerusalem,
  coming down out of heaven from God,
  prepared as a bride adorned for her
    husband.
I heard a loud voice from the throne
    saying,
  "Behold, God's dwelling is with the
    human race.
He will dwell with them and they will be
    his people
  and God himself will always be with
    them as their God.
He will wipe every tear from their eyes,
  and there shall be no more death or
    mourning, wailing or pain,
  for the old order has passed away."

The One who sat on the throne said,
  "Behold, I make all things new."

About Liturgy

Intercessions for the dead at Mass: The categories given in GIRM 70 (for the church, world, needy, ourselves) do not include a specific intention praying for the dead, although the same paragraph does allow for other intentions to fit special occasions such as weddings and funerals. This does raise a question about whether it is good pastoral practice to always have an intention for the deceased. The four categories listed would suggest not, this because the church provides another time for praying for the dead (at Evening Prayer as part of the intercessions). Perhaps a pastorally sensitive balance might be to include an intercession for the dead when a parishioner has died, but on other Sundays to omit it (with the obvious caveat that in larger parishes or parishes with a larger elderly population someone might die almost every week).

About Liturgical Music

Hymn suggestions: An excellent hymn for the entrance procession or for the sprinkling rite this Sunday would be "We Know That Christ Is Raised and Dies No More" [CBW3, CH, RS, SS, WC, W3]. The text speaks of sharing by water in Jesus' death and new life. Especially apropos is verse 4, "A new creation comes to life and grows, As Christ's new body takes on flesh and blood. The universe restored and whole will sing." Another hymn that speaks of the new creation ushered in by Christ's resurrection is "Christ Is Risen! Shout Hosanna!" [G2, GC2, PMB, SS, WC, WS]. The text is full of the scriptural allusions and poetic imagery characteristic of Brian Wren's work. The catchy and upbeat tune would make the hymn work well either for the entrance procession or as a song of praise after Communion. A good choice for Communion would be James Chepponis's "Love One Another" [G2, GC, RS] or Bob Dufford's "Love One Another" [BB, JS2, OFUV].

✠ SPIRITUALITY

GOSPEL ACCLAMATION
John 14:23

R7. Alleluia, alleluia.
Whoever loves me will keep my word, says the
   Lord,
and my Father will love him and we will come
   to him.
R7. Alleluia, alleluia.

Gospel

John 14:23-29; L57C

Jesus said to his disciples:
   "Whoever loves me will
      keep my word,
   and my Father will love
      him,
   and we will come to
      him and make our
      dwelling with him.
Whoever does not love me
      does not keep my words;
   yet the word you hear is not mine
   but that of the Father who sent me.

"I have told you this while I am with
      you.
The Advocate, the Holy Spirit,
   whom the Father will send in my
      name,
   will teach you everything
   and remind you of all that I told you.
Peace I leave with you; my peace I give
      to you.
Not as the world gives do I give it to
      you.
Do not let your hearts be troubled or
      afraid.
You heard me tell you,
   'I am going away and I will come
      back to you.'
If you loved me,
   you would rejoice that I am going to
      the Father;
   for the Father is greater than I.
And now I have told you this before it
      happens,
   so that when it happens you may
      believe."

Reflecting on the Gospel

It seems hard for most of us to have the integrity to keep our own word and promises faithfully. Lo and behold, in this gospel Jesus takes this one step further: "Whoever loves me will keep *my* word . . ." In last Sunday's gospel Jesus admonished us to love not on our own terms but as he loves. This week he commands us to keep not our word but his word. If we have difficulty keeping our own word (and, realistically, sometimes we do), how in the world can we be successful in keeping *Jesus'* word? Besides, Jesus' word is much more than simply what Jesus said and taught. It is the way he lived. Jesus' words and deeds coalesce into the same reality, that is, a life of self-giving that brings salvation. It is the same life we are called to in this gospel.

This would seem a daunting task for us, and quite discouraging from the outset. However, we are not left powerless in the face of keeping Jesus' word. We are given the help of God's own presence. To enable us to keep his word, Jesus promises us a divine indwelling through which we are re-created as persons able to live and love as Jesus himself did. We are a new creation empowered to continue, in peace and fearlessness, the mission of Jesus in the world. To be created anew means that we share in the life of the risen Lord—in a very real way, we share in Jesus' identity. Indeed, this is the gift of baptism: that we are made members of the Body of Christ. Only because we share in Jesus' identity as members of his Body can we truly keep his word and carry on his saving mission. Keeping Jesus' word means that we open our hearts to his presence, allow him to change us, and grow in such a way that his integrity and identity are meshed with ours.

Jesus' word is a promise of a new relationship with him and his Father, where God comes and dwells within us through the power of the Holy Spirit. We keep his word, therefore, when we embody in our living the fearlessness and peace of Jesus that are evidence of the presence of the Spirit. We keep his word when we respond to indwelling divine Love with self-giving as modeled by Jesus. The truth and power of the word come from within, and it is the truth and power of the Holy Spirit. We are fearless not because of our own power but because of the Spirit dwelling within us.

Our Christian understanding of love rests precisely in the breadth of self-giving we are willing to offer. Keeping Jesus' word ultimately means that we make all the Gospel our own. This is surely no small task! But the reward—God's indwelling that brings us new life—is not small either.

Living the Paschal Mystery

Living the paschal mystery is as demanding as loving with the same self-sacrifice as Jesus and as easy as responding to God's indwelling as an intimate Friend who is always with us, never forsakes us, and at all times is there for us with care and strength. These Sundays before Pentecost when we celebrate the gift of the Spirit are so important for our daily Christian living: they remind us that as disciples we never have to feel like the whole task of living the gospel falls on our shoulders alone. God is always present, dwelling within us, to give us the strength we need to be faithful to Jesus' commands. Only in this way can our everyday lives be fruitful, can we keep Jesus' word as our own word.

Focusing the Gospel

Key words and phrases: keep my word, love, make our dwelling, peace, not . . . afraid

To the point: In last Sunday's gospel Jesus admonished us to love not on our own terms but as he loves. This week he commands us to keep not our word but his word. To enable us to keep his word, Jesus promises us a divine indwelling through which we are re-created as persons able to live and love as Jesus himself did. We are a new creation empowered to continue, in peace and fearlessness, the mission of Jesus in the world.

Connecting the Gospel

to the second reading: The radiant vision of God's dwelling among us (see second reading) is realized when disciples take up the practical way of life Jesus commands in the gospel: to love, keep his word, believe. To take up this daunting way of life Jesus sends his Spirit, gives his peace, and removes our fears.

to our experience: For almost fifty years now, since the Second Vatican Council, we have thought of the church as "the people of God." How easy it still is to think of God's dwelling place as a church building, and how difficult for us to believe God's dwelling is found among the people who follow Jesus!

Connecting the Responsorial Psalm

to the readings: Psalm 67 begins with part of the blessing of Aaron (Num 6:24-26). For the Israelite community, blessings were different from intercessory prayer in times of need or danger and were given at turning points in life such as weddings, deaths, and certain religious ceremonies. What is the turning point on this Sixth Sunday of Easter? For the early church the decision to eliminate certain identifying Jewish practices as requirements for entrance into the community was a huge shift (first reading). The understanding that Jerusalem was not a place on earth but a heavenly dwelling and that the temple was not a building but the very person of God was a radically new conceptualization (second reading). Love of Christ and fidelity to his word meant acceptance of a markedly new way of living (gospel).

Psalm 67 can be seen as our acknowledgment that the resurrection of Christ (and this Easter season) have brought our lives to a turning point. We are no longer who we were. Our understanding of salvation is more extensive, our concept of God broader, and our need to change deeper. May God bless us.

to psalmist preparation: Understanding that a blessing often marks a turning point in one's life casts this responsorial psalm in a whole new light. In singing it you are praying for what needs to come because of what has already happened. What has happened to the assembly because of Christ's resurrection? To you? What is the assembly being called to? What are you being called to?

ASSEMBLY & FAITH-SHARING GROUPS

- This Easter the word of Jesus that I am being called to keep is . . .
- When I am aware that God dwells with me, my daily living is like . . .
- I need the Holy Spirit to continue fearlessly Jesus' mission because . . .

PRESIDERS

- For me the connection between Jesus' word during the week and proclaiming that word on Sunday is . . .

DEACONS

- I embody the word of Jesus in my servant ministry when . . .

HOSPITALITY MINISTERS

- " . . . we will come to him and make our dwelling with him." I help God's people be ready for God's dwelling among them by . . .

MUSIC MINISTERS

- Sometimes in my music ministry I need to be more aware of God's dwelling within me because . . . I need to be more aware of God's dwelling with the assembly because . . .

ALTAR MINISTERS

- My serving others witnesses to the indwelling of the Holy Spirit ("whom the Father will send") when . . .

LECTORS

- When I approach the text and only worry about enunciation, my preparation is like . . . When I approach the text recalling that it is the Father's word sent to us, my preparation is like . . .

EXTRAORDINARY MINISTERS OF HOLY COMMUNION

- Jesus' eucharistic presence instills in us a peace so that our hearts need not be troubled or afraid. I am becoming that kind of presence for others when I . . .

Model Rite of Blessing and Sprinkling Holy Water

Presider: Dear friends, as we ask God to bless this water and we sprinkle it, may it help us to keep Jesus' word and live in peace with unafraid and untroubled hearts . . . [pause]

[continue with form C of the blessing of water]

Homily Points

• We respect persons who keep their word. They are models of integrity and reliability for there is no distinction between what they say and what they do. Such integrity gives them a "wholeness" that determines their relationships with others.

• "[K]eep my word" may seem to be a simplistic phrase in the gospel until we remember that Jesus is the Word made flesh who comes from the Father. What, then, is the word Jesus commands us to keep? His very way of life. His concern for others put into action every day by the way he related to all whom he met. The Word we keep is Jesus himself. And this shapes our relationships with others, too.

• In Jesus, the lame walked, the oppressed rejoiced, the poor had the Good News preached to them, and the dead were raised to new life. If we are to keep Jesus' word, then our life must be characterized by a speaking and doing that brings about these same transformations. This is the way of life for which the Spirit empowers us.

Model Prayer of the Faithful

Presider: Living the word of Jesus makes demands on us. Let us pray for strength to be faithful followers of Jesus.

Response:

Lord, hear our prayer.

Cantor:

we pray to the Lord,

That all members of the church may embody the integrity of Jesus . . . [pause]

That government leaders faithfully keep God's word, building peace and justice for all . . . [pause]

That those who are frightened and troubled may find peace in the loving concern of others . . . [pause]

That each of us here become more deeply aware of God's indwelling and make that presence known to others we meet . . . [pause]

Presider: Loving God, you dwell within us and enable us to keep your word: hear these our prayers that we might always be faithful disciples of your Son and one day dwell forever with you and the Holy Spirit, one God, for ever and ever. **Amen.**

OPENING PRAYER

Let us pray

Pause for silent prayer

Ever-living God,
help us to celebrate our joy
in the resurrection of the Lord
and to express in our lives
the love we celebrate.

Grant this through our Lord Jesus Christ,
        your Son,
who lives and reigns with you and the
        Holy Spirit,
one God, for ever and ever. **Amen.**

FIRST READING

Acts 15:1-2, 22-29

Some who had come down from Judea were
        instructing the brothers,
    "Unless you are circumcised according
        to the Mosaic practice,
    you cannot be saved."
Because there arose no little dissension
        and debate
    by Paul and Barnabas with them,
    it was decided that Paul, Barnabas, and
        some of the others
    should go up to Jerusalem to the
        apostles and elders
    about this question.

The apostles and elders, in agreement
        with the whole church,
    decided to choose representatives
    and to send them to Antioch with Paul
        and Barnabas.
The ones chosen were Judas, who was
        called Barsabbas,
    and Silas, leaders among the brothers.
This is the letter delivered by them:

"The apostles and the elders, your brothers,
    to the brothers in Antioch, Syria, and
        Cilicia
    of Gentile origin: greetings.
Since we have heard that some of our
        number
    who went out without any mandate
        from us
    have upset you with their teachings
    and disturbed your peace of mind,
    we have with one accord decided to
        choose representatives
    and to send them to you along with our
        beloved Barnabas and Paul,
    who have dedicated their lives to the
        name of our Lord Jesus Christ.

So we are sending Judas and Silas
who will also convey this same message
by word of mouth:
'It is the decision of the Holy Spirit and
of us
not to place on you any burden beyond
these necessities,
namely, to abstain from meat sacrificed
to idols,
from blood, from meats of strangled
animals,
and from unlawful marriage.
If you keep free of these,
you will be doing what is right. Farewell.'"

RESPONSORIAL PSALM

Ps 67:2-3, 5, 6, 8

R̊. (4) O God, let all the nations praise you!
    or:
R̊. Alleluia.

May God have pity on us and bless us;
    may he let his face shine upon us.
So may your way be known upon earth;
    among all nations, your salvation.

R̊. O God, let all the nations praise you!
    or:
R̊. Alleluia.

May the nations be glad and exult
    because you rule the peoples in equity;
    the nations on the earth you guide.

R̊. O God, let all the nations praise you!
    or:
R̊. Alleluia.

May the peoples praise you, O God;
    may all the peoples praise you!
May God bless us,
    and may all the ends of the earth fear
        him!

R̊. O God, let all the nations praise you!
    or:
R̊. Alleluia.

SECOND READING

Rev 21:10-14, 22-23

See Appendix A, p. 298.

Or, where the Ascension is celebrated on
Sunday, the second reading and gospel for
the Seventh Sunday of Easter may be used
on this Sunday.

Rev 22:12-14, 16-17, 20, p. 137.

John 17:20-26, p. 134.

About Liturgy

Mother's Day: This second Sunday of May is traditionally observed as Mother's Day. Although it would be inappropriate to focus the liturgy on mothers, two ritual elements are always appropriate.

1. The following model of intercession based on the gospel might be used as a fifth intercession during the prayer of the faithful: "That all mothers' self-giving love enables them to shine with the glory of God and receive strength from it . . . [pause]." Three other model intercessions are given in BofB chapter 55, no. 1727.

2. In BofB chapter 55, no. 1728, a prayer over the people is given and may replace the prayer over the people given in the Sacramentary for the Sixth Sunday of Easter.

God's indwelling: Divine indwelling has been part of our Catholic doctrine from the very beginning. In particular, the sacraments of initiation celebrate a divine love that is so great that God chooses to live within us and among us. In baptism we are plunged into the paschal mystery of Christ, dying to self so that we might rise to new life in Christ. We are sealed in baptism with the gift of the Holy Spirit and strengthened in confirmation to live this new life. In the Eucharist we are nourished by Christ's Body and Blood, and by eating and drinking so sublime a Food we become what we eat—the Body of Christ in whom God dwells in glory.

The challenge, of course, is that these sacraments remain not simply actions we go through but become dynamic ways of living. This is one reason why we celebrate liturgy each Sunday—so that we remember Jesus' words and deeds. One practice that might help us make this practical in our daily living—and over the years see real spiritual growth in ourselves—is to make sure we take one thought from each Sunday celebration that leads to particular action in our daily living. Questions to ask might be: How, this week, might I express to others that God dwells within me? How does this week's gospel challenge me to live?

About Liturgical Music

Hymn suggestions: "For Your Gift of God the Spirit" [HG] combines thanksgiving for the gift of the Spirit with proclamation about what this Spirit does within us—stirs life, interprets Scripture, gives strength to conquer evil, etc. Verse 3 is particularly relevant to this gospel: "He, himself the living Author, Wakes to life the sacred Word, Reads with us its holy pages, And reveals our risen Lord . . ." The final verse is a petition that God give this Spirit full sway in our hearts. HG suggests HYMN TO JOY as the tune, making this a strong processional hymn that would work well for the entrance. The hymn could also be used during the preparation of the gifts, provided this is long enough to accommodate all the verses. As a third option, the hymn would make a wonderful after-Communion song of praise for the assembly.

A hymn directly connected to the second reading is "I Want to Walk as a Child of the Light" [found in most hymnals]. The refrain concludes with "The Lamb is the light of the city of God. Shine in my heart, Lord Jesus." The song could be used at either the preparation of the gifts or after Communion.

SPIRITUALITY

GOSPEL ACCLAMATION
Matt 28:19a, 20b

℟. Alleluia, alleluia.
Go and teach all nations, says the Lord;
I am with you always, until the end of the
   world.
℟. Alleluia, alleluia.

Gospel

Luke 24:46-53; L58C

Jesus said to his disciples:
   "Thus it is written that the
      Christ would suffer
   and rise from the dead on the
      third day
   and that repentance, for the
      forgiveness of sins,
   would be preached in his name
   to all the nations, beginning from
      Jerusalem.
You are witnesses of these things.
And behold I am sending the promise
      of my Father upon you;
   but stay in the city
   until you are clothed with power from
      on high."

Then he led them out as far as Bethany,
   raised his hands, and blessed them.
As he blessed them he parted from
   them
   and was taken up to heaven.
They did him homage
   and then returned to Jerusalem with
      great joy,
   and they were continually in the
      temple praising God.

Reflecting on the Gospel

It's fairly easy and sometimes rather convenient to make a sharp distinction between the material world and "spirit" world in such terms as these: one is real, the other isn't; one is sensible, the other isn't; one is provable, the other isn't; one is under our control, the other isn't. Some people even try to negate the spirit world completely. They claim that we can't test it in a lab; we can't prove scientifically what a spirit is. Most of us, however, have a great deal of experience with the spirit world and believe firmly in it. A new idea pops into our heads that is just the right way to solve a problem. We catch school spirit at pep rallies. We talk about high-spirited adventures or being in low spirits. While none of this experience of the spirit world is tangible, we still act upon it as being very real. Not everything important to us is tangible and sensible. In fact, sometimes what is most real to us is spirit. Spirit is what can most motivate us, inspire us, bring us to insight and creative responses to situations that would otherwise perplex or even overwhelm us.

We might well imagine the disciples' perplexity and overwhelming sense of absence when Jesus ascended into heaven. The first reading account from Acts mentions that "as he was going" the disciples were "standing there looking at the sky." Maybe they wanted a last glimpse of Jesus. Maybe they were wishing that he wouldn't leave them. Maybe they were still trying to catch a last-minute something of his spirit so they wouldn't feel his absence so keenly.

As time will tell, Jesus' disappearance from sight does not mark an absence but marks a new kind of presence. In the "absence" left by his ascension, we his followers are commissioned to "preach[ ] in his name to all nations." What is it we preach? That suffering and even death lead to new life and that forgiveness will be granted to all who repent. His very ascension into heaven is our commissioning on earth because, "clothed with power from on high," we are now the visible presence of Jesus.

Think of that: his ascension itself is a commissioning. His absence brings a presence—the Holy Spirit who is the "power from on high" and who consecrates us to continue Jesus' saving mission. The very absence sends us forth to be and do as Jesus. We don't do this on our own, as Jesus promised. We can't set out to take up Jesus' mission to preach the Good News until we receive the Holy Spirit. This ensures us that our work isn't ours but Christ's. Ultimately our mission is to preach not simply events but a Person—Jesus Christ, the risen One. Even more: with the Spirit, we *are* the presence of the risen Lord. It's his Spirit we catch. And it is very real, indeed.

Living the Paschal Mystery

We are all familiar with the Catholic doctrine that the Holy Scriptures are the inspired word of God. Through the indwelling of the Holy Spirit, each of us is an inspired word of God when we are faithful to Jesus. This means, as the gospel suggests, that we are to preach and live as Jesus commanded. Repentance and forgiveness require that we first are willing to do as Jesus did—give ourselves over to the Spirit of God who heals and gives life. Having first experienced God's saving action, we can be that saving action for others.

Focusing the Gospel

Key words and phrases: suffer, rise, repentance, forgiveness, would be preached, clothed with power, parted from them

To the point: Jesus' disappearance from sight does not mark an absence but marks a new kind of presence. In the "absence" left by his ascension, we his followers are commissioned to "preach[ ] in his name to all nations." What is it we preach? That suffering and even death lead to new life and that forgiveness will be granted to all who repent. His very ascension into heaven is our commissioning on earth because, "clothed with power from on high," we are now the visible presence of Jesus.

Connecting the Gospel

to the first reading: The ascension account in the first reading makes even more concrete the "power from on high" that will be given us: the Holy Spirit who instructs us, in whom we are baptized, and who empowers us to continue Jesus' mission on earth.

to our experience: We've all had experiences during which insight or strength or power have come to us from "we know not where." We experience these energies coming both from a source outside ourselves as well as from within us. So is our experience of the Holy Spirit.

Connecting the Responsorial Psalm

to the readings: Psalm 47 was an enthronement psalm used when the ark of the covenant was carried in procession into the temple. It celebrated God's sovereignty over all heaven and earth. The song contains verses (omitted from this responsorial psalm) that express Israel's belief that choosing them as a special people was part of God's plan for establishing kingship over all nations. Verses 4-5, for example, acclaim, "He brings peoples under us, nations under our feet . . ."

Knowing the full text of this psalm brings its use on this solemnity into fuller perspective. The psalm is not just about the historical ascension of Jesus to the throne of God but includes our participation in his ascendancy. We, too, "have confidence of entrance into the sanctuary" (second reading). Though we do not know the time of the kingdom's coming, we do witness to its presence (first reading). We have been blessed by Christ to tell of it (gospel). By Jesus' ascension all humanity is raised to the glory of God. When we sing Psalm 47 on this solemnity, this is what we witness to, celebrate, and proclaim.

to psalmist preparation: On the surface you can interpret this psalm as a celebration of the historical event of Jesus' ascension. But it is about far more than that. The psalm is about the complete victory of the whole Body of Christ over the forces of sin and death. Who sits on the "holy throne"? The church does. This assembly does. You do. As you prepare to sing this psalm, you need to reflect on this fuller understanding so that you can move the assembly (and yourself) beyond historicizing Jesus' life and mission to participation in it.

**ASSEMBLY &
FAITH-SHARING GROUPS**

- I "preach" Jesus' dying and rising pattern in my life when . . .
- I continue Jesus' mission of repentance and forgiveness by . . .
- I experience being the visible presence of Jesus for others when . . .

PRESIDERS

- When I become "absent" in my presiding, Jesus becomes more present in that . . .

DEACONS

- My ordination commissions me to . . . I make Jesus present when I . . .

HOSPITALITY MINISTERS

- My hospitality witnesses to the assembly my faith that they are "clothed with power on high" when I . . .

MUSIC MINISTERS

- The assembly experiences the presence of Jesus through my music ministry when . . . The assembly offers me the presence of Jesus by . . .

ALTAR MINISTERS

- The suffering and dying to self that my ministry entails is . . .

LECTORS

- Sometimes I pray the readings and realize that I am not living them. At those moments what it means to me to hear Jesus say, ". . . stay . . . until you are clothed with power from on high" is . . .

**EXTRAORDINARY MINISTERS
OF HOLY COMMUNION**

- I distribute the presence of Jesus in Holy Communion. My daily living distributes the presence of Jesus in that . . .

Model Rite of Blessing and Sprinkling Holy Water

Presider: Dear friends, this water will be blessed and sprinkled to remind us of our baptism through which we receive the Holy Spirit. As we begin this liturgy, let us open ourselves to God's presence so that we can be this presence for others . . . [pause]

[continue with form C of the blessing of water]

Homily Points

• Persons' "spirits" often live on long after their death. Certain situations in our own lives trigger our memory of them. Recalling what they said or did, we are inspired to live up to the legacy they have left us. In this way their presence continues through our own words and actions.

• The gospels are products of the early communities' memories of Jesus, which keep alive the Good News of his words and deeds. Although Jesus absented himself after the ascension, he is still present among us through the Spirit who enlivens our memories and urges us to live as Jesus did.

• We are the visible presence of Jesus when we accept his commission to "preach": die to self, repent, forgive one another. We die to ourselves, for example, every time we put another's need above our own desires. We repent every time we recognize that we have hurt another and seek amends. We forgive every time we let go of a grudge. Our "preaching" is more than words; it is doing the very deeds Jesus did.

Model Prayer of the Faithful

Presider: Let us pray that we might be faithful in taking up Jesus' commission to be his followers.

Response:

Lord, hear our prayer.

Cantor:

we pray to the Lord,

Clothed with power from on high, may all members of the church make visible the presence of Jesus through the good works they do . . . [pause]

Clothed with power from on high, may the peoples of all nations forgive others and build a world of peace and justice . . . [pause]

Clothed with power from on high, may the poor and downtrodden be lifted up . . . [pause]

Clothed with power from on high, may each of us preach the Good News faithfully in both words and deeds . . . [pause]

Presider: Good and gracious God, your Son Jesus ascended into heaven so that we might receive the Holy Spirit: help us to be Jesus' presence and goodness for others. We ask this through that same Christ Jesus, our Lord. **Amen**.

OPENING PRAYER

Let us pray

Pause for silent prayer

God our Father,
make us joyful in the ascension of your
    Son Jesus Christ.
May we follow him into the new creation,
for his ascension is our glory and our
    hope.

We ask this through our Lord Jesus Christ,
    your Son,
who lives and reigns with you and the
    Holy Spirit,
one God, for ever and ever. **Amen**.

FIRST READING
Acts 1:1-11

In the first book, Theophilus,
    I dealt with all that Jesus did and taught
    until the day he was taken up,
    after giving instructions through the
        Holy Spirit
    to the apostles whom he had chosen.
He presented himself alive to them
    by many proofs after he had suffered,
    appearing to them during forty days
    and speaking about the kingdom of
        God.
While meeting with them,
    he enjoined them not to depart from
        Jerusalem,
    but to wait for "the promise of the
        Father
    about which you have heard me speak;
    for John baptized with water,
    but in a few days you will be baptized
        with the Holy Spirit."

When they had gathered together they
    asked him,
    "Lord, are you at this time going to
        restore the kingdom to Israel?"
He answered them, "It is not for you to
        know the times or seasons
    that the Father has established by his
        own authority.
But you will receive power when the Holy
        Spirit comes upon you,
    and you will be my witnesses in
        Jerusalem,
    throughout Judea and Samaria,
    and to the ends of the earth."
When he had said this, as they were
        looking on,
    he was lifted up, and a cloud took him
        from their sight.

While they were looking intently at the
  sky as he was going,
    suddenly two men dressed in white
    garments stood beside them.
They said, "Men of Galilee,
  why are you standing there looking at
    the sky?
This Jesus who has been taken up from
  you into heaven
    will return in the same way as you have
    seen him going into heaven."

RESPONSORIAL PSALM

Ps 47:2-3, 6-7, 8-9

R℣. (6) God mounts his throne to shouts of
joy: a blare of trumpets for the Lord.
  or:
R℣. Alleluia.

All you peoples, clap your hands,
  shout to God with cries of gladness,
for the LORD, the Most High, the awesome,
  is the great king over all the earth.

R℣. God mounts his throne to shouts of joy:
a blare of trumpets for the Lord.
  or:
R℣. Alleluia.

God mounts his throne amid shouts of joy;
  the LORD, amid trumpet blasts.
Sing praise to God, sing praise;
  sing praise to our king, sing praise.

R℣. God mounts his throne to shouts of joy:
a blare of trumpets for the Lord.
  or:
R℣. Alleluia.

For king of all the earth is God;
  sing hymns of praise.
God reigns over the nations,
  God sits upon his holy throne.

R℣. God mounts his throne to shouts of joy:
a blare of trumpets for the Lord.
  or:
R℣. Alleluia.

SECOND READING

Eph 1:17-23

or

Heb 9:24-28; 10:19-23

See Appendix A, p. 299.

About Liturgy

Choice of second reading for Ascension: Since the second reading from Ephesians is the only option given for year A, we suggest that reading be reserved for year A and the reading from the letter to the Hebrews be chosen for year C.

Silences during Mass: Several times during Mass it is appropriate to pause in silence. These silent times enable us to surrender ourselves to God's presence, to remember that the Spirit dwells within us and enables us to reverse the "absence" of the ascension: through the power of the Spirit within us the risen Christ is present.

First, both the rite of blessing and sprinkling holy water, and the penitential rite call for a brief period of silence and reflection. This time allows us to make the transition from our busy lives into God's presence, consciously surrender ourselves to God's action within us, and call to mind anything we have done that keeps us from giving ourselves over to taking up Jesus' saving mission. Although this time is brief (and in some cases so brief as to be nonexistent!) it is mightily important; this opens the door for our participation in the rest of Mass. We take much time to prepare for important events in our lives; surely this brief time is no less important!

Second, after Communion there may be a brief period of silence. Since we have just shared in eating and drinking the Body and Blood of Christ, this is time afforded us to appreciate more fully what we have shared and think about how we might be a better presence of the Body and Blood of Christ to others in our daily living. We might consider one specific way during the coming week when we will consciously be the presence of the risen Christ for someone else.

About Liturgical Music

Hymn suggestions: Hymns celebrating the ascension are designated in every hymnal. Look for ones that connect Jesus' ascension with the elevation of all humanity. Some Easter hymns do this; for example, "Up from the Earth" [G2, GC, RS]. Its style and energy suit it best either for the entrance procession or for a song of praise after Communion.

Another possibility for an assembly song after Communion would be a hymn praying for the descent of the Holy Spirit. For example, quietly singing the Taizé "Veni, Sancte Spiritus," with its suggested shifts in dynamic levels and harmonizations, would be an effective way to enter into the prayer and expectancy of the church as it awaits the day of Pentecost. A similar lovely piece with ostinato refrain is Paul Page's "Come, Spirit, Come" [in *Mantras for the Seasons*, WLP]. Although in general it is appropriate for the assembly to stand for the hymn after Communion, the meditative nature and purpose of either of these songs suggest it would be better to be seated, then to stand for the prayer after Communion. And, as always when singing a post-Communion hymn, it is preferable to omit a recessional hymn and go immediately to an instrumental postlude.

SPIRITUALITY

GOSPEL ACCLAMATION
cf. John 14:18

R̸. Alleluia, alleluia.
I will not leave you orphans, says the Lord.
I will come back to you, and your hearts
    will rejoice.
R̸. Alleluia, alleluia.

Gospel

John 17:20-26; L61C

Lifting up his eyes to heaven,
    Jesus prayed, saying:
    "Holy Father, I pray not only for
        them,
    but also for those who will
        believe in me through their
        word,
    so that they may all be one,
    as you, Father, are in me and I in you,
    that they also may be in us,
    that the world may believe that you
        sent me.
And I have given them the glory you
        gave me,
    so that they may be one, as we are
        one,
    I in them and you in me,
    that they may be brought to
        perfection as one,
    that the world may know that you
        sent me,
    and that you loved them even as you
        loved me.
Father, they are your gift to me.
I wish that where I am they also may
        be with me,
    that they may see my glory that you
        gave me,
    because you loved me before the
        foundation of the world.
Righteous Father, the world also does
        not know you,
    but I know you, and they know that
        you sent me.
I made known to them your name and I
        will make it known,
    that the love with which you loved me
    may be in them and I in them."

Reflecting on the Gospel

The Little Prince, by French author Antoine de Saint-Exupéry, is a classic work that tells the tale of a little prince from a far-off world who comes to earth searching for happiness. He finally chances upon a wise fox who teaches him about friendship. When the Little Prince is about ready to return to his planet, the fox says good-bye by telling him a secret: "It is only with the heart that one can see rightly; what is essential is invisible to the eye." For all the time Jesus has spent with his disciples (and, no doubt, he had many an intimate moment), perhaps the one recorded in this Sunday's gospel is the most telling. Jesus is preparing to say goodbye to his disciples, and he lets them through his prayer see intimately into his own heart. The "secret" Jesus reveals is how much he loves us and that he desires for us the same love and unity that he and the Father share.

Prayer reveals the deepest desire of our hearts and our truest selves. As Jesus prays in this gospel, we learn what is deepest in his heart. What is more, Jesus' prayer teaches us that in the unity we share as the one Body of Christ we already participate in Jesus' glory—this because by being the one Body of Christ we share in his identity and so also are already united with the Trinity in all its glory. Jesus' prayer reminds us that being a disciple means that we already share in Jesus' glory. Whether we are disciples who give our lives for Christ, as did Stephen in the first reading, or whether we are disciples who plod along as faithful witnesses to Christ in the ordinary circumstances of daily living, the result is the same: we are the Father's gift to Jesus, we are intimately loved into a union with God and each other, and we already share in divine glory.

In this intimate prayer of Jesus before his suffering and death, we see clearly how much Jesus sustains us in our discipleship. Our peek into what is deepest in Jesus' heart encourages us. The gift of the Spirit that we receive helps us see who we are to be as the one Body of Christ: those whose lives are spent in self-sacrificing surrender for the sake of others. Our glory lies in imitating Jesus, knowing that dying to self leads to risen life.

Truly, Jesus' prayer at the Last Supper is not only for the disciples who were present with him but also for us. In this very heartfelt prayer, Jesus reveals the intimacy he enjoys with his Father—the same intimacy he desires with and for his disciples (and us). Such a love! Such a unity! Such a gift! Such a life!

Living the Paschal Mystery

Most often when we think of living the paschal mystery we think in terms of the concrete self-surrendering acts we undertake in order to live the dying and rising mystery of Christ. The gospel for this Sunday affords us an opportunity to reflect on a completely different kind of self-surrender—that of giving ourselves over to God in the intimacy of prayer. Just as Jesus' prayer reveals us as sharing in his love for and unity with the Father, our prayer reveals both our love for and union with God and our love for and union with each other. Just as Jesus was prompted in his prayer to look not to himself but to the well-being of his disciples, our prayer draws us out of ourselves toward God and concern for others. Thus, prayer itself is a kind of self-sacrificing surrender for others.

Focusing the Gospel

Key words and phrases: Jesus prayed, may all be one, gift to me, love

To the point: Jesus' prayer at the Last Supper is not only for the disciples who were present with him but also for us. In this very heartfelt prayer, Jesus reveals the intimacy he enjoys with his Father—the same intimacy he desires with and for his disciples (and us). Such a love! Such a unity! Such a gift! Such a life!

Connecting the Gospel

to the first reading: It is only because Stephen is "filled with the Holy Spirit," that is, filled with the love of Jesus, that he is able to give his life to be in union with Jesus. Would that we be so filled with this love!

to our experience: Praying aloud is not only an expression of intimacy with God; it is also an occasion for intimacy among those who hear our prayer. The intimacy of shared prayer fosters the unity Jesus and the Father desire for us.

Connecting the Responsorial Psalm

to the readings: The responsorial psalm seems a strange follow-up to the recounting of Stephen's martyrdom until we read the entirety of Psalm 97 and discover its parallels with Stephen's story. Psalm 97 begins with a theophany (vv. 1-6) that concludes with the acclamation that "all peoples see [God's] glory." The psalm describes two responses to this epiphany of God's glory. False gods and those who worship them fall down in fear and defeat (v. 7), and believers faithful to God rejoice (v. 8). Verse 10 states that God guards the lives of these faithful ones and delivers them from the hand of the wicked.

In the account from Acts we have a theophany—Stephen sees the glory of God and of Christ in heaven—and the reaction of an unbelieving crowd. We also have a deliverance, for in freely giving his spirit over to Christ and in forgiving his killers, Stephen was glorified. His death was his resurrection. Stephen had seen the glory given him by Christ (gospel) and cried out, "Come" (second reading). In singing this psalm we acclaim that we, too, have seen the glory and that we, too, can stake our lives on it.

to psalmist preparation: It would be easy to skim over this responsorial psalm as a generic text about the glory of God and sing it perhaps in only a perfunctory way. But the context of Stephen's martyrdom for bearing witness to the glory of God and Jesus' prayer that we be one with him and the Father invites a much deeper interpretation. To see truly the glory of God means to discover the mystery of your own glory. To become truly one with Christ means to accept that such glorification can come only through death. To sing these verses is, like Stephen then, to lay down your life in surrender and belief. You sing no simple song.

**ASSEMBLY &
FAITH-SHARING GROUPS**

- As I listen to Jesus' prayer for me, what is most comforting is . . .
- One thing I need to change in order to conform my life more closely to Jesus' prayer is . . .
- I have experienced Jesus' love for me when . . .

PRESIDERS

- Generally when I look upon the people in my care I see them as . . . When I recall that they are God's "gift to me," my ministry looks like . . .

DEACONS

- My intimate love for others is expressed through my service ministry when . . .

HOSPITALITY MINISTERS

- Where I could bring about love and unity among those who are alienated (in my family or parish) is . . .

MUSIC MINISTERS

- My liturgical music making leads me— and the assembly—to union with Christ and one another when . . . What gets in the way of this union is . . .

ALTAR MINISTERS

- My serving others fulfills the desire of Jesus' prayer because . . .

LECTORS

- I proclaim Jesus' love for his disciples in my daily living when . . .

**EXTRAORDINARY MINISTERS
OF HOLY COMMUNION**

- "I pray . . . that they may all be one." I seek to bring about communion in my daily living when . . .

Model Rite of Blessing and Sprinkling Holy Water

Presider: Dear friends, we ask God to bless this water and we sprinkle it as a reminder of Jesus' intimate love for us. As we prepare to celebrate this feast of love, let us open ourselves to God's presence . . . [pause]

> *[continue with form C of the blessing of water]*

Homily Points

• Love is the most powerful human emotion. We seek it above all other goods. Sometimes our seeking love is right and healthy, for example, when we work to strengthen the bonds within our families. At other times seeking love is misguided and ultimately destructive, for example, when we seek our own satisfaction without regard for the other.

• Jesus in this gospel shows us that love is also the most powerful divine impulse. Divine love always seeks the good of others, always leads to unity, always generates new life.

• As Jesus prayed that his love might be known, so must we look into our hearts to discern the extent and kind of love that is there. Jesus' prayer and example invite us to root out any selfish love and to open ourselves more expansively to the kind of other-centered, divine love that brings new life to others.

Model Prayer of the Faithful

Presider: Let us unite our prayer with Jesus' prayer for us, asking God to help us to love more generously.

Response:

Lord, hear our prayer.

Cantor:

we pray to the Lord,

That all members of the church witness to the love with which God has first loved us . . . [pause]

That all peoples of the world share in a bond of unity that brings peace and justice for all . . . [pause]

That those who find it difficult to pray or don't take time to pray learn to enjoy the intimacy with God that prayer offers . . . [pause]

That each one of us always pray with the same intimacy and fervor as Jesus . . . [pause]

Presider: Glorious God, you invite us to share in your unity: hear these our prayers that we might one day share in your everlasting glory. We ask this through Christ our risen Savior. **Amen.**

OPENING PRAYER

Let us pray

Pause for silent prayer

Father,
help us keep in mind that Christ our Savior
lives with you in glory
and promised to remain with us until the end of time.

We ask this through our Lord Jesus Christ, your Son,
who lives and reigns with you and the Holy Spirit,
one God, for ever and ever. **Amen.**

FIRST READING

Acts 7:55-60

Stephen, filled with the Holy Spirit,
    looked up intently to heaven and saw
        the glory of God
    and Jesus standing at the right hand of God,
    and Stephen said, "Behold, I see the heavens opened
    and the Son of Man standing at the right hand of God."
But they cried out in a loud voice,
    covered their ears, and rushed upon him together.
They threw him out of the city, and began to stone him.
The witnesses laid down their cloaks
    at the feet of a young man named Saul.
As they were stoning Stephen, he called out,
    "Lord Jesus, receive my spirit."
Then he fell to his knees and cried out in a loud voice,
    "Lord, do not hold this sin against them";
    and when he said this, he fell asleep.

RESPONSORIAL PSALM

Ps 97:1-2, 6-7, 9

R̸. (1a and 9a) The Lord is king, the most high over all the earth.
or:
R̸. Alleluia.

The LORD is king; let the earth rejoice;
  let the many islands be glad.
Justice and judgment are the foundation of
    his throne.

R̸. The Lord is king, the most high over all the earth.
or:
R̸. Alleluia.

The heavens proclaim his justice,
  and all peoples see his glory.
All gods are prostrate before him.

R̸. The Lord is king, the most high over all the earth.
or:
R̸. Alleluia.

You, O LORD, are the Most High over all
    the earth,
  exalted far above all gods.

R̸. The Lord is king, the most high over all the earth.
or:
R̸. Alleluia.

SECOND READING

Rev 22:12-14, 16-17, 20

I, John, heard a voice saying to me:
  "Behold, I am coming soon.
I bring with me the recompense I will give
    to each
  according to his deeds.
I am the Alpha and the Omega, the first
    and the last,
  the beginning and the end."

Blessed are they who wash their robes
  so as to have the right to the tree of life
  and enter the city through its gates.

"I, Jesus, sent my angel to give you this
    testimony for the churches.
I am the root and offspring of David,
  the bright morning star."

The Spirit and the bride say, "Come."
Let the hearer say, "Come."
Let the one who thirsts come forward,
  and the one who wants it receive the gift
    of life-giving water.

The one who gives this testimony says,
  "Yes, I am coming soon."
Amen! Come, Lord Jesus!

✠ CATECHESIS

About Liturgy

The intimacy of prayer: We are comfortable praying together traditional prayers, such as the rosary or novenas, but we seldom are comfortable praying aloud spontaneously when others can hear us. Even people who belong to shared prayer groups and have much practice in this kind of prayer can find it unsettling. It makes us quite vulnerable! Yet one of the most precious gifts we can give to each other is a share in our prayer life.

This kind of shared prayer, when we pour out our hearts to God and allow others to witness it, is a wonderful gift of love to others. It says that we trust them and desire the same kind of unity with them that we have with God. Shared prayer between husband and wife and among family members, among parish staff, at parish meetings, etc., can all promote a new kind of tolerance for one another so the differences we naturally have seem less divisive.

Prayer as the gift of the elder members of the community: One of the most priceless gifts the elder members of our parish communities can give to others is the gift of prayer. Generally when we retire we have a bit more time on our hands. What better way to spend this time for the good of others than to pray for those in need! In a real way elder parish members can make up what is "lacking" in the prayer life of the busier members of the parish. This is another way we can witness to the unity of the one Body of Christ: all our prayers together help build up the Body.

About Liturgical Music

Music suggestion: In her collection *Sing a New Church* [OCP], Delores Dufner provides "Gospel Responses for the Easter Season." The verses in each set correspond chronologically with the gospel readings for each year of the Lectionary cycle. Dufner intends them to be used as sung responses to the gospel proclamation, but they could also be sung as a hymn. From the third Sunday onward appropriate sequences of verses could be sung for the entrance hymn or during the preparation of the gifts. This Sunday and again on Pentecost all the verses could be sung as the Communion hymn, recapping our gospel journey with Christ through the Easter season. Set to the familiar SURGIT IN HAEC DIES with alleluia refrain, the verses could be sung by cantor or choir alone, with the assembly joining in on the refrain.

MAY 16, 2010
SEVENTH SUNDAY OF EASTER or CELEBRATION OF ASCENSION

SPIRITUALITY

GOSPEL ACCLAMATION

℟. Alleluia, alleluia.
Come, Holy Spirit, fill the hearts of your faithful and kindle in them the fire of your love.
℟. Alleluia, alleluia.

Gospel John 14:15-16, 23b-26; L63C

Jesus said to his disciples:
"If you love me, you will keep my
commandments.
And I will ask the Father,
and he will give you another
Advocate to be with you
always.

"Whoever loves me will keep my word,
and my Father will love him,
and we will come to him and make our
dwelling with him.
Those who do not love me do not keep my
words;
yet the word you hear is not mine
but that of the Father who sent me.

"I have told you this while I am with you.
The Advocate, the Holy Spirit whom the
Father will send in my name,
will teach you everything
and remind you of all that I told you."

or John 20:19-23

On the evening of that first day of the
week,
when the doors were locked, where the
disciples were,
for fear of the Jews,
Jesus came and stood in their midst
and said to them, "Peace be with you."
When he had said this, he showed them
his hands and his side.
The disciples rejoiced when they saw the
Lord.
Jesus said to them again, "Peace be with
you.
As the Father has sent me, so I send you."
And when he had said this, he breathed
on them and said to them,
"Receive the Holy Spirit.
Whose sins you forgive are forgiven them,
and whose sins you retain are
retained."

Reflecting on the Gospel

We tend for many reasons to shun standing alone. The last one standing, waiting to be chosen to be on a side for a children's game, is never comfortable. Even standing alone for a principle can tend to sow seeds of doubt, anxiety, uncertainty. Conversely, we say and experience that there is strength in numbers. When others support us concerning a dearly held principle, we are encouraged. When others speak up on our behalf, we are relieved. When others help us with a daunting task, we are energized. There is solidarity in standing together that affirms, strengthens, and fortifies convictions and acts. We don't like to stand alone.

The gospel selection for this Pentecost Sunday is taken from Jesus' Last Supper farewell discourse to his disciples. He is preparing them for when he will no longer be with them. While Jesus is present, he is the advocate who teaches and models how the disciples should love him by keeping his commandments and word. After Jesus' ascension, the disciples no longer will have him present to them in the same way. Yet Jesus never leaves his disciples completely, for as the Father sent Jesus, so does the Father send the Spirit, a new Advocate who teaches and reminds disciples of all Jesus said and did.

With the sending of the Holy Spirit who is "another Advocate," we followers of Jesus are never bereft of divine presence. This new Advocate teaches us just as Jesus taught the first disciples. This new Advocate "calls" (L. *advocare* = to call) us to faithful discipleship and "supports" (G. *paráklētos* = helper) us in our efforts to love Jesus. This new Advocate enables us to love and live as Jesus did, continuing his saving mission and making him present through us.

God can give us no greater gift than a share in the very life of God's divine presence. This is what we celebrate on this solemnity of Pentecost—God dwells within us, giving us a share in divine life. Moreover, since we all share in the same life, the Spirit is the bond of unity among us. Pentecost is a celebration of both the gift of the Spirit and the effects of that gift—we are sharers in the one Body of Christ and take up Jesus' mission to preach the Good News of salvation.

We followers of Jesus never stand alone. We always have the Spirit who dwells within and among us. Moreover, we have each other. We all share in the same life, the same saving mission, the same love. There is strength in numbers. Our strength is the gift of the Spirit who binds us in love and unity as the one Body of Christ.

Living the Paschal Mystery

By this indwelling of the Holy Spirit we ourselves become advocates of God's presence for others. This gift of the Spirit, then, makes its demands on us. We must monitor the way we live so that others truly see us as advocates of God's presence bringing new life.

This new life that we share with others might be as simple as a reassuring touch or helping hand. It might be as great as making a sacrifice of time to join the parish choir or volunteering for some task that needs to be done for the good of all. Living the Gospel means that we bask in the good gift of God's life that the Spirit brings. Living the paschal mystery means that this good gift has its cost—we still must die to ourselves in order to be the true presence of Christ for others.

Focusing the Gospel

Key words and phrases: love me, another Advocate, we will . . . make our dwelling

To the point: With the sending of the Holy Spirit who is "another Advocate," we followers of Jesus are never bereft of divine presence. This new Advocate teaches us just as Jesus taught the first disciples. This new Advocate "calls" (L. *advocare* = to call) us to faithful discipleship and "supports" (G. *paráklētos* = helper) us in our efforts to love Jesus. This new Advocate enables us to love and live as Jesus did, continuing his saving mission and making him present through us.

Connecting the Gospel

to the sequence: This poetic hymn reminds us that by ourselves we cannot continue the saving mission of Jesus. It is the Spirit, "the soul's most welcome guest," who gives us the comfort, solace, Light, rest, healing, strength, guidance, and joys that we need to successfully bring to completion Jesus' mission.

to our experience: In our world the most important and wealthy people live in the best places. Wondrously, the Spirit of our God chooses to dwell within *us*, raising us to the dignity of being the "children of God" and "joint heirs with Christ" (see second reading from Romans).

Connecting the Responsorial Psalm

to the readings: Psalm 104 is a masterful hymn praising God for the creation of the cosmos. It unfolds in a seven-part structure paralleling the creation account in Genesis 1. In Hebrew thought the cause of creation is God's breath or spirit (*ruach*). Take breath away and creatures die; give them breath/spirit and they live (vv. 29-30).

In the first reading this breath of God comes like a "strong driving wind" that enables the disciples to witness to "the mighty acts of God." In the second reading this breath comes as a "spirit of adoption" making us sons and daughters of God. In the gospel this breath comes as Advocate sent in Jesus' name to teach us all things. This is the Spirit we ask God to send us in the responsorial psalm: the power pushing us forward in mission, the love that is God's very life within us, and the spokesperson reminding us of all that Jesus has taught— truly a breath that will re-create the universe!

to psalmist preparation: You pray in this responsorial psalm for renewal— the renewal of our knowledge of Christ (gospel), the renewal of our sense of identity as children of God (second reading), and the renewal of our commitment to mission (first reading). How during these past weeks of Easter celebration have you felt renewed in Christ? How have you seen the parish community become renewed?

ASSEMBLY & FAITH-SHARING GROUPS

- The way I experience the Spirit's indwelling is . . .
- In receiving the Spirit I become an advocate of God's presence. What that means to me is . . . This requires that I . . .
- My love for others expresses Jesus' continued presence among us in that . . .

PRESIDERS

- My ministry inspires the assembly to claim their dignity and role as advocates of God's presence in the world by . . .

DEACONS

- My service ministry makes visible the love of Jesus and the presence of the Spirit in that . . .

HOSPITALITY MINISTERS

- Everyone who gathers is a child of God, an heir with Christ (see the second reading from Romans). My hospitality honors this great dignity when I . . .

MUSIC MINISTERS

- Some things the Spirit has taught me through my music ministry have been . . . Some things the Spirit needs to remind me of are . . .

ALTAR MINISTERS

- I am an advocate of God's presence for others through my service when I . . .

LECTORS

- Where I need the Holy Spirit to enable me to *live* a better proclamation is . . .

EXTRAORDINARY MINISTERS OF HOLY COMMUNION

- My manner of distributing Holy Communion calls others to love Jesus more deeply when I . . .

Model Rite of Blessing and Sprinkling Holy Water

Presider: Dear friends, on this Pentecost Sunday we celebrate the gift of the Holy Spirit. We once again ask God to bless this water and we sprinkle it to remind us that God dwells within us and we must always be faithful to the gift we have been given . . . [pause]

[continue with form C of the blessing of water]

Homily Points

• At the beginning of their married life a couple's love seems full and completely satisfying. Yet as they live faithfully together and learn more about each other, they are called to deepen and strengthen their love. Even trials and difficulties in a marriage can strengthen the relationship and help love grow.

• At the end of Jesus' life on earth the disciples do not understand everything he has taught them nor do they fully realize what lies ahead of them as they pursue Jesus' mission. The role of the Holy Spirit, the Advocate, is to continue the formation of disciples Jesus has begun.

• As with marriage, discipleship is also a lifelong learning process. Each year of our Christian journey brings new insights, new challenges, new opportunities to grow in fidelity to Jesus and his teachings. We do not start the journey fully understanding all that it will entail. Yet we are never alone on this journey.

Model Prayer of the Faithful

Presider: Today we celebrate our receiving the gift of the Spirit. Let us pray fervently that we be a fitting dwelling place for God.

Response:

Lord, hear our prayer.

Cantor:

we pray to the Lord,

That all members of the church be faithful advocates of God's presence to the world . . . [pause]

That world leaders be advocates of peace and justice for all people . . . [pause]

That all those in need receive from the abundance of God's gift of creation . . . [pause]

That each of us listen to the Spirit who dwells within us and faithfully proclaim Jesus' Good News of salvation . . . [pause]

Presider: Saving God, you send your Spirit to dwell within us and make us your children: hear these our prayers that we might always be fitting dwelling places and bring your presence to all we meet. We ask this through your Son, Jesus Christ the risen Lord. **Amen**.

Let us pray

Pause for silent prayer

God our Father,
let the Spirit you sent on your Church
to begin the teaching of the gospel
continue to work in the world
through the hearts of all who believe.

We ask this through our Lord Jesus Christ,
    your Son,
who lives and reigns with you and the
    Holy Spirit,
one God, for ever and ever. **Amen.**

FIRST READING
Acts 2:1-11

When the time for Pentecost was fulfilled,
    they were all in one place together.
And suddenly there came from the sky
    a noise like a strong driving wind,
    and it filled the entire house in which
        they were.
Then there appeared to them tongues as
        of fire,
    which parted and came to rest on each
        one of them.
And they were all filled with the Holy Spirit
    and began to speak in different tongues,
    as the Spirit enabled them to proclaim.

Now there were devout Jews from every
        nation under heaven
        staying in Jerusalem.
At this sound, they gathered in a large
        crowd,
    but they were confused
    because each one heard them speaking
        in his own language.
They were astounded, and in amazement
        they asked,
    "Are not all these people who are
            speaking Galileans?
Then how does each of us hear them in
        his native language?
We are Parthians, Medes, and Elamites,
    inhabitants of Mesopotamia, Judea and
            Cappadocia,
    Pontus and Asia, Phrygia and Pamphylia,
    Egypt and the districts of Libya near
            Cyrene,
    as well as travelers from Rome,
    both Jews and converts to Judaism,
            Cretans and Arabs,
    yet we hear them speaking in our own
            tongues
    of the mighty acts of God."

RESPONSORIAL PSALM
Ps 104:1, 24, 29-30, 31, 34

℞. (cf. 30) Lord, send out your Spirit, and renew the face of the earth.
or: ℞. Alleluia.

Bless the LORD, O my soul!
    O LORD, my God, you are great indeed!
How manifold are your works, O LORD!
    The earth is full of your creatures.

℞. Lord, send out your Spirit, and renew the face of the earth.
or: ℞. Alleluia.

If you take away their breath, they perish
    and return to their dust.
When you send forth your spirit, they are created,
    and you renew the face of the earth.

℞. Lord, send out your Spirit, and renew the face of the earth.
or: ℞. Alleluia.

May the glory of the LORD endure forever;
    may the LORD be glad in his works!
Pleasing to him be my theme;
    I will be glad in the LORD.

℞. Lord, send out your Spirit, and renew the face of the earth.
or: ℞. Alleluia.

SECOND READING
Rom 8:8-17

or

1 Cor 12:3b-7, 12-13

See Appendix A, p. 299.

SEQUENCE

See Appendix A, pp. 299–300.

About Liturgy

Pentecost readings: For all three years in the Lectionary cycle, the first reading from Acts (relating the Pentecost account) and the responsorial psalm are the same. For years B and C, two choices are given for the second reading and gospel, but the first of those choices is proper for year A. Therefore, we suggest that the second reading and gospel proper for the respective year be used. This maximizes the use of Sacred Scripture on these great feasts.

The gospel for year C is similar to the one proclaimed just two weeks ago on the Sixth Sunday of Easter, but with different verses. These different verses and the Pentecost context suggest that our interpretation be different from that of two weeks ago. We stressed God's dwelling on both the Sixth Sunday of Easter and on Pentecost, but with a bit different twist: two weeks ago we focused on being re-created to carry forth Jesus' saving mission; on Pentecost we focus on *being* God's presence, being the advocates (teachers) of the Good News.

Pentecost—birthday of the church? We have customarily interpreted Pentecost as the birthday of the church. We must take care that we don't trivialize this (for example, using birthday cakes, singing happy birthday). The more demanding effect of the birth of the church through the coming of the Spirit who dwells in us and makes us one is that through the indwelling of the Spirit we become the missionary presence of the risen Christ—*we ourselves* are advocates of God's plan of salvation. Any "birthing" that happens is our openness to have the Spirit work through us to make God's life and saving grace present for others.

About Liturgical Music

Singing the sequence: In the Middle Ages myriads of sequences were added to the liturgy to expand on and explain the meaning of certain feasts and celebrations. Today only four remain: the obligatory ones on Easter and Pentecost, and optional ones on The Most Holy Body and Blood of Christ and Our Lady of Sorrows. Most often the sequences were attached to the gospel acclamation (hence, why the Easter one concludes with "Amen. Alleluia."). One can conjecture, then, that the sequences accompanied extended gospel processions.

To honor its original purpose, as well as to demonstrate the centrality of the gospel in the life of the church, the Pentecost sequence could be sung as part of an extended gospel procession using incense and moving among the people. Musical settings already exist in which cantor(s) or choir sing the verses and the assembly joins in on an alleluia refrain. "Come, Holy Spirit, on Us Shine" [PMB, WC, WS] uses the familiar tune O FILII ET FILIAE. "Come, Holy Spirit" [JS2] includes a refrain with alleluia; the verses could be split between women and men in the choir, with the assembly singing the refrain. "Come, O Holy Spirit" [BB, JS2, OFUV] is set to HYMN TO JOY. This setting could be framed beginning and end with the Mode VI Easter Alleluia. The choir could sing the first half of each verse, the assembly the second half, and everyone the concluding "Come, O Holy Spirit, come!"

Appropriate posture during the procession is to stand, just as we do for the gospel acclamation every Sunday.

Ordinary Time II

SPIRITUALITY

R℣. Alleluia, alleluia.
Glory to the Father, the Son, and the Holy Spirit;
to God who is, who was, and who is to come.
R℣. Alleluia, alleluia.

Gospel

John 16:12-15; L166C

Jesus said to his disciples:
  "I have much more to tell
      you, but you cannot
      bear it now.
But when he comes, the Spirit
      of truth,
  he will guide you to all truth.
He will not speak on his own,
  but he will speak what he hears,
  and will declare to you the things that
      are coming.
He will glorify me,
  because he will take from what is
      mine and declare it to you.
Everything that the Father has is mine;
  for this reason I told you that he will
      take from what is mine
  and declare it to you."

Reflecting on the Gospel

Experience tells us that the most successful smaller communities always have an even number of members. We are familiar with the "middle child syndrome" of families with three children. People in groups naturally tend to pair off. So when there are odd numbers, one person is always left out. This Sunday we celebrate the mystery of God as one but yet three. Unlike our human communities with an odd number of members, the Trinity is a perfectly harmonious, dynamic unity. We are unable to fully grasp with our intellect the mystery of divine Three-in-One. Nonetheless, our triune God is not a distant, uncaring deity. God desires to be personally encountered by us. God chooses to reveal the divine Self to us and be present to us.

The readings for this solemnity describe the majesty of God in the many ways we encounter the divine among us: in creation that is tangible and all around us, in Jesus of Nazareth who lived among us and is then the risen Lord who commands us to continue his saving mission, and in the Holy Spirit who is poured forth in our hearts. The glory of God's presence is encountered through creation, salvation, and each other! Perhaps, then, the greatest mystery of the Trinity is not so much how God can be Three-in-One but why this God chooses to be intimately present to us. Perhaps the greatest mystery is that the triune community of the Trinity wishes to dwell within the diverse community of humanity.

Surely this mystery of our God is so great that we "cannot bear it now" fully. Revelation is always gradual. The fullness of "all truth" would be overwhelming if we heard it in its full power, for the ultimate revelation—"all truth"—is the gift of the Trinity itself dwelling within and among us. This festival celebrates the mystery that the life and love of the Trinity "has been poured out into our hearts" (second reading). As we faithfully live Jesus' command to make known the Good News, we gradually become aware that no one of us can reveal God, but together, in community, we are that presence. The stronger the community in openness to encountering God, the clearer to us is the revelation of divine presence. We gradually learn from each other how much God loves us by the divine presence that we encounter and mediate for each other.

The majesty of the Trinity defies any intellectual unraveling of the mystery. An intellectual exercise is not what God reveals to us or asks of us. God gives triune Self to us simply so that we can encounter God's glory and share among us the grace, peace, and hope of divine presence.

Living the Paschal Mystery

As difficult as it is to grasp the mystery of God's triune majesty, it is even more difficult to grasp that God loves us enough to share divine life and glory with us. God chooses to dwell within and among us. Living the dying and rising of the paschal mystery means that we are faithful witnesses to the God within. Sometimes rather than witnessing through doing good works, we need to witness simply by appreciating ourselves and others for the wonderful gift of God's presence that we are. The readings this week challenge us to become more deeply aware of God's presence in creation, in Jesus, and in ourselves. We are invited to allow that awareness to overflow in thanksgiving and praise.

Focusing the gospel

Key words and phrases: cannot bear it now, all truth, the things that are coming

To the point: This mystery of our God is so great that we "cannot bear it now" fully. Revelation is always gradual. The fullness of "all truth" would be overwhelming if we heard it in its full power, for the ultimate revelation—"all truth"—is the gift of the Trinity itself dwelling within and among us. This festival celebrates the mystery that the life and love of the Trinity "has been poured out into our hearts" (second reading).

Connecting the Gospel

to the first and second readings: The majesty of God is revealed in creation (first reading and psalm), the glorified Jesus (gospel), and the Holy Spirit who is poured forth in our hearts (second reading). Through faith (second reading) we share in the glory of this creating, redeeming, and indwelling God.

to our experience: The dogma of the Trinity poses a great intellectual challenge. But to honor the Trinity we do not need to understand fully. All we need do is recognize that each of us reveals a facet of God's glory.

Connecting the Responsorial Psalm

to the readings: The wisdom the first reading speaks of is often interpreted as a figure of Christ. Preexisting forerunner, Christ participated in creation and danced for God's delight. Poured forth by God to play on the earth, he in turn found "delight in the human race." Thus it is through him that we are given access to grace and glory (second reading).

But such glory is too much for us to bear (gospel). With all that has already been revealed through creation and incarnation, the whole truth of who we are in God's sight is yet beyond imagining. For the whole truth is that God holds back nothing, pouring the very force of divine life—God's own love—"into our hearts" (second reading). For all its touting of our dignity, the responsorial psalm in fact understates the truth. We have not been created only "little less than the angels," but we are very like unto God. This the Spirit does, this the Spirit declares, and this the Spirit enables us to bear (second reading and gospel). Truly, we have much to sing about this Trinity who dances with us, delights in us, and brings us a share in divine life.

to psalmist preparation: This responsorial psalm is not so much about our greatness as human beings as about the beneficence of God who treats us with unimaginable dignity and grace. How this week might you treat those whom you meet with this same dignity and grace—at home? at work? on the street?

**ASSEMBLY &
FAITH-SHARING GROUPS**

- The revelation of God has been gradual in my life and I experience it . . .
- The revelation of God has come to me through . . . I am the revelation of God for others when . . .
- The truth of God's indwelling overwhelms me and . . .

PRESIDERS

- My openness to God's indwelling shapes how I minister in that . . .

DEACONS

- My service ministry helps others realize the gift of God's indwelling when . . .

HOSPITALITY MINISTERS

- My hospitality is a pouring of God's love into another's heart (see second reading) when I . . .

MUSIC MINISTERS

- My collaboration with others in the ministry of music reveals the presence and love of God by . . .

ALTAR MINISTERS

- God is revealed to me as I serve at the altar when . . .

LECTORS

- My proclamation is different when I am aware of God's indwelling because . . .

**EXTRAORDINARY MINISTERS
OF HOLY COMMUNION**

- I carry out my ministry in a way that reveals both God's majesty and God's intimacy among us by . . .

Model Act of Penitence

Presider: This Sunday when we celebrate the glory of our triune God, we also celebrate that God dwells within and among us. At the beginning of this liturgy let us open ourselves to this mystery of divine presence . . . [pause]

Lord Jesus, you are the glory of the Father: Lord . . .

Christ Jesus, your Spirit of truth dwells within us: Christ . . .

Lord Jesus, you are the revelation of divine presence: Lord . . .

Homily Points

• In learning we only gradually master bits and pieces of knowledge. Moreover, most of our learning relies on interaction with others; the most complete learning happens in a community of learners. The very presence of others is itself a continual learning process.

• We are assured of divine presence because Jesus promised that the Spirit would come to us. This Spirit and divine indwelling is God's gift at our baptism, which continues to deepen as we live out our Christian calling. Recognizing this divine presence within opens us to God's truth as well as to the richness of each other.

• The stronger the community, the greater God's presence is revealed among us. So what do we have to be for one another? The love of God poured out, the truth that guides, the joy that dances before creation. This is the glory of God revealed within and among us.

Model Prayer of the Faithful

Presider: With confidence let us pray for our needs to our triune God who dwells within us.

Response:

Lord, hear our prayer.

Cantor:

we pray to the Lord,

That each member of the church rejoice in being God's presence in the community . . . [pause]

That all people faithfully participate in God's life through acts of charity and justice that bring peace . . . [pause]

That those in need have confidence in God's nearness and generosity through others . . . [pause]

That each of us reflect the glory of God's presence within us by the way we live with and act toward others . . . [pause]

Presider: Triune God, you fill us with your grace and presence: hear these our prayers that one day we might share your glory for ever and ever. **Amen.**

ALTERNATIVE OPENING PRAYER

Let us pray
   [to our God who is Father, Son, and
   Holy Spirit]

Pause for silent prayer

God, we praise you:
Father all-powerful, Christ Lord and
   Savior, Spirit of love.
You reveal yourself in the depths of our
   being,
drawing us to share in your life and your
   love.
One God, three Persons,
be near to the people formed in your
   image,
close to the world your love brings to life.

We ask this, Father, Son, and Holy Spirit,
one God, true and living, for ever and ever.
   Amen.

FIRST READING
Prov 8:22-31

Thus says the wisdom of God:
"The LORD possessed me, the beginning of
   his ways,
   the forerunner of his prodigies of long
      ago;
from of old I was poured forth,
   at the first, before the earth.
When there were no depths I was brought
   forth,
   when there were no fountains or springs
      of water;
before the mountains were settled into
   place,
   before the hills, I was brought forth;
while as yet the earth and fields were not
   made,
   nor the first clods of the world.

"When the Lord established the heavens
   I was there,
   when he marked out the vault over the
      face of the deep;
when he made firm the skies above,
   when he fixed fast the foundations of
      the earth;
when he set for the sea its limit,
   so that the waters should not transgress
      his command;
then was I beside him as his craftsman,
   and I was his delight day by day,
playing before him all the while,
   playing on the surface of his earth;
   and I found delight in the human race."

RESPONSORIAL PSALM

Ps 8:4-5, 6-7, 8-9

R̸. (2a) O Lord, our God, how wonderful
your name in all the earth!

When I behold your heavens, the work of
        your fingers,
    the moon and the stars which you set in
        place—
what is man that you should be mindful
        of him,
    or the son of man that you should care
        for him?

R̸. O Lord, our God, how wonderful your
name in all the earth!

You have made him little less than the
        angels,
    and crowned him with glory and honor.
You have given him rule over the works of
        your hands,
    putting all things under his feet.

R̸. O Lord, our God, how wonderful your
name in all the earth!

All sheep and oxen,
    yes, and the beasts of the field,
the birds of the air, the fishes of the sea,
    and whatever swims the paths of the
        seas.

R̸. O Lord, our God, how wonderful your
name in all the earth!

SECOND READING

Rom 5:1-5

Brothers and sisters:
Therefore, since we have been justified by
        faith,
    we have peace with God through our
        Lord Jesus Christ,
    through whom we have gained access
        by faith
    to this grace in which we stand,
    and we boast in hope of the glory of God.
Not only that, but we even boast of our
        afflictions,
    knowing that affliction produces
        endurance,
    and endurance, proven character,
    and proven character, hope,
    and hope does not disappoint,
    because the love of God has been
        poured out into our hearts
    through the Holy Spirit that has been
        given to us.

About Liturgy

Making the sign of the cross: Because we sign ourselves in the form of a cross, this traditional Catholic gesture is probably more readily connected with Christ and his paschal mystery than with the mystery of the Trinity. Yet the words of the gesture—"In the name of the Father, and of the Son, and of the Holy Spirit"—clearly connect this gesture with the whole triune mystery of God.

We begin and end each Mass with the sign of the cross. When we make it at the beginning of Mass, we are prompted to remember that this celebration is God's invitation to be in God's triune presence. Mass isn't primarily *our* celebration, but God's gift of self to us in which we are transformed into being more perfect images of the Body of Christ. It is well that we make this sign slowly and deliberately at the beginning of Mass and ask God to help us to surrender ourselves to this great mystery of God's presence to us.

When we are blessed and sent forth at the end of Mass, we are prompted to remember that we are dismissed to be God's presence to all those we meet in the ordinary circumstances of our daily lives. By signing ourselves with the cross in blessing, we also make a commitment to live in such a way that others might see the goodness in us that is God's presence. Further, this signing and blessing remind us that in our ordinary actions we are to carry on the work of our triune God; that is, to re-create our world in newness of life, to redeem our world from the evil that besets it, and to bring God's glory and holiness to all we meet. Through the indwelling God we participate in God's loving work on behalf of all.

About Liturgical Music

Music suggestions: Two hymns that connect well with this year's Trinity Sunday readings are "How Wonderful the Three-in-One" [BB, G2, GC, GC2, JS2, PMB, WC, RS] and "May God's Love Be Fixed above You" [HG]. The former captures very well the imagery of the first reading: "How wonderful the Three-in-One, Whose energies of dancing light, Are undivided, pure and good, Communing love in shared delight. Before the flow of dawn and dark, Creation's lover dreamed of earth, And with a caring deep and wise, All things conceived and brought to birth." Since the tune will most likely be unfamiliar to the assembly, the choir could sing the hymn as a prelude or during the preparation of the gifts with the assembly joining in on the last verse.

The second hymn is an extended blessing asking that God's love be "fixed above you . . . advance before you . . . be close beside you . . . remain upon you." The suggested tune (LAUDA ANIMA) is well known and perfect for the text. This hymn would make an excellent song after Communion through which the assembly could express their prayer for one another as they reenter Ordinary Time in the grace of the Trinity.

MAY 30, 2010
THE SOLEMNITY OF
THE MOST HOLY TRINITY

✠ SPIRITUALITY

GOSPEL ACCLAMATION
John 6:51

R̷. Alleluia, alleluia.
I am the living bread that came down from heaven,
says the Lord; whoever eats this bread will live
forever.
R̷. Alleluia, alleluia.

Gospel   Luke 9:11b-17; L169C

Jesus spoke to the crowds
    about the kingdom of
        God,
    and he healed those who
        needed to be cured.
As the day was drawing to a
        close,
    the Twelve approached him
        and said,
    "Dismiss the crowd
    so that they can go to the
        surrounding villages
        and farms
    and find lodging and provisions;
    for we are in a deserted place here."
He said to them, "Give them some food
        yourselves."
They replied, "Five loaves and two fish
        are all we have,
    unless we ourselves go and buy food
        for all these people."
Now the men there numbered about
        five thousand.
Then he said to his disciples,
    "Have them sit down in groups of
        about fifty."
They did so and made them all sit down.
Then taking the five loaves and the two
        fish,
    and looking up to heaven,
    he said the blessing over them, broke
        them,
    and gave them to the disciples to set
        before the crowd.
They all ate and were satisfied.
And when the leftover fragments were
        picked up,
    they filled twelve wicker baskets.

Reflecting on the Gospel

There is perhaps no more heart-wrenching sight than the malnourished and starving. We receive pamphlets in the mail, see images on TV, bring nonperishable food staples to church to offer during the presentation of the gifts. These sights demand a response from us. We know there is food in abundance. We know that often the world hunger problem is tied into politics. We know all these facts. And so when we celebrate this particular feast day and hear these particular readings, we are once more challenged to respond. Our own share in God's abundant gifts demands that those gifts spill out for those in need.

But the plight of the needy extends beyond food, and our response must extend beyond providing food because this festival is about more than even the sublime gift of Jesus giving himself to us in the Eucharist. This festival is about handing over life.

Jesus' gospel command is clear: we are to feed others. We give to others not from the "deserted place" of our own hearts but from the "leftover fragments" of God's blessings (see first reading). God's abundant nourishment is most startlingly given in the handing over of Jesus' life (see second reading)—on the cross, in the bread and wine. As Jesus' followers we are to be God's abundant nourishment for others by our own self-gift of life. God's abundant giving continues in our own self-giving lives.

The Twelve apparently still haven't quite gotten this message of abundance and self-giving. They approach Jesus with the instruction to "dismiss the crowd"; this is clearly a practical response to a practical situation—a hungry, tired, large crowd. Jesus' response makes clear God's intention for us: "Give them some food yourselves." Perhaps the amazement of this gospel and festival is that God so willingly chooses us humans to make known divine superabundance and blessing.

The gospel moves from the practical, tangible level of feeding hungry people to the mystery of God's abundance and excess; the gospel moves from our being in control to an invitation to surrender ourselves so that God provides in excess through us. On our own we will always lack; when we surrender ourselves to God and let God act in and through us, we will have all we need in abundance.

This solemnity celebrates God's graciousness to us—a gift of superabundance. We are invited to participate in God's graciousness by passing on his abundance. Our lives, then, must witness to the intersection of need and generosity. Our self-gift makes present divine generosity.

Living the Paschal Mystery

The first reading relates the priest Melchizedek's bringing out gifts of bread and wine and blessing Abram. The last line of the reading records Abram's response: "Then Abram gave him a tenth of everything." Like Abram, we've been given many gifts, surely not least being the Eucharist. Our response, like Abram, must be to "tithe" ourselves, to share those gifts with others. We proclaim the death of the Lord when we are the "body that is for [others]." Death leading to new life lies in giving of ourselves. If we dare to share in the sublime gift of Jesus' Body and Blood, then we must also dare to die to ourselves and share our abundance with others. Gift demands response. Sublime gift demands ultimate response—dying to ourselves so that we might share eucharistic life with the world.

Focusing the gospel

Key words and phrases: deserted place, Give them some food yourselves, leftover fragments

To the point: Jesus' command is clear: we are to feed others. We give to others not from the "deserted place" of our own hearts but from the "leftover fragments" of God's blessings (see first reading). God's abundant nourishment is most startlingly given in the handing over of Jesus' life (see second reading)—on the cross, in the bread and wine, and in our own self-gift to others.

Connecting the Gospel

to Trinity Sunday: The good news of Trinity Sunday is our participation in the mystery of God's life. This solemnity of the Most Holy Body and Blood of Christ also celebrates our participation in divine life: we eat the Bread of blessing and drink the Wine of self-gift, the risen Lord's very presence.

to our experience: We tend to narrow our consideration of the Eucharist to the sacramental elements of bread and wine. Eucharist is more—our own commitment to give ourselves to others as Jesus gives himself to us.

Connecting the Responsorial Psalm

to the readings: Psalm 110 was a royal psalm used at the coronation ceremony of a king descended from the line of David. The text promised the king a place of honor next to God, victory over enemies, and a priestly role before the people. In the first reading Melchizedek, "a priest of God Most High," gives food, drink, and blessing to Abram. In the gospel Jesus heals those in need and feeds the starving crowd, creating an amazing abundance out of a meager supply. In the second reading Paul reminds us that the food and drink Jesus gives us is his very Body and Blood. In singing this psalm we recognize what Jesus does and who Jesus is. He is the one victorious over all that impedes fullness of life. He is the one who feeds us with his very self. He is the completion of the Davidic line and a "priest forever, in the line of Melchizedek."

to psalmist preparation: The psalm you sing this Sunday acclaims the power and priesthood of Christ, both most evident to us in the gift of his Body and Blood for food. What might you do this week to affirm your personal faith in Jesus and express your gratitude for what he does in giving us the Eucharist?

ASSEMBLY & FAITH-SHARING GROUPS

- What is most important to me about the Eucharist is . . .
- Where Jesus could say to me, "Give them some food yourselves," is . . .
- Where God has satisfied me with abundance is . . . My response to such abundance has been . . . my response should be . . .

PRESIDERS

- At times when I feel like I only have "leftover fragments," the assembly fills me with abundance by . . .

DEACONS

- A time when I was abundantly satisfied by serving others was . . .

HOSPITALITY MINISTERS

- The occasions when I am tempted to "dismiss" the needs of others are . . . Where I have witnessed to God's abundance through my welcome care is . . .

MUSIC MINISTERS

- My ministry of music is self-gift that feeds others when . . .

ALTAR MINISTERS

- In serving others I am "proclaiming the death of the Lord until he comes" (second reading) because . . .

LECTORS

- Proclamation is one way I hand on what I received from the Lord (see second reading). My daily living is another way when I . . .

EXTRAORDINARY MINISTERS OF HOLY COMMUNION

- My ministry of distributing Holy Communion at Mass urges me to distribute my self to those in need by . . .

Model Act of Penitence

Presider: Today we celebrate God's gracious gift of abundance to us in the gift of Christ's Body and Blood for our nourishment. Let us open ourselves to this great mystery and prepare to receive this abundance from our God . . . [pause]

> Lord Jesus, you are the abundant Gift of God to us: Lord . . .

> Christ Jesus, you nourish us with your Body and Blood: Christ . . .

> Lord Jesus, you call us to give to each other as you have given to us: Lord . . .

Homily Points

• In the midst of the Great Depression of the 1930s, President Roosevelt gave a powerful radio speech during which he stressed that the only thing that could really hurt us as a nation was hoarding. Our very existence depends upon making available whatever we have for the good of others.

• Jesus' feeding the crowd to the point of satisfaction with some left over is a metaphor for an even deeper mystery. In the Eucharist Jesus continues to feed us, not on a bread that does not last, but on the Bread of eternal life. In Jesus' kingdom, everyone is satisfied fully even now.

• Jesus' gift of abundant bread is revelation of the kingdom of God. In the kingdom, the meager resources we possess become superabundant nourishment for others when we hand them over to the power of Jesus. We are to be eucharistic self-gift for others—the risen Lord's very Body.

Model Prayer of the Faithful

Presider: Our God is gracious and abundantly gives us all we need. We are encouraged to pray to such a good God.

Response:

Lord, hear our prayer.

Cantor:

we pray to the Lord,

That all members of the church celebrate Eucharist ever more fervently as a gift of God and a sign of the presence of God's reign . . . [pause]

That all peoples share equitably in the abundance of the world's resources and conserve them for future generations . . . [pause]

That the hungry be fed and lifted out of their poverty . . . [pause]

That each of us here always be generous with the gifts God has given us . . . [pause]

Presider: Gracious God, you give us all good things in abundance: hear our prayers that your gift of Eucharist might transform us into being ever more perfect members of the Body of Christ. We ask this through Christ our Lord. **Amen.**

ALTERNATIVE OPENING PRAYER

Let us pray
[for the willingness to make present in our world the love of Christ shown to us in the eucharist]

Pause for silent prayer

Lord Jesus Christ,
we worship you living among us
in the sacrament of your body and blood.
May we offer to our Father in heaven
a solemn pledge of undivided love.
May we offer our brothers and sisters
a life poured out in loving service of that kingdom
where you live with the Father and the Holy Spirit,
one God, for ever and ever. **Amen.**

FIRST READING
Gen 14:18-20

In those days, Melchizedek, king of Salem, brought out bread and wine,
and being a priest of God Most High,
he blessed Abram with these words:
"Blessed be Abram by God Most High,
the creator of heaven and earth;
and blessed be God Most High,
who delivered your foes into your hand."
Then Abram gave him a tenth of everything.

RESPONSORIAL PSALM

Ps 110:1, 2, 3, 4

R⁊. (4b) You are a priest forever, in the line of Melchizedek.

The LORD said to my Lord: "Sit at my right hand
    till I make your enemies your footstool."

R⁊. You are a priest forever, in the line of Melchizedek.

The scepter of your power the LORD will stretch forth from Zion:
    "Rule in the midst of your enemies."

R⁊. You are a priest forever, in the line of Melchizedek.

"Yours is princely power in the day of your birth, in holy splendor;
    before the daystar, like the dew, I have begotten you."

R⁊. You are a priest forever, in the line of Melchizedek.

The LORD has sworn, and he will not repent:
    "You are a priest forever, according to the order of Melchizedek."

R⁊. You are a priest forever, in the line of Melchizedek.

SECOND READING

1 Cor 11:23-26

Brothers and sisters:
I received from the Lord what I also
    handed on to you,
    that the Lord Jesus, on the night he was
        handed over,
    took bread, and, after he had given
        thanks,
    broke it and said, "This is my body that
        is for you.
Do this in remembrance of me."
In the same way also the cup, after supper,
    saying,
    "This cup is the new covenant in my
        blood.
Do this, as often as you drink it, in
    remembrance of me."
For as often as you eat this bread and
    drink the cup,
    you proclaim the death of the Lord until
        he comes.

OPTIONAL SEQUENCE

See Appendix A, p. 300.

About Liturgy

Breadth of the eucharistic mystery: We rightly think of the Eucharist as God's gift of nourishment for us when we share in the Body and Blood of the Lord and recognize this as a sublime gift that Jesus has left us. The readings for this solemnity also help us think of the eucharistic mystery in even broader terms.

First, by sharing in the Body and Blood of Christ we are *transformed* into being more perfect members of the Body of Christ. Thus, sharing in Eucharist is our way of growing more deeply into our own baptismal identity. Second, the eucharistic mystery includes continually establishing God's reign, which is evidenced by healing, reconciling, and feeding others. Third, the eucharistic mystery calls forth from us practical, everyday actions by which we help establish God's reign by dying to ourselves for the sake of others. Fourth, the eucharistic mystery demands a response, and so we "tithe" the gifts given to us for the sake of others less fortunate. In a real sense the eucharistic mystery begins at Mass, reaches a high point during Communion, and then extends beyond the ritual moment to our everyday lives when we live its self-sacrificing demand-response.

About Liturgical Music

Music suggestions: Eucharistic hymns that express our participation in Jesus' feeding of the hungry would be especially appropriate this Sunday. Marty Haugen's litanic "Bread to Share" [RS] is uplifting with its repetition of "You have plenty to share, you have plenty of bread to share." Thomas Porter's "Let Us Be Bread" [G2, GC, GC2, RS] offers the refrain, "Let us be bread, broken and shared, life for the world. Let us be wine, love freely poured. Let us be one in the Lord." Rory Cooney's "Bread of Life/Pan de Vida" [BB, GC, GC2, OFUV] uses the refrain, "I myself am the bread of life. You and I are the bread of life, taken and blessed, broken and shared by Christ that the world might live." Delores Dufner's "We Come with Joy" [HG] combines narration of the story of Jesus' feeding the crowd with the call that we do likewise, "For Christ will bless our bit of bread, The loaves our hands provide, Till empty baskets overflow, And all are satisfied." This hymn could be sung during the preparation of the gifts, during the Communion procession, or after Communion as a song of praise.

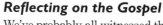

✝ SPIRITUALITY

GOSPEL ACCLAMATION
Matt 11:29ab

℟. Alleluia, alleluia.
Take my yoke upon you, says the Lord;
and learn from me, for I am meek and humble
    of heart.
℟. Alleluia, alleluia.

or

1 John 4:10b

℟. Alleluia, alleluia.
God first loved us
and sent his Son as expiation
    for our sins.
℟. Alleluia, alleluia.

Gospel

Luke 15:3-7; L172C

**Jesus addressed this
        parable to the
        Pharisees and scribes:
"What man among you having a
        hundred sheep and losing one of
        them
    would not leave the ninety-nine in the
        desert
    and go after the lost one until
        he finds it?
And when he does find it,
    he sets it on his shoulders with great
        joy
    and, upon his arrival home,
    he calls together his friends and
        neighbors and says to them,
    'Rejoice with me because I have
        found my lost sheep.'
I tell you, in just the same way
    there will be more joy in heaven over
        one sinner who repents
    than over ninety-nine righteous
        people
    who have no need of repentance."**

See Appendix A, p. 301, for other readings.

Reflecting on the Gospel

We've probably all witnessed the following scene in a supermarket. A testy child wanders off to fetch something that catches his or her eye and the parent rushes to find the child, grabs the little one by the scruff of the neck, then drags the screaming child back to the shopping cart without much show of tenderness. What a contrast this gospel makes to our human responses when patience is tried! We glimpse here some of the tenderness, care, and love of our Good Shepherd. We encounter the solicitude, persistency, and joy of the Sacred Heart.

In the gospel parable, instead of punishing the errant sheep, the Good Shepherd puts it on his shoulders and tenderly carries it back to the fold. No grabbing by the scruff of the neck here! The single sheep is treated with inestimable worth. Our good God carries us with the same solicitude and care, and grants us the same inestimable worth. All we need do is repent of our wandering, and God celebrates "with great joy." It is such tenderness, love, and joy flowing from the Sacred Heart that we celebrate this day. This festival reminds us that God's heart is large enough to welcome the stranger and tender enough to search out the lost and straying. This festival reminds us that we ourselves are still to be counted among the lost, among those whom Jesus is persistent to search after, caring enough to forgive, and loving enough to embrace with joy.

Whenever we wander, the Good Shepherd seeks us with persistence and love. The Good Shepherd doesn't grab us by the scruff of the neck to drag us back to the fold when we are sinful. Rather, there is always gentle invitation to repent (see the first reading: "The lost I will seek out . . . shepherding them rightly"), always ample reminders of God's desire to be in relationship with us (see the second reading: we are reconciled through "the death of his Son"), always joy (see gospel: in heaven, no less!) when we allow God to carry us toward wholeness and new life. The Sacred Heart is a powerful image for us because it captures so completely the loving sacrifice of the Son, God's regard for our worth, and the persistence of God's saving mission.

Living the Paschal Mystery

Jesus' image of the persistent sheep owner who leaves ninety-nine to find the one lost sheep is a model for paschal mystery living. We often speak of dying to self. One way to die to self is to search out the "one" among the "ninety-nine." Who among us is lonely? Reach out to that person. Is someone being neglected because of age, religion, social status, economic status? Reach out to that person. Do the physically or mentally challenged leave us uncomfortable? Find out enough about them that we can be comfortable reaching out with a friendly word or gesture.

If we open our eyes and look, we will no doubt discover many among us who seem isolated and alone. Emulating the sacred, tender heart of Jesus means that we make room in our own hearts for everyone, not just those who are naturally close to us or with whom we are most comfortable. This doesn't mean that we don't have a justified predilection for our family and friends. It does mean that we are willing to break out of our usual family, work, and social groups to be present to those who seem alone or lost. Dying to self can mean caring enough to have room in our own hearts for all who come.

Focusing the gospel

Key words and phrases: the lost one, sets it on his shoulders, great joy, sinner who repents

To the point: Instead of punishing the errant sheep, the Good Shepherd puts it on his shoulders and tenderly carries it back to the fold. Our good God carries us with the same solicitude and care. All we need do is repent of our wandering, and God celebrates "with great joy." It is such tenderness, love, and joy flowing from the Sacred Heart that we celebrate this day.

Model Act of Penitence

Presider: Jesus is persistent in searching out the lost and tenderly gathers them close to his Sacred Heart. We pause at the beginning of this liturgy to see how we have strayed from Jesus' embrace and open ourselves to his loving presence . . . [pause]

Lord Jesus, you lovingly seek the lost: Lord . . .

Christ Jesus, you carry us in our weakness: Christ . . .

Lord Jesus, your heart overflows with joy at our repentance: Lord . . .

Model Prayer of the Faithful

Presider: Let us confidently commend our needs to the heart of a loving and caring God.

Response:

Lord, hear our prayer.

Cantor:

we pray to the Lord,

That the church be the visible presence of Jesus' loving heart . . . [pause]

That government leaders lead rightly and bring their peoples together in unity and joy . . . [pause]

That the lost and forsaken find comfort in Jesus' Sacred Heart . . . [pause]

That each one of us have the compassion to reach out to the lonely, the wounded, the alienated . . . [pause]

Presider: Loving and caring God, the Sacred Heart of your Son Jesus embraces the lost and those who have strayed: hear these our prayers that we might rest everlastingly in your loving embrace. We ask this through that same Son, Jesus Christ our Lord. **Amen.**

OPENING PRAYER

Let us pray

Pause for silent prayer

Father,
we rejoice in the gifts of love
we have received from the heart of Jesus
    your Son.
Open our hearts to share his life
and continue to bless us with his love.

We ask this through our Lord Jesus Christ,
    your Son,
who lives and reigns with you and the Holy
    Spirit,
one God, for ever and ever. **Amen.**

FOR REFLECTION

- The image of the heart of Jesus emphasizes for me . . .
- When I look upon "him whom they have pierced," I . . . I am willing to let my heart be pierced for the sake of others when . . .
- The self-giving of Jesus which touches me the most is . . .
- I have encountered the love of Jesus in . . . through . . . by . . .

Homily Points

- Parents readily identify with the imagery the prophet Hosea uses in the first reading to try and capture the deep, intimate love God has for us: calls us children; teaches us to walk; hugs, feeds, heals us. While no human can express the "breadth and length and height and depth" of God's love for us, this divine love remains the call to us to love each other.

- Divine love is incarnated and fully expressed in Jesus' self-giving—perfectly summed up in the "sacred heart." This love now manifested through us is spilled out from our hearts aflame with the love of God.

✠ SPIRITUALITY

GOSPEL ACCLAMATION
1 John 4:10b

℞. Alleluia, alleluia.
God loved us and sent his Son
as expiation for our sins.
℞. Alleluia, alleluia.

Gospel

Luke 7:36–8:3; L93C

A Pharisee invited Jesus to
  dine with him,
  and he entered the
    Pharisee's house and
    reclined at table.
Now there was a sinful
  woman in the city
  who learned that he was at
    table in the house of
    the Pharisee.
Bringing an alabaster flask of ointment,
  she stood behind him at his feet
    weeping
  and began to bathe his feet with her
    tears.
Then she wiped them with her hair,
  kissed them, and anointed them with
    the ointment.
When the Pharisee who had invited
  him saw this he said to
  himself,
  "If this man were a prophet,
  he would know who and what sort of
    woman this is who is touching
    him,
  that she is a sinner."
Jesus said to him in reply,
  "Simon, I have something to say to
    you."
"Tell me, teacher," he said.
"Two people were in debt to a certain
    creditor;
  one owed five hundred days' wages
    and the other owed fifty.
Since they were unable to repay the
    debt, he forgave it for both.
Which of them will love him more?"

Continued in Appendix A, p. 302.

Reflecting on the Gospel

We bathe others when they are in need. Parents bathe babies and toddlers because they are not yet able to do it for themselves. Hospital aides bathe patients when they are too sick to do it for themselves. Nursing home aides bathe the very elderly, assisting them in their frailty and forgetfulness. In all these cases bathing another is a very tender, loving, and generous act. In addition to making another clean, the act also cements a connection, a relationship. Bathing another can have multiple layers of meaning. Perhaps nowhere is this clearer than in this Sunday's gospel.

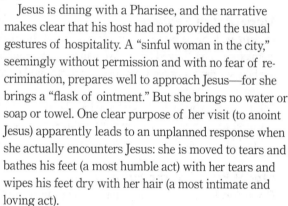

Jesus is dining with a Pharisee, and the narrative makes clear that his host had not provided the usual gestures of hospitality. A "sinful woman in the city," seemingly without permission and with no fear of recrimination, prepares well to approach Jesus—for she brings a "flask of ointment." But she brings no water or soap or towel. One clear purpose of her visit (to anoint Jesus) apparently leads to an unplanned response when she actually encounters Jesus: she is moved to tears and bathes his feet (a most humble act) with her tears and wipes his feet dry with her hair (a most intimate and loving act).

The Pharisee's response is indignation. But was he concerned about the woman, or embarrassed because she provided what he neglected to—cleansing water, a welcoming kiss, a reverent anointing revealing regard for the dignity of another? Contrary to what the Pharisee was thinking, Jesus was a most profound prophet, for he was able to see into the woman's heart and forgive her. He looks into the heart of the Pharisee, and sees there a lack of love. The deeper issue of true hospitality this incident raises is *how* we see others, encounter them, and respond to their needs with care.

Jesus asks, "Do you see this woman?" The Pharisee looks at her and sees only a sinner. Jesus looks at her and sees a sinner who repents. He sees her tremendous humility, her great sorrow, her desire to minister to him in his need, her "great love," her saving faith. The woman sees Jesus as One whom she can love and who loves her in return. This relationship brings her salvation and peace. Jesus is able to do for the sinful woman what he might have done for the Pharisee, who needed only to truly encounter Jesus for who he is.

While the woman and her actions seem to be the centerpiece of this gospel, what is really central is openness to others, accepting them for who they are, and seeing rightly into our own hearts before we judge the heart of another. Jesus is the model for seeing rightly. What does Jesus see when he looks at us? What do we see when we look at one another?

Living the Paschal Mystery

The Pharisee neglected to see Jesus' need for hospitality and the sinful woman's need for forgiveness and salvation. It is so easy to miss seeing the needs of others! Part of seeing is to forget self so that we can truly encounter the other. If we are wrapped up in our own needs, it is impossible to see the needs of others. One way to live this gospel is to practice every day reaching out to another with a simple gesture of kindness or hospitality. This can be as simple as saying hello to someone we pass in a hallway, smiling at someone who seems depressed, or lending a helping hand to someone who seems burdened.

Focusing the gospel

Key words and phrases: sinful woman, weeping, bathe his feet, anointed, Do you see this woman? great love, faith has saved

To the point: "Do you see this woman?" The Pharisee looks at her and sees only a sinner. Jesus looks at her and sees a sinner who repents. He sees her tremendous humility, her great sorrow, her desire to minister to him, her "great love," her saving faith. What does Jesus see when he looks at us? What do we see when we look at one another?

Connecting the Gospel

to the first reading: No number of sins or heinousness of deeds is too great for God to forgive. God, through Nathan the prophet, forgives David's sins of adultery and murder. Jesus, himself the prophet, forgives the "sinful woman."

to our experience: We tend to find it easier to stereotype people than to look into their hearts and really see them for who they are. As followers of Jesus we are called to see others as he does.

Connecting the Responsorial Psalm

to the readings: This Sunday's responsorial psalm celebrates the renewed life and joy that come from confessing sin and experiencing God's mercy. Missing from these verses, however, are the lines in Psalm 32 where the person praying admits having initially refused to acknowledge any sin or guilt. The person kept both self and God at a distance. When he or she did finally repent and confess, the experience of God's forgiveness was overwhelming. The Lectionary could omit these verses because their content is dramatically relayed in the first reading and the gospel. Confronted by Nathan, David confesses his heinous sin and is forgiven. Encountering Jesus, the sinful woman weeps and is forgiven. Above self-recrimination, the Pharisee misses both the point and the experience. How often is this same story told dramatically in our own lives? How often has honest admission of sinfulness led us to new life in the embrace of our forgiving God? This psalm, first reading, and gospel call us to acknowledge our sinfulness so that we might experience the forgiveness of God. Like David, like the weeping woman, like the psalmist, we will find that the latter far surpasses the former.

to psalmist preparation: Spend some time this week reflecting on the overwhelming mercy of God, who longs to forgive no matter what the sin. What moves you to ask for this forgiveness? What sometimes moves you to resist it?

ASSEMBLY & FAITH-SHARING GROUPS

- I see family members, closest friends, colleagues at work as . . .
- What I need to see in myself in order to repent is . . .
- Jesus sees in me . . .

PRESIDERS

- When I am presiding at the altar, I look at the assembly and see . . .

DEACONS

- When I serve others, I see them as . . .

HOSPITALITY MINISTERS

- As I welcome those gathering for liturgy, I see . . .

MUSIC MINISTERS

- When I look into my own singing heart, I see . . . Jesus sees . . . the assembly sees . . .

ALTAR MINISTERS

- My ministry by its very nature is unobtrusive. Jesus sees . . . others see . . .

LECTORS

- When I proclaim God's word, others see in me . . . In my daily living, others see in me . . .

EXTRAORDINARY MINISTERS OF HOLY COMMUNION

- My manner of distributing Holy Communion lets others see in me . . . I see in them . . .

Model Act of Penitence

Presider: In today's gospel we hear the story of the repentant woman who washes Jesus' feet with her tears. As we prepare to celebrate this liturgy, let us open ourselves to the God who washes away our sins . . . [pause]

> Lord Jesus, you forgive those who turn to you: Lord . . .
>
> Christ Jesus, you save us and give us peace: Christ . . .
>
> Lord Jesus, you look compassionately into our hearts: Lord . . .

Homily Points

• Our vantage point determines what we see. From one perspective, we might see another as weak, inadequate, beneath us. From a different perspective, we might see another as having worth and goodness—a child of God. How we see others determines our response to them.

• Jesus always sees into the hearts of others. He seeks the good, calls forth the best in them, and frees them by forgiving any wrong they may have done. We need only come to him and touch him with our love and sorrow.

• While Jesus always forgives those who come to him, this gospel points out that we must be willing to come to Jesus. The woman comes to him without asking and ministers without permission. Jesus sees the woman for who she is, but the woman also sees the truth of her own life. Because of her honesty, she comes to a new self-realization, is forgiven, and is saved by her faith. Like her, we are called to the same honesty about self and the willingness to come to Jesus for forgiveness. Then does Jesus' merciful response shape our attitudes and responses toward one another.

Model Prayer of the Faithful

Presider: Let us place before our loving and forgiving God all that we need.

Response:

Lord, hear our prayer.

Cantor:

we pray to the Lord,

That all members of the church may be honest with themselves and come to Jesus for forgiveness and mercy . . . [pause]

That all peoples of the world may see one another as having dignity and worth . . . [pause]

That outcasts and sinners might be embraced by the love and mercy of others . . . [pause]

That all of us gathered here may see others with the eyes of Jesus . . . [pause]

Presider: Merciful God, you look into our hearts and forgive the wrong we have done: hear our prayers that one day we might rejoice forever with you. We ask this through Christ our Lord. **Amen.**

ALTERNATIVE OPENING PRAYER

Let us pray

Pause for silent prayer

God our Father,
we rejoice in the faith that draws us
    together,
aware that selfishness can drive us apart.
Let your encouragement be our constant
    strength.
Keep us one in the love that has sealed our
    lives,
help us to live as one family
the gospel we profess.

We ask this through Christ our Lord.
    Amen.

FIRST READING

2 Sam 12:7-10, 13

Nathan said to David:
"Thus says the LORD God of Israel:
  'I anointed you king of Israel.
I rescued you from the hand of Saul.
I gave you your lord's house and your
    lord's wives for your own.
I gave you the house of Israel and of
    Judah.
And if this were not enough, I could count
    up for you still more.
Why have you spurned the LORD and done
    evil in his sight?
You have cut down Uriah the Hittite with
    the sword;
    you took his wife as your own,
    and him you killed with the sword of
      the Ammonites.
Now, therefore, the sword shall never
    depart from your house,
    because you have despised me
    and have taken the wife of Uriah to be
      your wife.'"
Then David said to Nathan,
  "I have sinned against the LORD."
Nathan answered David:
  "The LORD on his part has forgiven your
    sin:
  you shall not die."

RESPONSORIAL PSALM
Ps 32:1-2, 5, 7, 11

R⁊. (cf. 5c) Lord, forgive the wrong I have done.

Blessed is the one whose fault is taken
    away,
    whose sin is covered.
Blessed the man to whom the LORD
    imputes not guilt,
    in whose spirit there is no guile.

R⁊. Lord, forgive the wrong I have done.

I acknowledged my sin to you,
    my guilt I covered not.
I said, "I confess my faults to the LORD,"
    and you took away the guilt of my sin.

R⁊. Lord, forgive the wrong I have done.

You are my shelter; from distress you will
    preserve me;
    with glad cries of freedom you will ring
    me round.

R⁊. Lord, forgive the wrong I have done.

Be glad in the LORD and rejoice, you just;
    exult, all you upright of heart.

R⁊. Lord, forgive the wrong I have done.

SECOND READING
Gal 2:16, 19-21

Brothers and sisters:
 We who know that a person is not
    justified by works of the law
    but through faith in Jesus Christ,
    even we have believed in Christ Jesus
    that we may be justified by faith in
        Christ
    and not by works of the law,
    because by works of the law no one will
        be justified.
For through the law I died to the law,
    that I might live for God.
I have been crucified with Christ;
    yet I live, no longer I, but Christ lives
        in me;
    insofar as I now live in the flesh,
    I live by faith in the Son of God
    who has loved me and given himself up
        for me.
I do not nullify the grace of God;
    for if justification comes through the
        law,
    then Christ died for nothing.

About Liturgy

Hospitality at liturgy: We usually think of liturgy and hospitality in terms of the obvious liturgical ministry. Greeters welcome us and help us feel at home. Ushers take care of making sure the space is well prepared and comfortable, and seat us if the church is crowded. Hospitality ministers help us find restrooms, get help if we are ill, direct us to where the coffee and donuts are after Mass. All this ministry is important. It helps us become a caring community. It takes care of our needs.

There is another angle to liturgical hospitality, however. And this approach is much less tangible than what we mentioned above, yet even so much more important. The other side of hospitality is what all assembly members must minister.

Liturgical hospitality includes opening ourselves to encounter God and each other, becoming transparent enough so that others can see us as wanting to be part of this community, letting go of any expectations we might have with regard to how we want the liturgy to be celebrated. Liturgical hospitality might mean that we must quiet ourselves when we come to liturgy agitated over the pressures and demands of life. It might mean that we are willing to encounter the stranger—to greet someone we don't know, to help someone who is disabled, to volunteer when the parish needs additional liturgical ministers or workers for social events or justice actions. Above all, liturgical hospitality means that we see in the face of others the Christ whom we have come to liturgy to encounter.

About Liturgical Music

Music suggestions: Appropriate this Sunday would be songs celebrating God's life-giving mercy and our need to admit sinfulness and seek forgiveness. Examples include "Amazing Grace" [in most hymnals]; "Grant to Us, O Lord" [PMB, RS, WC, WS]; "There's a Wideness in God's Mercy" [in most hymnals]; "With the Lord" [BB, JS2, OFUV]; "Hosea" [BB, G2, GC, GC2, JS2, OFUV]; "Softly and Tenderly Jesus Is Calling" [BB, JS2, OFUV, RS]; "Come, You Sinners, Poor and Needy" [RS, W3]. Also appropriate would be songs that call us to offer the same forgiving mercy to one another, such as "The Master Came to Bring Good News" [GC, GC2, RS, W3].

JUNE 13, 2010
ELEVENTH SUNDAY
IN ORDINARY TIME

SPIRITUALITY

GOSPEL ACCLAMATION
John 10:27

℟. Alleluia, alleluia.
My sheep hear my voice, says the Lord;
I know them, and they follow me.
℟. Alleluia, alleluia.

Gospel

Luke 9:18-24; L96C

Once when Jesus was praying in
    solitude,
    and the disciples were with him,
    he asked them, "Who do the
        crowds say that I am?"
They said in reply, "John the
        Baptist;
    others, Elijah;
    still others, 'One of the ancient
        prophets has arisen.'"
Then he said to them, "But who do you
        say that I am?"
Peter said in reply, "The Christ of
        God."
He rebuked them
    and directed them not to tell this to
        anyone.

He said, "The Son of Man must suffer
        greatly
    and be rejected by the elders, the
        chief priests, and the scribes,
    and be killed and on the third day be
        raised."

Then he said to all,
    "If anyone wishes to come after me,
        he must deny himself
    and take up his cross daily and follow
        me.
For whoever wishes to save his life will
        lose it,
    but whoever loses his life for my sake
        will save it."

Reflecting on the Gospel

Anyone involved with youth (parents, youth ministers, teachers, counselors) knows that the question of identity is paramount for them. They are trying to find out who they are in terms of talents, potential career choices, how they relate to others. All this is a positive step in their maturing process, during which they identify their strengths and weaknesses, consider their assets, and bond with others who help them in this sometimes painful process. When asked about who they are, virtually no one would answer in terms of pain, suffering, death. In this Sunday's gospel Jesus asks his disciples about his identity. They reply with good answers that they have heard from others, part of the Jewish psyche of the time about the Messiah.

Jesus asks again a pretty simple question about his identity. Now Peter answers, but a surprise lies in how Jesus clarifies the meaning of "the Christ." He is to "suffer greatly," "be rejected," "be killed." This is the way Jesus becomes who he really is—the risen One. To realize our own truest identity, we must daily die to ourselves. This is the way we become who we truly are to be—followers of Jesus who daily die to ourselves and daily share more and more in the life of the risen Lord.

Jesus is so much in touch with his ultimate *mission*—to "suffer greatly," "be rejected," "be killed," and "be raised"—that he actually defines his identity in terms of it. His mission is an extension of who Jesus is—Savior. We usually think of Jesus' mission as teaching and preaching, healing and working miracles, and so it was. But underlying these activities is the ultimate one—his suffering, death, and resurrection. So it is with us.

Through baptism we share in Jesus' identity and mission—we are plunged into the waters of baptism, dying to self and rising to new life in Christ and thus are made members of the Body of Christ. Our own identity and mission is that of Jesus: to die to self so that we are raised to new life. Following Jesus has its cost. The statement in the gospel is true: we save our lives by losing them. We know this is true because Jesus showed us the way.

Living the Paschal Mystery

The first reading from the prophet Zechariah mentions "a fountain to purify from sin and uncleanness." As Christians we naturally think of the baptismal font that purifies and cleanses us. Two points might be made.

First, these waters of baptism don't flow just once. The ritual is an action that aptly describes an ongoing sacramental reality in our lives: we are constantly being washed clean. One way to do this, of course, is through confessing our sins either in prayer itself or in sacramental confession. We sometimes forget, though, that good works also cleanse us of our sins! So, the denying self and carrying our daily cross mentioned in the gospel are cleansing activities that lead us to forgiveness and new life.

Second, baptismal purification is also tied to our Christian identity. We not only are freed from sin but also are made members of Christ's Body. As such, we might expect that the same things that happened to Jesus will also happen to us. To be practical, that means that when we live our baptismal promises we can expect to be misunderstood, ridiculed, shunned, etc. Paschal mystery living has its demands (dying to self) and rewards (new life). Self-giving is always life-giving.

Focusing the gospel

Key words and phrases: The Christ of God, suffer greatly, be rejected, be killed, be raised, follow me

To the point: Jesus asks a pretty simple question about his identity. Peter answers, but the surprise lies in how Jesus clarifies the meaning of "the Christ." He is to "suffer greatly," "be rejected," "be killed." This is the way Jesus becomes who he really is—the risen One. To realize our truest identity, we must daily die to ourselves. This is the way we become who we truly are to be—followers of Jesus who daily die to ourselves and daily share more and more in the life of the risen Lord.

Connecting the Gospel

to the first reading: The prophecy of Zechariah referring to the fate of Israel's king can be applied to Jesus the Messiah King whose side is pierced on the cross and for whom we all mourn.

to our experience: Suffering and death are experiences we avoid. The gospel challenges us to embrace them as the way to new life.

Connecting the Responsorial Psalm

to the readings: In the first reading God pours onto the people a "spirit of grace and petition." Their prayer moves them to acknowledge their sinfulness, mourn what they have done, and receive purification. The gospel also relates a moment of prayer, one in which Jesus leads the disciples to acknowledge who he is and to accept the suffering that he, and they with him, must undergo.

The responsorial psalm reminds us that prayer—thirsting for God—is the fountainhead of redemption. On the one hand, prayer is a gift from God (first reading). On the other, it is a choice on our part (gospel). It is always a relationship that reveals both who God is and who we are. Prayer teaches us that we are souls in need of divine nourishment (psalm), sinners in need of repentance and purification (first reading), and disciples called to acknowledge Christ and carry the cross (gospel). Prayer also teaches us that God is our greatest good and ultimate satisfaction, that God acts to bring us to repentance, and that God in Christ takes up the cross ahead of us. May we know for whom we thirst, and may we drink deeply and be transformed.

to psalmist preparation: In the context of this Sunday's readings, this responsorial psalm is a courageous, and confident, prayer to make. Jesus pours out his thirst for God as he seeks the reassurance he needs to bear the suffering and death incumbent upon him (gospel). You lead the assembly in joining Jesus in this prayer and the commitment it implies. Do you accept where thirsting for God will ultimately lead you? Do you believe that only carrying the cross will bring ultimate satisfaction?

ASSEMBLY & FAITH-SHARING GROUPS

- For me, Jesus is . . . My understanding of Jesus has grown in these ways . . .
- The cross that I face in my life is . . . What I must "deny" in order to take it up is . . .
- "Whoever loses his life for my sake will save it." The ways I experience this as true are . . .

PRESIDERS

- My truest identity is . . .

DEACONS

- As I serve others what I "lose" is . . . what is "saved" in me is . . .

HOSPITALITY MINISTERS

- My hospitality supports others to carry their daily cross by . . .

MUSIC MINISTERS

- In order for my music ministry to lead the assembly to Christ, I must die to myself by . . .

ALTAR MINISTERS

- As Christ's "anointed," serving others is not what I do but who I am. What this means to me is . . .

LECTORS

- The readings direct me to "look on him whom they have pierced" (first reading). I direct others to "look on him" whenever . . .

EXTRAORDINARY MINISTERS OF HOLY COMMUNION

- We recognize Jesus in the Body and Blood. The way I recognize Jesus in denying self and taking up the cross is . . .

Model Act of Penitence

Presider: Jesus invites us to follow him but also tells us that discipleship has its cost: we must deny ourselves and take up our cross daily. During this liturgy let us ask God to strengthen us on our Christian journey . . . [pause]

Lord Jesus, you are the Christ of God: Lord . . .

Christ Jesus, you suffered greatly, were rejected, killed, and raised on the third day: Christ . . .

Lord Jesus, you are the Savior of the world: Lord . . .

Homily Points

• Without realizing it, many people faithfully take up their daily cross. Parents, for example, lose a night's sleep to care for a sick child. Teachers spend long hours correcting papers, planning lessons, and working with students who struggle to learn. We are patient with clerks who are in training. These simple, everyday instances of relating with one another are opportunities to grow in the life of the risen Christ.

• The daily demands on us to be good to others are daunting. Jesus stands before us as the model of dying to self and the promise of the new life this dying to self brings.

• Our truest identity is deepened by our self-giving and our care for others. We humans have a compelling drive to connect with one another. Self-giving and care for others are life-giving precisely because they bond us with one another.

Model Prayer of the Faithful

Presider: God demands great things of us who are Jesus' followers. With God's help we can be faithful to the call to die daily to self. And so we pray.

Response:

Lord, hear our prayer.

Cantor:

we pray to the Lord,

For the members of the church, the Body of Christ, called to deny themselves, take up their cross, and follow Jesus . . . [pause]

For all peoples of the world, called to lose their lives for the sake of others . . . [pause]

For all those in need, saved by Jesus' life, death, and resurrection . . . [pause]

For ourselves, strengthened by the bonds of community with one another to be faithful disciples of Jesus . . . [pause]

Presider: Gracious God, you strengthen those who call to you in need: hear these our prayers that one day we might enjoy everlasting life with you. We ask this through your Son, Jesus Christ our Lord. **Amen**.

OPENING PRAYER

Let us pray
[to God whose fatherly love keeps us safe]

Pause for silent prayer

Father,
guide and protector of your people,
grant us an unfailing respect for your name,
and keep us always in your love.

Grant this through our Lord Jesus Christ, your Son,
who lives and reigns with you and the Holy Spirit,
one God, for ever and ever. **Amen.**

FIRST READING
Zech 12:10-11; 13:1

Thus says the LORD:
I will pour out on the house of David
and on the inhabitants of Jerusalem
a spirit of grace and petition;
and they shall look on him whom they have pierced,
and they shall mourn for him as one mourns for an only son,
and they shall grieve over him as one grieves over a firstborn.

On that day the mourning in Jerusalem shall be as great
as the mourning of Hadadrimmon in the plain of Megiddo.

On that day there shall be open to the house of David
and to the inhabitants of Jerusalem,
a fountain to purify from sin and uncleanness.

RESPONSORIAL PSALM
Ps 63:2, 3-4, 5-6, 8-9

R. My soul is thirsting for you, O Lord my God.

O God, you are my God whom I seek;
for you my flesh pines and my soul thirsts
like the earth, parched, lifeless and without water.

R. My soul is thirsting for you, O Lord my God.

Thus have I gazed toward you in the sanctuary
to see your power and your glory,
for your kindness is a greater good than life;
my lips shall glorify you.

R. My soul is thirsting for you, O Lord my God.

Thus will I bless you while I live;
  lifting up my hands, I will call upon
      your name.
As with the riches of a banquet shall my
    soul be satisfied,
  and with exultant lips my mouth shall
      praise you.

R⃰. My soul is thirsting for you, O Lord my
God.

You are my help,
  and in the shadow of your wings I
      shout for joy.
My soul clings fast to you;
  your right hand upholds me.

R⃰. My soul is thirsting for you, O Lord my
God.

SECOND READING
Gal 3:26-29

Brothers and sisters:
Through faith you are all children of God
    in Christ Jesus.
For all of you who were baptized into
    Christ
  have clothed yourselves with Christ.
There is neither Jew nor Greek,
  there is neither slave nor free person,
  there is not male and female;
  for you are all one in Christ Jesus.
And if you belong to Christ,
  then you are Abraham's descendant,
  heirs according to the promise.

About Liturgy

Father's Day: The Mass of the Sunday is to be respected even if this Sunday is Father's Day. A fifth intercession might be added to the general intercessions at the prayer of the faithful (see BofB 1732), and a blessing for the fathers may be given in place of the prayer over the people for the Sunday (see BofB 1733).

The cross: The cross has been a Christian symbol of self-denial, self-sacrifice, redemption, and identity with Christ from at least the fourth century. It has become the primary symbol of Christianity. The cross leads processions (GIRM 117, 119, and 122) and is venerated with incense (GIRM 49 and 277), as are the altar and paschal candle. A cross with a corpus is to be on or near the altar during Mass (GIRM 117 and 308), which helps us relate the sacrifice of the Mass to the sacrifice of Calvary.

In the Eastern church the custom has been to use a cross rather than a crucifix (a cross with a corpus), often studded with jewels or richly decorated. Sometimes an image of Christ the High Priest may be used. The cross in this context celebrates Christ's victory over death and sin and is a symbol of triumph. In the Western church the custom has been to use a crucifix with an image of the dying or dead Jesus. The cross in this context reminds us of Jesus' self-sacrificing love demonstrated through his passion and death.

About Liturgical Music

Music suggestions: In this Sunday's gospel the disciples grow in their awareness of who Jesus is, and they are confronted with the challenge of the cross. Songs about Jesus' identity as Messiah and the necessity of his suffering and death would fit the liturgy well. Examples include: "Let Kings and Prophets Yield Their Name" [HG] for either the entrance or the preparation of the gifts; "Jesus Christ, by Faith Revealed" [PMB, WC, WS] for the entrance procession; "There in God's Garden" [WC] for the Communion procession. Songs that call us to take up the cross as Jesus' disciples would also be appropriate. Examples include: "Only This I Want" [BB, G2, GC, GC2, JS2, OFUV] for the preparation of the gifts or Communion; "Take Up Your Cross" [in most hymnals] for the preparation of the gifts; Bernadette Farrell's "Unless a Grain of Wheat" [BB, G2, GC, GC2, JS2, OFUV, RS] for Communion. Owen Alstott's "We Have No Glory" [JS2] reminds us that our identity, "our only glory" and "our only name," are found in Jesus Christ; this hymn would work well either during the preparation of the gifts or Communion.

JUNE 20, 2010
TWELFTH SUNDAY
IN ORDINARY TIME

✝ SPIRITUALITY

GOSPEL ACCLAMATION
cf. Luke 1:76

R℣. Alleluia, alleluia.
You, child, will be called prophet of the Most High,
for you will go before the Lord to prepare his way.
R℣. Alleluia, alleluia.

Gospel   Luke 1:57-66, 80; L587

When the time arrived for Elizabeth
    to have her child
    she gave birth to a son.
Her neighbors and relatives heard
    that the Lord had shown his great
        mercy toward her,
    and they rejoiced with her.
When they came on the eighth day to
    circumcise the child,
    they were going to call him Zecha-
        riah after his father,
    but his mother said in reply,
"No. He will be called John."
But they answered her,
    "There is no one among your relatives
        who has this name."
So they made signs, asking his father what
    he wished him to be called.
He asked for a tablet and wrote, "John is his
    name,"
    and all were amazed.
Immediately his mouth was opened, his
    tongue freed,
    and he spoke blessing God.
Then fear came upon all their neighbors,
    and all these matters were discussed
    throughout the hill country of Judea.
All who heard these things took them to
    heart, saying,
"What, then, will this child be?"
For surely the hand of the Lord was with him.

The child grew and became strong in spirit,
    and he was in the desert until the day
    of his manifestation to Israel.

*See Appendix A, pp. 302–303, for the other
readings.*

Reflecting on the Gospel

A car parked in the doctors' parking lot at a hospital had the "vanity" license plate "Stork 1." It doesn't take a rocket scientist to figure out that it must have been a car belonging to an obstetrician! No doubt this doctor is happy to announce in so public a way that he is in a profession that almost always is filled with pleasant outcomes and the joyful welcoming of new life. Conception and birth are usually causes for great rejoicing and wonder, today as well as in the society at the time of John the Baptist's birth. New life always brings new possibilities. New life always brings changes: one more person in the family, schedule interruptions by the demands of a helpless and vulnerable infant, endless hours of watching the little bit of life grow and become strong.

Zechariah and Elizabeth had been barren, and now they have a newborn son. God has blessed them and "shown great mercy" toward them. How much joy they must have felt when their boy was born! The "neighbors and relatives" were rejoicing, too, and they already had a name picked out for this new blessing and life: "they were going to call him Zechariah after his father." How startled they were when Elizabeth announced his name would be John! Doubting her, they pressed Zechariah about "what he wished him to be called." Now they were "amazed." And then fearful, as Zechariah's "mouth was opened . . . and he spoke blessing God." Such an amazing array of emotions are displayed in this gospel: joy, amazement, fear. All this points to a birth that holds meaning beyond the events described, goes beyond a whole gamut of emotions evoked at a birth. The meaning of this birth is still told "throughout the hill country" and through time even to today.

The centerpiece of the gospel is rejoicing not so much at the blessing of a newborn but at the obedience of Elizabeth and Zechariah to God's word in naming their newborn son John. The name John was cause for great amazement among the people who wondered, "What, then, will this child be?" We know that John became the forerunner of the One who would come to save us. Being saved takes as a given obedience to God's word—obedience by Elizabeth and Zechariah, by John, by Jesus, by us.

Something new is happening—God continues Jesus' saving work through us when we, too, obediently listen for and act upon God's word. In this way we ourselves are both precursor and the presence of Christ in the world. Never before has this happened, even in John's time. We announce Jesus and *are* the presence of the risen Christ. No wonder we are amazed. No wonder we rejoice. And no wonder we, too, are just a bit fearful. Such an awesome task God entrusts to us: to cooperate in fulfilling the divine plan of salvation.

Living the Paschal Mystery

John could point his disciples to Jesus as the Savior. We, too, point to the presence of the risen Christ among us. More than by words, we do so by our obedience to God. We do so by living the paschal mystery in such a way that our own actions and way of living are so filled with love, so radically new—so radically different—that people are moved to ask of us, "What, then, is this person?" This doesn't mean that we leave all and go out into a desert. It does mean that we allow ourselves to grow "strong in the spirit" and live as those who have been baptized into Christ the Savior.

Focusing the gospel

Key words and phrases: he will be called; his name is; What, then, will this child be?

To the point: The centerpiece of the gospel is the obedience of Elizabeth and Zechariah to God's word in naming their newborn son John. The name John was cause for great amazement among the people who wondered, "What, then, will this child be?" We know that John became the forerunner of the One who would come to save us. Being saved takes as a given obedience to God's word—obedience by Elizabeth and Zechariah, by John, by Jesus, by us.

Model Act of Penitence

Presider: John the Baptist was the forerunner of our Lord. As we begin this liturgy, let us open ourselves to the Lord announcing his presence to us . . . [pause]

Lord Jesus, you are the Savior of the world: Lord . . .

Christ Jesus, you are the Presence John announced: Christ . . .

Lord Jesus, you are the Word of salvation: Lord . . .

Model Prayer of the Faithful

Presider: From the beginning of creation God has desired all humanity to be saved. We are confident that such a loving God will hear our prayers and answer our needs.

Response:

Lord, hear our prayer.

Cantor:

we pray to the Lord,

That each member of the church point to the presence of Christ in our world as did John the Baptist . . . [pause]

That leaders of nations be agents of righteousness and peace . . . [pause]

That those who are in need receive from God what they ask . . . [pause]

That each one of us be faithful to our own mission to make known Christ in the world . . . [pause]

Presider: Saving God, you hear the prayers of your obedient people: grant us what we need so that one day we might share everlasting life with you. We ask this through Christ our Lord. **Amen.**

FOR REFLECTION
- What, then, is this child John to me?
- The people who are like John and herald Christ's presence to me are . . .
- Obedience to God's word is easiest for me when . . . hardest for me when . . .

Homily Points

• Parents usually spend a great deal of time choosing a name for their unborn child. It is such a joy and pleasure that they suggest all kinds of names—some good ones, some really way off. Elizabeth and Zechariah's joy and pleasure at the naming lay in something quite different—in being obedient to the name God gave John.

• Elizabeth and Zechariah handed on their gift of obedience to John, who himself was obedient to his call to be the Savior's forerunner. Obedience also guided Jesus through his public ministry to death and resurrection. Obedience guides us to . . .

✚ SPIRITUALITY

GOSPEL ACCLAMATION
1 Sam 3:9; John 6:68c

R̸. Alleluia, alleluia.
Speak, Lord, your servant is listening;
you have he words of everlasting life.
R̸. Alleluia, alleluia.

Gospel   Luke 9:51-62; L99C

When the days for Jesus'
    being taken up were
    fulfilled,
  he resolutely determined to
    journey to Jerusalem,
  and he sent messengers
    ahead of him.
On the way they entered a
    Samaritan village
  to prepare for his reception there,
  but they would not welcome him
  because the destination of his journey
    was Jerusalem.
When the disciples James and John saw this
    they asked,
  "Lord, do you want us to call down fire
    from heaven
  to consume them?"
Jesus turned and rebuked them, and they
    journeyed to another village.

As they were proceeding on their journey
    someone said to him,
  "I will follow you wherever you go."
Jesus answered him,
  "Foxes have dens and birds of the sky
    have nests,
  but the Son of Man has nowhere to rest
    his head."

And to another he said, "Follow me."
But he replied, "Lord, let me go first and
    bury my father."
But he answered him, "Let the dead bury
    their dead.
But you, go and proclaim the kingdom of
    God."
And another said, "I will follow you, Lord,
  but first let me say farewell to my family
    at home."
To him Jesus said, "No one who sets a hand
    to the plow
  and looks to what was left behind is fit for
    the kingdom of God."

Reflecting on the Gospel

Many of us need a push to dive into something demanding, be it an unpleasant task, a tediously long and boring job, or patching up a relationship gone awry. Sometimes just trying to motivate ourselves for various kinds of tasks is a hard sell. This is so common that we have any number of sayings we use in this regard: bite the bullet; go, team, go; set our hand to the plow; move, darn it. Motivation and persistence aren't traits that come naturally to many of us. We need an extra "push" to get moving. The gospel for this Sunday is about a journey, but the end isn't something anyone would choose. It truly takes motivation to undergo this journey and stay the course. It definitely takes a push to get started, and much more than that to keep going. What kind of a journey is this?

The beginning of the gospel sets the tone for this selection: Jesus "resolutely determined to journey to Jerusalem." This might seem like a pleasant enough journey until we consider that here "Jerusalem" is a metaphor for death, the end of our life's journey—but also for new life. Jesus invites us on this journey. We know the cost, even as we also know the new life that awaits us. We need to get started, and help to stay on an unswerving path. Jesus is there to be that help.

This gospel depicts various responses to and interactions with Jesus: some refuse him entrance into their village, some naively swear to follow wherever he leads, some put the exigencies of life ahead of following him. Each response suggests that people have some sense of the cost of following Jesus. Throughout, Jesus consistently indicates that those who follow him must separate themselves from anything that hinders their resolutely journeying with him through death to new life. The price is high but so are the stakes and so is the reward.

The challenge of this gospel is for us to be resolutely determined to accept the dying to self that is necessary to follow Jesus and cooperate with him in establishing God's reign, just as Jesus was resolutely determined to go to his own suffering and death. We can be neither naive nor self-excusing. To be "fit for the kingdom of God" we must keep our eyes on Jesus and our destiny. We must let him be our motivation to stay the course. The course: Jerusalem. The price: dying. The stakes: new life. This is surely all the motivation we could possibly need: following Jesus brings new life.

Living the Paschal Mystery

The context for this Sunday's gospel is that Jesus is "resolutely determined" to go to Jerusalem, and this sets the tone for the next months of Ordinary Time. On our own journey to the end of the liturgical year in November (hardly on our minds at this point in June!) we must be resolute about hearing the gospel faithfully and following Jesus, even when that means we, too, are going to "Jerusalem," which symbolizes the ongoing dying to self that is what living the paschal mystery really is.

We hear the gospel faithfully when that gospel is lived in our everyday circumstances. Hearing is more than words going into our ears; it demands of us resolute action. The gospels often are challenging. This one challenges us to go to Jerusalem with Jesus, and by being his faithful followers "the kingdom of God" is at hand through us. This ought to be all the motivation we need!

Focusing the gospel

Key words and phrases: resolutely determined to journey to Jerusalem, the destination of his journey was Jerusalem, follow me, kingdom of God

To the point: This gospel depicts various responses to and interactions with Jesus: some refuse him entrance into their village, some naively swear to follow wherever he leads, some put the exigencies of life ahead of following him. Throughout, Jesus consistently indicates that those who follow him must separate themselves from anything that hinders their resolutely journeying with him through death to new life. The price is high but so are the stakes and so is the reward.

Connecting the Gospel

to the first reading: In order to answer Elijah's invitation to succeed him as prophet, Elisha must first relinquish his former way of life ("die"), symbolized by the destruction of his plowing equipment and oxen.

to our experience: Every journey has its purpose, for example, business, pleasure, refuge, diversion, etc. The Christian journey has a singular purpose—making present "the kingdom of God"—about which we must be resolute.

Connecting the Responsorial Psalm

to the readings: Confronted with the urgency of God's call, Elisha abandoned everything and followed Elijah without hesitation, leaving no possessions intact, not stopping even to bid his parents good-bye (first reading). Similarly, the gospel reveals how radically pressing the journey to Jerusalem is for Jesus. Jesus waits for nothing and no one, wastes no time on those unable to receive him, and cuts no slack for those who hesitate to follow him. For Jesus the urgency of the kingdom overrides everything else.

The responsorial psalm reveals what enables Jesus and Elisha to abandon all so freely for the sake of the kingdom. They can relinquish everything, even what seems necessary for a safe and happy life (home and homeland, family and possessions), because they know they possess the very person of God (psalm refrain). They abandon all because they have been given even more. In this gospel Jesus asks us to make the same choice. Full of divine promise and presence, the psalm gives us the motivation to say yes. May it become our journey-to-Jerusalem song.

to psalmist preparation: In singing this psalm you testify that what you have given up in order to follow Jesus is nothing compared with what you have been given in return: the very person of God as your inheritance. How have you come to know this? Who has shown you? How might you continue to show others?

ASSEMBLY & FAITH-SHARING GROUPS

- Jesus "resolutely determined to journey to Jerusalem." To me what this entails is . . . In general my life is headed toward . . .
- Ways that I am already "following" Jesus to Jerusalem are . . .
- One thing I could alter in order to journey to Jerusalem with Jesus more faithfully is . . .

PRESIDERS

- What I need to leave behind in order to preside well is . . .

DEACONS

- The kind of service I must render on my journey to Jerusalem is . . . What helps me journey faithfully is . . .

HOSPITALITY MINISTERS

- Hospitality is not a haven *from* the journey to Jerusalem but reassurance for those *on* the journey. The way I live/minister this for others is . . .

MUSIC MINISTERS

- In order to follow Jesus to Jerusalem through my music ministry, some things I have to abandon are . . .

ALTAR MINISTERS

- The way I am assisting others on their journey to Jerusalem is . . .

LECTORS

- My daily living proclaims "the kingdom of God" when . . . This helps me when I proclaim Scripture because . . .

EXTRAORDINARY MINISTERS OF HOLY COMMUNION

- The way even the eucharistic banquet directs me toward Jerusalem is . . .

Model Act of Penitence

Presider: Today's gospel challenges us to follow Jesus on his journey to Jerusalem, where he will suffer, die, and be raised to new life. Let us prepare ourselves to hear this call and answer resolutely . . . [pause]

Lord Jesus, you were resolutely determined to journey to Jerusalem: Lord . . .
Christ Jesus, you call us to walk with you on this journey: Christ . . .
Lord Jesus, you are the way to new life: Lord . . .

Homily Points

• What does it take to be totally resolute about something? Maybe it takes intense pressure from an outside influence or a domineering individual. Maybe it takes the threat of legal consequences. Maybe it actually takes an obsessive-compulsive disorder! None of these describes Jesus' resolute determination to journey to Jerusalem.

• Jesus' resoluteness comes from his radical commitment to the will of the Father, to his mission to establish "the kingdom of God," to bringing salvation. Neither frustration nor fatigue, disappointment nor rejection, nor even death, can deter him from acting in accord with who he is—"Jesus," the Savior.

• None of us is as resolute as Jesus. Frustration and fatigue, disappointment and rejection can all stop us dead in our tracks. Even so, Jesus is very patient with our weak resolve and gives us the strength we need—in spite of meandering from the path of life—to continue the journey. This strength comes through the love and support of family and friends, through gradually learning to let go of less important things, by experiencing the good that comes from our self-giving. The Good News is that to be totally resolute we need to rely, not on ourselves, but on Jesus, who is with us to the end of our journey.

Model Prayer of the Faithful

Presider: We need strength on our Christian journey and so we make our needs known to God.

Response:

Lord, hear our prayer.

Cantor:

we pray to the Lord,

That all members of the church resolutely follow Jesus on the journey through death to new life . . . [pause]

That leaders of nations resolutely lead their people to justice and peace . . . [pause]

That those who falter on the journey of life might be guided in God's ways . . . [pause]

That each of us further God's reign by being faithful to the gospel's demands of dying to self for the good of others . . . [pause]

Presider: Gracious God, you desire that your kingdom of justice and peace be established throughout the world: hear these our prayers that one day we might enjoy everlasting life in the kingdom of heaven. We ask this through Christ our Lord. **Amen.**

OPENING PRAYER

Let us pray

Pause for silent prayer

Father,
you call your children
to walk in the light of Christ.
Free us from darkness
and keep us in the radiance of your truth.

We ask this through our Lord Jesus Christ,
  your Son,
who lives and reigns with you and the
  Holy Spirit,
one God, for ever and ever. **Amen.**

FIRST READING
1 Kgs 19:16b, 19-21

The LORD said to Elijah:
  "You shall anoint Elisha, son of Shaphat
    of Abel-meholah,
  as prophet to succeed you."

Elijah set out and came upon Elisha, son
    of Shaphat,
  as he was plowing with twelve yoke of
    oxen;
  he was following the twelfth.
Elijah went over to him and threw his
    cloak over him.
Elisha left the oxen, ran after Elijah,
    and said,
  "Please, let me kiss my father and
    mother goodbye,
  and I will follow you."
Elijah answered, "Go back!
Have I done anything to you?"
Elisha left him and, taking the yoke of
    oxen, slaughtered them;
  he used the plowing equipment for fuel
    to boil their flesh,
  and gave it to his people to eat.
Then Elisha left and followed Elijah as his
    attendant.

RESPONSORIAL PSALM
Ps 16:1-2, 5, 7-8, 9-10, 11

R̸. (cf. 5a) You are my inheritance, O Lord.

Keep me, O God, for in you I take refuge;
    I say to the LORD, "My Lord are you.
O LORD, my allotted portion and my cup,
    you it is who hold fast my lot."

R̸. You are my inheritance, O Lord.

I bless the LORD who counsels me;
    even in the night my heart exhorts me.
I set the LORD ever before me;
    with him at my right hand I shall not be
      disturbed.

R̸. You are my inheritance, O Lord.

Therefore my heart is glad and my soul
    rejoices,
    my body, too, abides in confidence
because you will not abandon my soul to
    the netherworld,
    nor will you suffer your faithful one to
      undergo corruption.

R̸. You are my inheritance, O Lord.

You will show me the path to life,
    fullness of joys in your presence,
    the delights at your right hand forever.

R̸. You are my inheritance, O Lord.

SECOND READING
Gal 5:1, 13-18

Brothers and sisters:
For freedom Christ set us free;
    so stand firm and do not submit again
      to the yoke of slavery.

For you were called for freedom, brothers
    and sisters.
But do not use this freedom
    as an opportunity for the flesh;
    rather, serve one another through love.
For the whole law is fulfilled in one
    statement,
    namely, *You shall love your neighbor as
      yourself.*
But if you go on biting and devouring one
    another,
    beware that you are not consumed by
      one another.

I say, then: live by the Spirit
    and you will certainly not gratify the
      desire of the flesh.
For the flesh has desires against the Spirit,
    and the Spirit against the flesh;
    these are opposed to each other,
    so that you may not do what you want.
But if you are guided by the Spirit, you are
    not under the law.

About Liturgy

Processions at Mass: Processions are like mini journeys—they lead us from one place to another. They always have a goal. During Mass there are actually four processions, each with its own goal. Although the General Instruction of the Roman Missal refers to the four processions (see GIRM 44, 47, 73, 86, 119, 133), it gives no explanation or theology for them. The following comments may help fill in this lacuna.

1. Entrance procession. This procession at the beginning of Mass is symbolic of the gathering of all the people into a unity for a common purpose of worship and transformation. The entrance procession symbolizes our journey from being individual *members* of the Body of Christ to *being* the Body of Christ gathered around the one Head, Christ made visible in the church.

2. Gospel procession. The procession with the gospel book (usually from the altar to the ambo) is an opportunity for the assembly to acclaim the presence of Christ in the proclaimed word. It also is a symbolic expression of their journey from *hearing* God's word to putting it into practice. We are now invited to turn toward the gospel book and follow its journey to the place of proclamation (see GIRM 133) as a sign of respect.

3. Procession with the gifts. The procession and presentation of the gifts symbolize the gift of ourselves presented to God for transformation into being more perfect members of the Body of Christ, just as the bread and wine are transformed into being the Real Presence of Christ. As the gifts are placed on the altar, we place ourselves on the altar and offer ourselves with Christ in sacrifice. It is symbolic of the ongoing journey of self-sacrifice that characterizes Christian living.

4. Communion procession. The Communion procession symbolizes our journey to the messianic table, that heavenly banquet where we already share by partaking in Jesus' Body and Blood at Communion, and also which we will forever share when we die and go to heaven. This procession most clearly proclaims what it means when the Communion lines actually move forward toward the altar.

About Liturgical Music

Music suggestions: Reflecting on this Sunday's gospel in light of the responsorial psalm reveals intersecting themes: to follow Jesus we must leave all other goods behind; if we do so, we will be given an even greater good in return—lasting life, joys in God's presence, God's very Self as our inheritance. "The Love of the Lord" [G2, GC, GC2, RS] combines these themes and would be a good choice for either the preparation of the gifts or Communion. "Seek Ye First the Kingdom of God" [BB, G2, GC, GC2, JS2, OFUV, RS, W3] also promises great reward for placing discipleship above all other goods and would be appropriate for the preparation of the gifts. Reminding us that when we serve Jesus, the Father will honor us, "Whenever You Serve Me" [PMB, WC] would be a fitting song for Communion.

JUNE 27, 2010
THIRTEENTH SUNDAY IN ORDINARY TIME

SPIRITUALITY

GOSPEL ACCLAMATION
Matt 16:18

℟. Alleluia, alleluia.
You are Peter and upon this rock I will build my church,
and the gates of the netherworld shall not prevail against it.
℟. Alleluia, alleluia.

Gospel   Matt 16:13-19; L591

When Jesus went into the region of Caesarea Philippi
   he asked his disciples,
   "Who do people say that the Son of Man is?"
They replied, "Some say John the Baptist, others Elijah,
   still others Jeremiah or one of the prophets."
He said to them, "But who do you say that I am?"
Simon Peter said in reply,
   "You are the Christ, the Son of the living God."
Jesus said to him in reply, "Blessed are you, Simon son of Jonah.
For flesh and blood has not revealed this to you, but my heavenly Father.
And so I say to you, you are Peter,
   and upon this rock I will build my Church,
   and the gates of the netherworld shall not prevail against it.
I will give you the keys to the Kingdom of heaven.
Whatever you bind on earth shall be bound in heaven;
   and whatever you loose on earth shall be loosed in heaven."

See Appendix A, pp. 303–304, for the other readings.

Reflecting on the Gospel

The first two readings for this solemnity record attempts to thwart the spread of the Gospel. All those chains and guards (see first reading), all those lions (see second reading)—how strong was the attempt to shackle the proclamation of the Gospel, the growth of the church! From this we can take a clue that this solemnity not only honors these two greatest saints (these are the only two apostles who have a festival with the rank of solemnity on our liturgical calendar), but the readings unquestionably direct our attention to God and what God is accomplishing through them—the establishment of Jesus' church. Thus, while this festival is about two great apostles of Jesus, the readings direct us to God's actions on behalf of the church that Jesus founds. In the gospel it is God who reveals to Peter who Jesus really is. In the first and second readings it is God who rescues both Peter and Paul from death. Nothing can "prevail against" God's plan for the growth and endurance of the community of the church.

The first reading's context is "the feast of Unleavened Bread" or "Passover." Peter is to be brought to trial after the festival; he is rescued the night before trial. Clearly there is a parallel with Jesus' own arrest and coming to trial; Jesus suffers and dies while Peter's demise is delayed until he has completed his apostolic work of being instrumental in establishing the church. Paul is nearing the end of his apostolic mission and readily acknowledges that he has "competed well" and "finished the race" because "the Lord stood by me and gave me strength." Both apostles were successful because they surrendered to God's action within them and made clear that their mission was not their own but Christ's. The gospel reminds us that we can't come to any true sense of who Jesus is or be successful in our efforts to carry on Jesus' mission except through the hand of God.

Both of these great apostles "kept the faith." And this is what they share with us. We, too, have been given the same faith in Christ Jesus as Peter and Paul. Because of this we can be as extraordinary as they were. All we need do is surrender ourselves like they did to the mystery of God's actions on behalf of the church. We honor Peter and Paul as the two apostles upon whom the universal mission of the church rests; this feast challenges us to accept that this same mission is continued in our own efforts to be faithful to Jesus' Gospel. Yes, John, Peter, and Paul are amazing and cause for wonder. Because we share in their same mission to make known Christ in the world, so can our efforts be amazing and cause for wonder. Like these apostles, we need only acknowledge that Jesus is the Christ and resolve to follow him wherever he leads. We are the church. We are the manifestation of God's mighty acts of salvation. We are the new pillars upon which this church continues to be built.

Living the Paschal Mystery

Being great apostles of Christ isn't a matter of doing great things; it is a matter of keeping faith in Christ Jesus. By recognizing ourselves as church—the Body of Christ—all our actions are truly God's actions on behalf of the church. It is through us that the proclamation of the Good News of Jesus' death and resurrection is being completed. And, like these two great apostles, the Lord will give us strength to carry on the mission, will rescue us from evil, and bring us safely "to his heavenly kingdom."

Focusing the gospel

Key words and phrases: You are the Christ, revealed . . . to you, build my church, shall not prevail against

To the point: While this festival is about two great apostles of Jesus, the readings direct us to God's actions on behalf of the church that Jesus founds. In the gospel it is God who reveals to Peter who Jesus really is. In the first and second readings it is God who rescues both Peter and Paul from death. Nothing can "prevail against" God's plan for the growth and endurance of the community of the church.

Model Act of Penitence

Presider: We honor today Saints Peter and Paul because they were faithful to preaching the Gospel and cooperating with Christ in establishing his church. Let us prepare ourselves to celebrate this liturgy by surrendering ourselves to God's action within us so that we, too, can be faithful disciples . . . [pause]

Lord Jesus, you are the Christ: Lord . . .

Christ Jesus, you are the Son of the living God: Christ . . .

Lord Jesus, you build your church upon your faithful disciples: Lord . . .

Model Prayer of the Faithful

Presider: Let us pray that Christ's church will always prevail against evil and bring us all to everlasting life.

Response:

Lord, hear our prayer.

Cantor:

we pray to the Lord,

That all members of the church may be models of faithful discipleship like Peter and Paul . . . [pause]

That all leaders of the world's nations guide their people in righteousness . . . [pause]

That those who are imprisoned unjustly might be freed . . . [pause]

That each of us take up our own role in establishing Christ's church . . . [pause]

Presider: Caring God, you strengthen all faithful disciples to carry on your Son's mission of establishing your kingdom: hear our prayers that one day we might also receive a "crown of righteousness." We pray through the intercession of Saints Peter and Paul and ask this through Jesus Christ our Lord. **Amen**.

OPENING PRAYER
Let us pray
Pause for silent prayer

God our Father,
today you give us the joy
of celebrating the feast of the apostles
     Peter and Paul.
Through them your Church first received
     the faith.
Keep us true to their teaching.

Grant this through our Lord Jesus Christ,
     your Son,
who lives and reigns with you and the Holy
     Spirit,
one God, for ever and ever. **Amen.**

FOR REFLECTION

- As I ponder the lives of Peter and Paul, some things I can learn from them are . . .

- Like Peter, an example of where Christ is building his church through me is . . .

- Like Paul, a time when "the Lord stood by me and gave me strength" (second reading) was . . .

Homily Points

• All too often the word "church" brings to mind only the institutional aspect. This solemnity of Peter and Paul reminds us that the church is a community of persons brought together by Christ and held together in the hands of God.

• Peter and Paul were two very different personalities: Peter was impetuous; Paul was determined. Peter immediately left his nets to follow Jesus; Paul first persecuted the church before he turned to Jesus. Peter was hurt when Jesus challenged him ("Do you love me?"); Paul challenged others to love Jesus. These two were very human, yet they were pillars of the church. We, too, are very human, yet God continues to build the church on us.

✝ SPIRITUALITY

GOSPEL ACCLAMATION
Col 3:15a, 16a

℟. Alleluia, alleluia.
Let the peace of Christ control your hearts;
let the word of Christ dwell in you richly.
℟. Alleluia, alleluia.

Gospel   Luke 10:1-12, 17-20; L102C

At that time the Lord appointed
   seventy-two others
   whom he sent ahead of him in
      pairs
   to every town and place he
      intended to visit.
He said to them,
   "The harvest is abundant but
      the laborers are few;
   so ask the master of the harvest
   to send out laborers for his harvest.
Go on your way;
   behold, I am sending you like lambs
      among wolves.
Carry no money bag, no sack, no
      sandals;
   and greet no one along the way.
Into whatever house you enter, first say,
   'Peace to this household.'
If a peaceful person lives there,
   your peace will rest on him;
   but if not, it will return to you.
Stay in the same house and eat and
      drink what is offered to you,
   for the laborer deserves his payment.
Do not move about from one house to
      another.
Whatever town you enter and they
      welcome you,
   eat what is set before you,
   cure the sick in it and say to them,
   'The kingdom of God is at hand for
      you.'
Whatever town you enter and they do
      not receive you,
   go out into the streets and say,
   'The dust of your town that clings to
      our feet,
   even that we shake off against you.'

Continued in Appendix A, p. 304.

Reflecting on the Gospel

Birthdays are always times to celebrate life, to reminisce about growing up, to take stock of where we are and where we want to go. These kinds of reflections are a bit more difficult to do as a nation, but the Fourth of July does help us to pause and be grateful for all that we have as a country founded on principles of equality and freedom. Truly, we have had an abundant harvest as a nation: supermarkets stacked to the ceiling with food; freedom of speech, press, assembly; blessings of resources, talents, strengths. At the same time we are well aware that not everyone shares equally in all this abundance—we still face appalling poverty, ghastly prejudices, gross abuse of power. Our abundance or lack of it is measured by such things as wealth, power, peace; poverty, oppression, discord. The gospel doesn't talk about a country but about a "kingdom." This kingdom is of God and, though very different from our country, it is just as "at hand."

In this Sunday's gospel Jesus refers three times to an abundant harvest. The nature of this harvest is evident through the ministry of the disciples Jesus sends forth: peace, stability, nourishment, healing, rejoicing. This is no ordinary harvest of the fruits of the earth. This harvest is the fruit of God's kingdom "at hand" through the very ministry of Jesus and his disciples. Moreover, the harvest is being reaped today through us who continue to go forth in Jesus' name.

Note that some of the abundant harvest goes to the laborer-disciples who are sent forth: they have the power to heal, are nourished, are welcomed, cast out demons, and rejoice. Some of the abundant harvest goes to those who receive the ministry: peace and healing. The abundant harvest of both laborers and recipients is a sign of God's presence. And where God is present, there is God's kingdom. Rather than being measured by spacious skies, prairies of ripe wheat, majestic mountains, sobering deserts, rivers and lakes replete with commerce, God's kingdom is measured by the abundance of goodness, care for others, growth toward new life.

Living the Paschal Mystery

In our own times we are not as conscious of personified evil as in the time of Jesus. Demons represent a worldview; God's kingdom breaks in on this evil and establishes a new world order in which evil's grasp is broken. The establishment of God's reign is already an in-breaking of the final glory that will be ours—our "names are [already] written in heaven." References to the abundance of the end times are captured in the "harvest" metaphor Jesus uses. Jesus looks at the harvest and sees abundance, fulfillment. Some of this abundance and fulfillment is surely realized when we take up Jesus' mission to bring peace, heal, and dispel evil. The challenge of the gospel is that we don't get so lost in doing Jesus' mission that we forget that being faithful disciples is in itself already an in-breaking of God's reign. It is in Christ's presence through us that peace and joy are spread.

Living the paschal mystery means believing in what God has made us—members of his Body sent forth to be God's presence. It means that we are as satisfied with the presence we bring as we are with the good that we can do. Mission is being sent to *be* Christ for others. Only when we act out of our identity can anything we do help establish God's reign.

Focusing the gospel

Key words and phrases: harvest, Go on your way, peace, cure, kingdom of God is at hand, rejoicing

To the point: In this Sunday's gospel Jesus refers three times to an abundant harvest. The nature of this harvest is evident through the ministry of the disciples Jesus sends forth: peace, stability, nourishment, healing, rejoicing. This is no ordinary harvest of the fruits of the earth. This harvest is the fruit of God's kingdom "at hand" through the very ministry of Jesus and his disciples. Moreover, the harvest is being reaped today through us who continue to go forth in Jesus' name.

Connecting the Gospel

to the first reading: Isaiah foresees the kingdom restored after the exile in Babylon: there will be comfort, rejoicing, abundance, prosperity. This prophecy was fulfilled when God's people returned to Israel. In the ministry of Jesus and his disciples a new and even more desirable kingdom of God is at hand.

to our experience: When we think of having an abundance, we usually think in terms of larger income, bigger homes, nicer cars. Isaiah and Jesus announce that God is bringing about a kingdom where abundance is measured not by possessions but by the quality of our relationships.

Connecting the Responsorial Psalm

to the readings: In these verses from Psalm 66 the psalmist calls the entire earth to come and see the marvelous works of the Lord and to shout praises for God who has wrought such "tremendous . . . deeds!" In the first reading it is the Lord who calls the people to rejoice over marvelous deeds done on behalf of Jerusalem. In her arms the people will be fed and comforted and will discover how God has acted to save and restore. In the gospel Jesus sends his disciples out to proclaim the same message: God is acting to save, the kingdom is at hand. Some will welcome this message, others will reject it. But regardless of the response, the coming of the kingdom of God will not be thwarted: evil will be destroyed, healing will come, and peace will prevail. In this psalm we "cry out . . . with joy" over the abundant works of God for the salvation of the world.

to psalmist preparation: In this Sunday's gospel Jesus sends the disciples on mission to announce his coming. Your singing of the responsorial psalm is part of that mission, for it is a hymn of praise telling of God's saving deeds. Where have you experienced these deeds in your own life? In the lives of others? How have you announced them to the world?

ASSEMBLY & FAITH-SHARING GROUPS

* The abundance of "the kingdom of God is at hand" for me when . . .
* Jesus is sending me to announce the kingdom in my daily life. Some obstacles are . . . Ways that I am manifesting the kingdom's presence are . . .
* God is harvesting in me . . . through me . . .

PRESIDERS

* The harvest my ministry encourages is . . . discourages is . . .

DEACONS

* My daily life and ministry embodies that "the kingdom of God is at hand" when . . .

HOSPITALITY MINISTERS

* Genuine hospitality manifests how God's kingdom is at hand because . . .

MUSIC MINISTERS

* What helps my music ministry announce the presence of the kingdom within the assembly is . . . What impedes this announcement is . . .

ALTAR MINISTERS

* The harvest my service ministry makes visible is . . .

LECTORS

* I proclaim that "the kingdom of God is at hand" in my daily living when . . .

EXTRAORDINARY MINISTERS OF HOLY COMMUNION

* The eucharistic banquet manifests God's abundance. I have experienced this abundance when . . . I extend it toward others when . . .

Model Act of Penitence

Presider: In today's gospel Jesus sends forth the seventy-two disciples to minister in his name and reap the abundant harvest of the presence of the kingdom of God. As we prepare for this liturgy, let us open ourselves to God's presence and mercy . . . [pause]

Lord Jesus, your presence brings peace and healing: Lord . . .

Christ Jesus, you give us the power to further God's reign: Christ . . .

Lord Jesus, you send us forth to reap an abundant harvest: Lord . . .

Homily Points

• We reap what we sow. If we take on a task and do it only halfheartedly, the outcome will be deficient. If we sow seeds of discord, the community in which we live or work will be fragmented. In the gospel Jesus warns us that our response to his sending us out to minister must be single-minded and wholehearted.

• In the gospel God is reaping what God has sown. To reap the abundant harvest of the presence of God's kingdom, Jesus commands his disciples to take up this task without getting bogged down, sidetracked, distracted, or discouraged. Their success is dependent upon their ministering in Jesus' name and with his power.

• When we pray in the Our Father "thy kingdom come," exactly what are we praying for? Is it only for heaven? Or is the kingdom, as Jesus says in this gospel, "at hand," and what does that look like? Jesus promises this: the kingdom of God is wherever peace, healing, justice, overcoming evil, and rejoicing are. In response to Jesus' command that we disciples go forth, we must live in such a way that our words and actions assure this "abundant harvest."

Model Prayer of the Faithful

Presider: Jesus sends us forth as disciples to make present the blessings of God's kingdom. Let us pray for what we need to be faithful to this mission.

Response:

Lord, hear our prayer.

Cantor:

we pray to the Lord,

That all members of the church manifest the presence of God's kingdom through the goodness of their lives . . . [pause]

That all peoples live in the justice and peace of God's kingdom . . . [pause]

That the sick and those in need of healing be touched by the presence of Christ . . . [pause]

That each of us, on this day when we celebrate the founding of our nation, further by the way we live the ideals of freedom and dignity for all . . . [pause]

Presider: God of abundance, you give us all good things in order that your kingdom may be firmly established: hear these our prayers that one day we might share in your everlasting kingdom of heaven. We pray through Jesus Christ our Lord. **Amen.**

OPENING PRAYER

Let us pray

Pause for silent prayer

Father,
through the obedience of Jesus,
your servant and your Son,
you raised a fallen world.
Free us from sin
and bring us the joy that lasts for ever.

We ask this through our Lord Jesus Christ,
    your Son,
who lives and reigns with you and the
        Holy Spirit,
one God, for ever and ever. **Amen.**

FIRST READING
Isa 66:10-14c

Thus says the LORD:
Rejoice with Jerusalem and be glad
        because of her,
    all you who love her;
exult, exult with her,
    all you who were mourning over her!
Oh, that you may suck fully
    of the milk of her comfort,
that you may nurse with delight
    at her abundant breasts!
    For thus says the LORD:
Lo, I will spread prosperity over Jerusalem
        like a river,
    and the wealth of the nations like an
        overflowing torrent.
As nurslings, you shall be carried in her
        arms,
    and fondled in her lap;
as a mother comforts her child,
    so will I comfort you;
    in Jerusalem you shall find your
        comfort.

When you see this, your heart shall rejoice
    and your bodies flourish like the grass;
the LORD's power shall be known to his
    servants.

RESPONSORIAL PSALM

Ps 66:1-3, 4-5, 6-7, 16, 20

R⁊. (1) Let all the earth cry out to God with joy.

Shout joyfully to God, all the earth,
    sing praise to the glory of his name;
    proclaim his glorious praise.
Say to God, "How tremendous are your
    deeds!"

R⁊. Let all the earth cry out to God with joy.

"Let all on earth worship and sing praise
    to you,
    sing praise to your name!"
Come and see the works of God,
    his tremendous deeds among the
    children of Adam.

R⁊. Let all the earth cry out to God with joy.

He has changed the sea into dry land;
    through the river they passed on foot.
Therefore let us rejoice in him.
    He rules by his might forever.

R⁊. Let all the earth cry out to God with joy.

Hear now, all you who fear God,
    while I declare what he has done for me.
Blessed be God who refused me not
    my prayer or his kindness!

R⁊. Let all the earth cry out to God with joy.

SECOND READING

Gal 6:14-18

Brothers and sisters:
May I never boast except in the cross of
    our Lord Jesus Christ,
    through which the world has been
        crucified to me,
    and I to the world.
For neither does circumcision mean
    anything, nor does uncircumcision,
    but only a new creation.
Peace and mercy be to all who follow this
    rule
    and to the Israel of God.

From now on, let no one make troubles
    for me;
    for I bear the marks of Jesus on my
    body.

The grace of our Lord Jesus Christ be
    with your spirit,
    brothers and sisters. Amen.

About Liturgy

July 4th: This Sunday is July 4th and there is always a pastoral temptation on such days to blend the Sunday liturgy with the national holiday. Good liturgical planning would enable the Sunday liturgy to take precedence but still acknowledge the holiday. For example, the last petition in the model prayer of the faithful takes into consideration the holiday. Some comments might be made in the presider's introduction. There is a proper Mass for July 4th given in the US Sacramentary, but it may not replace the proper Mass for this Sunday.

Choosing the longer or shorter form of a reading: Sometimes the Lectionary offers a longer or shorter form of a reading, and which to use is left to the pastoral discretion of liturgy planners. It is not good to assume that the shorter reading is always best; often it is the longer reading that fills out and completes an important message of the Liturgy of the Word.

In the case of the gospel for this Sunday, for example, the longer form adds that, as disciples sent on mission, we act in Jesus' name (not our own), with Jesus' power (not our own), and are given eschatological reward (our names are "written in heaven").

When would one use the shorter form? Some pastoral situations (for example, in a children's Liturgy of the Word) might demand simpler readings. Or when the specific point that is being developed in the homily and carried through the prayer of the faithful does not benefit from the extra Scripture verses. The point is, choices must be made deliberately, carefully, and with good reason.

About Liturgical Music

Hymn suggestion: Because of its origins, "Battle Hymn of the Republic"/"Mine Eyes Have Seen the Glory" is generally considered more a patriotic song than a religious hymn. But its text heralds more than national victory over enemies (in this case the Union army over the Confederacy). On a deeper, eschatological level the text celebrates the ultimate victory of the kingdom of God over all opposing forces. Furthermore, the fourth verse lays down the ultimate challenge of discipleship: that we give our lives that this kingdom come. In light of its theology this hymn connects well, then, with this Sunday's gospel and would make an appropriate recessional song. The hymn needs to be used cautiously, however. An assembly that does not grasp its eschatological meaning will sing it only as a patriotic hymn celebrating July 4th. It is important that they understand this hymn is not a battle cry for national victory in war but a testimony that the kingdom of God will triumph no matter what forces vie against it. To this end it might be wise to run a blurb in the bulletin explaining the hymn's deeper religious meaning and its connection with this Sunday's gospel.

JULY 4, 2010
FOURTEENTH SUNDAY
IN ORDINARY TIME

SPIRITUALITY

GOSPEL ACCLAMATION
cf. John 6:63c, 68c

Ry. Alleluia, alleluia.
Your words, Lord, are Spirit
and life;
you have the words of
everlasting life.
Ry. Alleluia, alleluia.

Gospel
Luke 10:25-37; L105C

There was a scholar of
the law who stood
up to test Jesus and said,
"Teacher, what must I do to inherit
eternal life?"
Jesus said to him, "What is written in
the law?
How do you read it?"
He said in reply,
"You shall love the Lord, your God,
with all your heart,
with all your being,
with all your strength,
and with all your mind,
and your neighbor as
yourself. "
He replied to him, "You have
answered correctly;
do this and you will live."

But because he wished to justify
himself, he said to Jesus,
"And who is my neighbor?"
Jesus replied,
"A man fell victim to robbers
as he went down from Jerusalem to
Jericho.
They stripped and beat him and went
off leaving him half-dead.
A priest happened to be going down
that road,
but when he saw him, he passed by
on the opposite side.
Likewise a Levite came to the place,
and when he saw him, he passed by
on the opposite side.

Continued in Appendix A, p. 304.

Reflecting on the Gospel

"How far is it to the moon?" children like to ask. We could answer with a specific number of miles (average distance of about 238,600 miles), which makes the moon seem far, far away. But at a time when astronauts have been to the moon and even brought back lunar rocks for us to see, this same moon doesn't seem quite so very far away. For many things the question of "how far?" is relative. Today's gospel raises the same question about love, but there is nothing relative about how far we must go in our loving. We must go the distance.

Jesus' huge commandment of love is not impossibly far beyond us, because his own life manifests concretely here and now how to live loving relationships with others. At first glance the gospel this Sunday is about keeping the two great commandments—love of God and neighbor. By answering the lawyer's question with a parable, Jesus shows us a more expansive understanding: that of giving up personal gain for the good of another. Jesus teaches us how far we must go in loving others.

The lawyer puts an important question to Jesus, but it is insincere because he is really posing the question "to test" him. Jesus takes his question at face value and gives a right and all-embracing answer about how we "inherit eternal life." We must make love of God and neighbor the guiding focus of our lives here and now. The Good Samaritan parable admirably and clearly illustrates this kind of love. Our challenge: to go *this far* in our loving. "This far" has no limits, as Jesus himself illustrated by his own life. He loved, even to dying for us out of that love. Our loving one another must go this far, too. This kind of boundless love redefines who our neighbor is (everyone in need) and sets no limits on our time or care for others. Further, we show our love for God "with all [our] heart[s]" precisely when we love our neighbor "this far."

Ironically, the way we inherit eternal life (to go back to the lawyer's first question) is by dying to self for the sake of another. The Samaritan in the parable isn't moved to help the stricken traveler because of a commandment but because he was a person of loving compassion and mercy—he illustrates unbounded love. This is the law written within our hearts (see first reading)—not details about keeping specific commandments but a positive regard for the other that arises out of genuine love. "This far" must be as wide as our universe and embrace all God's beloved. Only by going "this far" can we truly be neighbor. Only by going "this far" can love truly become the guiding force in our lives. Only by going "this far" can we, like God, be defined as love.

Living the Paschal Mystery

In our society and church today we probably need to become more aware of the value of keeping laws. Our reflection does alert us to the fact that simply keeping laws and commandments isn't enough. All our actions must be directed to the good of others. Keeping laws promotes good order in any community; doing good for others promotes right relationships in those same communities.

Law is something external to us, rather easily measured. Mercy and compassion are internal to us and can be measured only in terms of the good we actually do for others. Laws are internalized—written in our hearts—when they are kept for the sake of others. We are to do as the Samaritan in the parable: let the law of love and compassion guide us and gain for us eternal life.

Focusing the gospel

Key words and phrases: test Jesus, love . . . God . . . neighbor, compassion, Go and do likewise

To the point: The lawyer puts an important question to Jesus, but it is insincere because he is really posing the question "to test" him. Jesus takes his question at face value and gives a right and all-embracing answer about how we "inherit eternal life." We must make love of God and neighbor the guiding focus of our lives here and now. The Good Samaritan parable illustrates this kind of love. Our challenge: to go *this far* in our loving.

Connecting the Gospel

to the first reading: God's law "is not too mysterious and remote" for us—it is "already in [our] mouths and in [our] hearts." In the gospel the lawyer proves the truth of these words of Moses when he readily quotes the law. Jesus, echoing Moses, urges the lawyer to do what he already knows: "carry it out."

to our experience: In our legal culture we are very aware that law cannot legislate love or compassion. Yet loving God and others and acting compassionately *are* God's law.

Connecting the Responsorial Psalm

to the readings: At first glance the verses of Psalm 69 used for this responsorial psalm seem unrelated to either the first reading or the gospel. But further reflection reveals a rich and rewarding connection.

In the first reading Moses counsels the people that the commandments are not beyond them but within them. In the gospel Jesus teaches that the commandments to love God and neighbor are not hazy but clear and applicable: to love God means to love the immediate neighbor in need. Psalm 69 reminds us that whenever we have been in need God has responded without hesitation. We know God's law of love because we have experienced God's loving us—directly and personally. And we know who the neighbor in need is because we have been that neighbor. It is this knowledge that fills our hearts and inspires us to act compassionately toward others. Psalm 69 grounds our ability to love in the One who has first loved us.

to psalmist preparation: In the responsorial psalm you exhort the assembly to turn to God in their need. In this you are a beacon of hope, for you reveal they are saved not because of their strength but because of God's mercy. They have only to ask and God will respond with the gift of life. In what ways do you turn to God when you are in need? In what ways has God responded?

ASSEMBLY & FAITH-SHARING GROUPS

- What I find challenging about Jesus' reply to "who is my neighbor?" is . . . What is comforting to me is . . .
- In loving God, I have gone this far . . . In loving my neighbor I have gone this far . . .
- In light of this parable, I [my parish] must "go and do" . . .

PRESIDERS

- Times when I have tried to "test" Jesus or "justify" myself to him were . . . The way Jesus responded to me was . . . What this teaches me about ministry is . . .

DEACONS

- The Samaritan was "moved" not by the Law but by compassion. In my ministry I am moved by . . .

HOSPITALITY MINISTERS

- Times when my hospitality was merely a formality are . . . The difference in my hospitality when I embody compassion is . . .

MUSIC MINISTERS

- My music ministry enables me to love God by . . . love my neighbor by . . .

ALTAR MINISTERS

- Serving others is forming me into a "good Samaritan" because . . .

LECTORS

- The word that is "very near" me and that Jesus is asking me to "carry" out (first reading) is . . .

EXTRAORDINARY MINISTERS OF HOLY COMMUNION

- Looking at my daily life, my answer to "who is my neighbor?" has been . . . and is reflected in my Communion ministry in that . . .

Model Act of Penitence

Presider: The Good Samaritan is a familiar parable reminding us to love and care for each other. As we prepare this liturgy, let us open ourselves to God's love and care for us . . . [pause]

Lord Jesus, you are the love of the Father: Lord . . .

Christ Jesus, you are compassionate and merciful: Christ . . .

Lord Jesus, you are our teacher and guide: Lord . . .

Homily Points

• We live with all kinds of boundaries and limits, some of them necessary and healthy, some of them prejudicial and harmful. For example, people with highly contagious diseases are quarantined; all too many of our neighborhoods are still virtually segregated. While these boundaries might make us feel safe and protected, they also separate us from one another and limit our capacity to love.

• In the Good Samaritan parable Jesus challenges the boundaries we place between ourselves and certain other people. Furthermore, Jesus challenges us with more than the words of this parable: his very life and ministry incarnated love and compassion. How often did Jesus touch lepers, speak with women, eat with sinners, embrace little children? How far did Jesus go in expressing his love for us? To the limits of giving his very life.

• The commandment to love our neighbor is "not up in the sky" nor "is it across the sea," but it is "something very near to you" (first reading). We see it incarnated in the unselfish attentiveness of parents to a sick child, in the vigil a spouse keeps at the bedside of a dying partner, in the sensitivity of hospitality ministers at church who reach out to make strangers feel at home among us. In these ways we see faithful disciples of Jesus express that love is not distant but near, not pie-in-the-sky but down-to-earth and practical, not limited to the comfortable or familiar but all-inclusive and expansive.

Model Prayer of the Faithful

Presider: Our God is compassionate and merciful and so surely hears the prayers of those who cry out in need.

Response:

Lord, hear our prayer.

Cantor:

we pray to the Lord,

That all members of the church model love of God and neighbor . . . [pause]

That all peoples remove boundaries that separate . . . [pause]

That those who are downtrodden or in need be treated with compassion and mercy . . . [pause]

That we deepen our love of others as the guiding focus of our lives . . . [pause]

Presider: Loving God, you hear the prayers of those who cry out to you: hear us today that one day we might enjoy our eternal inheritance with you in everlasting joy. We ask this through Christ our Lord. **Amen.**

OPENING PRAYER

Let us pray

Pause for silent prayer

God our Father,
your light of truth
guides us to the way of Christ.
May all who follow him
reject what is contrary to the gospel.

We ask this through our Lord Jesus Christ,
    your Son,
who lives and reigns with you and the
    Holy Spirit,
one God, for ever and ever. **Amen.**

FIRST READING
Deut 30:10-14

Moses said to the people:
    "If only you would heed the voice of the
        LORD, your God,
    and keep his commandments and
        statutes
    that are written in this book of the law,
    when you return to the LORD, your God,
    with all your heart and all your soul.

"For this command that I enjoin on you
        today
    is not too mysterious and remote for
        you.
It is not up in the sky, that you should say,
    'Who will go up in the sky to get it for
        us
    and tell us of it, that we may carry it
        out?'
Nor is it across the sea, that you should
        say,
    'Who will cross the sea to get it for us
    and tell us of it, that we may carry it
        out?'
No, it is something very near to you,
    already in your mouths and in your
        hearts;
    you have only to carry it out."

RESPONSORIAL PSALM
Ps 69:14, 17, 30-31, 33-34, 36, 37

℟. (cf. 33) Turn to the Lord in your need, and you will live.

I pray to you, O LORD,
    for the time of your favor, O God!
In your great kindness answer me
    with your constant help.
Answer me, O LORD, for bounteous is your
        kindness:
    in your great mercy turn toward me.

℟. Turn to the Lord in your need, and you will live.

I am afflicted and in pain;
    let your saving help, O God, protect me.
I will praise the name of God in song,
    and I will glorify him with
        thanksgiving.

R⁊. Turn to the Lord in your need, and you
will live.

"See, you lowly ones, and be glad;
    you who seek God, may your hearts
        revive!
For the LORD hears the poor,
    and his own who are in bonds he spurns
        not."

R⁊. Turn to the Lord in your need, and you
will live.

For God will save Zion
    and rebuild the cities of Judah.
The descendants of his servants shall
        inherit it,
    and those who love his name shall
        inhabit it.

R⁊. Turn to the Lord in your need, and you
will live.

OR

RESPONSORIAL PSALM
Ps 19:8, 9, 10, 11

See Appendix A, p. 304.

SECOND READING
Col 1:15-20

Christ Jesus is the image of the invisible
        God,
    the firstborn of all creation.
For in him were created all things in
        heaven and on earth,
    the visible and the invisible,
    whether thrones or dominions or
        principalities or powers;
    all things were created through him and
        for him.
He is before all things,
    and in him all things hold together.
He is the head of the body, the church.
He is the beginning, the firstborn from the
        dead,
    that in all things he himself might be
        preeminent.
For in him all the fullness was pleased to
        dwell,
    and through him to reconcile all things
        for him,
    making peace by the blood of his cross
    through him, whether those on earth or
        those in heaven.

About Liturgy

Choice of responsorial psalm: This Sunday the Lectionary gives us two choices for a responsorial psalm, and which one is chosen for use will depend upon the approach taken to the readings and gospel. The verses selected from Psalm 69 are a better choice for the approach we have taken in these reflections because they focus on God's mercy as a model for our own mercy. The verses selected from Psalm 19 focus more on the preciousness of the law itself and how the law brings life.

Liturgical law: enslavement or freedom? Some liturgists, liturgy committees, and segments of the church get so caught up in keeping every detail of liturgical law that the celebration of liturgy is robbed of any focus on our love and worship of God and concern for others. We are careful to pay attention to liturgical laws but equally careful that our liturgies unfold as prayer and worship, as making present the paschal mystery, as celebrations of God's word and sacrament that transform us into being better members of Christ's Body who live with compassion and mercy toward all. If our adherence to liturgical law does not aid in this transformation, then we have missed its point. We have made the law external rubrics to be followed for their own sake rather than something written in our hearts. This skews the real purpose of liturgical law—to ensure that liturgy remains the liturgy of the whole church making present Christ's mystery, and not just an idiosyncratic ritual of a few.

About Liturgical Music

Role of the responsorial psalm, part 1: One way to look at the role of the responsorial psalm is to see it as a bridge between the first reading and the gospel. The image of a bridge conveys both movement forward and connectedness, and accords with the principle that the climax of the Liturgy of the Word is the gospel for which the preceding elements prepare us (see the Introduction to the Lectionary for Mass, no. 13).

The movement forward aspect of the bridge metaphor implies that we begin the Liturgy of the Word in one place and cross over to another. There is a journey here. The connectedness aspect of the metaphor indicates that the beginning and ending of this journey are related. The starting point and the ending point form opposing shorelines. What we cross over in between varies; sometimes it is moving water, sometimes it is a valley bursting with grain, and sometimes it is a dry gulch or even a frighteningly deep canyon.

The crossing over is not a journey through time from the Old Testament to the New Testament but a journey of transformation. We begin the Liturgy of the Word standing on the threshold of a new moment of encounter with the word of God, and we cross over to a new level of self-understanding as Body of Christ. The structural element that carries us from one way of being to another is the responsorial psalm.

✝ SPIRITUALITY

GOSPEL ACCLAMATION
cf. Luke 8:15

R. Alleluia, alleluia.
Blessed are they who have kept the word with a
  generous heart
and yield a harvest through perseverance.
R. Alleluia, alleluia.

Gospel

Luke 10:38-42; L108C

**Jesus entered a village
  where a woman whose name was
    Martha welcomed him.
She had a sister named Mary
  who sat beside the Lord at his feet
    listening to him speak.
Martha, burdened with much serving,
    came to him and said,
"Lord, do you not care
  that my sister has left me by myself
    to do the serving?
Tell her to help me."
The Lord said to her in reply,
  "Martha, Martha, you are anxious
    and worried about many things.
There is need of only one thing.
Mary has chosen the better part
  and it will not be taken from her."**

Reflecting on the Gospel

Hearing this familiar gospel story might lead us to jump to a hasty, either-or kind of interpretation: Mary's "better part" of listening, being taught, reflecting is a better choice than taking care of the usual daily chores! Jesus couldn't have been negating hospitality and taking care of the needs of others, however. After all, he had to eat, too! Perhaps a less hasty and more reflective interpretation of this gospel lies in another, more integrative direction: that "listening" must be more than sitting at Jesus' feet—it includes seeing and hearing him in all the activities and circumstances of life. Sometimes we listen when we are being taught. Sometimes we listen when we are serving. The point is, we must listen: to Jesus, to each other.

What is each of the people in the gospel story doing? Martha is serving; Mary is listening; Jesus is teaching. While Jesus says that Mary has the "better part," this doesn't necessarily mean that listening to Jesus is either the only or the easier part. Listening to Jesus with a heart truly able to hear is difficult, indeed. Listening to Jesus is the "better part" only when it leads us to serve and teach as Jesus himself did. The effectiveness of our serving (and teaching, being disciples, caring for others, fulfilling our daily duties) is determined by the way we listen—to others, to Jesus through others.

The gospel is about hosts and guest and hospitality, but Jesus puts an unparalleled twist on the notion of hospitality. Martha's "hospitality" was made edgy because of her becoming burdened with the cooking and serving and focusing only on that, losing sight of Jesus. Martha is settling to be only a servant (and complaining about it at that!), while Jesus is looking for disciples. Mary's hospitality was more gracious than Martha's because she focused her attention on Jesus: "sat beside the Lord at his feet listening to him." The surprise is that Jesus affirms that the "better part" is to listen, the stance of a disciple. The "better part" is to be disciple, attuned to the Master!

A welcoming hospitality implies an "at-homeness" and belonging that parallels the unique relationship of disciple to Master. This kind of discipleship hospitality always brings new life. The "better part" Jesus promises is not just listening and being a disciple, but it is also sharing the new life that Jesus offers with others. Discipleship and listening cannot be separated. Neither can listening and serving.

Living the Paschal Mystery

Before we can carry on the mission of Jesus, we must become disciples by sitting at the feet of Jesus listening to him. In our time, we can hardly invite Jesus over for dinner. But there are ways that Jesus is present to us if we take the time to be present to him.

We usually address living the paschal mystery in terms of how we die to ourselves in our everyday living. This gospel suggests a radically different—and complementary—way of living the paschal mystery: taking the time to listen to Jesus. Practically speaking, this means being attentive to the proclamation of the Scriptures (especially the gospel) during Mass. It means taking the time to be with Jesus in prayer—not just saying prayers but being quiet and listening to how Jesus speaks to our hearts. It means hearing Jesus in the cry of another for help. There is truly a great deal of self-sacrificing in letting go of our busyness in order to listen to Jesus and see him in all circumstances of our daily living!

Focusing the gospel

Key words and phrases: burdened with much serving, listening to him, The Lord said, better part

To the point: What is each of the people in the gospel story doing? Martha is serving; Mary is listening; Jesus is teaching. While Jesus says that Mary has the "better part," this doesn't necessarily mean that listening to Jesus is either the only or the easier part. Listening to Jesus with a heart truly able to hear is difficult, indeed. Listening to Jesus is the "better part" only when it leads us to serve and teach as Jesus himself did.

Connecting the Gospel

to the first reading: The first reading cautions us not to conclude that Mary's part, though called "better" by Jesus, is the only way to be attentive to God. Abraham greets the strangers and serves them, and for these hospitable actions he is promised a son.

to our experience: We tend to be "either-or" in our thinking. This is also how we tend to interpret this gospel. Jesus is not saying hospitality and serving are unimportant; he is inviting us to reflect on how and when we listen to him.

Connecting the Responsorial Psalm

to the readings: Psalm 15 was part of a ritual followed whenever a person wished to gain admittance to the temple. Because the temple was God's dwelling, one could not enter without permission. Instead, the person was questioned at the gate by a priest who would ask, "Who, Lord, may dwell in your tent?" (v. 1 of the psalm, omitted in the Lectionary). The person then answered by reciting the subsequent verses of Psalm 15: one who does justice, thinks truth, slanders not, etc. This ritual expressed Israel's understanding that entrance into God's dwelling place required right living.

In the first reading Abraham stands as a type of the right living that grants entrance into the divine presence. He receives strangers with hospitality and is blessed for it. That he responds so immediately to their needs, however, indicates he was already living "in the presence of the Lord" (psalm refrain). Such was the consistent orientation of his life. This is the orientation to which the psalm calls us and to which Jesus calls us when he praises Mary's choice of the "better part" in the gospel. May our central desire be to live in the presence of God and may that presence be the source of our manner of living.

to psalmist preparation: In preparing to sing this responsorial psalm, spend some time reflecting on how you choose to live in the presence of God and how that choice shapes your manner of living. When and how do you take time to be with God? How, in concrete ways, do you let God's presence challenge your living?

**ASSEMBLY &
FAITH-SHARING GROUPS**

- When entertaining guests I am more like Martha or Mary . . . because . . .
- When attending to my relationship with God, I am more like Martha or Mary . . . because . . .
- I understand the "better part" chosen by Mary to mean . . . For me to embrace this teaching of Jesus more deeply I need to . . .

PRESIDERS

- My homilies are more effective when I listen to . . .

DEACONS

- My reason for being "burdened with much serving" is . . . The "one thing" that Jesus is asking of me is . . .

HOSPITALITY MINISTERS

- By my hospitality ministry, I serve when . . . I listen when . . . I teach when . . .

MUSIC MINISTERS

- The "better part" of my music ministry is . . .

ALTAR MINISTERS

- While tending to the "many things" necessary in serving others, the way I keep in mind the Guest for whom I serve is . . .

LECTORS

- I listen to God's word in my daily life in these ways . . . This helps my proclamation in that . . .

**EXTRAORDINARY MINISTERS
OF HOLY COMMUNION**

- At Eucharist Christ is the Host, Guest, and Food. I go to the Host anticipating . . . I prepare for the Guest by . . . The Food nourishes me for . . .

Model Act of Penitence

Presider: Today's gospel shows us Mary busy about listening to Jesus while Martha remains busy about serving him. Let us open our hearts to listen to God's word and to serve God by our obedience to that word . . . [pause]

Lord Jesus, you are the Guest in our hearts: Lord . . .

Christ Jesus, you are the One who speaks and we listen: Christ . . .

Lord Jesus, you are the Teacher who calls us to discipleship: Lord . . .

Homily Points

• It's very unsatisfying when we are invited to dinner and the hosts are so concerned with serving us a perfect meal that they neglect to make us feel at home through their hospitality, listening, and care. In the gospel Jesus upbraids Martha for being so anxious about serving that she seems not only to neglect him but also to be asking that Mary neglect him. Good hosts, no matter how busy with the details of a meal, never lose sight of their guests.

• The issue here isn't with serving; after all, Jesus calls us to service over and over in the gospels. The real issue is that the service disciples offer must flow from being truly attentive to the person of Jesus—to his words, his teachings, his values, his manner of receiving and caring for others. Good disciples, no matter how busy with the demands of discipleship, never lose sight of Jesus.

• Our service must be done with the stance of Mary, with contemplative hearts focused on Jesus. Such contemplation—the "better part"— will lead us to acts of service, but it will be service truly modeled on the Master. Listening to Jesus, for example, will lead us to listen to one another more openly; heeding Jesus' words will open us to truth spoken by all sorts of people; sitting at the feet of Jesus will ready us to jump up and serve whoever is in need.

Model Prayer of the Faithful

Presider: God always welcomes us and hears our prayers. Let us pray for the needs of our church and world.

Response:

Lord, hear our prayer.

Cantor:

we pray to the Lord,

That all members of the church listen to Jesus with open hearts . . . [pause]

That all peoples of the world share in the hospitality of God's generosity . . . [pause]

That those who are burdened with the cares of life might take time to be attentive to God's presence . . . [pause]

That each of us here never lose sight of Jesus as the center of our lives . . . [pause]

Presider: Gracious God, you call us to listen to Jesus and serve him in one another: hear our prayers that we might enjoy everlasting life with you. We ask this through Christ our Lord. **Amen.**

ALTERNATIVE OPENING PRAYER
Let us pray

Pause for silent prayer

Father,
let the gift of your life
continue to grow in us,
drawing us from death to faith, hope, and
    love.
Keep us alive in Christ Jesus.
Keep us watchful in prayer
and true to his teaching
till your glory is revealed in us.

Grant this through Christ our Lord.
    Amen.

FIRST READING
Gen 18:1-10a

The LORD appeared to Abraham by the
        terebinth of Mamre,
    as he sat in the entrance of his tent,
    while the day was growing hot.
Looking up, Abraham saw three men
        standing nearby.
When he saw them, he ran from the
        entrance of the tent to greet them;
    and bowing to the ground, he said:
    "Sir, if I may ask you this favor,
    please do not go on past your servant.
Let some water be brought, that you may
        bathe your feet,
    and then rest yourselves under the tree.
Now that you have come this close to your
        servant,
    let me bring you a little food, that you
        may refresh yourselves;
    and afterward you may go on your
        way."
The men replied, "Very well, do as you
        have said."

Abraham hastened into the tent and told
        Sarah,
    "Quick, three measures of fine flour!
        Knead it and make rolls."
He ran to the herd, picked out a tender,
        choice steer,
    and gave it to a servant, who quickly
        prepared it.
Then Abraham got some curds and milk,
    as well as the steer that had been
        prepared,
    and set these before the three men;
    and he waited on them under the tree
        while they ate.

They asked Abraham, "Where is your wife
        Sarah?"
He replied, "There in the tent."
One of them said, "I will surely return to
        you about this time next year,
    and Sarah will then have a son."

RESPONSORIAL PSALM

Ps 15:2-3, 3-4, 5

℞. (1a) He who does justice will live in the presence of the Lord.

One who walks blamelessly and does
    justice;
  who thinks the truth in his heart
  and slanders not with his tongue.

℞. He who does justice will live in the presence of the Lord.

Who harms not his fellow man,
  nor takes up a reproach against his
    neighbor;
by whom the reprobate is despised,
  while he honors those who fear the
    LORD.

℞. He who does justice will live in the presence of the Lord.

Who lends not his money at usury
  and accepts no bribe against the
    innocent.
One who does these things
  shall never be disturbed.

℞. He who does justice will live in the presence of the Lord.

SECOND READING

Col 1:24-28

Brothers and sisters:
Now I rejoice in my sufferings for your
    sake,
  and in my flesh I am filling up
  what is lacking in the afflictions of
    Christ
  on behalf of his body, which is the
    church,
  of which I am a minister
  in accordance with God's stewardship
    given to me
  to bring to completion for you the word
    of God,
  the mystery hidden from ages and from
    generations past.
But now it has been manifested to his holy
    ones,
  to whom God chose to make known the
    riches of the glory
  of this mystery among the Gentiles;
  it is Christ in you, the hope for glory.
It is he whom we proclaim,
  admonishing everyone and teaching
    everyone with all wisdom,
  that we may present everyone perfect
    in Christ.

About Liturgy

Hospitality ministers: Most parishes and liturgical communities have hospitality ministers—whether they are called that or greeters or ushers or some combination of all these. Although we Catholics could certainly take some lessons in church hospitality from our Protestant brothers and sisters (it is only in recent church renovations that we are providing for such simple human necessities as restrooms and cloakrooms!), we must also take care that our hospitality ministry doesn't limit what the gospel for this Sunday implies.

Hospitality at church is far more than a pleasant greeting and welcome (although surely these are important aspects of the ministry). Hospitality ministers must understand themselves first of all as disciples and, like Mary in the gospel, must assume in their lives and ministry a listening stance toward Jesus. The ministry points to Christ's presence in the community, emphasizes all are welcome because all are members of the Body of Christ, and helps the assembling church members prepare to *listen* to Jesus speak to their hearts during the liturgy. Hospitality ministry is more than a practical convenience or a social nicety; it is an expression of Jesus' ministry that recognizes the other's dignity as members of the Body of Christ.

About Liturgical Music

Role of the responsorial psalm, part 2: How does the responsorial psalm act as bridge between the first reading and the gospel? How does the psalm help us surrender to the transformation the gospel calls for? Part of what happens is that the movement within the psalm text itself—its internal changes of mood, focus, content, and metaphor—parallel the movement meant to take place within us as we respond to the word of God. There is an integral relationship between the process of transformation and conversion within the heart, mind, and behavior of the original psalmist as he or she was responding to the actions of God and the change that takes place within us as we pray that psalm within the context of this Liturgy of the Word. One of the implications here is that the role of the cantor is very important. The cantor must personally embody the transformation unfolding in the psalm and call us to that transformation. This is no small task and certainly one that involves far more than the singing of a nice song.

Each week "Connecting the Responsorial Psalm to the readings" (on the second page for each Sunday or solemnity) explores the relationship between the psalm and the readings of the day. Sometimes the connection is obvious, other times it is not so clear, but it is always there. Identifying this connection and reflecting on it deepens our appreciation of the role of the psalm. Only then can we sing it with understanding and surrender to its transformative power.

✢ SPIRITUALITY

GOSPEL ACCLAMATION
Rom 8:15bc

R̸. Alleluia, alleluia.
You have received a Spirit of adoption,
through which we cry, Abba, Father.
R̸. Alleluia, alleluia.

Gospel
Luke 11:1-13; L111C

Jesus was praying in a certain place,
  and when he had finished,
  one of his disciples said to him,
  "Lord, teach us to pray just as John
    taught his disciples."
He said to them, "When you pray, say:
  Father, hallowed be your name,
  your kingdom come.
  Give us each day our daily bread
  and forgive us our sins
  for we ourselves forgive everyone in
    debt to us,
  and do not subject us to the final
    test."

And he said to them, "Suppose one of
  you has a friend
to whom he goes at midnight and
  says,
'Friend, lend me three loaves of
  bread,
for a friend of mine has arrived at
  my house from a journey
and I have nothing to offer him,'
and he says in reply from within,
'Do not bother me; the door has
  already been locked
and my children and I are already in
  bed.
I cannot get up to give you anything.'
I tell you,
  if he does not get up to give the
    visitor the loaves
  because of their friendship,
  he will get up to give him whatever
    he needs
  because of his persistence.

Continued in Appendix A, p. 305.

Reflecting on the Gospel

Little children can be amazingly persistent about some things. If they want a new toy, they ask, and ask, and ask—often to the point of greatly annoying the parents. They might be shown how to stack up building blocks, then sit for hours doing it over and over again. They try over and over again to learn to tie their shoe laces and keep at it until they succeed. Children (and we) learn through persistence. They (and we) achieve through persistence. In fact, per-

sistence is something that can serve us throughout our whole lives. The important thing to remember, though, is that the point isn't the persistence itself; the point is gaining what is desired. The first reading and gospel this Sunday each speaks of persistence. In both readings what is important is not the persistence but the result: fruitful prayer. The readings focus on where prayer takes us—the thrust of prayer is life, which ultimately leads to eternal life.

In this gospel Jesus "teach[es] us to pray." Most important, he teaches us to whom we pray: God who is a generous and caring Father. He also teaches us for what we should pray: not just for immediate needs ("daily bread") but, more important, for ultimate needs: the furthering of God's kingdom, the gift of forgiveness, and protection from anything that would take us from God. It is persistence in prayer that brings us deeper into our relationship with God and opens us to receive these "good gifts" God offers us. It is persistence in prayer that establishes and maintains the kind of relationship with God that assures us of the ultimate goal of life: eternal happiness with our divine Lover.

The two examples that Jesus uses (neighborly friendship and father-son kinship) reveal that what is always granted through prayer is deeper relationship with God and others. Jesus teaches us that the One to whom we pray is our "Father" whose love and care for us is unlimited. This deeply intimate and personal relationship with God inspires in us the confidence ("how much more . . .") to pray with "persistence" and the realization that what we pray for is not as important as the fact that we address God in such intimate terms. The prayer always deepens our relationship with God and this is already an answer to what we need.

Living the Paschal Mystery

There is nothing wrong with praying for specific needs; after all, we do it at every Mass at the prayer of the faithful, not to mention our own personal and daily prayers of petition. This gospel challenges us to go beyond specific needs and get the larger picture, to focus on the gifts God offers us always in prayer, and often in surprising and unexpected ways. What inspires confidence in us is not whether God gives us what we specifically ask for in prayer; our confidence comes from the Spirit who dwells within and establishes a most intimate relationship between God and us—shared life.

Unlike small children who seem to have a capacity to stay endlessly with some tasks, most of us need to develop a habit of daily prayer. With such busy schedules, this can be difficult. Choosing a specific time and being persistent about honoring that time for prayer helps.

Focusing the gospel

Key words and phrases: Father, kingdom come, daily bread, forgive, do not subject us, persistence, good gifts, Father in heaven

To the point: In this gospel Jesus "teach[es] us to pray." Most important, he teaches us to whom we pray: God who is a generous and caring Father. He also teaches us for what we should pray: not just for immediate needs ("daily bread") but, more important, for ultimate needs: the furthering of God's kingdom, the gift of forgiveness, and protection from anything that would take us from God. It is persistence in prayer that brings us deeper into our relationship with God and opens us to receive these "good gifts" God offers us.

Connecting the Gospel

to the first reading: Abraham's persistence may not have obtained the ultimate deliverance of Sodom and Gomorrah, but it did reveal to Abraham something about God: the One who is compassionate and just.

to our experience: We often use prayer as an opportunity to tell God what we need. Prayer is also the opportunity God takes to reveal to us who God is (Father) and how God acts toward us (with compassion and care).

Connecting the Responsorial Psalm

to the readings: In the gospel Jesus responds on several levels to the disciples' request that he show them how to pray: he teaches them the Our Father, he encourages them to be persistent, he subtly suggests what it is they are to pray for (the gift of the Holy Spirit), and he calls them to ground their prayer in the goodness of God who is their Father. The first reading gives us a dramatic example of such prayer. Abraham persists in his petition. He remains humble yet audacious, speaking to God directly and forcefully. Finally, what he prays for is righteous judgment and protection of the innocent. On the divine side, the story reveals that God waits for such prayer. God stands directly in front of Abraham and invites the conversation. God listens each time Abraham speaks and grants his request. Clearly this is a God who desires salvation for us and who seeks human collaboration in bringing it about.

The responsorial psalm confirms that what grounds confidence in prayer is the nature of God who is great in kindness and true to every promise. God will answer when we call; God will complete the work of salvation begun in us. We need have no hesitation to petition such a God. We need only to discern carefully for what it is we ask.

to psalmist preparation: When you sing the responsorial psalm, what the assembly hears more than the beauty of your voice is the sound of your praying. Ask Christ this week to teach you how to *pray* the psalm.

ASSEMBLY & FAITH-SHARING GROUPS

- Jesus' Our Father reveals God as . . . It discloses my deepest self as . . . It characterizes my relationship with God as . . .
- What is most comforting about praying is . . . most difficult is . . .
- The part "persistence" plays in my prayer life is . . .

PRESIDERS

- Like Abraham (see first reading), my ministry is a persistent intercession for the benefit of others when I . . .

DEACONS

- My ministry manifests the "how much more will the Father in heaven give" by . . .

HOSPITALITY MINISTERS

- My hospitality helps create an environment conducive for prayer when I . . .

MUSIC MINISTERS

- My music ministry helps me pray by . . . My music ministry is prayer when . . .

ALTAR MINISTERS

- My serving others is prayer when . . . My service aids the prayer of others by . . .

LECTORS

- The fruit of remaining persistent with God's word is . . . The way my proclamation shares that fruit with the assembly is . . .

EXTRAORDINARY MINISTERS OF HOLY COMMUNION

- The ways I give "daily bread" to my family, neighbors, coworkers, those who are infirm, etc., are . . .

Model Act of Penitence

Presider: In today's gospel the disciples ask Jesus to teach them to pray. Let us surrender ourselves to God so that we can truly pray during this liturgy and open our hearts to a God who gives us all good things . . . [pause]

Lord Jesus, you are the good Gift of the Father to us: Lord . . .

Christ Jesus, you reveal the love and compassion of the Father for us: Christ . . .

Lord Jesus, you teach us how to pray: Lord . . .

Homily Points

• There is a difference between finding and searching. For example, we can focus on finding a very specific seashell on the beach, or we can search the whole expanse of sand and allow it to yield a surprising variety of gifts. When we pray, we ought not to be so focused on specific requests that we miss the multiplicity of gifts God offers. Prayer is more about searching than finding.

• Jesus opens our hearts to the deepest possibilities of prayer: personal relationship with God as loving Father, receiving the gift of the Holy Spirit, being given many gifts for our daily needs. The words Jesus gives us in the Our Father express exactly the way Jesus himself lived and prayed: in intimate union with and trust in the Father, in furthering God's kingdom, and in surrender to God's will, which brings life.

• Prayer is more about searching for God and divine presence than about finding answers to specific needs. During our inevitable struggles with praying well, have we ever put to God the request the disciples put to Jesus: "Lord, teach us to pray"? We need only ask, and God will do so.

Model Prayer of the Faithful

Presider: Jesus taught us to pray to our loving Father, and so we confidently ask God for what we need.

Response:

Lord, hear our prayer.

Cantor:

we pray to the Lord,

That all members of the church grow through prayer in their relationship with God and each other . . . [pause]

That leaders of nations respond justly to the needs of their people . . . [pause]

That those who lack their daily bread may receive what they need . . . [pause]

That each one of us learn to pray with perseverance and seek God's will . . . [pause]

Presider: O good God, you give us all we need to come to everlasting happiness: hear these our prayers that we might be a sign of your presence to all we meet. We ask this through Christ our Lord. **Amen.**

OPENING PRAYER

Let us pray

Pause for silent prayer

God our Father and protector,
without you nothing is holy,
nothing has value.
Guide us to everlasting life
by helping us to use wisely
the blessings you have given to the world.

We ask this through our Lord Jesus Christ,
    your Son,
who lives and reigns with you and the
    Holy Spirit,
one God, for ever and ever. **Amen.**

FIRST READING
Gen 18:20-32

In those days, the LORD said: "The outcry
    against Sodom and Gomorrah is so
    great,
  and their sin so grave,
  that I must go down and see whether or
    not their actions
  fully correspond to the cry against them
    that comes to me.
I mean to find out."

While Abraham's visitors walked on
    farther toward Sodom,
  the LORD remained standing before
    Abraham.
Then Abraham drew nearer and said:
  "Will you sweep away the innocent with
    the guilty?
Suppose there were fifty innocent people
    in the city;
  would you wipe out the place, rather
    than spare it
  for the sake of the fifty innocent people
    within it?
Far be it from you to do such a thing,
    to make the innocent die with the guilty
  so that the innocent and the guilty
    would be treated alike!
Should not the judge of all the world act
    with justice?"
The LORD replied,
  "If I find fifty innocent people in the
    city of Sodom,
  I will spare the whole place for their
    sake."
Abraham spoke up again:
  "See how I am presuming to speak to
    my Lord,
  though I am but dust and ashes!
What if there are five less than fifty
    innocent people?
Will you destroy the whole city because of
    those five?"
He answered, "I will not destroy it, if I find
    forty-five there."
But Abraham persisted, saying, "What if
    only forty are found there?"

He replied, "I will forbear doing it for the
sake of the forty."
Then Abraham said, "Let not my Lord
grow impatient if I go on.
What if only thirty are found there?"
He replied, "I will forbear doing it if I can
find but thirty there."
Still Abraham went on,
"Since I have thus dared to speak to my
Lord,
what if there are no more than twenty?"
The LORD answered, "I will not destroy it,
for the sake of the twenty."
But he still persisted:
"Please, let not my Lord grow angry if I
speak up this last time.
What if there are at least ten there?"
He replied, "For the sake of those ten, I will
not destroy it."

RESPONSORIAL PSALM
Ps 138:1-2, 2-3, 6-7, 7-8

R. (3a) Lord, on the day I called for help,
you answered me.

I will give thanks to you, O LORD, with all
my heart,
    for you have heard the words of my
        mouth;
    in the presence of the angels I will sing
        your praise;
I will worship at your holy temple
    and give thanks to your name.

R. Lord, on the day I called for help, you
answered me.

Because of your kindness and your truth;
    for you have made great above all things
    your name and your promise.
When I called you answered me;
    you built up strength within me.

R. Lord, on the day I called for help, you
answered me.

The LORD is exalted, yet the lowly he sees,
    and the proud he knows from afar.
Though I walk amid distress, you preserve
    me;
    against the anger of my enemies you
        raise your hand.

R. Lord, on the day I called for help, you
answered me.

Your right hand saves me.
    The LORD will complete what he has
        done for me;
    your kindness, O LORD, endures forever;
        forsake not the work of your hands.

R. Lord, on the day I called for help, you
answered me.

SECOND READING
Col 2:12-14

See Appendix A, p. 305.

About Liturgy

Liturgy as prayer: We call liturgy a celebration, a ritual act, the communal worship of the people. We process during liturgy, sing, acclaim, proclaim. Liturgy is filled with many different kinds of activities. This Sunday's gospel challenges us to consider whether we approach liturgy as *prayer*. True, we pray the Our Father just before Communion, the prayer that Jesus taught us and we hear about in this Sunday's gospel. Since this is the prayer that Jesus taught, we rightly think of its preeminence. At the same time we cannot forget that *all* of liturgy is prayer, from the beginning sign of the cross to the concluding blessing. A prayerful attitude should mark how we celebrate liturgy.

Why is it important to insist that liturgy is prayer? An attitude of prayer keeps us focused on the relationship we share with God. It helps us realize that we celebrate liturgy not because of any power we have but because God invites us and gives us the Spirit who enables us to respond with praise and thanksgiving.

True, different kinds of prayer mark our liturgies. Sometimes we pray aloud together, such as during the responsorial psalm and the Our Father. Sometimes we are given silent time to very personally pour out our hearts to God in prayer, such as in the quiet time after the readings and after Communion. Sometimes we actively listen as another voices our prayer, such as during the presidential prayers (opening prayer, prayer over the gifts, prayer after Communion) and the eucharistic prayer. Surely our acclaiming and hymn singing is also prayer. But for all these (and other) types of prayer during Mass, the real challenge is to make the *whole Mass* the *one prayer* of the one Body of Christ.

About Liturgical Music

Role of the responsorial psalm, part 3: The primary transformation taking place in us as we respond to the Liturgy of the Word is deeper surrender to the paschal mystery. The Word issues a prophetic challenge that we be true to the ideal that stands before us in the gospel, the person of Christ. The Word reminds us that we are the Body of Christ, and our mission is to heal the sick, feed the hungry, clothe the naked, and forgive those who injure us. The Word confronts us with how far we fall short of that ideal and reassures us that God forgives this failure and continues to call us forward. What we hear in the proclamation of Scripture, then, is a continuously fresh presentation of the reality of God's faithfulness and of the ideal of faithfulness to which we are summoned in response.

When we sing the responsorial psalm, we express our surrender to the paschal mystery in song and voice. The cantor leads the surrender, embodying it in breath and melody, and mirroring through gesture the dialogue taking place between Christ and his assembled church. When we, the assembly, respond, we sacramentalize our assent, that is, we make our surrender audibly, visibly, physically apparent. In other words, we are doing far more in the responsorial psalm than merely singing a song. We are saying yes to the ideal being placed before us. Moreover, that ideal is not a set of directives but a living Person calling us to die to self that we might have new and fuller life.

✝ SPIRITUALITY

GOSPEL ACCLAMATION
Matt 5:3

℞. Alleluia, alleluia.
Blessed are the poor in spirit,
for theirs is the kingdom of heaven.
℞. Alleluia, alleluia.

Gospel

Luke 12:13-21; L114C

Someone in the crowd said to
　　Jesus,
　"Teacher, tell my brother to
　　　share the inheritance with
　　　me."
He replied to him,
　"Friend, who appointed me as
　　　your judge and arbitrator?"
Then he said to the crowd,
　"Take care to guard against all greed,
　for though one may be rich,
　one's life does not consist of
　　　possessions."

Then he told them a parable.
"There was a rich man whose land
　　　produced a bountiful harvest.
He asked himself, 'What shall I do,
　for I do not have space to store my
　　　harvest?'
And he said, 'This is what I shall do:
　I shall tear down my barns and build
　　　larger ones.
There I shall store all my grain and
　　　other goods
　and I shall say to myself, "Now as for
　　　you,
　you have so many good things stored
　　　up for many years,
　rest, eat, drink, be merry!"'
But God said to him,
　'You fool, this night your life will be
　　　demanded of you;
　and the things you have prepared, to
　　　whom will they belong?'
Thus will it be for all who store up
　　　treasure for themselves
　but are not rich in what matters to
　　　God."

Reflecting on the Gospel

More and more people are choosing to live in apartments and condos. As these kinds of dwellings become more popular, we see springing up a plethora of self-storage units. These become necessary, as smaller dwellings cannot hold what some formerly put in basements and garages. We do, indeed, store up possessions in great quantities! So, in many ways we are not totally unlike the rich man in this Sunday's gospel parable. He has enough in his present storehouses; ironically, by wanting more than he needs, he builds more and larger storehouses only to die and not enjoy his abundance anyway.

The rich man is a fool because he mistakenly thinks his future happiness is guaranteed by his possessions. Even had his life not been demanded of him, those possessions could not have bought him happiness. Jesus cautions us to "guard against" such greed and turn our attention to where our real inheritance lies: in the fullness of life God wishes to give us. How mistaken the rich man is to identify good living with material things and miss "[W]hat matters to God"!

We work hard for what we think is important to us, but we may end up with nothing because we have missed the whole point: life. Both the first reading and gospel speak of inheritance; what we struggle all our lives to learn is that life does not consist of possessions or our perceived security. Our true inheritance is not more possessions or security but life with God. The only security we truly possess is a loving relationship with God—and this is surely what matters most to God. It should matter most to us as well.

Even with all our Christian living and reflection, we still struggle with what God graciously offers us—not more possessions but fullness of life. The gospel challenges us to make all our work directed to a quality of life that has as its basis growing in our relationship with God and each other. Even our possessions and how we use them have this end, to bring us to right relationship with God and each other so that in the end we possess what really counts—God's life. God offers us what matters most—fullness of life and the secure happiness that only a share in God's life can bring.

Living the Paschal Mystery

If most of us take time to think about the way we live, we would have to admit that the pressures of everyday life tend to be our main focus. We are concerned about calendars and schedules, bills and getting ahead, sickness and health. Our lives tend to be so busy that our immediate goal is to get through another day. What would happen if we would truly take some time to think about what we possess (and where we store it all!) and what possesses us?

It takes conscious effort to ask the question, to whom do *we* belong? In some sense this is a question about priorities and putting God truly at the center of our lives. The answer must be more than an intellectual commitment to grow in our relationship with God and have God as our center. We must stop building (using) larger storage barns and begin changing the way we live so that our priorities are evident. Practically speaking, this probably means settling for fewer possessions. But with God at center, we really gain everything—fullness of life.

Focusing the gospel

Key words and phrases: inheritance, guard against all greed, one's life does not consist of possessions, what matters to God

To the point: The rich man is a fool because he mistakenly thinks his future happiness is guaranteed by his possessions. Even had his life not been demanded of him, those possessions could not have bought him happiness. Jesus cautions us to "guard against" such greed and turn our attention to where our real inheritance lies: in the fullness of life God wishes to give us. How mistaken the rich man is to identify good living with material things and miss "[W]hat matters to God"!

Connecting the Gospel

to the first reading: The first reading expresses the wisdom that the rich man in the gospel lacks. Qoheleth recognizes the vanity (fleetingness) of acquiring more and more things.

to our experience: The rich man's reality is everyone's dream: to have more than we really need. Prudently providing for our future is responsible planning. The gospel's challenge, however, is that the future is not made secure by possessions but is secured in God alone.

Connecting the Responsorial Psalm

to the readings: Psalm 90, from which this responsorial psalm is taken, contrasts the stability and steadfastness of God with the uncertainty and transience of human life. The verses used in the Lectionary express Israel's prayer that God teach them true assessment of their life and work. As the reading from Ecclesiastes indicates, they already realize hard work and physical possessions give no sure value. What is worth possessing is the kind and gracious care of God (psalm). Jesus affirms this stance when he challenges his hearers to turn from evaluating their worth based on physical possessions to evaluating it based on being "rich in what matters to God" (gospel).

It is significant that the psalm refrain is taken, not from Psalm 90, but from Psalm 95, a psalm that refers to the infidelity of Israel's ancestors during their desert exodus from slavery to the Promised Land. No matter how much God gave them (water, manna), they constantly whined that they did not have enough. The Lectionary's choice of this refrain is acknowledgment that reckoning our days and assessing our worth in God's terms is always a challenge. May this be the work God prospers in us.

to psalmist preparation: The refrain for this responsorial psalm is particularly challenging. Sometimes when you hear God's voice, your heart hardens. When do you experience this happening for yourself? How does God help you hear in spite of your resistance?

ASSEMBLY & FAITH-SHARING GROUPS

- Where I am often tempted to build "larger barns" is . . . At such times trusting in God to me means . . .
- If I knew that "this night [my] life would be demanded of [me]" I would . . .
- For me being "rich in what matters to God" means . . . My richness (or poverty) in what matters to God is revealed by . . .

PRESIDERS

- I witness to my people "what matters to God" by . . . They witness to me "what matters to God" by . . .

DEACONS

- Where greed shows its face in my life or ministry is . . . I am reminded to remain "rich in what matters to God" in my ministry by . . .

HOSPITALITY MINISTERS

- My ministry reminds me that "what matters to God" are these people gathering for worship. I show this by . . .

MUSIC MINISTERS

- My music ministry focuses me on "what matters to God" by . . . Sometimes I struggle with keeping this focus because . . .

ALTAR MINISTERS

- Serving is "toil and anxiety of heart" (first reading) when I . . . Serving embodies what it means to be "rich in what matters to God" when I . . .

LECTORS

- My proclamation bespeaks God's desire that we have a rich inheritance when . . .

EXTRAORDINARY MINISTERS OF HOLY COMMUNION

- The way I distribute Holy Communion helps others see the fullness of life God wishes for them by . . .

Model Act of Penitence

Presider: In today's gospel Jesus challenges us to focus on what matters to God. We place ourselves in God's presence at the beginning of this liturgy and open ourselves to the fullness of life God wishes for us . . . [pause]

Lord Jesus, you are the fullness of God's love and life: Lord . . .

Christ Jesus, you give us all good things: Christ . . .

Lord Jesus, you call us to be rich in what matters to God: Lord . . .

Homily Points

• As human beings we "hunger" to be satisfied. Since our hunger knows no bounds, we are naturally driven to possess more and more. We are satisfied with the latest widescreen TV until a newer model with more features appears. Is anyone ever satisfied with his or her salary? It seems that the more we have, the more we want. Jesus teaches us that we've already got more than we can imagine—the fullness of life at our fingertips.

• In the gospel Jesus seems curt and perturbed at the question about inheritance put to him by someone in the crowd. He is not the judge and arbitrator of such mundane things. He is, however, the judge and arbitrator of what matters most—lasting happiness and the fullness of life.

• Many of us are so caught up in the things and demands of daily living that it is hard for us to assess where our focus lies. We need to reflect on what we say matters most to us and what our manner of living says matters most to us. Then we need to reflect on what Jesus says matters most and what God is offering us.

Model Prayer of the Faithful

Presider: Let us pray that we might always be in loving relationship with God and each other and gain what is most valuable—fullness of life.

Response:

Lord, hear our prayer.

Cantor:

we pray to the Lord,

That all members of the church support one another in seeking what matters most to God . . . [pause]

That all leaders of nations focus in their deliberations on what matters most to God . . . [pause]

That those who devalue life through violence might respect life as God's precious gift to us . . . [pause]

That each of us gathered here share with others what we have been given by God . . . [pause]

Presider: Loving God, life is your most precious gift to us: hear these our prayers that one day we might all enjoy everlasting life with you. We ask this through Jesus Christ our Lord. **Amen.**

ALTERNATIVE OPENING PRAYER

Let us pray

Pause for silent prayer

God our Father,
gifts without measure flow from your
    goodness
to bring us your peace.
Our life is your gift.
Guide our life's journey,
for only your love makes us whole.
Keep us strong in your love.

We ask this through Christ our Lord.
    Amen.

FIRST READING
Eccl 1:2; 2:21-23

Vanity of vanities, says Qoheleth,
    vanity of vanities! All things are vanity!

Here is one who has labored with wisdom
    and knowledge and skill,
    and yet to another who has not labored
        over it,
    he must leave property.
This also is vanity and a great misfortune.
For what profit comes to man from all the
        toil and anxiety of heart
    with which he has labored under the
        sun?
All his days sorrow and grief are his
        occupation;
    even at night his mind is not at rest.
This also is vanity.

RESPONSORIAL PSALM
Ps 90:3-4, 5-6, 12-13, 14 and 17

℟. (8) If today you hear his voice, harden
not your hearts.

You turn man back to dust,
    saying, "Return, O children of men."
For a thousand years in your sight
    are as yesterday, now that it is past,
    or as a watch of the night.

℟. If today you hear his voice, harden not
your hearts.

You make an end of them in their sleep;
    the next morning they are like the
        changing grass,
which at dawn springs up anew,
    but by evening wilts and fades.

℟. If today you hear his voice, harden not
your hearts.

Teach us to number our days aright,
    that we may gain wisdom of heart.
Return, O LORD! How long?
    Have pity on your servants!

℞. If today you hear his voice, harden not your hearts.

Fill us at daybreak with your kindness,
    that we may shout for joy and gladness
      all our days.
And may the gracious care of the LORD
    our God be ours;
    prosper the work of our hands for us!
    Prosper the work of our hands!

℞. If today you hear his voice, harden not your hearts.

SECOND READING
Col 3:1-5, 9-11

Brothers and sisters:
If you were raised with Christ, seek what
    is above,
    where Christ is seated at the right hand
      of God.
Think of what is above, not of what is on
    earth.
For you have died,
    and your life is hidden with Christ in
      God.
When Christ your life appears,
    then you too will appear with him in
      glory.

Put to death, then, the parts of you that
    are earthly:
    immorality, impurity, passion, evil
      desire,
    and the greed that is idolatry.
Stop lying to one another,
    since you have taken off the old self
      with its practices
    and have put on the new self,
    which is being renewed, for knowledge,
    in the image of its creator.
Here there is not Greek and Jew,
    circumcision and uncircumcision,
    barbarian, Scythian, slave, free;
    but Christ is all and in all.

About Liturgy

Liturgy's true focus: With our everyday lives and all the possessions we have it is easy to lose sight of the true focus; so it is with liturgy itself. Without realizing it we can get so completely caught up in the *doing* of liturgy that subtly we put ourselves at the center. For example, we can be so concerned about hospitality that we forget this isn't a simple gathering of the folks but an assembly gathered to hear God's call to be in divine presence. Or we can be so caught up in doing good music that we forget that music's purpose is to draw us into the ritual action to be transformed into being more perfect members of Christ's Body, the church. Or we can be so caught up in our own need for private prayer time that we can easily forget that at liturgy we surrender ourselves and our own needs in order to be an assembly called into God's presence.

Each Sunday it would be a good practice for each assembly member to examine *why* he or she comes to celebrate liturgy. Ultimately we come to respond to God's call and to give praise and thanks for God's tremendous gifts of life and self to us. At each liturgy committee/commission meeting it would be a good practice to ask what exactly is the parish's focus of liturgy? What are the subtle ways we place ourselves and our own needs at the center? How faithful are we to the church's practice of liturgy that draws us into God's presence for transformation?

About Liturgical Music

Music suggestions: An appropriate song for either the entrance procession or the preparation of the gifts would be "O God, Our Help in Ages Past" [in most hymnals] in which we sing of the fleetingness of human life and proclaim our confidence in God who is our ultimate hope and eternal home. In "Seek Ye First" [BB, G2, GC, GC2, JS2, OFUV, RS, W3] we challenge one another to pursue first and foremost the things of God; this song would work well during the preparation of the gifts. A good choice for either the preparation of the gifts or Communion would be "The Love of the Lord" [G2, GC, GC2, RS] in which we profess that "faith in the promise of Christ" is worth more to us than any riches, honors, or "earthly delights." In "Only This I Want" [BB, G2, GC, GC2, JS2, OFUV] we claim as loss everything but the cross of Christ; this song would be suitable during the preparation of the gifts or Communion.

AUGUST 1, 2010
EIGHTEENTH SUNDAY
IN ORDINARY TIME

✠ SPIRITUALITY

GOSPEL ACCLAMATION
Matt 24:42a, 44

R̸. Alleluia, alleluia.
Stay awake and be ready!
For you do not know on what day the Son of
    Man will come.
R̸. Alleluia, alleluia.

Gospel
Luke 12:32-48; L117C

Jesus said to his disciples:
   "Do not be afraid any longer, little
      flock,
   for your Father is pleased to give
      you the kingdom.
Sell your belongings and give alms.
Provide money bags for yourselves
      that do not wear out,
   an inexhaustible treasure in
      heaven
   that no thief can reach nor moth
      destroy.
For where your treasure is, there also
      will your heart be.

"Gird your loins and light your lamps
   and be like servants who await their
      master's return from a wedding,
   ready to open immediately when he
      comes and knocks.
Blessed are those servants
   whom the master finds vigilant on his
      arrival.
Amen, I say to you, he will gird
      himself,
   have them recline at table, and
      proceed to wait on them.
And should he come in the second or
      third watch
   and find them prepared in this way,
   blessed are those servants.
Be sure of this:
   if the master of the house had known
      the hour
   when the thief was coming,
   he would not have let his house be
      broken into.

Continued in Appendix A, p. 305.

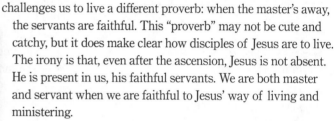

Reflecting on the Gospel

The proverb "When the cat's away, the mouse will play" dates back many centuries. A fourteenth-century French variation has it, "Where there is no cat, the rat is king." Shakespeare used it in *Henry V*: "mows lordchypythe ther a cat ys nawt." Simply put, when an authority figure is absent, those under the authority tend to do what they want. Human beings must not change much, because in the gospel for this Sunday we see that Jesus had raised the same issue: in the delayed return of the master, a servant acts perversely. Jesus challenges us to live a different proverb: when the master's away, the servants are faithful. This "proverb" may not be cute and catchy, but it does make clear how disciples of Jesus are to live. The irony is that, even after the ascension, Jesus is not absent. He is present in us, his faithful servants. We are both master and servant when we are faithful to Jesus' way of living and ministering.

Jesus makes clear that the blessed servant is the one who does the master's will even when the master is absent. Being prepared for the master's presence is not a matter of calculating time; it is a matter of faithfulness. In the master's absence, the faithful servant acts as the master himself would—caring for others, giving them all they need. Doing the master's will and remaining faithful is *being* the master in his absence. Of such is discipleship.

What Jesus intimates in the parable is that we followers are being vigilant for the *master*, that is, Jesus himself, and our vigilance is expressed in doing as our Master would do. To have our hearts where our treasure is means to "act in accord with [Jesus'] will." This is our ultimate treasure: to give up our own wills and conform them to Jesus. This is our ultimate blessedness: to act responsibly, to treat others with dignity and care, to live righteously and faithfully.

Living the Paschal Mystery

The final line of this gospel is most demanding and directly applicable to our daily paschal mystery living: "Much will be required of the person entrusted with much, and still more will be demanded of the person entrusted with more." We've been entrusted with much: furthering Jesus' mission of bringing the Good News of salvation to all as his disciples. We have been entrusted with *even more*: we are not simply servants, but because of our baptism and being plunged into the paschal mystery we become members of the Body of Christ. We are to be the presence of the Master himself, continuing his gracious ministry on behalf of others. Our faithfulness is measured by even more than doing God's will; it is measured by our *being* the presence of the risen Christ for all those we meet.

The real surprise of the gospel is that we ourselves, in our daily paschal mystery living of dying to ourselves for the sake of others, become more perfectly that presence of the very Master for whom we are vigilant. In a sense our vigilance is less about looking for Someone and more about being Someone. Our vigilance is for our own faithfulness.

If we are preoccupied by possessions, schedules, work, sports, entertainment, etc., our hearts are already filled with exhaustible, insecure, and corruptible matters. The challenge of this gospel is to redirect our hearts to what is our true treasure, Jesus, and then be faithful disciples. The gift is great. Our treasure is Jesus.

Focusing the gospel

Key words and phrases: servants who await their master's return, Blessed are those servants, faithful, distribute the food

To the point: The blessed servant is the one who does the master's will even when the master is absent. Being prepared for the master's presence is not a matter of calculating time; it is a matter of faithfulness. In the master's absence, the faithful servant acts as the master himself would—caring for others, giving them all they need. Doing the master's will and remaining faithful is *being* the master in his absence. Of such is discipleship.

Connecting the Gospel

to the first reading: For the Hebrews, "the night of the passover was known beforehand" and so they took courage in God's fidelity to the oaths made on their behalf. We who do not know the hour of the Lord's return are likewise confident of God's care and called to respond with the same fidelity.

to our experience: The master-servant relationship described in the gospel is not really part of our everyday experience. Nonetheless, we are to be both master and servant in following Jesus.

Connecting the Responsorial Psalm

to the readings: Jesus tells us in this Sunday's gospel that where our treasure is, there will be our heart. Along this very line the responsorial psalm says something remarkable about God: we are God's treasure, chosen as "his own inheritance." And where God's treasure is, God's heart will be.

This is the reason we can wait with hope and "sure knowledge" for the deliverance promised us, whether we know the hour of its arrival (first reading) or not (gospel). God has chosen us and already given us the kingdom (gospel). Our response is to keep our eyes turned toward the God whose eyes are fixed upon us (psalm) by being faithful servants who fulfill the Lord's will in season and out (gospel). We are but returning the gift.

to psalmist preparation: Preparing to sing the responsorial psalm involves more than learning the words and the music. On a deeper level, it involves readying yourself for the coming of Christ in the Liturgy of the Word. No matter how many times you have sung a particular psalm, no matter how many times you have heard the proclamation of a particular gospel, there is always a new coming of Christ. How might this awareness shape your manner of preparing the psalm?

**ASSEMBLY &
FAITH-SHARING GROUPS**

- To be vigilant until the "master's return" means to me . . . Ways that I am preparing for the Master's return are . . .

- In the Master's absence, I continue his work by . . .

- What encourages me to remain faithful in the Master's absence is . . . What impedes my faithfulness is . . .

PRESIDERS

- I find myself calculating time when . . . This impedes my faithfulness when . . .

DEACONS

- What my serving others teaches them about *vigilance* is . . .

HOSPITALITY MINISTERS

- Good hospitality requires vigilance. This helps those assembling to be attentive to the Master's presence in that . . .

MUSIC MINISTERS

- What encourages me to be faithful to the duties of my music ministry is . . .

ALTAR MINISTERS

- By serving others I am becoming a "faithful and prudent steward" because . . .

LECTORS

- My proclamation reveals how I am faithful to the Master's presence in that . . .

**EXTRAORDINARY MINISTERS
OF HOLY COMMUNION**

- My ministry witnesses to my faithfulness to the Master when . . .

Model Act of Penitence

Presider: Today's gospel reminds us that we are to be faithful servants of the Lord Jesus. As we prepare to celebrate this liturgy, let us open ourselves to God's presence and help . . . [pause]

Lord Jesus, you are the caring Master who blesses us for our faithfulness: Lord . . .

Christ Jesus, you call us to be vigilant for your abiding presence: Christ . . .

Lord Jesus, you entrust us to be your presence to one another: Lord . . .

Homily Points

• We live by the clock. Time is money. We calculate time minutely because of overfilled schedules, too little sleep, too many demands. We hardly have the time to consider our responses—we just go, go, go. This gospel contrasts calculating time with considered faithfulness.

• The gospel reminds us that, as servants of Jesus, we must be vigilant and faithful always. We must show Jesus' care and concern for others, and we seek to do this as Jesus himself did. Our mission is not to calculate when the Master will return but to live in and be his abiding presence now.

• We not only calculate time spent on everyday tasks but we often calculate time spent on discipleship as well. Faithful discipleship cannot be calculated only by time spent in church, how much we give to the poor, time spent in personal prayer. Faithful discipleship must also include vigilant response to others, genuine care for them, and reaching out as Jesus himself would. Because of this kind of fidelity, the Master is never really absent.

Model Prayer of the Faithful

Presider: Let us pray that we might be faithful servants until the Master returns.

Response:

Cantor:

That all members of the church be vigilant in doing God's will and always remain faithful disciples . . . [pause]

That leaders of the world's nations be faithful in executing the responsibilities entrusted to them . . . [pause]

That those in need receive an abundance of the Master's care . . . [pause]

That each of us be a faithful presence of Jesus for each other . . . [pause]

Presider: Loving God, you give us the gift of your divine Son and ask us to be faithful to his gospel: hear these our prayers that one day we might enjoy lasting treasure with you in heaven. We ask this through that same Son, Jesus Christ our Lord. **Amen.**

Let us pray

Pause for silent prayer

Almighty and ever-living God,
your Spirit made us your children,
confident to call you Father.
Increase your Spirit within us
and bring us to our promised inheritance.

Grant this through our Lord Jesus Christ,
    your Son,
who lives and reigns with you and the
    Holy Spirit,
one God, for ever and ever. **Amen.**

FIRST READING
Wis 18:6-9

The night of the passover was known
    beforehand to our fathers,
    that, with sure knowledge of the oaths
        in which they put their faith,
    they might have courage.
Your people awaited the salvation of the
    just
    and the destruction of their foes.
For when you punished our adversaries,
    in this you glorified us whom you had
        summoned.
For in secret the holy children of the good
        were offering sacrifice
    and putting into effect with one accord
        the divine institution.

✝ CATECHESIS

RESPONSORIAL PSALM
Ps 33:1, 12, 18-19, 20-22

℟. (12b) Blessed the people the Lord has chosen to be his own.

Exult, you just, in the LORD;
    praise from the upright is fitting.
Blessed the nation whose God is the LORD,
    the people he has chosen for his own
        inheritance.

℟. Blessed the people the Lord has chosen to be his own.

See, the eyes of the LORD are upon those
    who fear him,
    upon those who hope for his kindness,
to deliver them from death
    and preserve them in spite of famine.

℟. Blessed the people the Lord has chosen to be his own.

Our soul waits for the LORD,
    who is our help and our shield.
May your kindness, O LORD, be upon us
    who have put our hope in you.

℟. Blessed the people the Lord has chosen to be his own.

SECOND READING
Heb 11:1-2, 8-19

Brothers and sisters:
Faith is the realization of what is hoped
    for
    and evidence of things not seen.
Because of it the ancients were well attested.

By faith Abraham obeyed when he was
    called to go out to a place
    that he was to receive as an inheritance;
    he went out, not knowing where he was
        to go.
By faith he sojourned in the promised land
    as in a foreign country,
    dwelling in tents with Isaac and Jacob,
        heirs of the same promise;
    for he was looking forward to the city
        with foundations,
    whose architect and maker is God.
By faith he received power to generate,
    even though he was past the normal age
    —and Sarah herself was sterile—
    for he thought that the one who had
        made the promise was trustworthy.

Continued in Appendix A, p. 306.

About Liturgy

Stewardship, faithfulness, and liturgy: Many parishes next month (September) have various stewardship activities. Often this includes filling out a form indicating monetary gifts to the parish as well as how one will contribute time and expertise during the next year. Our reflections on the gospel for this Sunday raise some issues about stewardship. Our hearts can be distracted in many ways, and if our hearts are distracted, then we may lose sight of our true treasure, Jesus.

For the good management of a parish, of course, there must be monetary and time donations. This is part of the "faithfulness" of good disciples. At the same time we must always caution ourselves that we don't become so involved in *doing* that we neglect the way we encounter our Treasure in good celebration of liturgy. Our hearts must always be tuned into the praise and thanksgiving that is liturgy.

It is easy to be distracted during liturgy by the demands of *doing* ministry. Vigilance for our truest Treasure means that we must always bring ourselves back to full, conscious, and active participation in the liturgy that makes present the greatest gift God has given us—Jesus. Celebration of good liturgy makes demands on our energy (it takes more energy to make sure that our minds remain focused on the celebration) and calls us to vigilance (how God is transforming each of us into being richer members of the Body of Christ). Ultimately, the most important stewardship is not the money or time we donate but surrendering ourselves to being transformed. Our ultimate stewardship is how faithful we are to being Jesus' disciples.

About Liturgical Music

Selecting musical settings of the responsorial psalm, part 1: The first principle guiding the selection of the responsorial psalm setting is found in GIRM 61, which directs that the psalm should "as a rule, be taken from the Lectionary." Because the psalm text has been deliberately chosen to accord with the readings of the day, paraphrased texts taken from other sources compromise the psalm's capacity to act as interpretive bridge between the readings. The issue here is not the poetic beauty of the paraphrase or the quality of the music but the capability of the setting to fulfill its liturgical role.

A second principle for selecting a psalm setting is that the text of the psalm ought to predominate over the music. If the music is so chorally or instrumentally elaborate that it overshadows the text, then the setting will interfere with the function of the psalm. The setting may be rhythmically or harmonically complex, but this complexity should support the text, not compete with it.

AUGUST 8, 2010

NINETEENTH SUNDAY IN ORDINARY TIME

✛ SPIRITUALITY

GOSPEL ACCLAMATION

R⁊. Alleluia, alleluia.
Mary is taken up to heaven;
a chorus of angels exults.
R⁊. Alleluia, alleluia.

Gospel Luke 1:39-56; L622

Mary set out
and traveled to the hill country in
haste
to a town of Judah,
where she entered the house of
Zechariah
and greeted Elizabeth.
When Elizabeth heard Mary's
greeting,
the infant leaped in her womb,
and Elizabeth, filled with the Holy
Spirit,
cried out in a loud voice and said,
"Blessed are you among women,
and blessed is the fruit of your womb.
And how does this happen to me,
that the mother of my Lord should
come to me?
For at the moment the sound of your
greeting reached my ears,
the infant in my womb leaped for joy.
Blessed are you who believed
that what was spoken to you by the Lord
would be fulfilled."

And Mary said:
"My soul proclaims the greatness of
the Lord;
my spirit rejoices in God my Savior
for he has looked with favor on his
lowly servant.
From this day all generations will call
me blessed:
the Almighty has done great things
for me,
and holy is his Name.
He has mercy on those who fear him
in every generation.
He has shown the strength of his arm,
and has scattered the proud in their
conceit.

Continued in Appendix A, p. 306.

Reflecting on the Gospel

Even before the dawn of feminism and rising consciousness about the dignity of women, great women have done great things and history has been kind to their memory. We have, for example, Esther, Ruth, and Judith from the Old Testament; pagan societies had goddesses as well as gods; Troy had Helen and France had Joan; Constantine had Helena and Augustine had Monica; Florence Nightingale, Dorothy Day, and Mother Teresa have all left their indelible marks.

It is no surprise, then, that we also find a great woman remembered at the very heart of Christianity—Mary, the mother of our Lord.

This solemnity celebrates the "great things" God has done for Mary. God, who has "lifted up" his "lowly servant" Mary, lifts up all the lowly not only because they are faithful but because God is faithful to the promise of divine mercy. Mary's assumption of body and soul into heaven celebrates the mercy of God and the promise to us of a share in that same mercy. It is God who does great things because God has promised mercy. The great thing Mary does is say *yes* to being an instrument of God's promise. The great thing God does for us is invite us to share in that same promise—everlasting life.

Jesus' birth ushers in a new age of "great things" that are manifested in the *Magnificat*'s reversals: the conceited are scattered, the mighty are cast down, the lowly are lifted up, the hungry are filled, the rich are sent away empty. In her *Magnificat* Mary already announces the new age to come, which is established through faithful discipleship. God's kingdom of the new age is brought to completion when all are gathered into a sharing in eternal life. Mary's assumption—this festival—is a sign of the completion already coming about. This is why we might think of Mary's assumption as a festival of mercy: Mary "returned to her home" when she completed her mission of being an instrument of God's promise, a home that is to be with God for all eternity. The assumption is a sign of God's mercy being fulfilled. It is also a sign that our true home is with God.

Living the Paschal Mystery

Mary remained with Elizabeth "about three months." Mary remains with the church (with us) always, to be a sign of the "great things" God continues to do. Her discipleship continues in that she is a sign of hope and mercy. So it is with us. One way our own discipleship is expressed is through our being a sign of God's mercy.

Mercy in the gospel is shown not only in the forgiveness of sins but also in the fulfillment of promises. Therefore, one important aspect of discipleship is to live in such a way as to witness to God's promise of mercy being fulfilled. Practically speaking, this means that we carry ourselves with dignity and bestow that same dignity on others. No one is beneath us or too "lowly" or insignificant to deserve our attention and respect. This is easier said than done!

Dying to self means treating the other as one deserving and receiving God's mercy. First of all, this means that we don't judge others. Our judgments of each other are usually much more unkind than God's merciful judgment of us! This also means that we are careful never to speak negatively of others. Diminishing others surely doesn't raise them up and ultimately diminishes even ourselves. Finally, paschal mystery living means that we treat the other as one blessed by God.

Focusing the gospel

Key words and phrases: lowly servant, great things, lifted up, promise of mercy

To the point: This solemnity celebrates the "great things" God has done for Mary. God, who has "lifted up" his "lowly servant" Mary, lifts up all the lowly not only because they are faithful but because God is faithful to the promise of divine mercy. Mary's assumption of body and soul into heaven celebrates the mercy of God and the promise to us of a share in that same mercy.

Connecting the Gospel

to the second reading: The second reading rehearses the entire history of God's promise of mercy: death came through Adam; life came through Christ. Mary's assumption foreshadows the destiny of all "those who belong to Christ."

to our experience: In our news-dominated culture we tend to view events historically. From this viewpoint the solemnity of the assumption celebrates what happened to Mary in the past. Liturgy does more than recall a past event, however; it draws us into divine mystery where that event is present now.

Connecting the Responsorial Psalm

to the readings: Psalm 45 was a nuptial psalm used by the Israelites in the wedding ceremony between their king and his bride. The people called upon the bride to forget her family and homeland and embrace a new and more glorious relationship. She chose to do so, but not alone: with "gladness and joy" an entire retinue followed her.

By accepting her role in the incarnation, Mary chose to embody the cosmic struggle between the forces of evil and the saving power of God (first reading). Blessed is she for believing in the power and promise of God even when these seemed hidden from view (gospel). Blessed is she for not clinging to past and present and venturing in hope into an unseen future. Now the victory of Christ over sin and death is completed in her (second reading) and God celebrates her beauty (psalm). In her, the lowly have been lifted up and the hungering satisfied with salvation (gospel). In her, humanity has been wedded to God. And we belong to the retinue.

to psalmist preparation: As you sing this responsorial psalm, you celebrate your own entrance into heaven, for the entire church is borne with Mary into God's kingdom. How can you prepare yourself to sing such promise and glory? How can you imitate Mary more fully in her choice to cooperate with God's plan for salvation?

**ASSEMBLY &
FAITH-SHARING GROUPS**

- Mary's blessedness is revealed by her being assumed body and soul into heaven. My blessedness is revealed by . . .
- The "great things" God did for Mary are . . . God does for me are . . .
- Mary recognizes the source of her blessedness as "the Almighty." I am reminded that God is the source of my blessedness when . . . A way I direct others to God as the source of blessedness is . . .

PRESIDERS

- A way my ministry participates in fulfilling God's "promise of mercy" is . . .

DEACONS

- A way my service points others to heaven as a Christian's "final goal" (see opening prayer) is . . .

HOSPITALITY MINISTERS

- Elizabeth experiences being blessed in welcoming Mary. A blessing for me whenever I welcome another is . . .

MUSIC MINISTERS

- My music ministry celebrates the mercy of God and the blessedness of Mary by . . . It honors the blessedness of the assembly when . . .

ALTAR MINISTERS

- When I serve others as a response to the "great things" God has done, my service looks like . . .

LECTORS

- My reading "proclaims the greatness of the Lord" when . . .

**EXTRAORDINARY MINISTERS
OF HOLY COMMUNION**

- The Eucharist makes me, like Mary, an instrument of God's promise of mercy for others. I witness to this whenever . . .

Model Act of Penitence

Presider: Today we celebrate the assumption of Mary into heaven. The promise of God's divine mercy is fulfilled as Mary joins her divine Son in everlasting glory. Let us pause and prepare ourselves to celebrate these great mysteries and ask God's help in being faithful as Mary was faithful . . . [pause]

> Lord Jesus, your mother Mary is blessed among all women: Lord . . .
>
> Christ Jesus, you are the fulfillment of God's mercy: Christ . . .
>
> Lord Jesus, you are God our Savior: Lord . . .

Homily Points

• We tend to put people who do "great things" on pedestals, making them better than us, more worthy than us, heroes beyond us. For example, we think we can never be as holy as Mother Teresa; we can never be as courageous as the police and firefighters who lost their lives in the World Trade Center; we can never be as principled as Martin Luther King Jr. Nor do we think that we can be as close to God as Mary.

• God did "great things" for Mary—chose her to be the mother of Jesus, assumed her body and soul into heaven—and we tend to think she is beyond us. This solemnity reminds us that God does "great things" for all God's beloved, that God shows mercy to all the faithful, that God looks upon all the lowly with favor, and that God promises all of us a share in divine life. Like Mary, we also receive "great things" from God.

• Mary was a simple maiden from Nazareth: a woman who gave birth, a wife who cared for her family and home, a refugee in a foreign land, a caring relative who visited her pregnant cousin, a mother who suffered. Mary surely is not beyond us in these ordinary, everyday things. In all things she responded faithfully to God; we are called to do the same. Mary is our model of fidelity.

Model Prayer of the Faithful

Presider: Let us place our needs before God through the intercession of Mary.

Response:

Lord, hear our prayer.

Cantor:

we pray to the Lord,

That the church, like Mary, remain a faithful witness to God's promise of mercy for all . . . [pause]

That those in leadership positions be avenues of God's mercy so all may have justice and peace . . . [pause]

That the lowly be lifted up, the hungry be fed, and the poor have dignity . . . [pause]

That each one of us model our lives after Mary's faithfulness . . . [pause]

Presider: Merciful God, you assumed Mary body and soul into heaven: hear these our prayers that through her intercession we might one day also live in glory with you. We ask this through the divine Son, Christ our Lord. **Amen.**

OPENING PRAYER
Let us pray

Pause for silent prayer

All-powerful and ever-living God,
you raised the sinless Virgin Mary, mother
    of your Son,
body and soul to the glory of heaven.
May we see heaven as our final goal
and come to share her glory.

We ask this through our Lord Jesus Christ,
    your Son,
who lives and reigns with you and the
    Holy Spirit,
one God, for ever and ever. **Amen.**

FIRST READING
Rev 11:19a; 12:1-6a, 10ab

God's temple in heaven was opened,
    and the ark of his covenant could be
        seen in the temple.

A great sign appeared in the sky, a woman
        clothed with the sun,
    with the moon under her feet,
    and on her head a crown of twelve
        stars.
She was with child and wailed aloud in
        pain as she labored to give birth.
Then another sign appeared in the sky;
    it was a huge red dragon, with seven
        heads and ten horns,
    and on its heads were seven diadems.
Its tail swept away a third of the stars in
        the sky
    and hurled them down to the earth.
Then the dragon stood before the woman
        about to give birth,
    to devour her child when she gave birth.
She gave birth to a son, a male child,
    destined to rule all the nations with an
        iron rod.
Her child was caught up to God and his
        throne.
The woman herself fled into the desert
    where she had a place prepared by God.

Then I heard a loud voice in heaven say:
    "Now have salvation and power come,
        and the Kingdom of our God
        and the authority of his Anointed
            One."

RESPONSORIAL PSALM

Ps 45:10, 11, 12, 16

R℣. (10bc) The queen stands at your right hand, arrayed in gold.

The queen takes her place at your right
    hand in gold of Ophir.

R℣. The queen stands at your right hand, arrayed in gold.

Hear, O daughter, and see; turn your ear,
    forget your people and your father's
        house.

R℣. The queen stands at your right hand, arrayed in gold.

So shall the king desire your beauty;
    for he is your lord.

R℣. The queen stands at your right hand, arrayed in gold.

They are borne in with gladness and joy;
    they enter the palace of the king.

R℣. The queen stands at your right hand, arrayed in gold.

SECOND READING

1 Cor 15:20-27

Brothers and sisters:
Christ has been raised from the dead,
    the firstfruits of those who have fallen
        asleep.
For since death came through man,
    the resurrection of the dead came also
        through man.
For just as in Adam all die,
    so too in Christ shall all be brought to
        life,
    but each one in proper order:
    Christ the firstfruits;
    then, at his coming, those who belong
        to Christ;
    then comes the end,
    when he hands over the Kingdom to his
        God and Father,
    when he has destroyed every
        sovereignty
    and every authority and power.
For he must reign until he has put all his
    enemies under his feet.
The last enemy to be destroyed is death,
    for "he subjected everything under his
        feet."

About Liturgy

Sundays and solemnities. When August 15 falls on a Sunday, as it does this year, the celebration of the solemnity of the Assumption of the Blessed Virgin Mary replaces the respective Sunday in Ordinary Time. There are fewer than a score of solemnities celebrated during our liturgical year; the small number testifies that these are our major festivals, carefully chosen because they celebrate an event important to the saving mission of Jesus or celebrate someone who was key in unfolding those events. This is one way that the liturgical calendar continually keeps before us the major aspects of the paschal mystery. We celebrate a Marian festival, but since it falls on Sunday it is also a happy reminder that any celebration of the saints is always a celebration of Christ.

Each Sunday is a celebration of resurrection—a "little Easter." On this first day of the week the whole church celebrates redemption; this is why we have a *Sunday* Mass obligation—it is the church's way to underscore that every Sunday is a salvation feast. When we have the coincidence of a saint's feast and Sunday, it is a kind of "double reminder" that salvation in Christ is such a great gift from God that we need at least a weekly, communal celebration.

This Sunday we also celebrate Jesus' first, faithful disciple—his mother Mary. Its falling on a Sunday is a "double reminder" that God's mighty deeds toward Mary always redound to her Son. Mary's assumption witnesses to God's bringing to completion the work of salvation; Mary's assumption into heaven is a promise to all of us that this is where our own fidelity leads. Each Sunday our celebration at Mass is a remembrance of God's fidelity to the promise of salvation that one day we, too, will dwell in God's everlasting kingdom of heaven.

About Liturgical Music

Hymn suggestions: A very appropriate hymn of praise after Communion would be the *Magnificat.* Many settings exist, but one paraphrase that gives fresh insight into the text is Rory Cooney's "Canticle of the Turning" [G2, GC, GC2, RS]. Choir or cantor(s) could sing the verses, with the assembly joining in on the refrain. The refrain is set to a simple, easily learned SAB arrangement. Its energetic Irish melody and the intriguing metaphor that unifies the text ("the world is about to turn") make this setting especially appealing. Another fresh paraphrase is Alan Hommerding and Steven Warner's "My Soul Flies Free" [WLP octavo #007220]. Choir or cantor(s) could sing the verses, with the assembly singing the refrain. Marty Haugen's "My Soul Proclaims" [GC2] offers a joyful verse-refrain, call-response setting. Led by a cantor, the assembly will delight in singing their dance-like responses.

AUGUST 15, 2010

THE ASSUMPTION OF
THE BLESSED VIRGIN MARY

SPIRITUALITY

GOSPEL ACCLAMATION
John 14:6

℟. Alleluia, alleluia.
I am the way, the truth and the life, says the
    Lord;
no one comes to the Father, except through me.
℟. Alleluia, alleluia.

Gospel
Luke 13:22-30; L123C

Jesus passed through towns and
    villages,
    teaching as he went and making
        his way to Jerusalem.
Someone asked him,
    "Lord, will only a few people be
        saved?"
He answered them,
    "Strive to enter through the narrow
        gate,
    for many, I tell you, will attempt to
        enter
    but will not be strong enough.
After the master of the house has arisen
    and locked the door,
    then will you stand outside knocking
        and saying,
    'Lord, open the door for us.'
He will say to you in reply,
    'I do not know where you are from.'
And you will say,
    'We ate and drank in your company
        and you taught in our streets.'
Then he will say to you,
    'I do not know where you are from.
Depart from me, all you evildoers!'
And there will be wailing and grinding of
    teeth
    when you see Abraham, Isaac, and Jacob
    and all the prophets in the kingdom of
        God
    and you yourselves cast out.
And people will come from the east and
    the west
    and from the north and the south
    and will recline at table in the kingdom
        of God.
For behold, some are last who will be first,
    and some are first who will be last."

Reflecting on the Gospel

The shortest distance between two points is a straight line. Take the path of least resistance. In these and other ways we try to capture how we achieve goals without putting out any more effort than is necessary. All our modern conveniences are geared toward accomplishing life's tasks in the easiest way possible and in the least amount of time. We like our life to be streamlined and relatively effortless. The gospel this Sunday invites us on a journey, but this journey is hardly easy. The destination is Jerusalem—a metaphor reminding us that to walk with Jesus means that we walk with him through death to new life. We know the destination and cost of our Christian journey to Jerusalem, but in our wildest imagination we can hardly know the fullness of life and joy God has in store for us.

Jesus was asked in the gospel about how many would be saved. The issue, however, is not how many but *who*. The saved are those who don't merely accompany Jesus but who freely choose to follow him "to Jerusalem"—and all that this destination entails. The door of salvation will be open only to all those who have chosen to pass through the "narrow gate" of self-surrender. As we can see, Jesus' answer is neither streamlined nor indicative of relative ease, as we like our life to be. In fact, Jesus' answer indicates quite the opposite. So, why would we choose this journey? Because the immediate destination (Jerusalem, with its promised death) is the way to a greater destination (new and eternal life).

By "making his way to Jerusalem" Jesus is being faithful to his own mission; by going to Jerusalem he fulfills his Father's will even when that means he must suffer and die. Jesus walks the journey with us and shows us the way to what we desire most for our lives—salvation. Our salvation is a great gift from God, but it is not without cost. We must pass through the "narrow gate" of conforming ourselves to Jesus and participating in his dying and rising. Being disciples of Jesus, then, demands more than being in Jesus' company (for example, being faithful to personal prayer and celebrating liturgy); it means we must take up the mission of Jesus to die and rise, that is, we must be on the way to Jerusalem.

What limits the scope of salvation is not God's reach (which is to east, west, north, and south—that is, salvation is offered to all people) but *our response*. We do not gain eternal salvation by walking in a straight line or by taking the path of least resistance. We gain eternal salvation, rather, by the difficult and demanding path of following Jesus on his way to Jerusalem; we do this by dying to self and being faithful disciples. The surprise of the gospel is that all are offered salvation, but this isn't enough. We must also know Jesus well enough to be faithful in following him.

Living the Paschal Mystery

We all claim to know Jesus; after all, we are for the most part faithful church-goers who weekly eat and drink in his company. This gospel warns us that this isn't enough. There is an urgency about our paschal mystery living; we don't have forever to make up our minds to respond to God's offer of salvation. Each day we must take up our own cross, die to self, and live for the sake of others. This is how we enter through the narrow gate and how we get to know Jesus intimately enough to receive salvation: we must *live and act like Jesus*. Becoming least is a metaphor for dying to self. This is what Jesus asks: that the first become the last. Yes, what limits the scope of salvation is not God's reach but our response.

Focusing the gospel

Key words and phrases: making his way to Jerusalem, be saved, enter through the narrow gate, open the door

To the point: Jesus was asked about how many would be saved. The issue, however, is not how many but *who*. The saved are those who don't merely accompany Jesus but who freely choose to follow him "to Jerusalem"—and all this destination entails. The door of salvation will be open only to all those who have chosen to pass through the "narrow gate" of self-surrender.

Connecting the Gospel

to the first reading: Both the first reading and gospel reinforce salvation's wide reach: "from all the nations" and "from the east and the west and from the north and the south." All anyone need do is follow Jesus to Jerusalem, through death to life.

to our experience: Every journey requires self-discipline and stamina because there are always unexpected things encountered: a broken-down car, a closed road, a lost hotel reservation. Our Christian journey also has unexpected things: temptations, suffering, disappointments. It also requires self-discipline and stamina to finish the journey and receive the gift of salvation.

Connecting the Responsorial Psalm

to the readings: In this Sunday's gospel Jesus challenges us with the harsh reality that not everyone will be admitted to the kingdom of God. His message, however, is for those who have heard the Good News of salvation, not for those who have "never heard of [God's] name, or seen [God's] glory" (first reading). To these God will send messengers to tell them the Good News and gather them to the holy dwelling, Jerusalem. For those who have already heard, radical demands are in place (Jesus has been spelling these out in previous Sundays' gospels). And the responsorial psalm gives yet another command: we are to be the messengers who spread the Good News of God's salvation to all the world. The psalm reminds us that we are a necessary part of God's plan of salvation for all. It also suggests that we cannot recline at God's table if we have not invited everyone else to be there with us.

to psalmist preparation: In singing this psalm you command the assembly to tell the world the Good News of salvation. Who in your life is especially in need of hearing this news? How do you tell them?

ASSEMBLY & FAITH-SHARING GROUPS

- To be like Jesus and make my "way to Jerusalem" means to me . . .
- The people and/or practices that enable me to "strive to enter through the narrow gate" are . . .
- The self-discipline required of me to continue my journey to salvation is . . . What gives me stamina on the journey is . . .

PRESIDERS

- The door of salvation is open now! My ministry communicates this invitation and its urgency by . . .

DEACONS

- My Christian living goes beyond mere familiarity with Jesus ("we ate and drank in your company") to following him to Jerusalem because . . .

HOSPITALITY MINISTERS

- My hospitality embodies God's all-inclusive invitation to enter God's kingdom by . . .

MUSIC MINISTERS

- My music ministry is one way I "eat and drink in Jesus' company" because . . . It is also a way I accept the challenge to follow him to Jerusalem because . . .

ALTAR MINISTERS

- The way my service goes beyond attending to vessels and rubrics to supporting others on the way to Jerusalem is . . .

LECTORS

- My proclamation is a word of encouragement and hope on the journey of salvation when . . .

EXTRAORDINARY MINISTERS OF HOLY COMMUNION

- The way I am God's food that aids and encourages others to enter through the narrow gate is . . .

Model Act of Penitence

Presider: In the gospel Jesus invites us to journey to salvation through a narrow gate. As we prepare to celebrate this liturgy, let us ask God for the grace to be faithful to this journey . . . [pause]

Lord Jesus, you give us the strength to journey with you to Jerusalem: Lord . . .

Christ Jesus, you call all people into the kingdom of God: Christ . . .

Lord Jesus, you are the open door to salvation: Lord . . .

Homily Points

• Every year over a hundred people attempt to scale Mount Everest. On average only four people make it to the top and two lose their lives on the way. What motivates climbers to take up this perilous journey with its threat of possible death is the thrill of the triumph of standing on the summit. What motives us on our Christian journey of salvation is the joy of the triumph of receiving everlasting life.

• Jesus makes clear to us that this journey of salvation is hard, demanding, and always requires dying to self. We are never alone on this difficult journey, however; Jesus is walking with us, teaching us, and strengthening us with his abiding presence.

• Because the triumph of salvation is not as concrete as the triumph of reaching a mountain top, it is easy to stray from the path. To encourage us to stay the course, we need to look for the signs of new life occurring along the way. For example, we move beyond self to seek reconciliation with another; we find the stamina to accompany a dying spouse; we reach out in compassion to a neighbor in need. In all these ways we are already glimpsing the mountaintop.

Model Prayer of the Faithful

Presider: Let us place our needs before God, so that we might have the strength to walk faithfully with Jesus on the journey of salvation.

Response:

Lord, hear our prayer.

Cantor:

we pray to the Lord,

That all members of the church may follow Jesus faithfully through death to new life . . . [pause]

That world leaders may open the doors of justice and peace . . . [pause]

That those in need may have their fill of this world's abundance . . . [pause]

That all of us here support one another on our Christian journey in times of discouragement or fatigue . . . [pause]

Presider: Loving God, you offer salvation to all who come to you: hear these our prayers that one day we might enter through the narrow gate into your everlasting glory. We ask this through Jesus Christ our Lord. **Amen.**

OPENING PRAYER
Let us pray

Pause for silent prayer

Father,
help us to seek the values
that will bring us lasting joy in this
changing world.
In our desire for what you promise
make us one in mind and heart.

Grant this through our Lord Jesus Christ,
your Son,
who lives and reigns with you and the
Holy Spirit,
one God, for ever and ever. **Amen.**

FIRST READING
Isa 66:18-21

Thus says the LORD:
I know their works and their thoughts,
and I come to gather nations of every
language;
they shall come and see my glory.
I will set a sign among them;
from them I will send fugitives to the
nations:
to Tarshish, Put and Lud, Mosoch,
Tubal and Javan,
to the distant coastlands
that have never heard of my fame, or
seen my glory;
and they shall proclaim my glory
among the nations.
They shall bring all your brothers and
sisters from all the nations
as an offering to the LORD,
on horses and in chariots, in carts, upon
mules and dromedaries,
to Jerusalem, my holy mountain, says
the LORD,
just as the Israelites bring their offering
to the house of the LORD in clean
vessels.
Some of these I will take as priests and
Levites, says the LORD.

RESPONSORIAL PSALM
Ps 117:1, 2

R⁷. (Mark 16:15) Go out to all the world and tell the Good News.
  or:
R⁷. Alleluia.

Praise the Lord, all you nations;
  glorify him, all you peoples!

R⁷. Go out to all the world and tell the Good News.
  or:
R⁷. Alleluia.

For steadfast is his kindness toward us,
  and the fidelity of the Lord endures
    forever.

R⁷. Go out to all the world and tell the Good News.
  or:
R⁷. Alleluia.

SECOND READING
Heb 12:5-7, 11-13

Brothers and sisters,
You have forgotten the exhortation
  addressed to you as children:
"My son, do not disdain the discipline
    of the Lord
  or lose heart when reproved by him;
  for whom the Lord loves, he disciplines;
    he scourges every son he
      acknowledges."
Endure your trials as "discipline";
  God treats you as sons.
For what "son" is there whom his father
    does not discipline?
At the time,
  all discipline seems a cause not for joy
      but for pain,
  yet later it brings the peaceful fruit of
    righteousness
  to those who are trained by it.

So strengthen your drooping hands and
    your weak knees.
Make straight paths for your feet,
  that what is lame may not be disjointed
    but healed.

About Liturgy

Prefaces: During Ordinary Time there are eight prefaces given in the Sacramentary for Sundays. Because these prefaces are used with a wide variety of Sunday Lectionary readings, they tend to be "generic," speaking more generally of the mystery of salvation. On festivals the prefaces always open up the mystery being celebrated.

The dialogue before the preface proper begins is one of the oldest of all liturgical texts. The dialogue invites the assembly to prayer but does so much more elaborately than the usual "Let us pray" that begins the opening prayer and prayer after Communion. First of all, the invitation to pray the eucharistic prayer is truly a dialogue between presider and assembly. The dialogue unfolds in three parts: greeting ("The Lord be with you"), command to a specific prayer sentiment or stance ("Lift up your hearts"), and an invitation to pray in a particular way ("Let us give thanks to the Lord our God"). The eucharistic prayer is our great thanksgiving to God for the work of salvation.

The body of the preface then unfolds as an act of thanksgiving and praise and includes reasons why we have these sentiments toward God. Often the preface includes mention of God as creator, of Jesus as redeemer, and of the Holy Spirit as sanctifier.

Originally the Latin word we translate as preface (*praefatio*) meant "proclamation" and was sometimes ascribed to the whole eucharistic prayer. Our English translation can get in the way here; rather than being merely "preliminary" (like the preface in a book, which can be skipped over or discarded), the preface to the eucharistic prayer is the first invitation, and reason to give God praise and thanks.

About Liturgical Music

Changing service music: Because Jesus clearly makes the turn toward Jerusalem in this Sunday's gospel, this would be an appropriate Sunday to switch to another Ordinary Time setting of service music. Changing this music is one way to express the choice to turn with Jesus and accept the challenge of discipleship: to walk with him toward the ultimate fulfillment of his mission in passion, death, and resurrection.

Selecting musical settings of the responsorial psalm, part 2: A third principle guiding the selection of a musical setting of the responsorial psalm is that the psalm should not overshadow the readings themselves. If the setting is so long or so embellished that the assembly continues mentally humming the refrain during the subsequent readings, then the psalm has overstepped its bounds. The psalm is meant to lead to the readings, not to itself. (Sometimes the problem, however, is not that the psalm setting is too elaborate but that the proclamation of the readings is too weak. The need, then, is not to tone down the psalm but to improve the proclamation.)

This is not to say that we never use an elaborate musical setting of a responsorial psalm. This is more than appropriate on solemnities like Christmas, Easter, Pentecost, Christ the King, etc. On these occasions highly embellished musical settings with perhaps more than one cantor or the choir as a whole singing the verses in harmony and with solo instrument(s) added communicate the high festivity of the day, in contrast with the less festive periods of the year. These solemnities call for more elaborate music. But highly ornamented psalm settings lose their festive capability if they are used on a regular basis, Sunday after Sunday.

✝ SPIRITUALITY

GOSPEL ACCLAMATION
Matt 11:29ab

R⁊. Alleluia, alleluia.
Take my yoke upon you, says the Lord;
and learn from me, for I am meek and humble
   of heart.
R⁊. Alleluia, alleluia.

Gospel   Luke 14:1, 7-14; L126C

On a sabbath Jesus went to dine
   at the home of one of the leading
      Pharisees,
   and the people there were observing
      him carefully.

He told a parable to those who had
      been invited,
   noticing how they were choosing the
      places of honor at the table.
"When you are invited by someone to a
      wedding banquet,
   do not recline at table in the place of
      honor.
A more distinguished guest than you
      may have been invited by him,
   and the host who invited both of you
      may approach you and say,
   'Give your place to this man,'
   and then you would proceed with
      embarrassment
to take the lowest place.
Rather, when you are invited,
   go and take the lowest place
   so that when the host comes to you
      he may say,
   'My friend, move up to a higher
      position.'
Then you will enjoy the esteem of your
      companions at the table.
For everyone who exalts himself will
      be humbled,
   but the one who humbles himself will
      be exalted."

Continued in Appendix A, p. 306.

Reflecting on the Gospel

The word "humility" derives from the Latin adjective *humilis,* which means on the ground, of the earth, earthy (noun: *humus,* ground, earth, soil). From this we understand humility as not being someone other than we are, just down-to-earth folks who know ourselves in both our gifts and our limitations. In the gospel today Jesus uses two very familiar social situations—dining at table and guest invitation lists—to teach us about true humility. From the point of view of being guest, humility is knowing one's place; from the point of view of being host, humility is knowing whom to invite (to be in relation with). The two parables prod us to see both of these as aspects of humility, of authentic Christian self-understanding.

The first parable about wedding guests invites us to reflect on humility as knowing ourselves in relation to others. The "wedding banquet" imagery of the gospel is eschatological imagery; that is, we might think of God as the host and the wedding banquet as the Lord's heavenly banquet. We are all invited to the banquet (offered salvation), but we must remember that it is *God who invites.* Our own relation to God is as those who are poor; we cannot "buy" our place in heaven. God invites us to this exalted position. God raises us up! Humility is recognizing that by God's choosing us we are raised up to share in divine riches and bestowed the great dignity of sharing in God's life. If this is how God relates to us, then this is how the disciple relates to others. As God has bestowed dignity on us, so do we shower others with dignity.

The second parable about hosts invites us to reflect on humility in terms of how we wish God to relate to us. We know we are poor (a metaphor for sinners). God extends an invitation to the banquet not only to those who seem worthy but also to all who would respond. No one is excluded from the banquet. Neither should we exclude others from our own attention and ministrations. If we wish God to invite us who are poor to the divine banquet, then we also extend ourselves to all others, regardless of social or economic class, religious affiliation, gender or sexual orientation.

In the gospel the people dining with Jesus were "observing him carefully." What Jesus says turns the tables by inviting the guests to look at themselves. Jesus challenges them to choose, not a "higher position," but a "lower place," teaching us who we are to be before God and each other. Jesus calls us to true humility: to know the truth about ourselves, to sit in right relationship with one another, and to allow ourselves to be lifted up by God.

Living the Paschal Mystery

Humility isn't a matter of beating our breast or putting ourselves down. Humility is recognizing that we are gifted, enriched, and nourished by God and then reaching out to others in the same way. If we wish God to raise us up ("repaid at the resurrection of the righteous"), then we must live our lives raising others up.

Each Sunday we are invited to God's banquet table. We are nourished at the same time that we are called to share the abundance of God's life by reaching out to others in need. We eat and drink in order to be gracious to others. This is the most profound humility!

Focusing the gospel

Key words and phrases: observing him carefully, noticing how they were choosing the places, lowest place, higher position, humbles, will be exalted

To the point: The people dining with Jesus were "observing him carefully." What Jesus says turns the tables by inviting the guests to look at themselves. Jesus challenges them to choose, not a "higher position," but a "lower place," teaching us who we are to be before God and each other. Jesus calls us to true humility: to know the truth about ourselves, to sit in right relationship with one another, and to allow ourselves to be lifted up by God.

Connecting the Gospel

to the first reading: The wisdom of Sirach invites us to know ourselves and, accordingly, make right choices. For example, choose neither what is too sublime nor beyond our strength, be attentive to wisdom. As did Jesus, Sirach shows us that those who are truly humble "find favor with God."

to our experience: We live in a society in which self-image, self-esteem, ego strength, positive self-regard, etc., have been exaggerated and made ends in themselves. Some tend to see humility as negative and ego-damaging. Humility, however, is authentic Christian self-understanding.

Connecting the Responsorial Psalm

to the readings: This Sunday's gospel tells us that the people were "observing [Jesus] carefully." The responsorial psalm invites us to the same observation of God, for the psalm shows God "[making] a home for the poor." When Jesus in the gospel advises us to invite to our table "the poor, the crippled, the lame, the blind," he is challenging us to model what we see God doing. And when we do so, we experience a remarkable reversal in our own position. Choosing to give up the first place so that room is made for the poor and needy exalts us. Our humility "finds favor with God" (first reading). Even more, we become like God. Our singing of this psalm is our prayer that we see the goodness of God toward the needy and act likewise.

to psalmist preparation: This psalm praises God for goodness to the poor and needy. Only those who recognize themselves among the poor and needy can see what God is doing to lift them up. How are you poor and needy? How is God lifting you up by inviting you to the banquet of Jesus' Body and Blood? How do you offer God praise for this great gift? How do you invite others to join you at this table?

ASSEMBLY & FAITH-SHARING GROUPS

- To be humble means to me . . . A time when I acted/lived humbly was . . .
- The truth about myself is . . .
- Occasions when I am prompted toward self-exaltation are . . . I have experienced God exalting me when . . .

PRESIDERS

- My ministry humbles me when . . . My ministry exalts me when . . .

DEACONS

- The blessing I receive (even now) whenever I minister to those who are unable to repay me is . . .

HOSPITALITY MINISTERS

- What is humbling—that is, realizing my rightful place in life and sensing the dignity of others—about hospitality is . . .

MUSIC MINISTERS

- Sometimes music ministry tempts me to grab for first place when . . . When this happens, Jesus calls me to humility by . . .

ALTAR MINISTERS

- A time when serving others was an occasion to grow in humility was . . .

LECTORS

- An occasion where I could better "conduct [my] affairs with humility" (first reading) is . . . This would affect my proclamation by . . .

EXTRAORDINARY MINISTERS OF HOLY COMMUNION

- My distributing Holy Communion is an example of taking a lower place when . . .

Model Act of Penitence

Presider: Each Sunday we gather here to dine at the Lord's table. Let us prepare ourselves to be nourished by word and sacrament by humbling ourselves before our generous God . . . [pause]

Lord Jesus, you invite us to share in your heavenly banquet: Lord . . .

Christ Jesus, you humbled yourself to live among us: Christ . . .

Lord Jesus, you call us to be humble: Lord . . .

Homily Points

• In Dickens's novel David Copperfield, Uriah Heep, "a very 'umble man," projected a false humility. For many, humility is expressed in belittling oneself and finding it hard to accept the compliments of others. This false humility does not allow them to act in full accord with the gifts God has given them. This is not the humility to which Jesus invites us in this Sunday's gospel.

• When Jesus says in the parable to take the "lowest place," he is not speaking literally but metaphorically. He is teaching us that taking our rightful place is an invitation and gift given to us, not something we choose. Humility is the virtue of accepting our gifts and rejoicing in them as God's blessings to be put at the service of those with whom we "recline at table."

• The crowd is carefully observing Jesus. What do we learn if we carefully observe him? In humility, Jesus abandoned the exaltation of heaven for the earthiness of living among us. In humility, Jesus reached out to the poor, the women, the sick and maimed, the outcasts. In humility, he freely gave his life for us. In humility, we treat others with respect and dignity. In humility, we reach out to those who are exhausted, left out, sick. In humility, we give ourselves over for the good of others.

Model Prayer of the Faithful

Presider: In humility, let us ask God for what we need.

Response:

Lord, hear our prayer.

Cantor:

we pray to the Lord,

For all members of the church to faithfully use God's gifts in the service of others . . . [pause]

For all world leaders to provide for those under their guidance with care and dignity . . . [pause]

For the poor and disadvantaged to be equitably included in the world's abundance . . . [pause]

For each of us to humble ourselves before our God who exalts us . . . [pause]

Presider: Gracious God, you provide us with all we need: hear these our prayers that all of us may one day share at your heavenly banquet. We ask this through Christ our Lord. **Amen.**

OPENING PRAYER
Let us pray

Pause for silent prayer

Almighty God,
every good thing comes from you.
Fill our hearts with love for you,
increase our faith,
and by your constant care
protect the good you have given us.

We ask this through our Lord Jesus Christ,
your Son,
who lives and reigns with you and the
Holy Spirit,
one God, for ever and ever. **Amen.**

FIRST READING
Sir 3:17-18, 20, 28-29

My child, conduct your affairs with
humility,
and you will be loved more than a giver
of gifts.
Humble yourself the more, the greater
you are,
and you will find favor with God.
What is too sublime for you, seek not,
into things beyond your strength search
not.
The mind of a sage appreciates proverbs,
and an attentive ear is the joy of the
wise.
Water quenches a flaming fire,
and alms atone for sins.

RESPONSORIAL PSALM
Ps 68:4-5, 6-7, 10-11

R℣. (cf. 11b) God, in your goodness, you have made a home for the poor.

The just rejoice and exult before God;
    they are glad and rejoice.
Sing to God, chant praise to his name;
    whose name is the LORD.

R℣. God, in your goodness, you have made a home for the poor.

The father of orphans and the defender of
    widows
    is God in his holy dwelling.
God gives a home to the forsaken;
    he leads forth prisoners to prosperity.

R℣. God, in your goodness, you have made a home for the poor.

A bountiful rain you showered down, O
    God, upon your inheritance;
    you restored the land when it
        languished;
your flock settled in it;
    in your goodness, O God, you provided
        it for the needy.

R℣. God, in your goodness, you have made a home for the poor.

SECOND READING
Heb 12:18-19, 22-24a

Brothers and sisters:
You have not approached that which could
    be touched
    and a blazing fire and gloomy darkness
    and storm and a trumpet blast
    and a voice speaking words such that
        those who heard
    begged that no message be further
        addressed to them.
No, you have approached Mount Zion
    and the city of the living God, the
        heavenly Jerusalem,
    and countless angels in festal gathering,
    and the assembly of the firstborn
        enrolled in heaven,
    and God the judge of all,
    and the spirits of the just made perfect,
    and Jesus, the mediator of a new
        covenant,
    and the sprinkled blood that speaks
        more eloquently than that of Abel.

About Liturgy
Eschatological turning point in Luke's gospel: Toward the end of the liturgical year—as our sequential reading of a Synoptic gospel brings events closer to Jerusalem and Jesus' passion and death—we begin to pick up Parousia (referring to Jesus' second coming) and eschatological themes. Often this begins toward the end of October or early November and culminates in the great eschatological festival, the solemnity of Christ the King. This year, however, themes that we would ordinarily be dealing with later in the liturgical year already show up in late August. This is because of the structure of Luke's gospel, about one-third of which focuses on Jesus' journey to Jerusalem. The prevailing journey theme is a reminder that our whole Christian life is a journey to our final union with Jesus in eschatological glory.

About Liturgical Music
Helping the assembly sing the responsorial psalm: The most important way to help an assembly sing the responsorial psalm is to choose a musical setting that is easy for them to sing. This norm will be relative to the ability of the cantor(s) and the assembly. What is the singing proficiency of this assembly? How used to singing the responsorial psalm are they? If watching and listening to a cantor is still new to them, using simpler musical settings is the way to begin. Another helpful approach is to use the seasonal psalm refrains and common seasonal psalms offered in the Lectionary (nos. 173–74). One of the added gains of this approach is that over time the people will learn to look at the cantor rather than at a line of music in the hymnal or missalette. The goal is eventually to move beyond these seasonal refrains and psalms to singing the psalm assigned for the day.

Another aid to helping the assembly participate more fully in the responsorial psalm is to print the upcoming Sunday psalm refrain in the same spot in the bulletin each week. This "spotlight" could include an invitation to make the refrain a prayer mantra throughout the week. It could also include one or two sentences about the relationship of the psalm to the readings of the day (see "Connecting the Responsorial Psalm" in this volume for ideas).

AUGUST 29, 2010
TWENTY-SECOND SUNDAY IN ORDINARY TIME

✝ SPIRITUALITY

GOSPEL ACCLAMATION
Ps 119: 135

℞. Alleluia, alleluia.
Let your face shine upon your servant;
and teach me your laws.
℞. Alleluia, alleluia.

Gospel   Luke 14:25-33; L129C

Great crowds were traveling with
      Jesus,
   and he turned and addressed
      them,
   "If anyone comes to me without
      hating his father and mother,
   wife and children, brothers and sisters,
   and even his own life,
   he cannot be my disciple.
Whoever does not carry his
      own cross and come after me
   cannot be my disciple.
Which of you wishing to construct a
      tower
   does not first sit down and calculate the
      cost
   to see if there is enough for its
      completion?
Otherwise, after laying the foundation
   and finding himself unable to finish the
      work
   the onlookers should laugh at him and
      say,
   'This one began to build but did not
      have the resources to finish.'
Or what king marching into battle would
      not first sit down
   and decide whether with ten thousand
      troops
   he can successfully oppose another
      king
   advancing upon him with twenty
      thousand troops?
But if not, while he is still far away,
   he will send a delegation to ask for
      peace terms.
In the same way,
   anyone of you who does not renounce
      all his possessions
   cannot be my disciple."

Reflecting on the Gospel

Most of us are bombarded every day with TV commercials, internet spam, newspaper ads with enticing announcements of something we can have for "free." Some of us get stung—we do what the ad asks and find out the "free" thing actually costs quite a lot. Or we are wary from the beginning, knowing that nothing in life comes free. If something is too good to be true, it isn't true; there's a catch someplace. We learn quickly to read the fine print of such offers. In this Sunday's gospel Jesus is very up front with us. He bluntly challenges the crowd to take up the demands of discipleship with eyes wide open. Jesus clearly spells out the fine print in large, large letters: disciples must put Jesus ahead of their families and even their own lives, carry their cross, and renounce all they have. Why would anyone make such a choice to be his follower? Because Jesus has shown us by his own choices that this is the only way to the fullness of life. Discipleship constantly demands of us radical and calculated choices. It offers incalculable fruits.

The gospel lays out three demands, and unless we meet those demands we "cannot be [Jesus'] disciple. First, we must hate father and mother. Obviously, Jesus doesn't mean this literally (over and over again Jesus tells us that we must love even our enemies). This hyperbole is a way for Jesus to stress that even family relationships (where we first receive life and preserve it) and our very own lives must not take precedence over following him. Why is the cost of discipleship so high that we give even our lives? Because we emulate Jesus, who gave his life. No less can be true for disciples. Second, we must carry our cross. This means the daily discipline of self-sacrifice for the sake of others. To follow Jesus means to take up the cross. Third, we must "renounce all . . . possessions." Again, this command must be taken in context. We must forego any thing or conduct that causes us to question discipleship or swerve from the path of following Jesus.

In three different ways in this gospel Jesus tries to help us calculate the cost of discipleship—it demands everything we are and everything we have. Jesus intends no surprises for those who choose discipleship. Here's the fine print: we have to die if we wish to follow Jesus. The cost of discipleship seems disproportionately high compared with anything we could want or value as humans. And this is the point: following Jesus to Jerusalem leads us beyond human expectations. It leads to death, to be sure, but a death that grants us a share in God's very divine life, an outcome worth any price.

Living the Paschal Mystery

The amazing thing is that we *know* the cost of discipleship, yet we spend our whole lives trying to figure it out! We know that we must hand our lives over to Jesus, we know that we are given wisdom and the Holy Spirit to be faithful (see the first reading), yet we aren't quite sure where the journey leads. We just follow.

It would be nice to say that we shouldn't start what we can't finish. If we calculated the cost, or had undo concern for what others think, or weighed the risks involved, we might never begin the journey of discipleship. But we have in fact already begun this journey at baptism. The challenge, then, is not to look at the cost but to keep our eyes on Jesus who is leading. In Jesus, death always leads to new life. This is the promise and it is worth the cost.

Focusing the gospel

Key words and phrases: hating . . . father and mother, cannot be my disciple, carry . . . own cross, calculate the cost, renounce all

To the point: Jesus bluntly challenges the crowd to take up the demands of discipleship with eyes wide open. Disciples must put Jesus ahead of their families and even their own lives, carry their cross, and renounce all they have. Why would anyone make such a choice? Because Jesus has shown us by his own choices that this is the only way to the fullness of life. Discipleship constantly demands of us radical and calculated choices.

Connecting the Gospel

to the first reading: To be faithful disciples we need God's help, for our "deliberations are timid, and unsure are our plans." Through the indwelling of the Holy Spirit, God gives us the wisdom and foresight we need.

to our experience: Achieving success as a professional athlete, musician, artist, or performer places incredible demands on a person's time and energy. Intense commitment is not outside human possibility. Discipleship demands even more: *total* commitment.

Connecting the Responsorial Psalm

to the readings: The first reading reminds us of a truth we are already familiar with: "the deliberations of mortals are timid and unsure." But Jesus challenges us in the gospel to be neither timid nor unsure when deliberating the cost of discipleship. It is total. Relationships must be abandoned, possessions must be renounced, the cross must be carried. The responsorial psalm promises, however, that we will not be left with only our own meager strength. God will grant us "wisdom" and will "prosper the work of our hands." God will give us both the wisdom to calculate the cost and the courage to pay it (first reading). God knows the all-encompassing cost of discipleship and will be with us when we need strength, support, encouragement, and mercy. In singing this psalm we profess our confidence in God, who knows even better than we do what will be exacted of us and who has promised to see us through.

to psalmist preparation: The cost of following Christ is radical, but in this psalm you remind the assembly they have more than themselves to depend upon: their discipleship will prosper because God underwrites it. You sing realistically of both the tenuousness of human strength and the steadfastness of God. May your singing give the assembly courage.

ASSEMBLY & FAITH-SHARING GROUPS

- When I hear Jesus demanding that I place him ahead of family and my own self, I understand Jesus is asking me to . . .
- An example of when I placed someone or something ahead of my discipleship was . . . The cost to me was . . .
- I am willing to pay the high cost of discipleship because . . . I am unwilling when . . .

PRESIDERS

- My preaching helps others understand the cost of discipleship by . . . My ministry encourages others to remain faithful to their discipleship by . . .

DEACONS

- Discipleship requires me to place Jesus ahead of family, self, and possessions. Where this is difficult for me is . . . What makes this possible for me is . . .

HOSPITALITY MINISTERS

- My hospitality (at church, at home, at work) helps others accept the demands of discipleship when . . .

MUSIC MINISTERS

- The unexpected cost of my choosing to be a music minister has been . . . What keeps me faithful is . . .

ALTAR MINISTERS

- What I must renounce in order to serve others faithfully is . . .

LECTORS

- Humanity's "deliberations" are "timid" and "unsure" (first reading). God's word brings wisdom to my everyday deliberations by . . . This strengthens my ministry in that . . .

EXTRAORDINARY MINISTERS OF HOLY COMMUNION

- Eucharist reveals the cost of discipleship by . . . Eucharist inspires and nourishes me to the pay the price until completion because . . .

Model Act of Penitence

Presider: The cost of discipleship is high, as we hear in today's gospel: we must lose our lives, carry our crosses, and renounce our possessions. Jesus speaks strong words to help us understand the cost of following him. Let us pray for wisdom and the Holy Spirit to help us be faithful . . . [pause]

Lord Jesus, you give your life for our salvation: Lord . . .

Christ Jesus, you carry the cross of our human weakness: Christ . . .

Lord Jesus, you give us the Spirit of wisdom and strength: Lord . . .

Homily Points

• The norm in the United States is that youngsters attend school for twelve or so years. This acknowledges our awareness that learning is a long process making continual demands on us. Moreover, learning is about more than acquiring facts; in the process, we grow into the persons we are capable of becoming. Such is even truer of discipleship.

• In this gospel Jesus lays out radical and nonnegotiable demands for discipleship. Meeting these demands, however, is not a prerequisite for discipleship but a road map marking the way of discipleship.

• Jesus invites us to follow him, lays out the demands, and walks with us on the journey as we grow into greater fidelity. The discipline of carrying the cross today strengthens us to carry it tomorrow. For example, not participating in negative gossip strengthens us to regard others with charity; reaching out to another in need when we are already overburdened with responsibilities strengthens our relationships with others. Such dying to self already raises us to new life: we are growing into the persons God has made us capable of becoming.

Model Prayer of the Faithful

Presider: Let us pray that we might be ever more faithful disciples who do not count the cost.

Response:

Lord,   hear our prayer.

Cantor:

we pray   to the Lord,

That all members of the church support one another in taking up our daily cross . . . [pause]

That all people of the world find salvation in God . . . [pause]

That those burdened with the cares of life find comfort in Jesus . . . [pause]

That each of us finish faithfully the work that Jesus has entrusted to us . . . [pause]

Presider: Faithful God, you offer us new life in Christ: hear these our prayers that we might remain faithful to the demands of discipleship and one day enjoy the promise of glory with you. We ask this through Christ our Lord. **Amen.**

OPENING PRAYER

Let us pray

Pause for silent prayer

God our Father,
you redeem us
and make us your children in Christ.
Look upon us,
give us true freedom
and bring us to the inheritance you
    promised.

Grant this through our Lord Jesus Christ,
    your Son,
who lives and reigns with you and the
    Holy Spirit,
one God, for ever and ever. **Amen.**

FIRST READING
Wis 9:13-18b

Who can know God's counsel,
    or who can conceive what the LORD
        intends?
For the deliberations of mortals are timid,
    and unsure are our plans.
For the corruptible body burdens the soul
    and the earthen shelter weighs down the
        mind that has many concerns.
And scarce do we guess the things on
    earth,
    and what is within our grasp we find
        with difficulty;
    but when things are in heaven, who can
        search them out?
Or who ever knew your counsel, except
    you had given wisdom
    and sent your holy spirit from on high?
And thus were the paths of those on earth
    made straight.

RESPONSORIAL PSALM
Ps 90:3-4, 5-6, 12-13, 14, 17

℟. (1) In every age, O Lord, you have been
our refuge.

You turn man back to dust,
    saying, "Return, O children of men."
For a thousand years in your sight
    are as yesterday, now that it is past,
    or as a watch of the night.

℟. In every age, O Lord, you have been
our refuge.

You make an end of them in their sleep;
   the next morning they are like the
      changing grass,
which at dawn springs up anew,
   but by evening wilts and fades.

R̹. In every age, O Lord, you have been
our refuge.

Teach us to number our days aright,
   that we may gain wisdom of heart.
Return, O LORD! How long?
   Have pity on your servants!

R̹. In every age, O Lord, you have been
our refuge.

Fill us at daybreak with your kindness,
   that we may shout for joy and gladness
      all our days.
And may the gracious care of the LORD
   our God be ours;
   prosper the work of our hands for us!
   Prosper the work of our hands!

R̹. In every age, O Lord, you have been
our refuge.

SECOND READING
Phlm 9-10, 12-17

I, Paul, an old man,
   and now also a prisoner for Christ Jesus,
   urge you on behalf of my child
      Onesimus,
   whose father I have become in my
      imprisonment;
I am sending him, that is, my own heart,
      back to you.
I should have liked to retain him for
      myself,
   so that he might serve me on your
      behalf
in my imprisonment for the gospel,
   but I did not want to do anything
      without your consent,
   so that the good you do might not be
      forced but voluntary.
Perhaps this is why he was away from you
      for a while,
   that you might have him back forever,
   no longer as a slave
   but more than a slave, a brother,
   beloved especially to me, but even more
      so to you,
   as a man and in the Lord.
So if you regard me as a partner, welcome
      him as you would me.

About Liturgy

Intercessory prayer: When we read gospels such as this Sunday's we could easily become discouraged at the demands of faithful discipleship. Although Jesus speaks in metaphors, he also is making clear to us that following him will cost us dearly. One way we gain the strength to be faithful is through prayer—for ourselves and for other disciples.

Usually when we think of intercessory or petitionary prayer we think of the specific prayer requests of our own that we send to God or those for which others have asked us to pray—perhaps for a sick family member, or success in the search for employment, or a friend who is suffering from depression. This kind of prayer is good and helps us connect with the everyday concerns of all of us. In the liturgy, however, most often the intercessory prayer is more general—both in intention and for the persons we pray. This more general intercessory prayer (the prayer of the faithful) helps us realize that we are all disciples together on the road to Jerusalem, and one strength we receive is the prayer we have for each other. None of us is ever forgotten in our need.

After the prayer of the faithful that concludes the Liturgy of the Word, intercessory prayer continues within the very heart of our great prayer of praise and thanksgiving, the eucharistic prayer. By continuing our intercessory prayer here, we are reminded that the ultimate praise and thanksgiving we can give God is the gift of our very lives in discipleship. Furthermore, when we are faithful disciples the church is fruitful in its mission. As we pray for the pope, bishops, ministers, and all God's people, we ought to be mindful of the seriousness of the task at hand. Our prayer is that we might not count the cost but look to the fruits of our faithfulness.

About Liturgical Music

Ministry of the psalmist, part 1: Ever since the liturgical reforms of Vatican II, we have generally used the term "cantor" to refer to both the leader of song and the one who sings the responsorial psalm. The U.S. bishops' 2007 document on liturgical music, *Sing to the Lord: Music in Divine Worship,* however, makes a distinction between the "cantor" and the "psalmist" (no. 34). The document makes this distinction in order to highlight the importance of both the responsorial psalm and the one who sings it. Being the psalmist requires skills beyond purely musical ones. In addition to singing ability, the psalmist must also possess the ability to communicate the text of the psalm with "clarity, conviction, and sensitivity to the text, the musical setting, and those who are listening" (no. 35). The ministry requires a spiritual depth and a personal presence that are gifts of the Spirit. Part of selecting persons to be psalmists, then, involves discerning who has been given these gifts.

SEPTEMBER 5, 2010
TWENTY-THIRD SUNDAY
IN ORDINARY TIME

✝ SPIRITUALITY

GOSPEL ACCLAMATION
2 Cor 5:19

R̥. Alleluia, alleluia.
God was reconciling the world to himself in
Christ
and entrusting to us the message of
reconciliation.
R̥. Alleluia, alleluia.

Gospel
Luke 15:1-32; L132C

Tax collectors and
sinners were all
drawing near to
listen to Jesus,
but the Pharisees
and scribes began to complain,
saying,
"This man welcomes sinners and
eats with them."
So to them he addressed this parable.
"What man among you having a
hundred sheep and losing one of
them
would not leave the ninety-nine in the
desert
and go after the lost one until he
finds it?
And when he does find it,
he sets it on his shoulders with great
joy
and, upon his arrival home,
he calls together his friends and
neighbors and says to them,
'Rejoice with me because I have
found my lost sheep.'
I tell you, in just the same way
there will be more joy in heaven over
one sinner who repents
than over ninety-nine righteous people
who have no need of repentance.

"Or what woman having ten coins and
losing one
would not light a lamp and sweep the
house,
searching carefully until she finds it?

Continued in Appendix A, p. 307.

Reflecting on the Gospel

Since Amber Alerts have been introduced, they have greatly helped to find lost children more quickly. But whether a child is lost a short time or a long time, the anguish of the parents is the same until the child is found. It is heart-wrenching to see notices of people who have been missing for many years. Seeking the lost is something we humans do out of deep compassion and love. Even when a total stranger is lost, we take notice. Often times, for example, when there is news of a toddler straying into the woods, we hear of hundreds of people turning up to begin the search. And what rejoicing occurs when someone is found! If this is true of us as humans, how much truer is it of our loving God! In this Sunday's gospel Jesus uses not one but three parables to tell

us how much God seeks us when we are lost, how much God (and all of heaven!) rejoices when we are found.

Jesus uses three situations (a lost sheep, a lost coin, a lost son) to dramatize that whenever we stray from God's steadfast compassion and love (become lost), God always seeks to find us and show us divine mercy. For our part, we must realize we are lost, recognize our need for God, and begin the journey home to be embraced by divine mercy. When God's offer of mercy is met by our repentance, all in heaven rejoice. God's feast is about rejoicing over us humans who stray from God but repent and are welcomed back.

When he returns to his father's house, the younger son doesn't deserve such lavish behavior on the part of the prodigal father. Yet the father is just that—prodigal, lavish in his love and compassion for this lost son. No calculating person would risk ninety-nine or nine for one, or have a feast for one who has squandered so much. No one today would turn a house upside down to find a lost penny (we probably wouldn't even know we lost it). But God does not act like us calculating humans—God always acts with the utmost compassion and love. God always knows when we are lost and gives us every means to come back. God desires that no one be lost. For this we rejoice and feast.

Living the Paschal Mystery

If God is so compassionate and loving with us, then as faithful followers of Jesus we must risk being so compassionate and loving with others. First of all, this means that we don't judge whether the other is worth our compassion and love. God shows us that all are—even outcasts and sinners. Second, we don't earn compassion and love. Since it is a free gift of God to us, it is a gift we freely give to others. We don't wait until someone wrongs us to show compassion and love—we offer these gifts simply because the other is a beloved of God.

It's much easier for us to be compassionate and loving when the end situation is better for us. For example, we might forgive a family member some wrongdoing because we want peace in the family. It is far more risky to be compassionate when there is no immediate gain for us in sight. As those who follow Jesus we are called to be compassionate simply because this is the way Jesus is. Living the paschal mystery means that we feast well and often because we realize that God unfailingly extends compassion and love without calculating whether or not we deserve it. All we need do is repent.

Focusing the gospel
Key words and phrases: lost, go after, found, filled with compassion, celebrate and rejoice

To the point: Jesus uses three situations (a lost sheep, a lost coin, a lost son) to dramatize that whenever we stray from God's steadfast compassion and love (become lost), God always seeks to find us and show us divine mercy. For our part, we must realize we are lost, recognize our need for God, and begin the journey home to be embraced by divine mercy. When God's offer of mercy is met by our repentance, all in heaven rejoice.

Connecting the Gospel
to the first reading: Israel has indeed strayed from God and deserves punishment. Moses intercedes on behalf of the people by reminding God of all God has done on Israel's behalf. Moses appeals to God's steadfast compassion and love.

to our experience: When a calf is taken from the cow, when a deer loses her fawn, when a newborn kitten dies, the mother animals cry. How much more does God weep when we stray from the divine embrace.

Connecting the Responsorial Psalm
to the readings: In his choice to welcome and eat with sinners, Jesus reveals the deep mercy at the very heart of God (gospel). Faced with Israel's infidelity and depravity, God is nonetheless easily dissuaded from wreaking just punishment (first reading). The injured father gives no thought to punishing the Prodigal Son but instead throws him a banquet (gospel). Jesus' parables and his actions reveal the orientation of God who desires the restoration of what is lost and who rejoices over the return of even one sinner.

Our role in this reconciliation is revealed in the behavior of the Prodigal Son who makes the decision to return to his father. The responsorial psalm plays the same role. In the psalm we turn toward God, admit our sinfulness, and beg for restoration. The amazing thing is that once we make the decision to return, the rest of the work of restoration is done by God who washes away our guilt and re-creates our heart. In singing this psalm, then, we enter into the mercy of God. We discover we have a place at the banquet table. We come home, and God rejoices.

to psalmist preparation: Singing these verses from Psalm 51 is an act of public confession, for you stand before the assembly and admit sinfulness. But even more important, you confess the mercy of God who never spurns a contrite and humbled heart. As you prepare to sing this psalm, what forgiveness might you ask of God so that you will know this mercy?

**ASSEMBLY &
FAITH-SHARING GROUPS**
- When, like the tax collectors and sinners, I draw "near to listen to Jesus," what I hear is . . .
- What usually brings me to my "senses" (like the Prodigal Son) and calls me to return home to God is . . .
- I am most in need of God's steadfast compassion and love when . . .

PRESIDERS
- I help others through my ministry to encounter God and receive divine mercy when . . .

DEACONS
- My service reaches out to these who are lost . . . I bring God's compassion and love by . . .

HOSPITALITY MINISTERS
- My hospitality is a sign of God's steadfast compassion and love when . . .

MUSIC MINISTERS
- Whenever I find myself straying from the real purpose of music ministry, Jesus seeks me out and brings me back by . . .

ALTAR MINISTERS
- My service is a sign of God's steadfast care and love when . . .

LECTORS
- God's compassion is greater than the depravity of the stiff-necked people of God (first reading). I extend this compassion toward another when . . . This helps me proclaim God's word better in that . . .

**EXTRAORDINARY MINISTERS
OF HOLY COMMUNION**
- My ministry embodies Jesus' compassion and love for others in that . . .

Model Act of Penitence

Presider: Whenever we are lost or faltering on our Christian journey, God is there with divine compassion and love. As we prepare ourselves to celebrate this liturgy, let us open our hearts to such a lavish God . . . [pause]

Lord Jesus, you are compassionate and loving: Lord . . .

Christ Jesus, you are our feast of love: Christ . . .

Lord Jesus, you are the Good Shepherd who seeks us when we are lost: Lord . . .

Homily Points

• By using the image of a hound closing in on a hare, Francis Thompson's poem "The Hound of Heaven" illustrates how God relentlessly pursues us even when we persist in running from God's presence. Ultimately God's steadfast compassion and love draw us back to life.

• The parables Jesus tells in the gospel all describe God as "The Hound of Heaven" who lovingly pursues us when we are lost or running. Jesus not only tells us about God's love but he himself sought out the lost: ate with sinners, treated women with dignity, reached out to the sick and poor. While God is steadfast in pursuing us, we, however, do have a part to play.

• Our part has a number of steps on our journey of repenting and receiving mercy. First we must stop running. Second, we must be ruthlessly honest about why and how we have run away from God. Then we must stop long enough to hear God's invitation to repent and return home. Finally, we must seek to restore the relationships with others that have been hurt by our running from God.

Model Prayer of the Faithful

Presider: God is full of compassion and love, and listens to our cries for mercy.

Response:

Lord, hear our prayer.

Cantor:

we pray to the Lord,

That the church be quick to search out the lost with compassion and love . . . [pause]

That all peoples of the world be brought to the feast of God's lavish table . . . [pause]

That the poor and outcasts find their home in the loving embrace of God . . . [pause]

That each of us rejoice that God is relentless in pursuing us and bringing us home . . . [pause]

Presider: Compassionate and loving God, you are ever faithful to your promise of salvation: hear these our prayers that one day we might feast at your everlasting banquet table. We ask this through Christ our Lord. **Amen.**

OPENING PRAYER

Let us pray
 [that God will keep us faithful in his
 service]

Pause for silent prayer

Almighty God,
our creator and guide,
may we serve you with all our heart
and know your forgiveness in our lives.

We ask this through our Lord Jesus Christ,
 your Son,
who lives and reigns with you and the
 Holy Spirit,
one God, for ever and ever. **Amen.**

FIRST READING
Exod 32:7-11, 13-14

The LORD said to Moses,
 "Go down at once to your people,
 whom you brought out of the land of
 Egypt,
 for they have become depraved.
They have soon turned aside from the way
 I pointed out to them,
 making for themselves a molten calf
 and worshiping it,
 sacrificing to it and crying out,
 'This is your God, O Israel,
 who brought you out of the land of
 Egypt!'
I see how stiff-necked this people is,"
 continued the LORD to Moses.
"Let me alone, then,
 that my wrath may blaze up against
 them to consume them.
Then I will make of you a great nation."

But Moses implored the LORD, his God,
 saying,
 "Why, O LORD, should your wrath blaze
 up against your own people,
 whom you brought out of the land of
 Egypt
 with such great power and with so
 strong a hand?
Remember your servants Abraham, Isaac,
 and Israel,
 and how you swore to them by your
 own self, saying,
 'I will make your descendants as
 numerous as the stars in the sky;
 and all this land that I promised,
I will give your descendants as their
 perpetual heritage.'"
So the LORD relented in the punishment
 he had threatened to inflict on his
 people.

RESPONSORIAL PSALM
Ps 51:3-4, 12-13, 17, 19

R/. (Luke 15:18) I will rise and go to my father.

Have mercy on me, O God, in your
    goodness;
  in the greatness of your compassion
    wipe out my offense.
Thoroughly wash me from my guilt
  and of my sin cleanse me.

R/. I will rise and go to my father.

A clean heart create for me, O God,
  and a steadfast spirit renew within me.
Cast me not out from your presence,
  and your Holy Spirit take not from me.

R/. I will rise and go to my father.

O Lord, open my lips,
  and my mouth shall proclaim your
    praise.
My sacrifice, O God, is a contrite spirit;
  a heart contrite and humbled, O God,
    you will not spurn.

R/. I will rise and go to my father.

SECOND READING
1 Tim 1:12-17

Beloved:
I am grateful to him who has strengthened
    me, Christ Jesus our Lord,
  because he considered me trustworthy
  in appointing me to the ministry.
I was once a blasphemer and a persecutor
    and arrogant,
  but I have been mercifully treated
  because I acted out of ignorance in my
    unbelief.
Indeed, the grace of our Lord has been
    abundant,
  along with the faith and love that are in
    Christ Jesus.
This saying is trustworthy and deserves
    full acceptance:
  Christ Jesus came into the world to save
    sinners.
Of these I am the foremost.
But for that reason I was mercifully
    treated,
  so that in me, as the foremost,
  Christ Jesus might display all his
    patience as an example
  for those who would come to believe in
    him for everlasting life.
To the king of ages, incorruptible,
    invisible, the only God,
  honor and glory forever and ever. Amen.

About Liturgy

God's prodigality in liturgy: There can be no more concrete expression of God's lavish compassion and love for us than in the celebration of liturgy's sacred mysteries, especially the Eucharist. God's prodigality takes many special symbolic forms during Mass. Here are some examples.

1. *Gifts for the poor.* It is always acceptable and to be encouraged to bring gifts for the poor to be offered along with the bread and wine. These food staples and monetary gifts are concrete expressions of the solidarity we have with others in the Body of Christ as well as a concrete way that we can share God's lavish gifts with others who are less fortunate.

2. *Intercessions.* There are a number of instances at Mass where we are invited to pray for others—after the "Let us pray" invitations, during the prayer of the faithful, at the prayers for the living and dead during the eucharistic prayer, during the Our Father, in the quiet meditation time after Communion (just to name a few of the obvious and communal times for intercessory prayer). Our prayer for each other is an aspect of discipleship and one way we express the worth of all others.

3. *Sign of peace.* The sign of peace is an embrace given in compassion and love. GIRM no. 82 specifies that the sign of peace is offered to those nearby. It doesn't say to family members and friends, but to those nearby. We don't judge whether the person is sinner or saint, wealthy or poor, lost or found—we simply offer this gift of peace because God has first given it to us. The dignity of the sign indicates the dignity of both the giver and receiver.

4. *Communion.* God invites us to the messianic banquet where we rejoice and feast on the very Body and Blood of God's only-begotten Son. There is no discrimination in how the line is formed and who may come; indeed, ministers are not to judge who may receive Communion but simply offer it to all those who come. Especially important is the sign of the one bread and the one cup, for in the Body of Christ we are all beloved in God's eyes.

About Liturgical Music

Ministry of the psalmist, part 2: Whether the members of the assembly are novices or veterans at singing their part of the responsorial psalm, the psalmist must make it obvious that his or her attention is focused on them and their prayer rather than being caught up with self. One of the most important criteria for selecting psalmists, then, is the quality of other-centeredness. Vocal competency and audience poise are only surface aspects of this ministry. The heart of the ministry is the ability to give self to God and to others.

A second vital requirement of this ministry is that the psalmist understand the psalms. Reading about the psalms, reflecting on their meaning, and using them in personal prayer must be regular activities for the psalmist. One way to make praying the psalms routine is to pray Morning and Evening Prayer of the church on a regular basis. One way to grow in understanding the psalms and their meaning is to read at least one book a year on the subject. Books of particular value in this regard include Walter Brueggemann's *The Message of the Psalms* (Minneapolis: Augsburg, 1984); Walter Brueggemann's *The Psalms and the Life of Faith (*Minneapolis: Fortress, 1995); Patrick Miller's *Interpreting the Psalms* (Philadelphia: Fortress, 1986); and V. Steven Parrish's *A Story of the Psalms: Conversation, Canon, and Congregation* (Collegeville, MN: Liturgical Press, 2003).

SEPTEMBER 12, 2010
TWENTY-FOURTH SUNDAY IN ORDINARY TIME

✠ SPIRITUALITY

GOSPEL ACCLAMATION
2 Cor 8:9

℟. Alleluia, alleluia.
Though our Lord Jesus Christ was rich, he
   became poor,
so that by his poverty you might become
   rich.
℟. Alleluia, alleluia.

Gospel
Luke 16:1-13; L135C

Jesus said to his disciples,
   "A rich man had a steward
   who was reported to him for
      squandering his property.
He summoned him and said,
   'What is this I hear about you?
Prepare a full account of your
      stewardship,
   because you can no longer be
      my steward.'
The steward said to himself,
   'What shall I do,
   now that my master is taking
      the position of steward away
      from me?
I am not strong enough to dig and I am
      ashamed to beg.
I know what I shall do so that,
   when I am removed from the
      stewardship,
   they may welcome me into their
      homes.'
He called in his master's debtors one
      by one.
To the first he said,
   'How much do you owe my master?'
He replied, 'One hundred measures of
      olive oil.'
He said to him, 'Here is your
      promissory note.
Sit down and quickly write one for
      fifty.'
Then to another the steward said, 'And
      you, how much do you owe?'
He replied, 'One hundred kors of wheat.'

Continued in Appendix A, p. 308.

Reflecting on the Gospel
Dishonesty seems to have become a way of life for all too many people. Some corporate leaders have amassed great wealth at the expense of stockholders, sometimes even to the point of companies going bankrupt. Substance abuse has made stealing a way of life for others. Cheating on income taxes has become a badge of honor for still others. Dishonesty always robs us—the dishonest one of dignity, the hurt party of deserved wealth. In this Sunday's gospel, a dishonest servant cheats his master for personal gain. He thinks he has secured a future for himself; in fact, he has secured nothing, as Jesus tells us.

This odd-sounding gospel isn't about Jesus commending the steward's dishonesty; dishonesty is just that, and is never virtuous. Jesus does, however, commend the steward's shrewdness in cleverly ensuring a secure future for himself, albeit not the future Jesus is trying to teach his disciples about. Disciples must be equally shrewd as the steward but make very different choices: choosing trustworthy service over dishonesty for personal gain, choosing concern for others over personal needs, choosing eternal happiness above security in this world at any cost. In these very choices, disciples serve God and God alone. Only by serving God alone can we ever secure for ourselves a sure future: being "welcomed into eternal dwellings."

We must handle the things of this world and our daily actions in relation to what is eternal and with prudent decisiveness. This means that there can be no split between our spiritual/religious lives (for example, going to Mass on Sunday) and our daily living. Christianity is better expressed as a *way of life* than as practices to be fulfilled. Prudent decisiveness about our future means that "religion" is an expression of our relationship to God that is shown in the simple choices of our daily living. To put it simply, prudent decisiveness about our future means that God is truly at the center of our lives. Truly, we serve God and God alone.

Living the Paschal Mystery
When it comes to paschal mystery living, we often squander opportunities to gain "true wealth." The thrust of the gospel is that we act prudently in this life in order to "be welcomed into eternal dwellings." Prudence demands that we not squander opportunities to be charitable and just toward others. Prudence demands that we not squander opportunities to die to self. Prudence demands that we not squander opportunities to be trustworthy with the ministry of discipleship that we take on each time we say yes to our baptismal commitment.

Most of us are serious about our paschal mystery living. We honestly try to live good lives. When opportunities present themselves to act in a Christian way, most of us respond appropriately most of the time. This gospel challenges us to take this one step further. Paschal mystery living isn't simply a matter of *surrendering* to the self-sacrificing possibilities that come our way simply in the normal course of daily living. With an eye to the future, we must also *surrender* ourselves to actually *searching out* opportunities to live the paschal mystery. There is such an urgency about discipleship and proclaiming the Good News of salvation that we cannot be passive in any way. Just as Jesus did all he needed to do to make his message known, even when that led to Jerusalem and the cross, so must we be as proactive in our own discipleship.

Focusing the gospel

Key words and phrases: commended . . . for acting prudently, trustworthy, welcomed into eternal dwellings, serve . . . God

To the point: Jesus does not commend the steward's dishonesty; he does commend his shrewdness in cleverly ensuring a secure future for himself. Disciples must be equally shrewd but make very different choices: choosing trustworthy service over dishonesty for personal gain, choosing concern for others over personal needs, choosing eternal happiness above security in this world at any cost. In these very choices, disciples serve God and God alone.

Connecting the Gospel

to the first reading: This reading from Amos shows the consequences of making choices for selfish personal gain and losing sight of how we are to be in relation to each other.

to our experience: To protect ourselves and our families and to have enough to get ahead in this life, we must be shrewd about many things. To win eternal life, shrewdness is not enough. We must care for others, be honest and trustworthy, maintain single-minded focus on God.

Connecting the Responsorial Psalm

to the readings: The connection of the responsorial psalm to the first reading is obvious. In the first reading God swears never to forget an injustice done to the poor. In the psalm God redresses such wrongs and raises the poor from dust to nobility. The relationship of the psalm to the gospel, however, is not so clear. Both the first reading and the gospel relate incidences of unjust and dishonest behavior pursued for the sake of personal gain. The intimation is that these stories exemplify the choice to serve mammon rather than God. Yet while Jesus condemns dishonest behavior, he commends the dishonest steward for pursuing it.

What Jesus invites, however, is not emulation of the behavior but emulation of the shrewdness that motivates it. We are to act in service of what is true and just. The role of the psalm, then, becomes clear. Our real model of behavior is God who redresses wrongs and raises up the poor. In praying this psalm we are singing the praises of the One we wish to be like. We are choosing our Master.

to psalmist preparation: In singing this psalm you invite the assembly to praise God for acting on behalf of the poor and oppressed. By implication you also invite them to imitate God in their own manner of acting. In what ways do you choose God as your Master and guide? In what ways do you struggle with this choice? How might Christ help you?

ASSEMBLY & FAITH-SHARING GROUPS

- If Jesus were to say to me "Prepare a full account of your stewardship," my response would be . . .
- The steward acted decisively and prudently at a critical moment. For a disciple each moment in every day is critical because . . .
- I am trustworthy in serving God and others when . . .

PRESIDERS

- I am serving mammon whenever I . . . I am serving God whenever I . . . The impact each has on my ministry is . . .

DEACONS

- My ministry embodies "the Lord who lifts up the poor" (psalm) whenever I . . .

HOSPITALITY MINISTERS

- In my ministry, putting others' needs ahead of my personal gain is a challenge when . . . is a joy when . . .

MUSIC MINISTERS

- Sometimes in my music ministry I find myself divided between serving more than one master. I know I am serving God when . . . I know I am serving another master when . . .

ALTAR MINISTERS

- My serving God at the altar helps me better serve others in need because . . .

LECTORS

- When I serve God faithfully in my living, my proclamation is like . . . When I am self-serving in my daily living, my proclamation is like . . .

EXTRAORDINARY MINISTERS OF HOLY COMMUNION

- My manner of distributing Holy Communion reveals that God is the center of my life in that . . .

Model Act of Penitence

Presider: In today's gospel Jesus reminds us that we cannot serve both God and money. We must make a choice. Let us open our hearts to encounter Jesus who helps us make good choices as his followers . . . [pause]

Lord Jesus, you teach us the way to fullness of life: Lord . . .

Christ Jesus, you live in eternal glory: Christ . . .

Lord Jesus, you call us to serve God with singleness of mind and heart: Lord . . .

Homily Points

• The issue of financial manipulation at the expense of others is a rampant problem. For example, CEOs embezzle funds from their companies; individuals overspend, then declare bankruptcy to avoid paying debts; businesses charge exorbitantly high interest rates on credit cards and advance check cashing. The kind of manipulative behavior of the dishonest steward in the gospel parable, then, is not all that uncommon even today. What is perhaps too uncommon is the behavior to which Jesus calls us who are his disciples.

• Jesus acknowledges by his examples in the gospel that faithful disciples every day face issues dealing with self-interest, trustworthiness, honesty. These issues force us to make choices revealing our real goals for life. The foundation for all our choices must be that God holds first place in our hearts.

• When we choose to give God first place in our hearts, this is what happens: we live simpler lives dependent upon fewer material things, we experience serving others as serving God, we find that being trustworthy and honest is its own reward. These ways of living and relating show the kind of shrewdness Jesus praises and bring us to eternal happiness.

Model Prayer of the Faithful

Presider: We turn to the God whom we serve and make known our needs.

Response:

Lord, hear our prayer.

Cantor:

we pray to the Lord,

That all members of the church deepen their choice to serve God and God alone . . . [pause]

That leaders of the world's nations faithfully serve the needs of their people . . . [pause]

That those threatened by an insecure future find support in the care of others . . . [pause]

That each of us remain trustworthy and faithful in following Jesus . . . [pause]

Presider: Merciful God, you hear the prayers of those who call out to you: help us to be prudent about the affairs of this life so that we might enjoy the richness of your eternal glory. We ask this through Christ our Lord. **Amen.**

OPENING PRAYER

Let us pray
[that we may grow in the love of God
and of one another]

Pause for silent prayer

Father,
guide us, as you guide creation
according to your law of love.
May we love one another
and come to perfection
in the eternal life prepared for us.

Grant this through our Lord Jesus Christ,
your Son,
who lives and reigns with you and the
Holy Spirit,
one God, for ever and ever. **Amen.**

FIRST READING
Amos 8:4-7

Hear this, you who trample upon the
needy
and destroy the poor of the land!
"When will the new moon be over," you
ask,
"that we may sell our grain,
and the sabbath, that we may display
the wheat?
We will diminish the ephah,
add to the shekel,
and fix our scales for cheating!
We will buy the lowly for silver,
and the poor for a pair of sandals;
even the refuse of the wheat we will
sell!"
The LORD has sworn by the pride of Jacob:
Never will I forget a thing they have
done!

RESPONSORIAL PSALM
Ps 113:1-2, 4-6, 7-8

R̸. (cf. 1a, 7b) Praise the Lord, who lifts up
the poor.
or:
R̸. Alleluia.

Praise, you servants of the LORD,
praise the name of the LORD.
Blessed be the name of the LORD
both now and forever.

R̸. Praise the Lord, who lifts up the poor.
or:
R̸. Alleluia.

High above all nations is the LORD;
　above the heavens is his glory.
Who is like the LORD, our God, who is
　　enthroned on high
　and looks upon the heavens and the
　　earth below?

R⁄. Praise the Lord, who lifts up the poor.
　or:
R⁄. Alleluia.

He raises up the lowly from the dust;
　from the dunghill he lifts up the poor
to seat them with princes,
　with the princes of his own people.

R⁄. Praise the Lord, who lifts up the poor.
　or:
R⁄. Alleluia.

SECOND READING
1 Tim 2:1-8

Beloved:
First of all, I ask that supplications,
　　prayers,
　petitions, and thanksgivings be offered
　　for everyone,
　for kings and for all in authority,
　that we may lead a quiet and tranquil
　　life
　in all devotion and dignity.
This is good and pleasing to God our
　　savior,
　who wills everyone to be saved
　and to come to knowledge of the truth.
　　For there is one God.
　　There is also one mediator between God
　　　and men,
　　the man Christ Jesus,
　　who gave himself as ransom for all.
This was the testimony at the proper time.
For this I was appointed preacher and
　　apostle
　—I am speaking the truth, I am not
　　lying—,
　teacher of the Gentiles in faith and
　　truth.

It is my wish, then, that in every place the
　　men should pray,
　lifting up holy hands, without anger
　　or argument.

✠ CATECHESIS

About Liturgy

Praying always: One way to thwart compartmentalizing our religion is to develop a habit of praying always (see, for example, 1 Thess 5:17). Even if our liturgical prayer is very rich and satisfying—and this is the goal of every parish—we also need our own personal, devotional prayer to complement liturgical prayer. If the only time of the week we think about God is during Sunday Mass, it will be quite difficult, if not impossible, to grasp that our daily decisions are really expressions of our commitment to be followers of Jesus who serve God alone.

Since Vatican II there has been something of a negative attitude about devotional prayer. Some of this derives from the historical fact that in the past not all devotions were good ones. The Constitution on the Sacred Liturgy gives criteria for good devotional prayer: it should help to draw us into the various liturgical seasons, lead us to a better celebration of liturgy, help us to live liturgy in our daily lives (no. 13). One sure way to accomplish this is to prepare for liturgy ahead of Sunday, especially by reflecting on the readings. Perhaps one might take the response to the psalm and make that a kind of mantra that is recited throughout the week, especially when difficult decisions come our way. If we are singers we might even sing it when we are driving somewhere or while we are doing work at home. It might begin and end our meals.

Meals could be another way of praying always. Families might have to make a concerted effort to eat at least one or two meals together during the week. Then during the meal there might be conscious sharing about each one's successes and failures, about how members of the family are trying to live the gospel, about the good each one sees in the other. At first this might seem awkward and uncomfortable, especially if family members haven't shared in this way before. With time, each family will find what works best for them. Over time, members will see how more and more of their daily lives are lived with an eye to God.

About Liturgical Music

Ministry of the psalmist, part 3: It is important that the psalmist prepare the singing of the responsorial psalm in the context of the readings and gospel of the day. Before looking at the psalm, the psalmist needs to read the gospel and first reading (and the second reading during festal seasons and on solemnities) and spend some time reflecting on and praying over them. Only then should the psalmist look at the text of the psalm and see how it is connected to the first reading and gospel. The purpose of "Connecting the Responsorial Psalm" in this volume is to help the psalmist (and everyone in the assembly) make this connection and apply it to daily living.

A psalmist who has a sense of how the psalm is connected to the first reading and gospel, as well as to his or her daily living, will have a better sense of how to sing the psalm. The psalmist will realize his or her singing is actually a dialogue with God that mirrors the dialogue going on between God and the assembly in the Liturgy of the Word. A dimension will emerge that is deeper than the music alone, that is nothing less than the working of God leading the psalmist to surrender to the paschal mystery. It is this surrender that the assembly members will hear and to which they will respond.

SEPTEMBER 19, 2010
TWENTY-FIFTH SUNDAY
IN ORDINARY TIME

✝ SPIRITUALITY

GOSPEL ACCLAMATION
2 Cor 8:9

R̸. Alleluia, alleluia.
Though our Lord Jesus Christ was rich, he became poor,
so that by his poverty you might become rich.
R̸. Alleluia, alleluia.

Gospel
Luke 16:19-31; L138C

Jesus said to the Pharisees:
  "There was a rich man who
      dressed in purple garments
      and fine linen
    and dined sumptuously each
      day.
  And lying at his door was a poor
      man named Lazarus, covered
      with sores,
    who would gladly have eaten his
      fill of the scraps
    that fell from the rich man's table.
  Dogs even used to come and lick his
      sores.
  When the poor man died,
    he was carried away by angels to the
      bosom of Abraham.
  The rich man also died and was buried,
    and from the netherworld, where he
      was in torment,
    he raised his eyes and saw Abraham
      far off
    and Lazarus at his side.
  And he cried out, 'Father Abraham, have
      pity on me.
  Send Lazarus to dip the tip of his finger
      in water and cool my tongue,
    for I am suffering torment in these
      flames.'
  Abraham replied,
    'My child, remember that you received
    what was good during your lifetime
    while Lazarus likewise received what
      was bad;
    but now he is comforted here, whereas
      you are tormented.

Continued in Appendix A, p. 308.

Reflecting on the Gospel
Every day we are bombarded with the "needy" at our door—we receive telephone, mail, door-to-door solicitations for donations to various charitable organizations, and other kinds of requests for help. Often, if a fire destroys a family's home with all their belongings, the news lists the banks where one can make a donation to help. An accidental death that makes the news sometimes includes information on where to send donations to help defray funeral expenses. Clearly, we cannot respond to all requests for help or help all the needy of the world.

Daily we are faced with choices, sometimes difficult ones. This Sunday's gospel is a parable about the needy at our door, with an admonition to *listen*. We are faced with a question: how does listening open up the insight to see needs? Ultimately, this is a question about how we become more compassionate and caring people.

Jesus addresses this parable specifically to the Pharisees. This is telling. The Pharisees were the "professional" teachers in Jesus' time. They knew the law and what is demanded in order to be faithful to the covenant with each other. However, they have become complacent in neglecting what they *know*—Moses and the prophets have urged Israel to care for the poor and needy. Jesus had come with the same message; they weren't listening to him either. Had the Pharisees had an attitude of *listening*, they would have been open to Jesus. Without this openness, even rising "from the dead" would not persuade.

We are so inundated with requests for donations that we can turn a deaf ear to them; it is so easy to live oblivious to the needs of others. Jesus makes clear at the end of this parable, however, that we are given everything we need to set our values and relationships right. We have the words of "Moses and the prophets." Even more, unlike the rich man in the parable, we *do* have Someone among us who has "rise[n] from the dead." We need only listen. This is how we gain the insight to see those in need at our own door and choose how to respond.

There is a great "chasm" between selfishness and self-surrender, between evil and good, between the lost and saved. This chasm is a metaphor for *listening* to God's word and allowing ourselves to be guided by its demands. The time to respond decisively to God and others is *now*; after death it is too late.

Living the Paschal Mystery
There is no need to be frightened about eternal life if we daily allow God's word to guide us in our responses to others in need. Thus do we prepare for eternal life. This is what is amazing about choosing to help others, no matter how insignificant the help might seem: whatever we do for others is a preparation for eternal life.

God's word comes to us in more ways than the proclamations at Sunday Mass or taking time to read the Bible—as important as both of those are. God's word also comes to us through others. It can be presented as someone in need. God's word might come in some challenge to our self-centeredness or values. It might come through another's encouragement. In all these ways and countless others we are invited to *listen*. Listening is guidance for how to respond with compassion and care for others.

Focusing the gospel

Key words and phrases: lying at his door, Moses and the prophets, listen, not listen, someone should rise from the dead

To the point: We can so easily live oblivious to the needs of others. Jesus makes clear at the end of this parable, however, that we are given everything we need to set our values and relationships right. We have the words of "Moses and the prophets." Even more, unlike the rich man in the parable, we *do* have Someone among us who has "rise[n] from the dead." We need only listen. This is how we gain the insight to see those in need at our own door.

Connecting the Gospel

to the first reading: The first reading exemplifies what happens to those who heed not the words of Moses and the prophets: exile and destruction.

to our experience: For all kinds of reasons, we can be blind to the needs of others, even those who are suffering greatly. What opens our eyes is an encounter with Jesus who moves us to "pity."

Connecting the Responsorial Psalm

to the readings: Both the first reading and the gospel relate stories of indifference to human suffering. In the first reading the complacent revel in wine and music while society collapses around them. In the gospel the rich man gorges himself while the beggar dies of hunger at his gate. Had they heeded Moses and the prophets (gospel), they would have lived differently and secured a different future for themselves. The responsorial psalm relates a contrasting story. In the psalm, God secures justice for the oppressed, feeds the hungry, raises up the poor, and cares for those in need.

In a sense the psalm is our message from Moses and the prophets. By praising God for never being indifferent to human suffering, the psalm challenges us to act likewise. We have been sent the message, then; it is for us to hear and heed. May our singing of this psalm be a sign that we have heard and have chosen to heed. And may we reign with God forever (psalm).

to psalmist preparation: As with last Sunday's psalm, this psalm holds God up as the model of behavior for faithful disciples. The church is called to act on behalf of the poor and suffering just as God does. In singing this psalm you invite the assembly to respond to this call. In what ways are you responding? In what ways do you need to grow in response?

ASSEMBLY & FAITH-SHARING GROUPS

- The rich man did not heed the warnings from "Moses and the prophets." What makes me face the demanding truth of God's word is . . .
- I listen to the risen Jesus when . . . This changes my relationships to others by . . .
- A Lazarus to whom I need to respond is . . .

PRESIDERS

- Amos condemns the complacent for not heeding the suffering within the tribe of Joseph (see first reading). My ministry awakens others to the suffering of the disadvantaged by . . .

DEACONS

- I find myself listening to "Moses and the prophets" when . . . This helps me see those in need around me because . . .

HOSPITALITY MINISTERS

- My hospitality must include listening to others by . . . seeing others' needs when . . . responding in compassion to . . .

MUSIC MINISTERS

- My music ministry helps me listen better to God's word because . . . What in my ministry can interfere with this listening is . . .

ALTAR MINISTERS

- The last time I served "Lazarus" was . . . What this taught me about serving at the altar was …

LECTORS

- An example of God's word shattering my neglect of the needs of others is . . .

EXTRAORDINARY MINISTERS OF HOLY COMMUNION

- When I distribute Holy Communion I am "listening" to the needs of others in that . . .

Model Act of Penitence

Presider: Let us open ourselves to God's presence and prepare to listen to God's word, that we might respond to others with generosity and compassion . . . [pause]

Lord Jesus, you call us to listen to your words of truth: Lord . . .

Christ Jesus, you are the One raised from the dead: Christ . . .

Lord Jesus, you show us the way of compassion and care: Lord . . .

Homily Points

• A Korean proverb states, "As the twig is bent, so grows the tree." Every day many forces and influences bend us this way and that: peer pressure, advertising, job stress, financial worries, interpersonal tensions. What keeps us growing strong and straight is the voice of Jesus, the One risen from the dead who leads us to true life and happiness.

• The One who has risen from the dead offers us a share in his risen life. We are in turn to share this fullness of life with one another, especially with those most suffering from what we might call "lack of life," the "Lazaruses" among us. We learn this way of sharing life as we listen to Jesus speak to us every day.

• We hear the voice of Jesus not only in the proclamation of the Scriptures but also in many other ways: through the good work of others, through our own experience of doing good for others, in the cry of the poor and needy. Such listening opens us to a much wider world and develops in us attitudes of compassion and care.

Model Prayer of the Faithful

Presider: Let us pray that we might see and respond to those in need.

Response:

Lord, hear our prayer.

Cantor:

we pray to the Lord,

That the church proclaim boldly and listen attentively to God's word . . . [pause]

That all peoples of the world listen attentively to voices calling them to justice and peace . . . [pause]

That the poor and the hungry be met with compassion and care . . . [pause]

That this community continue to grow in listening to the voice of Jesus and reaching out to those in need . . . [pause]

Presider: Merciful God, you send your word of truth to lead us to everlasting life: hear these our prayers that we might become more faithful disciples of your Son who lives and reigns with you and the Holy Spirit, one God for ever and ever. **Amen.**

OPENING PRAYER

Let us pray

Pause for silent prayer

Father,
you show your almighty power
in your mercy and forgiveness.
Continue to fill us with your gifts of love.
Help us to hurry toward the eternal life
    you promise
and come to share in the joys of your
    kingdom.

Grant this through our Lord Jesus Christ,
    your Son,
who lives and reigns with you and the
    Holy Spirit,
one God, for ever and ever. **Amen.**

FIRST READING

Amos 6:1a, 4-7

Thus says the LORD, the God of hosts:
Woe to the complacent in Zion!
Lying upon beds of ivory,
    stretched comfortably on their couches,
they eat lambs taken from the flock,
    and calves from the stall!
Improvising to the music of the harp,
    like David, they devise their own
        accompaniment.
They drink wine from bowls
    and anoint themselves with the best oils;
    yet they are not made ill by the collapse
        of Joseph!
Therefore, now they shall be the first to go
    into exile,
    and their wanton revelry shall be done
        away with.

RESPONSORIAL PSALM
Ps 146:7, 8-9, 9-10

R̸. (1b) Praise the Lord, my soul!
or:
R̸. Alleluia.

Blessed is he who keeps faith forever,
    secures justice for the oppressed,
    gives food to the hungry.
The LORD sets captives free.

R̸. Praise the Lord, my soul!
or:
R̸. Alleluia.

The LORD gives sight to the blind.
    The LORD raises up those who were
        bowed down.
The LORD loves the just;
    the LORD protects strangers.

R̸. Praise the Lord, my soul!
or:
R̸. Alleluia.

The fatherless and the widow he sustains,
    but the way of the wicked he thwarts.
The LORD shall reign forever;
    your God, O Zion, through all
        generations. Alleluia.

R̸. Praise the Lord, my soul!
or:
R̸. Alleluia.

SECOND READING
1 Tim 6:11-16

But you, man of God, pursue righteousness,
    devotion, faith, love, patience, and
        gentleness.
Compete well for the faith.
Lay hold of eternal life, to which you were
    called
        when you made the noble confession in
            the presence of many witnesses.
I charge you before God, who gives life to
    all things,
    and before Christ Jesus,
    who gave testimony under Pontius
        Pilate for the noble confession,
    to keep the commandment without stain
        or reproach
    until the appearance of our Lord Jesus
        Christ
    that the blessed and only ruler
    will make manifest at the proper time,
    the King of kings and Lord of lords,
    who alone has immortality, who dwells
        in unapproachable light,
    and whom no human being has seen or
        can see.
To him be honor and eternal power. Amen.

About Liturgy

Purple and Advent: This gospel's description of the rich man has him "dressed in purple garments and fine linen." The mention of the color isn't simply a nice detail about a man whose favorite color was purple. Purple dye was very expensive at that time, when there were no inexpensive substitutes for natural dyes and so only the wealthy could afford clothes dyed purple. Purple clothing, then, proclaimed a status in society. Because purple was also frequently associated with emperors and kings, it likewise became a color associated with Jesus (see Mark 15:17 and John 19:2, where Jesus is clothed in a purple cloak during his scourging in mockery). When we celebrate Jesus as King (which we will do on the Thirty-fourth Sunday in Ordinary Time, the solemnity of Christ the King) we recall Jesus' victory and reign of glory. Purple, then, is a liturgical color that reminds us of eschatological glory and the end times when Jesus will come again to reign forever.

We make the distinction between royal purple (blue-purple) and violet purple (red-purple). We use the royal purple during Advent because it is a season that celebrates Jesus' victory and eternal reign. Already in these gospels from Matthew our attention is turned toward the end times and Jesus' eschatological victory.

About Liturgical Music

Music suggestions: The rich man who ignored the poor man dying on his doorstep finds himself condemned to eternal torment after his own death, when it is too late to change the choices he made in life. There are a number of songs available that call us to act now on behalf of the poor and needy in our midst. "God of Day and God of Darkness" [BB, G2, GC, GC2, RS, SS, WC, WS] offers an excellent text; its length indicates it might work best during the preparation of the gifts. "Abundant Life" [GC2] calls us to live in such a way "that all may have abundant life"; its gentle melody and tempo would be best suited for the preparation of the gifts. The energy of "Let Justice Roll Like a River" [GC2] suggests its suitability for the entrance or recessional; its length however, might work better during the preparation of the gifts or Communion. Finally, a superb choice for either the entrance or the recessional would be "God Whose Purpose Is to Kindle" [GC, GC2, RS] in which we ask God to "overcome our sinful calmness" and "disturb" the "complacency" we feel in face of "our neighbor's misery."

SEPTEMBER 26, 2010
TWENTY-SIXTH SUNDAY
IN ORDINARY TIME

✠ SPIRITUALITY

GOSPEL ACCLAMATION
1 Pet 1:25

℟. Alleluia, alleluia.
The word of the Lord remains forever.
This is the word that has been proclaimed to
    you.
℟. Alleluia, alleluia.

Gospel

Luke 17:5-10; L141C

The apostles said to the Lord,
    "Increase our faith."
The Lord replied,
  "If you have faith the size of a
      mustard seed,
  you would say to this mulberry tree,
  'Be uprooted and planted in the sea,'
      and it would obey you.

"Who among you would say to
      your servant
  who has just come in from plowing or
      tending sheep in the field,
  'Come here immediately and take
      your place at table'?
Would he not rather say to him,
  'Prepare something for me to eat.
Put on your apron and wait on me while
      I eat and drink.
You may eat and drink when I am
      finished'?
Is he grateful to that servant because
      he did what was commanded?
So should it be with you.
When you have done all you have been
      commanded,
  say, 'We are unprofitable servants;
  we have done what we were obliged
      to do.'"

Reflecting on the Gospel

Many of us have had the experience of driving on a highway and passing a semitrailer loaded with a mobile home. We have the ability to build a house and then move it to wherever we want it. A few years ago a three-story, century-old brick building on the campus of Saint John's University was hoisted up, loaded onto trailers, and moved to another part of campus. What an awesome sight! This stalwart building was picked up and moved—rather quickly, with seemingly little effort. We now have the hydraulics knowledge and enough power to practically move mountains if we want. Move a mulberry tree? No problem! When Jesus in the gospel suggests that a little bit of faith can move a mulberry tree, he's not suggesting that we hire hydraulic equipment! He's suggesting that we recognize that the power to be faithful disciples is not found in "how much" but in how obedient we are to responsibility.

The apostles' request of Jesus to "increase [their] faith" is made in the face of the seemingly impossible demands of discipleship. The issue is to take what we have—whether little or great—and *act*. If we wait until we think we have enough faith, we will never act. In the first example about the mulberry tree, Jesus is saying that even a little faith is enough to move this tree. The point about faith that Jesus makes is not that it be measured; active and fruitful faith is not a matter of "how much." But we must use what we do have, because even a little bit gives us great power to accomplish God's work. This is the great encouragement of the gospel. We have enough to be faithful disciples. We must have faith in who we are: God's servants empowered to carry on Jesus' saving mission.

Though the apostles ask Jesus to "increase [their] faith," what he gives them instead is greater confidence in the power of the faith they already have. What is this faith? It is obedience to responsibility, a matter of willingness to undertake decisive action for the sake of God's kingdom. Even faith that "feels" small possesses great power. Faithfulness is doing all we have been commanded. "Faith-filledness" is *acting* decisively. The faithful and faith-filled disciple is the one who doesn't wait for enough faith but continues to respond to the everyday and never-ending demands of discipleship. The Master demands our service. And then gives us the faith to perform it well.

Living the Paschal Mystery

When we think of people of great faith, we often mention people like Gandhi or Mother Teresa. These were great religious leaders who obviously had great faith and accomplished great things. We make a mistake, however, if we identify faith only with doing great things. Jesus reminds us in this gospel that our everyday actions, performed in loving service, are expressions of our faith.

The faith-filled person puts in an honest day's work. That person is gracious to those they encounter. That person is ready to reach out and help another, even beyond one's own workload. The faith-filled person sees Jesus in the other and responds to the situation with Jesus' love and care. Faith is obedience to responsibility. It is obedience to discipleship. It is obedience to our Master who encourages us, helps us, never abandons us.

Focusing the gospel

Key words and phrases: Increase our faith, did what was commanded

To the point: In this Sunday's gospel the apostles ask Jesus to "increase [their] faith." What he gives them instead is greater confidence in the power of the faith they already have. What is this faith? It is obedience to responsibility, a matter of willingness to undertake decisive action for the sake of God's kingdom. Even faith that "feels" small possesses great power.

Connecting the Gospel

to the first reading: Habakkuk laments because he is faced with so much violence and evil. God, however, has a longer view of history—these immediate events do not tell the full story of God's saving vision. Whereas Jesus describes the responsibility of faith, Habakkuk describes where our faith leads: "the just one . . . shall live."

to our experience: We sometimes think people of great faith are those who do big things for God and church. Faith is as readily expressed in simple acts of everyday service.

Connecting the Responsorial Psalm

to the readings: When the disciples ask Jesus to increase their faith, his answer seems unrelated to their request (gospel). The first reading, however, puts his answer in context. To have faith means to maintain hope in God's promise despite the long delay in its fulfillment (first reading). To have faith means to keep working at the task of discipleship even when we think that surely the task has been completed (gospel).

The responsorial psalm adds the dimension that having faith means to keep trudging on the journey to the Promised Land even when the going is rough and the goal far off. The first two strophes of the psalm have us arriving at the goal with joyful song. The final strophe, however, reminds us we are still on the journey and that the temptation to give up faith and quit the task—as did many Israelites in the desert—is real. May we not harden our hearts when God calls us to keep moving. May we keep working and keep maintaining faith.

to psalmist preparation: The harsh shift between the beginning of this responsorial psalm and its conclusion makes sense only when you acknowledge how easy it is to give up on the task of faithful discipleship. In the refrain you call the assembly to remain faithful despite setbacks and hardships. Where in your own life do you struggle with these setbacks and hardships? What do you hear God saying to you at these times? What helps you listen and respond with faith?

ASSEMBLY & FAITH-SHARING GROUPS

- Times when I plead to God for an increase of faith are . . .
- The circumstances where I am regularly required to "put my apron on" after a long day and continue serving is . . . This expresses my faith in that . . .
- I have experienced the power of faith when . . .

PRESIDERS

- I empower those whom I serve to have greater confidence in their faith when . . . by . . . They empower me when . . . by . . .

DEACONS

- My serving is an obedience to responsibility in that . . . It strengthens my faith when . . .

HOSPITALITY MINISTERS

- Extending hospitality to others has increased my faith when . . . has increased their faith when . . .

MUSIC MINISTERS

- The faithful discipleship I expect of myself in music ministry is . . . The faithful discipleship God expects is . . .

ALTAR MINISTERS

- My unobtrusive service is, indeed, an expression of great faith in that . . .

LECTORS

- My manner of proclaiming the Word enables listeners to see God's vision clearly (see first reading) when . . .

EXTRAORDINARY MINISTERS OF HOLY COMMUNION

- Distributing the Eucharist strengthens my faith in that . . .

Model Act of Penitence

Presider: As we begin this liturgy let us pray for the faith to remain decisive in following Jesus. Let us open ourselves to God's presence that our faith may grow stronger . . . [pause]

Lord Jesus, you strengthen our faith in you: Lord . . .

Christ Jesus, you are the risen One who lives forever: Christ . . .

Lord Jesus, you call us to be faithful disciples: Lord . . .

Homily Points

• What "mulberry trees" need to be moved in our lives? These "mulberry trees" are whatever big things seem insurmountable to us. Some examples might be overcoming our fear of reconciling with another who has hurt us deeply, dealing with some addiction, feeding the world's hungers, establishing lasting world peace, having patience with a teenager who seems to be choosing the wrong path. We tend to labor under the misconception that we can deal successfully with these issues if we only have more faith. Jesus tells us, however, that even the smallest bit of faith gives us the power to tackle whatever challenges life brings.

• Faith is measured not by problem solving but by being obedient servants of God. This faith enables us to move beyond our own limited vision and embrace instead God's vision of how the world is to be—a world free of violence, misery, strife, and discord. Moreover, God promises us that this vision will "surely come" to fulfillment.

• What holds us back from the task of moving "mulberry trees"? It may be that we lack confidence in our own power. Or maybe that we insist on doing the job alone. Or that, despite our problems with where the tree stands, we are comfortable with the fact that it's always been there. Jesus calls us to faith in who we are: God's servants empowered to make a difference in the world because God makes a difference in us.

Model Prayer of the Faithful

Presider: We make our needs known to the God who calls us to confident faith and obedient service.

Response:

Lord, hear our prayer.

Cantor:

we pray to the Lord,

That all members of the church express their faith in service of others . . . [pause]

That world leaders collaborate in bringing about God's vision for the world . . . [pause]

That the poor and the needy be lifted up . . . [pause]

That each of us model great faith by performing our daily tasks well . . . [pause]

Presider: Gracious God, you give us the strength and faith to be diligent disciples: hear these our prayers that one day we might live with you forever. We ask this through Christ our Lord. **Amen.**

ALTERNATIVE OPENING PRAYER

Let us pray
[before the face of God in trusting faith]

Pause for silent prayer

Almighty and eternal God,
Father of the world to come,
your goodness is beyond what our spirit
    can touch
and your strength is more than the mind
    can bear.
Lead us to seek beyond our reach
and give us the courage to stand before
    your truth.
We ask this through Christ our Lord.
    Amen.

FIRST READING
Hab 1:2-3; 2:2-4

How long, O LORD? I cry for help
    but you do not listen!
I cry out to you, "Violence!"
    but you do not intervene.
Why do you let me see ruin;
    why must I look at misery?
Destruction and violence are before me;
    there is strife, and clamorous discord.
Then the LORD answered me and said:
    Write down the vision clearly upon the
        tablets,
    so that one can read it readily.
For the vision still has its time,
    presses on to fulfillment, and will not
        disappoint;
if it delays, wait for it,
    it will surely come, it will not be late.
The rash one has no integrity;
    but the just one, because of his faith,
        shall live.

RESPONSORIAL PSALM

Ps 95:1-2, 6-7, 8-9

R⁊. (8) If today you hear his voice, harden not your hearts.

Come, let us sing joyfully to the LORD;
   let us acclaim the Rock of our salvation.
Let us come into his presence with
    thanksgiving;
   let us joyfully sing psalms to him.

R⁊. If today you hear his voice, harden not your hearts.

Come, let us bow down in worship;
   let us kneel before the LORD who made
    us.
For he is our God,
   and we are the people he shepherds, the
    flock he guides.

R⁊. If today you hear his voice, harden not your hearts.

Oh, that today you would hear his voice:
   "Harden not your hearts as at Meribah,
   as in the day of Massah in the desert,
where your fathers tempted me;
   they tested me though they had seen my
    works."

R⁊. If today you hear his voice, harden not your hearts.

SECOND READING

2 Tim 1:6-8, 13-14

Beloved:
I remind you to stir into flame
   the gift of God that you have through the
    imposition of my hands.
For God did not give us a spirit of
    cowardice
   but rather of power and love and
    self-control.
So do not be ashamed of your testimony
    to our Lord,
   nor of me, a prisoner for his sake;
   but bear your share of hardship for the
    gospel
with the strength that comes from God.

Take as your norm the sound words that
    you heard from me,
   in the faith and love that are in Christ
    Jesus.
Guard this rich trust with the help of the
    Holy Spirit
   that dwells within us.

About Liturgy

Ministry as service: We usually think of service in terms of doing for others. A very special kind of "doing for others" is the ministry each of us undertakes at any given liturgy. The General Instruction of the Roman Missal states in no. 95: "In the celebration of Mass the faithful form a holy people, a people whom God has made his own, a royal priesthood, so that they may give thanks to God and offer the spotless Victim not only through the hands of the priest but also together with him, and so that they may learn to offer themselves. They should, moreover, endeavor to make this clear by their deep religious sense and their charity toward brothers and sisters who participate with them in the same celebration." There is a direct link between our ministry at liturgy and our service of each other.

The most important ministry at Mass is that of the assembly. This means, first, that all present have an active, decisive ministry. To be assembly means to surrender ourselves to God's presence and in that surrender we become church made visible. Our very act of surrender, then, is an expression of faith. This is made concrete in the common responses, gestures, postures, and singing we do at liturgy. Faith is also made concrete in the active listening to God's word proclaimed, in heartfelt giving of praise and thanks during the eucharistic prayer, in genuine gift of self to others in the sign of peace, and in walking together in procession to God's banquet table where we are nourished for the demands of discipleship.

Each of the specific, visible ministries at liturgy (presider, deacon, hospitality ministers, altar ministers, musicians, lectors, extraordinary ministers of Holy Communion) is, of course, also an opportunity to express faith through service. But we must never forget that the most important ministry is to surrender to being church made visible. This is the most demanding service because it requires us to lose ourselves in something bigger than ourselves. This is how faith the size of the mustard seed can move mulberry trees—we are not alone, but our service is always with the other members of the Body of Christ.

About Liturgical Music

Music suggestions: Fred Pratt Green's "The Church of Christ in Every Age" [GC2, JS2, RS, SS, WC, W3] fits the parable in this Sunday's gospel when it calls the "servant Church" to rise and carry on the task of salvation because "We have no mission but to serve In full obedience to our Lord." The hymn would work well for the entrance procession. A song that captures the hope we maintain despite the sufferings and struggles of life (see first reading) is "Eye Has Not Seen" [BB, CBW3, G1, G2, GC, GC2, RS, SS, WC, WS], which would work well for the preparation of the gifts or the Communion procession. Finally, "The Love of the Lord" [RS, G1, G2, GC, GC2] speaks of hope grounded in the life and love of the Lord (refrain) and of faith as our greatest possession (v. 4). This song could be used during the preparation of the gifts, the Communion procession, or could be sung as a choir prelude.

✦ SPIRITUALITY

℟. Alleluia, alleluia.
In all circumstances, give thanks,
for this is the will of God for you in Christ Jesus.
℟. Alleluia, alleluia.

Gospel

Luke 17:11-19; L144C

As Jesus continued his journey to
Jerusalem,
he traveled through Samaria and
Galilee.
As he was entering a village, ten lepers
met him.
They stood at a distance from him and
raised their voices, saying,
"Jesus, Master! Have pity on us!"
And when he saw them, he said,
"Go show yourselves to the priests."
As they were going they were cleansed.
And one of them, realizing he had been
healed,
returned, glorifying God in a loud
voice;
and he fell at the feet of Jesus and
thanked him.
He was a Samaritan.
Jesus said in reply,
"Ten were cleansed, were they not?
Where are the other nine?
Has none but this foreigner returned to
give thanks to God?"
Then he said to him, "Stand up and go;
your faith has saved you."

Reflecting on the Gospel

We all experience at different times in our lives various kinds of alienation, for example, receiving the silent treatment from another, being shown a cold shoulder, holding an unpopular opinion. In all these cases, the alienation can be overcome; we can usually talk out misunderstandings and hurts. This Sunday's gospel records an extreme kind of alienation that could not be overcome by talking things out. Ten lepers, from "a distance," cry out to Jesus for pity. How did the ten lepers, who cannot take part in the social and religious activities of the community, know Jesus well enough to address him by name ("Jesus, Master!")? No doubt, word of Jesus' healing miracles spread even to these outcasts. No doubt, they clutched a straw of hope that Jesus could heal them and erase their separation. Jesus did just this—and so much more for one of them.

One leper is very different from the other nine, although all are healed. He alone returned to Jesus to give thanks for being healed. But the gospel is telling us even more: the leper's return revealed a depth of faith that Jesus acknowledged as a sign of salvation ("your faith has saved you"). This faith led him to turn from the command of Jesus ("Go show yourselves to the priests"), which would have fulfilled the ancient law concerning restoration of lepers to the community. Instead, the Samaritan leper returns to the Source of his healing. Jesus is not only the One who healed him of his leprosy but, more important, he is the One who drew him to act on the faith that assured him of the new life of restoration and salvation. Faith is discovering who Jesus is; salvation is the lifelong journey of returning to and encountering him.

Both the first reading and the gospel present a foreign leper who asks for healing, obeys what is commanded, experiences healing, and then worships God. The distinctive element is found in the gospel where encounter with Jesus leads to the declaration, "your faith has saved you." Salvation is not freedom from disease but relationship with Christ.

Living the Paschal Mystery

The leper was healed while "Jesus continued his journey to Jerusalem." This is what happens to us when by paschal mystery living we walk with Jesus to Jerusalem: on the way we are healed of our infirmities. We are healed each time we come to Eucharist to give praise and thanks to God, and in this act of worship we become more perfect members of the Body of Christ. We are healed each time we put others ahead of ourselves, and in these simple acts we strengthen our faith. We are healed each time we pause a few seconds to "give thanks to God" for the many blessings of each day because by giving thanks to *God* we acknowledge that God has acted in Christ. Gratitude is an expression of paschal mystery living because by giving thanks we acknowledge our own indebtedness—we are poor and everything we are and are becoming is because God has raised us up.

God gives us so much (salvation) and asks so little of us in return (faith and thankfulness). This is but another reminder that our relationship to God isn't between equals—God's gifts are lavish, far more than anything we could earn or accomplish on our own. This is why paschal mystery living makes such good sense. By living Jesus' dying and rising in our own simple everyday tasks, we render God the greatest thanks and worship because our lives become like that of the divine Son. Our thanks is manifestation of God's salvation.

Focusing the gospel

Key words and phrases: returned, your faith has saved you

To the point: What made this one leper different from the other nine? He alone returned to Jesus to give thanks for being healed. But the gospel is telling us even more: the leper's return revealed a depth of faith that Jesus acknowledged as a sign of salvation. Faith is discovering who Jesus is; salvation is the lifelong journey of returning to and encountering him.

Connecting the Gospel

to the first reading: Because of his cure from leprosy, Naaman experiences the power of God to heal, and this brings him to worship the God of Israel. In the gospel the Samaritan leper encounters God's power in Jesus and is brought to worship him.

to our experience: Expressing gratitude is more than a simple social grace; it deepens the relationship between giver and receiver. For us as Christians, giving thanks to Jesus strengthens our most important relationship: faith in God.

Connecting the Responsorial Psalm

to the readings: Psalm 98, from which this responsorial psalm is taken, is about the completion of God's saving plan for Israel. All the forces that threaten God's chosen people—depicted in various psalms as enemy nations, roaring seas, evildoers, famine, disease, etc.—have been put to rout by God. The whole world sees what God has done for Israel and rejoices.

The healing stories in the first reading and gospel are concrete dramatizations of God's saving deeds as well as of the faith responses these deeds engender. Surprisingly, it is foreigners (Naaman, the Samaritan leper, the entire world in the psalm) who acknowledge what God has done and members of the chosen people (the other nine lepers) who do not. Together the psalm and readings challenge us, then, to examine our faith response to God. As members of the church do we offer God thanks through worship and faith-filled discipleship, or do we simply take salvation for granted? Do we lead the world in offering God praise for salvation, or do we sit back and assume others will do so? Offering God our thanks is an expression of faith, and it is this faith, Jesus tells us, that leads to salvation (gospel).

to psalmist preparation: In this responsorial psalm you proclaim God's saving deeds and invite the assembly to acknowledge and give thanks for them. As preparation for singing this psalm, you might look each day for an example of salvation and consciously give God thanks for it.

ASSEMBLY & FAITH-SHARING GROUPS

- The Samaritan, "realizing he had been healed," returns to give thanks to God. What helps me recognize God's hand in my life is . . . The manner in which I give thanks to God is . . .
- Times when my faith has brought me to encounter Jesus are . . .
- My journey of salvation has led me to . . .

PRESIDERS

- The depth of my faith leads those to whom I minister to encounter Jesus when . . . by . . .

DEACONS

- Surprisingly the foreign leper is the model of faith. An unorthodox model of faith for me has been . . . This has strengthened me in my resolve to serve others in that . . .

HOSPITALITY MINISTERS

- The friendliness of my greeting helps others encounter Jesus more deeply in that . . .

MUSIC MINISTERS

- My music ministry has led me to deeper encounter with Jesus when . . . by . . .

ALTAR MINISTERS

- Since Elisha would not accept a gift, Naaman's gratitude was directed to worshiping God (see first reading). The way my service directs others to worship God is . . .

LECTORS

- Like Naaman, I know that "there is no other God in all the earth" (first reading). I communicate this belief to others by . . .

EXTRAORDINARY MINISTERS OF HOLY COMMUNION

- While distributing Holy Communion, I witness others coming to Jesus in faith. This deepens my faith in that . . .

Model Act of Penitence

Presider: In today's gospel one leper returns to Jesus to give thanks for being healed. As we prepare to celebrate this liturgy, let us open our hearts in gratitude for God's presence and healing power . . . [pause]

Lord Jesus, you are the divine Healer: Lord . . .

Christ Jesus, you are our salvation and hope: Christ . . .

Lord Jesus, you lead us to deeper faith: Lord . . .

Homily Points

• We've all witnessed this scene: little children who haven't seen parents or grandparents for a while excitedly run and jump into their arms. This joyful encounter is born of their previous experiences of love, care, goodness. The Samaritan leper in the gospel exemplifies the same kind of exuberant response to Jesus.

• By law, the lepers in the gospel "stood at a distance" from others. By healing them, Jesus closes this distance. But only one of the lepers chooses to respond and come face-to-face with the One who has healed him. His faith enables him to encounter Jesus so closely that, in fact, he crosses over the greatest distance of all: coming to salvation.

• What depth of faith leads us, like little children, to run toward Jesus with joyful expectation of being embraced, healed, and loved? How do we discover who Jesus is? Through others, yes. Through our own capacity to show care and love, yes. Through the many surprising ways God's goodness comes to us, yes. In all these ways our faith grows and brings us face-to-face with Jesus along our journey to salvation.

Model Prayer of the Faithful

Presider: Let us make our needs known to our caring and loving God who heals us and draws us to encounter the divine Son Jesus.

Response:

Lord, hear our prayer.

Cantor:

we pray to the Lord,

That all members of the church deepen their faith through loving care for others . . . [pause]

That all peoples of the world be open to God's offer of salvation . . . [pause]

That those who are alienated be restored to a loving community . . . [pause]

That we recognize Jesus in one another and be strengthened on our journey to salvation . . . [pause]

Presider: Gracious God, you are worthy of all glory and gratitude: hear these our prayers that we might one day enjoy eternal life with you. We ask this through Christ our Lord. **Amen.**

Let us pray

Pause for silent prayer

Father in heaven,
the hand of your loving kindness
powerfully yet gently guides all the
  moments of our day.
Go before us in our pilgrimage of life,
anticipate our needs and prevent our
  falling.
Send your Spirit to unite us in faith,
that sharing in your service,
we may rejoice in your presence.

We ask this through Christ our Lord.
  Amen.

FIRST READING
2 Kgs 5:14-17

Naaman went down and plunged into the
  Jordan seven times
  at the word of Elisha, the man of God.
His flesh became again like the flesh of a
  little child,
  and he was clean of his leprosy.

Naaman returned with his whole retinue
  to the man of God.
On his arrival he stood before Elisha and
  said,
  "Now I know that there is no God in all
    the earth,
  except in Israel.
Please accept a gift from your servant."

Elisha replied, "As the LORD lives whom
  I serve, I will not take it";
  and despite Naaman's urging, he still
    refused.
Naaman said: "If you will not accept,
  please let me, your servant, have two
    mule-loads of earth,
  for I will no longer offer holocaust or
    sacrifice
  to any other god except to the LORD."

RESPONSORIAL PSALM

Ps 98:1, 2-3, 3-4

R̂. (cf. 2b) The Lord has revealed to the nations his saving power.

Sing to the LORD a new song,
  for he has done wondrous deeds;
his right hand has won victory for him,
  his holy arm.

R̂. The Lord has revealed to the nations his saving power.

The LORD has made his salvation known:
  in the sight of the nations he has
    revealed his justice.
He has remembered his kindness and his
    faithfulness
  toward the house of Israel.

R̂. The Lord has revealed to the nations his saving power.

All the ends of the earth have seen
  the salvation by our God.
Sing joyfully to the LORD, all you lands:
  break into song; sing praise.

R̂. The Lord has revealed to the nations his saving power.

SECOND READING

2 Tim 2:8-13

Beloved:
Remember Jesus Christ, raised from the
    dead, a descendant of David:
  such is my gospel, for which I am
      suffering,
    even to the point of chains, like a
      criminal.
But the word of God is not chained.
Therefore, I bear with everything for the
    sake of those who are chosen,
  so that they too may obtain the
      salvation that is in Christ Jesus,
    together with eternal glory.
This saying is trustworthy:
  If we have died with him
    we shall also live with him;
  if we persevere
    we shall also reign with him.
  But if we deny him
    he will deny us.
  If we are unfaithful
    he remains faithful,
    for he cannot deny himself.

About Liturgy

Eucharist—faithfulness and thankfulness: Eucharist defines Catholic worship and even Christians themselves because, in Christ, God has given us the most profound gift of sharing in divine life. Our only response can be faithfulness and thankfulness.

Faithfulness. The divine gift of Eucharist calls us to be faithful in its celebration. Faithfulness means that we rejoice in God's most gracious gift and make every effort to participate fully, actively, and consciously. Faithful celebration, in turn, strengthens us for faithful discipleship. The Word and Food of Eucharist is a continual renewal of God's presence that invites us to an encounter with the One who heals and saves.

Thankfulness. Gratitude in face of God's great gifts to us is a recognition of indebtedness that can be adequately expressed only in worship. Each celebration of Eucharist is a profound acknowledgment that all we have is from God and that God still gives us even more. Without an attitude of thankfulness we cannot continually open up the capacity within ourselves to receive God's gifts. Thankfulness, then, is more than saying "thanks." It is opening ourselves to God by worship and self-surrender. Ultimately, gratitude also includes encounter.

Eucharist defines Catholic worship and Christian living because this is the only way we can adequately express what God desires of us—salvation in Christ. Eucharist not only changes the bread and wine into the Body and Blood of Christ, it changes us into the Body of Christ. This is how we are saved—by encountering Christ and being transformed.

About Liturgical Music

Music suggestion: This might be a good Sunday for the assembly to sing a hymn of praise and thanksgiving after Communion. For example, Marty Haugen's setting of Psalm 136 [G2, GC, GC2, and in GIA's *Psalms for the Church Year*, Volume 2] has the people responding energetically to a cantor's litany of God's saving deeds. The choir harmonization adds dimension and the use of percussion instruments would also add intensity. The Presbyterian publication *The Psalter—Psalms and Canticles for Singing* [Louisville, KY: Westminster/John Knox Press, 1993] has reprinted the Gelineau setting of Psalm 136 with a suggestion for an amended, inclusive-language refrain. The SATB arrangement is not difficult, but the syncopations that give it life require sure-footedness on the part of the choir.

OCTOBER 10, 2010
TWENTY-EIGHTH SUNDAY IN ORDINARY TIME

SPIRITUALITY

GOSPEL ACCLAMATION
Heb 4:12

R⁊. Alleluia, alleluia.
The word of God is living and effective,
discerning reflections and thoughts of the heart.
R⁊. Alleluia, alleluia.

Gospel   Luke 18:1-8; L147C

Jesus told his disciples a parable
    about the necessity for them to pray
        always without becoming weary.
He said, "There was a judge in a certain
    town
    who neither feared God nor respected
        any human being.
And a widow in that town used to come to
    him and say,
    'Render a just decision for me against
        my adversary.'
For a long time the judge was unwilling,
    but eventually he thought,
    'While it is true that I neither fear God
        nor respect any human being,
    because this widow keeps bothering me
    I shall deliver a just decision for her
    lest she finally come and strike me.'"
The Lord said, "Pay attention to what the
    dishonest judge says.
Will not God then secure the rights of his
    chosen ones
    who call out to him day and night?
Will he be slow to answer them?
I tell you, he will see to it that justice is
    done for them speedily.
But when the Son of Man comes, will he
    find faith on earth?"

Reflecting on the Gospel

The first reading includes an image that we witness every time we celebrate Mass. It tells of Moses keeping "his hands raised up." Hands uplifted is an ancient posture of prayer. The presider lifts his hands (and arms) during Mass when he lifts the community's prayers to God (during the presidential prayers and the eucharistic prayer, for example). For Moses, who was engaged in battle with enemies, uplifted hands was also a posture of vulnerability, for such a position makes it impossible to defend oneself from attack. During prayer we, too, are quite vulnerable, giving ourselves to God and what God wants for us. Persistence in this gospel context does not refer to bullheadedness about what we want. It is about aligning ourselves with what God desires for us. Ultimately, persistent prayer is faith-filled prayer.

In this gospel Jesus relates persistence in prayer and faith to his second coming ("when the Son of Man comes"). Persistence in prayer is not only about asking for what we need now but is also about maintaining hope that God will persist in bringing about final justice. Moreover, there is no real prayer without faith. Faith gives prayer a longer view and a broader vision—the view and vision of Jesus himself. In this, Jesus is teaching us that while our prayer tends to be about immediate needs, our life is about ultimate justice. Our persistence in prayer really is about a faith relationship with God that reveals we are God's "chosen ones" who are in right relationship with God. This righteousness leads to eternal life.

In the first reading Aaron and Hur support Moses' arms when he grows weary. The widow was supported only by her own persistence and conviction about her right to justice; she was upheld by her belief that God is the just One and will make justice happen. It ought to be encouraging to us that we are often supported in prayer by our faith community. Because of our Christian community we are never alone. Others can provide support, yet the community support must be complemented by a faith that comes from within us, sustaining us and encouraging us in persistence. This very persistence is a kind of steadfast relationship to God, a kind of prayer.

The gospel's legal language of judge, judgment, and justice bring to mind the final judgment Jesus renders at his second coming. One way to prepare for this second coming and alleviate any fears we might have is to be persistent in faith-filled prayer. Our faith grows through persistence in prayer because through this kind of prayer we build a stronger relationship with God. When Jesus comes again, "will he find faith on earth?" Yes, if we are persistent in praying "always without becoming weary." It seems persistence in prayer is a small price to pay for salvation and everlasting glory!

Living the Paschal Mystery

For many, setting aside any definite time for prayer during the day may seem all but impossible, especially if we are talking about ten or fifteen uninterrupted minutes. Persistence in praying always might need to take the form in our lives of developing the habit of being aware of God's abiding presence and blessings even in our busyness. It might mean that we learn to catch little moments for prayer (like we sometimes are able to catch moments for catnaps)—while driving to pick up the youngsters or waiting in a checkout line. The place and manner of prayer aren't nearly as important as the fact that we pray—always and without ceasing. And with deep faith in a God who loves us and cares for us.

Focusing the gospel

Key words and phrases: pray always, justice is done, when the Son of Man comes, faith

To the point: In this gospel Jesus relates persistence in prayer and faith to his second coming. Persistence in prayer is not only about asking for what we need now but also about maintaining hope that God will persist in bringing about final justice. Moreover, there is no real prayer without faith. Faith gives prayer a longer view and a broader vision—the view and vision of Jesus himself.

Connecting the Gospel

to the first reading: Sometimes we, in fact, grow weary in prayer. Like Moses, what sustains us in such times is other members of the faith community.

to religious experience: All of us at times experience dryness in prayer, and the temptation is to give up on prayer. At these times we need to remember that our very persistence is a kind of prayer.

Connecting the Responsorial Psalm

to the readings: Psalm 121, used in its entirety for this Sunday's responsorial psalm, is a pilgrimage song. Having journeyed to Jerusalem for festival, the Israelites must now travel back home. They see the mountains that surround them as a threat—the hideout of thieves and enemies, the home of wild animals. The psalm is a prayer of confidence in God's protection, perhaps said in blessing over them by the temple priest as the pilgrims began their journey home. What undergirds the psalm is surety about God who will always answer the prayer of those who have been faithful to the covenant and the cry of those who call for justice (gospel). For our part we must persist in prayer even when we have lost the strength for it (first reading, gospel). Such is the faithfulness the Son of Man hopes to find on his return (gospel). Psalm 121 indicates we can count on the faithfulness of God. May our praying of it indicate God can count on our faithfulness in return.

to psalmist preparation: When you sing this responsorial psalm, you are like the temple priest blessing the people as they begin their journey homeward. The people are the Body of Christ; the journey, that of faithful discipleship; the homeland, God's kingdom. How in your singing can you assure the assembly of God's presence and protection on the way? How outside of Sunday Eucharist can you persist in your prayer for them?

**ASSEMBLY &
FAITH-SHARING GROUPS**

- Jesus' teaching to "pray always without becoming weary" means to me . . . The wearisome part of praying for me is . . . What keeps me persistent in praying is . . .
- Faith affects my prayer in that . . . Prayer affects the depth of my faith when . . .
- The longer view and broader vision faith and prayer bring me are . . .

PRESIDERS

- The faith Jesus finds on earth when he hears my prayer is . . . when he observes my ministry is . . . when he watches my daily life is . . .

DEACONS

- My ministry is part of God's answer to the plea for justice; the way my ministry "secures the rights of [God's] chosen ones" is . . .

HOSPITALITY MINISTERS

- Like Aaron and Hur (first reading), my ministry of hospitality upholds and enables the prayer of others by . . .

MUSIC MINISTERS

- My music ministry becomes a way of "praying always" when I . . . My music ministry helps the assembly remain in prayer when I . . .

ALTAR MINISTERS

- In my serving others, God finds "faith on earth" because . . .

LECTORS

- Preparing to proclaim God's word deepens my faith and encourages my persistence in prayer because . . .

**EXTRAORDINARY MINISTERS
OF HOLY COMMUNION**

- As I distribute Holy Communion to each one who comes, my persistent prayer is . . .

Model Act of Penitence

Presider: In today's gospel Jesus calls us to be persistent in prayer. As we prepare for this liturgy, let us be persistent in seeking God in word and sacrament . . . [pause]

Lord Jesus, you teach us to pray always: Lord . . .

Christ Jesus, you will come to gather your faithful ones into glory: Christ . . .

Lord Jesus, you call us to deepen our faith and hope in you: Lord . . .

Homily Points

• How often children badger parents for something they want when, for example, they see a toy advertised on TV or their favorite junk food on the grocery store shelf. By their persistence they hope to change their parents' minds about what is good for them. The same is often true with our prayer. We pray to change God's will, that is, we pray for what we think we need or want and hope we can convince God to give it to us.

• In the gospel Jesus does encourage persistence in prayer. True persistence, however, is not badgering God for what we want. True persistence in prayer wells up from a deep faith and brings out the hope that leads us to the longer view and broader vision of Jesus. Our persistence in prayer—even for what we need now—brings us to new and, ultimately, eternal life.

• Persistence in prayer isn't relentlessly nagging God for what we want. Prayer informed by deep faith is openness to what God wants for us, which always leads to a greater good than we can now know or imagine. Jesus assures us that we can count on God. But can God count on us?

Model Prayer of the Faithful

Presider: Let us be persistent in our prayer, knowing God answers us with justice and mercy.

Response:

Lord, hear our prayer.

Cantor:

we pray to the Lord,

That all members of the church live in such a way that they witness to deep faith and persistent prayer . . . [pause]

That all peoples of the world have faith that leads to eternal life . . . [pause]

That the downtrodden and oppressed may receive justice . . . [pause]

That each of us pray always, growing in our relationship with God and with each other . . . [pause]

Presider: Just and merciful God, you hear the prayers of those who cry out to you: grant our needs and bring us to be with you one day in everlasting glory. We ask this through Christ our Lord. **Amen.**

OPENING PRAYER

Let us pray
[for the gift of simplicity and joy in our service of God and man]

Pause for silent prayer

Almighty and ever-living God,
our source of power and inspiration,
give us strength and joy
in serving you as followers of Christ,
who lives and reigns with you and the
Holy Spirit,
one God, for ever and ever. **Amen.**

FIRST READING
Exod 17:8-13

In those days, Amalek came and waged
war against Israel.
Moses, therefore, said to Joshua,
"Pick out certain men,
and tomorrow go out and engage
Amalek in battle.
I will be standing on top of the hill
with the staff of God in my hand."
So Joshua did as Moses told him:
he engaged Amalek in battle
after Moses had climbed to the top of
the hill with Aaron and Hur.
As long as Moses kept his hands raised
up,
Israel had the better of the fight,
but when he let his hands rest,
Amalek had the better of the fight.
Moses' hands, however, grew tired;
so they put a rock in place for him to
sit on.
Meanwhile Aaron and Hur supported his
hands,
one on one side and one on the other,
so that his hands remained steady till
sunset.
And Joshua mowed down Amalek and his
people
with the edge of the sword.

RESPONSORIAL PSALM
Ps 121:1-2, 3-4, 5-6, 7-8

R⁊. (cf. 2) Our help is from the Lord, who
made heaven and earth.

I lift up my eyes toward the mountains;
whence shall help come to me?
My help is from the LORD,
who made heaven and earth.

R⁊. Our help is from the Lord, who made
heaven and earth.

May he not suffer your foot to slip;
　　may he slumber not who guards you:
indeed he neither slumbers nor sleeps,
　　the guardian of Israel.

R︘. Our help is from the Lord, who made heaven and earth.

The LORD is your guardian; the LORD is
　　your shade;
he is beside you at your right hand.
The sun shall not harm you by day,
　　nor the moon by night.

R︘. Our help is from the Lord, who made heaven and earth.

The LORD will guard you from all evil;
　　he will guard your life.
The LORD will guard your coming and
　　your going,
both now and forever.

R︘. Our help is from the Lord, who made heaven and earth.

SECOND READING
2 Tim 3:14–4:2

Beloved:
Remain faithful to what you have learned
　　and believed,
　　because you know from whom you
　　　　learned it,
　　and that from infancy you have known
　　　　the sacred Scriptures,
　　which are capable of giving you
　　　　wisdom for salvation
　　through faith in Christ Jesus.
All Scripture is inspired by God
　　and is useful for teaching, for refutation,
　　　　for correction,
　　and for training in righteousness,
　　so that one who belongs to God may be
　　　　competent,
　　equipped for every good work.

I charge you in the presence of God and of
　　Christ Jesus,
　　who will judge the living and the dead,
　　and by his appearing and his kingly
　　　　power:
proclaim the word;
be persistent whether it is convenient or
　　inconvenient;
convince, reprimand, encourage through
　　all patience and teaching.

About Liturgy

Liturgy as prayer: Of course we all understand that liturgy is prayer. There are a number of indicators within the liturgy itself. For example, before the opening prayer and at the post-Communion prayer the presider specifically invites us to pray: "Let us pray." The heart of the Liturgy of the Eucharist is called the eucharistic *prayer*. The *prayer* of the faithful concludes the Liturgy of the Word. We pray together the Our Father, probably one of the first prayers we learned as children. How is it, though, that liturgy is more than just a stringing together of prayers? How is the liturgy itself a single, seamless prayer?

In the liturgy we pray as *one body*, the Body of Christ. By praying with one voice, we lift up a single prayer to God. Because we are this community, the liturgical prayer doesn't depend on any one individual's ability to pray or not during a particular liturgy. It is as though we are holding each other up and enabling one another to remain strong and persistent in prayer. The constant repetition of liturgy throughout the world is a constant reminder of the persistence of the prayer of the Body of Christ.

Another consideration for understanding liturgy as a single, seamless prayer is that the liturgy has an invariable structure. Individual elements may change and vary somewhat from liturgy to liturgy, but the essential structure is the same. This invariability enables us to surrender to the action, and in that surrender both encounter with God and the visibility of the church as the Body of Christ become possible.

Finally, and perhaps most important, the overall sentiments of liturgy are praise and thanksgiving. With these attitudes we glorify God and offer our worship. All the individual prayer—yes, even the petitionary prayer—redounds to praise and thanksgiving. All prayer converges on our acknowledging God's splendor and being grateful for the gift of divine presence.

About Liturgical Music

Music suggestions: "O God Our Help in Ages Past" parallels the content of the responsorial psalm and affirms the faith that inspires persistence in prayer. The hymn would be appropriate for the entrance procession or the preparation of the gifts. Another traditional hymn similar in meaning but very different in musical style is "Praise to the Lord, the Almighty," which praises God for keeping us safe, sustaining us, attending us with goodness and mercy. This hymn would be excellent for the entrance procession. Two hymns that ask God to teach us how to pray are "Lord, Teach Us How to Pray" and "Eternal Spirit of the Living Christ," both found in HG. Either would be appropriate during the preparation of the gifts. Finally, quiet repetitions of the Taizé "O Lord, Hear My Prayer" could be an appropriate choral prelude, with choir and assembly singing together.

✚ SPIRITUALITY

GOSPEL ACCLAMATION
2 Cor 5:19

R̷. Alleluia, alleluia.
God was reconciling the world to himself in
    Christ
and entrusting to us the message of salvation.
R̷. Alleluia, alleluia.

Gospel   Luke 18:9-14; L150C

Jesus addressed this parable
    to those who were convinced of their
        own righteousness
    and despised everyone else.
"Two people went up to the temple area
        to pray;
    one was a Pharisee and the other was a
        tax collector.
The Pharisee took up his position and
        spoke this prayer to himself,
    'O God, I thank you that I am not like
        the rest of humanity—
    greedy, dishonest, adulterous—or even
        like this tax collector.
I fast twice a week, and I pay tithes on
        my whole income.'
But the tax collector stood off at a
        distance
    and would not even raise his eyes to
        heaven
    but beat his breast and prayed,
    'O God, be merciful to me a sinner.'
I tell you, the latter went home justified,
        not the former;
    for whoever exalts himself will be
        humbled,
    and the one who humbles himself will
        be exalted."

Reflecting on the Gospel

A familiar saying warns us that pride goes before the fall. Aesop tells the fable of two roosters who were fighting fiercely to see who would be the barnyard champion. Finally one was defeated and went to hide behind the barn in shame. The victor flew atop the house and crowed loudly so everyone would know about his victory. Then a hawk swooped down, clutched him in his talons, and carried him off for dinner, whereby the defeated rooster came out from behind the barn and took possession of the barnyard. The gospel this Sunday isn't about two roosters fighting but about a Pharisee and a tax collector praying. Jesus warns us that pride goes before the fall.

In the parable the Pharisee's prayer is praise for himself that he is "not like the rest of humanity." The tax collector, on the other hand, identifies himself with all of humanity as a sinner in need of God's mercy. The former is taken up with what he does for God (fasts, pays tithes). The latter is overcome by awareness of what he needs from God (mercy). The Pharisee justified himself; the tax collector "went home justified" by God. Jesus tells us that we are "justified" when we know who we are before God and open ourselves in humility to receive God's mercy.

There's hope for all of us in this gospel, for we are all sinners. The tax collector would hardly be numbered among the righteous by any stretch of the imagination. Tax collectors were hated and known for their unscrupulous practices. They lined their own pockets at others' expense. Yet, it is the tax collector who "stood off at a distance and would not even raise his eyes to heaven," a posture indicating he recognized his sinfulness and unworthiness before God. His prayer says something true about God (who is merciful) and himself (who is a sinner). The tax collector's prayer allows God to be God and show mercy. The tax collector's prayer reveals both an understanding of God and the desire to be in right relation with God. The tax collector stands far off, but his prayer draws him near to God.

Justification is knowing who God is and what our relationship to God is. It is addressing God as God and letting God be God. It is acknowledging humbly who we are before God: sinners in need of mercy. The exaltation at the end of time is determined by whether we are justified, that is, humble and in right relationship to God. Good works alone don't justify us—it is right relationship with God. Humility in face of our all-holy and merciful God brings exaltation.

Living the Paschal Mystery

In practice, most of us are probably not totally like the Pharisee or the tax collector. So both can teach us something. The Pharisee can teach us that religious practices are important but not enough. They must always be performed in humility and with the goal of deepening our relationship with God. The tax collector can teach us that God doesn't offer salvation to the perfect but to those who acknowledge their sinfulness and cry out for God's mercy. At the same time, some of us are so busy beating our breasts about our sinfulness that even this can be a form of pride. Like the tax collector, we must let God be God and receive the mercy offered. God exalts those who are in right relationship, though they may be sinners. Rather than focus unduly on our own sinfulness, we need turn to God and ask for mercy.

Focusing the gospel

Key words and phrases: not like the rest of humanity, be merciful to me a sinner, went home justified

To the point: In this parable the Pharisee's prayer is praise for himself that he is "not like the rest of humanity." The tax collector, on the other hand, identifies himself with all of humanity as a sinner in need of God's mercy. The former is taken up with what he does for God. The latter is overcome by awareness of what he needs from God. The Pharisee justified himself; the tax collector "went home justified" by God.

Connecting the Gospel

to the first reading: The first reading instills great hope in that God hears the prayer of the lowly, affirms them in their prayer, and does not delay in bringing them justice.

to our experience: The hope the gospel offers is that justification comes not to the perfect but to those who acknowledge their need for God's mercy.

Connecting the Responsorial Psalm

to the readings: God hears the prayer not of the self-righteous (gospel) but of those "crushed in spirit" (responsorial psalm). It is not that God who "knows no favorites" (first reading) is closed to the rich, but that the self-satisfied are closed to God. The Pharisee is so full of himself he keeps God at a distance (gospel). When the tax collector, on the other hand, begs for mercy, he allows God to draw close. In this Sunday's responsorial psalm we identify ourselves with the poor, the brokenhearted, the lowly. We acknowledge our true relationship with God—that of dependency, of humility, of need for mercy. We allow God to come close, and we are justified (gospel).

to psalmist preparation: In singing this responsorial psalm you encourage the assembly in their prayer. You assure them that when they come to God crushed and broken, their prayer is at its best. As part of your preparation you might spend some time this week reflecting on your own prayer and your own need for God's mercy.

**ASSEMBLY &
FAITH-SHARING GROUPS**

- When I am "convinced of [my] own righteousness," what ends up humbling me is . . .
- What I most need from God is . . .
- My prayer brings me closer to God when . . . because . . .

PRESIDERS

- The occasions for self-exaltation within my ministry are . . . What keeps me standing alongside the humble tax collector is . . .

DEACONS

- When serving others, I act like the Pharisee when . . . like the tax collector when . . .

HOSPITALITY MINISTERS

- When my welcome, care, and concern convey that "I am . . . like the rest of humanity," I go "home justified" (that is, in right relationship) with God and others because . . .

MUSIC MINISTERS

- My music ministry brings me to focus on praising myself when . . . What refocuses me on God and the assembly is . . .

ALTAR MINISTERS

- What is humbling about serving others is . . . God exalts me for . . .

LECTORS

- My proclamation conveys hope in God's mercy when I . . .

**EXTRAORDINARY MINISTERS
OF HOLY COMMUNION**

- My distributing Holy Communion keeps me humble because . . .

Model Act of Penitence

Presider: In today's gospel Jesus contrasts the prayer of the proud Pharisee with that of the humble tax collector. We prepare ourselves to celebrate this liturgy by humbly opening our hearts to God's mercy . . . [pause]

Lord Jesus, you hear the prayer of those who are humble: Lord . . .

Christ Jesus, you are exalted at the right hand of the Father: Christ . . .

Lord Jesus, you are full of mercy and compassion: Lord . . .

Homily Points

• In some ways we are all tempted to be like the Pharisee in this gospel story. For example, we might look down on those we consider less successful, those we consider scatterbrained, those we consider different from us in any way. In some ways we are also like the tax collector. For example, we are aware of our needs and inadequacies, acknowledge our faults, apologize when we hurt others. Jesus invites us to the truth of who we are before God and others.

• Although seemingly a pious person, the Pharisee's practices of fasting and tithing did not bring him closer to God or others. Simply doing religious practices is not enough. These must be accompanied by a heart turned to God in true humility.

• The noted spiritual author C. S. Lewis once wrote, "A proud man is always looking down on things and people; and, of course, as long as you're looking down, you can't see something that's above you." When our lives are focused on ourselves or when our attitudes and behaviors separate us from others, we cannot be lifted by God or others beyond where we are. Rather than focusing on ourselves, we must look beyond ourselves to God and others. Such humility promises gifts and growth.

Model Prayer of the Faithful

Presider: Let us stand humbly before our God and present our needs.

Response:

Lord, hear our prayer.

Cantor:

we pray to the Lord,

That all members of the church humbly acknowledge their needs before God and others . . . [pause]

That all peoples of the world be in right relationship with God and each other . . . [pause]

That the proud be humbled and the humble be exalted . . . [pause]

That each of us open our heart more widely to God's mercy . . . [pause]

Presider: Merciful God, you hear the cry of the poor: hear these our prayers that one day we might be exalted with you forever. We ask this through Christ our Lord. **Amen.**

ALTERNATIVE OPENING PRAYER

Let us pray
[in humble hope for salvation]

Pause for silent prayer

Praised be you, God and Father of our
    Lord Jesus Christ.
There is no power for good
which does not come from your covenant,
and no promise to hope in,
that your love has not offered.
Strengthen our faith to accept your
    covenant
and give us the love to carry out your
    command.
We ask this through Christ our Lord.
    Amen.

FIRST READING
Sir 35:12-14, 16-18

The LORD is a God of justice,
    who knows no favorites.
Though not unduly partial toward the
    weak,
    yet he hears the cry of the oppressed.
The LORD is not deaf to the wail of the
    orphan,
    nor to the widow when she pours out
        her complaint.
The one who serves God willingly is
    heard;
    his petition reaches the heavens.
The prayer of the lowly pierces the clouds;
    it does not rest till it reaches its goal,
nor will it withdraw till the Most High
    responds,
    judges justly and affirms the right,
and the LORD will not delay.

RESPONSORIAL PSALM
Ps 34:2-3, 17-18, 19, 23

R̸. (7a) The Lord hears the cry of the poor.

I will bless the LORD at all times;
 his praise shall be ever in my mouth.
Let my soul glory in the LORD;
 the lowly will hear me and be glad.

R̸. The Lord hears the cry of the poor.

The LORD confronts the evildoers,
 to destroy remembrance of them from
  the earth.
When the just cry out, the LORD hears
  them,
 and from all their distress he rescues
  them.

R̸. The Lord hears the cry of the poor.

The LORD is close to the brokenhearted;
 and those who are crushed in spirit he
  saves.
The LORD redeems the lives of his
  servants;
 no one incurs guilt who takes refuge in
  him.

R̸. The Lord hears the cry of the poor.

SECOND READING
2 Tim 4:6-8, 16-18

Beloved:
I am already being poured out like a
  libation,
 and the time of my departure is at
  hand.
I have competed well; I have finished the
  race;
 I have kept the faith.
From now on the crown of righteousness
  awaits me,
 which the Lord, the just judge,
 will award to me on that day, and not
  only to me,
 but to all who have longed for his
  appearance.

At my first defense no one appeared on
  my behalf,
 but everyone deserted me.
May it not be held against them!
But the Lord stood by me and gave me
  strength,
 so that through me the proclamation
  might be completed
 and all the Gentiles might hear it.
And I was rescued from the lion's mouth.
The Lord will rescue me from every evil
  threat
 and will bring me safe to his heavenly
  kingdom.
To him be glory forever and ever. Amen.

About Liturgy

Humility and liturgy: We have inherited a spirituality from the past that has not always portrayed humility in the best light. When we hear in this Sunday's gospel Jesus admonish us to humble ourselves, we can hear that as putting ourselves down, degrading ourselves, not acknowledging our gifts and talents. This is really a false humility.

Humility comes from the Latin word *humus*, which means "ground" or "soil." It reminds us of the second creation account (see Gen 2:7) in which God forms the first human beings from the dust of the ground and breathes life into them. The implication is that true humility is an admission of who we are: formed by God who breathes life into us. Humility is the down-to-earth recognition that God desires to be in relationship with us, loves us, and gives us all good gifts. Humility is rejoicing in who God has called us to be. Humility also leads us to readily acknowledge our weaknesses and failures and ask for God's mercy, as does the tax collector in this Sunday's gospel.

Celebrating liturgy well requires of us a good dose of humility. Liturgy is an awesome gift—God desires to nourish us in word and sacrament, comes to us, transforms us to be more faithful members of the Body of Christ. None of this we deserve. Yet God gives us these good gifts simply out of divine love. Our stance in liturgy, then, ought to be one of openness and acceptance of what God offers us, surrender to God's action, and joy in who God makes us to be. True humility, as this gospel tells us, leads to exaltation—not by us but by the God who created us, saves us, and loves us.

About Liturgical Music

Music suggestions: When consecutive gospel readings are as clearly interrelated as are the ones for this Sunday and last Sunday, repeating a hymn helps support the connection. Repeating either "Lord, Teach Us How to Pray" [HG] or "Eternal Spirit of the Living Christ" [HG] during the preparation of the gifts would be appropriate. Likewise, repeating quiet repetitions of the Taizé "O Lord, Hear My Prayer" as a choral prelude, with choir and assembly singing together, would be good. Songs expressing humility before God and one another include Lucien Deiss's setting of Psalm 131, "My Soul Is Longing" [PMB, WC, WS], which would be an excellent Communion song; the spiritual "Give Me a Clean Heart" [LMGM], which would also be a good Communion song; and the Shaker hymn "'Tis the Gift to Be Simple" [GC2, RS provide only the original verse; JS2, PMB, WC, WS include the additional verses written by Joyce Merman], which would be appropriate during the preparation of the gifts.

OCTOBER 24, 2010
THIRTIETH SUNDAY
IN ORDINARY TIME

✦ SPIRITUALITY

GOSPEL ACCLAMATION
John 3:16

℟. Alleluia, alleluia.
God so loved the world that he gave his only Son,
so that everyone who believes in him might have
    eternal life.
℟. Alleluia, alleluia.

Gospel Luke 19:1-10; L153C

At that time, Jesus came to
    Jericho and intended to
    pass through the town.
Now a man there named
    Zacchaeus,
    who was a chief tax collector
        and also a wealthy man,
    was seeking to see who Jesus
        was;
    but he could not see him
        because of the crowd,
    for he was short in stature.
So he ran ahead and climbed a sycamore
    tree in order to see Jesus,
    who was about to pass that way.
When he reached the place, Jesus looked
    up and said,
    "Zacchaeus, come down quickly,
    for today I must stay at your house."
And he came down quickly and received
    him with joy.
When they all saw this, they began to
    grumble, saying,
    "He has gone to stay at the house of a
        sinner."
But Zacchaeus stood there and said to the
    Lord,
    "Behold, half of my possessions, Lord,
        I shall give to the poor,
    and if I have extorted anything from
        anyone
    I shall repay it four times over."
And Jesus said to him,
    "Today salvation has come to this
        house
    because this man too is a descendant of
        Abraham.
For the Son of Man has come to seek
    and to save what was lost."

Reflecting on the Gospel

This Sunday's gospel tells us that on his way to Jerusalem Jesus "intended to pass through the town" of Jericho. Surely he would not plan "to stay at the house of" the chief tax collector, of all people! Ever faithful to his mission "to seek and to save what was lost," however, Jesus allows even his resolve to go to Jerusalem to be interrupted by a "short in stature" sinner who desired to see him. Even more than his resolve to go to Jerusalem is Jesus' resolve to encounter people with the kind of mercy and compassion that bring salvation. Zacchaeus desired to *see* Jesus; Jesus desired that he be saved.

Zacchaeus finds himself up the proverbial tree—both physically and metaphorically. In this gospel episode Zacchaeus is the epitome of the despised person—chief tax collector, wealthy, a sinner. And yet he is the one person in the crowd in whose house Jesus chooses to stay. Encountering Jesus does not depend upon goodness of life, but encountering him can bring about conversion of life: Zacchaeus undergoes dramatic change (he sets his affairs right and gives to the poor). His newfound concern for others is a sign of encounter with Jesus who brings salvation. Our own encounters with Jesus can bring about just as dramatic a change in our lives. We need only be willing to go to ever greater heights to "see him."

All sinners are *invited* to salvation. Those are saved who seek Jesus (Zacchaeus made the first step when he climbed the sycamore tree to see Jesus) and are open to being sought by him (Jesus stayed at his house). Those are saved who change their lives when they encounter Jesus. Seeing Jesus isn't enough. Encounter must lead to a faith relationship that makes a difference in our lives. Moreover, since Jesus continues his saving mission through us, his followers, we must be equally responsive to others. We must put our own affairs in order and care for those in any need. We must also live in such a way that when others encounter us, they encounter Jesus.

Zacchaeus is the last person Luke's gospel mentions before Jesus enters Jerusalem—it is as though Luke saves the worst for last in order to make his point: "For the Son of Man has come to seek and to save what was lost." If even for this sinner "salvation has come," then who would ever be excluded?

Living the Paschal Mystery

Most of us don't have to be so creative or go to the extreme of climbing a tree to encounter Jesus. However, this gospel forewarns us that we should not be complacent about our spiritual lives. Zacchaeus reminds us that we must also be willing to change and grow and be vigilant about our relationships with others, for these are barometers of our relationship with God.

Creativity in seeking Jesus might mean that we are innovative in our personal prayer life rather than continually reciting the prayers we might have learned long ago. What prayers might better meet our spiritual needs now so that we can grow in our relationships? It might mean that we keep certain days of the year (perhaps the days of the Triduum or some days during Advent) as a "mini retreat" in order to diligently seek Jesus and a better relationship with him. It might mean that we don't wait for people to come to us and ask for help but that we notice others' needs and offer to help before they ask. In these and countless other ways we encounter Jesus—and salvation comes to our house.

Focusing the gospel

Key words and phrases: see him, climbed a sycamore tree, stay at your house, give to the poor . . . extorted . . . repay it, salvation has come

To the point: In this gospel episode Zacchaeus is the epitome of the despised person—chief tax collector, wealthy, a sinner. And yet he is the one person in the crowd in whose house Jesus chooses to stay. Encountering Jesus does not depend upon goodness of life, but encountering him can bring about conversion of life: Zacchaeus undergoes dramatic change. Our encounters with Jesus can bring about just as dramatic a change in our own lives. We need only be willing to go to ever greater heights to "see him."

Connecting the Gospel

to the first reading: Jesus is doing in the gospel exactly what Wisdom reveals about the LORD: showing mercy, overlooking sins, loving all things, etc.

to our experience: We tend to paint people into a corner by labeling them. Rather than labeling people, we need to give them room to change, like Jesus does in the gospel.

Connecting the Responsorial Psalm

to the readings: Psalm 145 is an acrostic hymn, meaning that each verse begins with a successive letter of the Hebrew alphabet. Consequently, the psalm does not develop any theme in depth but simply offers God general praise. The verses chosen for this Sunday praise God for showing mercy and compassion rather than anger, and for lifting up those who have fallen. The reading from Wisdom confirms this attitude of God when it proclaims that the Lord "overlooks people's sins" and gently coaxes offenders back to right living. Clearly God prefers reconciliation to condemnation.

In his encounter with Zacchaeus Jesus is the living embodiment of this orientation of God (gospel). Jesus has come to "seek and to save what was lost." Zacchaeus recognizes his errant ways and transforms his behavior. In singing this psalm we are the living embodiment of Zacchaeus's response. We recognize ourselves as sinners and shout praise to the One who comes to save us.

to psalmist preparation: Psalm 145 praises God for all that God does, but in the context of the first reading and gospel the praise is particularly for God's mercy to sinners. For what have you been shown this mercy? How have you praised God for it?

ASSEMBLY & FAITH-SHARING GROUPS

- Like Zacchaeus, the greater heights to which I would go to see Jesus are . . .
- A change in me that encountering Jesus needs to bring about is . . .
- I experience Jesus' abiding presence (staying at my "house") when . . .

PRESIDERS

- My ministry brings people to encounter Jesus and conversion of life when . . .

DEACONS

- The greatest kind of service is assisting others to change their lives. I help others to turn from sin and find salvation by . . .

HOSPITALITY MINISTERS

- As a minister of Christ's hospitality I am required to embrace and serve all, especially the Zacchaeuses within my community. Whenever I do, salvation comes to my house, too, because . . .

MUSIC MINISTERS

- In my music ministry I seek to see who Jesus is by . . . Having seen him, I have chosen to change by . . .

ALTAR MINISTERS

- Zacchaeus put his life in order when Jesus decided to stay at his house. Serving others is the way I get my life in order for Jesus because . . .

LECTORS

- Like Zacchaeus's encounter with Jesus, my encounter with God's word calls me to change my life, for example, by . . . The effect this has on my proclamation is . . .

EXTRAORDINARY MINISTERS OF HOLY COMMUNION

- As I distribute Holy Communion, I see others encounter Jesus. This changes me in that . . .

Model Act of Penitence

Presider: In today's gospel episode Zacchaeus climbs a tree in order to see Jesus. Let us open our hearts to encounter Jesus in this celebration and be changed by his presence . . . [pause]

    Lord Jesus, you seek and save the lost: Lord . . .

    Christ Jesus, you are gracious and merciful: Christ . . .

    Lord Jesus, you call us to conversion of life: Lord . . .

Homily Points

• Zacchaeus is not that different from us in terms of how far we might go to encounter a celebrity of the moment. For example, people press to the front of a crowd to see a famous person passing by, and long lines form at theater doors and sports arenas to get autographs of stars. But Zacchaeus was different from the people in these examples because of who he was, whom he sought, and what happened to him.

• Zacchaeus, the despised tax collector, went to great heights to see Jesus. Jesus did more than fulfill Zacchaeus's curiosity, however: he stayed at his house and led him to a complete change of life. This same, transforming mission of Jesus is at work among us today.

• Every day the "Son of Man" continues "to seek and to save" us by coming to us ("stay at your house") and moving us beyond where we are. We respond to his presence through the everyday opportunities that present themselves, for example, when we seek reconciliation with a loved one we have hurt, reach out to the stranger or alienated among us, overcome our fears and risk speaking out in the face of injustice. Then our joy, like that of Zacchaeus, arises from receiving Jesus and letting ourselves be transformed by him.

Model Prayer of the Faithful

Presider: Let us make our needs known to the God who seeks us and saves us.

Response:

Lord, hear our prayer.

Cantor:

we pray to the Lord,

That each member of the church continually be open to encounters with Jesus and his transforming love . . . [pause]

That each person of the world embrace change and enter into a deeper relationship with God . . . [pause]

That the lost be found and those who seek God encounter the richness and grace of divine presence . . . [pause]

That each of us here open our heart to receive Jesus as our guest . . . [pause]

Presider: Saving God, you exclude no one from your grace and blessings: hear these our prayers that one day we might share everlasting life with you. We ask this through Christ our Lord. **Amen.**

ALTERNATIVE OPENING PRAYER

Let us pray

Pause for silent prayer

Father in heaven, God of power and Lord of mercy,
from whose fullness we have received,
direct our steps in everyday efforts.
May the changing moods of the human heart
and the limits which our failings impose on hope
never blind us to you, source of every good.
Faith gives us the promise of peace
and makes known the demands of love.
Remove the selfishness that blurs the vision of faith.

Grant this through Christ our Lord.
    Amen.

FIRST READING
Wis 11:22–12:2

Before the LORD the whole universe is as a grain from a balance
    or a drop of morning dew come down upon the earth.
But you have mercy on all, because you can do all things;
    and you overlook people's sins that they may repent.
For you love all things that are
    and loathe nothing that you have made;
    for what you hated, you would not have fashioned.
And how could a thing remain, unless you willed it;
    or be preserved, had it not been called forth by you?
But you spare all things, because they are yours,
    O LORD and lover of souls,
    for your imperishable spirit is in all things!
Therefore you rebuke offenders little by little,
    warn them and remind them of the sins they are committing,
    that they may abandon their wickedness and believe in you, O LORD!

RESPONSORIAL PSALM
Ps 145:1-2, 8-9, 10-11, 13, 14

℟. (cf. 1) I will praise your name forever, my king and my God.

I will extol you, O my God and King,
    and I will bless your name forever and
        ever.
Every day will I bless you,
    and I will praise your name forever and
        ever.

R̸. I will praise your name forever, my
king and my God.

The LORD is gracious and merciful,
    slow to anger and of great kindness.
The LORD is good to all
    and compassionate toward all his
        works.

R̸. I will praise your name forever, my
king and my God.

Let all your works give you thanks, O
    LORD,
    and let your faithful ones bless you.
Let them discourse of the glory of your
        kingdom
    and speak of your might.

R̸. I will praise your name forever, my
king and my God.

The LORD is faithful in all his words
    and holy in all his works.
The LORD lifts up all who are falling
    and raises up all who are bowed down.

R̸. I will praise your name forever, my
king and my God.

SECOND READING
2 Thess 1:11—2:2

Brothers and sisters:
We always pray for you,
    that our God may make you worthy of
        his calling
    and powerfully bring to fulfillment
        every good purpose
    and every effort of faith,
    that the name of our Lord Jesus may be
        glorified in you,
    and you in him,
    in accord with the grace of our God and
        Lord Jesus Christ.

We ask you, brothers and sisters,
    with regard to the coming of our Lord
        Jesus Christ
    and our assembling with him,
    not to be shaken out of your minds
        suddenly, or to be alarmed
    either by a "spirit," or by an oral
        statement,
    or by a letter allegedly from us
    to the effect that the day of the Lord is
        at hand.

About Liturgy

Change and liturgy: Change is generally a good thing—it indicates growth and desire for new directions and accomplishments. Even change in liturgy is good because the need for change is a witness that the liturgical assembly has grown deeper in their relationship with God and each other. Change is a fact of life and of liturgy! Change is good and necessary. But too much change too often can actually work against fruitful liturgy.

After change (especially something rather major) we must give ourselves time to "settle in" and make the change a natural part of the rhythm of our ritual celebrations. If we are always adjusting to something new, it is very difficult to internalize the fruits of liturgy. We must give ourselves time to settle in, not in the sense of becoming complacent or resting easy (liturgy is always hard work) or getting sloppy, but in the sense of having the luxury of fine-tuning what changes we have introduced. As we grow in familiarity with our rituals we are free to enter more deeply into the liturgical mystery itself.

While change is necessary and good for the rhythm of our liturgies, novelty and innovation (especially for their own sakes or just to hold people's interest) generally work against good liturgy. We must always remember that liturgy is given an essential ritual structure that has been tested through the centuries of tradition, and this structure must be respected. It ensures that we are maximizing liturgy's purpose to make present the paschal mystery and that we are celebrating with the whole church.

About Liturgical Music

Change and liturgical music: The same principles given above about the pace of change in liturgical ritual apply to changes in liturgical music, but with some further comments that are specifically musical. First, we must always remember that music stands in a secondary, supporting role. Its purpose is to enable the assembly to surrender to the liturgical ritual. When we change the music too much or too often, we divert the assembly's energies from the ritual demands. We sidetrack the liturgy. When we change the music for its own sake, we give it a position that doesn't belong to it by making it primary. Again, we sidetrack the liturgy.

Second, the demands of the ritual are intense, and repetition and consistency in the music are meant to ease the task of surrender. For the average assembly this means introducing two or three new songs or hymns in a year's time is enough. In a year when a new setting of the Mass is being introduced, that alone is sufficient. Any change in service music or introduction of a new song must be related to the goal of enabling deeper participation in the rite, not to the mistaken goal of keeping people "entertained."

Honoring these principles takes discipline. New music should be introduced to support the assembly's liturgical and musical growth. But it is their growth (and the demands of the rite) that must dictate the changes, not the desire for novelty.

GOSPEL ACCLAMATION
Matt 11:28

R⁊. Alleluia, alleluia.
Come to me, all you who labor and are burdened
and I will give you rest, says the Lord.
R⁊. Alleluia, alleluia.

Gospel   Matt 5:1-12a; L667

When Jesus saw the crowds, he went
    up the mountain,
and after he had sat down, his
    disciples came to him.
He began to teach them, saying:
    "Blessed are the poor in spirit,
        for theirs is the Kingdom of
        heaven.
    Blessed are they who mourn,
        for they will be comforted.
    Blessed are the meek,
        for they will inherit the land.
    Blessed are they who hunger and thirst
        for righteousness,
        for they will be satisfied.
    Blessed are the merciful,
        for they will be shown mercy.
    Blessed are the clean of heart,
        for they will see God.
    Blessed are the peacemakers,
        for they will be called children of God.
    Blessed are they who are persecuted
        for the sake of righteousness,
        for theirs is the Kingdom of heaven.
    Blessed are you when they insult you
        and persecute you
        and utter every kind of evil against
            you falsely because of me.
    Rejoice and be glad,
        for your reward will be great in
        heaven."

See Appendix A, p. 309, for the other readings.

Reflecting on the Gospel

There has been some controversy in recent years over nicknames for sports teams. Some nicknames have been derogatory toward ethnic groups (especially Native Americans), and teams have changed them out of sensitivity to the dignity of others. Isn't it interesting, though, that a professional football team retains the nickname "Saints"? Football is a physically punishing sport. It is about overpowering and reaching the goal, even when it means walking and falling all over others. Could any image be further from what we celebrate on this solemnity? At the same time, football does have something in common with the saints we honor— all are single-minded about their goal: football players, to get a piece of leather across a line; the saints, to give God "Blessing and glory, wisdom and thanksgiving, honor, power, and might . . . forever and ever."

On this solemnity we honor all those saints in heaven who have "washed their robes and made them white in the blood of the lamb" (first reading). There is a paradox of imagery here. We all know that blood stains clothes red. Yet, for those immersed in Christ, his blood stains *white*—the color of new life. This solemnity, then, is about life—the eternal life of the saints in heaven and the life in Christ we share here on earth. The saints are models for a way of living that brings us, too, to eternal life.

Throughout their lives the saints faithfully opened themselves to the transforming action of Christ within them. This transforming action strengthened their identity as God's children (see second reading and gospel) and enabled them to embody the Beatitudes as a way of living. For us who share this same identity and way of living, the reward will not only be with the saints in heaven but is already on earth: we are even now the blessed of God bathed in comfort, mercy, and peace. The paradox of the Beatitudes is that we already *are* what we try to live: those blessed in God.

As "children of God" washed "in the blood of the Lamb," we are "blood relatives," so to speak, because we share the same identity. The most telling mark of being children of God is that we are "blessed." This is *who* we are—those who belong to God, are loved by God, are blessed by God. More than describing the identity of those who have been immersed in Christ, the Beatitudes also require of us a way of living. We have to *do* the Beatitudes. They describe a way to live consistent with our identity as God's children immersed in Christ. In Christ, who we are and how we live come together as one.

The saints stand out as models who give us courage and strength that we, too, can be faithful to the demands that the Beatitudes lay out for us. We know some saints by name (those who have been canonized). There are countless others (our deceased relatives and friends, even football players!) whom we know by name in a different way. This multitude of faithful followers of Christ beckons us to hear what Jesus teaches in this gospel: "Blessed are [you] . . . your reward will be great in heaven."

Living the Paschal Mystery

At first glance the Beatitudes seem an impossible blueprint for Christian living; most of us aren't near at all to the ideal that they express. But nine times is the word "blessed" addressed to us. When our blessedness is our focus, then fidelity to our Gospel way of life is no ideal, but becomes a way of expressing who we are in Christ—blessed.

Focusing the gospel

Key words and phrases: Blessed, children of God, great in heaven

To the point: On this solemnity we honor all those saints in heaven who have "washed their robes and made them white in the blood of the lamb" (first reading). Throughout their lives they faithfully opened themselves to the transforming action of Christ within them. This transforming action strengthened their identity as God's children (see second reading and gospel) and enabled them to embody the Beatitudes as a way of living. For us who share this same identity and way of living, the reward will not only be with the saints in heaven but is already on earth: we are even now the blessed of God bathed in comfort, mercy, and peace.

Model Rite of Blessing and Sprinkling Holy Water

Presider: Dear friends, this water reminds us of our baptism when we were blessed by God and made children of God. May we remain faithful to our baptismal promises as were the saints whom we honor today . . . [pause]

[continue with form A or B of the blessing of water]

Model Prayer of the Faithful

Presider: Our merciful and comforting God hears the prayers of those who cry out. And so we are encouraged to pray.

Response:

Lord, hear our prayer.

Cantor:

we pray to the Lord,

That all members of the church faithfully immerse themselves in Christ and his way of life . . . [pause]

That all peoples respond to God's call to blessedness and express it in loving service to others . . . [pause]

That those who are poor be cared for, those who are mourning be comforted, those who are hungry be filled . . . [pause]

That each of us here more fully embrace the Beatitudes by showing others mercy, promoting peace, and doing justice . . . [pause]

Presider: Loving God, you receive the praise of the angels and saints who are with you in everlasting glory: through their intercession hear these our prayers that one day we might share in that same everlasting glory. We pray through the Lamb, Jesus Christ our Lord. **Amen.**

FOR REFLECTION

- To be a child of God means to me . . . This affects my way of living in that . . .
- The Beatitude most comforting to me is . . . The one most challenging to me is . . .
- The impact the saints have on my faith life is . . . Saints I know are . . .

Homily Points

- In sports the typical objective is to overcome, overpower, conquer one's opponent. Surfers, however, take a different approach. They know that to have a wonderful ride, they must work with the wave rather than fight it. In the Beatitudes Jesus takes a similar approach, calling us to work with and cooperate with him and others.

- Living the Beatitudes means putting aside our tendencies toward controlling and dominating others. It means adopting a different way of regarding our lives and relationships—giving ourselves over for the good of others. When we immerse ourselves in Christ and surrender to the demands of Christian living, we find ourselves offering mercy by forgiving others, bringing peace into tension-filled situations, acting justly even when there is a personal price to pay.

✝ SPIRITUALITY

GOSPEL ACCLAMATION
cf. John 6:40

This is the will of my Father, says the Lord,
that everyone who sees the Son and believes in
   him
may have eternal life.

Gospel

John 6:37-40; L668

Jesus said to the crowds:
"Everything that the Father gives
      me will come to me,
   and I will not reject anyone
         who comes to me,
   because I came down from
         heaven not to do my own
         will
   but the will of the one who sent me.
And this is the will of the one who sent
      me,
   that I should not lose anything of
         what he gave me,
   but that I should raise it on the last
         day.
For this is the will of my Father,
   that everyone who sees the Son and
         believes in him
   may have eternal life,
   and I shall raise him on the last day."

See Appendix A, p. 310, for the other readings.

*Other readings in L668 may be chosen or those
given in the Masses for the Dead, L1011–1016.*

Reflecting on the Gospel

Parents sometimes tease their little children when passing a cemetery with the question, "How many dead people are in there?" The children try to count tombstones as the car or van all too quickly speeds by. The joke's answer is, "All of them are dead." This is not true, however; in fact, all of them are alive! This is what we celebrate this day: those who are faithful followers of Jesus never die. Those who follow him into death follow him into new life (see second reading). As Jesus is glorified, so will they be.

This festival commemorating the faithful departed is a popular one among many people. It is also comforting, reassuring, and hope-filled. It is comforting in that Jesus rejects no one the Father has given to him (see gospel) and raises to new life those who have been buried with him in baptism (see second reading). It is reassuring in that "the just are in the hand of God" (first reading). It is hope-filled because it "is the will" of the Father that anyone who believes in Jesus will "have eternal life" (gospel). We celebrate this festival confident of the Good News that our beloved faithful departed are within the embrace of God.

We must keep in mind on this festival that we are celebrating, in a real sense, another All Saints' Day. These souls that we commemorate today are not damned in hell; they have remained faithful to their baptismal promises and so also have the promise of eternal glory. No doubt our scriptural image of purifying fires (how we have come to image the soul's time in purgatory) has roused our piety and prompted us to pray for the poor souls. In addition to the purifying benefits of such prayers for the faithful departed, there may be benefits for us as well. Certainly, remembering our departed loved ones in our prayers is an admirable way for us to keep them close to us. We might even suggest that praying for the dead (and to the dead) is an important part of the grieving process—just as we grew in our relationships with our loved ones during their lifetime, so do we continue to deepen our love for them as we remember them in prayer after their death. Praying for the dead reminds us that death isn't an end but a beginning of a new life. Our prayers can be a concrete expression of our belief in everlasting life.

The only thing that can separate anyone from Christ and sharing in everlasting life is to refuse to follow Jesus into his death. Our deceased loved ones are awaiting the fullness of life with Jesus. This festival reminds us to be faithful in our own call to follow Jesus so that one day we will share in his fullness of life. It's not death that is the worst of things; it's being separated from Jesus that is the worst thing.

Living the Paschal Mystery

Following Jesus means being willing to enter into his death; this is the only way to share in Jesus' eternal glory. Although November 2 and the entire month of November have been the church's time for commemorating the faithful departed, we would do well to remember the deceased throughout the year because they are constant reminders that death leads to life. It might be good practice in our Gospel living not only to keep Fridays as days of penance but also to pray regularly on this day for the faithful departed. This is a kind of service, too—that we never forget those who have touched our lives and whom we have loved and who have loved us.

Focusing the gospel

Key words and phrases: gives me, not lose anything, have eternal life

To the point: This festival commemorating the faithful departed is comforting, reassuring, and hope-filled. It is comforting in that Jesus rejects no one the Father has given to him (see gospel) and raises to new life those who have been buried with him in baptism (see second reading). It is reassuring in that "the just are in the hand of God" (first reading). It is hope-filled because it "is the will" of the Father that anyone who believes in Jesus will "have eternal life" (gospel). We celebrate this festival confident of the Good News that our beloved faithful departed are within the embrace of God.

Model Act of Penitence

Presider: We gather today to pray for the faithful departed. Let us open ourselves to the Good News that Jesus who has conquered death will raise us up on the last day . . . [pause]

> Lord Jesus, you have power over death: Lord . . .
>
> Christ Jesus, you promise to those who are faithful everlasting life: Christ . . .
>
> Lord Jesus, you reject no one who comes to you: Lord . . .

Model Prayer of the Faithful

Presider: Through our prayer and intercession let us ask God to be merciful to the faithful departed.

Response:

Lord, hear our prayer.

Cantor:

we pray to the Lord,

For all members of the church, that they may find comfort in Jesus' promise of fullness of life to the faithful departed . . . [pause]

For all people of the world, that they may come to salvation in God . . . [pause]

For those who have died and have no one to pray for them . . . [pause]

For each of us, that we may be confident in Jesus' love for us and be filled with the hope of being reunited with those who have gone before us . . . [pause]

Presider: Glorious God, you call us from death into eternal life: hear these our prayers that the faithful departed might have eternal rest and we might one day be with them in everlasting glory. We ask this through that same Son, our Lord Jesus Christ. **Amen.**

**OPENING PRAYER
(FROM THE FIRST MASS)**
Let us pray

Pause for silent prayer

Merciful Father,
hear our prayers and console us.
As we renew our faith in your Son,
whom you raised from the dead,
strengthen our hope that all our departed
    brothers and sisters
will share in his resurrection,
who lives and reigns with you and the Holy
    Spirit,
one God, for ever and ever. **Amen.**

FOR REFLECTION
- What is comforting for me about praying for the dead is . . .
- What is reassuring about this festival for me is . . .
- What gives me hope that one day I will be with Jesus forever in heaven is . . .

Homily Points

- Every year we remember those who have died, for example, on Memorial Day, Veterans' Day, 9/11, anniversaries, birthdays, etc. By so remembering, these loved ones are never really gone from us. Neither are the loved ones who have "grown into union with" (second reading) Christ and have died in him.

- What we celebrate this day is different from our secular or personal days of remembering. We are doing more than recalling people and events. We are celebrating the promise of Jesus to bring our beloved faithful departed to the fullness of life with him. It is his promise to us, too.

✝ SPIRITUALITY

GOSPEL ACCLAMATION
Rev 1:5a, 6b

℟. Alleluia, alleluia.
Jesus Christ is the firstborn of the dead;
to him be glory and power, forever and ever.
℟. Alleluia, alleluia.

Gospel
Luke 20:27-38; L156C

Some Sadducees, those
    who deny that there
    is a resurrection,
    came forward and put
        this question to
        Jesus, saying,
"Teacher, Moses wrote for us,
If someone's brother dies leaving a wife
    but no child,
his brother must take the wife
and raise up descendants for his brother.
Now there were seven brothers;
    the first married a woman but
        died childless.
Then the second and the third married her,
    and likewise all the seven died childless.
Finally the woman also died.
Now at the resurrection whose wife will
    that woman be?
For all seven had been married to her."
Jesus said to them,
    "The children of this age marry and
        remarry;
    but those who are deemed worthy to
        attain to the coming age
    and to the resurrection of the dead
    neither marry nor are given in marriage.
They can no longer die,
    for they are like angels;
    and they are the children of God
    because they are the ones who will rise.
That the dead will rise
    even Moses made known in the passage
        about the bush,
    when he called out 'Lord,'
    the God of Abraham, the God of Isaac,
        and the God of Jacob;
    and he is not God of the dead, but of the
        living,
    for to him all are alive."

or Luke 20:27, 34-38 in Appendix A, p. 311.

Reflecting on the Gospel
Some important days in our history have *names*, for example, Pearl Harbor Day, D-Day, Thanksgiving Day. Very few observances are named by the *date* on which they happened. Fourth of July is one such day, when we celebrate the independence of our country; 9/11 is another, when we honor the heroic values of so many who gave their lives trying to save others. We admire people who have such absolute convictions in their beliefs that they live them out no matter what the personal cost. We hear of missionaries who sacrifice everything to bring the message of Christ to others. We *do* sacrifice our lives for the good of others. We *do* know for what we would die. We *do* know why we would go to such extremes—because God wills that we have an abundance of life now and forever.

The gospel is really not about marriage but about resurrection and the categorically new life it brings. The first reading isn't so much about martyrdom as it is about the resolute convictions of the brothers to keep God's laws, couched in their absolute hope for resurrection. The Sadducees in this gospel suggest a preposterous example to ridicule belief in the resurrection. With supreme confidence Jesus counters that God "is not God of the dead, but of the living." We do, indeed, live forever. Like the brothers in the first reading, like Jesus himself, we believe in God's promise of resurrection. It is the bedrock of our hope and the inspiration for our fidelity to the living God.

Resurrection is much more than simply a theological issue worthy of debate. Resurrection is a way of living, witnessing to our belief that there is more to life than what meets the eye. The basis for this belief is *hope*. Although hope always has a future orientation about it, when we have confidence in God's grace to bring about change in us, when we have patience with ourselves while that change comes about, we already have something of the future in the present—we already are living this new, risen life that is characterized by faithful relationship with God. The relationship enabled by risen life is that of being "children of God" in an everlasting relationship with the living God.

With the promise of risen life, the suffering we face now seems nothing in comparison. In order for this to be really true for us, we must have zeal for God and God's ways that are, for us, a way of living. God is a God of the living. This is the core of our hope, borne out by the daily choices we make to be faithful followers of Jesus.

Living the Paschal Mystery
Paschal mystery living means that we live this life in a way that infuses it with the life that is to come. The dying part of the mystery always reminds us that suffering and death pale in comparison to the categorically new life that God offers us in Christ.

When we faithfully live our Christian life, like the brothers in the first reading, we will meet with controversy. In fact, controversy may be a sign of integrity since truly living the gospel always precipitates conflict. This doesn't mean that we go out looking for controversy; it does mean that when controversy happens because of the authenticity of our Christian living, we see through the controversy with hope for eternal life. This hope is what gives us the courage of our convictions and helps us remain steadfast even to death.

Focusing the gospel

Key words and phrases: deny . . . resurrection, the dead will rise, God . . . of the living

To the point: The Sadducees in this gospel suggest a preposterous example to ridicule belief in the resurrection. With supreme confidence Jesus counters that God "is not God of the dead, but of the living." We do, indeed, live forever. Like the brothers in the first reading, like Jesus himself, we believe in God's promise of resurrection. It is the bedrock of our hope and the inspiration for our fidelity to the living God.

Connecting the Gospel

to the end of the liturgical year: As we approach the end of the church year, the Lectionary always directs our attention to Jesus' second coming and the promise of resurrection. This focus is reinforced by the cluster of festivals (All Saints, All Souls, Christ the King) we celebrate at this time.

to our experience: The death of a loved one is an occasion when our thoughts consciously turn to the hope of life after death. The readings this Sunday reassure us that this hope in new life after death is well founded.

Connecting the Responsorial Psalm

to the readings: On this Sunday, when the church begins to focus on the end times and the second coming of Christ, both the first reading and the gospel speak directly of God's promise to raise the just to new life after death. The martyred brothers in the first reading remain faithful to the covenant even to death, for they believe that the giver of life and limb will never take back what has been bestowed. As Jesus asserts in the gospel, "the dead will rise," for God is "God of the living."

Like the brothers in the first reading, Jesus knows that he will be put to death for remaining faithful to the call of God. In the responsorial psalm we align ourselves with these brothers and Jesus. We state our hope that on "waking" from death we shall find ourselves in the presence of God. And we make our commitment that we will remain "steadfast in [the] path" of discipleship. As we celebrate this Eucharist and sing this psalm, we look to the glory of Christ to come and know that we shall share in that glory just as we have shared in its price.

to psalmist preparation: In this responsorial you proclaim your faith in God's promise of eternal life and your choice to remain faithful to discipleship no matter what its costs. This is no small thing considering the cost will be your life. What conversation might you have with Christ this week to give you courage and strengthen your hope?

**ASSEMBLY &
FAITH-SHARING GROUPS**

- I am confident in Jesus' promise of life after death when . . . I struggle with belief in everlasting life when . . .
- I show my fidelity to the God of the living when . . .
- My belief in being raised from the dead makes a difference in my daily living in that . . .

PRESIDERS

- My ministry embodies hope in new life and gives courage to those struggling with the future by . . .

DEACONS

- In my serving others, I have marveled at the hope and courage of their faith (first reading) when . . . This has changed me by . . .

HOSPITALITY MINISTERS

- The manner of my welcoming of others reminds them of God's enduring love and promise of new life when . . .

MUSIC MINISTERS

- My music ministry strengthens my relationship with the living God by . . .

ALTAR MINISTERS

- My faithful and unobtrusive service expresses my belief in God's promise of everlasting life in that . . .

LECTORS

- Just as I am inspired by the behavior of the brothers in the first reading, my life inspires others by . . .

**EXTRAORDINARY MINISTERS
OF HOLY COMMUNION**

- The manner of my distributing Holy Communion helps others realize that they are participating in the new life Jesus brings when . . .

Model Act of Penitence

Presider: In today's gospel Jesus promises everlasting life to those who are faithful. As we prepare for this liturgy, let us open ourselves to the living God who comes to save . . . [pause]

Lord Jesus, you will appear in glory: Lord . . .

Christ Jesus, you are the God of the living: Christ . . .

Lord Jesus, you promise to those who are faithful everlasting life: Lord . . .

Homily Points

• None of us likes to have our selves or our ideas ridiculed. For example, we don't like our profession, our race or ethnic background, our religious affiliation to be the butt of a joke. The Sadducees in the gospel ridicule Jesus and everyone who believes in life after death. Rather than putting them down with a nasty retort, Jesus uses the opportunity to teach about what is fundamental to his life and mission.

• Jesus lived and ministered as one fully in tune with the "God . . . of the living." All his encounters with others were life-giving. His promise of new life and our own hope of sharing in eternal life are based on the very way he lived—seeing life even where others thought there was only death.

• Jesus reached out to those whom others considered "dead": lepers, sinners, outcasts. His relationship with the "God . . . of the living" enabled him to bring even these people in touch with new life. Like Jesus, we also must spend our lives deepening our relationship with the God of life and sharing this with others. We do so through concrete choices and actions directed to their good. We thus attest to God's life acting through us now— the promise and hope of future glory within us.

Model Prayer of the Faithful

Presider: We pray to our living God, confident that God hears the prayer of those who share in the divine life.

Response:

Lord, hear our prayer.

Cantor:

we pray to the Lord,

That the church be a bedrock of hope for those who seek better life . . . [pause]

That people live the conviction of their faith in God and one day enjoy everlasting life . . . [pause]

That those who are suffering and dying for their beliefs may be comforted by the living God . . . [pause]

That each of us grow in our relationship with the living God and share the divine life given us through the good works we do . . . [pause]

Presider: Saving God, you are the God of the living: hear these our prayers that one day we might enjoy everlasting life with you. We ask this through Christ our Lord. **Amen.**

OPENING PRAYER

Let us pray

Pause for silent prayer

God of power and mercy,
protect us from all harm.
Give us freedom of spirit
and health in mind and body
to do your work on earth.

We ask this through our Lord Jesus Christ,
    your Son,
who lives and reigns with you and the
    Holy Spirit,
one God, for ever and ever. **Amen.**

FIRST READING 2 Macc 7:1-2, 9-14

It happened that seven brothers with their
    mother were arrested
    and tortured with whips and scourges
        by the king,
    to force them to eat pork in violation of
        God's law.
One of the brothers, speaking for the
    others, said:
    "What do you expect to achieve by
        questioning us?
We are ready to die rather than transgress
    the laws of our ancestors."

At the point of death he said:
    "You accursed fiend, you are depriving
        us of this present life,
    but the King of the world will raise us
        up to live again forever.
It is for his laws that we are dying."

After him the third suffered their cruel sport.
He put out his tongue at once when told
        to do so,
    and bravely held out his hands, as he
        spoke these noble words:
    "It was from Heaven that I received these;
    for the sake of his laws I disdain them;
    from him I hope to receive them again."
Even the king and his attendants marveled
    at the young man's courage,
    because he regarded his sufferings as
        nothing.

After he had died,
    they tortured and maltreated the fourth
        brother in the same way.
When he was near death, he said,
    "It is my choice to die at the hands of
        men
    with the hope God gives of being raised
        up by him;
    but for you, there will be no resurrection
        to life."

RESPONSORIAL PSALM

Ps 17:1, 5-6, 8, 15

℞. (15b) Lord, when your glory appears,
my joy will be full.

Hear, O LORD, a just suit;
　attend to my outcry;
　hearken to my prayer from lips without
　　deceit.

℞. Lord, when your glory appears, my joy
will be full.

My steps have been steadfast in your
　　paths,
　my feet have not faltered.
I call upon you, for you will answer me,
　O God;
　incline your ear to me; hear my word.

℞. Lord, when your glory appears, my joy
will be full.

Keep me as the apple of your eye,
　hide me in the shadow of your wings.
But I in justice shall behold your face;
　on waking I shall be content in your
　　presence.

℞. Lord, when your glory appears, my joy
will be full.

SECOND READING

2 Thess 2:16–3:5

Brothers and sisters:
May our Lord Jesus Christ himself and
　God our Father,
　who has loved us and given us
　　everlasting encouragement
　and good hope through his grace,
　encourage your hearts and strengthen
　　them in every good deed and word.

Finally, brothers and sisters, pray for us,
　so that the word of the Lord may speed
　　forward and be glorified,
　as it did among you,
　and that we may be delivered from
　　perverse and wicked people,
　for not all have faith.
But the Lord is faithful;
　he will strengthen you and guard you
　　from the evil one.
We are confident of you in the Lord that
　　what we instruct you,
　you are doing and will continue to do.
May the Lord direct your hearts to the love
　of God
　and to the endurance of Christ.

About Liturgy

Resurrection of the dead: Easter, of course, is the prime time of the year when we think about Jesus' resurrection from the dead. The end of the liturgical year, when the liturgy invites us to look to the Parousia or Christ's second coming, is another time when we think of resurrection and this time as it also applies to ourselves. Our hope in resurrection, naturally, is based in Jesus' being raised from the dead to new life. To put this another way (and perhaps make it a bit more concrete and easier to grasp): in his resurrection Jesus was taken into eternity by his Father. Resurrection, then, is less a mystery and more a statement of belief that what happened to Jesus will happen to his faithful disciples as well—we will one day be with God in eternal glory.

Each time we recite the Creed we include a statement of our belief in the resurrection from the dead. This is a doctrine that we Christians have held since apostolic times. Moreover, it is more than belief that the soul will live forever; we also believe that at the general resurrection at Christ's second coming somehow our bodies will also be united with our souls. Just as Jesus' glorified body was different from his body before the resurrection (he could go through doors, was not immediately recognized, etc.), so will our glorified bodies be different from these, our earthly bodies.

Resurrection and cremation: In the past the church disallowed cremation in view of the resurrection of the body. Now the church allows cremation so long as it isn't chosen out of disbelief in the resurrection of the body. Under all circumstances the church wants to preserve dignity for our earthly bodies since they have been created by God and are holy. Similar to Mary's, our bodies have been temples of the Holy Spirit.

About Liturgical Music

Music suggestions: The readings and psalm this Sunday speak of hope in the resurrection but also of the challenge to be faithful to the demands of discipleship. "A Multitude Comes from the East and the West" [W3] speaks of many who will join Abraham, Isaac, and Jacob (gospel) at the "feast of salvation" and receive the crown of victory. The text with its lovely E-minor tune would work well during the preparation of the gifts. Both "We Shall Rise Again" [G2, GC, GC2, RS] and "We Will Rise Again" [BB, G2, JS2, OFUV] speak of the weariness and dangers that accompany discipleship and the certainty we hold in God's promise of resurrection. These verse-refrain songs would work well during the Communion procession. Another excellent choice for Communion would be "Come, All You Blessed Ones" [PMB, WC, WS], which combines a refrain about the promise of eternal joy for those "blest of a loving God" with verses based on Psalm 23 and Psalm 34. "Want to Go to Heaven When I Die" [LMGM] sings of longing and of hope to join those loved ones who have preceded us to risen glory. This song would work well either as a choral prelude or as an assembly song of praise after Communion.

SPIRITUALITY

GOSPEL ACCLAMATION
Luke 21:28

R⁊. Alleluia, alleluia.
Stand erect and raise your heads
because your redemption is at hand.
R⁊. Alleluia, alleluia.

Gospel
Luke 21:5-19; L159C

While some people were
    speaking about
    how the temple was
        adorned with
        costly stones and
        votive offerings,
Jesus said, "All that
    you see here—
the days will come when there will
    not be left
a stone upon another stone that will
    not be thrown down."

Then they asked him,
    "Teacher, when will this happen?
And what sign will there be when all
    these things are about to happen?"
He answered,
"See that you not be deceived,
    for many will come in my name,
        saying,
    'I am he,' and 'The time has come.'
Do not follow them!
When you hear of wars and
    insurrections,
    do not be terrified; for such things
        must happen first,
    but it will not immediately be the
        end."
Then he said to them,
    "Nation will rise against nation, and
        kingdom against kingdom.
There will be powerful earthquakes,
    famines, and plagues
    from place to place;
    and awesome sights and mighty signs
        will come from the sky.

Continued in Appendix A, p. 311.

Reflecting on the Gospel

Archaeology teaches us that things last (they tell stories for people living far into the future) and that all things come to an end. Historians of ancient cultures painstakingly sift through sand and earth to tease out artifacts, outlines of buildings, sometimes even preserved bodies that give us insight into past peoples and cultures long after these have ceased to exist. The Wailing Wall is all that is left of the splendid temple in Jerusalem, of which this Sunday's gospel speaks; stone upon stone barely is left, but the way of living that Jesus taught is still lived and witnessed among us, preserved in the faithful lives of his disciples. The gospel predicts end times; our challenge is to live faithfully *now*.

The signs of the end times that Jesus names (wars, insurrection, earthquakes, famine, plagues, etc.) describe human history as it has *always* been. Jesus assures us that the end is not immediate. The challenge for us as faithful followers is to face persecution with courage *now*, testify to Jesus' name *now*, open ourselves *now* to the wisdom given us by Jesus. Embracing this way of living gives us hope and confidence that, no matter when the end times come, our lives are secure.

We might ask, then, what will be so different at the end times? In one sense every day is already the beginning of the end time. The signs we observe of human calamities bid us to testify to all that Jesus taught us—that there is more to life than we can see. We must live faithfully *now*. By our perseverance as faithful followers testifying to Jesus' name, we secure everlasting life. Every day is an opportunity to live discipleship fully and confidently. Every day is an opportunity to grow in our relationship with Jesus, the one who promises life to his faithful ones.

If we are able to look to the end time without fear, it is because we live in constant preparedness for Jesus' second coming. We don't prepare by stockpiling supplies or creating time capsules for future generations. We prepare by the very way we live now: we follow Jesus (rather than others who might lead us astray) and testify to his message of salvation. For when all is said and done, unity with Jesus now is the only thing that guarantees unity with Jesus for all eternity. Unity with Jesus now is what secures our lives.

Living the Paschal Mystery

The signs of the end time alert us to the fact that our striving to be faithful disciples has *cosmic* proportions. Living the paschal mystery has consequences not just for us but also for all others. When we break out of a chronological understanding of time (that is, time as duration with past, present, and future) and break into God's eternal time (time without duration in which everything just *is*), we can begin to understand how even the little acts of kindness and self-sacrifice we perform each day affect all that is. Our unity with Jesus is deepened by striving to care for others, help others, shower others with dignity and respect.

Here is a sobering thought: the way we care for the children, are honest at the workplace, take leisure time to care for ourselves affect our whole world and everyone in it. This is the privilege of discipleship: we can make a difference! This is the effect of faithful discipleship: the world is a better place—we have readied it for Christ's second coming at the end of time by our faithful and grace-filled living *now*.

Focusing the gospel

Key words and phrases: not immediately be the end, awesome sights and mighty signs, persecute you, testimony, wisdom, secure your lives

To the point: The signs of the end times that Jesus names (wars, insurrection, earthquakes, famine, plagues, etc.) describe human history as it has *always* been. Jesus assures us that the end is not immediate. The challenge for us as faithful followers is to face persecution with courage *now*, testify to Jesus' name *now*, open ourselves *now* to the wisdom given us by Jesus. Embracing this way of living gives us hope and confidence that, no matter when the end times come, our lives are secure.

Connecting the Gospel

to the first reading: In face of fearsome events described in both the gospel and first reading, the faithful have nothing to fear, for they will be protected by "the sun of justice with its healing rays."

to our experience: The general populace thinks of the end times in terms of cosmic, catastrophic events that are yet to come. Consequently, we think the end times concern future generations, not us. The truth, however, is that the end times, no matter when they come, do help us reflect on how we need to live now.

Connecting the Responsorial Psalm

to the readings: The day is coming, says the Lord, when the faithful will see justice (first reading). But "before this happens," Jesus tells us, we will experience the destruction wrought by natural disasters and human will; we will suffer persecution for being disciples; we will be called to testify to the vision we have been granted in him (gospel). And our perseverance will gain us life.

We find the source of our perseverance in the words of the responsorial psalm: the Lord will come to rule the world with justice. This declaration is the hope that sustains us, the vision of the future we see now with the eyes of faith. It is the assurance that gives us courage to continue in discipleship knowing we face persecution, even death. It is the faith to which we testify before the world. As we sing this psalm, may we feel the presence of Christ filling us with his wisdom, his courage, and his faithfulness.

to psalmist preparation: When you sing this responsorial psalm, you stand before the assembly testifying to a vision of the future in which God reigns with justice. Do you believe in this future? Are you looking for it? Will you stake your life on it?

**ASSEMBLY &
FAITH-SHARING GROUPS**

• I need courage to live and proclaim the gospel when . . .

• I am called to testify to Jesus' name when . . .

• The wisdom that secures my life is . . .

PRESIDERS

• I lead the assembly to hope and confidence in the future when I . . .

DEACONS

• To those troubled and burdened, my ministry embodies "the sun of justice with its healing rays" (first reading) by . . .

HOSPITALITY MINISTERS

• The manner of my greeting helps those gathering for liturgy to hand the concerns of their daily living over to God in hope and confidence when . . .

MUSIC MINISTERS

• My music ministry helps me hope in the coming of the Lord because . . . It calls me to persevere in discipleship by . . .

ALTAR MINISTERS

• Perseverance in faithful ministry gives me hope, confidence, and security in God because . . .

LECTORS

• " . . . I myself shall give you a wisdom . . ." An example of the wisdom I have been given through prayerful attention to God's word is . . .

**EXTRAORDINARY MINISTERS
OF HOLY COMMUNION**

• Like the gift of the Eucharist itself, my ministry offers others strength, courage, and hope by . . .

Model Act of Penitence

Presider: The gospel invites us today not to look to cosmic events such as wars, earthquakes, and famine for signs of the end of the world but to look to the faithfulness of our own discipleship. Let us pray during this liturgy for perseverance . . . [pause]

Lord Jesus, you come to rule the earth with justice: Lord . . .

Christ Jesus, you give us your wisdom and strength: Christ . . .

Lord Jesus, you secure for us eternal life: Lord . . .

Homily Points

• We tend to bank on security by installing alarm systems, building up reserves of money, having a plentiful supply of food and drink on hand. While these external measures may be necessary for our material well-being, the secure lives Jesus promises us in the gospel derive from within ourselves and from living in a way consistent with who we are as his followers.

• How reassuring it is to have Jesus tell us that "not a hair on [our] head will be destroyed" if we are faithful to discipleship. The source of our confidence and trust that we can live in the way Jesus asks is Jesus himself. By his teaching and by the example of his way of living, Jesus gives us the wisdom we need to face any and all adversity.

• The secure life Jesus is talking about doesn't mean that everything in our lives is going to be easy or the way we want it. We will, in fact, face many "deaths," as Jesus did—we will be misunderstood, criticized, taken for granted, taken advantage of, sometimes even face physical death in our pursuit of Jesus' way of living. No matter what "deaths" we face, our lives are secure in Jesus.

Model Prayer of the Faithful

Presider: Let us pray for strength and perseverance to be faithful followers of Jesus.

Response:

Cantor:

That all members of the church may persevere through death to new life . . . [pause]

That the world may live in peace and justice . . . [pause]

That those who face persecution for faithfully living the gospel be given strength and courage . . . [pause]

That all of us here ground our security in Jesus who gives us wisdom and perseverance . . . [pause]

Presider: God of life, you protect us and care for us: hear these our prayers and strengthen us to persevere as your Son's followers so that one day we might live forever with you and our Lord Jesus Christ. **Amen.**

Let us pray

Pause for silent prayer

Father of all that is good,
keep us faithful in serving you,
for to serve you is our lasting joy.

We ask this through our Lord Jesus Christ,
    your Son,
who lives and reigns with you and the
    Holy Spirit,
one God, for ever and ever. **Amen.**

Mal 3:19-20a

Lo, the day is coming, blazing like an oven,
    when all the proud and all evildoers will
        be stubble,
and the day that is coming will set them
    on fire,
    leaving them neither root nor branch,
    says the LORD of hosts.
But for you who fear my name, there will
    arise
    the sun of justice with its healing rays.

RESPONSORIAL PSALM

Ps 98:5-6, 7-8, 9

R̸. (cf. 9) The Lord comes to rule the earth with justice.

Sing praise to the LORD with the harp,
   with the harp and melodious song.
With trumpets and the sound of the horn
   sing joyfully before the King, the LORD.

R̸. The Lord comes to rule the earth with justice.

Let the sea and what fills it resound,
   the world and those who dwell in it;
let the rivers clap their hands,
   the mountains shout with them for joy.

R̸. The Lord comes to rule the earth with justice.

Before the LORD, for he comes,
   for he comes to rule the earth;
he will rule the world with justice
   and the peoples with equity.

R̸. The Lord comes to rule the earth with justice.

SECOND READING

2 Thess 3:7-12

Brothers and sisters:
You know how one must imitate us.
For we did not act in a disorderly way
   among you,
   nor did we eat food received free from
   anyone.
On the contrary, in toil and drudgery,
   night and day
   we worked, so as not to burden any of
   you.
Not that we do not have the right.
Rather, we wanted to present ourselves as
   a model for you,
   so that you might imitate us.
In fact, when we were with you,
   we instructed you that if anyone was
     unwilling to work,
   neither should that one eat.
We hear that some are conducting
   themselves among you in a disorderly
   way,
   by not keeping busy but minding the
   business of others.
Such people we instruct and urge in the
   Lord Jesus Christ to work quietly
   and to eat their own food.

About Liturgy

Ministry of the assembly: When we speak about cosmic dimensions of our discipleship (as in the reflection section, Living the Paschal Mystery), it seems a bit too much for us to grasp. A reflection on the ministry of the assembly might help us make this more concrete.

When we think of "liturgical ministries" we usually think of the visible ministries, for example, hospitality ministers, lectors, altar ministers, etc. We can easily lose sight of an important ministry that has no "assignment sheet": the ministry of the assembly, a ministry we all share each time we gather. The basic ministry of the assembly is to make visible the church, members united with Head. This is how we can begin to grasp the cosmic dimension of our discipleship: we are never acting alone, but always as *church*.

Jesus promised that where two or three are gathered *in his name*, he is present. What is key here is not just the gathering, but the gathering *in his name*. When we gather as liturgical assembly, we unite the various members of Christ's Body with the Head. The very idea of gathering, then, is an expression of who we are: the Body of Christ. All ministry is from the body to the Body.

When we absent ourselves from the assembly without good reason, we make a difference in how the Body is manifested. In other words, coming together for liturgical prayer is far more than fulfilling obligation. The liturgical assembly bids us to surrender ourselves to the transforming action of the liturgy. This generous self-giving is the first step in faithful discipleship and is what church is really all about. It is necessary in order for church to be concretely and most assuredly visible. It is necessary if the Body of Christ is to be built up, to come to full stature. Our presence in and to the assembly is indispensable, for we are all members of the church, the one Body. When the membership of the liturgical assembly is diminished, the Body is diminished. Our presence makes a difference. It is the first expression of faithful discipleship. It is a concrete expression of the cosmic dimension of faithful discipleship—Jesus' kingdom is present through the whole world throughout all times because we (all of us) gather.

About Liturgical Music

Music suggestions: "In the Day of the Lord" [BB, JS2, OFUV] is an energetic verse-refrain song whose meter shifts from 4/4 to 6/8, adding rhythmic interest in just the right places. This would make an excellent entrance song. The Advent song "Now Is the Time Approaching" [WC] speaks of the end of war and strife in the kingdom of the Prince of Peace. Its final verse is especially applicable to this Sunday: "O long expected dawning, Come with your cheering ray! Yet shall the morning brighten, The shadows flee away. O sweet anticipation! It cheers the watchers on, To pray and hope and labor, Till dark of night be gone." This would make an excellent post-Communion or recessional hymn. Another Advent song fitting for this Sunday is "City of God, Jerusalem" [RS, W3]. The canonic repetition of the melody in the bass line intensifies the hymn's forward movement, and the chromatic rise in the final phrase captures the hope of the church. This would work well as a post-Communion or a recessional hymn.

✠ SPIRITUALITY

GOSPEL ACCLAMATION
Mark 11:9, 10

℟. Alleluia, alleluia.
Blessed is he who comes in the name of
    the Lord!
Blessed is the kingdom of our father
    David that is to come!
℟. Alleluia, alleluia.

Gospel

Luke 23:35-43; L162C

The rulers sneered at Jesus and
    said,
    "He saved others, let him save
        himself
    if he is the chosen one, the
        Christ of God."
Even the soldiers jeered at him.
As they approached to offer him wine
    they called out,
    "If you are King of the Jews, save
        yourself."
Above him there was an inscription
    that read,
    "This is the King of the Jews."

Now one of the criminals hanging there
    reviled Jesus, saying,
    "Are you not the Christ?
Save yourself and us."
The other, however, rebuking him, said
    in reply,
    "Have you no fear of God,
    for you are subject to the same
        condemnation?
And indeed, we have been condemned
    justly,
    for the sentence we received
        corresponds to our crimes,
    but this man has done nothing
        criminal."
Then he said,
    "Jesus, remember me when you come
        into your kingdom."
He replied to him,
    "Amen, I say to you,
    today you will be with me in
        Paradise."

Reflecting on the Gospel

One theory about the origin of the word "king" is that it is from the Old English *cyning*, from which we derive our word "kin." The king is the one to whom authority and leadership within a tribe, nation, or group is passed down because of family lineage. The king's position is dependent not upon his personal abilities, goodness, or virtues but upon his kinship line. His position is one of status through inheritance. This Sunday we celebrate Christ as our King. Christ is no ordinary ruler, however. His kingship is dependent not upon human bloodline but upon his relationship to his heavenly Father. Through him we become "kin," members of his Body, the church. He leads this Body with vision and promise, hope and new life, and to those who are faithful he grants the inheritance of eternal life in paradise.

How does using the image "king" to refer to Christ shape our relationship to him? By naming him "king" we acknowledge him and his way of living as the wellspring of our goodness and salvation. We acknowledge our status as his "subjects" called to relate to others as he did. We acknowledge our shared inheritance as the "holy ones" (second reading) who receive life through him. By naming Christ our King we identify him as the One who offers us the fullness of life in his kingdom both now and forever. By naming Christ our King we also accept the responsibility to be faithful to the demands required of those who follow him. This is the relationship to which the image "king" challenges us: we are our King's "kin." We inherit from him what is his to give: life. That inheritance has its cost.

Although Jesus' kingdom is established from the very beginning of creation (see second reading) and through the Davidic kingship (see the first reading), his reign is not one of power but of mercy, not one of self-service but of self-giving, not one of material wealth but of eternal salvation. His throne is a cross. Such a King the world has never seen.

The cross is where we least expect a king to be. Yet this is where we find Jesus. The cross is where we least want to be. Yet this is how God's kingdom is established and where our discipleship begins: allowing ourselves to be crucified on the cross of self-giving. Jesus demonstrates his kingship not by saving himself but by saving others. Jesus demonstrates his kingship not by power but by loving reassurance that paradise awaits faithful disciples. Only by beginning here, on the cross, can our discipleship end like the Good Thief's, hearing Jesus say to us, "Amen, I say to you, today you will be with me in paradise."

Living the Paschal Mystery

The Good Thief said, "Jesus, remember me when you come into your kingdom." This solemnity celebrates Christ as King. His kingdom has come. *We* are living in God's kingdom *now*. But we are called not to simply pay homage to our exalted King, but to do as he did. This means that each day we must live in a self-giving way because only through goodness expressed in reaching out to others is God's reign at hand. Living the paschal mystery means living the cross. Just as the cross was the means to Jesus' exaltation, so is the cross the means to our own entry into paradise. When self-giving seems to swallow us up and we are tempted to choose a self-serving attitude, all we need do is remember that the cross is the door to paradise. The only way.

Focusing the gospel

Key words and phrases: He saved, King, into your kingdom

To the point: How does using the image "king" to refer to Christ shape our relationship to him? By naming him "king" we acknowledge him and his way of living as the wellspring of our goodness and salvation. We acknowledge our status as his "subjects," called to relate to others as he did. We acknowledge our shared inheritance as the "holy ones" (second reading) who receive life through him. By naming Christ our King we identify him as the One who offers us the fullness of life in his kingdom both now and forever.

Connecting the Gospel

to the other readings: Jesus is a King who "shepherds [his] people" (first reading), delivers them, and bestows an unimaginable inheritance on them (see second reading).

to our experience: In the political world a king is wealthy, powerful, the center of attention and adulation. In this Sunday's gospel Jesus is a king who relinquishes wealth and power and who, even at the moment of his own death, turns attention not to himself but to someone else who is calling out in need.

Connecting the Responsorial Psalm

to the readings: Israelites arriving at the gates of Jerusalem for annual worship sang Psalm 122. It was a song of great joy, for entering Jerusalem meant encountering God. It meant celebrating membership in God's people. It meant reaffirming who they were and who God was for them. On this solemnity of Christ the King we, too, celebrate who we are and who God is for us. We are the people forgiven by God through Christ's redeeming death (second reading). We are the very "bone and flesh" (first reading) of Christ, members of the Body of which he is the head (second reading). We are the ones remembered by Christ and called to his kingdom (gospel). Let us enter with rejoicing!

to psalmist preparation: In singing this responsorial psalm you invite the assembly to enter the kingdom of God. They have journeyed through all of Ordinary Time. They have struggled, they have been faithful. Bring them in with joy.

**ASSEMBLY &
FAITH-SHARING GROUPS**

- What this gospel teaches me about Jesus as king is . . . What this gospel teaches me about being Jesus' "subject" is . . .
- The goodness I have received from Christ the King is . . . I share this goodness with others by . . .
- I experience the fullness of life in Christ's kingdom when . . .

PRESIDERS

- Over the past liturgical year my ministry has helped the assembly realize their "inheritance [as] the holy ones in light" (second reading) by . . .

DEACONS

- Jesus' kingship demanded that he be emptied unto death on a cross. Times when my diaconal service required self-emptying were . . . The glory I have found in such moments is . . .

HOSPITALITY MINISTERS

- The manner of my greeting enables those gathering to see themselves as the "holy ones" of Christ's kingdom when . . .

MUSIC MINISTERS

- Through my music ministry I have not "saved" myself but, like Christ, have given myself for others when . . . I feel remembered by Christ for this and called into his kingdom when . . .

ALTAR MINISTERS

- My ministry truly serves Christ my King through serving others when . . .

LECTORS

- The word I proclaim declares Christ as King and the life I live proclaims Christ as King in that . . .

**EXTRAORDINARY MINISTERS
OF HOLY COMMUNION**

- When I distribute Holy Communion, I am drawn to think about Christ as my King when . . .

Model Act of Penitence

Presider: As we prepare ourselves to celebrate well these sacred mysteries, let us ask Christ our King to strengthen our resolve to imitate him through a life of self-giving for the good of others . . . [pause]

Lord Jesus, you are King of all creation: Lord . . .

Christ Jesus, you reign with justice and bring peace: Christ . . .

Lord Jesus, you bring your faithful followers into the fullness of life: Lord . . .

Homily Points

• In our fantasies the possibility of being a king or queen is pretty appealing. We'd be the center of attention, everyone would wait on us hand and foot, we would have everything we want with no financial worries. Best of all, we would never have to do any work. We mistakenly think living this way would be the fullness life offers. Jesus, however, shows us otherwise.

• The fullness of life Jesus offers cannot be provided by money or power, but only by giving ourselves over for the good of others. Jesus himself modeled such self-giving when, on the cross, he responded to the Good Thief's cry for compassion and mercy.

• While we don't encounter someone dying on a cross asking for compassion and mercy, every day we do meet the bedraggled parent with a fussy child, the belligerent teen, the frustrated coworker. Here is where we encounter our King: in the face of others in need. Here is how we really are kings and queens: by responding to others. This is fullness of life. One question remains: how do we respond to others?

Model Prayer of the Faithful

Presider: Let us confidently make known our needs to Christ our King who invites us to fullness of life.

Response:

Lord, hear our prayer.

Cantor:

we pray to the Lord,

That all members of the church faithfully follow Christ the King by caring for others . . . [pause]

That all peoples of the world come into God's kingdom and live in peace and justice . . . [pause]

That those who are suffering and dying be comforted by Christ the King's promise of fullness of life . . . [pause]

That each one of us celebrate in joy this festival in honor of Christ our King . . . [pause]

Presider: God of goodness and holiness, you offer us fullness of life in the kingdom of your Son: hear these our prayers that one day we might live with you forever. We ask this through Our Lord Jesus Christ our King. **Amen.**

ALTERNATIVE OPENING PRAYER
Let us pray

Pause for silent prayer

Father all-powerful, God of love,
you have raised our Lord Jesus Christ from
   death to life,
resplendent in glory as King of creation.
Open our hearts,
free all the world to rejoice in his peace,
to glory in his justice, to live in his love.
Bring all mankind together in Jesus Christ
   your Son,
whose kingdom is with you and the Holy
   Spirit,
one God, for ever and ever. **Amen.**

FIRST READING
2 Sam 5:1-3

In those days, all the tribes of Israel came
   to David in Hebron and said:
   "Here we are, your bone and your flesh.
In days past, when Saul was our king,
   it was you who led the Israelites out and
   brought them back.
And the LORD said to you,
   'You shall shepherd my people Israel
   and shall be commander of Israel.'"
When all the elders of Israel came to
   David in Hebron,
   King David made an agreement with
   them there before the LORD,
   and they anointed him king of Israel.

RESPONSORIAL PSALM
Ps 122:1-2, 3-4, 4-5

℟. (cf. 1) Let us go rejoicing to the house
of the Lord.

I rejoiced because they said to me,
   "We will go up to the house of the
   LORD."
And now we have set foot
   within your gates, O Jerusalem.

℟. Let us go rejoicing to the house of the
Lord.

Jerusalem, built as a city
  with compact unity.
To it the tribes go up,
  the tribes of the Lord.

R̂. Let us go rejoicing to the house of the Lord.

According to the decree for Israel,
  to give thanks to the name of the Lord.
In it are set up judgment seats,
  seats for the house of David.

R̂. Let us go rejoicing to the house of the Lord.

SECOND READING
Col 1:12-20

Brothers and sisters:
Let us give thanks to the Father,
  who has made you fit to share
  in the inheritance of the holy ones in
    light.
He delivered us from the power of
    darkness
  and transferred us to the kingdom of
    his beloved Son,
  in whom we have redemption, the
    forgiveness of sins.

He is the image of the invisible God,
  the firstborn of all creation.
For in him were created all things in
    heaven and on earth,
  the visible and the invisible,
  whether thrones or dominions or
    principalities or powers;
  all things were created through
    him and for him.
He is before all things,
  and in him all things hold together.
He is the head of the body, the
    church.
He is the beginning, the firstborn
    from the dead,
  that in all things he himself might
    be preeminent.
For in him all the fullness was
    pleased to dwell,
  and through him to reconcile all
    things for him,
  making peace by the blood of his
    cross
  through him, whether those on
    earth or those in heaven.

About Liturgy

Discipleship and victory: For months now we have been traveling with Jesus through the proclamation of Luke's gospel. This festival of Christ the King is the last Sunday and culmination of the whole liturgical year. Next Sunday we begin Advent and thus begin again yet another paschal mystery journey through a liturgical year. This annual celebration reminds us that the difficulties of discipleship are always rewarded by the joy of victory. The cross leads to risen life. As we embrace the cross in our own journey of discipleship each day, we are spurred on to faithfulness by remembering that it all culminates in this victory.

Each year we begin and end the same journey. Why isn't this cyclic pattern of our liturgical celebrations tedious? The answer lies in our taking the time to recognize our growth in discipleship and our personal relationship with Jesus our King during this past year. Since judgment is one of the themes of the end times, it might be good to take some time this week to judge our own growth and preparedness to enter paradise with Jesus. Without such self-reflection we run the risk of every liturgical year simply being like all others for us. Endings and beginnings always give us an opportunity to assess growth and recommit ourselves to faithful discipleship. True, the cross is not something we would naturally choose for ourselves. But the end of this liturgical year and the beginning of the new one when we encounter our victorious Christ is exactly what we need in order to be faithful to the disciple's life of self-giving for the good of others.

About Liturgical Music

Liturgical music and growth in discipleship: The solemnity of Christ the King is a good time to assess how we have grown this past year in and through liturgical music. How through our music have we more clearly become the Body of Christ given for the redemption of the world?

For assembly members: How have we grown in singing well together, that is, with willing heart and full voice? How have we grown in listening to each other as we sing, in becoming one Body rather than individuals singing "our own thing"?

For cantors and choir members: How have we grown in focusing on Christ rather than making ourselves the "star" of the liturgy? How have we grown in treating each other as members of the one Body of Christ? How have we grown in unselfishness because of the disciplines required for our ministry?

For music directors: How have we grown in our understanding of the role of music in liturgy? How have we stayed faithful to keeping liturgy central and music secondary and supporting? How have we grown through this ministry in our relationship with Christ and in our ability to see the assembly as Body of Christ? How have we helped psalmists, cantors, and choir members grow in these ways?

NOVEMBER 21, 2010
THE SOLEMNITY OF OUR LORD JESUS CHRIST THE KING

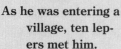

SPIRITUALITY

GOSPEL ACCLAMATION

℟. Alleluia, alleluia.
In all circumstances, give thanks,
for this is the will of God for you in Christ Jesus.
℟. Alleluia, alleluia.

Gospel Luke
17:11-19; L947.6

As Jesus continued
    his journey to
    Jerusalem,
he traveled
    through Sa-
    maria and
    Galilee.
As he was entering a
    village, ten lep-
    ers met him.
They stood at a distance from him and
    raised their voices, saying,
    "Jesus, Master! Have pity on us!"
And when he saw them, he said,
    "Go show yourselves to the priests."
As they were going they were cleansed.
And one of them, realizing he had been
    healed,
    returned, glorifying God in a loud voice;
    and he fell at the feet of Jesus and
    thanked him.
He was a Samaritan.
Jesus said in reply,
    "Ten were cleansed, were they not?
Where are the other nine?
Has none but this foreigner returned to
    give thanks to God?"
Then he said to him, "Stand up and go;
    your faith has saved you."

See Appendix A, p. 311, for the other readings.

Reflecting on the Gospel

This is an interesting day: even though it is a civic holiday it has a proper Mass in our U.S. Sacramentary. We have a strong sense that on a day when we celebrate the abundances of our country and its blessings, we naturally want to turn to God. This holiday takes many of us back to our immigrant roots and the Native Americans who helped our ancestors survive the difficult times of adjusting to this new land. Those first immigrants' grateful response to graciousness and hospitality came out of the religious grounding that brought them to this new land in the first place. Deep down we were—and still are—a religious people. We have a natural sense that generosity can be properly repaid only by turning to the One who is all and gives all, just as the Samaritan leper in the gospel returned to Jesus to give thanks.

The act of thanksgiving by the Samaritan leper expresses the frame of heart and mind we bring to the liturgical celebration on Thanksgiving Day. The civil observance of Thanksgiving Day calls us to gratitude for such gifts as abundant crops, natural resources, and civil liberties. Our liturgical observance of this day calls us to turn to God as the origin of all our blessings. Jesus announced that the Samaritan leper received salvation. This salvation is not simply the human wholeness that comes from his being healed. Gathering to offer God thanks acknowledges our dependency upon God for the fullness of life given to us through Christ Jesus. The fullness of life salvation brings is the divine presence and our attentiveness to it.

This gospel reminds us that salvation itself is located in the act of thanksgiving directed to God. An attitude of thanksgiving reorients us from focusing on a gift received to encountering the gift-giver. In the gospel story the grateful leper returns to Jesus to encounter him in a new way. An act of giving thanks, then, is always a kind of conversion. No matter how wonderful a gift is—whether it is being healed from a terrible disease, or being given the abundant crops, natural resources, and civil liberties that we celebrate this day—the full value of a gift is realized when it turns us to the giver. Especially so, when it turns us to the divine Giver.

Living the Paschal Mystery

Thanksgiving comes once a year. We ought not wait until the fourth Thursday of November, however, to give thanks for all God has given us. The very life of Christians is one of putting on the habit of thankfulness, because this habit of thankfulness orients us to God as the One who bestows on us abundant blessings.

God forbid that Jesus would ever address to us, "Where are the other nine?" As we die to ourselves and come to new life in living daily the paschal mystery, we want to grow in a stance of gratitude before our God. Even if our own personal circumstances don't seem to leave much room for thankfulness (hurt or broken relationships, economic hard times, sickness and death, etc.), today and every day we are called to acknowledge all God has given us. Our very life is a gift. Our health, such as it may be, is a gift. Our loved ones and friends are gifts. Even our ability to encounter God and recognize the divine blessings in our lives are gifts.

Each day we ought to pause and recognize the gifts given to us. And let each blessing orient us to God with hearts filled with love and gratitude.

Focusing the gospel

Key words and phrases: realizing he had been healed, returned, feet of Jesus, thanked him

To the point: An attitude of thanksgiving reorients us from focusing on a gift received to encountering the gift-giver. In the gospel story the grateful leper returns to Jesus to encounter him in a new way. No matter how wonderful a gift is—whether being healed from a terrible disease, or the abundant crops, natural resources, and civil liberties that we celebrate this day—the full value of a gift is realized when it turns us to the giver. Especially so, when it turns us to the divine Giver.

Model Act of Penitence

Presider: We come together today to celebrate God's many blessings and gifts to us. Let us pause at the beginning of this liturgy to open our hearts in gratitude to God, the divine gift-giver . . . [pause]

> Lord Jesus, you are God's healing Gift to us: Lord . . .
>
> Christ Jesus, you are our Savior: Christ . . .
>
> Lord Jesus, you are worthy of all praise and thanksgiving: Lord . . .

Model Prayer of the Faithful

Presider: God has blessed us with abundance. We are confident that God will hear our prayers and continue to bless us with all we need.

Response:

Lord, hear our prayer.

Cantor:

we pray to the Lord,

That all members of the church raise grateful hearts always and everywhere for God's abundant blessings . . . [pause]

That all peoples of the world share equitably in the abundant fruits of this earth . . . [pause]

That the poor be raised up, the hungry be fed, and those deprived of liberty be freed . . . [pause]

That each of us share the gifts we have—whether small or great—with those less fortunate as a sign of our gratitude to God for all the blessings bestowed on us . . . [pause]

Presider: Gracious God, you give us abundant gifts and especially your own Son, Jesus Christ; hear these our prayers that all might share in your goodness and come to everlasting life. We ask this through that same Son, our Lord Jesus Christ. **Amen.**

FOR REFLECTION

- What I am doing to foster a habit of thankfulness in myself is . . .

- Of the gifts I've been given, the ones that bring me most surely to give thanks to the divine Giver are . . .

- What helps me realize the full value of the gifts in my life is . . .

Homily Points

- Cell phones and internet access have made it easy to say thanks. When we do so in person, however, we experience the power that gratitude unleashes between gift-giver and gift-receiver. Gratitude is more than a social convention and polite expression. It is a personal encounter that brings new life. The encounter retold in this gospel is a poignant example.

- Jesus' healing of the lepers revealed his personal care and regard for them. The expression of gratitude from the Samaritan leper revealed his personal care and regard for Jesus. The leper had already recognized the gift of having been healed; the full value of this gift became evident only when he knelt at the feet of Jesus in gratitude. This encounter brought the leper the new life that only a divine Gift-giver can give: "your faith has saved you."

Readings *(continued)*

The Immaculate Conception of the Blessed Virgin Mary, *December 8, 2009*

Gospel (cont.)
Luke 1:26-38; L689

But Mary said to the angel,
　"How can this be,
　　since I have no relations with a man?"
And the angel said to her in reply,
　"The Holy Spirit will come upon you,
　　and the power of the Most High will overshadow you.
Therefore the child to be born
　will be called holy, the Son of God.
And behold, Elizabeth, your relative,
　has also conceived a son in her old age,
　and this is the sixth month for her who was called barren;
　for nothing will be impossible for God."
Mary said, "Behold, I am the handmaid of the Lord.
May it be done to me according to your word."
Then the angel departed from her.

FIRST READING
Gen 3:9-15, 20

After the man, Adam, had eaten of the tree,
　the LORD God called to the man and asked
　　him, "Where are you?"
He answered, "I heard you in the garden;
　but I was afraid, because I was naked,
　so I hid myself."
Then he asked, "Who told you that you were
　naked?
You have eaten, then,
　from the tree of which I had forbidden you
　　to eat!"
The man replied, "The woman whom you put
　here with me—
　she gave me fruit from the tree, and so I
　　ate it."
The LORD God then asked the woman,
　"Why did you do such a thing?"
The woman answered, "The serpent tricked
　me into it, so I ate it."

Then the LORD God said to the serpent:
　"Because you have done this, you shall be
　　banned
　　from all the animals
　　and from all the wild creatures;
　on your belly shall you crawl,
　　and dirt shall you eat
　　all the days of your life.
I will put enmity between you and the
　woman,
　and between your offspring and hers;
he will strike at your head,
　while you strike at his heel."

The man called his wife Eve,
　because she became the mother of all the
　　living.

RESPONSORIAL PSALM
Ps 98:1, 2-3, 3-4

℟. (1a) Sing to the Lord a new song, for he has
done marvelous deeds.

Sing to the LORD a new song,
　for he has done wondrous deeds;
his right hand has won victory for him,
　his holy arm.

℟. Sing to the Lord a new song, for he has
done marvelous deeds.

The LORD has made his salvation known:
　in the sight of the nations he has revealed
　　his justice.
He has remembered his kindness and his
　faithfulness
　toward the house of Israel.

℟. Sing to the Lord a new song, for he has
done marvelous deeds.

All the ends of the earth have seen
　the salvation by our God.
Sing joyfully to the LORD, all you lands;
　break into song; sing praise.

℟. Sing to the Lord a new song, for he has
done marvelous deeds.

SECOND READING
Eph 1:3-6, 11-12

Brothers and sisters:
Blessed be the God and Father of our Lord
　Jesus Christ,
　who has blessed us in Christ
　with every spiritual blessing in the
　　heavens,
　as he chose us in him, before the foundation
　　of the world,
　to be holy and without blemish before him.
In love he destined us for adoption to himself
　through Jesus Christ,
　in accord with the favor of his will,
　for the praise of the glory of his grace
　that he granted us in the beloved.

In him we were also chosen,
　destined in accord with the purpose of the
　　One
　who accomplishes all things according to
　　the intention of his will,
　so that we might exist for the praise of his
　　glory,
　we who first hoped in Christ.

Gospel (cont.)
Matt 1:1-25; L13ABC

David became the father of Solomon,
    whose mother had been the wife of Uriah.
Solomon became the father of Rehoboam,
    Rehoboam the father of Abijah,
    Abijah the father of Asaph.
Asaph became the father of Jehoshaphat,
    Jehoshaphat the father of Joram,
    Joram the father of Uzziah.
Uzziah became the father of Jotham,
    Jotham the father of Ahaz,
    Ahaz the father of Hezekiah.
Hezekiah became the father of Manasseh,
    Manasseh the father of Amos,
    Amos the father of Josiah.
Josiah became the father of Jechoniah and his brothers
    at the time of the Babylonian exile.

After the Babylonian exile,
    Jechoniah became the father of Shealtiel,
    Shealtiel the father of Zerubbabel,
    Zerubbabel the father of Abiud.
Abiud became the father of Eliakim,
    Eliakim the father of Azor,
    Azor the father of Zadok.
Zadok became the father of Achim,
    Achim the father of Eliud,
    Eliud the father of Eleazar.
Eleazar became the father of Matthan,
    Matthan the father of Jacob,
    Jacob the father of Joseph, the husband of Mary.
Of her was born Jesus who is called the Christ.

Thus the total number of generations
    from Abraham to David
    is fourteen generations;
    from David to the Babylonian exile,
    fourteen generations;
    from the Babylonian exile to the Christ,
    fourteen generations.

Now this is how the birth of Jesus Christ came about.
When his mother Mary was betrothed to Joseph,
    but before they lived together,
    she was found with child through the Holy Spirit.
Joseph her husband, since he was a righteous man,
    yet unwilling to expose her to shame,
    decided to divorce her quietly.

Such was his intention when, behold,
    the angel of the Lord appeared to him in a dream and said,
    "Joseph, son of David,
    do not be afraid to take Mary your wife into your home.
For it is through the Holy Spirit
    that this child has been conceived in her.
She will bear a son and you are to name him Jesus,
    because he will save his people from their sins."
All this took place to fulfill
    what the Lord had said through the prophet:
        Behold, the virgin shall conceive and bear a son,
            and they shall name him Emmanuel,
        which means "God is with us."
When Joseph awoke,
    he did as the angel of the Lord had commanded him
    and took his wife into his home.
He had no relations with her until she bore a son,
    and he named him Jesus.

or Matt 1:18-25

This is how the birth of Jesus Christ came about.
When his mother Mary was betrothed to Joseph,
    but before they lived together,
    she was found with child through the Holy Spirit.
Joseph her husband, since he was a righteous man,
    yet unwilling to expose her to shame,
    decided to divorce her quietly.
Such was his intention when, behold,
    the angel of the Lord appeared to him in a dream and said,
    "Joseph, son of David,
    do not be afraid to take Mary your wife into your home.
For it is through the Holy Spirit
    that this child has been conceived in her.
She will bear a son and you are to name him Jesus,
    because he will save his people from their sins."
All this took place to fulfill
    what the Lord had said through the prophet:
        Behold, the virgin shall conceive and bear a son,
            and they shall name him Emmanuel,
        which means "God is with us."
When Joseph awoke,
    he did as the angel of the Lord had commanded him
    and took his wife into his home.
He had no relations with her until she bore a son,
    and he named him Jesus.

FIRST READING
Isa 62:1-5

For Zion's sake I will not be silent,
    for Jerusalem's sake I will not be quiet,
until her vindication shines forth like the dawn
    and her victory like a burning torch.

Nations shall behold your vindication,
    and all the kings your glory;
you shall be called by a new name
    pronounced by the mouth of the LORD.
You shall be a glorious crown in the hand of
        the LORD,
    a royal diadem held by your God.
No more shall people call you "Forsaken,"
    or your land "Desolate,"
but you shall be called "My Delight,"
    and your land "Espoused."
For the LORD delights in you
    and makes your land his spouse.
As a young man marries a virgin,
    your Builder shall marry you;
and as a bridegroom rejoices in his bride
    so shall your God rejoice in you.

RESPONSORIAL PSALM
Ps 89:4-5, 16-17, 27, 29

R̸. (2a) Forever I will sing the goodness of the
Lord.

I have made a covenant with my chosen one,
    I have sworn to David my servant:
forever will I confirm your posterity
    and establish your throne for all
        generations.

R̸. Forever I will sing the goodness of the Lord.

Blessed the people who know the joyful shout;
    in the light of your countenance, O LORD,
        they walk.
At your name they rejoice all the day,
    and through your justice they are exalted.

R̸. Forever I will sing the goodness of the Lord.

He shall say of me, "You are my father,
    my God, the Rock, my savior."
Forever I will maintain my kindness toward
        him,
    and my covenant with him stands firm.

R̸. Forever I will sing the goodness of the Lord.

SECOND READING
Acts 13:16-17, 22-25

When Paul reached Antioch in Pisidia and
        entered the synagogue,
    he stood up, motioned with his hand, and
        said,
    "Fellow Israelites and you others who are
        God-fearing, listen.
The God of this people Israel chose our
        ancestors
    and exalted the people during their sojourn
        in the land of Egypt.
With uplifted arm he led them out of it.
Then he removed Saul and raised up David
        as king;
    of him he testified,
    'I have found David, son of Jesse, a man
        after my own heart;
    he will carry out my every wish.'
From this man's descendants God, according
        to his promise,
    has brought to Israel a savior, Jesus.
John heralded his coming by proclaiming a
        baptism of repentance
    to all the people of Israel;
    and as John was completing his course, he
        would say,
    'What do you suppose that I am? I am not he.
Behold, one is coming after me;
    I am not worthy to unfasten the sandals of
        his feet.'"

Gospel (cont.)
Luke 2:1-14; L14ABC

Now there were shepherds in that region living in the fields
    and keeping the night watch over their flock.
The angel of the Lord appeared to them
    and the glory of the Lord shone around them,
    and they were struck with great fear.
The angel said to them,
    "Do not be afraid;
    for behold, I proclaim to you good news of great joy
    that will be for all the people.
For today in the city of David
    a savior has been born for you who is Christ and Lord.
And this will be a sign for you:
    you will find an infant wrapped in swaddling clothes
    and lying in a manger."
And suddenly there was a multitude of the heavenly host with the
        angel,
    praising God and saying:
        "Glory to God in the highest
            and on earth peace to those on whom his favor rests."

The Nativity of the Lord, December 25, 2009 (Mass at Midnight)

FIRST READING
Isa 9:1-6

The people who walked in darkness
    have seen a great light;
upon those who dwelt in the land of gloom
    a light has shone.
You have brought them abundant joy
    and great rejoicing,
as they rejoice before you as at the harvest,
    as people make merry when dividing
        spoils.
For the yoke that burdened them,
    the pole on their shoulder,
and the rod of their taskmaster
    you have smashed, as on the day of Midian.
For every boot that tramped in battle,
    every cloak rolled in blood,
    will be burned as fuel for flames.
For a child is born to us, a son is given us;
    upon his shoulder dominion rests.
They name him Wonder-Counselor, God-Hero,
    Father-Forever, Prince of Peace.
His dominion is vast
    and forever peaceful,
from David's throne, and over his kingdom,
    which he confirms and sustains
by judgment and justice,
    both now and forever.
The zeal of the LORD of hosts will do this!

RESPONSORIAL PSALM
Ps 96:1-2, 2-3, 11-12, 13

R̸. (Luke 2:11) Today is born our Savior,
Christ the Lord.

Sing to the LORD a new song;
    sing to the LORD, all you lands.
Sing to the LORD; bless his name.

R̸. Today is born our Savior, Christ the Lord.

Announce his salvation, day after day.
    Tell his glory among the nations;
    among all peoples, his wondrous deeds.

R̸. Today is born our Savior, Christ the Lord.

Let the heavens be glad and the earth rejoice;
    let the sea and what fills it resound;
    let the plains be joyful and all that is in
        them!
Then shall all the trees of the forest exult.

R̸. Today is born our Savior, Christ the Lord.

They shall exult before the LORD, for he
    comes;
    for he comes to rule the earth.
He shall rule the world with justice
    and the peoples with his constancy.

R̸. Today is born our Savior, Christ the Lord.

SECOND READING
Titus 2:11-14

Beloved:
The grace of God has appeared, saving all
    and training us to reject godless ways and
        worldly desires
    and to live temperately, justly, and
        devoutly in this age,
    as we await the blessed hope,
    the appearance of the glory of our great
        God
    and savior Jesus Christ,
    who gave himself for us to deliver us from
        all lawlessness
    and to cleanse for himself a people as his
        own,
    eager to do what is good.

The Nativity of the Lord, December 25, 2009 (Mass at Dawn)

FIRST READING
Isa 62:11-12

See, the LORD proclaims
    to the ends of the earth:
say to daughter Zion,
    your savior comes!
Here is his reward with him,
    his recompense before him.
They shall be called the holy people,
    the redeemed of the LORD,
and you shall be called "Frequented,"
    a city that is not forsaken.

RESPONSORIAL PSALM
Ps 97:1, 6, 11-12

R̸. A light will shine on us this day: the Lord
is born for us.

The LORD is king; let the earth rejoice;
    let the many isles be glad.
The heavens proclaim his justice,
    and all peoples see his glory.

R̸. A light will shine on us this day: the Lord
is born for us.

Light dawns for the just;
    and gladness, for the upright of heart.
Be glad in the LORD, you just,
    and give thanks to his holy name.

R̸. A light will shine on us this day: the Lord
is born for us.

SECOND READING
Titus 3:4-7

Beloved:
When the kindness and generous love
    of God our savior appeared,
not because of any righteous deeds we had
        done
    but because of his mercy,
he saved us through the bath of rebirth
    and renewal by the Holy Spirit,
whom he richly poured out on us
    through Jesus Christ our savior,
so that we might be justified by his grace
    and become heirs in hope of eternal life.

Gospel (cont.)
John 1:1-18; L16ABC

The true light, which enlightens everyone,
  was coming into the world.

He was in the world,
    and the world came to be through him,
    but the world did not know him.
He came to what was his own,
    but his own people did not accept him.

But to those who did accept him
    he gave power to become children of God,
    to those who believe in his name,
    who were born not by natural generation
    nor by human choice nor by a man's decision
    but of God.

And the Word became flesh
    and made his dwelling among us,
    and we saw his glory,
    the glory as of the Father's only Son,
    full of grace and truth.

John testified to him and cried out, saying,
    "This was he of whom I said,
    'The one who is coming after me ranks ahead of me
    because he existed before me.'"
From his fullness we have all received,
    grace in place of grace,
    because while the law was given through Moses,
    grace and truth came through Jesus Christ.
No one has ever seen God.
The only Son, God, who is at the Father's side,
    has revealed him.

or John 1:1-5, 9-14

In the beginning was the Word,
    and the Word was with God,
    and the Word was God.
He was in the beginning with God.
All things came to be through him,
    and without him nothing came to be.
What came to be through him was life,
    and this life was the light of the human race;
    the light shines in the darkness,
    and the darkness has not overcome it.

The true light, which enlightens everyone,
    was coming into the world.

He was in the world,
    and the world came to be through him,
    but the world did not know him.
He came to what was his own,
    but his own people did not accept him.

But to those who did accept him
    he gave power to become children of God,
    to those who believe in his name,
    who were born not by natural generation
    nor by human choice nor by a man's decision
    but of God.

And the Word became flesh
    and made his dwelling among us,
    and we saw his glory,
    the glory as of the Father's only Son,
    full of grace and truth.

FIRST READING
Isa 52:7-10

How beautiful upon the mountains
    are the feet of him who brings glad tidings,
announcing peace, bearing good news,
    announcing salvation, and saying to Zion,
    "Your God is King!"

Hark! Your sentinels raise a cry,
    together they shout for joy,
for they see directly, before their eyes,
    the LORD restoring Zion.
Break out together in song,
    O ruins of Jerusalem!
For the LORD comforts his people,
    he redeems Jerusalem.
The LORD has bared his holy arm
    in the sight of all the nations;
all the ends of the earth will behold
    the salvation of our God.

RESPONSORIAL PSALM
Ps 98:1, 2-3, 3-4, 5-6

R̸. (3c) All the ends of the earth have seen the saving power of God.

Sing to the LORD a new song,
    for he has done wondrous deeds;
his right hand has won victory for him,
    his holy arm.

R̸. All the ends of the earth have seen the saving power of God.

The LORD has made his salvation known:
    in the sight of the nations he has revealed
        his justice.
He has remembered his kindness and his
        faithfulness
    toward the house of Israel.

R̸. All the ends of the earth have seen the saving power of God.

All the ends of the earth have seen
    the salvation by our God.
Sing joyfully to the LORD, all you lands;
    break into song; sing praise.

R̸. All the ends of the earth have seen the saving power of God.

Sing praise to the LORD with the harp,
    with the harp and melodious song.
With trumpets and the sound of the horn
    sing joyfully before the King, the LORD.

R̸. All the ends of the earth have seen the saving power of God.

The Nativity of the Lord, *December 25, 2009 (Mass During the Day)*

SECOND READING
Heb 1:1-6

Brothers and sisters:
In times past, God spoke in partial and
    various ways
    to our ancestors through the prophets;
    in these last days, he has spoken to us
        through the Son,
    whom he made heir of all things
    and through whom he created the universe,
    who is the refulgence of his glory, the very
        imprint of his being,
    and who sustains all things by his
        mighty word.
When he had accomplished purification
    from sins,
he took his seat at the right hand of the
    Majesty on high,
    as far superior to the angels
        as the name he has inherited is more
        excellent than theirs.

For to which of the angels did God ever say:
    You are my son; this day I have begotten
        you?
Or again:
    I will be a father to him, and he shall be a
        son to me?
And again, when he leads the firstborn into
    the world, he says:
    Let all the angels of God worship him.

The Holy Family of Jesus, Mary, and Joseph, *December 27, 2009*

Gospel (cont.)
Luke 2:41-52; L17C

When his parents saw him,
    they were astonished,
    and his mother said to him,
    "Son, why have you done this to us?
Your father and I have been looking for you
    with great anxiety."
And he said to them,
    "Why were you looking for me?
Did you not know that I must be in my
    Father's house?"
But they did not understand what he said to
    them.
He went down with them and came to
    Nazareth,
    and was obedient to them;
    and his mother kept all these things in her
        heart.
And Jesus advanced in wisdom and age and
    favor
    before God and man.

FIRST READING
Sir 3:2-6, 12-14

God sets a father in honor over his children;
    a mother's authority he confirms over her
        sons.
Whoever honors his father atones for sins,
    and preserves himself from them.
When he prays, he is heard;
    he stores up riches who reveres his mother.
Whoever honors his father is gladdened by
    children,
    and, when he prays, is heard.
Whoever reveres his father will live a long
    life;
    he who obeys his father brings comfort to
        his mother.

My son, take care of your father when he is old;
    grieve him not as long as he lives.
Even if his mind fail, be considerate of him;
    revile him not all the days of his life;
kindness to a father will not be forgotten,
    firmly planted against the debt of your sins
    —a house raised in justice to you.

RESPONSORIAL PSALM
Ps 128:1-2, 3, 4-5

℞. (cf. 1) Blessed are those who fear the Lord
and walk in his ways.

Blessed is everyone who fears the LORD,
    who walks in his ways!
For you shall eat the fruit of your handiwork;
    blessed shall you be, and favored.

℞. Blessed are those who fear the Lord and
walk in his ways.

Your wife shall be like a fruitful vine
    in the recesses of your home;
your children like olive plants
    around your table.

℞. Blessed are those who fear the Lord and
walk in his ways.

Behold, thus is the man blessed
    who fears the LORD.
The LORD bless you from Zion:
    may you see the prosperity of Jerusalem
    all the days of your life.

℞. Blessed are those who fear the Lord and
walk in his ways.

The Holy Family of Jesus, Mary, and Joseph, *December 27, 2009*

SECOND READING
Col 3:12-21

Brothers and sisters:
Put on, as God's chosen ones, holy and beloved,
    heartfelt compassion, kindness, humility,
        gentleness, and patience,
    bearing with one another and forgiving one
        another,
    if one has a grievance against another;
    as the Lord has forgiven you, so must you
        also do.
And over all these put on love,
    that is, the bond of perfection.
And let the peace of Christ control your hearts,
    the peace into which you were also called in
        one body.
And be thankful.
Let the word of Christ dwell in you richly,
    as in all wisdom you teach and admonish
        one another,

singing psalms, hymns, and spiritual songs
    with gratitude in your hearts to God.
And whatever you do, in word or in deed,
    do everything in the name of the Lord Jesus,
    giving thanks to God the Father through him.

Wives, be subordinate to your husbands,
    as is proper in the Lord.
Husbands, love your wives,
    and avoid any bitterness toward them.
Children, obey your parents in everything,
    for this is pleasing to the Lord.
Fathers, do not provoke your children,
    so they may not become discouraged.

or

Col 3:12-17

Brothers and sisters:
Put on, as God's chosen ones, holy and beloved,
    heartfelt compassion, kindness, humility,

gentleness, and patience,
    bearing with one another and forgiving one
        another,
    if one has a grievance against another;
    as the Lord has forgiven you, so must you
        also do.
And over all these put on love,
    that is, the bond of perfection.
And let the peace of Christ control your hearts,
    the peace into which you were also called in
        one body.
And be thankful.
Let the word of Christ dwell in you richly,
    as in all wisdom you teach and admonish
        one another,
    singing psalms, hymns, and spiritual songs
    with gratitude in your hearts to God.
And whatever you do, in word or in deed,
    do everything in the name of the Lord Jesus,
    giving thanks to God the Father through him.

Solemnity of the Blessed Virgin Mary, Mother of God, *January 1, 2010*

FIRST READING
Num 6:22-27

The LORD said to Moses:
    "Speak to Aaron and his sons and tell them:
    This is how you shall bless the Israelites.
Say to them:
    The LORD bless you and keep you!
    The LORD let his face shine upon
        you, and be gracious to you!
    The LORD look upon you kindly and
        give you peace!
So shall they invoke my name upon the
    Israelites,
    and I will bless them."

RESPONSORIAL PSALM
Ps 67:2-3, 5, 6, 8

R̸. (2a) May God bless us in his mercy.

May God have pity on us and bless us;
    may he let his face shine upon us.
So may your way be known upon earth;
    among all nations, your salvation.

R̸. May God bless us in his mercy.

May the nations be glad and exult
    because you rule the peoples in equity;
    the nations on the earth you guide.

R̸. May God bless us in his mercy.

May the peoples praise you, O God;
    may all the peoples praise you!
May God bless us,
    and may all the ends of the earth fear him!

R̸. May God bless us in his mercy.

SECOND READING
Gal 4:4-7

Brothers and sisters:
When the fullness of time had come, God sent
    his Son,
    born of a woman, born under the law,
    to ransom those under the law,
    so that we might receive adoption as sons.
As proof that you are sons,
    God sent the Spirit of his Son into our
        hearts,
    crying out, "Abba, Father!"
So you are no longer a slave but a son,
    and if a son then also an heir, through God.

The Epiphany of the Lord, *January 3, 2010*

Gospel (cont.)
Matt 2:1-12; L20ABC

And behold, the star that they had seen at its rising preceded them,
    until it came and stopped over the place where the child was.
They were overjoyed at seeing the star,
    and on entering the house
    they saw the child with Mary his mother.

They prostrated themselves and did him homage.
Then they opened their treasures
    and offered him gifts of gold, frankincense, and myrrh.
And having been warned in a dream not to return to Herod,
    they departed for their country by another way.

267

SECOND READING (cont.)

Titus 2:11-14; 3:4-7

When the kindness and generous love
    of God our savior appeared,
not because of any righteous deeds we had
        done
    but because of his mercy,
he saved us through the bath of rebirth
    and renewal by the Holy Spirit,
whom he richly poured out on us
    through Jesus Christ our savior,
so that we might be justified by his grace
    and become heirs in hope of eternal life.

or

FIRST READING

Isa 42:1-4, 6-7

Thus says the LORD:
Here is my servant whom I uphold,
    my chosen one with whom I am pleased,
upon whom I have put my spirit;
    he shall bring forth justice to the nations,
not crying out, not shouting,
    not making his voice heard in the street.
A bruised reed he shall not break,
    and a smoldering wick he shall not quench,
until he establishes justice on the earth;
    the coastlands will wait for his teaching.

I, the LORD, have called you for the victory of
        justice,
    I have grasped you by the hand;

I formed you, and set you
    as a covenant of the people,
    a light for the nations,
to open the eyes of the blind,
    to bring out prisoners from confinement,
    and from the dungeon, those who live in
        darkness.

RESPONSORIAL PSALM

Ps 29:1-2, 3-4, 3, 9-10

℟. (11b) The Lord will bless his people with
peace.

Give to the LORD, you sons of God,
    give to the LORD glory and praise,
give to the LORD the glory due his name;
    adore the LORD in holy attire.

℟. The Lord will bless his people with peace.

The voice of the LORD is over the waters,
    the LORD, over vast waters.
The voice of the LORD is mighty;
    the voice of the LORD is majestic.

℟. The Lord will bless his people with peace.

The God of glory thunders,
    and in his temple all say, "Glory!"
The LORD is enthroned above the flood;
    the LORD is enthroned as king forever.

℟. The Lord will bless his people with peace.

SECOND READING

Acts 10:34-38

Peter proceeded to speak to those gathered
    in the house of Cornelius, saying:
    "In truth, I see that God shows no
        partiality.
Rather, in every nation whoever fears him
        and acts uprightly
    is acceptable to him.
You know the word that he sent to the
        Israelites
    as he proclaimed peace through Jesus
        Christ, who is Lord of all,
    what has happened all over Judea,
    beginning in Galilee after the baptism
    that John preached,
    how God anointed Jesus of Nazareth
    with the Holy Spirit and power.
He went about doing good
    and healing all those oppressed by the
        devil,
    for God was with him."

Third Sunday in Ordinary Time, *January 24, 2010*

Gospel (cont.)

Luke 1:1-4; 4:14-21; L69C

He has sent me to proclaim liberty to captives
    and recovery of sight to the blind,
    to let the oppressed go free,
    and to proclaim a year acceptable to the Lord.
Rolling up the scroll, he handed it back to the attendant and sat down,
    and the eyes of all in the synagogue looked intently at him.
He said to them,
    "Today this Scripture passage is fulfilled in your hearing."

Third Sunday in Ordinary Time, *January 24, 2010*

SECOND READING
1 Cor 12:12-30

Brothers and sisters:
As a body is one though it has many parts,
  and all the parts of the body, though many,
    are one body,
so also Christ.
For in one Spirit we were all baptized into one
  body,
  whether Jews or Greeks, slaves or free
    persons,
  and we were all given to drink of one Spirit.

Now the body is not a single part, but many.
If a foot should say,
  "Because I am not a hand I do not belong to
    the body,"
  it does not for this reason belong any less
    to the body.
Or if an ear should say,
  "Because I am not an eye I do not belong to
    the body,"
  it does not for this reason belong any less
    to the body.
If the whole body were an eye, where would
  the hearing be?

If the whole body were hearing, where would
  the sense of smell be?
But as it is, God placed the parts,
  each one of them, in the body as he
    intended.
If they were all one part, where would the
  body be?
But as it is, there are many parts, yet one
  body.
The eye cannot say to the hand, "I do not need
  you,"
  nor again the head to the feet, "I do not
    need you."
Indeed, the parts of the body that seem to be
  weaker
  are all the more necessary,
  and those parts of the body that we
    consider less honorable
  we surround with greater honor,
  and our less presentable parts are treated
    with greater propriety,
  whereas our more presentable parts do not
    need this.
But God has so constructed the body
  as to give greater honor to a part that is
    without it,

so that there may be no division in the
  body,
  but that the parts may have the same
    concern for one another.
If one part suffers, all the parts suffer with it;
  if one part is honored, all the parts share
    its joy.

Now you are Christ's body, and individually
  parts of it.
Some people God has designated in the
  church
  to be, first, apostles; second, prophets;
    third, teachers;
  then, mighty deeds;
  then gifts of healing, assistance,
    administration,
  and varieties of tongues.
Are all apostles? Are all prophets? Are all
  teachers?
Do all work mighty deeds? Do all have gifts
  of healing?
Do all speak in tongues? Do all interpret?

Fourth Sunday in Ordinary Time, *January 31, 2010*

SECOND READING
1 Cor 12:31–13:13

Brothers and sisters:
Strive eagerly for the greatest spiritual gifts.
But I shall show you a still more excellent way.

If I speak in human and angelic tongues,
  but do not have love,
  I am a resounding gong or a clashing cymbal.
And if I have the gift of prophecy,
  and comprehend all mysteries and all
    knowledge;
  if I have all faith so as to move mountains,
  but do not have love, I am nothing.
If I give away everything I own,
  and if I hand my body over so that I may
    boast,
  but do not have love, I gain nothing.

Love is patient, love is kind.
It is not jealous, it is not pompous,
  it is not inflated, it is not rude,
  it does not seek its own interests,
  it is not quick-tempered, it does not brood
    over injury,
    it does not rejoice over wrongdoing
  but rejoices with the truth.
It bears all things, believes all things,
  hopes all things, endures all things.
Love never fails.
If there are prophecies, they will be brought
  to nothing;
  if tongues, they will cease;
  if knowledge, it will be brought to
    nothing.
For we know partially and we prophesy
  partially,

but when the perfect comes, the partial will
  pass away.
When I was a child, I used to talk as a child,
  think as a child, reason as a child;
  when I became a man, I put aside childish
    things.
At present we see indistinctly, as in a mirror,
  but then face to face.
At present I know partially;
  then I shall know fully, as I am fully
    known.
So faith, hope, love remain, these three;
  but the greatest of these is love.

Gospel (cont.)
Luke 5:1-11; L75C

When Simon Peter saw this, he fell at the knees of Jesus and said,
"Depart from me, Lord, for I am a sinful man."
For astonishment at the catch of fish they had made seized him
and all those with him,
and likewise James and John, the sons of Zebedee,
who were partners of Simon.
Jesus said to Simon, "Do not be afraid;
from now on you will be catching men."
When they brought their boats to the shore,
they left everything and followed him.

SECOND READING
1 Cor 15:1-11

I am reminding you, brothers and sisters,
of the gospel I preached to you,
which you indeed received and in which
you also stand.
Through it you are also being saved,
if you hold fast to the word I preached to
you,
unless you believed in vain.
For I handed on to you as of first importance
what I also received:
that Christ died for our sins
in accordance with the Scriptures;
that he was buried;
that he was raised on the third day
in accordance with the Scriptures;
that he appeared to Cephas, then to the
Twelve.

After that, he appeared to more
than five hundred brothers at once,
most of whom are still living,
though some have fallen asleep.
After that he appeared to James,
then to all the apostles.
Last of all, as to one born abnormally,
he appeared to me.
For I am the least of the apostles,
not fit to be called an apostle,
because I persecuted the church of God.
But by the grace of God I am what I am,
and his grace to me has not been
ineffective.
Indeed, I have toiled harder than all of them;
not I, however, but the grace of God that is
with me.
Therefore, whether it be I or they,
so we preach and so you believed.

Ash Wednesday, *February 17, 2010*

FIRST READING
Joel 2:12-18

Even now, says the LORD,
 return to me with your whole heart,
 with fasting, and weeping, and mourning;
Rend your hearts, not your garments,
 and return to the LORD, your God.
For gracious and merciful is he,
 slow to anger, rich in kindness,
 and relenting in punishment.
Perhaps he will again relent
 and leave behind him a blessing,
Offerings and libations
 for the LORD, your God.

Blow the trumpet in Zion!
 proclaim a fast,
 call an assembly;
Gather the people,
 notify the congregation;
Assemble the elders,
 gather the children
 and the infants at the breast;
Let the bridegroom quit his room
 and the bride her chamber.
Between the porch and the altar
 let the priests, the ministers of the LORD,
 weep,
And say, "Spare, O LORD, your people,
 and make not your heritage a reproach,
 with the nations ruling over them!
Why should they say among the peoples,
 'Where is their God?'"

Then the LORD was stirred to concern for his
 land
 and took pity on his people.

RESPONSORIAL PSALM
Ps 51:3-4, 5-6ab, 12-13, 14, and 17

R̂. (see 3a) Be merciful, O Lord, for we have
sinned.

Have mercy on me, O God, in your goodness;
 in the greatness of your compassion wipe
 out my offense.
Thoroughly wash me from my guilt
 and of my sin cleanse me.

R̂. Be merciful, O Lord, for we have sinned.

For I acknowledge my offense,
 and my sin is before me always:
"Against you only have I sinned,
 and done what is evil in your sight."

R̂. Be merciful, O Lord, for we have sinned.

A clean heart create for me, O God,
 and a steadfast spirit renew within me.
Cast me not out from your presence,
 and your Holy Spirit take not from me.

R̂. Be merciful, O Lord, for we have sinned.

Give me back the joy of your salvation,
 and a willing spirit sustain in me.
O Lord, open my lips,
 and my mouth shall proclaim your praise.

R̂. Be merciful, O Lord, for we have sinned.

SECOND READING
2 Cor 5:20–6:2

Brothers and sisters:
We are ambassadors for Christ,
 as if God were appealing through us.
We implore you on behalf of Christ,
 be reconciled to God.
For our sake he made him to be sin who did
 not know sin,
 so that we might become the righteousness
 of God in him.

Working together, then,
 we appeal to you not to receive the grace of
 God in vain.
For he says:

 In an acceptable time I heard you,
 and on the day of salvation I helped you.

Behold, now is a very acceptable time;
 behold, now is the day of salvation.

First Sunday of Lent, *February 21, 2010*

SECOND READING
Rom 10:8-13

Brothers and sisters:
What does Scripture say?
 The word is near you,
 in your mouth and in your heart
 —that is, the word of faith that we preach—,
 for, if you confess with your mouth that Jesus is Lord
 and believe in your heart that God raised him from the dead,
 you will be saved.
For one believes with the heart and so is justified,
 and one confesses with the mouth and so is saved.
For the Scripture says,
 No one who believes in him will be put to shame.
For there is no distinction between Jew and Greek;
 the same Lord is Lord of all,
 enriching all who call upon him.
For "everyone who calls on the name of the Lord will be saved."

Second Sunday of Lent, *February 28, 2010*

SECOND READING
Phil 3:20–4:1

Brothers and sisters:
Our citizenship is in heaven,
 and from it we also await a savior, the Lord Jesus Christ.
He will change our lowly body
 to conform with his glorified body
 by the power that enables him also
 to bring all things into subjection to himself.

Therefore, my brothers and sisters,
 whom I love and long for, my joy and crown,
 in this way stand firm in the Lord, beloved.

SECOND READING

1 Cor 10:1-6, 10-12

I do not want you to be unaware, brothers and
    sisters,
    that our ancestors were all under the cloud
    and all passed through the sea,
    and all of them were baptized into Moses
    in the cloud and in the sea.
All ate the same spiritual food,
    and all drank the same spiritual drink,
    for they drank from a spiritual rock that
        followed them,
    and the rock was the Christ.
Yet God was not pleased with most of them,
    for they were struck down in the desert.

These things happened as examples for us,
    so that we might not desire evil things, as
        they did.
Do not grumble as some of them did,
    and suffered death by the destroyer.
These things happened to them as an
        example,
    and they have been written down as a
        warning to us,
    upon whom the end of the ages has come.
Therefore, whoever thinks he is standing
        secure
    should take care not to fall.

Gospel

John 4:5-15, 19b-26, 39a, 40-42; L28A

Jesus came to a town of Samaria called Sychar,
    near the plot of land that Jacob had given to his son Joseph.
Jacob's well was there.
Jesus, tired from his journey, sat down there at the well.
It was about noon.

A woman of Samaria came to draw water.
Jesus said to her,
    "Give me a drink."
His disciples had gone into the town to buy food.
The Samaritan woman said to him,
    "How can you, a Jew, ask me, a Samaritan woman, for a drink?"
—For Jews use nothing in common with Samaritans.—
Jesus answered and said to her,
    "If you knew the gift of God
    and who is saying to you, 'Give me a drink,'
    you would have asked him
    and he would have given you living water."
The woman said to him,
    "Sir, you do not even have a bucket and the cistern is deep;
    where then can you get this living water?
Are you greater than our father Jacob,
    who gave us this cistern and drank from it himself
    with his children and his flocks?"
Jesus answered and said to her,
    "Everyone who drinks this water will be thirsty again;
    but whoever drinks the water I shall give will never thirst;
    the water I shall give will become in him
    a spring of water welling up to eternal life."
The woman said to him,
    "Sir, give me this water, so that I may not be thirsty
    or have to keep coming here to draw water.

"I can see that you are a prophet.
Our ancestors worshiped on this mountain;
    but you people say that the place to worship is in Jerusalem."
Jesus said to her,
    "Believe me, woman, the hour is coming
    when you will worship the Father
    neither on this mountain nor in Jerusalem.
You people worship what you do not understand;
    we worship what we understand,
    because salvation is from the Jews.
But the hour is coming, and is now here,
    when true worshipers will worship the Father in Spirit and truth;
    and indeed the Father seeks such people to worship him.
God is Spirit, and those who worship him
    must worship in Spirit and truth."
The woman said to him,
    "I know that the Messiah is coming, the one called the Christ;
    when he comes, he will tell us everything."
Jesus said to her,
    "I am he, the one who is speaking with you."

Many of the Samaritans of that town began to believe in him.
When the Samaritans came to him,
    they invited him to stay with them;
    and he stayed there two days.
Many more began to believe in him because of his word,
    and they said to the woman,
    "We no longer believe because of your word;
    for we have heard for ourselves,
    and we know that this is truly the savior of the world."

Gospel

John 4:5-42; L28A

Jesus came to a town of Samaria called Sychar,
near the plot of land that Jacob had given to his son Joseph.
Jacob's well was there.
Jesus, tired from his journey, sat down there at the well.
It was about noon.

A woman of Samaria came to draw water.
Jesus said to her,
"Give me a drink."
His disciples had gone into the town to buy food.
The Samaritan woman said to him,
"How can you, a Jew, ask me, a Samaritan woman, for a drink?"
—For Jews use nothing in common with Samaritans.—
Jesus answered and said to her,
"If you knew the gift of God
and who is saying to you, 'Give me a drink,'
you would have asked him
and he would have given you living water."
The woman said to him,
"Sir, you do not even have a bucket and the cistern is deep;
where then can you get this living water?
Are you greater than our father Jacob,
who gave us this cistern and drank from it himself
with his children and his flocks?"
Jesus answered and said to her,
"Everyone who drinks this water will be thirsty again;
but whoever drinks the water I shall give will never thirst;
the water I shall give will become in him
a spring of water welling up to eternal life."
The woman said to him,
"Sir, give me this water, so that I may not be thirsty
or have to keep coming here to draw water."

Jesus said to her,
"Go call your husband and come back."
The woman answered and said to him,
"I do not have a husband."
Jesus answered her,
"You are right in saying, 'I do not have a husband.'
For you have had five husbands,
and the one you have now is not your husband.
What you have said is true."
The woman said to him,
"Sir, I can see that you are a prophet.
Our ancestors worshiped on this mountain;
but you people say that the place to worship is in Jerusalem."
Jesus said to her,
"Believe me, woman, the hour is coming
when you will worship the Father
neither on this mountain nor in Jerusalem.
You people worship what you do not understand;
we worship what we understand,
because salvation is from the Jews.

But the hour is coming, and is now here,
when true worshipers will worship the Father in Spirit and truth;
and indeed the Father seeks such people to worship him.
God is Spirit, and those who worship him
must worship in Spirit and truth."
The woman said to him,
"I know that the Messiah is coming, the one called the Christ;
when he comes, he will tell us everything."
Jesus said to her,
"I am he, the one who is speaking with you."

At that moment his disciples returned,
and were amazed that he was talking with a woman,
but still no one said, "What are you looking for?"
or "Why are you talking with her?"
The woman left her water jar
and went into the town and said to the people,
"Come see a man who told me everything I have done.
Could he possibly be the Christ?"
They went out of the town and came to him.
Meanwhile, the disciples urged him, "Rabbi, eat."
But he said to them,
"I have food to eat of which you do not know."
So the disciples said to one another,
"Could someone have brought him something to eat?"
Jesus said to them,
"My food is to do the will of the one who sent me
and to finish his work.
Do you not say, 'In four months the harvest will be here'?
I tell you, look up and see the fields ripe for the harvest.
The reaper is already receiving payment
and gathering crops for eternal life,
so that the sower and reaper can rejoice together.
For here the saying is verified that 'One sows and another reaps.'
I sent you to reap what you have not worked for;
others have done the work,
and you are sharing the fruits of their work."

Many of the Samaritans of that town began to believe in him
because of the word of the woman who testified,
"He told me everything I have done."
When the Samaritans came to him,
they invited him to stay with them;
and he stayed there two days.
Many more began to believe in him because of his word,
and they said to the woman,
"We no longer believe because of your word;
for we have heard for ourselves,
and we know that this is truly the savior of the world."

Third Sunday of Lent, *March 7, 2010*

FIRST READING
Exod 17:3-7

In those days, in their thirst for water,
  the people grumbled against Moses,
  saying, "Why did you ever make us leave
    Egypt?
Was it just to have us die here of thirst
  with our children and our livestock?"
So Moses cried out to the LORD,
  "What shall I do with this people?
A little more and they will stone me!"
The LORD answered Moses,
  "Go over there in front of the people,
  along with some of the elders of Israel,
  holding in your hand, as you go,
  the staff with which you struck the river.
I will be standing there in front of you on the
    rock in Horeb.
Strike the rock, and the water will flow from it
  for the people to drink."
This Moses did, in the presence of the elders
  of Israel.
The place was called Massah and Meribah,
  because the Israelites quarreled there
  and tested the LORD, saying,
  "Is the LORD in our midst or not?"

RESPONSORIAL PSALM
Ps 95:1-2, 6-7, 8-9

R̸. (8) If today you hear his voice, harden not
your hearts.

Come, let us sing joyfully to the LORD;
  let us acclaim the Rock of our salvation.
Let us come into his presence with
    thanksgiving;
  let us joyfully sing psalms to him.

R̸. If today you hear his voice, harden not
your hearts.

Come, let us bow down in worship;
  let us kneel before the LORD who made us.
For he is our God,
  and we are the people he shepherds, the
    flock he guides.

R̸. If today you hear his voice, harden not
your hearts.

Oh, that today you would hear his voice:
  "Harden not your hearts as at Meribah,
  as in the day of Massah in the desert,
where your fathers tempted me;
  they tested me though they had seen my
    works."

R̸. If today you hear his voice, harden not
your hearts.

SECOND READING
Rom 5:1-2, 5-8

Brothers and sisters:
Since we have been justified by faith,
  we have peace with God through our Lord
    Jesus Christ,
  through whom we have gained access by
    faith
  to this grace in which we stand,
  and we boast in hope of the glory of God.

And hope does not disappoint,
  because the love of God has been poured
    out into our hearts
  through the Holy Spirit who has been given
    to us.
For Christ, while we were still helpless,
  died at the appointed time for the ungodly.
Indeed, only with difficulty does one die for a
    just person,
  though perhaps for a good person one
    might even find courage to die.
But God proves his love for us
  in that while we were still sinners Christ
    died for us.

Fourth Sunday of Lent, *March 14, 2010*

Gospel (cont.)
Luke 15:1-3, 11-32; L33C

I no longer deserve to be called your son;
  treat me as you would treat one of your hired workers."'
So he got up and went back to his father.
While he was still a long way off,
  his father caught sight of him, and was filled with compassion.
He ran to his son, embraced him and kissed him.
His son said to him,
  'Father, I have sinned against heaven and against you;
  I no longer deserve to be called your son.'
But his father ordered his servants,
  'Quickly bring the finest robe and put it on him;
  put a ring on his finger and sandals on his feet.
Take the fattened calf and slaughter it.
Then let us celebrate with a feast,
  because this son of mine was dead, and has come to life again;
  he was lost, and has been found.'
Then the celebration began.
Now the older son had been out in the field
  and, on his way back, as he neared the house,
  he heard the sound of music and dancing.
He called one of the servants and asked what this might mean.

The servant said to him,
  'Your brother has returned
  and your father has slaughtered the fattened calf
  because he has him back safe and sound.'
He became angry,
  and when he refused to enter the house,
  his father came out and pleaded with him.
He said to his father in reply,
  'Look, all these years I served you
  and not once did I disobey your orders;
  yet you never gave me even a young goat to feast on with
    my friends.
But when your son returns
  who swallowed up your property with prostitutes,
  for him you slaughter the fattened calf.'
He said to him,
  'My son, you are here with me always;
  everything I have is yours.
But now we must celebrate and rejoice,
  because your brother was dead and has come to life again;
  he was lost and has been found.'"

Gospel
John 9:1-41; L31A

As Jesus passed by he saw a man blind from birth.
His disciples asked him,
    "Rabbi, who sinned, this man or his parents,
    that he was born blind?"
Jesus answered,
    "Neither he nor his parents sinned;
    it is so that the works of God might be made visible through him.
We have to do the works of the one who sent me while it is day.
Night is coming when no one can work.
While I am in the world, I am the light of the world."
When he had said this, he spat on the ground
    and made clay with the saliva,
    and smeared the clay on his eyes, and said to him,
    "Go wash in the Pool of Siloam"—which means Sent—.
So he went and washed, and came back able to see.

His neighbors and those who had seen him earlier as a beggar said,
    "Isn't this the one who used to sit and beg?"
Some said, "It is,"
    but others said, "No, he just looks like him."
He said, "I am."
So they said to him, "How were your eyes opened?"
He replied,
    "The man called Jesus made clay and anointed my eyes
    and told me, 'Go to Siloam and wash.'
So I went there and washed and was able to see."
And they said to him, "Where is he?"
He said, "I don't know."

They brought the one who was once blind to the Pharisees.
Now Jesus had made clay and opened his eyes on a sabbath.
So then the Pharisees also asked him how he was able to see.
He said to them,
    "He put clay on my eyes, and I washed, and now I can see."
So some of the Pharisees said,
    "This man is not from God,
    because he does not keep the sabbath."
But others said,
    "How can a sinful man do such signs?"
And there was a division among them.
So they said to the blind man again,
    "What do you have to say about him,
    since he opened your eyes?"
He said, "He is a prophet."

Now the Jews did not believe
    that he had been blind and gained his sight
    until they summoned the parents of the one who had gained his
        sight.
They asked them,
    "Is this your son, who you say was born blind?
How does he now see?"
His parents answered and said,
    "We know that this is our son and that he was born blind.
We do not know how he sees now,
    nor do we know who opened his eyes.
Ask him, he is of age;
    he can speak for himself."

His parents said this because they were afraid
    of the Jews, for the Jews had already agreed
    that if anyone acknowledged him as the Christ,
    he would be expelled from the synagogue.
For this reason his parents said,
    "He is of age; question him."

So a second time they called the man who had been blind
    and said to him, "Give God the praise!
We know that this man is a sinner."
He replied,
    "If he is a sinner, I do not know.
One thing I do know is that I was blind and now I see."
So they said to him,
    "What did he do to you?
    How did he open your eyes?"
He answered them,
    "I told you already and you did not listen.
Why do you want to hear it again?
Do you want to become his disciples, too?"
They ridiculed him and said,
    "You are that man's disciple;
    we are disciples of Moses!
We know that God spoke to Moses,
    but we do not know where this one is from."
The man answered and said to them,
    "This is what is so amazing,
    that you do not know where he is from, yet he opened my eyes.
We know that God does not listen to sinners,
    but if one is devout and does his will, he listens to him.
It is unheard of that anyone ever opened the eyes of a person born
        blind.
If this man were not from God,
    he would not be able to do anything."
They answered and said to him,
    "You were born totally in sin,
    and are you trying to teach us?"
Then they threw him out.

When Jesus heard that they had thrown him out,
    he found him and said, "Do you believe in the Son of Man?"
He answered and said,
    "Who is he, sir, that I may believe in him?"
Jesus said to him,
    "You have seen him,
    and the one speaking with you is he."
He said,
    "I do believe, Lord," and he worshiped him.
Then Jesus said,
    "I came into this world for judgment,
    so that those who do not see might see,
    and those who do see might become blind."

Some of the Pharisees who were with him heard this
    and said to him, "Surely we are not also blind, are we?"
Jesus said to them,
    "If you were blind, you would have no sin;
    but now you are saying, 'We see,' so your sin remains."

Gospel

John 9:1, 6-9, 13-17, 34-38; L31A

As Jesus passed by he saw a man blind from birth.
He spat on the ground and made clay with the saliva,
    and smeared the clay on his eyes, and said to him,
    "Go wash in the Pool of Siloam"—which means Sent—.
So he went and washed, and came back able to see.

His neighbors and those who had seen him earlier as a beggar said,
    "Isn't this the one who used to sit and beg?"
Some said, "It is,"
    but others said, "No, he just looks like him."
He said, "I am."

They brought the one who was once blind to the Pharisees.
Now Jesus had made clay and opened his eyes on a sabbath.
So then the Pharisees also asked him how he was able to see.
He said to them,
    "He put clay on my eyes, and I washed, and now I can see."
So some of the Pharisees said,
    "This man is not from God,
    because he does not keep the sabbath."
But others said,
    "How can a sinful man do such signs?"

And there was a division among them.
So they said to the blind man again,
    "What do you have to say about him,
    since he opened your eyes?"
He said, "He is a prophet."

They answered and said to him,
    "You were born totally in sin,
    and are you trying to teach us?"
Then they threw him out.

When Jesus heard that they had thrown him out,
    he found him and said, "Do you believe in the Son of Man?"
He answered and said,
    "Who is he, sir, that I may believe in him?"
Jesus said to him,
    "You have seen him,
    and the one speaking with you is he."
He said,
    "I do believe, Lord," and he worshiped him.

FIRST READING   1 Sam 16:1b, 6-7, 10-13a

The LORD said to Samuel:
    "Fill your horn with oil, and be on your way.
I am sending you to Jesse of Bethlehem,
    for I have chosen my king from among his sons."

As Jesse and his sons came to the sacrifice,
    Samuel looked at Eliab and thought,
    "Surely the LORD's anointed is here before him."
But the LORD said to Samuel:
    "Do not judge from his appearance or from his lofty stature,
    because I have rejected him.
Not as man sees does God see,
    because man sees the appearance
    but the LORD looks into the heart."
In the same way Jesse presented seven sons
    before Samuel,
    but Samuel said to Jesse,
    "The LORD has not chosen any one of these."
Then Samuel asked Jesse,
    "Are these all the sons you have?"
Jesse replied,
    "There is still the youngest, who is tending the sheep."
Samuel said to Jesse,
    "Send for him;
    we will not begin the sacrificial banquet until he arrives here."
Jesse sent and had the young man brought to them.
He was ruddy, a youth handsome to behold

and making a splendid appearance.
The LORD said,
    "There—anoint him, for this is the one!"
Then Samuel, with the horn of oil in hand,
    anointed David in the presence of his brothers;
    and from that day on, the spirit of the LORD rushed upon David.

RESPONSORIAL PSALM   Ps 23:1-3a, 3b-4, 5, 6

R̸. (1) The Lord is my shepherd; there is nothing I shall want.

The LORD is my shepherd; I shall not want.
    In verdant pastures he gives me repose;
beside restful waters he leads me;
    he refreshes my soul.

R̸. The Lord is my shepherd; there is nothing I shall want.

He guides me in right paths
    for his name's sake.
Even though I walk in the dark valley
    I fear no evil; for you are at my side
with your rod and your staff
    that give me courage.

R̸. The Lord is my shepherd; there is nothing I shall want.

You spread the table before me
    in the sight of my foes;
you anoint my head with oil;
    my cup overflows.

R̸. The Lord is my shepherd; there is nothing I shall want.

Only goodness and kindness follow me
    all the days of my life;
and I shall dwell in the house of the LORD
    for years to come.

R̸. The Lord is my shepherd; there is nothing I shall want.

SECOND READING
Eph 5:8-14

Brothers and sisters:
You were once darkness,
    but now you are light in the Lord.
Live as children of light,
    for light produces every kind of goodness
    and righteousness and truth.
Try to learn what is pleasing to the Lord.
Take no part in the fruitless works of darkness;
    rather expose them, for it is shameful even to mention
    the things done by them in secret;
    but everything exposed by the light becomes visible,
    for everything that becomes visible is light.
Therefore, it says:
    "Awake, O sleeper,
    and arise from the dead,
    and Christ will give you light."

Gospel
Matt 1:16, 18-21, 24a; L543

Jacob was the father of Joseph, the husband of Mary.
Of her was born Jesus who is called the Christ.

Now this is how the birth of Jesus Christ came about.
When his mother Mary was betrothed to Joseph,
    but before they lived together,
    she was found with child through the Holy Spirit.
Joseph her husband, since he was a righteous man,
    yet unwilling to expose her to shame,
    decided to divorce her quietly.
Such was his intention when, behold,
    the angel of the Lord appeared to him in a dream and said,
    "Joseph, son of David,
    do not be afraid to take Mary your wife into your home.
For it is through the Holy Spirit
    that this child has been conceived in her.
She will bear a son and you are to name him Jesus,
    because he will save his people from their sins."
When Joseph awoke,
    he did as the angel of the Lord had commanded him
    and took his wife into his home.

FIRST READING
2 Sam 7:4-5a, 12-14a, 16

The LORD spoke to Nathan and said:
"Go, tell my servant David,
    'When your time comes and you rest with
        your ancestors,
    I will raise up your heir after you, sprung
        from your loins,
    and I will make his kingdom firm.
It is he who shall build a house for my name.
And I will make his royal throne firm forever.
I will be a father to him,
    and he shall be a son to me.
Your house and your kingdom shall endure
      forever before me;
    your throne shall stand firm forever.'"

RESPONSORIAL PSALM
Ps 89:2-3, 4-5, 27, and 29

R̸. (37) The son of David will live forever.

The promises of the LORD I will sing forever,
    through all generations my mouth will
        proclaim your faithfulness,
For you have said, "My kindness is
    established forever";
    in heaven you have confirmed your
    faithfulness.

R̸. The son of David will live forever.

"I have made a covenant with my chosen one;
    I have sworn to David my servant:
Forever will I confirm your posterity
    and establish your throne for all
      generations."

R̸. The son of David will live forever.

"He shall say of me, 'You are my father,
    my God, the Rock, my savior!'
Forever I will maintain my kindness toward
    him,
    my covenant with him stands firm."

R̸. The son of David will live forever.

SECOND READING
Rom 4:13, 16-18, 22

Brothers and sisters:
It was not through the law
    that the promise was made to Abraham
      and his descendants
    that he would inherit the world,
    but through the righteousness that comes
      from faith.
For this reason, it depends on faith,
    so that it may be a gift,
    and the promise may be guaranteed to all
      his descendants,
    not to those who only adhere to the law
    but to those who follow the faith of Abraham,
    who is the father of all of us, as it is written,
    I have made you father of many nations.
He is our father in the sight of God,
    in whom he believed, who gives life to the
      dead
    and calls into being what does not exist.
He believed, hoping against hope,
    that he would become *the father of many*
      nations,
    according to what was said, *Thus shall*
      your descendants be.
That is why *it was credited to him as*
    righteousness.

Gospel

John 11:1-45; L34A

Now a man was ill, Lazarus from Bethany,
  the village of Mary and her sister Martha.
Mary was the one who had anointed the Lord with perfumed oil
  and dried his feet with her hair;
  it was her brother Lazarus who was ill.
So the sisters sent word to Jesus saying,
  "Master, the one you love is ill."
When Jesus heard this he said,
  "This illness is not to end in death,
  but is for the glory of God,
  that the Son of God may be glorified through it."
Now Jesus loved Martha and her sister and Lazarus.
So when he heard that he was ill,
  he remained for two days in the place where he was.
Then after this he said to his disciples,
  "Let us go back to Judea."
The disciples said to him,
  "Rabbi, the Jews were just trying to stone you,
  and you want to go back there?"
Jesus answered,
  "Are there not twelve hours in a day?
If one walks during the day, he does not stumble,
  because he sees the light of this world.
But if one walks at night, he stumbles,
  because the light is not in him."
He said this, and then told them,
  "Our friend Lazarus is asleep,
  but I am going to awaken him."
So the disciples said to him,
  "Master, if he is asleep, he will be saved."
But Jesus was talking about his death,
  while they thought that he meant ordinary sleep.
So then Jesus said to them clearly,
  "Lazarus has died.
And I am glad for you that I was not there,
  that you may believe.
Let us go to him."
So Thomas, called Didymus, said to his fellow disciples,
  "Let us also go to die with him."

When Jesus arrived, he found that Lazarus
  had already been in the tomb for four days.
Now Bethany was near Jerusalem, only about two miles away.
And many of the Jews had come to Martha and Mary
  to comfort them about their brother.
When Martha heard that Jesus was coming,
  she went to meet him;
  but Mary sat at home.
Martha said to Jesus,
  "Lord, if you had been here,
  my brother would not have died.
But even now I know that whatever you ask of God,
  God will give you."
Jesus said to her,
  "Your brother will rise."
Martha said to him,
  "I know he will rise,
  in the resurrection on the last day."
Jesus told her,

"I am the resurrection and the life;
  whoever believes in me, even if he dies, will live,
  and everyone who lives and believes in me will never die.
Do you believe this?"
She said to him, "Yes, Lord.
I have come to believe that you are the Christ, the Son of God,
  the one who is coming into the world."

When she had said this,
  she went and called her sister Mary secretly, saying,
  "The teacher is here and is asking for you."
As soon as she heard this,
  she rose quickly and went to him.
For Jesus had not yet come into the village,
  but was still where Martha had met him.
So when the Jews who were with her in the house comforting her
  saw Mary get up quickly and go out,
  they followed her,
  presuming that she was going to the tomb to weep there.
When Mary came to where Jesus was and saw him,
  she fell at his feet and said to him,
  "Lord, if you had been here,
  my brother would not have died."
When Jesus saw her weeping and the Jews who had come with her
    weeping,
  he became perturbed and deeply troubled, and said,
  "Where have you laid him?"
They said to him, "Sir, come and see."
And Jesus wept.
So the Jews said, "See how he loved him."
But some of them said,
  "Could not the one who opened the eyes of the blind man
  have done something so that this man would not have died?"

So Jesus, perturbed again, came to the tomb.
It was a cave, and a stone lay across it.
Jesus said, "Take away the stone."
Martha, the dead man's sister, said to him,
  "Lord, by now there will be a stench;
  he has been dead for four days."
Jesus said to her,
  "Did I not tell you that if you believe
  you will see the glory of God?"
So they took away the stone.
And Jesus raised his eyes and said,
  "Father, I thank you for hearing me.
I know that you always hear me;
  but because of the crowd here I have said this,
  that they may believe that you sent me."
And when he had said this,
  he cried out in a loud voice,
  "Lazarus, come out!"
The dead man came out,
  tied hand and foot with burial bands,
  and his face was wrapped in a cloth.
So Jesus said to them,
  "Untie him and let him go."

Now many of the Jews who had come to Mary
  and seen what he had done began to believe in him.

Gospel

John 11:3-7, 17, 20-27, 33b-45; L34A

The sisters of Lazarus sent word to Jesus, saying,
  "Master, the one you love is ill."
When Jesus heard this he said,
  "This illness is not to end in death,
  but is for the glory of God,
  that the Son of God may be glorified through it."
Now Jesus loved Martha and her sister and Lazarus.
So when he heard that he was ill,
  he remained for two days in the place where he was.
Then after this he said to his disciples,
  "Let us go back to Judea."

When Jesus arrived, he found that Lazarus
  had already been in the tomb for four days.
When Martha heard that Jesus was coming,
  she went to meet him;
  but Mary sat at home.
Martha said to Jesus,
  "Lord, if you had been here,
  my brother would not have died.
But even now I know that whatever you ask of God,
  God will give you."
Jesus said to her,
  "Your brother will rise."
Martha said,
  "I know he will rise,
  in the resurrection on the last day."
Jesus told her,
  "I am the resurrection and the life;
  whoever believes in me, even if he dies, will live,
  and everyone who lives and believes in me will never die.
Do you believe this?"
She said to him, "Yes, Lord.
I have come to believe that you are the Christ, the Son of God,
  the one who is coming into the world."

He became perturbed and deeply troubled, and said,
  "Where have you laid him?"
They said to him, "Sir, come and see."
And Jesus wept.
So the Jews said, "See how he loved him."
But some of them said,
  "Could not the one who opened the eyes of the blind man
  have done something so that this man would not have died?"

So Jesus, perturbed again, came to the tomb.
It was a cave, and a stone lay across it.
Jesus said, "Take away the stone."
Martha, the dead man's sister, said to him,
  "Lord, by now there will be a stench;
  he has been dead for four days."
Jesus said to her,
  "Did I not tell you that if you believe
  you will see the glory of God?"
So they took away the stone.
And Jesus raised his eyes and said,
  "Father, I thank you for hearing me.
I know that you always hear me;
  but because of the crowd here I have said this,
  that they may believe that you sent me."
And when he had said this,
  he cried out in a loud voice,
  "Lazarus, come out!"
The dead man came out,
  tied hand and foot with burial bands,
  and his face was wrapped in a cloth.
So Jesus said to them,
  "Untie him and let him go."

Now many of the Jews who had come to Mary
  and seen what he had done began to believe in him.

FIRST READING
Ezek 37:12-14

Thus says the Lord GOD:
 O my people, I will open your graves
  and have you rise from them,
  and bring you back to the land of Israel.
 Then you shall know that I am the LORD,
  when I open your graves and have you rise
   from them,
  O my people!
 I will put my spirit in you that you may live,
  and I will settle you upon your land;
  thus you shall know that I am the LORD.
 I have promised, and I will do it, says the
  LORD.

RESPONSORIAL PSALM
Ps 130:1-2, 3-4, 5-6, 7-8

R̖. (7) With the Lord there is mercy and fullness of redemption.

Out of the depths I cry to you, O LORD;
 Lord, hear my voice!
Let your ears be attentive
 to my voice in supplication.

R̖. With the Lord there is mercy and fullness
of redemption.

If you, O LORD, mark iniquities,
 Lord, who can stand?
But with you is forgiveness,
 that you may be revered.

R̖. With the Lord there is mercy and fullness
of redemption.

I trust in the LORD;
 my soul trusts in his word.
More than sentinels wait for the dawn,
 let Israel wait for the LORD.

R̖. With the Lord there is mercy and fullness
of redemption.

For with the LORD is kindness
 and with him is plenteous redemption;
and he will redeem Israel
 from all their iniquities.

R̖. With the Lord there is mercy and fullness
of redemption.

SECOND READING
Rom 8:8-11

Brothers and sisters:
Those who are in the flesh cannot please God.
But you are not in the flesh;
 on the contrary, you are in the spirit,
 if only the Spirit of God dwells in you.
Whoever does not have the Spirit of Christ
 does not belong to him.
But if Christ is in you,
 although the body is dead because of sin,
 the spirit is alive because of righteousness.
If the Spirit of the One who raised Jesus from
  the dead dwells in you,
 the One who raised Christ from the dead
 will give life to your mortal bodies also,
 through his Spirit dwelling in you.

FIRST READING
Isa 7:10-14; 8:10

The LORD spoke to Ahaz, saying:
Ask for a sign from the LORD, your God;
 let it be deep as the netherworld, or high as
  the sky!
But Ahaz answered,
 "I will not ask! I will not tempt the LORD!"
Then Isaiah said:
 Listen, O house of David!
Is it not enough for you to weary people,
 must you also weary my God?
Therefore the Lord himself will give you this
  sign:
 the virgin shall conceive, and bear a son,
 and shall name him Emmanuel,
 which means "God is with us!"

RESPONSORIAL PSALM
Ps 40:7-8a, 8b-9, 10, 11

R̖. (8a and 9a) Here am I, Lord; I come to do
your will.

Sacrifice or offering you wished not,
 but ears open to obedience you gave me.
Holocausts and sin-offerings you sought not;
 then said I, "Behold, I come."

R̖. Here am I, Lord; I come to do your will.

"In the written scroll it is prescribed for me.
To do your will, O God, is my delight,
 and your law is within my heart!"

R̖. Here am I, Lord; I come to do your will.

I announced your justice in the vast assembly;
 I did not restrain my lips, as you, O LORD,
  know.

R̖. Here am I, Lord; I come to do your will.

Your justice I kept not hid within my heart;
 your faithfulness and your salvation I have
  spoken of;
I have made no secret of your kindness and
  your truth
 in the vast assembly.

R̖. Here am I, Lord; I come to do your will.

SECOND READING
Heb 10:4-10

Brothers and sisters:
It is impossible that the blood of bulls and
  goats
 takes away sins.
For this reason, when Christ came into the
  world, he said:
 "Sacrifice and offering you did not desire,
  but a body you prepared for me;
 in holocausts and sin offerings you took no
  delight.
 Then I said, 'As is written of me in the scroll,
 behold, I come to do your will, O God.'"

First he says, "Sacrifices and offerings,
 holocausts and sin offerings,
 you neither desired nor delighted in."
These are offered according to the law.
Then he says, "Behold, I come to do your will."
He takes away the first to establish the
  second.
By this "will," we have been consecrated
 through the offering of the Body of Jesus
  Christ once for all.

Gospel at the Procession with Palms (cont.)
Luke 19:28-40; L37C

They proclaimed:
  "Blessed is the king who comes
    in the name of the Lord.
  Peace in heaven
    and glory in the highest."
Some of the Pharisees in the crowd said to him,
  "Teacher, rebuke your disciples."
He said in reply,
  "I tell you, if they keep silent,
    the stones will cry out!"

Gospel at Mass
Luke 22:14–23:56; L38ABC

When the hour came,
  Jesus took his place at table with the apostles.
He said to them,
  "I have eagerly desired to eat this Passover with you before I suffer,
  for, I tell you, I shall not eat it again
  until there is fulfillment in the kingdom of God."
Then he took a cup, gave thanks, and said,
  "Take this and share it among yourselves;
  for I tell you that from this time on
  I shall not drink of the fruit of the vine
  until the kingdom of God comes."
Then he took the bread, said the blessing,
  broke it, and gave it to them, saying,
  "This is my body, which will be given for you;
  do this in memory of me."
And likewise the cup after they had eaten, saying,
  "This cup is the new covenant in my blood,
  which will be shed for you.

"And yet behold, the hand of the one who is to betray me
  is with me on the table;
  for the Son of Man indeed goes as it has been determined;
  but woe to that man by whom he is betrayed."
And they began to debate among themselves
  who among them would do such a deed.

Then an argument broke out among them
  about which of them should be regarded as the greatest.
He said to them,
  "The kings of the Gentiles lord it over them
  and those in authority over them are addressed as 'Benefactors';
  but among you it shall not be so.
Rather, let the greatest among you be as the youngest,
  and the leader as the servant.
For who is greater:
  the one seated at table or the one who serves?
Is it not the one seated at table?
I am among you as the one who serves.
It is you who have stood by me in my trials;
  and I confer a kingdom on you,
  just as my Father has conferred one on me,
  that you may eat and drink at my table in my kingdom;
  and you will sit on thrones
  judging the twelve tribes of Israel.

"Simon, Simon, behold Satan has demanded
  to sift all of you like wheat,

but I have prayed that your own faith may not fail;
  and once you have turned back,
  you must strengthen your brothers."
He said to him,
  "Lord, I am prepared to go to prison and to die with you."
But he replied,
  "I tell you, Peter, before the cock crows this day,
  you will deny three times that you know me."

He said to them,
  "When I sent you forth without a money bag or a sack or sandals,
  were you in need of anything?"
"No, nothing," they replied.
He said to them,
  "But now one who has a money bag should take it,
  and likewise a sack,
  and one who does not have a sword
  should sell his cloak and buy one.
For I tell you that this Scripture must be fulfilled in me,
  namely, *He was counted among the wicked;*
  and indeed what is written about me is coming to fulfillment."
Then they said,
  "Lord, look, there are two swords here."
But he replied, "It is enough!"

Then going out, he went, as was his custom, to the Mount of Olives,
  and the disciples followed him.
When he arrived at the place he said to them,
  "Pray that you may not undergo the test."
After withdrawing about a stone's throw from them and kneeling,
  he prayed, saying, "Father, if you are willing,
  take this cup away from me;
  still, not my will but yours be done."
And to strengthen him an angel from heaven appeared to him.
He was in such agony and he prayed so fervently
  that his sweat became like drops of blood
  falling on the ground.
When he rose from prayer and returned to his disciples,
  he found them sleeping from grief.
He said to them, "Why are you sleeping?
Get up and pray that you may not undergo the test."

While he was still speaking, a crowd approached
  and in front was one of the Twelve, a man named Judas.
He went up to Jesus to kiss him.
Jesus said to him,
  "Judas, are you betraying the Son of Man with a kiss?"
His disciples realized what was about to happen, and they asked,
  "Lord, shall we strike with a sword?"
And one of them struck the high priest's servant
  and cut off his right ear.
But Jesus said in reply,
  "Stop, no more of this!"
Then he touched the servant's ear and healed him.
And Jesus said to the chief priests and temple guards
  and elders who had come for him,
  "Have you come out as against a robber, with swords and clubs?
Day after day I was with you in the temple area,
  and you did not seize me;
  but this is your hour, the time for the power of darkness."

After arresting him they led him away
  and took him into the house of the high priest;
  Peter was following at a distance.

They lit a fire in the middle of the courtyard and sat around it,
    and Peter sat down with them.
When a maid saw him seated in the light,
    she looked intently at him and said,
    "This man too was with him."
But he denied it saying,
    "Woman, I do not know him."
A short while later someone else saw him and said,
    "You too are one of them";
    but Peter answered, "My friend, I am not."
About an hour later, still another insisted,
    "Assuredly, this man too was with him,
    for he also is a Galilean."
But Peter said,
    "My friend, I do not know what you are talking about."
Just as he was saying this, the cock crowed,
    and the Lord turned and looked at Peter;
    and Peter remembered the word of the Lord,
    how he had said to him,
    "Before the cock crows today, you will deny me three times."
He went out and began to weep bitterly.
The men who held Jesus in custody were ridiculing and beating him.
They blindfolded him and questioned him, saying,
    "Prophesy! Who is it that struck you?"
And they reviled him in saying many other things against him.

When day came the council of elders of the people met,
    both chief priests and scribes,
    and they brought him before their Sanhedrin.
They said, "If you are the Christ, tell us,"
    but he replied to them, "If I tell you, you will not believe,
    and if I question, you will not respond.
But from this time on the Son of Man will be seated
    at the right hand of the power of God."
They all asked, "Are you then the Son of God?"
He replied to them, "You say that I am."
Then they said, "What further need have we for testimony?
We have heard it from his own mouth."

Then the whole assembly of them arose and brought him before Pilate.
They brought charges against him, saying,
    "We found this man misleading our people;
    he opposes the payment of taxes to Caesar
    and maintains that he is the Christ, a king."
Pilate asked him, "Are you the king of the Jews?"
He said to him in reply, "You say so."
Pilate then addressed the chief priests and the crowds,
    "I find this man not guilty."
But they were adamant and said,
    "He is inciting the people with his teaching
        throughout all Judea,
    from Galilee where he began even to here."

On hearing this Pilate asked if the man was a Galilean;
    and upon learning that he was under Herod's jurisdiction,
    he sent him to Herod who was in Jerusalem at that time.
Herod was very glad to see Jesus;
    he had been wanting to see him for a long time,
    for he had heard about him
    and had been hoping to see him perform some sign.
He questioned him at length,
    but he gave him no answer.

The chief priests and scribes, meanwhile,
    stood by accusing him harshly.
Herod and his soldiers treated him contemptuously and mocked him,
    and after clothing him in resplendent garb,
    he sent him back to Pilate.
Herod and Pilate became friends that very day,
    even though they had been enemies formerly.
Pilate then summoned the chief priests, the rulers, and the people
    and said to them, "You brought this man to me
    and accused him of inciting the people to revolt.
I have conducted my investigation in your presence
    and have not found this man guilty
    of the charges you have brought against him,
    nor did Herod, for he sent him back to us.
So no capital crime has been committed by him.
Therefore I shall have him flogged and then release him."

But all together they shouted out,
    "Away with this man!
    Release Barabbas to us."
—Now Barabbas had been imprisoned for a rebellion
    that had taken place in the city and for murder.—
Again Pilate addressed them, still wishing to release Jesus,
    but they continued their shouting,
    "Crucify him! Crucify him!"
Pilate addressed them a third time,
    "What evil has this man done?
    I found him guilty of no capital crime.
Therefore I shall have him flogged and then release him."
With loud shouts, however,
    they persisted in calling for his crucifixion,
    and their voices prevailed.
The verdict of Pilate was that their demand should be granted.
So he released the man who had been imprisoned
    for rebellion and murder, for whom they asked,
    and he handed Jesus over to them to deal with as they wished.

As they led him away
    they took hold of a certain Simon, a Cyrenian,
    who was coming in from the country;
    and after laying the cross on him,
    they made him carry it behind Jesus.
A large crowd of people followed Jesus,
    including many women who mourned and lamented him.
Jesus turned to them and said,
    "Daughters of Jerusalem, do not weep for me;
    weep instead for yourselves and for your children
    for indeed, the days are coming when people will say,
    'Blessed are the barren,
    the wombs that never bore
    and the breasts that never nursed.'
At that time people will say to the mountains,
    'Fall upon us!'
    and to the hills, 'Cover us!'
    for if these things are done when the wood is green
    what will happen when it is dry?"
Now two others, both criminals,
    were led away with him to be executed.

When they came to the place called the Skull,
    they crucified him and the criminals there,
    one on his right, the other on his left.

Then Jesus said,
   "Father, forgive them, they know not what they do."
They divided his garments by casting lots.
The people stood by and watched;
   the rulers, meanwhile, sneered at him and said,
   "He saved others, let him save himself
   if he is the chosen one, the Christ of God."
Even the soldiers jeered at him.
As they approached to offer him wine they called out,
   "If you are King of the Jews, save yourself."
Above him there was an inscription that read,
   "This is the King of the Jews."

Now one of the criminals hanging there reviled Jesus, saying,
   "Are you not the Christ?
   Save yourself and us."
The other, however, rebuking him, said in reply,
   "Have you no fear of God,
   for you are subject to the same condemnation?
And indeed, we have been condemned justly,
   for the sentence we received corresponds to our crimes,
   but this man has done nothing criminal."
Then he said,
   "Jesus, remember me when you come into your kingdom."
He replied to him,
   "Amen, I say to you,
   today you will be with me in Paradise."

It was now about noon and darkness came over the whole land
   until three in the afternoon
   because of an eclipse of the sun.
Then the veil of the temple was torn down the middle.
Jesus cried out in a loud voice,
   "Father, into your hands I commend my spirit";
   and when he had said this he breathed his last.

Here all kneel and pause for a short time.

The centurion who witnessed what had happened glorified God and said,
   "This man was innocent beyond doubt."
When all the people who had gathered for this spectacle
      saw what had happened,
   they returned home beating their breasts;
   but all his acquaintances stood at a distance,
   including the women who had followed him from Galilee
   and saw these events.

Now there was a virtuous and righteous man named Joseph who,
   though he was a member of the council,
   had not consented to their plan of action.
He came from the Jewish town of Arimathea
   and was awaiting the kingdom of God.
He went to Pilate and asked for the body of Jesus.
After he had taken the body down,
   he wrapped it in a linen cloth
   and laid him in a rock-hewn tomb
   in which no one had yet been buried.
It was the day of preparation,
   and the sabbath was about to begin.
The women who had come from Galilee with him followed behind,
   and when they had seen the tomb
   and the way in which his body was laid in it,
   they returned and prepared spices and perfumed oils.
Then they rested on the sabbath according to the commandment.

or Luke 23:1-49

The elders of the people, chief priests and scribes,
   arose and brought Jesus before Pilate.
They brought charges against him, saying,
   "We found this man misleading our people;
   he opposes the payment of taxes to Caesar
   and maintains that he is the Christ, a king."
Pilate asked him, "Are you the king of the Jews?"
He said to him in reply, "You say so."
Pilate then addressed the chief priests and the crowds,
   "I find this man not guilty."
But they were adamant and said,
   "He is inciting the people with his teaching
      throughout all Judea,
   from Galilee where he began even to here."

On hearing this Pilate asked if the man was a Galilean;
   and upon learning that he was under Herod's jurisdiction,
   he sent him to Herod who was in Jerusalem at that time.
Herod was very glad to see Jesus;
   he had been wanting to see him for a long time,
   for he had heard about him
   and had been hoping to see him perform some sign.
He questioned him at length,
   but he gave him no answer.
The chief priests and scribes, meanwhile,
   stood by accusing him harshly.
Herod and his soldiers treated him contemptuously and mocked him,
   and after clothing him in resplendent garb,
   he sent him back to Pilate.
Herod and Pilate became friends that very day,
   even though they had been enemies formerly.
Pilate then summoned the chief priests, the rulers, and the people
   and said to them, "You brought this man to me
   and accused him of inciting the people to revolt.
I have conducted my investigation in your presence
   and have not found this man guilty
   of the charges you have brought against him,
   nor did Herod, for he sent him back to us.
So no capital crime has been committed by him.
Therefore I shall have him flogged and then release him."

But all together they shouted out,
   "Away with this man!
   Release Barabbas to us."
—Now Barabbas had been imprisoned for a rebellion
   that had taken place in the city and for murder.—
Again Pilate addressed them, still wishing to release Jesus,
   but they continued their shouting,
   "Crucify him! Crucify him!"
Pilate addressed them a third time,
   "What evil has this man done?
   I found him guilty of no capital crime.
Therefore I shall have him flogged and then release him."
With loud shouts, however,
   they persisted in calling for his crucifixion,
   and their voices prevailed.
The verdict of Pilate was that their demand should be granted.
So he released the man who had been imprisoned
   for rebellion and murder, for whom they asked,
   and he handed Jesus over to them to deal with as they wished.

Gospel (cont.)
Luke 23:1-49

As they led him away
    they took hold of a certain Simon, a Cyrenian,
    who was coming in from the country;
    and after laying the cross on him,
    they made him carry it behind Jesus.
A large crowd of people followed Jesus,
    including many women who mourned and lamented him.
Jesus turned to them and said,
    "Daughters of Jerusalem, do not weep for me;
    weep instead for yourselves and for your children
    for indeed, the days are coming when people will say,
    'Blessed are the barren,
    the wombs that never bore
    and the breasts that never nursed.'
At that time people will say to the mountains,
    'Fall upon us!'
    and to the hills, 'Cover us!'
    for if these things are done when the wood is green
    what will happen when it is dry?"
Now two others, both criminals,
    were led away with him to be executed.

When they came to the place called the Skull,
    they crucified him and the criminals there,
    one on his right, the other on his left.
Then Jesus said,
    "Father, forgive them, they know not what they do."
They divided his garments by casting lots.
The people stood by and watched;
    the rulers, meanwhile, sneered at him and said,
    "He saved others, let him save himself
    if he is the chosen one, the Christ of God."
Even the soldiers jeered at him.

As they approached to offer him wine they called out,
    "If you are King of the Jews, save yourself."
Above him there was an inscription that read,
    "This is the King of the Jews."

Now one of the criminals hanging there reviled Jesus, saying,
    "Are you not the Christ?
    Save yourself and us."
The other, however, rebuking him, said in reply,
    "Have you no fear of God,
    for you are subject to the same condemnation?
And indeed, we have been condemned justly,
    for the sentence we received corresponds to our crimes,
    but this man has done nothing criminal."
Then he said,
    "Jesus, remember me when you come into your kingdom."
He replied to him,
    "Amen, I say to you,
    today you will be with me in Paradise."

It was now about noon and darkness came over the whole land
    until three in the afternoon
    because of an eclipse of the sun.
Then the veil of the temple was torn down the middle.
Jesus cried out in a loud voice,
    "Father, into your hands I commend my spirit";
    and when he had said this he breathed his last.

Here all kneel and pause for a short time.

The centurion who witnessed what had happened glorified God and said,
    "This man was innocent beyond doubt."
When all the people who had gathered for this spectacle
    saw what had happened,
    they returned home beating their breasts;
    but all his acquaintances stood at a distance,
    including the women who had followed him from Galilee
    and saw these events.

Gospel (cont.)

John 13:1-15; L39ABC

So when he had washed their feet
    and put his garments back on and reclined at table again,
    he said to them, "Do you realize what I have done for you?
You call me 'teacher' and 'master,' and rightly so, for indeed I am.
If I, therefore, the master and teacher, have washed your feet,
    you ought to wash one another's feet.
I have given you a model to follow,
    so that as I have done for you, you should also do."

FIRST READING

Exod 12:1-8, 11-14

The LORD said to Moses and Aaron in the
        land of Egypt,
    "This month shall stand at the head of your
        calendar;
    you shall reckon it the first month of the
        year.
Tell the whole community of Israel:
    On the tenth of this month every one of
        your families
    must procure for itself a lamb, one apiece
        for each household.
If a family is too small for a whole lamb,
    it shall join the nearest household in
        procuring one
    and shall share in the lamb
    in proportion to the number of persons who
        partake of it.
The lamb must be a year-old male and
        without blemish.
You may take it from either the sheep or the
        goats.
You shall keep it until the fourteenth day of
        this month,
    and then, with the whole assembly of Israel
        present,
    it shall be slaughtered during the evening
        twilight.
They shall take some of its blood
    and apply it to the two doorposts and the
        lintel
    of every house in which they partake of the
        lamb.
That same night they shall eat its roasted
        flesh
    with unleavened bread and bitter herbs.

"This is how you are to eat it:
    with your loins girt, sandals on your feet
        and your staff in hand,
    you shall eat like those who are in flight.

It is the Passover of the LORD.
For on this same night I will go through Egypt,
    striking down every firstborn of the land,
        both man and beast,
    and executing judgment on all the gods of
        Egypt—I, the LORD!
But the blood will mark the houses where you
        are.
Seeing the blood, I will pass over you;
    thus, when I strike the land of Egypt,
    no destructive blow will come upon you.

"This day shall be a memorial feast for you,
    which all your generations shall celebrate
    with pilgrimage to the LORD, as a perpetual
        institution."

RESPONSORIAL PSALM

Ps 116:12-13, 15-16bc, 17-18

R̼. (cf. 1 Cor 10:16) Our blessing-cup is a communion with the Blood of Christ.

How shall I make a return to the LORD
    for all the good he has done for me?
The cup of salvation I will take up,
    and I will call upon the name of the LORD.

R̼. Our blessing-cup is a communion with the
Blood of Christ.

Precious in the eyes of the LORD
    is the death of his faithful ones.
I am your servant, the son of your handmaid;
    you have loosed my bonds.

R̼. Our blessing-cup is a communion with the
Blood of Christ.

To you will I offer sacrifice of thanksgiving,
    and I will call upon the name of the LORD.
My vows to the LORD I will pay
    in the presence of all his people.

R̼. Our blessing-cup is a communion with the
Blood of Christ.

SECOND READING

1 Cor 11:23-26

Brothers and sisters:
I received from the Lord what I also handed
        on to you,
    that the Lord Jesus, on the night he was
        handed over,
    took bread, and, after he had given thanks,
    broke it and said, "This is my body that is
        for you.
Do this in remembrance of me."
In the same way also the cup, after supper,
        saying,
    "This cup is the new covenant in my blood.
Do this, as often as you drink it, in
        remembrance of me."
For as often as you eat this bread and drink
        the cup,
    you proclaim the death of the Lord until he
        comes.

Gospel (cont.)
John 18:1–19:42; L40ABC

So the band of soldiers, the tribune, and the Jewish guards seized Jesus,
bound him, and brought him to Annas first.
He was the father-in-law of Caiaphas,
who was high priest that year.
It was Caiaphas who had counseled the Jews
that it was better that one man should die rather than the people.

Simon Peter and another disciple followed Jesus.
Now the other disciple was known to the high priest,
and he entered the courtyard of the high priest with Jesus.
But Peter stood at the gate outside.
So the other disciple, the acquaintance of the high priest,
went out and spoke to the gatekeeper and brought Peter in.
Then the maid who was the gatekeeper said to Peter,
"You are not one of this man's disciples, are you?"
He said, "I am not."
Now the slaves and the guards were standing around a charcoal fire
that they had made, because it was cold,
and were warming themselves.
Peter was also standing there keeping warm.

The high priest questioned Jesus
about his disciples and about his doctrine.
Jesus answered him,
"I have spoken publicly to the world.
I have always taught in a synagogue
or in the temple area where all the Jews gather,
and in secret I have said nothing. Why ask me?
Ask those who heard me what I said to them.
They know what I said."
When he had said this,
one of the temple guards standing there struck Jesus and said,
"Is this the way you answer the high priest?"
Jesus answered him,
"If I have spoken wrongly, testify to the wrong;
but if I have spoken rightly, why do you strike me?"
Then Annas sent him bound to Caiaphas the high priest.

Now Simon Peter was standing there keeping warm.
And they said to him,
"You are not one of his disciples, are you?"
He denied it and said,
"I am not."
One of the slaves of the high priest,
a relative of the one whose ear Peter had cut off, said,
"Didn't I see you in the garden with him?"
Again Peter denied it.
And immediately the cock crowed.

Then they brought Jesus from Caiaphas to the praetorium.
It was morning.
And they themselves did not enter the praetorium,
in order not to be defiled so that they could eat the Passover.
So Pilate came out to them and said,
"What charge do you bring against this man?"
They answered and said to him,
"If he were not a criminal,
we would not have handed him over to you."
At this, Pilate said to them,
"Take him yourselves, and judge him according to your law."

The Jews answered him,
"We do not have the right to execute anyone,"
in order that the word of Jesus might be fulfilled
that he said indicating the kind of death he would die.
So Pilate went back into the praetorium
and summoned Jesus and said to him,
"Are you the King of the Jews?"
Jesus answered,
"Do you say this on your own
or have others told you about me?"
Pilate answered,
"I am not a Jew, am I?
Your own nation and the chief priests handed you over to me.
What have you done?"
Jesus answered,
"My kingdom does not belong to this world.
If my kingdom did belong to this world,
my attendants would be fighting
to keep me from being handed over to the Jews.
But as it is, my kingdom is not here."
So Pilate said to him,
"Then you are a king?"
Jesus answered,
"You say I am a king.
For this I was born and for this I came into the world,
to testify to the truth.
Everyone who belongs to the truth listens to my voice."
Pilate said to him, "What is truth?"

When he had said this,
he again went out to the Jews and said to them,
"I find no guilt in him.
But you have a custom that I release one prisoner to you at Passover.
Do you want me to release to you the King of the Jews?"
They cried out again,
"Not this one but Barabbas!"
Now Barabbas was a revolutionary.

Then Pilate took Jesus and had him scourged.
And the soldiers wove a crown out of thorns and placed it on his head,
and clothed him in a purple cloak,
and they came to him and said,
"Hail, King of the Jews!"
And they struck him repeatedly.
Once more Pilate went out and said to them,
"Look, I am bringing him out to you,
so that you may know that I find no guilt in him."
So Jesus came out,
wearing the crown of thorns and the purple cloak.
And he said to them, "Behold, the man!"
When the chief priests and the guards saw him they cried out,
"Crucify him, crucify him!"
Pilate said to them,
"Take him yourselves and crucify him.
I find no guilt in him."
The Jews answered,
"We have a law, and according to that law he ought to die,
because he made himself the Son of God."

Now when Pilate heard this statement,
he became even more afraid,
and went back into the praetorium and said to Jesus,
"Where are you from?"
Jesus did not answer him.
So Pilate said to him,
"Do you not speak to me?
Do you not know that I have power to release you
and I have power to crucify you?"
Jesus answered him,
"You would have no power over me
if it had not been given to you from above.
For this reason the one who handed me over to you
has the greater sin."
Consequently, Pilate tried to release him; but the Jews cried out,
"If you release him, you are not a Friend of Caesar.
Everyone who makes himself a king opposes Caesar."

When Pilate heard these words he brought Jesus out
and seated him on the judge's bench
in the place called Stone Pavement, in Hebrew, Gabbatha.
It was preparation day for Passover, and it was about noon.
And he said to the Jews,
"Behold, your king!"
They cried out,
"Take him away, take him away! Crucify him!"
Pilate said to them,
"Shall I crucify your king?"
The chief priests answered,
"We have no king but Caesar."
Then he handed him over to them to be crucified.

So they took Jesus, and, carrying the cross himself,
he went out to what is called the Place of the Skull,
in Hebrew, Golgotha.
There they crucified him, and with him two others,
one on either side, with Jesus in the middle.
Pilate also had an inscription written and put on the cross.
It read,
"Jesus the Nazorean, the King of the Jews."
Now many of the Jews read this inscription,
because the place where Jesus was crucified was near the city;
and it was written in Hebrew, Latin, and Greek.
So the chief priests of the Jews said to Pilate,
"Do not write 'The King of the Jews,'
but that he said, 'I am the King of the Jews.'"
Pilate answered,
"What I have written, I have written."

When the soldiers had crucified Jesus,
they took his clothes and divided them into four shares,
a share for each soldier.
They also took his tunic, but the tunic was seamless,
woven in one piece from the top down.
So they said to one another,
"Let's not tear it, but cast lots for it to see whose it will be,"
in order that the passage of Scripture might be fulfilled that says:
They divided my garments among them,
and for my vesture they cast lots.

This is what the soldiers did.
Standing by the cross of Jesus were his mother
and his mother's sister, Mary the wife of Clopas,
and Mary of Magdala.
When Jesus saw his mother and the disciple there whom he loved
he said to his mother, "Woman, behold, your son."
Then he said to the disciple,
"Behold, your mother."
And from that hour the disciple took her into his home.

After this, aware that everything was now finished,
in order that the Scripture might be fulfilled,
Jesus said, "I thirst."
There was a vessel filled with common wine.
So they put a sponge soaked in wine on a sprig of hyssop
and put it up to his mouth.
When Jesus had taken the wine, he said,
"It is finished."
And bowing his head, he handed over the spirit.

Here all kneel and pause for a short time.

Now since it was preparation day,
in order that the bodies might not remain
on the cross on the sabbath,
for the sabbath day of that week was a solemn one,
the Jews asked Pilate that their legs be broken
and that they be taken down.
So the soldiers came and broke the legs of the first
and then of the other one who was crucified with Jesus.
But when they came to Jesus and saw that he was already dead,
they did not break his legs,
but one soldier thrust his lance into his side,
and immediately blood and water flowed out.
An eyewitness has testified, and his testimony is true;
he knows that he is speaking the truth,
so that you also may come to believe.
For this happened so that the Scripture passage might be fulfilled:
Not a bone of it will be broken.
And again another passage says:
They will look upon him whom they have pierced.

After this, Joseph of Arimathea,
secretly a disciple of Jesus for fear of the Jews,
asked Pilate if he could remove the body of Jesus.
And Pilate permitted it.
So he came and took his body.
Nicodemus, the one who had first come to him at night,
also came bringing a mixture of myrrh and aloes
weighing about one hundred pounds.
They took the body of Jesus
and bound it with burial cloths along with the spices,
according to the Jewish burial custom.
Now in the place where he had been crucified there was a garden,
and in the garden a new tomb, in which no one had yet been
buried.
So they laid Jesus there because of the Jewish preparation day;
for the tomb was close by.

FIRST READING

Isa 52:13–53:12

See, my servant shall prosper,
   he shall be raised high and greatly exalted.
Even as many were amazed at him—
   so marred was his look beyond human
      semblance
   and his appearance beyond that of the sons
      of man—
so shall he startle many nations,
   because of him kings shall stand speechless;
for those who have not been told shall see,
   those who have not heard shall ponder it.

Who would believe what we have heard?
   To whom has the arm of the LORD been
      revealed?
He grew up like a sapling before him,
   like a shoot from the parched earth;
there was in him no stately bearing to make
      us look at him,
   nor appearance that would attract us to him.
He was spurned and avoided by people,
   a man of suffering, accustomed to infirmity,
one of those from whom people hide their faces,
   spurned, and we held him in no esteem.

Yet it was our infirmities that he bore,
   our sufferings that he endured,
while we thought of him as stricken,
   as one smitten by God and afflicted.
But he was pierced for our offenses,
   crushed for our sins;
upon him was the chastisement that makes
      us whole,
   by his stripes we were healed.
We had all gone astray like sheep,
   each following his own way;
but the LORD laid upon him
   the guilt of us all.

Though he was harshly treated, he submitted
   and opened not his mouth;
like a lamb led to the slaughter
   or a sheep before the shearers,
   he was silent and opened not his mouth.
Oppressed and condemned, he was taken away,
   and who would have thought any more of
      his destiny?
When he was cut off from the land of the living,
   and smitten for the sin of his people,
a grave was assigned him among the wicked
   and a burial place with evildoers,
though he had done no wrong
   nor spoken any falsehood.
But the LORD was pleased
   to crush him in infirmity.

If he gives his life as an offering for sin,
   he shall see his descendants in a long life,
   and the will of the LORD shall be
      accomplished through him.

Because of his affliction
   he shall see the light
   in fullness of days;
through his suffering, my servant shall justify
      many,
   and their guilt he shall bear.
Therefore I will give him his portion among
      the great,
   and he shall divide the spoils with the
      mighty,
because he surrendered himself to death
   and was counted among the wicked;
and he shall take away the sins of many,
   and win pardon for their offenses.

RESPONSORIAL PSALM

Ps 31:2, 6, 12-13, 15-16, 17, 25

R℘. (Luke 23:46) Father, into your hands I
commend my spirit.

In you, O LORD, I take refuge;
   let me never be put to shame.
In your justice rescue me.
Into your hands I commend my spirit;
   you will redeem me, O LORD, O faithful God.

R℘. Father, into your hands I commend my
spirit.

For all my foes I am an object of reproach,
   a laughingstock to my neighbors, and a
      dread to my friends;
   they who see me abroad flee from me.
I am forgotten like the unremembered dead;
   I am like a dish that is broken.

R℘. Father, into your hands I commend my
spirit.

But my trust is in you, O LORD;
   I say, "You are my God."
In your hands is my destiny; rescue me
   from the clutches of my enemies and my
      persecutors."

R℘. Father, into your hands I commend my
spirit.

Let your face shine upon your servant;
   save me in your kindness.
Take courage and be stouthearted,
   all you who hope in the LORD.

R℘. Father, into your hands I commend my
spirit.

SECOND READING

Heb 4:14-16; 5:7-9

Brothers and sisters:
Since we have a great high priest who has
      passed through the heavens,
   Jesus, the Son of God,
   let us hold fast to our confession.
For we do not have a high priest
   who is unable to sympathize with our
      weaknesses,
   but one who has similarly been tested in
      every way,
   yet without sin.
So let us confidently approach the throne of
      grace
   to receive mercy and to find grace for
      timely help.

In the days when Christ was in the flesh,
   he offered prayers and supplications with
      loud cries and tears
   to the one who was able to save him from
      death,
   and he was heard because of his reverence.
Son though he was, he learned obedience from
      what he suffered;
   and when he was made perfect,
   he became the source of eternal salvation
      for all who obey him.

FIRST READING
Gen 1:1–2:2

In the beginning, when God created the
    heavens and the earth,
    the earth was a formless wasteland, and
        darkness covered the abyss,
    while a mighty wind swept over the waters.

Then God said,
    "Let there be light," and there was light.
God saw how good the light was.
God then separated the light from the darkness.
God called the light "day," and the darkness
    he called "night."
Thus evening came, and morning followed—
    the first day.

Then God said,
    "Let there be a dome in the middle of the
        waters,
    to separate one body of water from the
        other."
And so it happened:
    God made the dome,
    and it separated the water above the dome
        from the water below it.
God called the dome "the sky."
Evening came, and morning followed—the
    second day.

Then God said,
    "Let the water under the sky be gathered
        into a single basin,
    so that the dry land may appear."
And so it happened:
    the water under the sky was gathered into
        its basin,
    and the dry land appeared.
God called the dry land "the earth,"
    and the basin of the water he called "the
        sea."
God saw how good it was.
Then God said,
    "Let the earth bring forth vegetation:
    every kind of plant that bears seed
    and every kind of fruit tree on earth
    that bears fruit with its seed in it."
And so it happened:
    the earth brought forth every kind of plant
        that bears seed
    and every kind of fruit tree on earth
    that bears fruit with its seed in it.
God saw how good it was.
Evening came, and morning followed—the
    third day.

Then God said:
    "Let there be lights in the dome of the sky,
    to separate day from night.
Let them mark the fixed times, the days and
    the years,
and serve as luminaries in the dome of the
    sky,
    to shed light upon the earth."
And so it happened:
    God made the two great lights,
    the greater one to govern the day,
    and the lesser one to govern the night;
    and he made the stars.
God set them in the dome of the sky,
    to shed light upon the earth,
    to govern the day and the night,
    and to separate the light from the darkness.
God saw how good it was.
Evening came, and morning followed—the
    fourth day.

Then God said,
    "Let the water teem with an abundance of
        living creatures,
    and on the earth let birds fly beneath the
        dome of the sky."
And so it happened:
    God created the great sea monsters
    and all kinds of swimming creatures with
        which the water teems,
    and all kinds of winged birds.
God saw how good it was, and God blessed
    them, saying,
    "Be fertile, multiply, and fill the water of
        the seas;
    and let the birds multiply on the earth."
Evening came, and morning followed—the
    fifth day.

Then God said,
    "Let the earth bring forth all kinds of living
        creatures:
    cattle, creeping things, and wild animals of
        all kinds."
And so it happened:
    God made all kinds of wild animals, all
        kinds of cattle,
    and all kinds of creeping things of the earth.
God saw how good it was.
Then God said:
    "Let us make man in our image, after our
        likeness.
Let them have dominion over the fish of the sea,
    the birds of the air, and the cattle,
    and over all the wild animals
    and all the creatures that crawl on the
        ground."
God created man in his image;
    in the image of God he created him;
    male and female he created them.
God blessed them, saying:
    "Be fertile and multiply;
    fill the earth and subdue it.
Have dominion over the fish of the sea, the
    birds of the air,
and all the living things that move on the
    earth."
God also said:
    "See, I give you every seed-bearing plant all
        over the earth
    and every tree that has seed-bearing fruit
        on it to be your food;
    and to all the animals of the land, all the
        birds of the air,
    and all the living creatures that crawl on
        the ground,
    I give all the green plants for food."
And so it happened.
God looked at everything he had made, and
    he found it very good.
Evening came, and morning followed—the
    sixth day.

Thus the heavens and the earth and all their
    array were completed.
Since on the seventh day God was finished
    with the work he had been doing,
    he rested on the seventh day from all the
        work he had undertaken.

or

Gen 1:1, 26-31a

In the beginning, when God created the
    heavens and the earth,
    God said: "Let us make man in our image,
        after our likeness.
Let them have dominion over the fish of the sea,
    the birds of the air, and the cattle,
    and over all the wild animals
    and all the creatures that crawl on the
        ground."
God created man in his image;
    in the image of God he created him;
    male and female he created them.
God blessed them, saying:
    "Be fertile and multiply;
    fill the earth and subdue it.
Have dominion over the fish of the sea, the
    birds of the air,
    and all the living things that move on the
        earth."
God also said:
    "See, I give you every seed-bearing plant all
        over the earth
    and every tree that has seed-bearing fruit
        on it to be your food;
    and to all the animals of the land, all the
        birds of the air,
    and all the living creatures that crawl on
        the ground,
    I give all the green plants for food."
And so it happened.
God looked at everything he had made, and
    found it very good.

RESPONSORIAL PSALM
Ps 104:1-2, 5-6, 10, 12, 13-14, 24, 35

R℣. (30) Lord, send out your Spirit, and renew
the face of the earth.

Bless the LORD, O my soul!
    O LORD, my God, you are great indeed!
You are clothed with majesty and glory,
    robed in light as with a cloak.

R℣. Lord, send out your Spirit, and renew the
face of the earth.

You fixed the earth upon its foundation,
    not to be moved forever;
with the ocean, as with a garment, you
        covered it;
    above the mountains the waters stood.

R℣. Lord, send out your Spirit, and renew the
face of the earth.

You send forth springs into the watercourses
    that wind among the mountains.
Beside them the birds of heaven dwell;
    from among the branches they send forth
        their song.

R℣. Lord, send out your Spirit, and renew the
face of the earth.

You water the mountains from your palace;
    the earth is replete with the fruit of your
        works.
You raise grass for the cattle,
    and vegetation for man's use,
producing bread from the earth.

R℣. Lord, send out your Spirit, and renew the
face of the earth.

How manifold are your works, O LORD!
    In wisdom you have wrought them all—
the earth is full of your creatures.
    Bless the LORD, O my soul!

R℣. Lord, send out your Spirit, and renew the
face of the earth.

or

Ps 33:4-5, 6-7, 12-13, 20 and 22

R℣. (5b) The earth is full of the goodness of the
Lord.

Upright is the word of the LORD,
    and all his works are trustworthy.
He loves justice and right;
    of the kindness of the LORD the earth is full.

R℣. The earth is full of the goodness of the Lord.

By the word of the LORD the heavens were
        made;
    by the breath of his mouth all their host.
He gathers the waters of the sea as in a
        flask;
    in cellars he confines the deep.

R℣. The earth is full of the goodness of the Lord.

Blessed the nation whose God is the LORD,
    the people he has chosen for his own
        inheritance.
From heaven the LORD looks down;
    he sees all mankind.

R℣. The earth is full of the goodness of the Lord.

Our soul waits for the LORD,
    who is our help and our shield.
May your kindness, O LORD, be upon us
    who have put our hope in you.

R℣. The earth is full of the goodness of the Lord.

SECOND READING
Gen 22:1-18

God put Abraham to the test.
He called to him, "Abraham!"
"Here I am," he replied.
Then God said:
    "Take your son Isaac, your only one, whom
        you love,
    and go to the land of Moriah.
There you shall offer him up as a holocaust
    on a height that I will point out to you."
Early the next morning Abraham saddled his
        donkey,
    took with him his son Isaac and two of his
        servants as well,
    and with the wood that he had cut for the
        holocaust,
    set out for the place of which God had told
        him.

On the third day Abraham got sight of the
        place from afar.
Then he said to his servants:
    "Both of you stay here with the donkey,
    while the boy and I go on over yonder.
We will worship and then come back to you."
Thereupon Abraham took the wood for the
        holocaust
    and laid it on his son Isaac's shoulders,
    while he himself carried the fire and the
        knife.
As the two walked on together, Isaac spoke to
        his father Abraham:
    "Father!" Isaac said.
"Yes, son," he replied.
Isaac continued, "Here are the fire and the
        wood,
    but where is the sheep for the holocaust?"
"Son," Abraham answered,
    "God himself will provide the sheep for the
        holocaust."
Then the two continued going forward.

When they came to the place of which God
        had told him,

Abraham built an altar there and arranged
        the wood on it.
Next he tied up his son Isaac,
    and put him on top of the wood on the altar.
Then he reached out and took the knife to
        slaughter his son.
But the LORD's messenger called to him from
        heaven,
    "Abraham, Abraham!"
"Here I am," he answered.
"Do not lay your hand on the boy," said the
        messenger.
"Do not do the least thing to him.
I know now how devoted you are to God,
    since you did not withhold from me your
        own beloved son."
As Abraham looked about,
    he spied a ram caught by its horns in the
        thicket.
So he went and took the ram
    and offered it up as a holocaust in place of
        his son.
Abraham named the site Yahweh-yireh;
    hence people now say, "On the mountain
        the LORD will see."

Again the LORD's messenger called to
        Abraham from heaven and said:
    "I swear by myself, declares the LORD,
    that because you acted as you did
    in not withholding from me your beloved
        son,
    I will bless you abundantly
    and make your descendants as countless
    as the stars of the sky and the sands of the
        seashore;
    your descendants shall take possession
    of the gates of their enemies,
    and in your descendants all the nations of
        the earth
        shall find blessing—
    all this because you obeyed my
        command."

or

Gen 22:1-2, 9a, 10-13, 15-18

God put Abraham to the test.
He called to him, "Abraham!"
"Here I am," he replied.
Then God said:
    "Take your son Isaac, your only one, whom
        you love,
    and go to the land of Moriah.
There you shall offer him up as a holocaust
    on a height that I will point out to you."

When they came to the place of which God
        had told him,
    Abraham built an altar there and arranged
        the wood on it.

Then he reached out and took the knife to
  slaughter his son.
But the LORD's messenger called to him from
  heaven,
  "Abraham, Abraham!"
"Here I am," he answered.
"Do not lay your hand on the boy," said the
  messenger.
"Do not do the least thing to him.
I know now how devoted you are to God,
  since you did not withhold from me your
  own beloved son."
As Abraham looked about,
  he spied a ram caught by its horns in the
  thicket.
So he went and took the ram
  and offered it up as a holocaust in place of
  his son.

Again the LORD's messenger called to
  Abraham from heaven and said:
"I swear by myself, declares the LORD,
  that because you acted as you did
  in not withholding from me your beloved son,
I will bless you abundantly
  and make your descendants as countless
  as the stars of the sky and the sands of the
  seashore;
  your descendants shall take possession
  of the gates of their enemies,
  and in your descendants all the nations of
  the earth
    shall find blessing—
  all this because you obeyed my command."

RESPONSORIAL PSALM

Ps 16:5, 8, 9-10, 11

R̮. (1) You are my inheritance, O Lord.

O LORD, my allotted portion and my cup,
  you it is who hold fast my lot.
I set the LORD ever before me;
  with him at my right hand I shall not be
  disturbed.

R̮. You are my inheritance, O Lord.

Therefore my heart is glad and my soul rejoices,
  my body, too, abides in confidence;
because you will not abandon my soul to the
  netherworld,
  nor will you suffer your faithful one to
  undergo corruption.

R̮. You are my inheritance, O Lord.

You will show me the path to life,
  fullness of joys in your presence,
  the delights at your right hand forever.

R̮. You are my inheritance, O Lord.

THIRD READING

Exod 14:15–15:1

The LORD said to Moses, "Why are you crying
  out to me?
Tell the Israelites to go forward.
And you, lift up your staff and, with hand
  outstretched over the sea,
  split the sea in two,
  that the Israelites may pass through it on
  dry land.
But I will make the Egyptians so obstinate
  that they will go in after them.
Then I will receive glory through Pharaoh
  and all his army,
  his chariots and charioteers.
The Egyptians shall know that I am the LORD,
  when I receive glory through Pharaoh
  and his chariots and charioteers."

The angel of God, who had been leading
  Israel's camp,
  now moved and went around behind them.
The column of cloud also, leaving the front,
  took up its place behind them,
  so that it came between the camp of the
  Egyptians
  and that of Israel.
But the cloud now became dark, and thus the
  night passed
  without the rival camps coming any closer
  together all night long.
Then Moses stretched out his hand over the
  sea,
  and the LORD swept the sea
  with a strong east wind throughout the night
  and so turned it into dry land.
When the water was thus divided,
  the Israelites marched into the midst of the
  sea on dry land,
  with the water like a wall to their right and
  to their left.

The Egyptians followed in pursuit;
  all Pharaoh's horses and chariots and
  charioteers went after them
  right into the midst of the sea.
In the night watch just before dawn
  the LORD cast through the column of the
  fiery cloud
  upon the Egyptian force a glance that
  threw it into a panic;
  and he so clogged their chariot wheels
  that they could hardly drive.
With that the Egyptians sounded the retreat
  before Israel,
  because the LORD was fighting for them
  against the Egyptians.

Then the LORD told Moses, "Stretch out your
  hand over the sea,
  that the water may flow back upon the
  Egyptians,
  upon their chariots and their charioteers."
So Moses stretched out his hand over the sea,
  and at dawn the sea flowed back to its
  normal depth.
The Egyptians were fleeing head on toward
  the sea,
  when the LORD hurled them into its midst.
As the water flowed back,
  it covered the chariots and the charioteers
  of Pharaoh's whole army
  which had followed the Israelites into the sea.
Not a single one of them escaped.
But the Israelites had marched on dry land
  through the midst of the sea,
  with the water like a wall to their right and
  to their left.
Thus the LORD saved Israel on that day
  from the power of the Egyptians.
When Israel saw the Egyptians lying dead on
  the seashore
  and beheld the great power that the LORD
  had shown against the Egyptians,
  they feared the LORD and believed in him
  and in his servant Moses.

Then Moses and the Israelites sang this song
  to the LORD:
  I will sing to the LORD, for he is gloriously
  triumphant;
  horse and chariot he has cast into the sea.

RESPONSORIAL PSALM

Exod 15:1-2, 3-4, 5-6, 17-18

R̮. (1b) Let us sing to the Lord; he has covered
himself in glory.

I will sing to the LORD, for he is gloriously
  triumphant;
  horse and chariot he has cast into the sea.
My strength and my courage is the LORD,
  and he has been my savior.
He is my God, I praise him;
  the God of my father, I extol him.

R̮. Let us sing to the Lord; he has covered
himself in glory.

The LORD is a warrior,
  LORD is his name!
Pharaoh's chariots and army he hurled into
  the sea;
  the elite of his officers were submerged in
  the Red Sea.

R̮. Let us sing to the Lord; he has covered
himself in glory.

The flood waters covered them,
  they sank into the depths like a stone.
Your right hand, O LORD, magnificent in
  power,
  your right hand, O LORD, has shattered the
    enemy.

R⁊. Let us sing to the Lord; he has covered
himself in glory.

You brought in the people you redeemed
  and planted them on the mountain of your
    inheritance—
the place where you made your seat, O
  LORD,
  the sanctuary, LORD, which your hands
    established.
The LORD shall reign forever and ever.

R⁊. Let us sing to the Lord; he has covered
himself in glory.

FOURTH READING
Isa 54:5-14

The One who has become your husband is
  your Maker;
  his name is the LORD of hosts;
your redeemer is the Holy One of Israel,
  called God of all the earth.
The LORD calls you back,
  like a wife forsaken and grieved in spirit,
  a wife married in youth and then cast off,
  says your God.
For a brief moment I abandoned you,
  but with great tenderness I will take you
    back.
In an outburst of wrath, for a moment
  I hid my face from you;
but with enduring love I take pity on you,
  says the LORD, your redeemer.
This is for me like the days of Noah,
  when I swore that the waters of Noah
  should never again deluge the earth;
so I have sworn not to be angry with you,
  or to rebuke you.
Though the mountains leave their place
  and the hills be shaken,
my love shall never leave you
  nor my covenant of peace be shaken,
  says the LORD, who has mercy on you.
O afflicted one, storm-battered and unconsoled,
  I lay your pavements in carnelians,
  and your foundations in sapphires;
I will make your battlements of rubies,
  your gates of carbuncles,
  and all your walls of precious stones.
All your children shall be taught by the LORD,
  and great shall be the peace of your children.

In justice shall you be established,
  far from the fear of oppression,
  where destruction cannot come near you.

RESPONSORIAL PSALM
Ps 30:2, 4, 5-6, 11-12, 13

R⁊. (2a) I will praise you, Lord, for you have
rescued me.

I will extol you, O LORD, for you drew me
    clear
  and did not let my enemies rejoice over me.
O LORD, you brought me up from the
    netherworld;
  you preserved me from among those going
    down into the pit.

R⁊. I will praise you, Lord, for you have
rescued me.

Sing praise to the LORD, you his faithful ones,
  and give thanks to his holy name.
For his anger lasts but a moment;
  a lifetime, his good will.
At nightfall, weeping enters in,
  but with the dawn, rejoicing.

R⁊. I will praise you, Lord, for you have
rescued me.

Hear, O LORD, and have pity on me;
  O LORD, be my helper.
You changed my mourning into dancing;
  O LORD, my God, forever will I give you
    thanks.

R⁊. I will praise you, Lord, for you have
rescued me.

FIFTH READING
Isa 55:1-11

Thus says the LORD:
All you who are thirsty,
  come to the water!
You who have no money,
  come, receive grain and eat;
come, without paying and without cost,
  drink wine and milk!
Why spend your money for what is not bread,
  your wages for what fails to satisfy?
Heed me, and you shall eat well,
  you shall delight in rich fare.
Come to me heedfully,
  listen, that you may have life.
I will renew with you the everlasting
    covenant,
  the benefits assured to David.
As I made him a witness to the peoples,
  a leader and commander of nations,
so shall you summon a nation you knew not,

and nations that knew you not shall run
    to you,
because of the LORD, your God,
  the Holy One of Israel, who has glorified you.

Seek the LORD while he may be found,
  call him while he is near.
Let the scoundrel forsake his way,
  and the wicked man his thoughts;
let him turn to the LORD for mercy;
  to our God, who is generous in forgiving.
For my thoughts are not your thoughts,
  nor are your ways my ways, says the LORD.
As high as the heavens are above the earth,
  so high are my ways above your ways
  and my thoughts above your thoughts.

For just as from the heavens
  the rain and snow come down
and do not return there
  till they have watered the earth,
  making it fertile and fruitful,
giving seed to the one who sows
  and bread to the one who eats,
so shall my word be
  that goes forth from my mouth;
my word shall not return to me void,
  but shall do my will,
  achieving the end for which I sent it.

RESPONSORIAL PSALM
Isa 12:2-3, 4, 5-6

R⁊. (3) You will draw water joyfully from the
springs of salvation.

God indeed is my savior;
  I am confident and unafraid.
My strength and my courage is the LORD,
  and he has been my savior.
With joy you will draw water
  at the fountain of salvation.

R⁊. You will draw water joyfully from the
springs of salvation.

Give thanks to the LORD, acclaim his name;
  among the nations make known his deeds,
  proclaim how exalted is his name.

R⁊. You will draw water joyfully from the
springs of salvation.

Sing praise to the LORD for his glorious
    achievement;
  let this be known throughout all the earth.
Shout with exultation, O city of Zion,
  for great in your midst
  is the Holy One of Israel!

R⁊. You will draw water joyfully from the
springs of salvation.

SIXTH READING
Bar 3:9-15, 32–4:4

Hear, O Israel, the commandments of life:
    listen, and know prudence!
How is it, Israel,
    that you are in the land of your foes,
    grown old in a foreign land,
defiled with the dead,
    accounted with those destined for the
        netherworld?
You have forsaken the fountain of wisdom!
    Had you walked in the way of God,
    you would have dwelt in enduring peace.
Learn where prudence is,
    where strength, where understanding;
that you may know also
    where are length of days, and life,
    where light of the eyes, and peace.
Who has found the place of wisdom,
    who has entered into her treasuries?

The One who knows all things knows her;
    he has probed her by his knowledge—
the One who established the earth for all
        time,
    and filled it with four-footed beasts;
he who dismisses the light, and it departs,
    calls it, and it obeys him trembling;
before whom the stars at their posts
    shine and rejoice;
when he calls them, they answer, "Here we
        are!"
    shining with joy for their Maker.
Such is our God;
    no other is to be compared to him:
he has traced out the whole way of
        understanding,
    and has given her to Jacob, his servant,
    to Israel, his beloved son.

Since then she has appeared on earth,
    and moved among people.
She is the book of the precepts of God,
    the law that endures forever;
all who cling to her will live,
    but those will die who forsake her.
Turn, O Jacob, and receive her:
    walk by her light toward splendor.
Give not your glory to another,
    your privileges to an alien race.
Blessed are we, O Israel;
    for what pleases God is known to us!

RESPONSORIAL PSALM
Ps 19:8, 9, 10, 11

℟. (John 6:68c) Lord, you have the words of
everlasting life.

The law of the LORD is perfect,
    refreshing the soul;

the decree of the LORD is trustworthy,
    giving wisdom to the simple.

℟. Lord, you have the words of everlasting life.

The precepts of the LORD are right,
    rejoicing the heart;
the command of the LORD is clear,
    enlightening the eye.

℟. Lord, you have the words of everlasting life.

The fear of the LORD is pure,
    enduring forever;
the ordinances of the LORD are true,
    all of them just.

℟. Lord, you have the words of everlasting life.

They are more precious than gold,
    than a heap of purest gold;
sweeter also than syrup
    or honey from the comb.

℟. Lord, you have the words of everlasting life.

SEVENTH READING
Ezek 36:16-17a, 18-28

The word of the LORD came to me, saying:
    Son of man, when the house of Israel lived
        in their land,
    they defiled it by their conduct and deeds.
Therefore I poured out my fury upon them
    because of the blood that they poured out
        on the ground,
    and because they defiled it with idols.
I scattered them among the nations,
    dispersing them over foreign lands;
    according to their conduct and deeds I
        judged them.
But when they came among the nations
        wherever they came,
    they served to profane my holy name,
    because it was said of them: "These are the
        people of the LORD,
    yet they had to leave their land."
So I have relented because of my holy name
    which the house of Israel profaned
    among the nations where they came.
Therefore say to the house of Israel: Thus
        says the Lord GOD:
    Not for your sakes do I act, house of Israel,
    but for the sake of my holy name,
    which you profaned among the nations to
        which you came.
I will prove the holiness of my great name,
    profaned among the nations,
    in whose midst you have profaned it.
Thus the nations shall know that I am the
        LORD, says the Lord GOD,
    when in their sight I prove my holiness
        through you.
For I will take you away from among the
        nations,

gather you from all the foreign lands,
    and bring you back to your own land.
I will sprinkle clean water upon you
    to cleanse you from all your impurities,
    and from all your idols I will cleanse you.
I will give you a new heart and place a new
        spirit within you,
    taking from your bodies your stony hearts
    and giving you natural hearts.
I will put my spirit within you and make you
        live by my statutes,
    careful to observe my decrees.
You shall live in the land I gave your fathers;
    you shall be my people, and I will be your
        God.

RESPONSORIAL PSALM
Ps 42:3, 5; 43:3, 4

℟. (42:2) Like a deer that longs for running
streams, my soul longs for you, my God.

Athirst is my soul for God, the living God.
    When shall I go and behold the face of God?

℟. Like a deer that longs for running streams,
my soul longs for you, my God.

I went with the throng
    and led them in procession to the house of
        God,
amid loud cries of joy and thanksgiving,
    with the multitude keeping festival.

℟. Like a deer that longs for running streams,
my soul longs for you, my God.

Send forth your light and your fidelity;
    they shall lead me on
and bring me to your holy mountain,
    to your dwelling-place.

℟. Like a deer that longs for running streams,
my soul longs for you, my God.

Then will I go in to the altar of God,
    the God of my gladness and joy;
then will I give you thanks upon the harp,
    O God, my God!

℟. Like a deer that longs for running streams,
my soul longs for you, my God.

or

Isa 12:2-3, 4bcd, 5-6

℟. (3) You will draw water joyfully from the
springs of salvation.

God indeed is my savior;
    I am confident and unafraid.
My strength and my courage is the LORD,
    and he has been my savior.
With joy you will draw water
    at the fountain of salvation.

℟. You will draw water joyfully from the
springs of salvation.

Give thanks to the LORD, acclaim his name;
  among the nations make known his deeds,
  proclaim how exalted is his name.

℞. You will draw water joyfully from the
springs of salvation.

Sing praise to the LORD for his glorious
  achievement;
  let this be known throughout all the earth.
Shout with exultation, O city of Zion,
  for great in your midst
  is the Holy One of Israel!

℞. You will draw water joyfully from the
springs of salvation.

or

Ps 51:12-13, 14-15, 18-19

℞. (12a) Create a clean heart in me, O God.

A clean heart create for me, O God,
  and a steadfast spirit renew within me.
Cast me not out from your presence,
  and your Holy Spirit take not from me.

℞. Create a clean heart in me, O God.

Give me back the joy of your salvation,
  and a willing spirit sustain in me.
I will teach transgressors your ways,
  and sinners shall return to you.

℞. Create a clean heart in me, O God.

For you are not pleased with sacrifices;
  should I offer a holocaust, you would not
  accept it.
My sacrifice, O God, is a contrite spirit;
  a heart contrite and humbled, O God, you
  will not spurn.

℞. Create a clean heart in me, O God.

EPISTLE
Rom 6:3-11

Brothers and sisters:
Are you unaware that we who were baptized
  into Christ Jesus
  were baptized into his death?
We were indeed buried with him through
  baptism into death,
  so that, just as Christ was raised from the
  dead
  by the glory of the Father,
  we too might live in newness of life.

For if we have grown into union with him
  through a death like his,
  we shall also be united with him in the
  resurrection.
We know that our old self was crucified with
  him,
  so that our sinful body might be done away
  with,
  that we might no longer be in slavery to sin.
For a dead person has been absolved from
  sin.
If, then, we have died with Christ,
  we believe that we shall also live with
  him.
We know that Christ, raised from the dead,
  dies no more;
  death no longer has power over him.
As to his death, he died to sin once and for
  all;
  as to his life, he lives for God.
Consequently, you too must think of
  yourselves as being dead to sin
  and living for God in Christ Jesus.

RESPONSORIAL PSALM
Ps 118:1-2, 16-17, 22-23

℞. Alleluia, alleluia, alleluia.

Give thanks to the LORD, for he is good,
  for his mercy endures forever.
Let the house of Israel say,
  "His mercy endures forever."

℞. Alleluia, alleluia, alleluia.

"The right hand of the LORD has struck with
  power;
  the right hand of the LORD is exalted.
I shall not die, but live,
  and declare the works of the LORD."

℞. Alleluia, alleluia, alleluia.

The stone which the builders rejected
  has become the cornerstone.
By the LORD has this been done;
  it is wonderful in our eyes.

℞. Alleluia, alleluia, alleluia.

Gospel

Luke 24:1-12; L41C

At daybreak on the first day of the week
    the women who had come from Galilee with Jesus
    took the spices they had prepared
    and went to the tomb.
They found the stone rolled away from the tomb;
    but when they entered,
    they did not find the body of the Lord Jesus.
While they were puzzling over this, behold,
    two men in dazzling garments appeared to them.
They were terrified and bowed their faces to the ground.
They said to them,
    "Why do you seek the living one among the dead?
He is not here, but he has been raised.
Remember what he said to you while he was still in Galilee,
that the Son of Man must be handed over to sinners
    and be crucified, and rise on the third day."
And they remembered his words.
Then they returned from the tomb
    and announced all these things to the eleven
    and to all the others.
The women were Mary Magdalene, Joanna, and Mary the mother of
      James;
    the others who accompanied them also told this to the apostles,
    but their story seemed like nonsense
    and they did not believe them.
But Peter got up and ran to the tomb,
    bent down, and saw the burial cloths alone;
    then he went home amazed at what had happened.

or, at an afternoon or evening Mass

Gospel

Luke 24:13-35; L46

That very day, the first day of the week,
    two of Jesus' disciples were going
    to a village seven miles from Jerusalem called Emmaus,
    and they were conversing about all the things that had occurred.
And it happened that while they were conversing and debating,
    Jesus himself drew near and walked with them,
    but their eyes were prevented from recognizing him.
He asked them,
    "What are you discussing as you walk along?"
They stopped, looking downcast.
One of them, named Cleopas, said to him in reply,
    "Are you the only visitor to Jerusalem
    who does not know of the things
    that have taken place there in these days?"
And he replied to them, "What sort of things?"
They said to him,
    "The things that happened to Jesus the Nazarene,
    who was a prophet mighty in deed and word
    before God and all the people,
    how our chief priests and rulers both handed him over
    to a sentence of death and crucified him.
But we were hoping that he would be the one to redeem Israel;
    and besides all this,
    it is now the third day since this took place.
Some women from our group, however, have astounded us:
    they were at the tomb early in the morning
    and did not find his body;
    they came back and reported
    that they had indeed seen a vision of angels
    who announced that he was alive.
Then some of those with us went to the tomb
    and found things just as the women had described,
    but him they did not see."

And he said to them, "Oh, how foolish you are!
How slow of heart to believe all that the prophets spoke!
Was it not necessary that the Christ should suffer these things
    and enter into his glory?"
Then beginning with Moses and all the prophets,
    he interpreted to them what referred to him
    in all the Scriptures.
As they approached the village to which they were going,
    he gave the impression that he was going on farther.
But they urged him, "Stay with us,
    for it is nearly evening and the day is almost over."
So he went in to stay with them.
And it happened that, while he was with them at table,
    he took bread, said the blessing,
    broke it, and gave it to them.
With that their eyes were opened and they recognized him,
    but he vanished from their sight.
Then they said to each other,
    "Were not our hearts burning within us
    while he spoke to us on the way and opened the Scriptures to us?"
So they set out at once and returned to Jerusalem
    where they found gathered together
    the eleven and those with them who were saying,
    "The Lord has truly been raised and has appeared to Simon!"
Then the two recounted
    what had taken place on the way
    and how he was made known to them in the breaking of bread.

Easter Sunday, *April 4, 2010*

FIRST READING
Acts 10:34a, 37-43

Peter proceeded to speak and said:
  "You know what has happened all over
    Judea,
  beginning in Galilee after the baptism
  that John preached,
  how God anointed Jesus of Nazareth
  with the Holy Spirit and power.
He went about doing good
  and healing all those oppressed by the devil,
  for God was with him.
We are witnesses of all that he did
  both in the country of the Jews and in
    Jerusalem.
They put him to death by hanging him on a
    tree.
This man God raised on the third day and
    granted that he be visible,
  not to all the people, but to us,
  the witnesses chosen by God in advance,
  who ate and drank with him after he rose
    from the dead.
He commissioned us to preach to the people
  and testify that he is the one appointed by
    God
  as judge of the living and the dead.
To him all the prophets bear witness,
  that everyone who believes in him
  will receive forgiveness of sins through his
    name."

RESPONSORIAL PSALM
Ps 118:1-2, 16-17, 22-23

R꓿. (24) This is the day the Lord has made; let
us rejoice and be glad.
  or:
R꓿. Alleluia.

Give thanks to the LORD, for he is good,
  for his mercy endures forever.
Let the house of Israel say,
  "His mercy endures forever."

R꓿. This is the day the Lord has made; let us
rejoice and be glad.
  or:
R꓿. Alleluia.

"The right hand of the LORD has struck with
    power;
  the right hand of the LORD is exalted.
I shall not die, but live,
  and declare the works of the LORD."

R꓿. This is the day the Lord has made; let us
rejoice and be glad.
  or:
R꓿. Alleluia.

The stone which the builders rejected
  has become the cornerstone.
By the LORD has this been done;
  it is wonderful in our eyes.

R꓿. This is the day the Lord has made; let us
rejoice and be glad.
  or:
R꓿. Alleluia.

SECOND READING
1 Cor 5:6b-8

Brothers and sisters:
Do you not know that a little yeast leavens all
    the dough?
Clear out the old yeast,
  so that you may become a fresh batch of
    dough,
  inasmuch as you are unleavened.
For our paschal lamb, Christ, has been
    sacrificed.

Therefore, let us celebrate the feast,
  not with the old yeast, the yeast of malice
    and wickedness,
  but with the unleavened bread of sincerity
    and truth.

or Col 3:1-4

Brothers and sisters:
If then you were raised with Christ, seek what
    is above,
  where Christ is seated at the right hand of
    God.
Think of what is above, not of what is on earth.
For you have died, and your life is hidden
    with Christ in God.
When Christ your life appears,
  then you too will appear with him in glory.

SEQUENCE *Victimae paschali laudes*

Christians, to the Paschal Victim
  Offer your thankful praises!
A Lamb the sheep redeems;
  Christ, who only is sinless,
  Reconciles sinners to the Father.
Death and life have contended in that combat
    stupendous:
  The Prince of life, who died, reigns immortal.
Speak, Mary, declaring
  What you saw, wayfaring.
"The tomb of Christ, who is living,
  The glory of Jesus' resurrection;
Bright angels attesting,
  The shroud and napkin resting.
Yes, Christ my hope is arisen;
  To Galilee he goes before you."
Christ indeed from death is risen, our new life
    obtaining.
  Have mercy, victor King, ever reigning!
  Amen. Alleluia.

Second Sunday of Easter (or Divine Mercy Sunday), *April 11, 2010*

Gospel (cont.)
John 20:19-31; L45C

Then he said to Thomas, "Put your finger here and see my hands,
  and bring your hand and put it into my side,
  and do not be unbelieving, but believe."
Thomas answered and said to him, "My Lord and my God!"
Jesus said to him, "Have you come to believe because you have seen
    me?
Blessed are those who have not seen and have believed."

Now Jesus did many other signs in the presence of his disciples
  that are not written in this book.
But these are written that you may come to believe
  that Jesus is the Christ, the Son of God,
  and that through this belief you may have life in his name.

Gospel (cont.)

John 21:1-19; L48C

When they climbed out on shore,
  they saw a charcoal fire with fish on it and bread.
Jesus said to them, "Bring some of the fish you just caught."
So Simon Peter went over and dragged the net ashore
  full of one hundred fifty-three large fish.
Even though there were so many, the net was not torn.
Jesus said to them, "Come, have breakfast."
And none of the disciples dared to ask him, "Who are you?"
  because they realized it was the Lord.
Jesus came over and took the bread and gave it to them,
  and in like manner the fish.
This was now the third time Jesus was revealed to his disciples
  after being raised from the dead.

When they had finished breakfast, Jesus said to Simon Peter,
  "Simon, son of John, do you love me more than these?"
Simon Peter answered him, "Yes, Lord, you know that I love you."
Jesus said to him, "Feed my lambs."
He then said to Simon Peter a second time,
  "Simon, son of John, do you love me?"
Simon Peter answered him, "Yes, Lord, you know that I love you."
Jesus said to him, "Tend my sheep."
Jesus said to him the third time,
  "Simon, son of John, do you love me?"
Peter was distressed that Jesus had said to him a third time,
  "Do you love me?" and he said to him,
  "Lord, you know everything; you know that I love you."
Jesus said to him, "Feed my sheep.
Amen, amen, I say to you, when you were younger,
  you used to dress yourself and go where you wanted;
  but when you grow old, you will stretch out your hands,
  and someone else will dress you
  and lead you where you do not want to go."
He said this signifying by what kind of death he would glorify God.
And when he had said this, he said to him, "Follow me."

or John 21:1-14; L48C

At that time, Jesus revealed himself again to his disciples at the Sea of
  Tiberias.
He revealed himself in this way.
Together were Simon Peter, Thomas called Didymus,
  Nathanael from Cana in Galilee,
  Zebedee's sons, and two others of his disciples.
Simon Peter said to them, "I am going fishing."
They said to him, "We also will come with you."
So they went out and got into the boat,
  but that night they caught nothing.
When it was already dawn, Jesus was standing on the shore;
  but the disciples did not realize that it was Jesus.
Jesus said to them, "Children, have you caught anything to eat?"
They answered him, "No."
So he said to them, "Cast the net over the right side of the boat
  and you will find something."
So they cast it, and were not able to pull it in
  because of the number of fish.
So the disciple whom Jesus loved said to Peter, "It is the Lord."
When Simon Peter heard that it was the Lord,
  he tucked in his garment, for he was lightly clad,
  and jumped into the sea.
The other disciples came in the boat,
  for they were not far from shore, only about a hundred yards,
  dragging the net with the fish.
When they climbed out on shore,
  they saw a charcoal fire with fish on it and bread.
Jesus said to them, "Bring some of the fish you just caught."
So Simon Peter went over and dragged the net ashore
  full of one hundred fifty-three large fish.
Even though there were so many, the net was not torn.
Jesus said to them, "Come, have breakfast."
And none of the disciples dared to ask him, "Who are you?"
  because they realized it was the Lord.
Jesus came over and took the bread and gave it to them,
  and in like manner the fish.
This was now the third time Jesus was revealed to his disciples
  after being raised from the dead.

Fourth Sunday of Easter, *April 25, 2010*

SECOND READING
Rev 7:9, 14b-17

I, John, had a vision of a great multitude,
    which no one could count,
    from every nation, race, people, and tongue.
They stood before the throne and before the
    Lamb,
    wearing white robes and holding palm
        branches in their hands.

Then one of the elders said to me,
    "These are the ones who have survived the
        time of great distress;
    they have washed their robes
    and made them white in the blood of the
        Lamb.

"For this reason they stand before God's
    throne
    and worship him day and night in his
        temple.
The one who sits on the throne will
    shelter them.
They will not hunger or thirst anymore,
    nor will the sun or any heat strike
        them.
For the Lamb who is in the center of the
    throne
    will shepherd them
    and lead them to springs of life-giving
        water,
    and God will wipe away every tear
        from their eyes."

Sixth Sunday of Easter, *May 9, 2010*

SECOND READING
Rev 21:10-14, 22-23

The angel took me in spirit to a great, high
    mountain
    and showed me the holy city Jerusalem
coming down out of heaven from God.
It gleamed with the splendor of God.
Its radiance was like that of a precious stone,
    like jasper, clear as crystal.
It had a massive, high wall,
    with twelve gates where twelve angels
        were stationed
    and on which names were inscribed,
    the names of the twelve tribes of the
        Israelites.

There were three gates facing east,
    three north, three south, and three west.
The wall of the city had twelve courses of
    stones as its foundation,
    on which were inscribed the twelve names
    of the twelve apostles of the Lamb.

I saw no temple in the city
    for its temple is the Lord God almighty and
        the Lamb.
The city had no need of sun or moon to shine
    on it,
    for the glory of God gave it light,
    and its lamp was the Lamb.

The Ascension of the Lord, *May 13, 2010 (Thursday) or May 16, 2010*

SECOND READING
Eph 1:17-23

Brothers and sisters:
May the God of our Lord Jesus Christ, the
    Father of glory,
    give you a Spirit of wisdom and revelation
    resulting in knowledge of him.
May the eyes of your hearts be enlightened,
    that you may know what is the hope that
        belongs to his call,
    what are the riches of glory
    in his inheritance among the holy ones,
    and what is the surpassing greatness of his
        power
    for us who believe,
    in accord with the exercise of his great
        might,
    which he worked in Christ,
    raising him from the dead
    and seating him at his right hand in the
        heavens,
    far above every principality, authority,
        power, and dominion,
    and every name that is named
    not only in this age but also in the one to
        come.

And he put all things beneath his feet
    and gave him as head over all things to the
        church,
    which is his body,
    the fullness of the one who fills all things in
        every way.

or

Heb 9:24-28; 10:19-23

Christ did not enter into a sanctuary made by
    hands,
    a copy of the true one, but heaven itself,
    that he might now appear before God on
        our behalf.
Not that he might offer himself repeatedly,
    as the high priest enters each year into the
        sanctuary
    with blood that is not his own;
    if that were so, he would have had to suffer
        repeatedly
    from the foundation of the world.
But now once for all he has appeared at the
    end of the ages
    to take away sin by his sacrifice.
Just as it is appointed that men and women
    die once,

and after this the judgment, so also Christ,
    offered once to take away the sins of many,
    will appear a second time, not to take away
        sin
    but to bring salvation to those who eagerly
        await him.

Therefore, brothers and sisters, since through
    the blood of Jesus
    we have confidence of entrance into the
        sanctuary
    by the new and living way he opened for us
        through the veil,
    that is, his flesh,
    and since we have "a great priest over the
        house of God,"
    let us approach with a sincere heart and in
        absolute trust,
    with our hearts sprinkled clean from an evil
        conscience
    and our bodies washed in pure water.
Let us hold unwaveringly to our confession
    that gives us hope,
    for he who made the promise is
        trustworthy.

Pentecost Sunday Mass During the Day, *May 23, 2010*

SECOND READING
Rom 8:8-17

Brothers and sisters:
Those who are in the flesh cannot please
    God.
But you are not in the flesh;
    on the contrary, you are in the spirit,
    if only the Spirit of God dwells in you.
Whoever does not have the Spirit of Christ
    does not belong to him.
But if Christ is in you,
    although the body is dead because of sin,
    the spirit is alive because of righteousness.
If the Spirit of the one who raised Jesus from
    the dead dwells in you,
    the one who raised Christ from the dead
    will give life to your mortal bodies also,
    through his Spirit that dwells in you.
Consequently, brothers and sisters,
    we are not debtors to the flesh,
    to live according to the flesh.
For if you live according to the flesh, you
    will die,
    but if by the Spirit you put to death the
        deeds of the body,
    you will live.

For those who are led by the Spirit of God are
    sons of God.
For you did not receive a spirit of slavery to
    fall back into fear,
    but you received a Spirit of adoption,
    through whom we cry, "Abba, Father!"
The Spirit himself bears witness with our
    spirit
    that we are children of God,
    and if children, then heirs,
    heirs of God and joint heirs with Christ,
    if only we suffer with him
    so that we may also be glorified with him.

or

1 Cor 12:3b-7, 12-13

Brothers and sisters:
No one can say, "Jesus is Lord," except by the
    Holy Spirit.

There are different kinds of spiritual gifts but
    the same Spirit;
    there are different forms of service but the
        same Lord;
    there are different workings but the same God
    who produces all of them in everyone.

To each individual the manifestation of the
    Spirit
    is given for some benefit.

As a body is one though it has many parts,
    and all the parts of the body, though many,
        are one body,
    so also Christ.
For in one Spirit we were all baptized into one
    body,
    whether Jews or Greeks, slaves or free
        persons,
    and we were all given to drink of one Spirit.

Pentecost Sunday Mass During the Day, May 23, 2010

SEQUENCE
Veni, Sancte Spiritus

Come, Holy Spirit, come!
And from your celestial home
   Shed a ray of light divine!
Come, Father of the poor!
Come, source of all our store!
   Come, within our bosoms shine.
You, of comforters the best;
You, the soul's most welcome guest;
   Sweet refreshment here below;
In our labor, rest most sweet;
Grateful coolness in the heat;
   Solace in the midst of woe.
O most blessed Light divine,
Shine within these hearts of yours,
   And our inmost being fill!

Where you are not, we have naught,
Nothing good in deed or thought,
   Nothing free from taint of ill.
Heal our wounds, our strength renew;
On our dryness pour your dew;
   Wash the stains of guilt away:
Bend the stubborn heart and will;
Melt the frozen, warm the chill;
   Guide the steps that go astray.
On the faithful, who adore
And confess you, evermore
   In your sevenfold gift descend;
Give them virtue's sure reward;
Give them your salvation, Lord;
   Give them joys that never end. Amen.
   Alleluia.

The Solemnity of the Most Holy Body and Blood of Christ, June 6, 2010

OPTIONAL SEQUENCE

Lauda Sion

Laud, O Zion, your salvation,
Laud with hymns of exultation,
   Christ, your king and shepherd true:

Bring him all the praise you know,
He is more than you bestow.
   Never can you reach his due.

Special theme for glad thanksgiving
Is the quick'ning and the living
   Bread today before you set:

From his hands of old partaken,
As we know, by faith unshaken,
   Where the Twelve at supper met.

Full and clear ring out your chanting,
Joy nor sweetest grace be wanting,
   From your heart let praises burst:

For today the feast is holden,
When the institution olden
   Of that supper was rehearsed.

Here the new law's new oblation,
By the new king's revelation,
   Ends the form of ancient rite:

Now the new the old effaces,
Truth away the shadow chases,
   Light dispels the gloom of night.

What he did at supper seated,
Christ ordained to be repeated,
   His memorial ne'er to cease:

And his rule for guidance taking,
Bread and wine we hallow, making
   Thus our sacrifice of peace.

This the truth each Christian learns,
Bread into his flesh he turns,
   To his precious blood the wine:

Sight has fail'd, nor thought conceives,
But a dauntless faith believes,
   Resting on a pow'r divine.

Here beneath these signs are hidden
Priceless things to sense forbidden;
   Signs, not things are all we see:

Blood is poured and flesh is broken,
Yet in either wondrous token
   Christ entire we know to be.

Whoso of this food partakes,
Does not rend the Lord nor breaks;
   Christ is whole to all that taste:

Thousands are, as one, receivers,
One, as thousands of believers,
   Eats of him who cannot waste.

Bad and good the feast are sharing,
Of what divers dooms preparing,
   Endless death, or endless life.

Life to these, to those damnation,
See how like participation
   Is with unlike issues rife.

When the sacrament is broken,
Doubt not, but believe 'tis spoken,

That each sever'd outward token
   doth the very whole contain.

Nought the precious gift divides,
Breaking but the sign betides
Jesus still the same abides,
   still unbroken does remain.

The shorter form of the sequence begins here.

Lo! the angel's food is given
To the pilgrim who has striven;
   See the children's bread from heaven,
   which on dogs may not be spent.

Truth the ancient types fulfilling,
Isaac bound, a victim willing,
   Paschal lamb, its lifeblood spilling,
   manna to the fathers sent.

Very bread, good shepherd, tend us,
Jesu, of your love befriend us,
   You refresh us, you defend us,
   Your eternal goodness send us
In the land of life to see.

You who all things can and know,
Who on earth such food bestow,
   Grant us with your saints, though lowest,
   Where the heav'nly feast you show,
Fellow heirs and guests to be. Amen. Alleluia.

FIRST READING
Ezek 34:11-16

Thus says the Lord GOD:
  I myself will look after and tend my sheep.
As a shepherd tends his flock
  when he finds himself among his scattered
    sheep,
  so will I tend my sheep.
I will rescue them from every place where
    they were scattered
  when it was cloudy and dark.
I will lead them out from among the peoples
  and gather them from the foreign lands;
  I will bring them back to their own country
  and pasture them upon the mountains of
    Israel
  in the land's ravines and all its inhabited
    places.
In good pastures will I pasture them,
  and on the mountain heights of Israel
  shall be their grazing ground.
There they shall lie down on good grazing
    ground,
  and in rich pastures shall they be pastured
  on the mountains of Israel.
I myself will pasture my sheep;
  I myself will give them rest, says the Lord
  GOD.
The lost I will seek out,
  the strayed I will bring back,
  the injured I will bind up,
  the sick I will heal,
  but the sleek and the strong I will destroy,
  shepherding them rightly.

RESPONSORIAL PSALM
Ps 23:1-3a, 3b-4, 5, 6

R̊. (1) The Lord is my shepherd; there is nothing I shall want.

The LORD is my shepherd; I shall not want.
  In verdant pastures he gives me repose;
beside restful waters he leads me;
  he refreshes my soul.

R̊. The Lord is my shepherd; there is nothing
I shall want.

He guides me in right paths
  for his name's sake.
Even though I walk in the dark valley
  I fear no evil; for you are at my side
with your rod and your staff
  that give me courage.

R̊. The Lord is my shepherd; there is nothing
I shall want.

You spread the table before me
  in the sight of my foes;
you anoint my head with oil;
  my cup overflows.

R̊. The Lord is my shepherd; there is nothing
I shall want.

Only goodness and kindness follow me
  all the days of my life;
and I shall dwell in the house of the LORD
  for years to come.

R̊. The Lord is my shepherd; there is nothing
I shall want.

SECOND READING
Rom 5:5b-11

Brothers and sisters:
The love of God has been poured out into our
    hearts
  through the Holy Spirit that has been given
    to us.
For Christ, while we were still helpless,
  died at the appointed time for the ungodly.
Indeed, only with difficulty does one die for a
    just person,
  though perhaps for a good person
  one might even find courage to die.
But God proves his love for us
  in that while we were still sinners Christ
    died for us.
How much more then, since we are now
    justified by his blood,
  will we be saved through him from the
    wrath.
Indeed, if, while we were enemies,
  we were reconciled to God through the
    death of his Son,
  how much more, once reconciled,
  will we be saved by his life.
Not only that,
  but we also boast of God through our Lord
    Jesus Christ,
  through whom we have now received
    reconciliation.

Gospel (cont.)
Luke 7:36–8:3; L93C

Simon said in reply,
  "The one, I suppose, whose larger debt was forgiven."
He said to him, "You have judged rightly."
Then he turned to the woman and said to Simon,
  "Do you see this woman?
When I entered your house, you did not give me water for my feet,
  but she has bathed them with her tears
  and wiped them with her hair.
You did not give me a kiss,
  but she has not ceased kissing my feet since the time I entered.
You did not anoint my head with oil,
  but she anointed my feet with ointment.
So I tell you, her many sins have been forgiven
  because she has shown great love.
But the one to whom little is forgiven, loves little."
He said to her, "Your sins are forgiven."
The others at table said to themselves,
  "Who is this who even forgives sins?"
But he said to the woman,
  "Your faith has saved you; go in peace."

Afterward he journeyed from one town and village to another,
  preaching and proclaiming the good news of the kingdom of God.
Accompanying him were the Twelve
  and some women who had been cured of evil spirits and infirmities,
  Mary, called Magdalene, from whom seven demons had gone out,
  Joanna, the wife of Herod's steward Chuza,
  Susanna, and many others who provided for them out of their
    resources.

or Luke 7:36-50

A Pharisee invited Jesus to dine with him,
  and he entered the Pharisee's house and reclined at table.
Now there was a sinful woman in the city
  who learned that he was at table in the house of the Pharisee.

Bringing an alabaster flask of ointment,
  she stood behind him at his feet weeping
  and began to bathe his feet with her tears.
Then she wiped them with her hair,
  kissed them, and anointed them with the ointment.
When the Pharisee who had invited him saw this he said to himself,
  "If this man were a prophet,
  he would know who and what sort of woman this is who is touching
    him,
  that she is a sinner."
Jesus said to him in reply,
  "Simon, I have something to say to you."
"Tell me, teacher," he said.
"Two people were in debt to a certain creditor;
  one owed five hundred day's wages and the other owed fifty.
Since they were unable to repay the debt, he forgave it for both.
Which of them will love him more?"
Simon said in reply,
  "The one, I suppose, whose larger debt was forgiven."
He said to him, "You have judged rightly."
Then he turned to the woman and said to Simon,
  "Do you see this woman?
When I entered your house, you did not give me water for my feet,
  but she has bathed them with her tears
  and wiped them with her hair.
You did not give me a kiss,
  but she has not ceased kissing my feet since the time I entered.
You did not anoint my head with oil,
  but she anointed my feet with ointment.
So I tell you, her many sins have been forgiven
  because she has shown great love.
But the one to whom little is forgiven, loves little."
He said to her, "Your sins are forgiven."
The others at table said to themselves,
  "Who is this who even forgives sins?"
But he said to the woman,
  "Your faith has saved you; go in peace."

The Nativity of St. John the Baptist, June 24, 2010

FIRST READING
Isa 49:1-6

Hear me, O coastlands,
  listen, O distant peoples.
The LORD called me from birth,
  from my mother's womb he gave me my
    name.
He made of me a sharp-edged sword
  and concealed me in the shadow of his arm.
He made me a polished arrow,
  in his quiver he hid me.
You are my servant, he said to me,
  Israel, through whom I show my glory.

Though I thought I had toiled in vain,
  and for nothing, uselessly, spent my strength,

yet my reward is with the LORD,
  my recompense is with my God.
For now the LORD has spoken
  who formed me as his servant from the
    womb,
that Jacob may be brought back to him
  and Israel gathered to him;
and I am made glorious in the sight of the LORD,
  and my God is now my strength!
It is too little, he says, for you to be my servant,
  to raise up the tribes of Jacob,
  and restore the survivors of Israel;
I will make you a light to the nations,
  that my salvation may reach to the ends of
    the earth.

The Nativity of St. John the Baptist, June 24, 2010

RESPONSORIAL PSALM
Ps 139:1b-3, 13-14ab, 14c-15

R̸. (14a) I praise you, for I am wonderfully made.

O LORD, you have probed me, you know me;
  you know when I sit and when I stand;
  you understand my thoughts from afar.
My journeys and my rest you scrutinize,
  with all my ways you are familiar.

R̸. I praise you, for I am wonderfully made.

Truly you have formed my inmost being;
  you knit me in my mother's womb.
I give you thanks that I am fearfully,
    wonderfully made;
  wonderful are your works.

R̸. I praise you, for I am wonderfully made.

My soul also you knew full well;
  nor was my frame unknown to you
When I was made in secret,
  when I was fashioned in the depths of the
    earth.

R̸. I praise you, for I am wonderfully made.

SECOND READING
Acts 13:22-26

In those days, Paul said:
  "God raised up David as their king;
  of him God testified,
  'I have found David, son of Jesse, a man after
    my own heart;
  he will carry out my every wish.'
From this man's descendants God, according to
  his promise,
has brought to Israel a savior, Jesus.
John heralded his coming by proclaiming a
    baptism of repentance
  to all the people of Israel;
  and as John was completing his course, he
    would say,
  'What do you suppose that I am? I am not he.
Behold, one is coming after me;
  I am not worthy to unfasten the sandals of
    his feet.'
"My brothers, sons of the family of Abraham,
  and those others among you who are God-
    fearing,
  to us this word of salvation has been sent."

SS. Peter and Paul, Apostles, June 29, 2010

FIRST READING
Acts 12:1-11

In those days, King Herod laid hands upon
    some members of the church to harm
    them.
He had James, the brother of John, killed by
    the sword,
  and when he saw that this was pleasing to
    the Jews
  he proceeded to arrest Peter also.
—It was the feast of Unleavened Bread.—
He had him taken into custody and put in
    prison
  under the guard of four squads of four
    soldiers each.
He intended to bring him before the people
    after Passover.
Peter thus was being kept in prison,
  but prayer by the church was fervently
    being made
  to God on his behalf.

On the very night before Herod was to bring
    him to trial,
  Peter, secured by double chains,
  was sleeping between two soldiers,
  while outside the door guards kept watch
    on the prison.
Suddenly the angel of the Lord stood by him
  and a light shone in the cell.
He tapped Peter on the side and awakened
    him, saying,
  "Get up quickly."
The chains fell from his wrists.

The angel said to him, "Put on your belt and
    your sandals."
He did so.
Then he said to him, "Put on your cloak and
    follow me."
So he followed him out,
  not realizing that what was happening
    through the angel was real;
  he thought he was seeing a vision.
They passed the first guard, then the second,
  and came to the iron gate leading out to
    the city,
  which opened for them by itself.
They emerged and made their way down an
    alley,
  and suddenly the angel left him.
Then Peter recovered his senses and said,
  "Now I know for certain
    that the Lord sent his angel
  and rescued me from the hand of Herod
  and from all that the Jewish people had
    been expecting."

RESPONSORIAL PSALM
Ps 34:2-3, 4-5, 6-7, 8-9

R̸. (8) The angel of the Lord will rescue those
who fear him.

I will bless the LORD at all times;
  his praise shall be ever in my mouth.
Let my soul glory in the LORD;
  the lowly will hear me and be glad.

R̸. The angel of the Lord will rescue those
who fear him.

Glorify the LORD with me,
  let us together extol his name.
I sought the LORD, and he answered me
  and delivered me from all my fears.

R̸. The angel of the Lord will rescue those
who fear him.

Look to him that you may be radiant with joy,
  and your faces may not blush with shame.
When the poor one called out, the LORD heard,
  and from all his distress he saved him.

R̸. The angel of the Lord will rescue those
who fear him.

The angel of the LORD encamps
  around those who fear him, and delivers
    them.
Taste and see how good the LORD is;
  blessed the man who takes refuge in him.

R̸. The angel of the Lord will rescue those
who fear him.

SS. Peter and Paul, Apostles, *June 29, 2010*

SECOND READING
2 Tim 4:6-8, 17-18

I, Paul, am already being poured out like a libation,
  and the time of my departure is at hand.
I have competed well; I have finished the race;
  I have kept the faith.
From now on the crown of righteousness awaits me,
  which the Lord, the just judge,
  will award to me on that day, and not only to me,
  but to all who have longed for his appearance.

The Lord stood by me and gave me strength,
  so that through me the proclamation might be completed
  and all the Gentiles might hear it.
And I was rescued from the lion's mouth.
The Lord will rescue me from every evil threat
  and will bring me safe to his heavenly kingdom.
To him be glory forever and ever. Amen.

Fourteenth Sunday in Ordinary Time, *July 4, 2010*

Gospel (cont.)
Luke 10:1-12, 17-20; L102C

Yet know this: the kingdom of God is at hand.
I tell you,
  it will be more tolerable for Sodom on that day than for that town."

The seventy-two returned rejoicing, and said,
  "Lord, even the demons are subject to us because of your name."
Jesus said, "I have observed Satan fall like lightning from the sky.
Behold, I have given you the power to 'tread upon serpents' and
    scorpions
  and upon the full force of the enemy and nothing will harm you.
Nevertheless, do not rejoice because the spirits are subject to you,
  but rejoice because your names are written in heaven."

or Luke 10:1-9; L102C

At that time the Lord appointed seventy-two others
  whom he sent ahead of him in pairs
  to every town and place he intended to visit.

He said to them,
  "The harvest is abundant but the laborers are few;
  so ask the master of the harvest
  to send out laborers for his harvest.
Go on your way;
  behold, I am sending you like lambs among wolves.
Carry no money bag, no sack, no sandals;
  and greet no one along the way.
Into whatever house you enter, first say,
  'Peace to this household.'
If a peaceful person lives there,
  your peace will rest on him;
  but if not, it will return to you.
Stay in the same house and eat and drink what is offered to you,
  for the laborer deserves his payment.
Do not move about from one house to another.
Whatever town you enter and they welcome you,
  eat what is set before you,
  cure the sick in it and say to them,
  'The kingdom of God is at hand for you.'"

Fifteenth Sunday in Ordinary Time, *July 11, 2010*

Gospel (cont.)
Luke 10:25-37; L105C

But a Samaritan traveler who came upon him
  was moved with compassion at the sight.
He approached the victim,
  poured oil and wine over his wounds and
      bandaged them.
  Then he lifted him up on his own animal,
  took him to an inn, and cared for him.
The next day he took out two silver coins
  and gave them to the innkeeper with the
      instruction,
  'Take care of him.
If you spend more than what I have given you,
  I shall repay you on my way back.'
Which of these three, in your opinion,
  was neighbor to the robbers' victim?"

He answered, "The one who treated him with
    mercy."
Jesus said to him, "Go and do likewise."

RESPONSORIAL PSALM
Ps 19:8, 9, 10, 11

℟. (9a) Your words, Lord, are Spirit and life.

The law of the LORD is perfect,
  refreshing the soul;
the decree of the LORD is trustworthy,
  giving wisdom to the simple.

℟. Your words, Lord, are Spirit and life.

The precepts of the LORD are right,
  rejoicing the heart;
the command of the LORD is clear,
  enlightening the eye.

℟. Your words, Lord, are Spirit and life.

The fear of the LORD is pure,
  enduring forever;
the ordinances of the LORD are true,
  all of them just.

℟. Your words, Lord, are Spirit and life.

They are more precious than gold,
  than a heap of purest gold;
sweeter also than syrup
  or honey from the comb.

℟. Your words, Lord, are Spirit and life.

Seventeenth Sunday in Ordinary Time, July 25, 2010

Gospel (cont.)
Luke 11:1-13; L111C

"And I tell you, ask and you will receive;
    seek and you will find;
    knock and the door will be opened to you.
For everyone who asks, receives;
    and the one who seeks, finds;
    and to the one who knocks, the door will be opened.
What father among you would hand his son a snake
    when he asks for a fish?
Or hand him a scorpion when he asks for an egg?
If you then, who are wicked,
    know how to give good gifts to your children,
    how much more will the Father in heaven
    give the Holy Spirit to those who ask him?"

SECOND READING
Col 2:12-14

Brothers and sisters:
You were buried with him in baptism,
    in which you were also raised with him
    through faith in the power of God,
    who raised him from the dead.
And even when you were dead
    in transgressions and the uncircumcision of your flesh,
    he brought you to life along with him,
    having forgiven us all our transgressions;
obliterating the bond against us, with its legal claims,
    which was opposed to us,
    he also removed it from our midst, nailing it to the cross.

Nineteenth Sunday in Ordinary Time, August 8, 2010

Gospel (cont.)
Luke 12:32-48; L117C

You also must be prepared, for at an hour you do not expect,
    the Son of Man will come."

Then Peter said,
    "Lord, is this parable meant for us or for everyone?"
And the Lord replied,
    "Who, then, is the faithful and prudent steward
    whom the master will put in charge of his servants
    to distribute the food allowance at the proper time?
Blessed is that servant whom his master on arrival finds doing so.
Truly, I say to you, the master will put the servant
    in charge of all his property.
But if that servant says to himself,
    'My master is delayed in coming,'
    and begins to beat the menservants and the maidservants,
    to eat and drink and get drunk,
    then that servant's master will come
    on an unexpected day and at an unknown hour
    and will punish the servant severely
    and assign him a place with the unfaithful.
That servant who knew his master's will
    but did not make preparations nor act in accord with his will
    shall be beaten severely;
    and the servant who was ignorant of his master's will
    but acted in a way deserving of a severe beating
    shall be beaten only lightly.
Much will be required of the person entrusted with much,
    and still more will be demanded of the person entrusted with more."

or Luke 12:35-40

Jesus said to his disciples:
"Gird your loins and light your lamps
    and be like servants who await their master's return from a
        wedding,
    ready to open immediately when he comes and knocks.
Blessed are those servants
    whom the master finds vigilant on his arrival.
Amen, I say to you, he will gird himself,
    have them recline at table, and proceed to wait on them.
And should he come in the second or third watch
    and find them prepared in this way,
    blessed are those servants.
Be sure of this:
    if the master of the house had known the hour
    when the thief was coming,
    he would not have let his house be broken into.
You also must be prepared, for at an hour you do not expect,
    the Son of Man will come."

SECOND READING

Heb 11:1-2, 8-19 *(cont.)*

So it was that there came forth from one man,
    himself as good as dead,
    descendants as numerous as the stars in
        the sky
    and as countless as the sands on the
        seashore.

All these died in faith.
They did not receive what had been promised
    but saw it and greeted it from afar
    and acknowledged themselves to be
        strangers and aliens on earth,
    for those who speak thus show that they
        are seeking a homeland.
If they had been thinking of the land from
    which they had come,
    they would have had opportunity to return.
But now they desire a better homeland, a
    heavenly one.
Therefore, God is not ashamed to be called
    their God,
    for he has prepared a city for them.

By faith Abraham, when put to the test,
    offered up Isaac,
    and he who had received the promises was
        ready to offer his only son,
    of whom it was said,
    "Through Isaac descendants shall bear
        your name."
He reasoned that God was able to raise even
    from the dead,
    and he received Isaac back as a symbol.

or Heb 11:1-2, 8-12

Brothers and sisters:
Faith is the realization of what is hoped for
    and evidence of things not seen.
Because of it the ancients were well attested.

By faith Abraham obeyed when he was called
    to go out to a place
    that he was to receive as an inheritance;
    he went out, not knowing where he was to
        go.
By faith he sojourned in the promised land as
    in a foreign country,

dwelling in tents with Isaac and Jacob,
    heirs of the same promise;
    for he was looking forward to the city with
        foundations,
    whose architect and maker is God.
By faith he received power to generate,
    even though he was past the normal age
    —and Sarah herself was sterile—
    for he thought that the one who had made
        the promise was trustworthy.
So it was that there came forth from one man,
    himself as good as dead,
    descendants as numerous as the stars in
        the sky
    and as countless as the sands on the
        seashore.

Gospel (cont.)

Luke 1:39-56; L622

He has cast down the mighty from their thrones,
    and has lifted up the lowly.
He has filled the hungry with good things,
    and the rich he has sent away empty.
He has come to the help of his servant Israel
    for he has remembered his promise of mercy,
    the promise he made to our fathers,
    to Abraham and his children forever."

Mary remained with her about three months
    and then returned to her home.

Gospel (cont.)

Luke 14:1, 7-14; L126C

Then he said to the host who invited him,
    "When you hold a lunch or a dinner,
    do not invite your friends or your brothers
    or your relatives or your wealthy neighbors,
    in case they may invite you back and you have repayment.
Rather, when you hold a banquet,
    invite the poor, the crippled, the lame, the blind;
    blessed indeed will you be because of their inability to repay you.
For you will be repaid at the resurrection of the righteous."

Gospel (cont.)
Luke 15:1-32; L132C

And when she does find it,
she calls together her friends and neighbors
and says to them,
'Rejoice with me because I have found the coin that I lost.'
In just the same way, I tell you,
there will be rejoicing among the angels of God
over one sinner who repents."

Then he said,
"A man had two sons, and the younger son said to his father,
'Father give me the share of your estate that should come to me.'
So the father divided the property between them.
After a few days, the younger son collected all his belongings
and set off to a distant country
where he squandered his inheritance on a life of dissipation.
When he had freely spent everything,
a severe famine struck that country,
and he found himself in dire need.
So he hired himself out to one of the local citizens
who sent him to his farm to tend the swine.
And he longed to eat his fill of the pods on which the swine fed,
but nobody gave him any.
Coming to his senses he thought,
'How many of my father's hired workers
have more than enough food to eat,
but here am I, dying from hunger.
I shall get up and go to my father and I shall say to him,
"Father, I have sinned against heaven and against you.
I no longer deserve to be called your son;
treat me as you would treat one of your hired workers."'
So he got up and went back to his father.
While he was still a long way off,
his father caught sight of him,
and was filled with compassion.
He ran to his son, embraced him and kissed him.
His son said to him,
'Father, I have sinned against heaven and against you;
I no longer deserve to be called your son.'
But his father ordered his servants,
'Quickly bring the finest robe and put it on him;
put a ring on his finger and sandals on his feet.
Take the fattened calf and slaughter it.
Then let us celebrate with a feast,
because this son of mine was dead, and has come to life again;
he was lost, and has been found.'
Then the celebration began.
Now the older son had been out in the field
and, on his way back, as he neared the house,
he heard the sound of music and dancing.
He called one of the servants and asked what this might mean.

The servant said to him,
'Your brother has returned
and your father has slaughtered the fattened calf
because he has him back safe and sound.'
He became angry,
and when he refused to enter the house,
his father came out and pleaded with him.
He said to his father in reply,
'Look, all these years I served you
and not once did I disobey your orders;
yet you never gave me even a young goat to feast on with my
friends. But when your son returns,
who swallowed up your property with prostitutes,
for him you slaughter the fattened calf.'
He said to him,
'My son, you are here with me always;
everything I have is yours.
But now we must celebrate and rejoice,
because your brother was dead and has come to life again;
he was lost and has been found.'"

or Luke 15:1-10

Tax collectors and sinners were all drawing near to listen to Jesus,
but the Pharisees and scribes began to complain, saying,
"This man welcomes sinners and eats with them."
So to them he addressed this parable.
"What man among you having a hundred sheep and losing one of them
would not leave the ninety-nine in the desert
and go after the lost one until he finds it?
And when he does find it,
he sets it on his shoulders with great joy
and, upon his arrival home,
he calls together his friends and neighbors and says to them,
'Rejoice with me because I have found my lost sheep.'
I tell you, in just the same way
there will be more joy in heaven over one sinner who repents
than over ninety-nine righteous people
who have no need of repentance.

"Or what woman having ten coins and losing one
would not light a lamp and sweep the house,
searching carefully until she finds it?
And when she does find it,
she calls together her friends and neighbors
and says to them,
'Rejoice with me because I have found the coin that I lost.'
In just the same way, I tell you,
there will be rejoicing among the angels of God
over one sinner who repents."

Twenty-Fifth Sunday in Ordinary Time, *September 19, 2010*

Gospel (cont.)
Luke 16:1-13; L135C

The steward said to him, 'Here is your promissory note;
write one for eighty.'
And the master commended that dishonest steward for acting
      prudently.

"For the children of this world
      are more prudent in dealing with their own generation
      than are the children of light.
I tell you, make friends for yourselves with dishonest wealth,
      so that when it fails, you will be welcomed into eternal dwellings.
The person who is trustworthy in very small matters
      is also trustworthy in great ones;
      and the person who is dishonest in very small matters
      is also dishonest in great ones.
If, therefore, you are not trustworthy with dishonest wealth,
      who will trust you with true wealth?
If you are not trustworthy with what belongs to another,
      who will give you what is yours?
No servant can serve two masters.
He will either hate one and love the other,
      or be devoted to one and despise the other.
You cannot serve both God and mammon."

or Luke 16:10-13

Jesus said to his disciples,
      "The person who is trustworthy in very small matters
      is also trustworthy in great ones;
      and the person who is dishonest in very small matters
      is also dishonest in great ones.
If, therefore, you are not trustworthy with dishonest wealth,
      who will trust you with true wealth?
If you are not trustworthy with what belongs to another,
      who will give you what is yours?
No servant can serve two masters.
He will either hate one and love the other,
      or be devoted to one and despise the other.
You cannot serve both God and mammon."

Twenty-Sixth Sunday in Ordinary Time, *September 26, 2010*

Gospel (cont.)
Luke 16:19-31; L138C

Moreover, between us and you a great chasm is established
      to prevent anyone from crossing who might wish to go
      from our side to yours or from your side to ours.'
He said, 'Then I beg you, father,
      send him to my father's house, for I have five brothers,
      so that he may warn them,
      lest they too come to this place of torment.'
But Abraham replied, 'They have Moses and the prophets.
Let them listen to them.'
He said, 'Oh no, father Abraham,
      but if someone from the dead goes to them, they will repent.'
Then Abraham said, 'If they will not listen to Moses and the prophets,
      neither will they be persuaded if someone should rise from the dead.'"

FIRST READING

Rev 7:2-4, 9-14

I, John, saw another angel come up from the
East,
holding the seal of the living God.
He cried out in a loud voice to the four angels
who were given power to damage the land
and the sea,
"Do not damage the land or the sea or the
trees
until we put the seal on the foreheads of the
servants of our God."
I heard the number of those who had been
marked with the seal,
one hundred and forty-four thousand
marked
from every tribe of the children of Israel.

After this I had a vision of a great multitude,
which no one could count,
from every nation, race, people, and tongue.
They stood before the throne and before the
Lamb,
wearing white robes and holding palm
branches in their hands.
They cried out in a loud voice:

"Salvation comes from our God,
who is seated on the throne,
and from the Lamb."
All the angels stood around the throne
and around the elders and the four living
creatures.
They prostrated themselves before the throne,
worshiped God, and exclaimed:

"Amen. Blessing and glory, wisdom and
thanksgiving,
honor, power, and might
be to our God forever and ever. Amen."

Then one of the elders spoke up and said to
me,
"Who are these wearing white robes, and
where did they come from?"
I said to him, "My lord, you are the one who
knows."
He said to me,
"These are the ones who have survived the
time of great distress;
they have washed their robes
and made them white in the Blood of the
Lamb."

RESPONSORIAL PSALM

Ps 24:1-2, 3-4, 5-6

℟. (cf. 6) Lord, this is the people that longs to
see your face.

The LORD's are the earth and its fullness;
the world and those who dwell in it.
For he founded it upon the seas
and established it upon the rivers.

℟. Lord, this is the people that longs to see
your face.

Who can ascend the mountain of the LORD?
or who may stand in his holy place?
One whose hands are sinless, whose heart is
clean,
who desires not what is vain.

℟. Lord, this is the people that longs to see
your face.

He shall receive a blessing from the LORD,
a reward from God his savior.
Such is the race that seeks for him,
that seeks the face of the God of Jacob.

℟. Lord, this is the people that longs to see
your face.

SECOND READING

1 John 3:1-3

Beloved:
See what love the Father has bestowed on us
that we may be called the children of God.
Yet so we are.
The reason the world does not know us
is that it did not know him.
Beloved, we are God's children now;
what we shall be has not yet been revealed.
We do know that when it is revealed we shall
be like him,
for we shall see him as he is.
Everyone who has this hope based on him
makes himself pure,
as he is pure.

All Souls, *November 2, 2010*

(Other options can be found in the Lectionary for Mass, L668.)

FIRST READING
Wis 3:1-9

The souls of the just are in the hand of God,
    and no torment shall touch them.
They seemed, in the view of the foolish, to be
    dead;
    and their passing away was thought an
        affliction
    and their going forth from us, utter
        destruction.
But they are in peace.
For if before men, indeed they be punished,
    yet is their hope full of immortality;
chastised a little, they shall be greatly blessed,
    because God tried them
    and found them worthy of himself.
As gold in the furnace, he proved them,
    and as sacrificial offerings he took them to
        himself.
In the time of their visitation they shall shine,
    and shall dart about as sparks through
        stubble;
they shall judge nations and rule over peoples,
    and the LORD shall be their King forever.
Those who trust in him shall understand
    truth,
    and the faithful shall abide with him in
        love:
because grace and mercy are with his holy
    ones,
    and his care is with his elect.

RESPONSORIAL PSALM
Ps 23:1-3a, 3b-4, 5, 6

R̝. (1) The Lord is my shepherd; there is
nothing I shall want.
    or:
R̝. (4ab) Though I walk in the valley of
darkness, I fear no evil, for you are with me.

The LORD is my shepherd; I shall not want.
    In verdant pastures he gives me repose;
beside restful waters he leads me;
    he refreshes my soul.

R̝. The Lord is my shepherd; there is nothing
I shall want.
    or:
R̝. Though I walk in the valley of darkness, I
fear no evil, for you are with me.

He guides me in right paths
    for his name's sake.
Even though I walk in the dark valley
    I fear no evil; for you are at my side
with your rod and your staff
    that give me courage.

R̝. The Lord is my shepherd; there is nothing
I shall want.
    or:
R̝. Though I walk in the valley of darkness, I
fear no evil, for you are with me.

You spread the table before me
    in the sight of my foes;
you anoint my head with oil;
    my cup overflows.

R̝. The Lord is my shepherd; there is nothing
I shall want.
    or:
R̝. Though I walk in the valley of darkness, I
fear no evil, for you are with me.

Only goodness and kindness follow me
    all the days of my life;
and I shall dwell in the house of the LORD
    for years to come.

R̝. The Lord is my shepherd; there is nothing
I shall want.
    or:
R̝. Though I walk in the valley of darkness, I
fear no evil, for you are with me.

SECOND READING
Rom 6:3-9; L1014.3

Brothers and sisters:
Are you unaware that we who were baptized
    into Christ Jesus
    were baptized into his death?
We were indeed buried with him through
    baptism into death,
    so that, just as Christ was raised from the
        dead
    by the glory of the Father,
    we too might live in newness of life.

For if we have grown into union with him
    through a death like his,
    we shall also be united with him in the
        resurrection.
We know that our old self was crucified with
    him,
    so that our sinful body might be done away
        with,
    that we might no longer be in slavery to sin.
For a dead person has been absolved from sin.
If, then, we have died with Christ,
    we believe that we shall also live with him.
We know that Christ, raised from the dead,
    dies no more;
    death no longer has power over him.

Thirty-Second Sunday in Ordinary Time,
November 7, 2010

Gospel
Luke 20:27, 34-38; L156C

Some Sadducees, those who deny that there is a resurrection,
    came forward.

Jesus said to them,
    "The children of this age marry and remarry;
    but those who are deemed worthy to attain to the coming age
    and to the resurrection of the dead
    neither marry nor are given in marriage.
They can no longer die,
    for they are like angels;
    and they are the children of God
    because they are the ones who will rise.
That the dead will rise
    even Moses made known in the passage about the bush,
    when he called out 'Lord,'
    the God of Abraham, the God of Isaac, and the God of Jacob;
    and he is not God of the dead, but of the living,
    for to him all are alive."

Thirty-Third Sunday in Ordinary Time,
November 14, 2010

Gospel (cont.)
Luke 21:5-19; L159C

"Before all this happens, however,
    they will seize and persecute you,
    they will hand you over to the synagogues and to prisons,
    and they will have you led before kings and governors
    because of my name.
It will lead to your giving testimony.
Remember, you are not to prepare your defense beforehand,
    for I myself shall give you a wisdom in speaking
    that all your adversaries will be powerless to resist or refute.
You will even be handed over by parents, brothers, relatives, and
        friends,
    and they will put some of you to death.
You will be hated by all because of my name,
    but not a hair on your head will be destroyed.
By your perseverance you will secure your lives."

Thanksgiving Day, November 25, 2010
(Other options can be found in the Lectionary for Mass, L943–947.)

FIRST READING
Sir 50:22-24; L943.2

And now, bless the God of all,
    who has done wondrous things on earth;
Who fosters people's growth from their
        mother's womb,
    and fashions them according to his will!
May he grant you joy of heart
    and may peace abide among you;
May his goodness toward us endure in Israel
    to deliver us in our days.

RESPONSORIAL PSALM
Psalm 138:1-2a, 2bc-3, 4-5; L945.3

R̞. (2bc) Lord, I thank you for your
faithfulness and love.

I will give thanks to you, O Lᴏʀᴅ, with all of
        my heart,
    for you have heard the words of my mouth;
    in the presence of the angels I will sing
        your praise;
I will worship at your holy temple.

R̞. Lord, I thank you for your faithfulness and
love.

I will give thanks to your name,
Because of your kindness and your truth.
When I called, you answered me;
    you built up strength within me.

R̞. Lord, I thank you for your faithfulness and
love.

All the kings of the earth shall give thanks to
        you, O Lᴏʀᴅ,
    when they hear the words of your mouth;
And they shall sing of the ways of the Lᴏʀᴅ:
    "Great is the glory of the Lᴏʀᴅ."

R̞. Lord, I thank you for your faithfulness and
love.

SECOND READING
1 Cor 1:3-9; L944.1

Brothers and sisters:
Grace to you and peace from God our Father
    and the Lord Jesus Christ.

I give thanks to my God always on your
        account
    for the grace of God bestowed on you in
        Christ Jesus,
    that in him you were enriched in every
        way,
    with all discourse and all knowledge,
    as the testimony to Christ was confirmed
        among you,
    so that you are not lacking in any spiritual
        gift
    as you wait for the revelation of our Lord
        Jesus Christ.
He will keep you firm to the end,
    irreproachable on the day of our Lord Jesus
        Christ.
God is faithful,
    and by him you were called to fellowship
        with his Son, Jesus Christ our Lord.

Choral Settings for the Prayer of the Faithful

Purchasers of this volume may reproduce these choral arrangements for use in their parish or community. The music must be reproduced as given below, with composer's name and copyright line.

ADVENT

we pray to the Lord,

Lord, hear our prayer.

Lord, hear our prayer.

Lord, hear our prayer.

Music: Kathleen Harmon, SNDdeN, ©1999, Institute for Liturgical Ministry, 4960 Salem Avenue, Dayton OH 45416. All rights reserved.

CHRISTMAS and EASTER

we pray to the Lord,

Lord, hear our prayer.

Lord, hear our prayer.

Music: Kathleen Harmon, SNDdeN, ©1999, Institute for Liturgical Ministry, 4960 Salem Avenue, Dayton OH 45416. All rights reserved.

LENT

we pray to the Lord,

Lord, hear our prayer.

Music: Kathleen Harmon, SNDdeN, ©1999, Institute for Liturgical Ministry, 4960 Salem Avenue, Dayton OH 45416. All rights reserved.

SOLEMNITIES

we pray to the Lord,

Lord, hear our prayer.

Lord, hear our prayer.

Music: Kathleen Harmon, SNDdeN, ©1999, Institute for Liturgical Ministry, 4960 Salem Avenue, Dayton OH 45416. All rights reserved.

ORDINARY TIME, WEEKS 2-6

Cantor:

we pray to the Lord,

SATB Response:

Descant

Lord, _____ hear our prayer.

Lord, _____ hear our prayer.

ORDINARY TIME, WEEKS 11-19

Cantor:

we pray to the Lord,

SATB Response:

Lord, hear _____ our prayer.

ORDINARY TIME, WEEKS 21-33

Cantor:

we pray _____ to the Lord,

SATB Response:

Lord, hear our prayer.

Lectionary Pronunciation Guide

Lectionary Word	Pronunciation
Aaron	EHR-uhn
Abana	AB-uh-nuh
Abednego	uh-BEHD-nee-go
Abel-Keramin	AY-b'l-KEHR-uh-mihn
Abel-meholah	AY-b'l-mee-HO-lah
Abiathar	uh-BAI-uh-ther
Abiel	AY-bee-ehl
Abiezrite	ay-bai-EHZ-rait
Abijah	uh-BAI-dzhuh
Abilene	ab-uh-LEE-neh
Abishai	uh-BIHSH-ay-ai
Abiud	uh-BAI-uhd
Abner	AHB-ner
Abraham	AY-bruh-ham
Abram	AY-br'm
Achaia	uh-KAY-yuh
Achim	AY-kihm
Aeneas	uh-NEE-uhs
Aenon	AY-nuhn
Agrippa	uh-GRIH-puh
Ahaz	AY-haz
Ahijah	uh-HAI-dzhuh
Ai	AY-ee
Alexandria	al-ehg-ZAN-dree-uh
Alexandrian	al-ehg-ZAN-dree-uhn
Alpha	AHL-fuh
Alphaeus	AL-fee-uhs
Amalek	AM-uh-lehk
Amaziah	am-uh-ZAI-uh
Amminadab	ah-MIHN-uh-dab
Ammonites	AM-uh-naitz
Amorites	AM-uh-raits
Amos	AY-muhs
Amoz	AY-muhz
Ampliatus	am-plee-AY-tuhs
Ananias	an-uh-NAI-uhs
Andronicus	an-draw-NAI-kuhs
Annas	AN-uhs
Antioch	AN-tih-ahk
Antiochus	an-TAI-uh-kuhs
Aphiah	uh-FAI-uh
Apollos	uh-PAH-luhs
Appius	AP-ee-uhs
Aquila	uh-KWIHL-uh
Arabah	EHR-uh-buh
Aram	AY-ram
Arameans	ehr-uh-MEE-uhnz
Areopagus	ehr-ee-AH-puh-guhs
Arimathea	ehr-uh-muh-THEE-uh
Aroer	uh-RO-er

Lectionary Word	Pronunciation
Asaph	AY-saf
Asher	ASH-er
Ashpenaz	ASH-pee-naz
Assyria	a-SIHR-ee-uh
Astarte	as-TAHR-tee
Attalia	at-TAH-lee-uh
Augustus	uh-GUHS-tuhs
Azariah	az-uh-RAI-uh
Azor	AY-sawr
Azotus	uh-ZO-tus
Baal-shalishah	BAY-uhl-shuh-LAI-shuh
Baal-Zephon	BAY-uhl-ZEE-fuhn
Babel	BAY-bl
Babylon	BAB-ih-luhn
Babylonian	bab-ih-LO-nih-uhn
Balaam	BAY-lm
Barabbas	beh-REH-buhs
Barak	BEHR-ak
Barnabas	BAHR-nuh-buhs
Barsabbas	BAHR-suh-buhs
Bartholomew	bar-THAHL-uh-myoo
Bartimaeus	bar-tih-MEE-uhs
Baruch	BEHR-ook
Bashan	BAY-shan
Becorath	bee-KO-rath
Beelzebul	bee-EHL-zee-buhl
Beer-sheba	BEE-er-SHEE-buh
Belshazzar	behl-SHAZ-er
Benjamin	BEHN-dzhuh-mihn
Beor	BEE-awr
Bethany	BEHTH-uh-nee
Bethel	BETH-el
Bethesda	beh-THEHZ-duh
Bethlehem	BEHTH-leh-hehm
Bethphage	BEHTH-fuh-dzhee
Bethsaida	behth-SAY-ih-duh
Beth-zur	behth-ZER
Bildad	BIHL-dad
Bithynia	bih-THIHN-ih-uh
Boanerges	bo-uh-NER-dzheez
Boaz	BO-az
Caesar	SEE-zer
Caesarea	zeh-suh-REE-uh
Caiaphas	KAY-uh-fuhs
Cain	kayn
Cana	KAY-nuh
Canaan	KAY-nuhn
Canaanite	KAY-nuh-nait
Canaanites	KAY-nuh-naits

Lectionary Word	Pronunciation
Candace	kan-DAY-see
Capernaum	kuh-PERR-nay-uhm
Cappadocia	kap-ih-DO-shee-u
Carmel	KAHR-muhl
carnelians	kahr-NEEL-yuhnz
Cenchreae	SEHN-kree-ay
Cephas	SEE-fuhs
Chaldeans	kal-DEE-uhnz
Chemosh	KEE-mahsh
Cherubim	TSHEHR-oo-bihm
Chislev	KIHS-lehv
Chloe	KLO-ee
Chorazin	kor-AY-sihn
Cilicia	sih-LIHSH-ee-uh
Cleopas	KLEE-o-pas
Clopas	KLO-pas
Corinth	KAWR-ihnth
Corinthians	kawr-IHN-thee-uhnz
Cornelius	kawr-NEE-lee-uhs
Crete	kreet
Crispus	KRIHS-puhs
Cushite	CUHSH-ait
Cypriot	SIH-pree-at
Cyrene	sai-REE-nee
Cyreneans	sai-REE-nih-uhnz
Cyrenian	sai-REE-nih-uhn
Cyrenians	sai-REE-nih-uhnz
Cyrus	SAI-ruhs
Damaris	DAM-uh-rihs
Damascus	duh-MAS-kuhs
Danites	DAN-aits
Decapolis	duh-KAP-o-lis
Derbe	DER-bee
Deuteronomy	dyoo-ter-AH-num-mee
Didymus	DID-I-mus
Dionysius	dai-o-NIHSH-ih-uhs
Dioscuri	dai-O-sky-ri
Dorcas	DAWR-kuhs
Dothan	DO-thuhn
dromedaries	DRAH-muh-dher-eez
Ebed-melech	EE-behd-MEE-lehk
Eden	EE-dn
Edom	EE-duhm
Elamites	EE-luh-maitz
Eldad	EHL-dad
Eleazar	ehl-ee-AY-zer
Eli	EE-lai
Eli Eli Lema MAH	AY-lee AY-lee luh-
Sabachthani	sah-BAHK-tah-nee

Lectionary Word	Pronunciation	Lectionary Word	Pronunciation	Lectionary Word	Pronunciation
Eliab	ee-LAI-ab	Gilead	GIHL-ee-uhd	Joppa	DZHAH-puh
Eliakim	ee-LAI-uh-kihm	Gilgal	GIHL-gal	Joram	DZHO-ram
Eliezer	ehl-ih-EE-zer	Golgotha	GAHL-guh-thuh	Jordan	DZHAWR-dn
Elihu	ee-LAI-hyoo	Gomorrah	guh-MAWR-uh	Joseph	DZHO-zf
Elijah	ee-LAI-dzhuh	Goshen	GO-shuhn	Joses	DZHO-seez
Elim	EE-lihm	Habakkuk	huh-BAK-uhk	Joshua	DZHAH-shou-ah
Elimelech	ee-LIHM-eh-lehk	Hadadrimmon	hay-dad-RIHM-uhn	Josiah	dzho-SAI-uh
Elisha	ee-LAI-shuh	Hades	HAY-deez	Jotham	DZHO-thuhm
Eliud	ee-LAI-uhd	Hagar	HAH-gar	Judah	DZHOU-duh
Elizabeth	ee-LIHZ-uh-bth	Hananiah	han-uh-NAI-uh	Judas	DZHOU-duhs
Elkanah	el-KAY-nuh	Hannah	HAN-uh	Judea	dzhou-DEE-uh
Eloi Eloi Lama	AY-lo-ee AY-lo-ee	Haran	HAY-ruhn	Judean	dzhou-DEE-uhn
Sabechthani	LAH-mah sah-	Hebron	HEE-bruhn	Junia	dzhou-nih-uh
	BAHK-tah-nee	Hermes	HER-meez	Justus	DZHUHS-tuhs
Elymais	ehl-ih-MAY-ihs	Herod	HEHR-uhd	Kephas	KEF-uhs
Emmanuel	eh-MAN-yoo-ehl	Herodians	hehr-O-dee-uhnz	Kidron	KIHD-ruhn
Emmaus	eh-MAY-uhs	Herodias	hehr-O-dee-uhs	Kiriatharba	kihr-ee-ath-AHR-buh
Epaenetus	ee-PEE-nee-tuhs	Hezekiah	heh-zeh-KAI-uh	Kish	kihsh
Epaphras	EH-puh-fras	Hezron	HEHZ-ruhn	Laodicea	lay-o-dih-SEE-uh
ephah	EE-fuh	Hilkiah	hihl-KAI-uh	Lateran	LAT-er-uhn
Ephah	EE-fuh	Hittite	HIH-tait	Lazarus	LAZ-er-uhs
Ephesians	eh-FEE-zhuhnz	Hivites	HAI-vaitz	Leah	LEE-uh
Ephesus	EH-fuh-suhs	Hophni	HAHF-nai	Lebanon	LEH-buh-nuhn
Ephphatha	EHF-uh-thuh	Hor	HAWR	Levi	LEE-vai
Ephraim	EE-fray-ihm	Horeb	HAWR-ehb	Levite	LEE-vait
Ephrathah	EHF-ruh-thuh	Hosea	ho-ZEE-uh	Levites	LEE-vaits
Ephron	EE-frawn	Hur	her	Leviticus	leh-VIH-tih-kous
Epiphanes	eh-PIHF-uh-neez	hyssop	HIH-suhp	Lucius	LOO-shih-uhs
Erastus	ee-RAS-tuhs	Iconium	ai-KO-nih-uhm	Lud	luhd
Esau	EE-saw	Isaac	AI-zuhk	Luke	look
Esther	EHS-ter	Isaiah	ai-ZAY-uh	Luz	luhz
Ethanim	EHTH-uh-nihm	Iscariot	ihs-KEHR-ee-uht	Lycaonian	lihk-ay-O-nih-uhn
Ethiopian	ee-thee-O-pee-uhn	Ishmael	ISH-may-ehl	Lydda	LIH-duh
Euphrates	yoo-FRAY-teez	Ishmaelites	ISH-mayehl-aits	Lydia	LIH-dih-uh
Exodus	EHK-so-duhs	Israel	IHZ-ray-ehl	Lysanias	lai-SAY-nih-uhs
Ezekiel	eh-ZEE-kee-uhl	Ituraea	ih-TSHOOR-ree-uh	Lystra	LIHS-truh
Ezra	EHZ-ruh	Jaar	DZHAY-ahr	Maccabees	MAK-uh-beez
frankincense	FRANGK-ihn-sehns	Jabbok	DZHAB-uhk	Macedonia	mas-eh-DO-nih-uh
Gabbatha	GAB-uh-thuh	Jacob	DZHAY-kuhb	Macedonian	mas-eh-DO-nih-uhn
Gabriel	GAY-bree-ul	Jairus	DZH-hr-uhs	Machir	MAY-kih
Gadarenes	GAD-uh-reenz	Javan	DZHAY-van	Machpelah	mak-PEE-luh
Galatian	guh-LAY-shih-uhn	Jebusites	DZHEHB-oo-zaits	Magdala	MAG-duh-luh
Galatians	guh-LAY-shih-uhnz	Jechoniah	dzhehk-o-NAI-uh	Magdalene	MAG-duh-lehn
Galilee	GAL-ih-lee	Jehoiakim	dzhee-HOI-uh-kihm	magi	MAY-dzhai
Gallio	GAL-ih-o	Jehoshaphat	dzhee-HAHSH-uh-fat	Malachi	MAL-uh-kai
Gamaliel	guh-MAY-lih-ehl	Jephthah	DZHEHF-thuh	Malchiah	mal-KAI-uh
Gaza	GAH-zuh	Jeremiah	dzhehr-eh-MAI-uh	Malchus	MAL-kuhz
Gehazi	gee-HAY-zai	Jericho	DZHEHR-ih-ko	Mamre	MAM-ree
Gehenna	geh-HEHN-uh	Jeroham	dzhehr-RO-ham	Manaen	MAN-uh-ehn
Genesis	DZHEHN-uh-sihs	Jerusalem	dzheh-ROU-suh-lehm	Manasseh	man-AS-eh
Gennesaret	gehn-NEHS-uh-reht	Jesse	DZHEH-see	Manoah	muh-NO-uh
Gentiles	DZHEHN-tailz	Jethro	DZHEHTH-ro	Mark	mahrk
Gerasenes	DZHEHR-uh-seenz	Joakim	DZHO-uh-kihm	Mary	MEHR-ee
Gethsemane	gehth-SEHM-uh-ne	Job	DZHOB	Massah	MAH-suh
Gideon	GIHD-ee-uhn	Jonah	DZHO-nuh	Mattathias	mat-uh-THAI-uhs

Lectionary Word	Pronunciation	Lectionary Word	Pronunciation	Lectionary Word	Pronunciation
Matthan	MAT-than	Parmenas	PAHR-mee-nas	Sabbath	SAB-uhth
Matthew	MATH-yoo	Parthians	PAHR-thee-uhnz	Sadducees	SAD-dzhoo-seez
Matthias	muh-THAI-uhs	Patmos	PAT-mos	Salem	SAY-lehm
Medad	MEE-dad	Peninnah	pee-NIHN-uh	Salim	SAY-lim
Mede	meed	Pentecost	PEHN-tee-kawst	Salmon	SAL-muhn
Medes	meedz	Penuel	pee-NYOO-ehl	Salome	suh-LO-mee
Megiddo	mee-GIH-do	Perez	PEE-rehz	Salu	SAYL-yoo
Melchizedek	mehl-KIHZ-eh-dehk	Perga	PER-guh	Samaria	suh-MEHR-ih-uh
Mene	MEE-nee	Perizzites	PEHR-ih-zaits	Samaritan	suh-MEHR-ih-tuhn
Meribah	MEHR-ih-bah	Persia	PER-zhuh	Samothrace	SAM-o-thrays
Meshach	MEE-shak	Peter	PEE-ter	Samson	SAM-s'n
Mespotamia	mehs-o-po-TAY-mih-uh	Phanuel	FAN-yoo-ehl	Samuel	SAM-yoo-uhl
Micah	MAI-kuh	Pharaoh	FEHR-o	Sanhedrin	san-HEE-drihn
Midian	MIH-dih-uhn	Pharisees	FEHR-ih-seez	Sarah	SEHR-uh
Milcom	MIHL-kahm	Pharpar	FAHR-pahr	Sarai	SAY-rai
Miletus	mai-LEE-tuhs	Philemon	fih-LEE-muhn	saraph	SAY-raf
Minnith	MIHN-ihth	Philippi	fil-LIH-pai	Sardis	SAHR-dihs
Mishael	MIHSH-ay-ehl	Philippians	fih-LIHP-ih-uhnz	Saul	sawl
Mizpah	MIHZ-puh	Philistines	fih-LIHS-tihnz	Scythian	SIH-thee-uihn
Moreh	MO-reh	Phinehas	FEHN-ee-uhs	Seba	SEE-buh
Moriah	maw-RAI-uh	Phoenicia	fee-NIHSH-ih-uh	Seth	sehth
Mosoch	MAH-sahk	Phrygia	FRIH-dzhih-uh	Shaalim	SHAY-uh-lihm
myrrh	mer	Phrygian	FRIH-dzhih-uhn	Shadrach	SHAY-drak
Mysia	MIH-shih-uh	phylacteries	fih-LAK-ter-eez	Shalishah	shuh-LEE-shuh
Naaman	NAY-uh-muhn	Pi-Hahiroth	pai-huh-HAI-rahth	Shaphat	Shay-fat
Nahshon	NAY-shuhn	Pilate	PAI-luht	Sharon	SHEHR-uhn
Naomi	NAY-o-mai	Pisidia	pih-SIH-dih-uh	Shealtiel	shee-AL-tih-ehl
Naphtali	NAF-tuh-lai	Pithom	PAI-thahm	Sheba	SHEE-buh
Nathan	NAY-thuhn	Pontius	PAHN-shus	Shebna	SHEB-nuh
Nathanael	nuh-THAN-ay-ehl	Pontus	PAHN-tus	Shechem	SHEE-kehm
Nazarene	NAZ-awr-een	Praetorium	pray-TAWR-ih-uhm	shekel	SHEHK-uhl
Nazareth	NAZ-uh-rehth	Priscilla	PRIHS-kill-uh	Shiloh	SHAI-lo
nazirite	NAZ-uh-rait	Prochorus	PRAH-kaw-ruhs	Shinar	SHAI-nahr
Nazorean	naz-aw-REE-uhn	Psalm	Sahm	Shittim	sheh-TEEM
Neapolis	nee-AP-o-lihs	Put	puht	Shuhite	SHOO-ait
Nebuchadnezzar	neh-byoo-kuhd-NEHZ-er	Puteoli	pyoo-TEE-o-lai	Shunammite	SHOO-nam-ait
Negeb	NEH-gehb	Qoheleth	ko-HEHL-ehth	Shunem	SHOO-nehm
Nehemiah	nee-hee-MAI-uh	qorban	KAWR-bahn	Sidon	SAI-duhn
Ner	ner	Quartus	KWAR-tuhs	Silas	SAI-luhs
Nicanor	nai-KAY-nawr	Quirinius	kwai-RIHN-ih-uhs	Siloam	sih-LO-uhm
Nicodemus	nih-ko-DEE-muhs	Raamses	ray-AM-seez	Silvanus	sihl-VAY-nuhs
Niger	NAI-dzher	Rabbi	RAB-ai	Simeon	SIHM-ee-uhn
Nineveh	NIHN-eh-veh	Rabbouni	ra-BO-nai	Simon	SAI-muhn
Noah	NO-uh	Rahab	RAY-hab	Sin (desert)	sihn
Nun	nuhn	Ram	ram	Sinai	SAI-nai
Obed	O-behd	Ramah	RAY-muh	Sirach	SAI-rak
Olivet	AH-lih-veht	Ramathaim	ray-muh-THAY-ihm	Sodom	SAH-duhm
Omega	o-MEE-guh	Raqa	RA-kuh	Solomon	SAH-lo-muhn
Onesimus	o-NEH-sih-muhs	Rebekah	ree-BEHK-uh	Sosthenes	SAHS-thee-neez
Ophir	O-fer	Rehoboam	ree-ho-BO-am	Stachys	STAY-kihs
Orpah	AWR-puh	Rephidim	REHF-ih-dihm	Succoth	SUHK-ahth
Pamphylia	pam-FIHL-ih-uh	Reuben	ROO-b'n	Sychar	SI-kar
Paphos	PAY-fuhs	Revelation	reh-veh-LAY-shuhn	Syene	sai-EE-nee
		Rhegium	REE-dzhee-uhm	Symeon	SIHM-ee-uhn
		Rufus	ROO-fuhs	synagogues	SIHN-uh-gahgz

Lectionary Word	Pronunciation	Lectionary Word	Pronunciation	Lectionary Word	Pronunciation
Syrophoenician	SIHR-o fee-NIHSH-ih-uhn	Timon	TAI-muhn	Zebedee	ZEH-beh-dee
		Titus	TAI-tuhs	Zebulun	ZEH-byoo-luhn
Tabitha	TAB-ih-thuh	Tohu	TO-hyoo	Zechariah	zeh-kuh-RAI-uh
Talitha koum	TAL-ih-thuh-KOOM	Trachonitis	trak-o-NAI-tis	Zedekiah	zeh-duh-KAI-uh
Tamar	TAY-mer	Troas	TRO-ahs	Zephaniah	zeh-fuh-NAI-uh
Tarshish	TAHR-shihsh	Tubal	TYOO-b'l	Zerah	ZEE-ruh
Tarsus	TAHR-suhs	Tyre	TAI-er	Zeror	ZEE-rawr
Tekel	TEH-keel	Ur	er	Zerubbabel	zeh-RUH-buh-behl
Terebinth	TEHR-ee-bihnth	Urbanus	er-BAY-nuhs	Zeus	zyoos
Thaddeus	THAD-dee-uhs	Uriah	you-RAI-uh	Zimri	ZIHM-rai
Theophilus	thee-AH-fih-luhs	Uzziah	yoo-ZAI-uh	Zion	ZAI-uhn
Thessalonians	theh-suh-LO-nih-uhnz	Wadi	WAH-dee	Ziph	zihf
Theudas	THU-duhs	Yahweh-yireh	YAH-weh-yer-AY	Zoar	ZO-er
Thyatira	thai-uh-TAI-ruh	Zacchaeus	zak-KEE-uhs	Zorah	ZAWR-uh
Tiberias	tai-BIHR-ih-uhs	Zadok	ZAY-dahk	Zuphite	ZUHR-ait
Timaeus	tai-MEE-uhs	Zarephath	ZEHR-ee-fath		